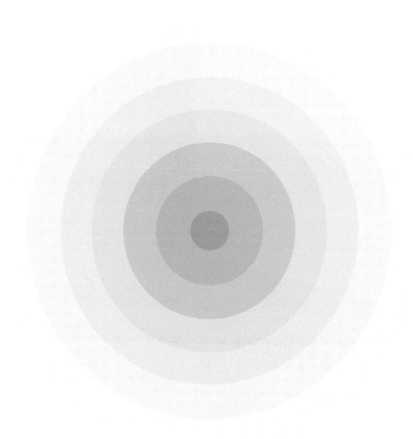

ORGANISATIONAL CHANGE

DEVELOPMENT AND TRANSFORMATION

7E

WADDELL
CREED
CUMMINGS
WORLEY

Organisational Change: Development and Transformation
7th Edition
Dianne M. Waddell
Andrew Creed
Thomas G. Cummings
Christopher G. Worley

Head of content management: Dorothy Chiu
Content manager: Rachael Pictor
Content developer: Samantha Brancatisano
Project editor: Raymond Williams
Project and cover designer: Nikita Bansal
Text designer: Watershed Art & Design (Leigh Ashforth)
Editor: Stephen Roche
Proofreader: James Anderson
Indexer: Julie King
Permissions/Photo researcher: Debbie Gallagher
Cover: Photo by Jason Leung on Unsplash
Typeset by Cenveo Publisher Services

Any URLs contained in this publication were checked for currency during the production process. Note, however, that the publisher cannot vouch for the ongoing currency of URLs.

Authorised adaptation of *Organizational Development and Change*, 11th edition by Thomas G. Cummings and Christopher G. Worley published by Cengage Learning, 2018 [9780357033906]

Sixth edition published 2017

For product information and technology assistance,
in Australia call 1300 790 853;
in New Zealand call 0800 449 725

For permission to use material from this text or product, please email aust.permissions@cengage.com

National Library of Australia Cataloguing-in-Publication Data
ISBN: 9780170424448
A catalogue record for this book is available from the National Library of Australia

Cengage Learning Australia
Level 7, 80 Dorcas Street
South Melbourne, Victoria Australia 3205

Cengage Learning New Zealand
Unit 4B Rosedale Office Park
331 Rosedale Road, Albany, North Shore 0632, NZ

For learning solutions, visit cengage.com.au

Printed in China by 1010 Printing International Limited.
1 2 3 4 5 6 7 23 22 21 20 19

BRIEF CONTENTS

CONTENTS

Guide to the text

As you read this text you will find a number of features in every chapter to enhance your study of Organisational Change and Development and help you understand how the theory is applied in the real world.

PART OPENING FEATURES

Understand how key concepts are connected across the text with the **Framework Diagram**.

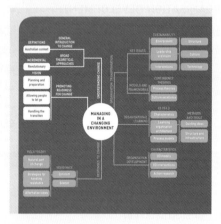

Meet real professionals in the **Practitioner Vignettes**, to gain an insight into how Organisational Change and Development theory informs their day-to-day practice.

FEATURES WITHIN CHAPTERS

Identify the key ideas that the chapter will cover with the **Learning Outcomes** at the start of each chapter.

Important **Key Terms** are marked in bold in the text and **defined in the margin** to help guide your understanding, and **Concept Links** will help you find related content in other chapters throughout the text.

FEATURES WITHIN CHAPTERS

Engage actively and personally with the material by completing the **Experiential Activities**, which help you assess your own knowledge, beliefs, traits and attitudes.

Relate chapter theory to real-world business environments by examining the organisational practices of local and international companies in the **Apply Your Learning Boxes**.

END-OF-CHAPTER FEATURES

At the end of each chapter you will find several tools to help you to review, practise and extend your knowledge of the key learning outcomes.

Review your understanding of the key chapter topics with the **Chapter Summary**.

Test your knowledge and consolidate your learning with the **Review Questions** and apply your skills with the **Extend Your Learning Activities**.

Conduct further research in the **Search Me! Management** database with the suggested key terms.

Guide to the online resources

FOR THE INSTRUCTOR

Cengage is pleased to provide you with a selection of resources that will help you prepare your lectures and assessments. These teaching tools are accessible via **cengage.com.au/instructors** for Australia or **cengage.co.nz/instructors** for New Zealand.

INSTRUCTOR'S MANUAL

The **Instructor's Manual** includes learning outcomes, solutions to questions in the text, additional activities, suggested class discussions and teaching ideas, websites and readings.

CASE DATABASE AND TEACHING NOTES

Access a **database of cases** extracted from this text and previous editions, including **case solutions** and **teaching notes**, which can be utilised on your LMS or in the classroom.

TEST BANK

A bank of questions has been developed in conjunction with the text for creating **quizzes**, **tests** and **exams** for your students. Create multiple test versions in an instant and deliver tests from your LMS, your classroom, or wherever you want using Cognero.

POWERPOINT™ PRESENTATIONS

Use the chapter-by-chapter **PowerPoint slides** to enhance your lecture presentations and handouts by reinforcing the key principles of your subject.

ARTWORK FROM THE TEXT

Add the digital files of **graphs**, **tables**, **pictures** and **flow charts** into your course management system, use them in student handouts, or copy them into your lecture presentations

FOR THE STUDENT

New copies of this text come with an access code that gives you a 12–month subscription to **Search Me! Management**. Visit **http://login.cengagebrain.com** and log in using the access code card.

SEARCH ME! MANAGEMENT

Search Me! is an online research library customised to your subject, that puts the information you need right at your fingertips. Content is updated daily from hundreds of scholarly and popular journals, eBooks and newspapers. Plus, 24-hour access means you won't be limited by library opening times! Log in using the code on the card inside the front cover.

PRACTITIONER VIGNETTES

APPLY YOUR LEARNING BOXES

EXPERIENTIAL ACTIVITIES

PREFACE

Organisational Change: Development and Transformation is a book describing change management as a challenge, particularly as the environment in which we work is in such a volatile state. The world of managing organisation development (OD), which is a planned process of change, continues to change dramatically as the terminology vacillates towards organisational transformation (OT), a more dramatic and unpredictable process. Leaders, and in particular change agents, are faced with conflicting challenges, such as understanding and motivating an increasingly diverse workforce, being open and accountable to a wide range of stakeholders, planning for the future in an increasingly chaotic environment, considering the ethical implications of decision making and many more unanticipated issues.

For students studying change management, the prospect of managing others in such a situation may be daunting. While it is interesting and somewhat straightforward to become a specialist in a specific field, such as OD, the added pressure of supervising or managing others can be stressful. This textbook is written with students in mind, preparing them for the challenges that lie ahead. Featuring current case studies, questions and activities and extensive support material, the book presents the challenges of change management from a real-life perspective. There is no 'one size fits all' method for being a successful change agent, so this book presents change management issues from different viewpoints.

The first author of this book in particular has taken advice from feedback given by her peers and has attempted to provide a comprehensive overview of the fundamental theory as well as its practical applications. Of particular significance is that this book assumes and encourages students to contribute their own understanding and experiences. Students are the beneficiaries of this expected exchange of expertise – as the book attempts to draw together the various views about change management, the emphasis is on heightening the learning experience for students. Students entering a change management position or contemplating being more proactive in their career as a change agent will be exposed to a variety of challenging management issues in this text. I must reiterate that this book is not designed to be prescriptive but a catalyst for further learning. It would be better to consider it to be a vehicle or language to assist in the articulation of ideas.

Students should appreciate the following quotation from George Bernard Shaw, which could well be their mantra in the future:

> Some men see things as they are and ask why. Others dream things that never were and ask why not.

ACKNOWLEDGEMENTS

Dianne M. Waddell

A special thanks must go to Andrew Creed. Although we have worked together over the years while at Deakin University, this is another foray into joint authorship and I have valued his support and camaraderie. It has certainly given us many opportunities to catch up for coffee, support and gossip.

This publication has been successful over the years mainly because it has mirrored its own philosophy of continuous improvement. Some changes have been incremental, whereas others have been significant; they have all been as a result of collaboration and, in some instances, negotiation. Peer reviewers have played a very significant role in helping refine the content and pedagogy of this book, and without their valuable contribution we would not be able to produce a publication of which we are proud.

Our special appreciation also extends to our case study authors; their texts give the book an extra dimension and a thematic approach to the issues. Thank you to Andrew Zur (University of Melbourne), Dr Shoaib Riaz (Monash University), Zane Diamond (Monash University), Scott Gardner (Murdoch University) and Karen Lin Mahar (Central Queensland University).

It would be remiss to not acknowledge the team at Cengage for their patience, understanding and, on many occasions, their persistence: our Content manager, Rachael Pictor; Samantha Brancatisano, Content developer, who has been persistent and resilient; and Debbie Gallagher, rights and Permissions researcher, who assisted me on the project by doing all the hard permissions work. Many thanks must also go to Raymond Williams, Project editor, as well as to Graphic designer Nikita Bansal for commissioning the cover and internal text design.

As writing a textbook bites considerably into the personal and family time of those involved, I would also like to thank the special people in my life. In particular, I would like to thank Denis for enduring 48 years of 'surprises' and not complaining about the cremated dinners. My children, Paul, Corinne and Suzanne, have also suffered because of my 'distractions', yet have survived the turmoil to become sane adults and have made me very proud. New members of the family, Megan and Edhi, are still in a state of shock while trying to adapt to the chaos, but hopefully time will help with their adjustment. My grandchildren, Kit, Anouk and Indie, think that their Nanna is a bit 'weird', but at least they now have something for show-and-tell.

Of course this project would not have been possible without the support and understanding of my past work colleagues and students, who were often the 'victims' of my experiments and vehicles for the testing of my ideas. Hopefully I have made a positive contribution to their work and learning and they have pleasant memories of our encounters.

Andrew Creed

There could be no better lead author on this project than Dianne Waddell. She was a cool colleague and a supportive mentor to me at Deakin University. Now she is working in other places and putting into practice, yet again, the change management principles from this book. I too have experienced much change during the creation of the new edition. Deepest, lasting thanks to my Mum and Dad, Nita and Trevor, with whom I have been privileged to share a journey on the ultimate life transition. There are other people, my children, family and friends, who all contributed to the thought and energy that went into this new edition. I appreciate you, everyone, and thank you for the experiences and interactions that fuelled the new concepts and cases I brought to the book. I also echo Di's thanks to the Cengage team. The end result is truly praiseworthy.

Cengage and the authors would also like to thank the following reviewers for their incisive and helpful feedback:

Jane Boeske (University of Southern Queensland)

Lisa Daniel (University of Adelaide Business School)

Erin C. Gallagher (University of Queensland)

Andrea Howell (Charles Sturt University)

Bernadette Lynch (University of Southern Queensland)

Tui McKeown (Monash Business School)

Mulyadi Robin (Alphacrucis College)

Gerardine Rudolphy (James Cook University)

Mohammad Saud Khan (Victoria University of Wellington)

ABOUT THE AUTHORS

Dianne M. Waddell is now semi-retired and occupying herself with some consulting in Higher Education, specialising in Quality Assurance in Higher Education. She was formerly Professor and Academic Director with two private providers in the tertiary sector. Before that she was an Associate Dean (Teaching and Learning) at Deakin University.

Dianne has been responsible for the development, implementation and evaluation of postgraduate and undergraduate courses and has been the coordinator of the Assurance of Learning processes for external accreditation with Tertiary Education Quality and Standards Agency (TEQSA). She has been on the list of Expert Reviewers for TEQSA. She has taught in the areas of management, quality management, change management and strategic management at a number of institutions, including Deakin University, Edith Cowan University, Monash University and Victoria University. She has taught in both the public and private education systems for many years, as well as presenting specially designed industry-based executive courses.

As well as significant external research-funded projects, her publications include eight books (of which two are textbooks), 15 book chapters, six research reports, 30 refereed journal articles and 76 conference papers. She has also written evaluation reports for various consultancies, including Australian and international universities. Dianne has received several professional awards, including the 2009 Vice Chancellor's Award for Outstanding Achievement in Teaching and Learning at Deakin University and in 2011 the Vice Chancellor's Award for Outstanding Achievement in Student and Staff Support as project leader for the implementation of the new Learning Management System.

Dianne holds a Graduate Certificate in Quality Assurance in Higher Education (Melbourne), PhD (Monash), Master of Education Administration (Melbourne), Bachelor of Education (Melbourne) and Bachelor of Arts (LaTrobe). She is an Affiliate with the International Network for Quality Assurance Agencies in Higher Education (INQAAHE) as well as Fellow with the Australian Organisation for Quality (AOQ). She was Chair of the Victorian Chapter of the Higher Education Research and Development Society.

Andrew Creed is an award-winning lecturer and writer at Deakin University, specialising in change management and organisational behaviour. His research interests include online management education, organisational learning and change, education for sustainable development, action research and relational ethics. He has published textbooks in the fields of organisational behaviour and business communication. He has authored more than 80 scholarly publications, with the highest impact including 10 book chapters, 17 technical manuals, 22 refereed journal articles and 17 conference papers. Other roles have included Adjunct Associate Professor in the online MBA course at University of Maryland University College; teacher and instructional designer in the TAFE and ACE sectors; owner-manager of a bookshop, publishing and consulting business; member of a family-run health care practice; and an area manager in south-west Victoria for the federal government's New

Enterprise Incentive Scheme (NEIS). Andrew has received several professional awards, including the 2006 and 2015 Vice Chancellor's Award and commendation for Teaching and Learning at Deakin University. Andrew holds a Graduate Certificate in Higher Education (Deakin), PhD (University of Exeter, UK), Master of Business Administration (University of Maryland University College) and Bachelor of Science (University of the State of New York). He is active in his local community and in global collaborations.

Thomas G. Cummings is Chair of the Department of Management and Organization and Professor of Management and Organization at the University of Southern California's Marshall School of Business in Los Angeles, California. He received his Bachelor of Science and MBA from Cornell University, and his PhD in sociotechnical systems from the University of California at Los Angeles. He was previously on the faculty at Case Western Reserve University. He has authored 13 books, written over 40 scholarly articles and given numerous invited papers at national and international conferences. He is associate editor of the *Journal of Organizational Behavior*, former editor-in-chief of the *Journal of Management Inquiry*, chairman of the Organizational Development and Change division of the Academy of Management and president of the Western Academy of Management. His major research and consulting interests include designing high-performing organisations and strategic change management. He has conducted several large-scale organisation design and change projects, and has consulted to a variety of private and public-sector organisations in the United States, Europe, Mexico and Scandinavia.

Dr Christopher G. Worley holds a joint appointment as a research scientist at the Center for Effective Organizations at the University of Southern California Marshall School of Business and as an associate professor at Pepperdine University. He is the former director of the Master of Science in Organization program at Pepperdine University, where he was awarded the Harriet and Charles Luckman Distinguished Teaching Fellowship between 1995 and 2000. Dr Worley also has taught undergraduate and graduate courses at the University of San Diego, University of Southern California and Colorado State University. He was chair of the Academy of Management's Organization Development and Change Division. Dr Worley received his PhD in strategic management from the University of Southern California, a Master of Science in organisation development from Pepperdine University, a Master of Science in environmental psychology from Colorado State University and a Bachelor of Science from Westminster College. He is a member of the Strategic Management Society, the Academy of Management, NTL and the Organization Development Network. He lives with his wife and three children in San Juan Capistrano, California.

BOOK OVERVIEW

This book presents the process and practice of organisation development in a logical sequence. In Part 1, Chapter 1 provides a comprehensive overview of organisation development (OD) that describes the process of planned change, those who perform the transition and the various types of interventions. This chapter sets the scene and includes a thought-provoking mind map on change management. It also introduces the concept of organisation transformation (OT). Part 2 covers an overview of change processes and concepts. In particular, Chapter 2 defines the term 'planned change' in the context of OD. All approaches to OD rely on some theory about planned change. Three theories are described and compared, and the chapter presents a general model of planned change that integrates recent conceptual developments in OD. Finally, several critiques of planned change are presented. Chapter 3 examines the people who perform OD in organisations and their role as leaders of change. A closer look at OD practitioners provides a more personal perspective on the field, and assists in the understanding of the essential character of OD as a helping profession, involving personal relationships between OD practitioners and organisation members. Chapter 4 presents two contentious issues facing change management practitioners: resistance to change, which is an inevitable response to any attempt to change, and fitting their organisational strategies, structures and processes to different organisational cultures. Chapter 5 presents an overview of the design, implementation and evaluation of interventions currently used in OD. It describes an intervention as a set of planned activities intended to help an organisation improve its performance and effectiveness. Effective interventions are designed to fit the needs of the organisation, are based on causal knowledge of intended outcomes and transfer competence to manage change to organisation members.

The book continues with Part 3, which gives further details regarding OD interventions. Chapter 6 describes interventions that enable organisations to change themselves continually. These change processes are particularly applicable for organisations facing turbulent environments where traditional sources of competitive advantage erode quickly. Chapter 7 discusses change programs relating to OD interventions, in particular people and processes. These change programs are among the earliest in OD and represent attempts to improve people's working relationships with one another. The interventions are aimed at helping group members to assess their interactions and to devise more effective ways of working together. Chapter 8 is concerned with interventions that are aimed at organisation and environment relationships. These change programs are relatively recent additions to the OD field that focus on helping organisations to relate better to their environments, and to achieve a better fit with those external forces that affect goal achievement and performance.

Part 4 presents the various views of OT. Chapter 9 presents interventions for transforming organisations; that is, for changing the basic character of the organisation, including how it is structured and how it relates to its environment. These frame-breaking and sometimes revolutionary interventions go beyond improving the organisation incrementally, focusing instead on changing the way it views itself. Chapter 10 describes the practice of change management in a chaotic and unpredictable environment, which is exhibited in international settings. It presents the contingencies and practice issues associated with change in organisations outside the host country, and worldwide organisations. Chapter 11 describes transformation interventions that help organisations implement strategies for both competing and collaborating with other organisations. They focus on helping organisations position themselves strategically in their social and economic environments and achieve a better fit with the external forces affecting goal achievement and performance.

Finally, Part 5 contains the concluding Chapters 12 and 13, which describe major trends within OD and trends driving change in OD's context. The future of OD is likely to be the result of the interactions among the traditional, pragmatic and scholarly trends as well as how the global economy evolves, technology develops, workforces engage and organisations structure themselves. Chapter 14 should be written by the readers of this book.

Organisational change: An integrated view

Organisational change affects all aspects of an organisation. Development and transformation cannot be a separate event happening in one place that does not affect the other parts. Structure and strategy are integral. Change is therefore a ripple with consequences. There is interdependency between organisational functions. However, the structure of this book collects chapters into parts to help organise our thinking about the management of change. Each part delineates a sector of the research and experience of change that is distinct yet interrelated to the other parts and chapters. Each part opening page shows you a chart of how these parts interrelate with each chapter. It would be helpful to consider change processes as being similar to a domino effect. Change one aspect, even a minor aspect, and it will lead to all sorts of consequences, both anticipated and/or unintended.

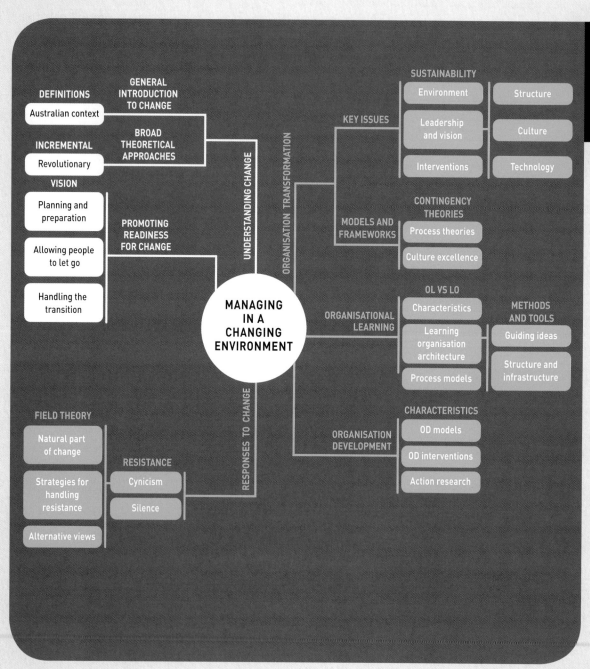

DEFINITIONS
Australian context

GENERAL
INTRODUCTION
TO CHANGE

INCREMENTAL
Revolutionary

BROAD
THEORETICAL
APPROACHES

VISION

Planning and
preparation

Allowing people
to let go

Handling the
transition

PROMOTING
READINESS
FOR CHANGE

UNDERSTANDING CHANGE

ORGANISATION TRANSFORMATION

KEY ISSUES

SUSTAINABILITY

Environment

Structure

Leadership
and vision

Culture

Interventions

Technology

MODELS AND
FRAMEWORKS

CONTINGENCY
THEORIES

Process theories

Culture excellence

MANAGING
IN A
CHANGING
ENVIRONMENT

ORGANISATIONAL
LEARNING

OL VS LO

Characteristics

METHODS
AND TOOLS

Learning
organisation
architecture

Guiding ideas

Structure and
infrastructure

Process models

RESPONSES TO CHANGE

ORGANISATION
DEVELOPMENT

CHARACTERISTICS

OD models

OD interventions

Action research

FIELD THEORY

Natural part
of change

Strategies for
handling
resistance

Alternative views

RESISTANCE

Cynicism

Silence

Source: Adapted from D. Waddell, *E-Business in Australia: Concepts and Cases*, Pearson Education Australia, 2002.

PART 1

INTRODUCTION

Part 1 comprises Chapter 1, which introduces themes dealing with evolution and trends in organisation development (OD). Such concepts are closely allied with material in Chapters 12 and 13. Part 1 also deals with the distinctive rise and characteristics of organisation transformation (OT), which is connected strongly to material covered in Chapter 9.

Bill Millard

Chief Executive/Moyne Shire Council

Roadmaps for organisation development

Source: Bill Millard.

Few people have the same breadth and intensity of experience of organisation development (OD) as Bill Millard, the current Chief Executive at Moyne Shire Council on Victoria's west coast and formerly a senior Director at Hobsons Bay City Council in inner-city Melbourne and at Warrnambool City Council. Bill has a unique managerial background in both regional and urban planning and development, in addition to qualifications and experience in sociology, human resources and business. Bill generously provides two recent roadmap examples of his experience of OD at Hobsons Bay City Council.

Example 1: Strategic roadmap

In late 2017, I presented to the International Economic Development Council (IEDC) conference (Toronto, Canada) with the topic 'Reconciling Objectives of Land Use Planners and Economic Developers'. City development is often highly contentious and triggers emotional responses from people who perceive themselves to be impacted negatively. Even high-quality proposals will be opposed vigorously, and passionate community members will galvanise against a project quickly. Developers often blame planning staff for delays and frustrations. As background to my presentation, I undertook a short survey of town planners in my network to uncover the 'Top 5 Gripes' of land use planners in dealing with development applications. Likewise, I surveyed economic development professionals and members of the development industry to understand their Top 5 Gripes of the planning process.

My survey showed that these myths about the planning process are heavily ingrained by all parties and new ways of engagement are needed. I suggest a practical approach for economic developers. In brief, the gripes of all parties are numerous. The Top 5 Gripes of land use planners in dealing with development applications were:

1 Not the right information to support development applications – inaccurate planning reports and/or technical information (a 'trust us' approach)
2 Lobbying CEO, Directors, state government – anyone who will listen to exert pressure when you are not giving them the answer they want to hear
3 Applicants who think their application is the only one that is being dealt with at that time
4 Being contacted (pressured and harassed) by several different parties relating to the same application to only give the same message

5 Higher consideration of the monetary contribution of a development as opposed to a net community benefit.

The Top 5 Gripes of the economic developers and proponents were:

1 Time frames – taking too long to make a decision
2 Planners not returning phone messages or responding to emails
3 Planners not being prepared to provide informal advice on whether an application is likely to be supported
4 Lack of coordination within Council or between Council and external referral agencies
5 Requiring reports and supporting documents that are not required and or referenced in the planning scheme; that is, social impact assessments, environmentally sustainable design reports and so on.

My guidance to development proponents and economic developers is to understand what drives town planners (planners are firstly people and skilled professionals), provide support (take away some of their pain), genuinely engage (teach, don't tell) and recognise (find subtle ways of recognising good work and close the loop when a development is finished). This approach can grow the confidence of all parties and lead to a highly engaged team approach to development facilitation with superior outcomes.

Example 2: Operational roadmap

In a change of role in 2017, and facing critical office space shortage, I decided to launch a demonstration project to test the theory that an 'open office' could be delivered seamlessly, with minimal disruption and improve relationships and productivity. Many organisations have struggled with this concept, and false starts are common. I applied an OD mindset in conceiving the project, achieving CEO buy-in and pitching the opportunity to the staff involved. This project was not a top-down direction, but it did have the following parameters:

1 Renew a traditional office space for 30 staff in an open office style.
2 Within the same physical footprint, add an additional eight seats.
3 A budget of $60 000.
4 Staff involved will plan, cost and deliver the project.
5 Management will have 'project approval' responsibility before any work starts.

In the first instance, I talked through the plan with the two managers involved, explaining the key role they would play in supporting the project parameters and enabling staff to deliver the outcome sought. Both managers immediately offered their existing offices as part of the renewal area. This was a brilliant signal that management were absolutely serious about supporting and enabling the change.

I then called a meeting of the team of staff and talked about the project, the drivers, and more importantly the opportunity for staff to plan, deliver and renew their office space. I took questions and then left the room, asking that staff let me know within a week whether they would like to take on the task.

Staff were back in my office in 20 minutes with a resounding yes! They had nominated a small project team but also allocated 30 minutes each week to work on design and logistics with the whole team over a morning tea. The project team visited other sites and sourced materials and ideas broadly. In addition, a planned upgrade to mobile IT was occurring with the change in office to an open style.

A brilliant project plan was signed off by the CEO and the project was delivered over a weekend and one working week. From my first discussion with the team to an 'official opening' took seven weeks. All parameters were met apart from the budget, which increased by $20 000 due to structural issues uncovered.

A year on, and managers and staff in the team reported improved relationships, better productivity and felt that work became in some way more enjoyable. Objectively, the team's staff engagement survey results post-change were strongly positive.

Bill Millard draws on these examples and others to explain OD from the most practical of perspectives. Bill's ultimate roadmap for developers is drawn from the application of OD principles: shared understanding, knowing the context, seeking clarity of roles, providing support for people and recognising good work. He is clear that, in complex planning matters or other organisational challenges or projects, emotionally charged, blaming circumstances are unlikely to result in either quick or quality outcomes.

1

INTRODUCTION

After studying this chapter, you should be able to:

1. Describe both organisation development (OD) and organisation transformation (OT), and explain their similarities and differences.
2. Explain the relevance of OD and its role within organisations.
3. Analyse the evolutionary historical context of OD and have an understanding of its future.
4. Assess the environment of OT and comment on its relevance in today's change environment.

Metaphor for change
Organisation development (OD)
Globalisation
Strategic alliance

Sensitivity training
Action research
Systematic collection

When one considers the events unfolding with each day, change remains one of the few constants in an increasingly unpredictable and complex environment and one of the more significant and demanding issues facing managers today. As the environment changes, organisations must adapt if they are to be successful. Under these pressures, companies are downsizing, re-engineering, flattening structures, going global and initiating more sophisticated technologies. A major challenge facing organisations today is to develop a management style and culture that will enable them to cope with the challenges and opportunities they face. Irrespective of whether the change has to do with introducing new technology, a reorganisation or new product development, it is important for leaders to have a sound understanding of change issues and theories to help guide their actions.[1]

Dr Nell Kimberley from Monash University has noted that there is no one universally accepted definition or model of organisational change.[2] Despite spanning a period of more than 60 years, the change literature remains complex and fragmented, characterised by a diversity of opinion, practices and models. Since the 1980s, numerous change models and frameworks have emerged, highlighting the need for greater macro environmental vigilance, organisational agility and radical forms of intervention.

The right-hand side of **Figure 1.1** identifies several common types of change models and frameworks. OD and action research emanated from Lewin's seminal work in the early 1950s. After much criticism in the 1980s surrounding OD's usefulness during times of uncertainty in the external business environment and the need for rapid transformation, numerous step models emerged. Various authors created step-by-step models, which typically reflected Lewin's 'before', 'during' and 'after' change processes. More recent contingency models reject prescriptive change models and take into account the impact of the external macro environment before determining the scale and type of change to be adopted. Other approaches, such as the processual model, emphasise the political aspects of change and the need for organisations to be more organic in their management of change. Complex adaptive systems approaches are also less prescriptive than the commonly used step models, highlighting management characteristics that enable organisations to actively adapt to dynamic and unpredictable environments.

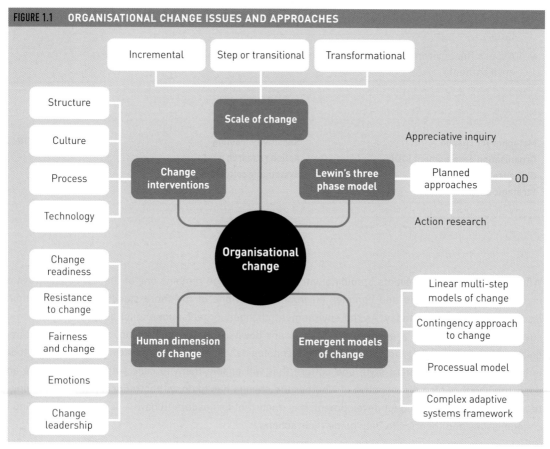

FIGURE 1.1   ORGANISATIONAL CHANGE ISSUES AND APPROACHES

Source: Professor Nell Kimberley, Monash University.

The left-hand side of the model reflects common organisational change management issues, such as the scale of change. How much change is required for an organisation to resolve a problem, such as poor customer service, or to adapt to competition and to grow? It also broadly identifies the types of change typically adopted in organisations, such as changes to structure or technology. The final and most important issue relates to the human dimension of change. It references the capabilities of leaders to establish a new direction and their ability to enable change. Effective change leadership also necessitates understanding the responses of employees who are the recipients of change, (the people who have to enact the change) and their responses to change in terms of their emotional reactions, perceptions of fairness and the extent to which they support or reject change initiatives.

It becomes apparent from the figure that, for the purposes of sustainability, organisations need to be able to implement both incremental and transformational change.[3] 'This requires organisational and management skills to compete in a mature market (where cost, efficiency and incremental innovation are key) and to develop new products and services (where radical innovation, speed and flexibility are critical).'[4] Thus, managers today are required to master both evolutionary and revolutionary change.

But in all probability managers have their own intuitive approaches to bringing about change – the change models they carry inside their heads. A personal theory of change would therefore include any assumptions, biases and paradigms that influence their beliefs about what should change and how change should occur. However, in order to successfully implement change, managers should at least be cognisant of various perspectives on change and the thinking that underpins them.

There is a **metaphor for change**: a pendulum that swings from incremental and planned change (organisation development) to dramatic and unplanned change (organisation transformation) **(Figure 1.2)**. Although organisation transformation (OT) receives headlines in the media, it is often **organisation development (OD)** that is the desired state for organisations. Where OT is a reactive, and sometimes dramatic, response to external pressures, OD is the preferred option for organisations that are introspective and wish to continually improve their products and services in an incremental manner.

Metaphor for change: a figure of speech or a current-day example; not literally applicable. For example, change is like the weather, always changing.

Organisation development (OD): a professional field of social action and an area of scientific inquiry.

This is a book predominantly about OD, the desired state: a process that applies behavioural science knowledge and practices to help organisations achieve greater effectiveness, including increased financial performance and improved quality of work life (QWL). It must also be noted that OD differs from other planned change efforts, such as technological innovation, training and development or new product development, in that the focus is on building the organisation's ability to assess its current functioning and to achieve its goals – OD is process-oriented, not outcome-oriented. Moreover, OD is oriented to improving the total system[5] – the organisation and its parts in the context of the larger environment that impacts on them.

On the other hand, OT may be perceived as volatile and reactive to environmental forces. In most instances, organisations tend to favour OD as it may be implemented proactively and therefore gradually minimise the disturbance within the organisation.

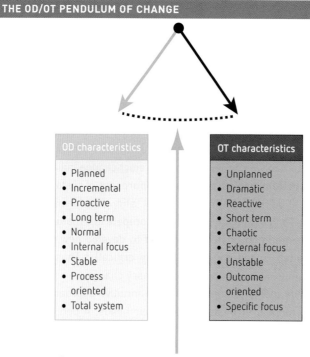

FIGURE 1.2   THE OD/OT PENDULUM OF CHANGE

OD characteristics	OT characteristics
• Planned	• Unplanned
• Incremental	• Dramatic
• Proactive	• Reactive
• Long term	• Short term
• Normal	• Chaotic
• Internal focus	• External focus
• Stable	• Unstable
• Process oriented	• Outcome oriented
• Total system	• Specific focus

Organisations will be at various stages on this spectrum
but would desire to be on the OD 'side'

Although this book presents both views of change, OT and OD, it is the latter that is often desired by organisations and planned accordingly. This book covers OD in more detail in preference to OT, as a basis and foundation for the ongoing debate surrounding change management processes.

WHAT IS ORGANISATION DEVELOPMENT?

This section starts consideration of change management by focusing on OD, describing the concept of OD itself and explaining why OD has expanded rapidly in the past 50 years, both in terms of people's needs to work with and through others in organisations and in terms of organisations' needs to adapt to a complex and changing world.[6] It briefly reviews the history of OD and describes its evolution into its current state. It is a comfortable start in order to become familiar with the change management terminology.

OD is both a professional field of social action and an area of scientific inquiry. The practice of OD covers a wide spectrum of activities, with seemingly endless variations upon them. Team building with top corporate management, structural change in a local council and job enrichment in a manufacturing firm are all examples of OD. Similarly, the study of OD addresses a broad range of topics, including the effects of change, the methods of organisational change and the factors that influence OD success.

A number of definitions of OD exist and are presented in **Table 1.1**. Each definition has a slightly different emphasis. For example, Burke's description focuses attention on culture as the target of change; French's definition is concerned with OD's long-term interest in, and use of, consultants; Beckhard's and Beer's definitions address the process of OD; while Dunphy and Stace refer to the 'soft' approaches. More recently, Burke and Bradford's definition broadens the range and interests of OD. Worley and Feyerherm suggested that for a process to be called OD, (1) it must focus on or result in the change of some aspect of the organisational system; (2) there must be learning or the transfer of knowledge or skill to the client system; and (3) there must be evidence of improvement in or an intention to improve the effectiveness of the client system.[7] The following definition incorporates most of these views and is used in this book:

> Organisation development is a system-wide application of behavioural science knowledge to the planned development and reinforcement of organisational strategies, structures and processes for improving an organisation's effectiveness.

TABLE 1.1	DEFINITIONS OF ORGANISATION DEVELOPMENT
Warner Burke[8]	OD is a planned process of change in an organisation's culture through the utilisation of behavioural science technology, research and theory.
Wendell French[9]	OD refers to a long-range effort to improve an organisation's problem-solving capabilities and its ability to cope with changes in its external environment with the help of external or internal behavioural-scientist consultants, or change agents, as they are sometimes called.
Richard Beckhard[10]	OD is an effort (1) planned, (2) organisation-wide and (3) managed from the top to (4) increase organisation effectiveness and health through (5) planned interventions in the organisation's 'processes', using behavioural science knowledge.
Michael Beer[11]	OD is a system-wide process of data collection, diagnosis, action planning, intervention and evaluation aimed at (1) enhancing congruence between organisational structure, process, strategy, people and culture; (2) developing new and creative organisational solutions; and (3) developing the organisation's self-renewing capacity. It occurs through the collaboration of organisation members working with a change agent using behavioural science theory, research and technology.
Dexter Dunphy and Doug Stace[12]	OD is a 'soft' approach that describes a process of change undertaken in small incremental steps managed participatively.
Warner Burke and David Bradford[13]	Based on (1) a set of values, largely humanistic; (2) application of the behavioural sciences; and (3) open systems theory, OD is a system-wide process of planned change aimed towards improving overall organisation effectiveness by way of enhanced congruence of such key organisation dimensions as external environment, mission, strategy, leadership, culture, structure, information and regard systems, and work policies and procedures.

This definition emphasises several features that differentiate OD from other singular approaches to organisational change and improvement, such as technological innovation, training and development, and organisation evolution.[14]

First, OD applies to an entire system, such as an organisation, a single plant of a multiplant firm, or a department or work group. This contrasts with approaches that focus on one or a few aspects of a system, such as a training and development model or a 'one off' technological innovation. In these approaches, attention is narrowed to individuals within a system or to the improvement of particular products or processes.

Second, OD is based on behavioural science knowledge and practice, including microconcepts such as leadership, group dynamics and work design, and macro-approaches such as strategy, organisation design and international relations. These subjects distinguish OD from such applications as technological innovation, which emphasise the technical and rational aspects of organisations. These latter approaches tend to neglect the personal and social characteristics of a system. In addition, the behavioural science approach to change acknowledges the individual's influence over an organisation's destiny. More deterministic perspectives, such as organisation evolution, discount the influence of organisation members on effectiveness.

Third, whereas OD is concerned with planned change, it is not, in the formal sense, typically associated with business planning or technological innovation[15] nor, in the deterministic sense, often associated with organisation evolution. Instead, OD is more an adaptive process for planning and implementing change than a blueprint for how things should be done. While it involves planning to diagnose and solve organisational problems, such plans are flexible and often revised as new information is gathered about the progress of the change program. If, for example, the performance of international managers was seen to be a concern, a reorganisation process might begin with plans to assess the current relationships between the international divisions and the corporate headquarters, and to redesign them if necessary. These plans would be modified should the assessment discover that most of the international managers' weak performance could be attributed to poor cross-cultural training prior to their international assignment.

Fourth, OD involves both the creation and the subsequent reinforcement of change. It moves beyond the initial efforts to implement a change program to a longer-term concern for stabilising and institutionalising new activities within the organisation. For example, the implementation of self-managed work teams might focus on ways by which supervisors could give workers more control over work methods. After the workers had been given more control, attention would shift to ensuring that supervisors continued to provide that freedom, including the possible rewarding of supervisors for managing in a participative style. This attention to reinforcement is similar to training and development approaches that address maintenance of new skills or behaviours, but differs from other change perspectives that do not address how a change can be institutionalised.

Fifth, OD encompasses strategy, structure and process changes (**Figure 1.3**), although different OD programs may focus more on one kind of change than another. A change program aimed at modifying organisation *strategy*, for example, might focus on how the organisation relates to a wider environment and on how those relationships can be improved. It might include changes in both the grouping of people to perform tasks (*structure*) and the methods of communicating and solving problems (*process*) used to support the changes in strategy. Similarly, an OD program directed at helping a top-management team become more effective might focus on interactions and problem-solving processes within the group. This focus might result in the improved ability of top management to solve company problems in strategy and structure. Other approaches to change, such as training and development, typically have a narrower focus on the skills and knowledge of organisation members.

FIGURE 1.3   THE INTERDEPENDENCIES BETWEEN CHANGE PROCESSES

It should be noted that ideally change should evolve from strategic intent and that structure and processes are required to facilitate smooth implementation of the change strategy. There is a strong interrelationship between these three components of change and, should one aspect be altered, there would be a domino effect and the other two components would also be affected. Therefore it is important to consider all contingencies when implementing change – even the unexpected.

Finally, OD is oriented towards improving organisational effectiveness. This involves two major assumptions. First, an effective organisation is able to solve its own problems and focus its attention and resources on achieving key goals. OD helps organisation members gain the skills and knowledge necessary to conduct these activities by involving them in the process. Second, an effective organisation has both high performance – including quality products and services, high productivity and continuous improvement – and a high quality of work life. The organisation's performance is responsive to the needs of external groups, such as stockholders, customers, suppliers and government agencies, which provide the organisation with resources and legitimacy. Moreover, it is able to attract and motivate effective employees who then perform at high levels.

This definition helps to distinguish OD from other applied fields, such as management consulting, operations management or new product development. It also furnishes a clear conception of organisational change, which is a related focus of this book. Organisational change is a broad phenomenon that involves a diversity of applications and approaches, including economic, political, technical and social perspectives. Change in organisations can be in response to external forces, such as market shifts, competitive pressures and radical new product technologies, or it can be internally motivated, such as by managers trying to improve existing methods and practices. Regardless of its origins, change does affect people and their relationships in organisations and so can have significant social consequences. For example, change may have a negative connotation or be poorly implemented. The behavioural sciences have developed useful concepts and methods for helping organisations deal with these problems. They help managers and administrators manage the change process. Many of these concepts and techniques are described in this book, particularly in relation to managing change.

OD can be applied to managing organisational change. However, it is primarily concerned with change that is oriented to transferring the knowledge and skills needed to build the capability to achieve goals, solve problems and manage change. It is intended to move the organisation in a particular direction, towards improved problem solving, responsiveness, quality of work life and effectiveness. Organisational change, in contrast, is more broadly focused and can apply to any kind of change, including technical, managerial and social innovations. These changes may or may not be directed at making the organisation more developed in the sense implied by OD.

WHY STUDY ORGANISATION DEVELOPMENT?

In the previous editions of this book, we argued that organisations must adapt to increasingly complex and uncertain technological, economic, political and cultural changes. We have also argued that OD can help an organisation create effective responses to these changes and, in many cases, proactively influence the strategic direction of the organisation. The rapidly changing conditions of the past few years confirm these arguments and accentuate their relevance. According to several observers, organisations are in the midst of unprecedented uncertainty and chaos, and nothing short of a management revolution will save them.[16] Three major trends are shaping change in organisations: **globalisation**, information technology and managerial innovation.[17]

Globalisation: the process by which businesses and other organisations develop international influence or start operating on an international scale.

First, globalisation is changing the markets and environments in which organisations operate as well as the way they function.[18] New governments, new leadership, new markets and new countries are emerging and creating a new global economy. The expansion of the European Union has developed and strengthened an internal market; the demise of the Soviet Union has allowed the progress of countries such as Kazakhstan, now a major provider of commercial minerals; and the growth of nationalism and religious fervour in Asia and the Middle East has had far-reaching, international effects resulting in economic and political uncertainty.

Second, information technology such as e-business is changing how work is performed and how knowledge is used. The way an organisation collects, stores, manipulates, uses and transmits information can lower costs or increase the value and quality of products. For example, the sharing of information occurs across a number of electronic platforms that enables global organisations to not only connect but effectively engage with its target audiences. This in turn provides new ways for people to shop, and organisations providing such a service have a competitive edge. In addition, the ability to move information easily and inexpensively throughout and between organisations has fuelled the downsizing, delayering and restructuring of firms. High-speed broadband, laptops and other mobile technologies continue to change the ways people can work, including telecommuting: organisation members can work from their homes or cars without ever going to the office. Finally, information technology is changing how knowledge is used. Information that is widely shared reduces the concentration of power at the top of the organisation. Decision making, once the exclusive province of senior managers who had key information, is shared by organisation members who now have the same information. The concept of work needs to be redefined and the relationship between business and customer is less delineated – business-to-business (B2B) versus business-to-consumer and now business-to-employee.

Third, managerial innovation has both responded to the globalisation and information technology trends and accelerated their impact on organisations. New organisational forms, such as networks, clusters, strategic alliances and virtual corporations, provide organisations with new ways of thinking about how to manufacture goods and deliver services. The **strategic alliance**,[19] for example, has emerged as one of the indispensable tools in strategy implementation. In addition, other methods of change, such as downsizing (right sizing, creating job opportunities, etc.) and re-engineering, have radically reduced the size of organisations and increased their flexibility, while large-group interventions, such as the search conference and open space, have increased the speed with which organisational change can take place.[20]

Strategic alliance: entering into an agreement between organisations for their mutual benefit.

Managers, OD practitioners and researchers argue that these forces are not only powerful in their own right but also interrelated. Their interaction makes for a highly uncertain and chaotic environment for all kinds of organisations, including manufacturing and service firms and those in the public and private sectors. There is no question that these forces are profoundly impacting on organisations.

Fortunately, a growing number of organisations are undertaking the kinds of organisational changes needed to survive and prosper in today's environment. They are making themselves more streamlined and nimble, and more responsive to external demands. They are involving employees in key decisions and paying for performance rather than time. They are taking the initiative in innovating and managing change, rather than simply responding to what has already happened.

OD is playing an increasingly important role in helping organisations change themselves. It is helping organisations to assess themselves and their environments and to revitalise and rebuild their strategies, structures and processes. OD is helping organisation members go beyond surface changes to transform the underlying assumptions and values that govern their behaviours. The different concepts and methods discussed in this book are increasingly finding their way into government agencies, manufacturing firms, multinational corporations, service industries, educational institutions and not-for-profit organisations. Perhaps at no other time has OD been more responsive and practically relevant to organisations' needs if they are to operate effectively in a highly complex and changing world.

OD is obviously important to those who plan a professional career in the field, either as an internal consultant employed by an organisation or as an external consultant practising in many organisations. A career in OD can be highly rewarding, providing challenging and interesting assignments that involve working with managers and employees to improve their organisations and their work lives. In today's environment, the demand for OD professionals is rising rapidly. Consulting continues to be a big growth area in Australia, representing up to 30 per cent of some accounting practices' total worldwide business. Many fast-growing companies are making more use of consultants, in some instances doubling their use and application of OD services, and expanding career opportunities in Australia and worldwide.

OD is also important to those who have no aspirations to become professional practitioners. All managers and administrators are responsible for supervising and developing subordinates and for improving their departments' performances. Similarly, all staff specialists, such as accountants, financial analysts, engineers, personnel specialists or market researchers, are responsible for offering advice and counsel to managers, and for introducing new methods and practices. Finally, OD is important to general managers and other senior executives as it can help the whole organisation be more flexible, adaptable and effective.

OD can help managers and staff personnel perform their tasks more effectively. It can provide the skills and knowledge necessary for establishing effective interpersonal and helping relationships. It can show personnel how to work effectively with others in diagnosing complex problems and devising appropriate solutions. It can help others become committed to the solutions, thereby increasing the chances of their successful implementation. In short, OD is highly relevant to anyone who has to work with and through others in organisations.

A SHORT HISTORY OF ORGANISATION DEVELOPMENT

A brief history of OD will help to clarify the evolution of the term as well as some of the problems and confusions that have surrounded its development. As currently practised, OD emerged from five major backgrounds or stems, as shown in **Figure 1.4**. The first stem was the growth of the National Training Laboratories (NTL) and the development of training groups, otherwise known as **sensitivity training** or T-groups. The second stem of OD was the classic work on action research conducted by social scientists who were interested in applying research to the management of change. An important feature of action research was a technique known as survey feedback. Kurt Lewin, a prolific theorist, researcher and practitioner in group dynamics and social change, was instrumental in the development of T-groups,

Sensitivity training: a program where small groups learn from their own interaction and evolving dynamics about particular issues.

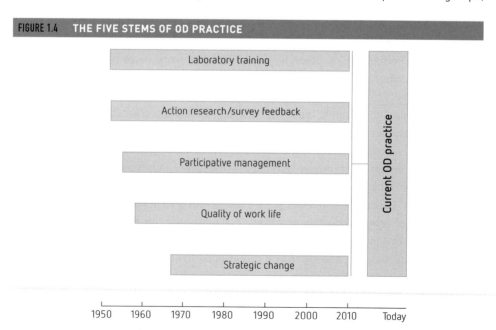

FIGURE 1.4   THE FIVE STEMS OF OD PRACTICE

Laboratory training

Action research/survey feedback

Participative management

Quality of work life

Strategic change

Current OD practice

1950   1960   1970   1980   1990   2000   2010   Today

survey feedback and action research. His work led to the initial development of OD and still serves as a major source of its concepts and methods. The third stem reflects the work of Rensis Likert and represents the application of participative management to organisational structure and design. The fourth background is the approach that focuses on productivity and the quality of work life. The fifth stem of OD, and the most recent influence on current practice, involves strategic change and organisational transformation.

LABORATORY TRAINING BACKGROUND

This stem of OD pioneered laboratory training or the T-group: a small, unstructured group in which participants learn from their own interactions and evolving dynamics about such issues as interpersonal relations, personal growth, leadership and group dynamics. Essentially, laboratory training began in the summer of 1946, when Kurt Lewin and his staff at the Research Center for Group Dynamics at the Massachusetts Institute of Technology (MIT) were asked by the Connecticut Interracial Commission and the Commission on Community Interrelations of the American Jewish Congress for help in research on training community leaders. A workshop was developed, and the community leaders were brought together to learn about leadership and discuss problems. At the end of each day, the researchers discussed privately what behaviours and group dynamics they had observed. The community leaders asked permission to sit in on these feedback sessions, to which the researchers finally gave their assent. Thus, the first T-group was formed, in which people reacted to data about their own behaviour. The researchers drew two conclusions about this first T-group experiment: (1) feedback about group interaction was a rich learning experience, and (2) the process of 'group building' had potential for learning that could be transferred to 'back-home' situations.[21]

A new phenomenon arose in 1950 when an attempt was made to have T-groups in the morning and cognitive-skill groups (A-groups)[22] in the afternoon. However, the staff found that the high level of carry-over from the morning sessions turned the afternoon A-groups into T-groups, despite the resistance of the afternoon staff members, who were committed to cognitive-skill development. This was the beginning of a decade of learning experimentation and frustration, especially in the attempt to transfer skills learned in the T-group setting to the 'back-home' situation.

Three trends emerged in the 1950s: (1) the emergence of regional laboratories, (2) the expansion of summer program sessions to year-round sessions and (3) the expansion of the T-group into business and industry, with NTL members becoming increasingly involved with industry programs. Applications of T-group methods at a number of major companies introduced the term 'organisation development' and led corporate personnel and industrial relations specialists to expand their roles to offer internal consulting services to managers.[23]

Applying T-group techniques to organisations gradually became known as 'team building': a process for helping work groups become more effective in accomplishing tasks and satisfying member needs. Team building is one of the most common OD interventions today.

ACTION RESEARCH AND SURVEY FEEDBACK BACKGROUND

Kurt Lewin was also involved in the second movement that led to OD's emergence as a practical field of social science. This second background refers to the processes of action research and survey feedback. The **action research** contribution began in the 1940s with studies conducted by social scientists John Collier, Kurt Lewin and William Whyte, who discovered that research needed to be closely linked to action if organisation members were to use it to manage change.

Action research: a process whereby research is needed to be closely linked to action and vice versa.

A collaborative effort was initiated between organisation members and social scientists to collect research data about an organisation's functioning, analyse it for causes of problems and devise and implement solutions. After implementation, further data were collected to assess the results, and the cycle of data collection and action often continued. The results of action research were twofold: members of organisations were able to use research on themselves to guide action and change, and social scientists were able to study that process to derive new knowledge that could be used elsewhere.

Systematic collection: gathering data in an organised and planned determined manner.

A key component of most action research studies was the **systematic collection** of survey data, which were subsequently fed back to the client organisation. Following Lewin's death in 1947, his Research Center for Group Dynamics at MIT moved to Michigan and joined with the Survey Research Center as part of the Institute for Social Research. The institute was headed by Rensis Likert, a pioneer in the development of scientific approaches to attitude surveys. Likert's doctoral dissertation at Columbia University, 'A technique for the measurement of attitudes', was the classic study in which he developed the widely used five-point 'Likert Scale'.[24]

In an early study of the institute, Likert and Floyd Mann administered a company-wide survey of management and employee attitudes at Detroit Edison.[25] Over a two-year period beginning in 1948, three sets of data were developed: (1) the viewpoints of 8000 non-supervisory employees about their supervisors, promotion opportunities and work satisfaction with fellow employees; (2) similar reactions from first- and second-line supervisors; and (3) information from higher levels of management.

The feedback process that evolved was an 'interlocking chain of conferences'. The major findings of the survey were first reported to the top management and then transmitted throughout the organisation. The feedback sessions were conducted in task groups, with supervisors and their immediate subordinates discussing the data together. Although there was little substantial research evidence, the researchers intuitively felt that this was a powerful process for change.

In 1950, eight accounting departments asked for a repeat of the survey, and this generated a new cycle of feedback meetings. Feedback approaches were used in four departments, but the method varied, with two of the remaining departments receiving feedback only at the departmental level. Because of changes in key personnel, nothing was done in two departments.

A third follow-up study indicated that more significant and positive changes (such as job satisfaction) had occurred in the departments that were receiving feedback than in the two departments that did not participate. From these findings, Likert and Mann derived several conclusions about the effects of survey feedback on organisational change, and this led to extensive applications of survey feedback methods in a variety of settings. The common pattern of data collection, data feedback, action planning, implementation and follow-up data collection in both action research and survey feedback can be seen in these examples.

PARTICIPATIVE MANAGEMENT BACKGROUND

The intellectual and practical advances from the laboratory training and action research/ survey feedback stems were followed closely by the belief that a human relations approach represented a 'one best way' to manage organisations. This belief was exemplified in research that associated Likert's participative management (System 4) style with organisational effectiveness.[26] This framework characterised organisations as having one of four types of management systems:[27]

→ *Exploitative authoritative*[28] systems (System 1) exhibit an autocratic, top-down approach to leadership. Employee motivation is based on punishment and occasional rewards. Communication is primarily downwards, and there is little lateral interaction or teamwork. Decision making and control reside primarily at the top of the organisation. System 1 results in mediocre performance.

→ *Benevolent authoritative*[29] systems (System 2) are similar to System 1, except that management is more paternalistic. Employees are allowed a little more interaction, communication and decision making, but within limited boundaries defined by management.

→ *Consultative* systems (System 3) increase employee interaction, communication and decision making. Although employees are consulted about problems and decisions, management still makes the final decisions. Productivity is good, and employees are moderately satisfied with the organisation.

→ *Participative* group systems (System 4) are almost the opposite of System 1. Designed around group methods of decision making and supervision, the participative group system fosters high degrees of member involvement and participation. Work groups are highly involved in setting goals, making decisions, improving methods and appraising results. Communication occurs both laterally and vertically, and decisions are linked throughout the organisation by overlapping group membership. Shown in **Figure 1.5**, this 'linking-pin' structure ensures continuity in communication and decision making across groups by means of people who are members of more than one group – the groups they supervise and the higher-level groups of which they are members. System 4 achieves high levels of productivity, quality and member satisfaction.

Likert applied System 4 management to organisations, using a survey feedback process. The intervention generally started with organisation members completing the profile of organisational characteristics. The survey asked members for their opinions about both the present and ideal conditions of six organisational features: leadership, motivation, communication, decisions, goals and control. In the second stage, the data were fed back to different work groups within the organisation. Group members examined the discrepancy between their present situation and their ideal, generally using System 4 as the ideal benchmark, and generated action plans to move the organisation towards System 4 conditions.

FIGURE 1.5   THE LINKING PIN

(The arrows indicate the linking-pin function.)

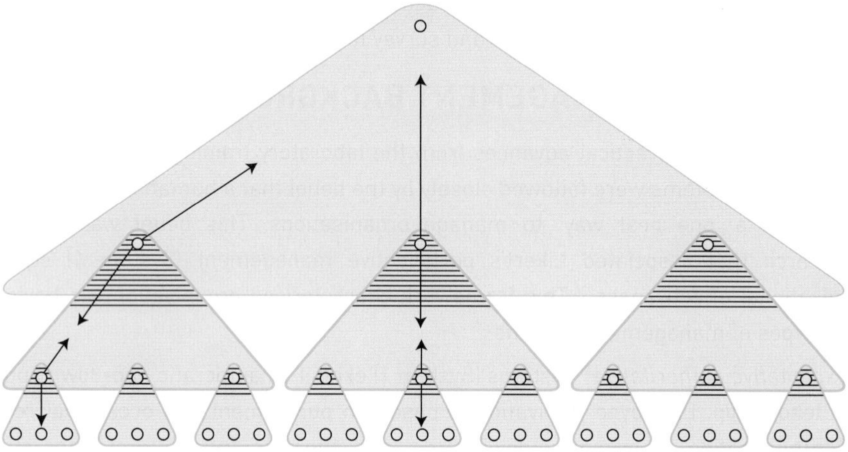

Source: R. Likert, *New Patterns of Management*, (New York: McGraw-Hill, 1961), p.113. Republished with permission of McGraw-Hill Education, permission conveyed through Copyright Clearance Center, Inc.

Despite some research support, the normative approach to change has given way to a contingency view that acknowledges the influence of the external environment, technology and other forces in determining the appropriate organisation design and management practices.

PRODUCTIVITY AND QUALITY OF WORK LIFE BACKGROUND

Projects to improve productivity and the quality of work life (QWL) were originally developed in Europe during the 1950s. Based on the research of Eric Trist and his colleagues at the Tavistock Institute of Human Relations in London, this approach examined the technical and human sides of organisations and how they interrelated.[30] It led to the development of the sociotechnical systems (STS) [31] methods of work design that underlie many of the employee involvement and empowerment efforts occurring in Australia today.

Early practitioners in the United Kingdom, Ireland, Norway and Sweden developed work designs that were aimed at better integrating technology and people. These QWL programs generally involved joint participation by unions and management in the design of work, and resulted in work designs that gave employees high levels of discretion, task variety and feedback about results. Perhaps the most distinguishing characteristic of these QWL programs was the development of self-managing work groups as a new form of work design. These groups were composed of multiskilled workers who were given the necessary autonomy and information to design and manage their own task performances.

Apply your learning 1.1 demonstrates how difficult it is to improve quality of work life through labour legislation in Nepal.

IMPROVING QUALITY OF WORK LIFE THROUGH LABOUR LEGISLATION

This research focuses on reviewing Nepalese labour laws, their implementation situation and examination of the present nature of jobs and expectations of trade union leaders in order to improve the quality of work life (QWL) situation of Nepalese employees.

Although there are provisions in labour laws and well-defined mechanisms to implement these provisions to ensure labour rights, at the organisational level there are a number of lapses. All three actors, governments, employers and unions, have, to a larger extent, failed to implement labour legislation.

In an opinion survey of 40 union leaders, it is revealed that most of the union leaders focus on the need for a proper mechanism for the enforcement of legislation and introduction of some other provisions that are not included in existing labour legislation. They still believe that the Nepalese organisations' pay and benefits and job security are considered the most important motivation factors to improve the level of the QWL situation. At the same time, consideration is needed to improve QWL through education, training and other skill development programs.

Source: Based on D.R. Adhikari and D.K. Gautam, 'Improving quality of worklife through labour legislation', https://www.ilo.org/legacy/english/protection/travail/pdf/rdwpaper12b.pdf, accessed 21 May 2018.

Critical thinking questions

1 What are the key findings of the paper?
2 In your opinion, can legislation assist in improving QWL?
3 Download the article and identify the difficulties that would impede a QWL culture.

Gradually, QWL programs expanded beyond individual jobs to include group forms of work and other features of the workplace that can affect employee productivity and satisfaction, such as reward systems, work flows, management styles and the physical work environment. This expanded focus resulted in larger-scale and longer-term projects than the early job-enrichment programs and shifted attention beyond the individual worker to work groups and the larger work context. Equally importantly, it added the critical dimension of organisational efficiency to what had been up to that time a predominant concern for the human dimension. The economic and human resource problems that faced Australia during the 1980s have further reinforced this focus upon organisational efficiency.

At one point, the productivity and QWL approach became so popular that it was called an ideological movement. International conferences were aimed at identifying a coalition of groups from among unions and management that supported QWL ideals of employee involvement, participative management and industrial democracy. Some Australian companies adopted the Japanese method of management and employee participation, which involved the spread of quality circles. Ford was one such company. Popularised in Japan, quality circles are groups of employees trained in problem-solving methods that meet regularly to resolve work environment, productivity and quality-control concerns and to develop more efficient ways of working.

Finally, the productivity and QWL approach has gained new momentum by joining forces with the total quality movement advocated by W. Edward Deming[32] and Joseph Juran.[33] In this approach, the organisation is viewed as a set of processes that can be linked to the quality of products and services, modelled through statistical techniques and continuously improved.[34] Quality efforts at Toyota, Sheraton and Ericsson, along with federal government support through the establishment of the Business Excellence Awards, have popularised this strategy of OD.

In Australia today, top management keeps employees motivated by a combination of good financial rewards, an interesting environment and challenging projects. The staff are also given feedback about their own work and kept informed about their company's situation.

STRATEGIC CHANGE BACKGROUND

The strategic change background is a recent influence on the evolution of OD. As organisations and their technological, political and social environments become more complex and more uncertain, the scale and intricacies of organisational change have increased. This trend has produced the need for a strategic perspective from OD and has encouraged planned change processes at the organisation level.[35]

Strategic change involves improving the alignment in an organisation's environment, strategy and organisation design.[36] Strategic change interventions include efforts to improve both the organisation's relationship to its environment and the fit between its technical, political and cultural systems.[37] The need for strategic change is usually triggered by some major disruption to the organisation, such as the lifting of regulatory requirements, a technological breakthrough or a new CEO from outside the organisation.[38]

One of the first applications of strategic change was Richard Beckhard's use of open systems planning (OSP).[39] He proposed that an organisation's environment and its strategy could be described and analysed. Based on the organisation's core mission, the differences between what the environment demanded and how the organisation responded could be reduced and performance improved. Since then, change agents have proposed a variety of large-scale or strategic change models.[40] Each of these models recognises that strategic change involves multiple levels of the organisation and a change in its culture, that it is often driven from the top by powerful executives and that it impacts significantly on performance.

The strategic change background has significantly influenced OD practice. For example, the implementation of strategic change requires OD practitioners to be familiar with competitive strategy, finance and marketing, as well as team building, action research and survey feedback. Together, these skills have improved OD's relevance to organisations and their managers.

Apply your learning 1.2 demonstrates how competitive advantage is the goal of strategic change at Nissan Motors.

EXAMPLES OF STRATEGIC CHANGE

APPLY YOUR LEARNING **1.2**

In March 1999, Renault Motors acquired the failing Nissan Motors of Japan. Japanese business culture is famous for its policy of life-long employment. In an interview for Harvard's 'Working Knowledge', Carlos Ghosn, the man Renault chose as CEO for Nissan, asked, 'How do you make head count reductions in Japan?' He had to reduce manufacturing overcapacity, get rid of the seniority system at Nissan and replace it with performance-based management. He focused his attention on cost reduction, sales of assets, eliminating the keiretsu, a Japanese term for interlocking business relationships to develop other kinds of suppliers. The result was a nearly complete strategic turn-around for Nissan, which went on to announce its biggest profit ever in May 2001 – only a year after it had posted its worst loss in the company's history.

Source: V. Duff, 'Examples of strategic change', https://smallbusiness.chron.com/examples-strategic-change-11467.html, accessed 21 May 2018.

Critical thinking questions

1 What does 'keiretsu' mean? Give an example.
2 List the major changes that were made by the organisation, which qualifies the changes to be strategic.
3 Search the internet and identify what has happened to the company since 2001.

EVOLUTION IN ORGANISATION DEVELOPMENT

Current practice in OD is strongly influenced by these five stems, as well as by the trends that shape change in organisations. The laboratory training, action research, survey feedback and participative management roots of OD are evident in the strong value focus that underlies its practice. The more recent influences (the quality of work life and strategic change stems) have greatly improved the relevance and rigour of OD practice. They have added financial and economic indicators of effectiveness to OD's traditional measures of work satisfaction and personal growth. All of the backgrounds support the transfer of knowledge and skill to the organisation so it can better manage change in the future.

Today, the field is being influenced by the globalisation and information technology trends described earlier. OD is being carried out in many more countries and in many more organisations that operate worldwide, and this is generating a whole new set of interventions as well as adaptations of traditional OD practice.[41] In addition, OD must adapt its methods to the technologies now being used in organisations. As information technology continues to influence organisational environments, strategies and structures, OD will need to manage change processes in cyberspace as well as face to face in the workplace. The diversity of this evolving discipline has led to tremendous growth in the number of professional practitioners, in the kinds of organisations involved with OD, in the range of countries within which OD is practised and in the kinds of interventions used to change and improve organisations.

The expansion of the OD network is one indication of this growth. OD divisions have been set up by many training and development organisations, and courses are being taught at Australian universities at postgraduate and undergraduate levels. For example, Victoria University offers the Bachelor of Business (Management and Innovation).

In addition to the growth of professional societies and educational programs in OD, the field continues to develop new theorists, researchers and practitioners who are building on the work of the early pioneers and extending it to contemporary issues and conditions. Included among the first generation of contributors are Chris Argyris, who developed a learning and action science approach to OD;[42] Warren Bennis, who tied executive leadership to strategic change;[43] Edgar Schein, who continues to develop process approaches to OD, including the key role of organisational culture in change management;[44] Richard Beckhard, who focused attention on the importance of managing transitions;[45] and Robert Tannenbaum, who continues to sensitise OD to the personal dimension of participants' lives.[46]

Among the second generation of contributors are Warner Burke, whose work has done much to make OD a professional field;[47] Larry Greiner, who has brought the ideas of power and evolution into the mainstream of OD;[48] Edward Lawler III, who has extended OD to reward systems and employee involvement;[49] Newton Margulies and Anthony Raia, who together have kept attention on the values underlying OD and what they mean for contemporary practice;[50] and Peter Vaill and Craig Lundberg, who continue to develop OD as a practical science.[51]

Among the newest generation of OD contributors are Dave Brown, whose work on action research and developmental organisations has extended OD into community and societal change;[52] Thomas Cummings, whose work on STS, self-designing organisations and transorganisational development (TD) has led OD beyond the boundaries of single organisations to groups of organisations and their environments;[53] Max Widen, whose international work in industrial democracy draws attention to the political aspects of OD;[54] William Pasmore and Jerry Porras, who have done much to put OD on a sound research and conceptual base;[55] and Peter Block, who has focused attention on consulting skills, empowerment processes and reclaiming our individuality.[56]

Other newcomers who are making important contributions to the field include Ken Murrell and Joanne Preston, who have focused attention on the internationalisation of OD;[57] Sue Mohrman and Gerry Ledford, who have explored team-based organisations and compensation;[58] and David Cooperrider, who has turned our attention towards the positive aspects of organisations.[59] In Australia there are such centres as the Centre for Sustainable Organisations and Work research clusters at RMIT University, which has actively contributed to the body of research. Academic contributors are joined by a large number of internal

OD practitioners and external consultants who lead organisational change, such as the Australian Institute of Training and Development.[60]

Many different organisations have undertaken a wide variety of OD efforts. Many have been at the forefront of innovating new change techniques and methods, as well as new organisational forms. Traditionally, much of this work was considered confidential and not publicised. Today, however, organisations have increasingly gone public with their OD efforts, sharing the lessons with others.

OD work is also being done in schools, communities and local, state and federal governments. A system that encouraged staff at Casey Institute of Technical and Further Education (TAFE) to learn from one another won its designer, Stuart Williams, a prestigious individual achievement recognition award from the Australian Human Resources Institute (AHRI). It required all departments to provide six hours of training to fellow staff members annually.[61] OD is increasingly international. As well as in South-East Asia, it has been applied in the United States, Canada, Sweden, Norway, Germany, Japan, Israel, South Africa, Mexico, Venezuela, the Philippines, China (including Hong Kong), Russia and the Netherlands. These efforts have involved such organisations as Saab (Sweden), Norsk Hydro (Norway), Imperial Chemical Industries (England), Royal Dutch Shell (Netherlands), Orrefors (Sweden) and Alcan Canada Products.

Although it is evident that OD has vastly expanded in recent years, relatively few of the total number of organisations in Australia are actively involved in formal OD programs. However, many organisations are applying OD approaches and techniques without knowing that such a term exists.

THE RISE OF ORGANISATION TRANSFORMATION

As a result of external forces, such as the global financial crisis that began in 2008–09 (the effects of which are still felt today), there has been a need to respond quickly in order to anticipate negative consequences and/or capture an opportunity for advancement. Later chapters (see Chapters 9–11) explain how OT is often perceived as observable and a 'quick fix', and as a result may even receive significant media coverage. It is also very evident in international contexts where the environment may be unpredictable and planning would be difficult.

This kind of change is often termed revolutionary, as distinct from evolutionary, which is the nature of OD. As a consequence, the alignment with factors (including internationalisation, environment and technology) will vary depending mainly on external forces, whereas OD has a predominantly internal focus. OT also requires a different leadership style, which would be more directional and/or charismatic, whereas OD requires a more transactional approach.

For further explanation of organisation transformation (OT), see Chapters 9–11.

Apply your learning 1.3 reports a longitudinal study that examined mergers between three large multi-site public-sector organisations.

APPLY
YOUR
LEARNING
1.3

THE IMPACT OF LEADERSHIP AND CHANGE MANAGEMENT STRATEGY ON ORGANIZATIONAL CULTURE AND INDIVIDUAL ACCEPTANCE OF CHANGE DURING A MERGER

Findings indicate that in many cases the change that occurs as a result of a merger is imposed on the leaders themselves, and it is often the pace of change that inhibits the successful re-engineering of the culture. In this respect, the success or otherwise of any merger hinges on individual perceptions about the manner in which the process is handled and the direction in which the culture is moved. Communication and a transparent change process are important, as this will often determine not only how a leader will be regarded, but who will be regarded as a leader. Leaders need to be competent and trained in the process of transforming organizations to ensure that individuals within the organization accept the changes prompted by a merger.

Source: M.H. Kavanagh and N.M. Ashkanasy, 'The impact of leadership and change management strategy on organizational culture and individual acceptance of change during a merger', *British Journal of Management*, 17:S1 (2006): S81–103.

Critical thinking questions	
1	According to this paper, what is the cause or catalyst for change?
2	What is important for successful change?
3	Do leaders need to be prepared? If so, what need to be the primary characteristics?
4	Download the article. It has a very good diagram (Figure 1). What is the pivotal role of leadership?

Despite the energy and resourcing commitment required in an OT change process, organisations naturally desire to 'return' to a stable state. Therefore, OT strategies tend to be short-term with the intention to stabilise in the long term, reverting back to using OD methodologies.

SUMMARY

This chapter begins with general observations about change management and utilises OD as a vehicle to familiarise ourselves with the terminology. The relevance of OD in today's business environment is introduced, bearing in mind the evolutionary nature of the concept. OT will be covered in more detail in later chapters and the reader will be introduced to various global perspectives and challenged to anticipate the future direction of change management.

ACTIVITIES

REVIEW QUESTIONS

1 Distinguish between OD and OT. What are the advantages and disadvantages of each? (LO1)

2 Likert's participative management system (System 4) suggests that organisations have one of four types of management systems. Provide examples from your own experiences of each management system and explain how it relates to the system chosen. (LO2)

3 Change processes can create a 'domino effect' where if anything changes it creates ongoing changes with other areas. Provide an example of how this can occur. (LO2 & 3)

4 Explain the difference between strategic change and OT. (LO4)

5 Do you agree with the metaphor of the pendulum? Explain your answer. (LO1)

EXTEND YOUR LEARNING

1 Explain the value of planned versus unplanned change. Use examples to reinforce your explanation. Is there a preferred process of change? (LO2 & 4)

2 What do you see as the future of change: planned or unplanned? Explain your answer using examples where appropriate. (LO3)

3 'As the environment changes, organisations need to adapt if they are to be successful.' Discuss. (LO2 & 4)

Search ⊕ Me! **Management**

Explore **Search Me! Management** for articles relevant to this chapter. Fast and convenient, **Search Me! Management** is updated daily and provides you with 24-hour access to full text articles from hundreds of scholarly and popular journals, eBooks and newspapers, including *The Australian* and *The New York Times*. Visit http://login.cengagebrain.com and use the access code that comes with this book for 12 months access to the **Search Me! Management** database. Try searching for the following keywords:

Keywords:

- Metaphor for change
- Organisation development
- Globalisation
- Strategic alliance
- Sensitivity training
- Action research
- Systematic collection

Search tip: **Search Me! Management** contains information from both local and international sources. To get the greatest number of search results, try using both Australian and American spellings in your searches; for example, 'globalisation' and 'globalization'; 'organisation' and 'organization'.

CRITICAL

REFERENCES

1 D. Waddell, *E-business in Australia: Concepts and Cases* (Sydney: Pearson Education Australia, 2002): 23.

2 See, for example, N. Kimberley and C. Hartel, 'A reversal of perspective: examining major change from employee perceptions of justice, emotions and trust', 2006, http://www.anzam.org/wp-content/uploads/pdf-manager/2170_KIMBERLEY.PDF.

3 'Incremental and transformational change', *Innovations Case Discussion*: Better Place, 4 (November 2009): 141–3.

4 M. Tushman and C. O'Reilly, 'Ambidextrous organisations: managing evolutionary and revolutionary change', *California Management Review*, 28 (Summer 1996): 11.

5 K.V. Siakas and E. Georgiadou, *Process Improvement: The Societal Iceberg*, University of North London and Technological Educational Institution of Thessaloniki, 2002, http://www.iscn.at/select_newspaper/people/unl.htm.

6 C.D. Lee, *Understanding Complex Ecologies in a Changing World* (Washington, DC, USA: American Educational Research Association, 2010).

7 C. Worley and A. Feyerherm, 'Reflections on the future of OD', *Journal of Applied Behavioral Science* 39 (2003): 97–115.

8 W. Burke, *Organization Development: Principles and Practices* (Boston, MA: Little Brown, 1982).

9 W. French, 'Organization development: objectives, assumptions, and strategies', *California Management Review*, 12 (February 1969): 23–34.

10 R. Beckhard, *Organization Development: Strategies and Models* (Reading, MA: Addison-Wesley, 1969).

11 M. Beer, *Organization Change and Development: A Systems View* (Santa Monica, CA: Goodyear Publishing, 1980).

12 D. Dunphy and D. Stace, *Beyond the Boundaries* (Sydney: McGraw-Hill, 1994).

13 C. Worley and A. Feyerherm, 'Reflections on the future of OD', op. cit.

14 T. Cummings and C. Cummings, 'Appreciating organization development: a comparative essay on divergent perspectives', *Human Resource Development Quarterly*, 25 (2014): 143.

15 *Technological Innovation and Cooperation for Foreign Information Access*, US Department of Education, http://www2.ed.gov/programs/iegpsticfia/index.html.

16 J. Naisbitt and P. Aburdene, *Re-inventing the Corporation* (New York: Warner Books, 1985); N. Tichy and M. Devanna, *The Transformational Leader* (New York: John Wiley and Sons, 1986); R. Kilmann and T. Covin, eds, *Corporate Transformation: Revitalizing Organizations for a Competitive World* (San Francisco: Jossey-Bass,

1988); T. Peters, *Thriving on Chaos: Handbook for a Management Revolution* (New York: Alfred A. Knopf, 1987); J. Kotter, *Leading Change* (Cambridge, MA: Harvard Business School Press, 1996).

17 T. Stewart, 'Welcome to the revolution', *Fortune* (13 December 1993): 66–80; C. Farrell, 'The new economic era', *Business Week* (18 November 1994); A. Church and W. Burke, 'Four trends shaping the future of organizations and organization development', *OD Practitioner*, 49 (2017): 14–22; M. Meehan, 'The top trends shaping business for 2017', *Forbes* (16 December 2016).

18 E. Greenberg, M. Hirt and S. Smit, 'The global forces inspiring a new narrative of progress', *McKinsey Quarterly* (April 2017).

19 B. Sims, 'Sustainable Power Corp., L.Sole' agrees to form strategic alliance', June 2008, http://www.biomassmagazine.com/article.jsp?article_id=1704.

20 L. Columbus, 'Roundup of cloud computing forecasts, 2017', *Forbes* (29 April 2017).

21 L. Bradford, 'Biography of an institution', *Journal of Applied Behavioral Science*, 3 (1967): 127; A. Marrow, 'Events leading to the establishment of the National Training Laboratories', *Journal of Applied Behavioral Science*, 3 (1967): 145–50.

22 A. Carnevale, 'The work place realities – in the new global workplace, what exactly do employees need and employers want?', American Association of School Administrators, http://www.aasa.org/SchoolAdministratorArticle.aspx?id=6000.

23 W. French, 'The emergence and early history of organization development with reference to influences upon and interactions among some of the key actors', in *Contemporary Organization Development: Current Thinking and Applications*, ed. D. Warrick (Glenview, IL: Scott, Foresman, 1985): 12–27.

24 R. Likert, 'A technique for the measurement of attitudes', 1932, http://www.voteview.com/pdf/Likert_1932.pdf.

25 F. Mann, 'Studying and creating change', in *The Planning of Change: Readings in the Applied Behavioral Sciences*, eds W. Bennis, K. Benne and R. Chin (New York: Holt, Rinehart and Winston, 1962): 605–15.

26 R. Likert, *The Human Organization* (New York: McGraw-Hill, 1967); S. Seashore and D. Bowers, 'Durability of organizational change', *American Psychologist*, 25 (1970): 227–33; D. Mosley, 'System Four revisited: some new insights', *Organization Development Journal*, 5 (Spring 1987): 19–24.

27 R. Likert, *The Human Organization*, op. cit.

28 M. Arab, M. Tajvar and F. Akbari, 'Selection an appropriate leadership style to direct hospital

manpower', *Iranian Journal of Public Health*, 35
(2006): 64–9.

29 C. Chambers Clark, *Creative Nursing Leadership
and Management* (Sudbury, MA: Jones and Bartlett
Publishers, 2009).

30 A. Rice, *Productivity and Social Organisation:
The Ahmedabad Experiment* (London: Tavistock
Publications, 1958); E. Trist and K. Bamforth, 'Some
social and psychological consequences of the
longwall method of coal-getting', *Human Relations*,
4 (January 1951): 1–38.

31 J. Husband, 'Will enterprise 2.0 drive management
innovation?', April 2008, http://www.backbonemag.
com/Backblog/1_01240801.asp.

32 M. Walton, *The Deming Management Method* (New
York: Dodd, Mead and Company, 1986).

33 J. Juran, *Juran on Leadership for Quality: An
Executive Handbook* (New York: Free Press, 1989).

34 'The quality imperative', *Business Week*, Special
Issue (25 October 1991).

35 M. Jelinek and J. Litterer, 'Why OD must become
strategic', in *Research in Organizational Change
and Development*, 2, eds W. Pasmore and R.
Woodman (Greenwich, CT: JAI Press, 1988):
135–62; P. Buller, 'For successful strategic change:
blend OD practices with strategic management',
Organizational Dynamics (Winter 1988): 42–55; C.
Worley, D. Hitchin and W. Ross, *Integrated Strategic
Change* (Reading, MA: Addison-Wesley, 1996).

36 Worley, Hitchin and Ross, *Integrated Strategic
Change*, op. cit.

37 R. Beckhard and R. Harris, *Organizational
Transitions: Managing Complex Change*, 2nd edn
(Reading, MA: Addison-Wesley, 1987); N. Tichy,
Managing Strategic Change (New York: John Wiley
and Sons, 1983); E. Schein, *Organizational Culture
and Leadership* (San Francisco: Jossey-Bass,
1985); C. Lundberg, 'Working with culture', *Journal
of Organizational Change Management*, 1 (1988):
38–47.

38 D. Miller and P. Freisen, 'Momentum and
revolution in organisation adaptation', *Academy
of Management Journal*, 23 (1980): 591–614;
M. Tushman and E. Romanelli, 'Organizational
evolution: a metamorphosis model of convergence
and reorientation', in *Research in Organizational
Behaviour*, 7, eds L. Cummings and B. Staw
(Greenwich, CT: JAI Press, 1985): 171–222.

39 Beckhard and Harris, *Organizational Transitions*,
op. cit.

40 T. Covin and R. Kilmann, 'Critical issues in large
scale organization change', *Journal of Organizational
Change Management*, 1 (1988): 59–72; A. Mohrman,
S. Mohrman, G. Ledford Jr, T. Cummings and E.
Lawler, eds, *Large Scale Organization Change* (San
Francisco: Jossey-Bass, 1989); W. Torbert, 'Leading
organizational transformation', in *Research in

Organizational Change and Development, 3, eds
R. Woodman and W. Pasmore (Greenwich, CT:
JAI Press, 1989): 83–116; J. Bartunek and M.
Louis, 'The interplay of organization development
and organization transformation', in *Research in
Organizational Change and Development*, 2, eds
W. Pasmore and R. Woodman (Greenwich, CT:
JAI Press, 1988): 97–134; A. Levy and U. Merry,
*Organizational Transformation: Approaches,
Strategies, Theories* (New York: Praeger, 1986).

41 A. Jaeger, 'Organization development and national
culture: where's the fit?', *Academy of Management
Review*, 11 (1986): 178; G. Hofstede, *Culture's
Consequences: International Differences in Work-
Related Values* (London: Sage, 1980); P. Sorensen Jr,
T. Head, N. Mathys, J. Preston and D. Cooperrider,
Global and International Organization Development
(Champaign, IL: Stipes, 1995).

42 C. Argyris and D. Schon, *Organizational Learning*
(Reading, MA: Addison-Wesley, 1978); C. Argyris,
R. Putnam and D. Smith, *Action Science* (San
Francisco: Jossey-Bass, 1985).

43 W. Bennis and B. Nanus, *Leaders* (New York:
Harper and Row, 1985).

44 E. Schein, *Process Consultation: Its Role in
Organization Development* (Reading, MA: Addison-
Wesley, 1969); E. Schein, *Process Consultation,
2: Lessons for Managers and Consultants*
(Reading, MA: Addison-Wesley, 1987); E. Schein,
Organizational Culture and Leadership, 2nd edn
(San Francisco: Jossey-Bass, 1992).

45 Beckhard and Harris, *Organizational Transitions*,
op. cit.

46 R. Tannenbaum and R. Hanna, 'Holding on, letting
go, and moving on: understanding a neglected
perspective on change', in *Human Systems
Development*, eds R. Tannenbaum, N. Margulies
and F. Massarik (San Francisco: Jossey-Bass,
1985): 95–121.

47 W. Burke, *Organization Development: Principles
and Practices* (Boston: Little, Brown, 1982);
W. Burke, *Organization Development: A Normative
View* (Reading, MA: Addison-Wesley, 1987);
W. Burke, 'Organization development: then, now,
and tomorrow', *OD Practitioner*, 27 (1995): 5–13.

48 L. Greiner and V. Schein, *Power and Organizational
Development: Mobilizing Power to Implement
Change* (Reading, MA: Addison-Wesley, 1988).

49 E. Lawler III, *Pay and Organization Development*
(Reading, MA: Addison-Wesley, 1981); E. Lawler
III, *High-Involvement Management* (San Francisco:
Jossey-Bass, 1986).

50 A. Raia and N. Margulies, 'Organization
development: issues, trends, and prospects', in
Human Systems Development, eds R. Tannenbaum,
N. Margulies and F. Massarik (San Francisco:
Jossey-Bass, 1985): 246–72; N. Margulies

and A. Raia, 'Some reflections on the values of organizational development', *Academy of Management OD Newsletter*, 1 (Winter 1988): 9–11.

51 P. Vaill, 'OD as a scientific revolution', in *Contemporary Organization Development: Current Thinking and Applications* (Glenview, IL: Scott, Foresman, 1985): 28–41; C. Lundberg, 'On organisation development interventions: a general systems–cybernetic perspective', in *Systems Theory for Organisational Development*, ed. T. Cummings (Chichester: John Wiley and Sons, 1980): 247–71.

52 L. Brown and J. Covey, 'Development organizations and organization development: toward an expanded paradigm for organization development', in *Research in Organizational Change and Development*, 1, eds R. Woodman and W. Pasmore (Greenwich, CT: JAI Press, 1987): 59–87.

53 T. Cummings and S. Srivastva, *Management of Work: A Socio-Technical Systems Approach* (San Diego: University Associates, 1977); T. Cummings, 'Transorganizational development', in *Research in Organizational Behavior*, 6, eds B. Staw and L. Cummings (Greenwich, CT: JAI Press, 1984): 367–422; T. Cummings and S. Mohrman, 'Self-designing organizations: towards implementing quality-of-work-life innovations', in *Research in Organizational Change and Development*, 1, eds R. Woodman and W. Pasmore (Greenwich, CT: JAI Press, 1987): 275–310.

54 M. Widen, 'Sociotechnical systems ideas as public policy in Norway: empowering participation through worker managed change', *Journal of Applied Behavioral Science*, 22 (1986): 239–55.

55 W. Pasmore, C. Haldeman and A. Shani, 'Sociotechnical systems: a North American reflection on empirical studies in North America', *Human Relations*, 32 (1982): 1179–204; W. Pasmore and J. Sherwood, *Sociotechnical Systems: A Source Book* (San Diego: University Associates, 1978); J. Porras, *Stream Analysis: A Powerful Way to Diagnose and Manage Organizational Change* (Reading, MA: Addison-Wesley, 1987); J. Porras, P. Robertson and L. Goldman, 'Organization development: theory, practice, and research', in *Handbook of Industrial and Organizational Psychology*, 2nd edn, ed. M. Dunnette (Chicago: Rand McNally, 1990).

56 P. Block, *Flawless Consulting* (Austin, TX: Learning Concepts, 1981); P. Block, *The Empowered Manager: Positive Political Skills at Work* (San Francisco:

Jossey-Bass, 1987); P. Block, *Stewardship* (San Francisco: Berrett-Koehler, 1994).

57 K. Murrell, 'Organization development experiences and lessons in the United Nations development program', *Organization Development Journal*, 12 (1994): 1–16; J. Vogt and K. Murrell, *Empowerment in Organizations* (San Diego: Pfeiffer and Company, 1990); J. Preston and L. DuToit, 'Endemic violence in South Africa: an OD solution applied to two educational settings', *International Journal of Public Administration*, 16 (1993): 1767–91; J. Preston, L. DuToit and I. Barber, 'A potential model of transformational change applied to South Africa', in *Research in Organizational Change and Development*, 9 (Greenwich, CT: JAI Press, 1998).

58 S. Mohrman, S. Cohen and A. Mohrman, *Designing Team-Based Organizations* (San Francisco: Jossey-Bass, 1995); S. Cohen and G. Ledford Jr, 'The effectiveness of self-managing teams: a quasi-experiment', *Human Relations*, 47 (1994): 13–43; G. Ledford and E. Lawler, 'Research on employee participation: beating a dead horse?', *Academy of Management Review*, 19 (1994): 633–6; G. Ledford, E. Lawler and S. Mohrman, 'The quality circle and its variations', in *Productivity in Organizations: New Perspectives from Industrial and Organizational Psychology*, eds J. Campbell, R. Campbell and associates (San Francisco: Jossey-Bass, 1988); A. Mohrman, G. Ledford Jr, S. Mohrman, E. Lawler III and T. Cummings, *Large Scale Organization Change* (San Francisco: Jossey-Bass, 1989).

59 D. Cooperrider and T. Thachankary, 'Building the global civic culture: making our lives count', in *Global and International Organization Development*, eds P. Sorensen Jr, T. Head, N. Mathys, J. Preston and D. Cooperrider (Champaign, IL: Stipes, 1995): 282–306; D. Cooperrider, 'Positive image, positive action: the affirmative basis for organising', in *Appreciative Management and Leadership*, eds S. Srivastva, D. Cooperrider and associates (San Francisco, CA: Jossey-Bass, 1990); D. Cooperrider and S. Srivastva, 'Appreciative inquiry in organizational life', in *Research in Organizational Change and Development*, 1, eds R. Woodman and W. Pasmore (Greenwich, CT: JAI Press, 1987): 129–70.

60 S. Marinos, 'Getting down to business beyond 2000', *The Age* (24 February 1998): 6.

61 C. Rance, 'Recognition for Casey learning system', *The Age* (20 September 1997): 12.60A; A. Hepworth, 'Yearning for more learning', *Australian Financial Review* (5 June 1984): 4.

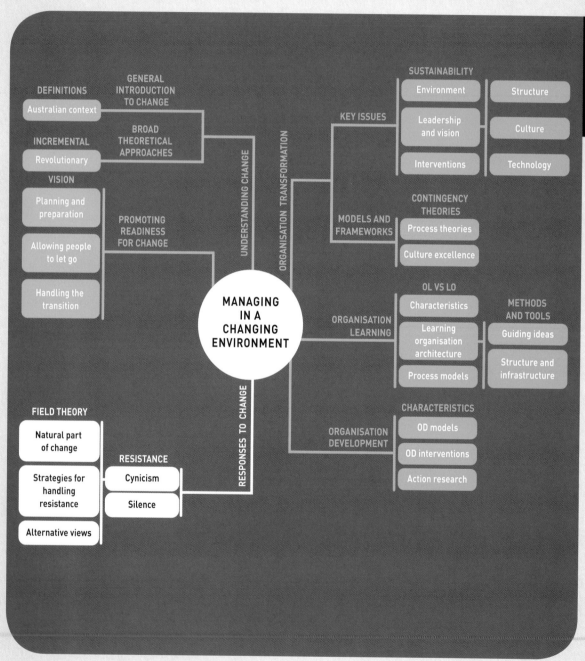

DEFINITIONS
Australian context

GENERAL
INTRODUCTION
TO CHANGE

BROAD
THEORETICAL
APPROACHES

INCREMENTAL
Revolutionary

VISION
Planning and
preparation

Allowing people
to let go

Handling the
transition

PROMOTING
READINESS
FOR CHANGE

UNDERSTANDING CHANGE

ORGANISATION TRANSFORMATION

MANAGING
IN A
CHANGING
ENVIRONMENT

KEY ISSUES

SUSTAINABILITY
Environment

Leadership
and vision

Interventions

Structure

Culture

Technology

MODELS AND
FRAMEWORKS

CONTINGENCY
THEORIES
Process theories

Culture excellence

ORGANISATION
LEARNING

OL VS LO
Characteristics

Learning
organisation
architecture

Process models

METHODS
AND TOOLS
Guiding ideas

Structure and
infrastructure

RESPONSES TO CHANGE

FIELD THEORY
Natural part
of change

Strategies for
handling
resistance

Alternative views

RESISTANCE
Cynicism

Silence

ORGANISATION
DEVELOPMENT

CHARACTERISTICS
OD models

OD interventions

Action research

Source: Adapted from D. Waddell, *E-Business in Australia: Concepts and Cases*, Pearson Education Australia, 2002.

PART 2

THE ENVIRONMENT
OF CHANGE

Part 2 comprises Chapters 2, 3, 4 and 5. The main concepts and themes emerge as shown in the table below, which also indicates main chapter linkages. Note that the links are within Part 2 and extend into each of Parts 3, 4 and 5 because change concepts generally interrelate through their causes and effects.

THEME OR CONCEPT	CONNECTED WITH MATERIAL IN OTHER CHAPTERS
Models of planned change	Ch 2, 5, 6, 7, 8, 9
Critique and resistance to change	Ch 2, 4, 6, 7, 8, 9
Organisation development (OD) practitioners	Ch 3, 5, 7
Values and ethics	Ch 3, 10, 11
Organisational culture	Ch 4, 6, 7, 9
Diagnosis and measurement	Ch 5, 8, 11

Colin May

Business Development Manager/
Suprico International

Sailing as a metaphor for change

Mounting the crest of a small wave in the Southern Ocean, half a kilometre off the coast of Port Fairy in Victoria, Colin May realises how similar the experience of navigating and negotiating changeable waters in a comparatively insignificant yacht is to the many sheers and shifts of his own global career. Of anyone's career, in fact.

Sailing was conceived and developed as an intricate art well before time clocks were invented. The very concept of time has historically been a general one emergent from natural rhythms and purely organic needs. The oceans spoke and sailors had to listen and adapt. It is only recently that mechanical time became embedded into the machines – digital machines – that now regulate most human systems around the globe and people have become bewitched into thinking that regimentation and control of the natural environment is how we are meant to handle change. Like a siren's song, the call of the computer today distracts the sailors of life into pursuits that can sometimes ignore the real challenges of their predicaments.

'That's the nature of boating,' Colin muses as another wave lifts our vessel and we plummet purposefully down into the subsequent trough. He adjusts his weight and strains on a sail rope to be sure the little craft is nosed in the best direction. 'I'm perfectly happy when circumstances dictate that change should occur, because I can then observe, adapt and make the necessary adjustments to ensure success in the new situation.' Just then, another crew on our boat, having not heard the conversation, calls to Colin from the stern suggesting a different way of tending to the sail. After some testing and further dialogue, a modified way of doing the job was settled upon. Afterwards, Colin's wry grin precedes further musings: 'So dealing with change imposed by the environment is something I'm comfortable with. But there is a different kind of change that frustrates the hell out of me, and that is when people change plans when it is not absolutely necessary. You're basically overlaying another change on top of the ones you have no choice over.' By now the boat is heading back towards shore and the conversation lapses until we are back on land in a cafe overlooking the same patch of ocean just sailed.

The turbulent sea of recent experience appears pristine from atop the dunes and behind the plate glass that protects our coffee and sandwiches from wind and sand. Colin explains more about his career and the changes he's had to navigate. One transition following the achievement of his Manchester Business School MBA was to move himself from his home in the United Kingdom to live and work in the United Arab Emirates in Dubai at the technology systems solution company Suprico International. He found himself managing systems contracts with banks, call centres and merchants of all kinds in Africa, the Middle East and parts of Asia. As Business Development Manager, responsible for information technology (IT) products and services, and associated customer relations, operations and strategy, he worked closely with IT and the very mechanical time we have just been musing about. This 15-year period of his life taught him much about the two types of change he mentioned on the boat. Adapting to the things imposed by the broader environment is strategic and manageable. Tending to the changes superimposed unnecessarily by others is also important though often stress-inducing.

We discuss IT programming and the cascading effects of changes made in IT systems. Often a programmer, without thinking through all the consequences, is tempted to 'improve' a system with a seemingly straightforward or trivial change. However, a ripple of confusion and frustration can affect all users of the system as they encounter the system's changed behaviour. Delays in routine tasks that unexpectedly become learning challenges, frantic requests for clarification, inaccuracies in labels, guides and training manuals, and general exasperation can take a significant toll on productivity and morale. This can be costly, perhaps dwarfing completely any benefits of the improvement. On the other hand, IT can solve some problems really effectively when it is properly designed, planned and implemented carefully with due consideration for the concerns and priorities of the people affected. Success can be as much about people and communication as about the technicalities.

Soon Colin reflects on his decision to move from Dubai to Australia. His first country move was when he was on his own, whereas this second life and career shift to Australia was a decision that included his life partner. Making a big change decision that would be life-changing for his spouse weighed heavily on his mind. All has turned out well, but the process for addressing the change situation with a significant other was markedly more intense than making the earlier life change with consequences mainly for himself.

Colin has worked in Australia as manager of adult education and community projects in local government and higher education sectors. He describes his career as a journey through life rather than something especially planned. However, the discussion moves to the very nature of change as it involves planned and unplanned aspects. The sailing metaphor emerges again. At the helm of the boat of his career, Colin is appropriately methodical and particular about the ways things are done. There are systems and procedures that ensure safety and allow for proper navigation of the turbulent environment. It is this very focus upon routine that enables a tempered expertise to enter in, especially in situations of sudden change when an immediate reaction is required. It is the fact of training and preparation that enables an appropriately measured response in the midst of any new situation of uncertainty and turbulence. So coping with chaos is dependent upon a precondition of systematic preparation. Even when the system itself has to be changed, it is knowledge of how systems are built and maintained that enables innovation or replacement of the system to happen successfully. Lives and livelihood depend upon getting the balance right.

As we finish the last crumbs on our plates and the clock on our phones tells us it is time to go, we gaze briefly again at the inscrutable ocean with its inexorable rhythms combined with flashes of turbulence. You plan what you can and you plan around what you can't. The lessons of yachting have been really useful today and probably for all times of change.

UNDERSTANDING CHANGE

After studying this chapter, you should be able to:

1   Understand and evaluate the theories of planned change.

2   Apply the general model of planned change to current situations.

3   Summarise and assess the relevance of the different types of planned change.

4   Critically analyse planned change and construct a contemporary definition of planned change.

KEY TERMS

Practitioner

Client

Consultant

Quasi-stationary equilibrium

Positive model

Behavioural science

Convention

Conceptualisation

The increasing pace of global, economic and technological development makes change an inevitable feature of organisational life. However, change that happens to an organisation can be distinguished from change that is planned by organisation members. In this book, the term 'change' generally refers to planned change. Organisation development[1] (OD) aims to bring about planned change in order to increase an organisation's effectiveness. It is generally initiated and implemented by managers, often with the help of an OD practitioner from inside or outside the organisation. Organisations can use planned change to solve problems, to learn from experience, to adapt to external environmental changes, to improve performance and to influence future changes.

All approaches to OD rely on some theory about planned change. These theories describe the different stages through which planned change[2] may be effected in organisations and explain the temporal process of applying OD methods to help organisation members manage change. In this chapter, we first describe and compare three major theories of organisation change: Lewin's change model, the action research model and the positive model. These three approaches, which have received considerable attention in the field, offer different concepts of planned change. Next, we present a general model of planned change that integrates the earlier models and incorporates recent conceptual developments in OD. This model has broad applicability to many types of planned change efforts. We then discuss different types of change, and how the change process can vary according to the situation. Finally, several critiques of planned change are presented.

THEORIES OF PLANNED CHANGE

Conceptions of planned change have tended to focus on how to implement change in organisations.[3] Called 'theories of changing', these frameworks describe the activities that must take place in order for people to initiate and carry out successful organisational change. In this section, we describe and compare three different theories of changing: Lewin's change model, the action research model and the positive model. These frameworks have received widespread attention in OD and serve as the primary basis for a general model of planned change.

LEWIN'S CHANGE MODEL

One of the early fundamental models of planned change was provided by Kurt Lewin.[4] He conceived of change as a modification of those forces that keep a system's behaviour stable; specifically, the level of behaviour at any moment in time is the result of two sets of forces: those striving to maintain the status quo and those pushing for change. When both sets of forces are about equal, current levels of behaviour are maintained in what Lewin termed a state of 'quasi-stationary equilibrium'. To change that state, one can increase those forces pushing for change, decrease those forces that maintain the current state or apply some combination of both. For example, in a government setting, outcomes or recommendations of Royal Commission reports will often challenge that 'quasi-stationary equilibrium': an expectation will be expressed that the level of performance of a departmental work group needs to rise, or that the level of accountability of a supervisor or a person in a position of influence needs to increase, or modify, thereby altering the status quo. A move in one direction will invariably prompt a similar shift in the other (the 'domino effect'). Lewin suggested that modifying those forces that maintain the status quo produces less tension and resistance than increasing forces for change, and consequently is a more effective strategy for change.

Lewin viewed this change process as consisting of three steps, which are shown in **Figure 2.1(A)**:

1 *Unfreezing.* This step usually involves reducing those forces that maintain the organisation's behaviour at its present level. Unfreezing is sometimes accomplished through a process of 'psychological disconfirmation'. By introducing information that shows discrepancies between the behaviours desired by organisation members and

those behaviours currently exhibited, members can be motivated to engage in change activities.[5] (To use a metaphor, it is like reducing an ice cube to water.)

2   *Moving.* This step shifts the behaviour of the organisation, department or individual to a new level. It involves the development of new behaviours, values and attitudes through changes in organisational structures and processes. (This is like placing the water into a mould.)

3   *Refreezing.* This step stabilises the organisation at a new state of equilibrium. It is frequently accomplished through the use of supporting mechanisms that reinforce the new organisational state, such as organisational culture, norms, policies and structures. (Here the water is refrozen into a particular shape of ice cube.)

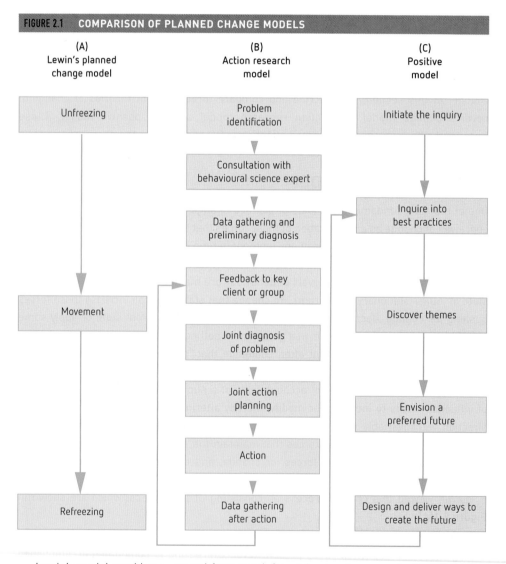

FIGURE 2.1   COMPARISON OF PLANNED CHANGE MODELS

Lewin's model provides a general framework for understanding organisational change. Because the three steps of change are relatively broad, considerable effort has gone into elaborating them. For example, the planning model (developed by Lippitt, Watson and Westley) arranges Lewin's model into seven steps: scouting, entry, diagnosis (unfreezing), planning, action (movement), stabilisation and evaluation, and termination of the process (refreezing).[6] However, this model remains closely identified with the field of OD, and is used to illustrate how other types of change can be implemented. For example, Lewin's three-step model has been used to explain how information technologies can be implemented more effectively.[7]

ACTION RESEARCH MODEL

The action research model[8] focuses on planned change as a cyclical process in which initial research about the organisation provides information to guide subsequent action. Then the results of the action are assessed to provide further information that will guide further action, and so on. This iterative cycle of research and action involves considerable collaboration between organisation members and OD practitioners. It places heavy emphasis on data gathering and diagnosis prior to action planning and implementation, as well as careful evaluation of the results after action has been taken. It is continuous: no action without research, no research without action.

Action research is traditionally aimed both at helping specific organisations to implement planned change and at developing more general knowledge that can be applied to other settings.[9] Although action research was originally developed to have this dual focus on change and knowledge, it has been adapted to OD efforts in which the major emphasis is on planned change.[10] **Figure 2.1(B)** shows the cyclical phases of planned change as defined by the action research model. There are eight main steps:

1 *Problem identification.* This stage usually begins when a key executive in the organisation, or someone with power and influence, senses that the organisation has one or more problems that might be alleviated with the help of an OD **practitioner** (the investigation for change can be internal or external). The transitioning of governments often provides the avenue for OD to take place, with OD practitioners (if appointed) at opposite ends of the spectrum competing to implement change that is designed to secure electorates for their respective parties.

   Practitioner: a person actively engaged in the change process, usually a member of the organisation.

   Client: a person/organisation using the services of a change agent either from within or outside the organisation.

2 *Consultation with a behavioural science expert.* During the initial contact, the OD practitioner and the **client** carefully assist each other. The practitioner has his or her own normative, developmental theory or frame of reference and must be conscious of those assumptions and values.[11] Sharing them with the client (an organisation may designate an individual within the organisation to take the role of OD change agent) from the beginning establishes an open and collaborative atmosphere.

3 *Data gathering and preliminary diagnosis.* This stage is usually completed by the OD practitioner, often in conjunction with organisation members. It involves gathering appropriate information and analysing it to determine the underlying causes of organisational problems. The four basic methods of gathering data are interviews, process observation, questionnaires and organisational performance data (unfortunately, often overlooked). One approach to diagnosis begins with observation, proceeds to a

semi-structured interview and concludes with a questionnaire to measure precisely the problems identified by the earlier steps.[12] When gathering diagnostic information, it is possible that OD practitioners may influence members from whom they are collecting data, especially if the change agent is a member of the organisation. In OD, 'every action on the part of the ... **consultant** constitutes an intervention' that will have some effect on the organisation.[13] While an important step in the process of change, involving members in order to collect data confirms that a potential problem has been identified and, unless communicated and managed well, may have a negative impact on the organisation. This step needs to be very carefully implemented as more 'damage' could occur.

Consultant: a person who provides expert advice professionally, usually outside an organisation.

4   *Feedback to key client or group.* Because action research is a collaborative activity, the diagnostic data are fed back to the client, usually in a group or team meeting. The feedback step, in which members are given the information gathered by the OD practitioner, helps them to determine the strengths and weaknesses of the organisation or the department under study – more importantly if the preliminary diagnosis is correct. The consultant provides the client with all relevant and useful data. Obviously, the practitioner will protect those sources of information and, where deemed necessary, withhold data if it is perceived that the information would make the client overly defensive. This may be considered as manipulation of data to suggest a preconceived conclusion.

5   *Joint diagnosis of problem.* At this point, members discuss the feedback and explore with the OD practitioner whether they want to work on identified problems. A close interrelationship exists among data gathering, feedback and diagnosis as the consultant summarises the basic data from the client members and presents the data to them for validation and further diagnosis. An important point to remember, as Schein suggests, is that the action research process is very different from the doctor–patient model, in which the consultant comes in, makes a diagnosis and prescribes a solution. Schein notes that the failure to establish a common frame of reference in the client–consultant relationship may lead to a faulty diagnosis or to a communications gap whereby the client is sometimes 'unwilling to believe the diagnosis or accept the prescription'. He believes 'most companies have drawers full of reports by consultants, each loaded with diagnoses and recommendations which are either not understood or not accepted by the "patient"'.[14] For some organisations, the process of recruiting an OD practitioner to undertake the action research model is sufficient to address the push for change; however, it is possible the client has no intention of following through or addressing the outcomes of that research. Hence the skill credibility of the change agent is extremely important and not to be used for political reasons.

6   *Joint action planning.* Next, the OD practitioner and the client members jointly agree on further actions to be taken. This is the beginning of the moving process (described in Lewin's change model), as the organisation decides on how best to reach a different **quasi-stationary equilibrium**. At this stage, the specific action to be taken depends on the culture, technology and environment of the organisation; the diagnosis of the problem; and the time and expense of the intervention. A 'needs analysis' should be done to determine the value of the change process.

Quasi-stationary equilibrium: appearing to be stable and unmoving but subtly changing.

7   *Action.* This stage involves the actual change from one organisational state to another. It may include installing new methods and procedures, reorganising structures and work designs and reinforcing new behaviours. These actions typically cannot be implemented immediately, but require a transition period as the organisation moves from the present to a desired future state.[15] Usually it is the most expensive part of the process as it is time-consuming, psychologically challenging and costly.

8   *Data gathering after action.* Because action research is a cyclical process, data must also be gathered after the action has been taken in order to measure and determine the effects of the action and to feed the results back to the organisation. This, in turn, should lead to rediagnosis and new action. This data gathering is an essential step for non-government organisations (NGOs), not only as a requirement for donors but also to inform business cases for continuing and/or identifying new projects.

Apply your learning 2.1 has extracts from a paper from two research academics who used action research in their studies.

IMPLEMENTING ORGANIZATIONAL CHANGE USING ACTION RESEARCH IN TWO ASIAN CULTURES

APPLY
YOUR
LEARNING
2.1

This paper is based on organizational change projects implemented by two managers, who used action research in their own organizations for their doctoral studies ... One project was carried out to prepare the engineering division of a Japanese multinational company in Singapore to expand its capability to carry out global projects by making large-scale changes in its structure and processes. The other project was carried out in a very large Indian bureaucracy to introduce total quality management in one part of this organization. The paper will first introduce the concepts of action research, action learning, and action science in management research.

...

The authors argue that action research, as an approach for organizational change, will find acceptance in societies that are systemic in their understanding of the world. Both Hindu and Buddhist philosophies are systemic ... and so in the countries where these philosophies are dominant, the employees will find action research an acceptable approach for learning in their organizations.

...

Action research has proved to be an effective and responsive methodology to implement organizational change in both cases, even though the ideas used to effect the change originated from the West ... The project management environment is becoming increasingly complex and often project managers have been asked to manage organizational change projects. While normative and reductionist approaches are useful in managing projects, it is becoming essential for project managers to learn holistic and responsive processes like action research and action learning to enhance their effectiveness as project managers and deliver benefits to stakeholders. Knowing about action science will also help them to improve their interpersonal effectiveness as leaders in a project environment.

»

»

Critical thinking questions

1   These authors compared their results from using action research in two different organisations in two different cultures. How did they go about this and what was their conclusion?

2   What do the terms 'normative' and 'reductionist' mean?

Contemporary adaptations to action research

The action research model underlies most current approaches to planned change and is often identified with the practice of OD. Action research has recently been extended to new settings and applications, and consequently researchers and practitioners have made the requisite adaptations to its basic framework.[16]

Trends in the application of action research include the movement from smaller subunits of organisations to total systems and communities.[17] In these larger contexts, action research is more complex and political than in smaller settings. Therefore, the action research cycle is coordinated across multiple change processes and includes a diversity of stakeholders who have an interest in the organisation.

Action research is also increasingly being applied in international settings, particularly in developing nations.[18] Embedded within the action research model, however, are Western assumptions about change. For example, action research traditionally views change more linearly than Eastern cultures, and it treats the change process more collaboratively than Latin American and African countries.[19] To achieve success in these settings, action research needs to be tailored to fit the organisations' cultural assumptions.

Finally, action research is increasingly being applied to promote social change and innovation.[20] This is demonstrated most clearly in community-development and global social-change projects.[21] These applications are heavily value-laden and seek to redress imbalances in power and resource allocations across different groups. Action researchers tend to play an activist role in the change process, which is often hectic and conflicted. An example of social-change projects is those that advocate for gender equality or providing access to education to vulnerable and/or minority groups. These action researchers use evidence-based literature to drive the change, which is significantly bigger than the capacity of the organisation to deliver on its own.

In view of these general trends, contemporary applications of action research have substantially increased the degree of member involvement in the change process. This contrasts with traditional approaches to planned change where consultants carried out most of the change activities, with the agreement and collaboration of management.[22] Although consultant-dominated change still persists in OD, there is a growing tendency to involve organisation members in learning about their organisation and how to change it. Referred to as 'participatory action research',[23] 'action learning',[24] 'action science'[25] or 'self-design',[26] this approach to planned change emphasises the need for organisation members to learn about it first-hand if they are to gain the knowledge and skills to change the organisation. In today's complex and changing business environment, some argue that

OD must go beyond solving particular problems to helping members gain the necessary competence to continually change and improve the organisation.[27]

In this modification of action research, the role of OD consultants[28] is to work with members to facilitate the learning process. Both parties are 'co-learners' in diagnosing the organisation, designing changes and implementing and assessing them.[29] Neither party dominates the change process. Rather, each participant brings unique information and expertise to the situation, and together they combine their resources to learn how to change the organisation. Consultants, for example, know how to design diagnostic instruments and OD interventions, while organisation members have 'local' knowledge about the organisation and how it functions. Each participant learns from the change process. Organisation members learn how to change their organisation, to refine and improve it. OD consultants learn how to facilitate complex organisational change and learning.

The action research model will continue to be the dominant methodological basis for planned change in the near future. But the basic philosophy of science on which traditional action research operates is also evolving and is described below.

THE POSITIVE MODEL

The third model of change, the **positive model**, is the promotion of a 'positive' approach to planned change.[30] This model focuses on what the organisation is doing right. It represents an important departure from Lewin's model and the action research process, which are primarily deficit-based, focusing on the organisation's problems and how they can be solved so it functions better. The positive application of planned change helps members understand their

> **Positive model**: a perspective of change that views change as constructive and uses an integrative approach to change. It uses current best practice from the organisation to help the change process.

organisation when it is working at its best and builds off those capabilities to achieve even better results. This approach to change suggests that all organisations are to some degree effective and that planned change should focus on the 'best of what is'.[31] It is consistent with a growing movement in the social sciences called 'positive organisational scholarship', which focuses on positive dynamics in organisations that give rise to extraordinary outcomes.[32] Considerable research on expectation effects supports this positive approach to planned change.[33] It suggests that people tend to act in ways that make their expectations occur; a positive vision of what the organisation can become can energise and direct behaviour to make that expectation come about.

The positive model has been applied to planned change primarily through a process called appreciative inquiry (AI).[34] As a 'reformist and rebellious' form of social constructionism, appreciative inquiry explicitly infuses a positive value orientation into analysing and changing organisations.[35] Social constructionism assumes that organisation members' shared experiences and interactions influence how they perceive the organisation and behave in it.[36] Because such shared meaning can determine how members approach planned change, appreciative inquiry encourages a positive orientation towards how change is conceived and managed. It promotes broad member involvement in creating a shared vision about the organisation's positive potential.[37] That shared appreciation provides a powerful and guiding image of what the organisation could be.

The positive model of planned change involves five phases that are depicted in **Figure 2.1(C)**.

1 *Initiate the inquiry.*[38] This first phase determines the subject of change. It emphasises member involvement to identify the organisational issue they have the most energy to address. For example, members can choose to look for successful male–female collaboration (as opposed to sexual discrimination), instances of customer satisfaction (as opposed to customer dissatisfaction), particularly effective work teams or product development processes that brought new ideas to market especially fast. If the focus of inquiry is real and vital to organisation members, the change process itself will take on these positive attributes.

2 *Inquiry into best practices.*[39] This phase involves gathering information about the 'best of what is' in the organisation. If the topic is organisational innovation, then members help to develop an interview protocol that collects stories of new ideas that were developed and implemented in the organisation. The interviews are conducted by organisation members; they interview each other and tell stories of innovation in which they have personally been involved. These stories are pulled together to create a pool of information describing the organisation as an innovative system.

3 *Discover the themes.* Here, members examine the stories, both large and small, to identify a set of themes representing the common dimensions of people's experiences. For example, organisations are now asking new employees, during their induction, to provide feedback on how they think the organisation is functioning and if there is anything they would be doing differently. If there are recurring themes, they use this information as a catalyst to generate further discussion. No theme is too small to be represented; it is important that all of the underlying mechanisms that helped to generate and support the themes are described. The themes represent the basis for moving from 'what is' to 'what could be'.

4 *Envision a preferred future.* Members then examine the identified themes, challenge the status quo and describe a compelling future. Based on the organisation's successful past, members collectively visualise the organisation's future and develop 'possibility propositions' – statements that bridge the organisation's current best practices with ideal possibilities for future organising. These propositions should present a truly exciting, provocative and possible picture of the future. Based on these possibilities, members identify the relevant stakeholders and critical organisation processes that must be aligned to support the emergence of the envisioned future. The vision becomes a statement of 'what should be'. As George Bernard Shaw has often been quoted as saying, some people see things as they are and ask why, whereas others see things as they should be and ask why not. Such an approach encourages people to think in terms of potential (or innovatively) rather than relying on the past.

5 *Design and deliver ways to create the future.* The final phase involves the design and delivery of ways to create the future. It describes the activities and creates the plans necessary to bring about the vision. It proceeds to action and assessment phases similar to those of action research described previously. Members make changes, assess the results, create necessary adjustments and so on as they move the organisation

towards the vision and sustain 'what will be'. The process is continued by renewing the conversations about the best of what is.

Yesterday's organisational structure is not necessarily appropriate for today's business environment. Markets change, as do client needs. Businesses need to ensure that their structures and skill sets are relevant to contemporary needs. To successfully implement change, it is vital that management is fully consulted and involved in the identification of market opportunities and planning of effective changes to take advantage of those opportunities;[40] for example, the emergence of STEM in education, which is to prepare the next generation for a more flexible workplace.

COMPARISONS OF CHANGE MODEL

All three models – Lewin's change model,[41] the action research model and the positive model – describe the phases by which planned change occurs in organisations.[42] As shown in **Figure 2.1**, the models overlap in that their emphases on action to implement organisational change are preceded by a preliminary stage (unfreezing, diagnosis or initiate the inquiry) and are followed by a closing stage (refreezing or evaluation). Moreover, all three approaches emphasise the application of **behavioural science** knowledge, involve organisation members in the change process and recognise that any interaction between a consultant and an organisation constitutes an intervention that may affect the organisation. However, Lewin's change model differs from the other two in that it focuses on the general process of planned change, rather than on specific OD activities.

Behavioural science: the scientific study of human behaviour.

Lewin's model and the action research model differ from the positive approach in terms of the level of involvement of the participants and the focus of change. Lewin's model and traditional action research models emphasise the role of the consultant with limited member involvement in the change process. Contemporary applications of action research and the positive model, on the other hand, treat both consultants and participants as co-learners who are heavily involved in planned change (more facilitative than directional). In addition, Lewin's model and action research are more concerned with outcomes (that is, fixing problems) than with focusing on what the organisation does well and leveraging those strengths (processes).

GENERAL MODEL OF PLANNED CHANGE

The three theories outlined above suggest a general framework for planned change, as shown in **Figure 2.2**. The framework describes the basic activities that practitioners and organisation members jointly carry out in OD. The arrows connecting the different activities in the model show the typical sequence of events, from entering and contracting, to diagnosing, to planning and implementing change, to evaluating and institutionalising change. The lines connecting the activities emphasise that organisational change is not a straightforward, linear process, but involves considerable overlap and feedback among the activities. These four major change activities are discussed in more detail in later chapters.

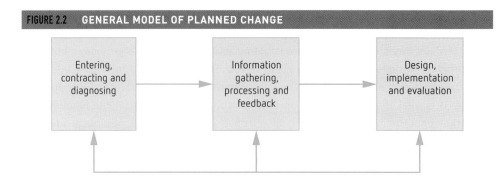

FIGURE 2.2   GENERAL MODEL OF PLANNED CHANGE

ENTERING AND CONTRACTING

The first set of activities in planned change concerns entering and contracting. These help managers decide whether they want to engage further in a planned change program and commit resources to such a process. Entering an organisation involves gathering initial data to understand the problems or opportunities facing the organisation. Once this information has been collected, the problems are discussed with managers and other organisation members in order to develop a contract or agreement to engage in planned change. The contract spells out future change activities, the resources that will be committed to the process and how OD practitioners and organisation members will be involved. In many cases, organisations do not get beyond this early stage of planned change because disagreements about the need for change surface, resource constraints are encountered or other methods for change appear more feasible. When OD is used in non-traditional and international settings, the entering and contracting process must be sensitive to the context in which the change is taking place.

DIAGNOSING

In this stage of planned change, the client system is unbiasedly and transparently studied. Diagnosis can focus on understanding organisational problems, including their causes and consequences, or on identifying the organisation's positive attributes. The diagnostic process is one of the most important activities in OD. It includes choosing an appropriate model for understanding the organisation, and gathering, analysing and feeding back information to managers and organisation members about the problems or opportunities. Even if a problem is not found, the process is part of the quality cycle.

For a detailed description of gathering, reviewing and analysing data, see Chapter 5.

Diagnostic models for analysing problems explore three levels of activities. Organisation problems represent the most complex level of analysis and involve the total system. Group-level problems are associated with departmental and group effectiveness, and individual-level problems involve how jobs are designed. Gathering, analysing and relaying data are the central change activities in diagnosis. Chapter 5 describes how data can be gathered through interviews, observations, survey instruments or from archival sources such as meeting minutes and organisation charts. It also explains how data can be reviewed and analysed, and the process of feeding back diagnostic data is described. Organisation members, often in collaboration with an OD practitioner, jointly discuss the data and their implications for change.

PLANNING AND IMPLEMENTING CHANGE

In this stage, organisation members and practitioners jointly plan and implement OD interventions. They design interventions to improve the organisation and make action plans to implement them. There are several criteria for designing interventions, including the organisation's readiness for change, its current change capability, its culture and power distributions, and the change agent's skills and abilities. Depending upon the outcomes of diagnosis, there are four major types of interventions in OD:

1   human process interventions at the individual, group and total system levels

2   interventions that modify an organisation's structure and technology

3   human resource interventions that seek to improve member performance and wellness

4   strategic interventions that involve managing the organisation's relationship to its external environment and the internal structure and processes necessary to support a business strategy.

Implementing interventions is concerned with managing the change process. It includes motivating change, creating a desired future vision of the organisation, developing political support, managing the transition towards the vision, and sustaining momentum for change and institutionalising the outcome with preparedness for ongoing processes and maintenance.

EVALUATING AND INSTITUTIONALISING CHANGE

This last stage in planned change involves an evaluation of the effects of the intervention and management of the institutionalisation of successful change programs. Feedback to organisation members about the intervention's results provides information about whether the changes should be continued, modified or suspended. Institutionalising successful changes involves reinforcing them through feedback, rewards and training. This is often the most important step, as it confirms the process and may be used as a stepping stone to ongoing improvement. Change never ends.

DIFFERENT TYPES OF PLANNED CHANGE

The general model of planned change describes how the OD process typically unfolds in organisations. In actual practice, the different phases are not nearly as orderly as the model implies. OD practitioners tend to modify or adjust the stages to fit the needs of the situation. Steps in planned change can be implemented in a variety of ways that depend on the client's needs and goals, the change agent's skills and values and the organisation's context. Therefore, it is clear that planned change can vary enormously from one situation to another.

To understand these differences better, planned change can be contrasted across situations on three key dimensions: the magnitude of organisational change, the degree to which the client system is organised and whether the setting is domestic or international.

MAGNITUDE OF CHANGE

Planned change efforts can be characterised as falling along a continuum, ranging from incremental changes that involve fine-tuning the organisation to quantum changes that entail fundamentally altering how it operates.[43] Incremental changes tend to involve limited dimensions and levels of the organisation, such as the decision-making processes of work groups. They occur within the context of the organisation's existing business strategy, structure and culture, and are aimed at improving the status quo. Quantum changes, on the other hand, are directed at significantly altering how the organisation operates. They tend to involve several organisational dimensions, including structure, culture, reward systems, information processes and work design. They also involve changing multiple levels of the organisation, from top-level management through departments and work groups to individual jobs.

Planned change has traditionally been applied in situations that involve incremental change, often when the environment is stable and all is going well. Organisations in the 1960s and 1970s were mainly concerned with fine-tuning their bureaucratic structures by resolving many of the social problems that emerged with increasing size and complexity. In these situations, planned change involves a relatively bounded set of problem-solving activities. OD practitioners are typically contracted by managers to help solve specific problems in particular organisational systems, such as poor communication among members of a work team or high absenteeism among shop-floor employees in a production facility. Diagnostic and change activities tend to be limited to these issues, although additional problems may be uncovered and may need to be addressed. Similarly, the change process tends to focus on those organisational systems that have specific problems, and it generally ends when the problems are resolved. Of course, the change agent may be contracted to help solve additional problems.

For a detailed description of planned change, see Chapter 1.

In recent years, OD has been increasingly concerned with quantum change: As the external environment becomes more chaotic and unpredictable, organisations need to be flexible and adaptive. As described in Chapter 1, the greater competitiveness and uncertainty of today's business environment have caused a growing number of organisations to drastically alter the way in which they operate. In these situations, planned change is more complex, extensive and long-term than when applied to incremental change.[44] Because quantum change involves most features and levels of the organisation, it is typically driven from the top of the organisation, where corporate strategy and values are set. Change agents help senior managers create a vision of a desired future organisation and energise movement in that direction. They also help executives develop structures for managing the transition from the present to the future organisation. This may include, for example, a variety of overlapping steering committees and redesign teams. Staff experts may also redesign many features of the organisation, such as performance measures, rewards, planning processes, work designs and information systems.

Because of the complexity and extensiveness of quantum change,[45] OD professionals often work in teams that consist of members with different yet complementary expertise. The consulting relationship persists over relatively long time periods and includes a great deal of renegotiation and experimentation among consultants and managers. The boundaries of the change effort are more uncertain and diffuse than in incremental change, making diagnosis and change seem more like discovery than problem solving. (Complex strategic and transformational types of change are described in more detail in later chapters.)

It is important to emphasise that quantum change may or may not be developmental in nature. Organisations may drastically alter their strategic direction and way of operating without significantly developing their capacity to solve problems and achieve both high performance and quality of work life. For example, firms may simply change their marketing mix, dropping or adding products, services or customers; they may drastically downsize by cutting out marginal businesses and laying off managers and workers; or they may tighten managerial and financial controls and attempt to more fully utilise the labour force. On the other hand, organisations may undertake quantum change from a developmental perspective. They may seek to make themselves more competitive by developing their human resources, by getting managers and employees more involved in problem solving and innovation and by promoting flexibility and direct, open communication. This OD approach to quantum change is particularly relevant in today's rapidly changing and competitive environment. To succeed in this setting, organisations such as General Electric, Kimberly-Clark, Asea Brown Boveri (ABB), IBM and Banca Intesa are transforming themselves from control-oriented bureaucracies to high-involvement organisations capable of continually changing and improving themselves.

DEGREE OF ORGANISATION

Planned change efforts can also vary according to the degree to which the organisation or client system is organised. In overorganised situations, such as in highly mechanistic, bureaucratic organisations, various dimensions such as leadership styles, job designs, organisation structure, and policies and procedures are too rigid and overly defined for effective task performance. Communication between management and employees is typically suppressed, conflicts are avoided and employees are apathetic. In underorganised organisations, on the other hand, there is too little constraint or regulation for effective task performance. Leadership, structure, job design and policy are ill-defined and fail to control task behaviours effectively. Communication is fragmented, job responsibilities are ambiguous and employees' energies are dissipated because of lack of direction. Underorganised situations are typically found in such areas as product development, project management and community development, where relationships among diverse groups and participants must be coordinated around complex, uncertain tasks.

In overorganised situations, where historically much of OD practice has taken place, planned change is generally aimed at loosening constraints on behaviour. Changes in leadership, job design, structure and other features are designed to liberate suppressed energy, to increase the flow of relevant information between employees and managers and to promote effective conflict resolution. The typical steps of planned change – entry, diagnosis, intervention and evaluation – are intended to penetrate a relatively closed organisation or department and make it increasingly open to self-diagnosis and revitalisation. The relationship between the OD practitioner and the management team attempts to model this loosening process. The consultant shares leadership of the change process with management, encourages open communication and confrontation of conflict and maintains flexibility when relating to the organisation.

When applied to organisations that face problems because of being underorganised, planned change is aimed at increasing organisation by clarifying leadership roles, structuring communication between managers and employees and specifying job and departmental responsibilities. These activities require a modification of the traditional phases of planned change and include the following four stages:[46]

1 *Identification.* This step identifies the relevant people or groups that need to be involved in the change program. In many underorganised situations, people and departments can be so disconnected that there is uncertainty about who should be included in the problem-solving process. For example, managers of different departments who have only limited interaction with each other might disagree or be confused about which departments should help develop a new product or service.

2 **Convention.** In this phase, the relevant people or departments in the company are brought together to begin organising for task performance. For example, department managers might be asked to attend a series of organising meetings to discuss the division of labour and the coordination required to introduce a new product.

Convention: gathering of like-minded professionals.

3 *Organisation.* Different organising mechanisms are created to structure the newly required interactions among people and departments. They might include creating new leadership positions, establishing communication channels and specifying appropriate plans and policies.

4 *Evaluation.* In this final step, the outcomes of the organisation phase are assessed. The evaluation might signal the need for adjustments in the organising process or for further identification, convention and organisation activities.

By carrying out these four stages of planned change in underorganised situations, the relationship between the OD practitioner and the client system attempts to reinforce the organising process. The consultant develops a well-defined leadership role, which might be autocratic during the early stages of the change program. Similarly, the consulting relationship is clearly defined and tightly specified. In effect, the interaction between the consultant and the client system supports the larger process of bringing order to the situation.

DOMESTIC VERSUS INTERNATIONAL SETTINGS

Developed in Western societies, OD reflects the underlying values and assumptions of these cultural settings, including quality, involvement and short-term time horizons. Under these conditions, it works quite well. In other societies, a different set of cultural values and assumptions can be operating and make the application of OD problematic. In contrast to

Western societies, for example, the cultures of most Asian countries are more hierarchical and status conscious, less open to discussing personal issues, more concerned with 'saving face' and have a longer time horizon for results.[47] These cultural differences can make OD more difficult to implement, especially for practitioners from Western countries; they simply may be unaware of the cultural norms and values that permeate the society.

The cultural values that guide OD practice in Australia or the United States include, for example, equality among people, individuality and achievement motives. An OD process that encourages openness among individuals, high levels of participation and actions that promote increased effectiveness is viewed favourably. The OD practitioner is also assumed to hold these values and to model them in the conduct of planned change. Most reported cases of OD involve Western-based organisations using practitioners trained in the traditional model, and raised and experienced in Western society.

When OD is applied outside of Western countries (and sometimes even within these settings), the action research process must be adapted to fit the cultural context. For example, the diagnostic phase, which is aimed at understanding the current drivers of organisation effectiveness, can be modified in a variety of ways. Diagnosis can involve many organisation members or include only senior executives, be directed from the top, conducted by an outside consultant or performed by internal consultants, or involve face-to-face interviews or organisational documents. Each step in the general model of planned change must be carefully mapped against the cultural context.

Conducting OD in international settings can be highly stressful for OD practitioners. To be successful, they must develop a keen awareness of their own cultural biases, be open to seeing a variety of issues from another perspective, be fluent in the values and assumptions of the host country and understand the economic and political context of business in the host country. Most OD practitioners are not able to meet all of those criteria and should consider partnering with a 'cultural guide', often a member of the client organisation, to help navigate the cultural, operational and political nuances of change in that society.

The article in **Apply your learning 2.2** asks various questions in relation to Australian companies expanding offshore.

AUSTRALIAN COMPANIES EXPANDING THEIR WINGS OFFSHORE

APPLY YOUR LEARNING
2.2

The latest corporate reporting season shows the risks and rewards of owning companies with an expanding international footprint. For every Australian company that delivers rapid offshore growth, many landmines lurk.

Yet investing in companies that can grow overseas has never been more important. Australia's small economy, challenged growth outlook and influx of foreign competition is encouraging more companies to look offshore.

...

IBIS World chairman Phil Ruthven says companies that resisted growing offshore face a challenging future. 'Australian companies that were not good enough to go overseas will get killed in our market. Very few of our retailers went overseas and

»

》

look what's happening to them now as Aldi and others increase their market share. Foreign competitors are coming.'

The good news, says Ruthven, is the emergence of younger Australian firms that suit international expansion. They tend to have capital-light business models, intellectual property and products or services that are scalable overseas.

'There's stacks of opportunity for clever Australian firms overseas,' says Ruthven. 'Those with products that are at, or preferably above, world's best practice have a real shot at cracking international markets because they need less capital to expand.'

Unique intellectual property is a trait of successful Australian companies overseas, says Ruthven. 'If the product is not unique by world standards, the company will get eaten alive offshore.'

Ruthven prefers Australian companies that expand in developed, rather than emerging, markets. 'There are always exceptions, but Asia has been a minefield for our companies. You need massive economies of scale to compete in markets as large as Asia. You have to take something unique to those markets that gives you a right of entry.'

Ruthven says Australian companies need deep pockets to win overseas. 'The company must be able to sustain the offshore divisions for a long time. When the product takes off, they need capital to grow the business very quickly, because foreign investors will chase hard if you have a good idea. You must keep innovating to stay head'.

Source: T. Featherstone, 'Australian companies expanding their wings offshore', *Australian Financial Review*, 12 August 2017.

| Critical thinking questions | 1 | This article encourages companies to go offshore. How can OD assist with their expansion? |
| | 2 | According to Phil Ruthven, what are the key characteristics for success? |

CRITIQUE OF PLANNED CHANGE

Conceptualisation: the action or process of forming a concept or idea of a change process.

Despite their continued refinement, the models and practices of planned change are still in a formative stage of development, and there is considerable room for improvement. Critics of OD[48] have pointed out several problems with the way planned change has been both **conceptualised** and practised.

CONCEPTUALISATION OF PLANNED CHANGE

Planned change typically has been characterised as involving a series of activities for carrying out effective change in organisations. Although current models outline a general set of steps that need to be followed, considerably more information is needed to guide how those steps should be performed in specific situations. In an extensive review and critique of planned change theory, Porras and Robertson argued that planned change activities should be guided by information about (1) the organisational features that can be changed, (2) the intended outcomes from making those changes, (3) the causal mechanisms by which those outcomes are achieved and (4) the contingencies upon which successful change depends.[49] In particular, they noted that the key to organisational change is change in the behaviour of each member and that the information available about the causal mechanisms that produce individual change is lacking. Overall, Porras and Robertson concluded that the information necessary for guiding change is only partially available and that a good deal more research and thinking are needed to fill the gaps.

Knowledge about how the stages of planned change differ across situations is a related area where current thinking about planned change is deficient. Most models specify a general set of prescribed steps that are intended to be applicable to most change efforts. However, the previous section of this chapter showed how change activities can vary, depending on such factors as the magnitude of change and the degree to which the client system is organised. Considerably more effort needs to be expended on identifying situational factors that may require modification of the general stages of planned change. This would probably lead to a rich array of planned change models, each geared to a specific set of situational conditions. Such contingency thinking is sorely needed in planned change.

Planned change also tends to be described as a rationally controlled, orderly process. Critics have argued that, although this view may be comforting, it is seriously misleading.[50] They point out that planned change has a more chaotic quality, often involving shifting goals, discontinuous activities, surprising events and unexpected combinations of changes. For example, managers often initiate changes without clear plans that clarify their strategies and goals. As change unfolds, new stakeholders may emerge and demand modifications that reflect previously unknown or unvoiced needs. These emergent conditions make planned change a far more disorderly and dynamic process than is customarily portrayed, and conceptions need to capture this reality.

Most descriptions of planned change typically describe a beginning, middle and end to the process. Critics have argued that planned change models that advocate evaluation and institutionalisation processes reinforce the belief that the organisation will 'refreeze' into some form of equilibrium following change.[51] In the face of increasing globalisation and technological change, it is unlikely that change will ever *be over*. Executives, managers and organisation members must be prepared for constant change in a variety of organisational features that are not obvious in most models of planned change.

Finally, the relationship between planned change and organisational performance and effectiveness is not well understood. OD has traditionally had problems assessing whether interventions are, in fact, producing observed results. The complexity of the change situation, the lack of sophisticated analyses and the long time periods for producing results have all contributed to a weak evaluation of OD efforts. In contrast, managers have often accounted for OD efforts with post-hoc testimonials, reports of possible future benefits and calls to support OD as the right thing to do.

In the absence of rigorous assessment and measurement, it is difficult to make resource-allocation decisions about change programs and to know which interventions are most effective in certain situations.

PRACTICE OF PLANNED CHANGE

Critics have suggested that there are several problems with the way planned change is carried out.[52] These concerns are not with the planned change model itself, but with how change takes place and with the qualifications and activities of OD practitioners.

A growing number of OD practitioners have acquired skills in specific techniques such as team building, total quality management, large-group interventions or gain sharing, and have chosen to specialise in those methods. Although such specialisation may be necessary, given the complex array of techniques that make up modern OD, it can lead to a certain myopia. Some OD practitioners favour particular techniques and ignore other OD strategies that might be more appropriate. They tend to interpret organisational problems as requiring the favoured technique. Thus, for example, it is not unusual to see consultants pushing such methods as diversity training, re-engineering, organisation learning (OL) or self-managing work teams as solutions to most organisational problems even though they may be inappropriate.

Effective change depends upon a careful diagnosis of how the organisation is functioning. Diagnosis identifies the underlying causes of organisational problems, such as poor product quality and employee dissatisfaction. It requires both time and money, and some organisations are not willing to make the necessary investment. They rely on preconceptions about what the problem is and hire consultants with appropriate skills for solving it. Managers may think, for example, that work design is the problem and hire an expert in job enrichment to implement a change program; however, the problem may be caused by other factors, such as poor reward practices, and job enrichment would be inappropriate. Careful diagnosis can help to avoid such mistakes.

In situations that require complex organisational changes, planned change is a long-term process involving considerable innovation and learning on-site. It requires a good deal of time and commitment and a willingness to modify and refine changes as the circumstances require. Some organisations demand more rapid solutions to their problems and seek 'quick fixes' from experts. Unfortunately, some OD consultants are more than willing to provide quick solutions. They may sell pre-packaged programs that tend to be appealing to managers as they typically include an explicit recipe to be followed, standard training materials and clear time and cost boundaries. However, these quick fixes have trouble gaining wide organisational support and commitment. They seldom produce the positive results that have been advertised because of the lack of adaptation to specific circumstances.

Other organisations have not recognised the systemic nature of change. Too often, they believe that intervention into one aspect or unit of the organisation will be sufficient to ameliorate the problems. They are unprepared for the other changes that may be necessary to support a particular intervention. For example, government departments at the federal, state or local level introduce a range of policies around industrial relations that, on the surface, may address identified programs within a particular department; however, these may not translate from a cross-functional point of view and could have far greater implications than originally estimated. Changing any one part or feature of an organisation often requires adjustments in other parts in order to maintain an appropriate alignment. Thus, although quick fixes and change programs that focus on only one part or aspect of the organisation may resolve some specific problems, they generally do not lead to complex organisational change, or increase members' capacity to carry out change.[53] Apply your learning 2.3 identifies opportunities for internal change agency.

APPLY YOUR LEARNING **2.3**

YOUR COMPANY'S SECRET CHANGE AGENTS

Organizational change has traditionally come about through top-down initiatives such as hiring experts or importing best-of-breed practices. Such methods usually result in companywide rollouts of templates mandated from on high. These do little to get people excited. But within every organization, there are a few individuals who find unique ways to look at problems that seem impossible to solve. Although these change agents start out with the same tools and access to resources as their peers, they are able to see solutions where others do not. They find a way to bridge the divide between what is happening and what is possible. These positive deviants are the key, the authors believe, to a better way of creating organizational change.

...

The positive-deviance approach has unearthed solutions to such complicated and diverse problems as malnutrition in Mali and human trafficking in East Java. This methodology can help solve even the most extreme dilemmas.

Source: R.T. Pascale and J. Sternin, 'Your company's secret change agents', *Harvard Business Review*, 83:5 (May 2005): 72–81, 153; abstract accessed at https://www.ncbi.nlm.nih.gov/pubmed/15929405.

Critical thinking questions		
	1	What is your understanding of the article?
	2	The article, which can be downloaded in full, lists the ways to implement change. What are the steps?
	3	Explain how the methodology has helped in Mali and East Java.

THE CONTINGENCY APPROACH TO CHANGE MANAGEMENT

Australian researchers Dexter Dunphy and Doug Stace argue that change management should be approached from a situational perspective. Their argument for contingency is as follows:

> [D]ramatically different approaches to change can work in different circumstances ... turbulent times create varied circumstances and demand different responses according to the needs of the situation. What is appropriate for one organisation may not be appropriate for another. So we need a model of change ... that indicates how to carry change strategies to achieve optimum fit with the changing environment.[54]

As a result of some seven years' research into change management techniques in Australia, Dunphy and Stace have derived a model of change that incorporates both 'soft' and 'hard' approaches. The model is a two-dimensional matrix that categorises the scale of change (from fine-tuning to corporate transformation) and the style of management that needs to be employed to facilitate the change (from collaborative to coercive). Four process change strategies or typologies may be identified from these dimensions.[55] See **Figure 2.3**.

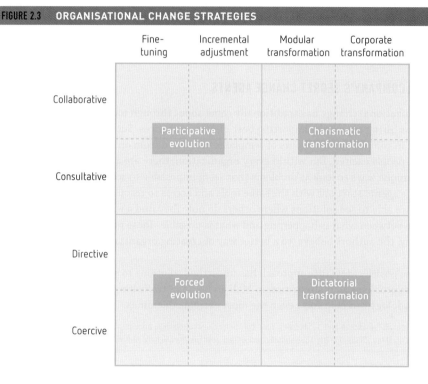

FIGURE 2.3   ORGANISATIONAL CHANGE STRATEGIES

Scale of change

→ *Fine-tuning:* Organisational change that is an ongoing process characterised by fine-tuning of the 'fit' or match between the organisation's strategy, structure, people and processes. Fine-tuning is typically manifested at departmental/divisional levels.

→ *Incremental adjustment:* Organisational change that is characterised by incremental adjustments to the changing environment. Such change involves distinct modifications (but not radical change) to corporate business strategies, structures and management processes.

→ *Modular transformation:* Organisational change that is characterised by major realignment of one or more departments/divisions. The process of radical change is focused on these subparts rather than on the organisation as a whole.

→ *Corporate transformation:* Organisational change that is corporation-wide, characterised by radical shifts in business strategy and revolutionary changes throughout the whole organisation.

Style of management

→ *Collaborative:* Widespread participation by employees in important decisions about the organisation's future and about the means of bringing about organisational change.

→ *Consultative:* Consultation with employees, primarily about the means of bringing about organisational change, with their possible limited involvement in goal setting that is relevant to their area of expertise or responsibility.

→ *Directive:* Use of managerial authority and direction as the main form of decision making about the organisation's future, and about the means of bringing about organisational change.

→ *Coercive:* Managers/executives or outside parties forcing or imposing change on key groups in the organisation.

Typology of change strategies and conditions for their use

→ *Participative evolution:* Used when the organisation is 'in fit' but needs minor adjustment, or is 'out of fit' but time is available and key interest groups favour change.

→ *Charismatic transformation:* Used when the organisation is 'out of fit' and there is little time for extensive participation, but there is support for radical change within the organisation.

→ *Forced evolution:* Used when the organisation is 'in fit' but needs minor adjustment, or is 'out of fit' but time is available. However, key interest groups oppose change.

→ *Dictatorial transformation:* Used when the organisation is 'out of fit', there is no time for extensive participation and no support within the organisation for radical change, but radical change is vital to organisational survival and fulfilment of the basic mission.

As with any paradigm, Dunphy and Stace's model has created considerable debate. There certainly are positive and negative aspects and issues of resistance, politics, the unpredictability of environment, ethical considerations and the unique characteristics of particular groups.

2.1

EXPERIENTIAL ACTIVITY

Understanding your beliefs about successful change managers

Read each of the following 10 statements and indicate your agreement or disagreement. If you fully agree with the statement, score 10. If you totally disagree, score 1. If you tend to agree more than you disagree, give a response between 6 and 9 depending on how much you agree. If you tend to disagree, give a response between 2 and 5.

1 Successful entrepreneur–change agents are often methodical and analytical individuals who carefully plan out what they are going to do and then do it.

2 The most successful entrepreneur–change agents are born with special characteristics, such as a high achievement drive and a winning personality, and these traits serve them well in their change endeavours.

3 Many of the characteristics needed for successful entrepreneurship–change agency can be learned through study and experience.

4 The most successful entrepreneur–change agents are those who invent a unique product or service.

5 Highly successful entrepreneur–change agents tend to have very little formal schooling.

»

6 Most successful entrepreneur–change agents admit that dropping out of school was the best thing they ever did.

7 Because they are unique and individualistic in their approach to business, most successful entrepreneur–change agents find it hard to socialise with others; they just do not fit in.

8 Research shows that although it is important to have adequate financing before beginning an entrepreneurial venture–change process, it is often more important to have managerial competence and proper planning.

9 Being a successful entrepreneur–change agent is more a matter of preparation and desire than luck.

10 Most successful entrepreneur–change agents do well in their first venture–change process, which encourages them to continue; failures tend to come later on as the enterprise grows and change becomes more complex.

Put your answers in the table below in this way:

   enter answers to numbers 1, 3, 8 and 9 just as they appear

   then subtract the answers to 2, 4, 5, 6, 7 and 10 from 11 before entering them here. Therefore, if you gave an answer of 8 to number 1, put an 8 after number 1 here. However, if you gave an answer of 7 to number 2, place a 4 after number 2 here. Then add both columns of answers and enter your total in the space provided.

SCORING BLOCK

As they appear	Subtract from 11
1	2
3	4
8	5
9	6
	7
	10
	Total of both columns

INTERPRETATION

This exercise measures how much you believe the myths of entrepreneurship change management. The lower your total, the stronger your beliefs; the higher your total, the less strong your beliefs. Numbers 1, 3, 8 and 9 are accurate statements; numbers 2, 4, 5, 6, 7 and 10 are inaccurate statements. Here is the scoring key:

   80–100 Excellent; you know the facts about entrepreneur–change agents.

   61–79 Good, but you still believe in a couple of myths.

   41–60 Fair; you need to review the chapter material on the myths of entrepreneurship and change agency.

   0–40 Poor; you need to reread the chapter material on the myths of entrepreneurship and change agency and study these findings.

SUMMARY

Theories of planned change describe the activities that are necessary in order to modify strategies, structures and processes to increase an organisation's effectiveness. Lewin's change model, the action research model and the positive model offer different views of the phases through which planned change occurs in organisations.

Lewin's change model views planned change as a three-step process of unfreezing, movement and refreezing. It provides a general description of the process of planned change. The action research model focuses on planned change as a cyclical process involving joint activities between organisation members and OD practitioners.[56] It consists of eight sequential steps that overlap and interact in practice: problem identification, consultation with a behavioural science expert, data gathering and preliminary diagnosis, feedback to key client or group, joint diagnosis of the problem, joint action planning, action and data gathering after action. The action research model places heavy emphasis on data gathering and diagnosis prior to action planning and implementation,[57] as well as on the assessment of results after action has been taken. In addition, change strategies are often modified on the basis of continued diagnosis, and termination of one OD program may lead to further work in other areas of the organisation. Trends in action research include the movement from smaller to larger systems, from domestic to international applications and from organisational issues to social change. As the name suggests, the positive model focuses on all that is good about the organisation. This constructive approach utilises the processes that are working and builds on their strengths.

These theories can be integrated into a general model of planned change. Four sets of activities – entering and contracting, diagnosing, planning and implementing, and evaluating and institutionalising – can be used to describe how change is accomplished in organisations. The general model has broad applicability to planned change; it identifies the steps that an organisation typically moves through in order to implement change and specifies the OD activities necessary for effecting the change.

Although the planned change models describe general stages of how the OD process unfolds, there are different types of change according to the situation. Planned change efforts can vary in terms of the magnitude of the change and the degree to which the client system is organised. When situations differ on these dimensions, planned change can vary greatly. Critics of OD have pointed out several problems with the way planned change has been conceptualised and practised. They point out specific areas where planned change can be improved.

ACTIVITIES

REVIEW QUESTIONS

1   'No action without research. No research without action'. Discuss. (LO1)

2   How are the five phases of the positive model similar to and/or different from the eight phases of action research? Is this an example of the evolution of change management theory or an entirely new concept? Explain your answer with examples. (LO1 & 2)

3   What are the major problems with planned change efforts? How may these be preempted or overcome? (LO3)

4 How useful is the Dunphy and Stace model when considering transformational change? What criticism or reservations do you have about the model? What adjustments would you make and how would you test the effectiveness of your recommendations? (LO4)

EXTEND YOUR LEARNING

1 One of the major problems in a 'change' relationship is the dependency of an organisation on the change agent. What could cause a problem and how can it be overcome? (LO4)

2 Compare and contrast the various approaches to planned change. Discuss the advantages and disadvantages of each. What would be the ideal scenario/model for planned change? (LO1 & 2)

Search Me! Management

Explore **Search Me! Management** for articles relevant to this chapter. Fast and convenient, **Search Me! Management** is updated daily and provides you with 24-hour access to full text articles from hundreds of scholarly and popular journals, eBooks and newspapers, including *The Australian* and *The New York Times*. Visit http://login.cengagebrain.com and use the access code that comes with this book for 12 months access to the **Search Me! Management** database. Try searching for the following keywords:

Keywords:
- Practitioner
- Client
- Consultant
- Quasi-stationary equilibrium
- Positive model
- Behavioural science
- Convention
- Conceptualisation

Search tip: **Search Me! Management** contains information from both local and international sources. To get the greatest number of search results, try using both Australian and American spellings in your searches; for example, 'globalisation' and 'globalization'; 'organisation' and 'organization'.

REFERENCES

1 Organisation Development Australia, 'What is ODA? Who is ODA for?', http://odaustralia.org.
2 M.F. Broom, PhD and E.W. Seashore, M.A., 'The meta-model of planned change', http://www.chumans.com/human-systems-resources/meta-model-planned-change.html, revised February 2009.
3 W. Bennis, *Changing Organizations* (New York: McGraw-Hill, 1966); J. Porras and P. Robertson, 'Organization development theory: a typology and evaluation', in *Research in Organizational Change and Development*, 1, eds R. Woodman and W. Pasmore (Greenwich, CT: JAI Press, 1987): 1–57.
4 K. Lewin, *Field Theory in Social Science* (New York: Harper and Row, 1951).
5 E. Schein, *Process Consultation*, 1 and 2 (Reading, MA: Addison-Wesley, 1987).
6 R. Lippitt, J. Watson and B. Westley, *The Dynamics of Planned Change* (New York: Harcourt, Brace and World, 1958).
7 R. Benjamin and E. Levinson, 'A framework for managing IT-enabled change', *Sloan Management Review* (Summer 1993): 23–33.

8 H. Knill-Griesser, *The Ontario Action Researcher*, Nipising University 2009, http://oar.nipissingu.ca/index.htm.

9 A. Shani and G. Bushe, 'Visionary action research: a consultation process perspective', *Consultation*, 6 (Spring 1987): 3–19; G. Sussman and R. Evered, 'An assessment of the scientific merit of action research', *Administrative Science Quarterly*, 12 (1978): 582–603.

10 W. French, 'Organization development: objectives, assumptions, and strategies', *California Management Review*, 12 (1969): 23–34; A. Frohman, M. Sashkin and M. Kavanagh, 'Action research as applied to organization development', *Organization and Administrative Sciences*, 7 (1976): 129–42; E. Schein, *Organizational Psychology*, 3rd edn (Englewood Cliffs, NJ: Prentice Hall, 1980); L. Rowell, C. Bruce, J. Shosh, and M. Riel, *Palgrave International Handbook of Action Research* (New York: Palgrave Macmillan, 2016).

11 N. Tichy, 'Agents of planned change: congruence of values, cognitions, and actions', *Administrative Science Quarterly*, 19 (1974): 163–82.

12 M. Beer, 'The technology of organization development', in *Handbook of Industrial and Organizational Psychology*, ed. M. Dunnette (Chicago: Rand McNally, 1976): 945.

13 E. Schein, *Process Consultation: Its Role in Organization Development* (Reading, MA: Addison-Wesley, 1969): 98.

14 ibid.: 6.

15 R. Beckhard and R. Harris, *Organizational Transitions*, 2nd edn (Reading, MA: Addison-Wesley, 1987).

16 M. Elden and R. Chisholm, 'Emerging varieties of action research: introduction to the special issue', *Human Relations*, 46 (1993): 121–42.

17 G. Ledford and S. Mohrman, 'Self-design for high involvement', *Human Relations*, 46 (1993): 143–68; B. Bunker and B. Alban, 'The large group intervention – a new social innovation?', *Journal of Applied Behavioral Science*, 28 (1992): 473–80.

18 R. Marshak, 'Lewin meets Confucius: a review of the OD model of change', *Journal of Applied Behavioral Science*, 29 (1993): 393–415; K. Murrell, 'Evaluation as action research: the case of the Management Development Institute in Gambia, West Africa', *International Journal of Public Administration*, 16 (1993): 341–56; J. Preston and L. DuToit, 'Endemic violence in South Africa: an OD solution applied to two educational settings', *International Journal of Public Administration*, 16 (1993): 1767–91.

19 D. Brown, 'Participatory action research for social change: collective reflections with Asian nongovernmental development organizations', *Human Relations*, 46:2 (1993): 208–27.

20 D. Cooperrider and S. Srivastva, 'Appreciative inquiry in organizational life', in *Research in Organizational Change and Development*, 1, eds R. Woodman and W. Pasmore (Greenwich, CT: JAI Press, 1987): 129–70.

21 D. Cooperrider and W. Pasmore, 'Global social change: a new agenda for social science?', *Human Relations*, 44 (1991): 1037–55.

22 W. Burke, *Organization Development: A Normative View* (Reading, MA: Addison-Wesley, 1987).

23 D. Greenwood, W. Whyte and I. Harkavy, 'Participatory action research as process and as goal', *Human Relations*, 46 (1993): 175–92.

24 J. Enderby and D. Phelan, 'Action learning groups as the foundation for cultural change', *Asia Pacific Journal of Human Resources*, 32 (1994).

25 C. Argyris, R. Putnam and D. Smith, *Action Science* (San Francisco: Jossey-Bass, 1985).

26 S. Mohrman and T. Cummings, *Self-designing Organizations: Learning How to Create High Performance* (Reading, MA: Addison-Wesley, 1989).

27 P. Senge, *The Fifth Discipline* (New York: Doubleday, 1990).

28 B. Braham PhD, Organizational Development Consultant, 'The inner arts of leadership', http://www.bbraham.com/organizational_development_consultant.html, 2006–11.

29 M. Weisbord, *Productive Workplaces* (San Francisco: Jossey-Bass, 1987).

30 D. Cooperrider, 'Positive image, positive action: the affirmative basis for organizing', in *Appreciative Management and Leadership*, eds S. Srivastva, D. Cooperrider and associates (San Francisco, CA: Jossey-Bass, 1990); D. Cooperrider, lecture notes, *Presentation to the MSOD Chi Class*, October 1995, Monterey, CA.

31 Cooperrider and Srivastva, 'Appreciative inquiry in organizational life', op. cit.

32 K. Cameron, J. Dutton and R. Quinn, eds, *Positive Organizational Scholarship: Foundations of a New Discipline* (New York: Berrett-Kohler, 2003).

33 D. Eden, 'Creating expectation effects in OD: applying self-fulfilling prophecy', in *Research in Organizational Change and Development*, 2, eds W. Pasmore and R. Woodman (Greenwich, CT: JAI Press, 1988); D. Eden, 'OD and self-fulfilling prophecy: boosting productivity by raising expectations', *Journal of Applied Behavioral Science*, 22 (1986): 1–13; Cooperrider, 'Positive image, positive action', op. cit.

34 D. Cooperrider and D. Whitney, 'A positive revolution in change: appreciative inquiry', in *Appreciative Inquiry: Rethinking Human Organization Toward a Positive Theory of Change*, eds. D. Cooperrider, P. Sorensen, D. Whitney and T. Yaeger (Champaign, Ill.: Stipes Publishing, 2000),

3–28; J. Watkins and B. Mohr, *Appreciative Inquiry* (San Francisco: Jossey-Bass, 2001).

35 I. Hacking, *The Social Construction of What?* (Cambridge: Harvard University Press, 1999).

36 P. Berger and T. Luckman, *The Social Construction of Reality* (New York: Anchor Books, 1967); K. Gergen, 'The social constructionist movement in modern psychology', *American Psychologist*, 40 (1985): 266–75; V. Burr, *An Introduction to Social Constructionism* (London: Routledge, 1995).

37 G. Bushe and R. Marshak, 'Revisioning organization development: diagnostic and dialogic premises and patterns of practice' *Journal of Applied Behavioral Science* 45 (2009): 348–68; G. Bushe and R. Marshak, eds, *Dialogic Organization Development* (Oakland, CA: Berrett-Koehler, 2015).

38 M. Zion and I. Sadeh, 'Curiosity and open inquiry learning', *Journal of Biological Education*, 41 (Autumn 2007): 162–9.

39 Youth Off the Streets, *Submission to the Inquiry into Disclosure Regimes for Charities and Not-for-Profit Organisations*, August 2008.

40 G. Roth and A. DiBella, *Systemic Change Management* (New York: Palgrave Macmillan, 2015).

41 K.A.S. Bahgel, 'A presentation on organizational change model', http://www.scribd.com/doc/6976882/A-Presentation-on-Organizational-Change-Model, 2008.

42 T. Cummings and C. Cummings, 'Appreciating organization development: a comparative essay on divergent perspectives', *Human Resource Development Quarterly*, 25 (2014): 141–54.

43 D. Nadler, 'Organizational frame-bending: types of change in the complex organization', in *Corporate Transformation*, eds R. Kilmann and T. Covin (San Francisco: Jossey-Bass, 1988): 66–83; P. Watzlawick, J. Weakland and R. Fisch, *Change* (New York: WW Norton, 1974); R. Golembiewski, K. Billingsley and S. Yeager, 'Measuring change and persistence in human affairs: types of change generated by OD designs', *Journal of Applied Behavioral Science*, 12 (1975): 133–57; A. Meyer, G. Brooks and J. Goes, 'Environmental jolts and industry revolutions: organizational responses to discontinuous change', *Strategic Management Journal*, 11 (1990): 93–110.

44 A. Mohrman, G. Ledford Jr, S. Mohrman, E. Lawler III and T. Cummings, *Large-Scale Organization Change* (San Francisco: Jossey-Bass, 1989).

45 C.F. Wordsworth, *Quantum Change Made Easy: Breakthroughs in Personal Transformation, Self-Healing and Achieving the Best of Who You Are* (Arizona, USA: Resonance Publishing, 2007).

46 F. Barrett and D. Cooperrider, 'Generative metaphor intervention: a new approach for working with systems divided by conflict and caught in defensive perception', *Journal of Applied Behavioral Science*, 26 (1990): 219–39.

47 G. Hofstede, *Culture's Consequences: Comparing Values, Behaviors, Institutions, and Organizations Across Nations* (Thousand Oaks, CA: Sage Publications, 2001).

48 T.G. Cummings and C.G. Worley, *Organization Development and Change*, 9th edn (Mason, OH: South-Western/Cengage Learning, 2009): 41.

49 J. Porras and P. Robertson, 'Organization development theory, practice, and research', in *Handbook of Industrial and Organizational Psychology*, 3, 2nd edn, eds M. Dunnette and M. Hough (Palo Alto, CA: Consulting Psychologists Press, 1992).

50 T. Cummings, S. Mohrman, A. Mohrman and G. Ledford, 'Organization design for the future: a collaborative research approach', in *Doing Research That Is Useful for Theory and Practice*, eds E. Lawler III, A. Mohrman, S. Mohrman, G. Ledford and T. Cummings (San Francisco: Jossey-Bass, 1985): 275–305.

51 E. Lawler and C. Worley, *Built to Change: How to Achieve Sustained Organizational Effectiveness* (San Francisco: Jossey-Bass, 2006).

52 A. Frohman, M. Sashkin and M. Kavanagh, 'Action research as applied to organization development', *Organization and Administrative Sciences*, 7 (1976): 129–42; S. Mohrman and T. Cummings, *Self-designing Organizations: Learning How to Create High Performance* (Reading, MA: Addison-Wesley, 1989); M. Beer, R. Eisenstat and B. Spector, 'Why change programs don't produce change', *Harvard Business Review*, 6 (November–December 1990): 158–66.

53 Beer, Eisenstat and Spector, 'Why change programs don't produce change', op. cit.

54 D. Dunphy and D. Stace, *Under New Management: Australian Organisations in Transition* (Sydney: McGraw-Hill, 1990): 82.

55 D. Dunphy and D. Stace, 'Strategies for organisational transition', *Centre for Corporate Change*, Paper 002, 1991, AGSM (University of New South Wales).

56 C. Worley and S. Mohrman, 'Is change management obsolete?', *Organizational Dynamics*, 43 (2014): 214–24.

57 G. Roth and A. DiBella, *Systemic Change Management* (New York: Palgrave Macmillan, 2015).

LEADERSHIP AND THE ROLE OF THE CHANGE AGENT

After studying this chapter, you should be able to:

1   Define the role, and provide examples, of organisation development (OD) practitioners.

2   Demonstrate an understanding of the characteristics of an OD change agent.

3   Summarise the process for developing a contract between change agent and client.

4   Compare and contrast the advantages and disadvantages of internal and external change agents.

5   Identify the need and importance of professional ethics in change management.

Humanistic values

Diagnostic phase

Contracting

Ground rules

Intrapersonal skills

Interpersonal skills

Marginality

Ethical dilemmas

Technical ineptitude

This chapter examines the people who perform OD in organisations. A closer look at OD practitioners can provide a more personal perspective on the field and help us to understand the essential character of OD as a helping profession, involving personal relationships between OD practitioners (whether internal or external) and organisation members.

Much of the literature about OD practitioners views them as internal or external consultants who provide professional services: diagnosing problems, developing solutions and helping to implement them. More recent perspectives expand the scope of OD practitioners to include professionals in related disciplines, such as industrial psychology and organisation theory, as well as line managers and human resource managers who have learned how to carry out OD in order to change and develop their departments.

A great deal of opinion and some research studies have focused on the necessary skills and knowledge of an effective OD practitioner. Studies provide a comprehensive list of basic skills and knowledge needed by all OD practitioners if they are to be effective.

Most of the relevant literature focuses on people who specialise in OD as a profession and addresses their roles and careers. The OD role can be described in relation to the position of OD practitioners: internal to the organisation, external to it or in a team composed of both internal and external consultants. The OD role can also be examined in terms of its marginality in organisations and where it fits along a continuum from client-centred to consultant-centred[1] functioning. Finally, OD is a profession that provides alternative opportunities for gaining competence and developing a career. However, the stressful nature of helping professions suggests that OD practitioners must cope with the possibility of professional burnout.

As in other helping professions, values and ethics play an important role in guiding OD practice and minimising the possibility of clients being neglected or abused.

WHO IS THE ORGANISATION DEVELOPMENT PRACTITIONER?

Throughout this text, the term 'organisation development (OD) practitioner'[2] refers to at least three kinds of people. The most obvious group of OD practitioners consists of those people who specialise in OD as a profession. They may be internal or external consultants who offer professional services to organisation clients, including top managers, functional department heads and staff groups. Traditionally OD professionals have shared a common set of **humanistic values**,[3] promoting open communications, employee involvement and personal growth and development. They tend to have common training, skills and experience in the social processes of organisations (for example, group dynamics, team building, decision making and communications). In recent years, OD professionals have expanded these traditional values and expertise to include more concern for organisational effectiveness, competitiveness and bottom-line results, and greater attention to the technical, structural and strategic parts of organisations. This expansion is mainly in response to the highly competitive demands that modern organisations face. It has resulted in a more diverse set of OD professionals geared to helping organisations cope with those pressures.[4]

Humanistic values: a rationalist outlook of thought attaching prime importance to human matters.

Next, the term 'OD practitioner' applies to people who specialise in fields related to OD, such as reward systems, organisation design, total quality management, information technology and business strategy. These content-oriented fields are increasingly becoming integrated with OD's process orientation, particularly as OD projects have become more comprehensive, involving multiple features and varying parts of organisations. A growing number of professionals in these related fields are gaining experience and competence in OD, mainly through working with OD professionals on large-scale projects and through attending OD training sessions. For example, Australia's 'Big Four' banks have diversified to promote change by addressing consumer expectations, packaging it as corporate social responsibility (CSR) and thereby enabling them to become more connected with the community in which they participate. In most cases, these related professionals or 'new' departments do not fully subscribe to traditional OD values, nor do they have extensive training and experience in OD. Rather, they have formal training and experience in their respective specialties, such as industrial relations, management consulting, control systems, health care and work design. They are OD practitioners in the sense that they apply their special competence within an OD-like process, typically by having OD professionals and managers help design and implement change programs.[5] They also practise OD when they apply their OD competence to their own specialties, thus diffusing an OD perspective into such areas as compensation practices, work design, labour relations and planning and strategy.[6]

Finally, the term 'OD practitioner' applies to the increasing number of managers and administrators who have gained competence in OD and who apply it to their own work areas. Managers can group under the general banner of OD, but it is not always done through an OD practitioner and where there are recognised OD people, their interventions and focus can be so varied that it is hard to link them as a profession.[7] It has been suggested that the faster pace of change affecting organisations today is highlighting the centrality of the manager in managing change. Consequently, OD must become a general management skill. Along these lines, the Centre for Sustainable Organisations and Work Research at RMIT University has studied a number of interrelated areas that provide evidence of the activity of OD within organisations.[8] They have gained the expertise to introduce change and innovation into the organisation with particular reference to the organisational benefits of social media.

Managers tend to gain competence in OD by interacting with OD professionals in actual change programs. This on-the-job training is frequently supplemented with more formal OD training, such as the variety of OD workshops offered by the Australian Institute of Management (AIM), Institution of Engineers Australia (IEAust), Australian Human Resource Institute (AHRI) and others. Line managers are increasingly attending such external programs. Moreover, a growing number of organisations, including ANZ Bank, offer all staff at least one day of paid volunteer leave per year to make a difference in their communities in the hope that the experience will translate to organisational growth, by bringing line managers 'closer' to their teams (see **http://www.anz.com/about-us/corporate-sustainability**). In practice, the distinction between the three kinds of OD practitioners is becoming blurred. A growing number of managers have moved, either temporarily or permanently, into the OD profession. For example, organisations such as Ambulance Victoria and Eastern Health are implementing OD initiatives and are expecting staff from various sections of the organisation to attend training in OD principles and then incorporate the learnings into existing job roles. Also, it is increasingly common to find OD practitioners and/or managers using their experience in OD to become external consultants (for example, The Coaching Institute, Fire Up Coaching), particularly in the employee involvement area.

More OD practitioners are gaining professional competence in related specialties, such as business process re-engineering, reward systems[9] and career planning and development. Conversely, many specialists in these related areas are achieving professional competence in OD. Cross-training and integration are producing a more comprehensive and complex kind of OD practitioner, who has a greater diversity of values, skills and experience than does the traditional OD practitioner.

In **Apply your learning 3.1**, the article looks at the field of OD, which has evolved during some difficult times since the 1940s, and has had to continuously adapt its practices because of its belief that 'context is everything'. The article gives a brief review of the macro

APPLY YOUR LEARNING 3.1

THE FUTURE OF THE ORGANISATION AND IMPLICATIONS FOR OD

Back in the 1990s Peter Drucker published a series of articles for *Management Today*, and some of them were compiled into a two-part book called *Managing for the Future*. There he touched on many challenges organisations would face in the future that leaders must deal with to survive.

Two decades later these areas remain current – even though the scale, scope, intensity, how they manifest and their impact have geared up significantly. Organisations worldwide have been facing the volatile interaction of the changing world economy; the rise and possible fall of economic integration through the European Union, the rise in the East, the gigantic economic powerhouse of China, and the emergence of a new international economic order supported by the rise of the knowledge society in which ICT and technology rule. These factors can be summed up as six key trends:

1   The scale of complexity in the environment …
2   Resource scarcity …
3   Technology breakthroughs …
4   Consumer/customer rights and the requirement for transparency …
5   Population movement and rapid urbanisation …
6   Demographic shift …

    …

The future of work patterns spans a wide spectrum. At the extreme more work is carried out by robots, services are provided by driverless cars, and the world of smart drugs enhances intelligence, memory, and work. Most firms, while not yet facing such radical adjustment, will need to make some sort of systemic preparation to be future-ready.

Source: M-Y. Cheung-Judge, 'The future of the organisation and implications for OD', *HR Magazine*, 28 February 2018.

Critical thinking questions

1   Does the author provide a convincing argument to prepare for the future?
2   What are the suggested six key trends? Explain your understanding of each and give current examples.

trends and their impact on the future of work, and how the discipline of OD can become more 'future-ready'.

THE OD PRACTITIONER AS LEADER OF CHANGE

Traditional, hierarchical organisations may once have made complex decisions about the organisation in-house. Changes in a business's competitive environment, as well as issues affecting the global economy, such as a global financial crisis, can create opportunities for OD practitioners to lead change within organisations.

Generally, in beginning the change process, a member of an organisation or unit contacts an OD practitioner about potential help in addressing an organisational issue.[10] The organisation member may be a manager, staff specialist or some other key participant, and the practitioner may be an OD professional from inside or outside the organisation. Determining whether the two parties should enter into an OD relationship typically involves clarifying the nature of the organisation's problem, the relevant client system for that issue and the 'appropriateness' of the particular OD practitioner.[11] In helping to assess these issues, the OD practitioner may need to collect preliminary data about the organisation. Similarly, the organisation may need to gather information about the practitioner's competence and experience.[12] This knowledge will help both parties determine whether they should proceed to develop a contract for working together.

This section describes the process of engaging an OD practitioner as organisational change agent: (1) clarifying the organisational issue, (2) determining the relevant client and (3) selecting an appropriate OD practitioner.

CLARIFYING THE ORGANISATIONAL ISSUE[13]

When seeking help from OD practitioners, organisations typically start with a presenting problem – the issue that has caused them to consider an OD process. It may be specific (decrease in market share, increase in absenteeism) or general ('we're growing too fast', 'we need to prepare for rapid changes'). The presenting problem often has an implied or stated solution. For example, managers may believe that, because members of their teams are in conflict, team building is the obvious answer. They may even state the presenting problem in the form of a solution: 'We need some team building.'

In many cases, however, the presenting problem is only a symptom of an underlying problem. For example, conflict among members of a team may result from several deeper causes, including ineffective reward systems, personality differences, inappropriate structure and poor leadership. The issue facing the organisation or department must be clarified early in the OD process so that subsequent diagnostic and intervention activities are focused on the right issue.[14]

For more information on team building, see Chapter 7.

Gaining a clearer perspective on the organisational issue may require the collection of preliminary data.[15] OD practitioners often examine company records and interview a few key members to gain an introductory understanding of the organisation, its context and the nature of the presenting problem. These data are gathered in a relatively short period of time, typically from a few hours to one or two days. They are intended to provide rudimentary knowledge of the organisational issue that will enable the two parties to make informed choices about proceeding with the contracting process.

Diagnostic phase: a process, practice or technique to identify change.

The **diagnostic phase** of OD involves a far more extensive assessment of the organisational issue than occurs during the entering and contracting stage.

The diagnosis might also discover other issues that need to be addressed, or it might lead to redefining the initial issue that was identified during the entering and contracting stage. This is a prime example of the emergent nature of the OD process, where things may change as new information is gathered and new events occur.

DETERMINING THE RELEVANT CLIENT

A second activity involved in entering an OD relationship is the definition of who is the relevant client for addressing the organisational issue.[16] Generally, the relevant client includes those organisation members who can directly impact on the change issue, whether it be solving a particular problem or improving an already successful organisation or department. Unless these members are identified and included in the entering and contracting process, they may withhold their support for, and commitment to, the OD process. In trying to improve the productivity and competitiveness of a leading bank, for example, the OD process is reliant on the customer as the client, as well as staff at every level representing every aspect of the organisation. It is not unusual for an OD project to fail because the relevant client was inappropriately defined.

Determining the relevant client can vary in complexity according to the situation. In those cases where the organisational issue can be addressed in a particular organisation unit, client definition[17] is relatively straightforward. Members of that unit constitute the relevant client. They or their representatives would need to be included in the entering and contracting process. For example, anyone positioned to benefit from the OD process can also be considered the relevant client/s. Unless they are actively involved in choosing an OD practitioner and defining the subsequent change process, there is little likelihood that OD will improve team decision making.

Determining the relevant client is more complex when the organisational issue cannot readily be addressed in a single organisation unit. Here, it may be necessary to expand the definition of the client to include members from multiple units, from different hierarchical levels and even from outside the organisation. For example, the manager of a production department may seek help in resolving conflicts between his or her unit and other departments in the organisation. The relevant client would transcend the boundaries of the production department because it alone cannot resolve the organisational issue. The client might include members from all departments involved in the conflict as well as the executive to whom all the departments report. If this interdepartmental conflict also involved key suppliers and customers from outside the business, the relevant client might also include members of those groups.

In these complex situations, OD practitioners may need to gather additional information about the organisation in order to determine the relevant client. This can be accomplished as part of the preliminary data collection that typically occurs when clarifying the organisational issue. When examining company records or interviewing personnel, practitioners can seek to identify the key members and organisational units that need to be involved in addressing the organisational issue. For example, they can ask organisation members such questions as: 'Who can directly affect the organisational issue?' 'Who has a vested interest in it?' 'Who has the power to approve or reject the OD effort?' Answers to these questions can help determine who is the relevant client for the entering and contracting stage. The relevant client may change, however, during the later stages of the OD process as new data are gathered and changes occur. If so, participants may have to return to this initial stage of the OD effort and modify it. The more the stages of the OD are present, the more likely it is to be a success.

SELECTING AN OD PRACTITIONER

The last activity involved in entering an OD relationship is selecting an OD practitioner who has the expertise and experience to work with members on the organisational issue. Unfortunately, little systematic advice is available on how to choose a competent OD professional, whether from inside or outside the organisation. Perhaps the best criteria for selecting, evaluating and developing OD practitioners are those suggested by the late Gordon Lippitt, a pioneering practitioner in the field.[18] Lippitt listed areas that managers should consider before selecting a practitioner, including the ability of the consultant to form sound interpersonal relationships, the degree of focus on the problem, the skills of the practitioner relative to the problem, the extent that the consultant clearly informs the client as to his or her role and contribution, and whether the practitioner belongs to a professional association. References from other clients are highly important. A client may not like the consultant's work, but it is critical to know the reasons for both pleasure and displeasure. One important consideration is whether the consultant approaches the organisation with openness and an insistence on diagnosis or whether the practitioner appears to have a fixed program that is applicable to almost any organisation.

Certainly, OD consulting is as much a person specialisation as it is a task specialisation. The OD professional must have not only a repertoire of technical skills but also the personality and interpersonal competence to be able to use himself or herself as an instrument of change. Regardless of technical training, the consultant must be able to maintain a boundary position, coordinating various units and departments and mixing disciplines, theories, technology and research findings in an organic rather than a mechanical way. The practitioner is potentially the most important OD technology available.

Thus, in the selection of an OD practitioner, perhaps the most important issue is the fundamental question: 'How effective has the person been in the past, with what kinds of organisations, using what kinds of techniques?' In other words, references must be checked. Interpersonal relationships are tremendously important, but even con artists have excellent interpersonal relationships and skills.

The burden of choosing an effective OD practitioner should not, however, rest entirely with the client organisation.[19] OD practitioners also bear a heavy responsibility for seeking an appropriate match between their skills and knowledge and what the organisation or department needs. Few managers are sophisticated enough to detect or understand subtle differences in expertise among OD professionals. They often do not understand the difference between consultants who specialise in different types of interventions. Thus, practitioners should help to educate potential clients. Consultants should be explicit about their strengths and weaknesses and about their range of competence. If OD professionals realise that a good match does not exist, they should inform managers and help them find more suitable help.

DEVELOPING A CONTRACT

The activities of entering an OD relationship – clarifying the organisational issue, determining who is the relevant client and deciding whether the practitioner is appropriate for helping the organisation – are a necessary prelude to developing an OD contract. They define the major focus for contracting, including the relevant parties. **Contracting** is a natural extension of the entering process and clarifies how the OD process will proceed. It typically establishes the expectations of the parties, the time and resources that will be expended and the ground rules under which the parties will operate.

Contracting: entering into a formal and legally binding agreement.

The goal of contracting is to make a good decision about how to carry out the OD process.[20] It can be relatively informal and involve only a verbal agreement between the client and OD practitioner.[21] A team leader with OD skills, for example, may voice his or her concerns to members about how the team is functioning. After some discussion, they might agree to devote one hour of future meeting time to diagnosing the team with the help of the leader. Here, entering and contracting are done together in an informal manner. In other cases, contracting can be more protracted and result in a formal document. This typically occurs when organisations employ outside OD practitioners. Government agencies, for example, generally have procurement regulations that apply to contracting with outside consultants.[22]

Regardless of the level of formality, all OD processes require some form of explicit contracting that results in either a verbal or written agreement. Such contracting clarifies the client's and the practitioner's expectations about how the OD process will take place. Unless there is mutual understanding and agreement about the OD process, there is considerable risk that someone's expectations will be unfulfilled.[23] This can lead to reduced commitment and support, to misplaced action or to premature termination of the process.

Ground rules: rules relating to the limits of actions during a change process.

The contracting step in OD generally addresses three key areas:[24] (1) what each party expects to gain from the OD process, (2) the time and resources that will be devoted to OD and (3) the **ground rules** for working together.

MUTUAL EXPECTATIONS

This part of the contracting process focuses on the expectations of the client and the OD practitioner. The client states the services and outcomes to be provided by the OD practitioner and describes what the organisation expects from the OD process and the consultant. Clients can usually describe the desired outcomes of the OD process, such as decreased turnover or higher job satisfaction. Encouraging them to state their wants in the form of outcomes, working relationships and personal accomplishments can facilitate the development of a good contract.[25]

The OD practitioner should also state what he or she expects to gain from the OD process. This can include the opportunity to try new OD interventions, report the results to other potential clients and receive appropriate compensation or recognition.

TIME AND RESOURCES

To accomplish change, the organisation and the OD practitioner must commit time and resources to the effort. Each must be clear about how much energy and resources will be dedicated to the change process. Failure to make explicit the necessary requirements of a change process can quickly ruin an OD effort. For example, a client may clearly state that the assignment involves diagnosing the causes of poor productivity in a work group. However, the client may expect the practitioner to complete the assignment without talking to the workers. Typically, clients want to know how much time will be necessary to complete the assignment, who needs to be involved, how much it will cost and so on.

Block has suggested that resources can be divided into two parts: essential and desirable requirements.[26] Essential requirements are things that are absolutely necessary if the change process is to be successful. From the practitioner's perspective, they can include access to key people or information, enough time to do the job properly and commitment from certain people. The organisation's essential requirements might include a speedy diagnosis or assurances that the project will be conducted at the lowest price. Being clear about the constraints on carrying out the assignment will facilitate the contracting process and improve the chances for success. Desirable requirements are the things that would be nice to have but are not absolutely necessary. They may include access to special resources and written (as opposed to verbal) reports.

GROUND RULES

The final part of the contracting process involves specifying how the client and the OD practitioner will work confidentially together. This includes such issues as confidentiality, if and how the OD practitioner will become involved in personal or interpersonal issues, how to terminate the relationship and whether the practitioner is supposed to make expert recommendations or help the manager make decisions. For internal consultants, organisational politics make it especially important to clarify issues of how to handle sensitive information and how to deliver 'bad news' if necessary.[27] These process issues are as important as the substantive changes to take place. Failure to address these concerns can mean that the client or the OD practitioner has inappropriate assumptions about how the process will unfold.

COMPETENCIES OF AN EFFECTIVE ORGANISATION DEVELOPMENT PRACTITIONER

Much of the literature about the skills and knowledge of an effective OD practitioner claims that a mixture of personality traits, experiences, kinds of knowledge and skills can be assumed to lead to effective practice. For example, research on the characteristics of successful change practitioners yields the following list of attributes and abilities: diagnostic ability, basic knowledge of behavioural science techniques, empathy, knowledge of the theories and methods within the consultant's own discipline, goal-setting ability, problem-solving ability, ability to do self-assessment, the ability to see things objectively, imagination, flexibility, honesty, consistency and trust.[28] Although these qualities and skills are certainly laudable, there has been relatively little consensus about their importance in effective OD practice.

Many consulting styles or approaches have been suggested, but each style usually varies according to its underlying character – shaped by the kinds of skills and techniques that the consultants use, the values they bring to their clients and the manner in which they carry out their assignments. Other research also examines the degree of emphasis that the consultant places upon two interrelated goals or dimensions of the change process. **Experiential activity 3.1** describes a classification that involves the consultant's orientation to the two interrelated dimensions:

1   the degree of emphasis upon effectiveness or goal accomplishment
2   the degree of emphasis upon relationships, morale and participant satisfaction.[29]

Two ongoing projects are attempting to define and categorise the skills and knowledge required of OD practitioners. In the first effort, a broad and growing list of well-known practitioners and researchers annually update a list of professional competencies. The most recent list has grown to 187 statements in nine areas of OD practice, including entry, start-up, assessment and feedback, action planning, intervention, evaluation, adoption,

---

EXPERIENTIAL ACTIVITY 3.1

Consultant styles matrix

Based upon two dimensions – an emphasis on morale and an emphasis on effectiveness – five different types of consultant styles or roles may be identified.

THE *STABILISER* STYLE:

- maintains a low profile
- is a survivalist – follows top management direction
- has learned to conform and suppress internal motivations, usually stemming from being situated in a large organisation where development programs may not be highly regarded by top management.

THE *CHEERLEADER* STYLE:

- is chiefly concerned with employee motivation and morale
- seeks warm working relationships and in general is more comfortable in non-confrontational situations
- assumes that high employee satisfaction equals high effectiveness (evidence, however, contradicts this assumption)
- avoids open conflict and attempts to maintain harmony by smoothing over differences.

»

FIGURE 3.1 CONSULTANT STYLES

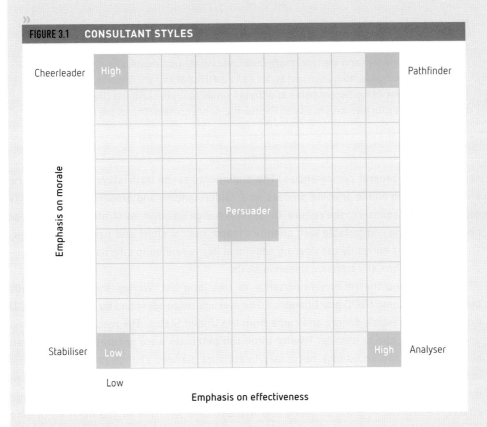

THE *ANALYSER* STYLE:

- emphasises efficiency over employee satisfaction
- is a rationalist – assumes the facts will lead to a solution
- may be confrontational, usually relying on authority to resolve conflict
- is a technical specialist – has the expertise, knowledge and experience to solve specific problems.

THE *PERSUADER* STYLE:

- tends to be low-risk, focusing on both effectiveness and moral dimensions
- is motivated primarily to satisfy; that is, to achieve something that is 'good enough'
- expends effort in satisfying differing forces, although the resulting change program may become 'watered down' or weakened.

THE *PATHFINDER* STYLE:

- seeks high degree of effectiveness and employee satisfaction, believing problems can be solved through teamwork
- is aware that confrontation and conflict may improve effectiveness
- uses collaborative problem solving and challenges the underlying patterns of employee behaviour.

>>

Most organisation problems are complex situations and may not be neatly solved by any one particular change, but will depend upon the particular consultant, the nature of the problem and the type of organisation climate that exists. The styles are not mutually exclusive. All consultant styles can be effective and are interrelated. A consultant may use different styles at different times to meet changing client system needs and deal with diverse situations. Frequently, some combination of the types may be applied.

separation and general competencies. The statements range from 'staying centred in the present, focusing on the ongoing process' and 'understanding and explaining how diversity will affect the diagnosis of the culture' to 'basing change on business strategy and business needs' and 'being comfortable with quantum leaps, radical shifts and paradigm changes'. The discussion is currently considering additional items related to international OD, large-group interventions and transorganisation skills.

To understand the relative importance of this long list, Worley and his colleagues collected data from 364 OD practitioners.[30] The average respondent had six to 10 years of OD experience, a master's degree and came from the United States. The results suggested an underlying structure to this list. Twenty-three competencies were generated that reflected both the skills and knowledge necessary to conduct planned change processes and the individual characteristics necessary to be an effective OD practitioner. Similar to other lists, the competencies included the ability to evaluate change, work with large-scale change efforts, create implementation plans and manage diversity. One of the most surprising results, however, was the emergence of 'self mastery' as the most important competence. The results supported the long-held belief that good OD practitioners know themselves and that such knowledge forms the basis of effective practice.

The second project, sponsored by the Organization Development and Change Division of the Academy of Management, seeks to develop a list of competencies to guide curriculum development in graduate OD programs. So far, more than 40 OD practitioners and researchers have worked to develop two competency lists (shown in **Table 3.1**). First, foundation competencies are oriented towards descriptions of an existing system. They include knowledge from organisation behaviour, psychology, group dynamics, management and organisation theory, research methods and business practices. Second, core competencies are aimed at how systems change over time. They include knowledge of organisation design, organisation research, system dynamics, OD history, and theories and models for change. They also involve the skills needed to manage the consulting process; analyse and diagnose systems; design and choose interventions; facilitate processes; develop clients' capability to manage their own change; and evaluate organisation change.

The information in **Table 3.1** applies primarily to people who specialise in OD as a profession. For those people, the list of skills and knowledge seems reasonable, especially in light of the growing diversity and complexity of interventions in OD. Gaining competence in those areas may take considerable time and effort, and it is questionable whether the

TABLE 3.1	KNOWLEDGE AND SKILL REQUIREMENTS OF OD PRACTITIONERS	
	Foundation competencies	Core competencies

Knowledge	1 Organisation behaviour
	  A Organisation culture
	  B Work design
	  C Interpersonal relations
	  D Power and politics
	  E Leadership
	  F Goal setting
	  G Conflict
	  H Ethics
	
	2 Individual psychology
	  A Learning theory
	  B Motivation theory
	  C Perception theory
	
	3 Group dynamics
	  A Roles
	  B Communication processes
	  C Decision-making process
	  D Stages of group development
	  E Leadership
	
	4 Management and organisation theory
	  A Planning, organising, leading and controlling
	  B Problem solving and decision making
	  C Systems theory
	  D Contingency theory
	  E Organisation structure
	  F Characteristics of environment and technology
	  G Models of organisation and system
	
	5 Research methods/statistics
	  A Measures of central tendency
	  B Measures of dispersion
	  C Basic sampling theory
	  D Basic experimental design
	  E Sample inferential statistics
	
	6 Comparative cultural perspectives
	  A Dimensions of natural culture
	  B Dimensions of industry culture
	  C Systems implications
	
	7 Functional knowledge of business and management principles and practice
		1 Organisation design: the decision process associated with formulating and aligning the elements of an organisational system, including but not limited to structural systems, human resource systems, information systems, reward systems, work design, political systems and organisation culture
		  A The concept of fit and alignment
		  B Diagnostic and design model for various subsystems that make up an organisation at any level of analysis, including the structure of work, human resources, information systems, reward systems, work design, political systems, and so on
		  C Key thought leaders in organisation design
		
		2 Organisation research: field research methods; interviewing; content analysis; design of questionnaires and interview protocol; designing change evaluation processes; longitudinal data collection and analysis; understanding and detecting alpha, beta and gamma change; and a host of quantitative and qualitative methods
		
		3 System dynamics: the description and understanding of how systems evolve and develop over time, how systems respond to exogenous and endogenous disruption as well as planned interventions (for example, evolution and revolution, punctuated equilibrium theory, chaos theory, catastrophe theory, incremental versus quantum change, transformation theory)
		
		4 History of organisation development and change: an understanding of the social, political, economic and personal forces that led to the emergence and development of organisation development and change, including the key thought leaders, the values underlying their writings and actions, the key events and writings, and related documentation
		  A Human relations movement
		  B NTL/T-groups/sensitivity training
		  C Survey research
		  D Quality of work life
		  E Tavistock Institute
		  F Key thought leaders
		  G Humanistic values
		  H Statement of ethics
		
		5 Theories and models for change: the basic action research model, participatory action research model, planning model, change typologies (for example, fast, slow, incremental, quantum, revolutionary), Lewin's model, transition models, and so on

»

	Foundation competencies	Core competencies
Skills	1 Interpersonal communication (listening, feedback and articulation) 2 Collaboration/working together 3 Problem solving 4 Using new technology 5 Conceptualising 6 Project management 7 Present/education	1 Managing the consulting process: the ability to enter, contract, diagnose, design appropriate interventions, implement those interventions, manage unprogrammed events and evaluate change process 2 Analysis/diagnosis: the abilities to conduct an inquiry into a system's effectiveness, to see the root cause(s) of a system's current level of effectiveness; the core skill is interpreted to include all systems – individual, group, organisation and multi-organisation – as well as the ability to understand and inquire into oneself 3 Designing/choosing appropriate, relevant interventions: understanding how to select, modify or design effective interventions that will move the organisation from its current state to its desired future state 4 Facilitation and process consultation: the ability to assist an individual or group towards a goal; the ability to conduct an inquiry into individual and group processes such that the client system maintains ownership of the issue, increases its capacity for reflection on the consequences of its behaviours and actions, and develops a sense of increased control and ability 5 Developing client capability: the ability to conduct a change process in such a way that the client is better able to plan and implement a successful change process in the future, using technologies of planned change in a values-based and ethical manner 6 Evaluating organisation change: the ability to design and implement a process to evaluate the impact and effects of change intervention, including control of alternative explanations and interpretation of performance outcomes

other two types of OD practitioners – managers and specialists in related fields – also need this full range of skills and knowledge. It seems more reasonable to suggest that some subset of the items listed in **Table 3.1** should apply to all OD practitioners, whether they are OD professionals, managers or related specialists. These items would constitute the basic skills and knowledge of an OD practitioner. Beyond this background, the three types of OD practitioners would probably differ in areas of concentration. OD professionals would extend their breadth of skills across the remaining categories in **Table 3.1**; managers would focus on the major management knowledge areas; and related specialists would concentrate on skills in their respective areas, such as those included in the major management and collateral knowledge areas.

Based on the data in **Table 3.1**, as well as on more recent studies of OD skills,[31] all OD practitioners should have the following basic skills and knowledge to be effective:

1   **Intrapersonal skills** *or 'self-management' competence.* Despite the growing knowledge base and sophistication of the field, OD is still a human craft. As the primary instrument of diagnosis and change, practitioners often must process complex, ambiguous information and make informed judgements about its relevance to organisational issues.

> **Intrapersonal skills:** relate to activity taking place within a person's mind, including awareness of their personal inner dialogue; for example, meditation, prayer, visualisation.

The core competency of analysis and diagnosis listed in **Table 3.1** includes the ability to inquire into oneself, and it remains one of the cornerstone skills in OD. Practitioners must also have the personal centring to know their own values, feelings and purposes and the integrity to behave responsibly in a helping relationship with others. Bob Tannenbaum, one of the founders of OD, argues that self-knowledge is the most central ingredient in OD practice and suggests that practitioners are becoming too enamoured of skills and techniques.[32] Because OD is a highly uncertain process that requires constant adjustment and innovation, practitioners need to have active learning skills and a reasonable balance between their rational and emotional sides. Finally, OD practice can be highly stressful and can lead to early burnout, so practitioners need to know how to manage their own stress.

2   **Interpersonal skills**. Practitioners must create and maintain effective relationships with individuals and groups within the organisation to help them gain the competence necessary to solve their own problems.

> **Interpersonal skills:** relate to relationships or communication between people.

Table 3.1 identifies group dynamics, comparative cultural perspectives and business function as foundation knowledge, plus managing the consulting process and facilitation as core skills. All of these interpersonal competencies promote effective helping relationships. Such relationships start with a grasp of the organisation's perspective and require listening to members' perceptions and feelings to understand how they see themselves and the organisation. This understanding provides a starting point for joint diagnosis and problem solving. Practitioners must establish trust and rapport with organisation members so that they can share pertinent information and work effectively together. This requires being able to converse in the members' own language and to exchange feedback about how the relationship is progressing.

To help members learn new skills and behaviours, practitioners must serve as concrete role models of what is expected.[33] They must act in ways that are credible to organisation members and provide them with the counselling and coaching necessary for development and change. Because the helping relationship is jointly determined, practitioners need to be able to negotiate an acceptable role and to manage changing expectations and demands.

3   *General consultation skills.* **Table 3.1** identifies the ability to manage the consulting process and the ability to design interventions as core competencies that all practitioners should possess. OD starts with diagnosing an organisation or department to understand the causes of its problems and to discover areas for further development. OD practitioners need to know how to carry out an effective diagnosis, at least at a rudimentary level. They should know how to engage organisation members in diagnosis,

how to help them ask the right questions and how to collect and analyse information. A manager, for example, should be able to work with subordinates to jointly find out how the organisation or department is functioning. The manager should know basic diagnostic questions, some methods for gathering information (such as interviews or surveys) and some techniques for analysing it, such as force-field analysis or statistical means and distributions.

In addition to diagnosis, OD practitioners should know how to design and execute and finalise an intervention. They need to be able to lay out an action plan and to gain commitment to the program. They also need to know how to tailor the intervention to the situation, using information about how the change is progressing in order to guide implementation (see Chapter 6). For example, managers should be able to develop action steps for an intervention with subordinates. They should be able to gain their commitment to the program (usually through participation), sit down with them and assess how it is progressing, and make modifications if necessary. Once completed, the organisation should be prepared for ongoing strategies.

For more information on how to tailor an intervention to a situation, see Chapter 6.

4   *OD theory.* The final basic tool that OD practitioners should have is a general knowledge of OD. They should have some appreciation for planned change, the action research model and contemporary approaches to managing change. They should have some familiarity with the range of available interventions and the need for assessing and institutionalising change programs. Perhaps most important is that OD practitioners should understand their own role in the emerging field of OD, whether as managers, OD professionals or specialists in related areas.

THE PROFESSIONAL ORGANISATION DEVELOPMENT PRACTITIONER

Most of the literature about OD practitioners has focused on people specialising in OD as a profession. Here we discuss the role and typical career paths of OD professionals.

THE ROLE OF ORGANISATION DEVELOPMENT PROFESSIONALS

This section specifically addresses the OD role, marginality, emotional demands, use of knowledge and experience, and career opportunities.

Position

OD professionals have positions that are either internal or external to the organisation. Internal consultants are members of the organisation, and may be located in the human resources department or report directly to a line manager. They may perform the OD role exclusively, or they may combine it with other tasks, such as compensation practices, training or labour relations.[34] Many large organisations have created specialised OD consulting groups, some with their human resources departments. Their internal consultants typically have a variety of clients within the organisation, serving both line and staff departments.

External consultants are not members of the client organisation; they typically work for a consulting firm, a university or themselves. Organisations generally hire external consultants to provide a particular expertise that is unavailable internally, and to bring a different and potentially more objective perspective into the OD process.

Table 3.2 describes the differences between these two roles at each stage of the action research process.

TABLE 3.2	THE DIFFERENCES BETWEEN EXTERNAL AND INTERNAL CONSULTING	
Stage of change	**External consultants**	**Internal consultants**
Entering	» Source clients » Build relationships » Learn company jargon » 'Presenting problem' challenge » Time-consuming » Stressful phase » Select project/client according to own criteria » Unpredictable outcome	» Ready access to clients » Ready relationships » Know company jargon » Understand root causes » Time efficient » Congenial phase » Obligated to work with everyone » Steady pay
Contracting	» Formal documents » Can terminate project at will » Guard against out-of-pocket expenses » Information confidential » Loss of contract at stake » Maintain third-party role	» Informal agreements » Must complete projects assigned » No out-of-pocket expenses » Information can be open or confidential » Risk of client retaliation and loss of job at stake » Acts as third party, driver (on behalf of client) or pair of hands
Diagnosing	» Meet most organisation members for the first time » Prestige from being external » Build trust quickly » Confidential data can increase political sensitivities	» Has relationships with many organisation members » Prestige determined by job rank and client stature » Sustain reputation as trustworthy over time » Data openly shared can reduce political intrigue
Intervening	» Insist on valid information, free and informed choice and internal commitment » Confine activities within boundaries of client organisation	» Insist on valid information, free and informed choice and internal commitment » Run interference for client across organisational lines to align support
Evaluating	» Rely on repeat business and customer referral as key measures of project success » Seldom see long-term results	» Rely on repeat business, pay raise and promotion as key measures of success » Can see change become institutionalised » Little recognition for job well done

Source: M. Lacey, 'Internal consulting: perspectives on the process of planned change', *Journal of Organizational Change Management*, 8 (1995):76. © Emerald Group Publishing Limited, all rights reserved.

During the entry process, internal consultants have clear advantages. They have ready access to and relationships with clients, know the language of the organisation and have insights about the root cause of many of its problems. This allows internal consultants to save time in identifying the organisation's culture, informal practices and sources of power. They have access to a variety of information, including rumours, company reports and direct observation. In addition, entry is more efficient and congenial, and their pay is not at risk. External consultants, however, have the advantage of being able to select the clients they want to work with according to their own criteria. The contracting phase is less formal for internal consultants and there is less worry about expenses, but there is less choice about whether to complete the assignment. Both types of consultants must address issues of confidentiality, risk project termination (and other negative consequences) by the client and fill a third-party role.

During the diagnosis process, internal consultants already know most organisation members and most would enjoy a basic level of rapport and trust. But external consultants often have higher status than internal consultants, which allows them to probe difficult issues and assess the organisation more objectively. In the intervention phase, both types of consultants must rely on valid information, free and informed choice and internal commitment for their success. However, an internal consultant's strong ties to the organisation may make him or her overly cautious, particularly when powerful others can affect a career. Internal consultants also may lack certain skills and experience in facilitating organisational change. Insiders may have some small advantages in being able to move around the system and cross key organisational boundaries. Finally, the measures of success and reward differ from those of the external practitioner in the evaluation process.

A promising approach to having the advantages of both internal and external OD consultants is to include them both as members of an internal–external consulting team.[35] External consultants can combine their special expertise and objectivity with the inside knowledge and acceptance of internal consultants. The two parties can provide complementary consulting skills, while sharing the workload and possibly accomplishing more than either would by operating alone.[36] Internal consultants, for example, can provide almost continuous contact with the client, while their external counterparts can periodically provide specialised services, perhaps on two or three days each month. External consultants can also help train their organisation partners, thus transferring OD skills and knowledge to the organisation.

Although little has been written on internal–external consulting teams, studies suggest that the effectiveness of such teams depends on the members developing strong, supportive, collegial relationships. They need to take time to develop the consulting team, confronting individual differences and establishing appropriate roles and exchanges. Members need to provide each other with continuous feedback and to make a commitment to learning from each other. In the absence of these team-building and learning features, internal–external consulting teams can be more troublesome and less effective than consultants working alone.

Marginality

A promising line of research on the professional OD role centres on the issue of marginality.[37] The marginal person is one who successfully straddles the boundary between two or more groups that have differing goals, value systems and behaviour patterns. In the past, the marginal role has always been seen as dysfunctional. Now marginality is seen in a more positive light. There are many examples of marginal roles in organisations: the salesperson, the buyer, the first-line supervisor, the integrator and the project manager.

Marginality: an amount of change included to be sure of success.

Evidence is mounting that some people are better at taking marginal roles than others. Those who are good at marginal roles seem to have personal qualities of low dogmatism, neutrality, open-mindedness, objectivity, flexibility and adaptable information-processing ability. Rather than being upset by conflict, ambiguity and stress, they thrive on it. Individuals with marginal orientations are more likely than others to develop integrative decisions that bring together and reconcile viewpoints between opposing organisational groups, and are more likely to remain neutral in controversial situations. Thus, the research suggests that the marginal role[38] can have positive effects when it is filled by a person with a marginal orientation. Such a person can be more objective and better able to perform successfully in linking, integrative or conflict-laden roles.[39]

A study of 89 external OD practitioners and 246 internal practitioners (response rates of 59 per cent and 54 per cent, respectively) showed that external OD professionals were more comfortable with the marginal role than were internal OD professionals. Internal consultants with more years of experience were more marginally oriented than were those with less experience.[40] These findings, combined with other research on marginal roles, suggest the importance of maintaining the OD professional's marginality, with its flexibility, independence and boundary-spanning characteristics.

Emotional demands

The OD practitioner role is emotionally demanding. The importance of understanding emotions and their impact on the practitioner's effectiveness has been evidenced by research and practice support.[41] The research on emotional intelligence in organisations suggests a set of abilities that can aid OD practitioners in conducting successful change efforts.[42] Emotional intelligence refers to the ability to recognise and express emotions appropriately, to use emotions in thought and decisions and to regulate emotion in oneself and in others. It is, therefore, a different kind of intelligence from problem-solving ability, engineering aptitude or the knowledge of concepts. In tandem with traditional knowledge and skill, emotional intelligence affects and supplements rational thought; emotions help prioritise thinking by directing attention to important information not addressed in models and theories. In that sense, some researchers argue that emotional intelligence is as important as cognitive intelligence.[43]

The importance of emotional intelligence in practice has been evidenced by OD practitioners' reports. From the client's perspective, OD practitioners must understand emotions well enough to relate to and help organisation members address resistance, commitment and ambiguity at each stage of planned change. Despite the predominant focus on rationality and efficiency, almost any change process must address important and difficult issues that raise emotions such as the fear of failure, rejection, anxiety and anger.[44] OD practitioners can provide psychological support, model appropriate emotional expression, reframe client perspectives and provide resources. The practitioners must also understand their own emotions. Ambiguity, unfamiliarity or denial of emotions can lead to inaccurate and untimely interventions. For example, a practitioner who is uncomfortable with conflict may intervene to defuse an argument between two managers because of the discomfort he or she feels, not because the conflict is destructive. In such a case, the practitioner is acting to address a personal need rather than intervening to improve the system's effectiveness.

Evidence suggests that emotional intelligence increases with age and experience.[45] Research also supports the conclusion that competence with emotions can be developed through personal growth processes such as sensitivity training, counselling and therapy. It seems reasonable to suggest that professional OD practitioners dedicate themselves to a long-term regime of development that includes acquiring both cognitive learning and emotional intelligence.

Use of knowledge and experience

The professional OD role has been described in terms of a continuum ranging from client-centred (using the client's knowledge and experience) to consultant-centred (using the consultant's knowledge and experience), as shown in **Figure 3.2**. Traditionally, OD consultants have worked at the client-centred end of the continuum. Relying mainly on sensitivity training, process consultation and team building, they have been expected to remain neutral, refusing to offer expert advice on organisational problems. Rather than contracting to solve specific problems, the consultant has tended to work with organisation

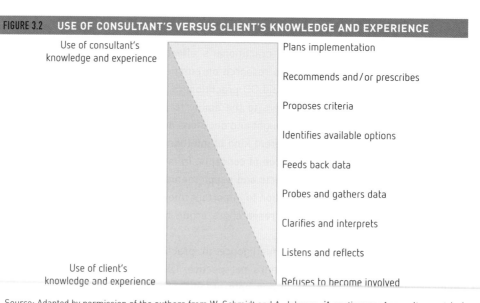

FIGURE 3.2   USE OF CONSULTANT'S VERSUS CLIENT'S KNOWLEDGE AND EXPERIENCE

Use of consultant's knowledge and experience

Plans implementation

Recommends and/or prescribes

Proposes criteria

Identifies available options

Feeds back data

Probes and gathers data

Clarifies and interprets

Listens and reflects

Use of client's knowledge and experience

Refuses to become involved

Source: Adapted by permission of the authors from W. Schmidt and A. Johnson, 'A continuum of consultancy styles', unpublished manuscript (July 1970), p. 1.

members to identify problems and potential solutions, to help them study what they are doing now and to consider alternative behaviours and solutions, and to help them discover whether in fact the consultant and they can learn to do things better. In doing this, the OD professional has generally listened and reflected upon members' perceptions and ideas, and helped clarify and interpret their communications and behaviours.

With the proliferation of OD interventions in the structural, human resource management and strategy areas, this limited definition of the professional OD role has expanded to include the consultant-centred end of the continuum. In many of these newer approaches, the consultant may have to take on a modified role of expert, with the consent and collaboration of organisation members. For example, if a consultant and managers were to try to bring about a major structural redesign, managers may not have the appropriate knowledge and expertise to create and manage the change. The consultant's role might be to present the basic concepts and ideas and then to struggle jointly with the managers to select an approach that might be useful to the organisation and decide how it might be best implemented. In this situation, the OD professional recommends or prescribes particular changes and is active in planning how to implement them. However, this expertise is always shared rather than imposed.

With the development of new and varied intervention approaches, the role of the OD professional needs to be seen as falling along the entire continuum from client-centred to consultant-centred. At times, the consultant will rely mainly on organisation members' knowledge and experiences to identify and solve problems. At other times, it may be more appropriate for the OD professional to take on the role of expert, withdrawing from this role as managers gain more knowledge and experience.

Careers of organisation development professionals

Unlike such occupations as medicine and law, OD is an emerging practice. It is still developing the characteristics of an established profession: a common body of knowledge, educational requirements, accrediting procedures, a recognised code of ethics, and rules and methods for governing conduct. This means that people can enter professional OD careers from a variety of educational and industry backgrounds. They do not have to follow an established career path, but rather have some choice about when to enter or leave an OD career and whether to be an internal or external consultant.[46]

Despite the looseness or flexibility of the OD profession, most OD professionals have had specific training in OD. This training can include relatively short courses (one day to two weeks) and programs or workshops conducted within organisations or at outside institutions, such as TAFE's 'Train the Trainer' programs. Training in OD can also be more formal and lengthy, including master's programs and doctoral training.

As might be expected, career choices widen as people gain training and experience in OD. Those with rudimentary training tend to be internal consultants, often taking on OD roles as temporary assignments on the way to higher managerial or staff positions. Holders of master's degrees are generally evenly split between internal and external consultants. Those with doctorates may join a university faculty and consult part-time, join a consulting firm or seek a position as a relatively high-level internal consultant.

External consultants tend to be more mature, to have more managerial experience and to spend more of their time in OD than do internal practitioners. Perhaps the most common career path is to begin as an internal consultant, gain experience and visibility through successful interventions or publishing and then become an external consultant. A field study found that internal consultants acquired greater competence by working with external consultants who deliberately helped to develop them. This development took place through a tutorial arrangement of joint diagnosis and intervention in the organisation, which gave the internal consultants a chance to observe and learn from the model furnished by the external consultants.[47]

There is increasing evidence that an OD career can be stressful, sometimes leading to burnout.[48] Burnout comes from taking on too many jobs, becoming overcommitted and, in general, working too hard. OD work often requires six-day weeks, with some days running up to 15 hours. Consultants may spend a week working with one organisation or department and then spend the weekend preparing for the next client. They may spend 50–75 per cent of their time travelling, living in planes, cars, hotels, meetings and restaurants. Indeed, one practitioner has suggested that the majority of OD consultants would repeat the phrase 'quality of work life for consultants' as follows: 'Quality of work life? For consultants?'[49]

OD professionals are increasingly taking steps to cope with burnout. They may shift jobs, moving from external to internal roles to avoid travel. They may learn to pace themselves better and to avoid taking on too much work.

PROFESSIONAL VALUES

Values have played an important role in OD from its beginning. Traditionally, OD professionals have promoted a set of humanistic and democratic values. They have sought to build trust and collaboration; to create an open, problem-solving climate; and to increase the self-control of organisation members. More recently, OD practitioners have extended those humanistic values to include a concern for improving organisational effectiveness (for example, to increase productivity or to reduce turnover) and performance (for example, to increase profitability). They have shown an increasing desire to optimise both human benefits and production objectives.[50]

The joint values of humanising organisations and improving their effectiveness have received widespread support in the OD profession, as well as increasing encouragement from managers, employees and union officials. Indeed, it would be difficult not to support these joint concerns. But, increasingly, questions have been raised about the possibility of simultaneously pursuing greater humanism and organisational effectiveness.[51] More practitioners are experiencing situations in which there is conflict between the employees' needs for greater meaning and the organisation's need for more effective and efficient use of its resources. For example, expensive capital equipment may run most efficiently if it is highly programmed and routinised; yet people may not derive satisfaction from working with such technology. Should efficiency be maximised at the expense of people's satisfaction? Can technology be changed to make it more humanly satisfying yet remain efficient? What compromises are possible? These are the value dilemmas often faced when trying to optimise both human benefits and organisational effectiveness.

In addition to value issues within organisations, OD practitioners are dealing more and more with value conflicts with powerful outside groups. Organisations are open systems and exist within increasingly turbulent environments. For example, educational institutes are facing complex and changing task environments. Australia has long had public-owned educational institutes and now these are being offered to private operators. This means a proliferation of external stakeholders with interests in the organisation's functioning, including students, suppliers, government regulation, employers, the government, shareholders, unions, the press and various interest groups. These external groups often have different and competing values for judging the organisation's effectiveness. For example, shareholders may judge the business in terms of price per share, the government in terms of compliance with Tertiary Education Quality and Standards Agency legislation, students in terms of quality of program. Because organisations must rely on these external groups for resources and legitimacy, they cannot simply ignore these competing values: they must somehow respond to them and try to reconcile the different interests.

It has been an ongoing debate as to how to support organisations in managing external relationships and the conclusion is always the need for new interventions and competence in OD.[52] Practitioners must not only have social skills (like those proposed in **Table 3.1**) but also political skills. They must understand the distribution of power, conflicts of interest and value dilemmas inherent in managing external relationships, and be able to manage their own role and values in respect to those dynamics. Interventions promoting collaboration and system maintenance may be ineffective in this larger arena, especially when there are power and dominance relationships between organisations, plus competition for scarce resources. Under these conditions, OD practitioners may need more power-oriented interventions, such as bargaining, coalition forming and pressure tactics.

For example, firms in the tobacco industry have waged an aggressive campaign against efforts of groups, such as the Australian Medical Association, the Royal Australasian College of General Practitioners, the Australian Cancer Society and the federal and state governments, to limit or ban the smoking of tobacco products. They have formed a powerful industry coalition to lobby against anti-smoking legislation, and they have spent enormous sums of money sponsoring leading sporting and cultural events, conducting public relations and refuting research that purportedly shows the dangers of smoking. These power-oriented strategies are intended to manage an increasingly hostile environment. They may be necessary for the industry's survival. People practising OD in such settings may need to help organisations implement such strategies if they are to manage their environments effectively. Apply your learning 3.2, presents an opinion on the role of ethics as part of the change process.

ETHICS AND ORGANIZATIONAL CHANGE MANAGEMENT

Change is inevitable at any organization and can arise from the need to improve resource allocation, reengineer business processes, tighten the budget, or other factors that require a restructuring of an organization. In order for organizational change to occur, a change agent must challenge the status quo by bringing a different perspective into the organizational environment. Change agents can be external, internal, or a hybrid of the two. External change agents can be consultants or other individuals who come from a third party organization, who utilize behavioral sciences techniques to initiate organizational change that is desired by executive management. Internal change agents are individuals, or occasionally departments, that are within the organization who know about the issues plaguing the organization, hence initiating the change from inside the organization. For complex issues, a combination of both external and internal change agents is required since a large knowledge base is needed to initiate change.

Regardless of the type of change agent initiating the change, there are many ethical issues that can arise during a change process. External change agents are hired by executive management to gather data and provide data analysis on an organizational issue. If the data analysis and proposed solution are not in alignment with the executive management agenda or show that poor performance was a result of executive management, the data could be manipulated. Manipulation of this data would be done to force the external agent's analysis to align with the executive management agenda or place blame for poor performance on low level employees. Since the change process is fundamentally initiated by executive management, there is a perception that change is based off power relationships within an organization. This can lead to purposefully misconstructed statements regarding the scope of change. Management can state that a change process is initiated with the purpose of increasing employee engagement, when in fact the true rationale behind the change process may be result based performance metrics that suffocate and scrutinize employee activities. Often times, change is not voluntary, and employee conformity to the change is required. This raises unethical concerns since employees will often be faced with the dilemma of forced conformity or being terminated.

Although there will always be change resistance, organizational management can promote ethical change initiatives by developing appropriate organizational culture. Organizational culture is shared set of principles, values, and beliefs that dictate how employees act. Managers who want to promote ethical change processes need to establish a culture of ethical behavior. It is best to lead by example, so managers need to act ethically themselves to promote ethical behavior as the norm throughout the organization. Ethical behavior includes department openness, constructive criticism, clear communication, conformity to policies, and workplace respect. Along with leading by example, management needs to create a code of ethics. An organizational code of ethics is a policy statement that binds employees to a set of organization wide value and ethical standards. This code will make employees hold

»

»

themselves and other accountable for acting in an ethical manner and promoting ethics throughout the organization. Through this ethical culture, change will be initiated ethically and resistance will be minimized.

Source: M. Botyarov, 'Ethics and organizational change management', 9 July 2016, https://www.linkedin.com/pulse/ethics-organizational-change-management-michael-botyarov, accessed 23 May 2018.

Critical thinking questions

1   What is an ethical behaviour? Give an example.

2   What is a code of ethics? Give an example of where an organisation or industry is bound by a code of ethics.

PROFESSIONAL ETHICS

Ethical issues in OD are concerned with how practitioners perform their helping relationship with organisation members. Inherent in any helping relationship is the potential for misconduct and client abuse. OD practitioners can let personal values stand in the way of good practice; they can use the power inherent in their professional role to abuse organisation members (possibly unintentionally) or favour one group of stakeholders at the expense of other stakeholders, or build a dependency of the organisation on OD.

ETHICAL GUIDELINES

To its credit, the field of OD has always shown concern for the ethical conduct of its practitioners. There have been several articles and conferences about ethics in OD. The Australasian Ethics Network held a three-day conference at the University of Sydney.[53] In addition, statements of ethics governing OD practice have been sponsored by many professional associations; for example, the Australian Association of Professional and Applied Ethics (AAPAE) comprises academics and professionals across a range of disciplines in a non-partisan and non-profit association, while Corporate Ethics is committed to helping business develop a strategic system that incorporates values and ethics.[54] The accounting industry is just one of many professions that has codes of ethics.[55] Both CPA Australia and Chartered Accountants Australia and New Zealand now follow the Code of Ethics for Professional Accountants (APES 110) as issued by the Accounting Professional and Ethical Standards Board (APESB). Visit **http://apesb.org.au** to view the Code.

ETHICAL DILEMMAS

Although adherence to statements of ethics helps prevent ethical problems from occurring, OD practitioners can still encounter **ethical dilemmas**. **Figure 3.3** is a process model that explains how ethical dilemmas can occur in OD. The antecedent conditions include an OD practitioner and a client system with different goals, values, needs, skills and abilities. During the entry and contracting

Ethical dilemma: a problem pertaining to the moral principles of the change process.

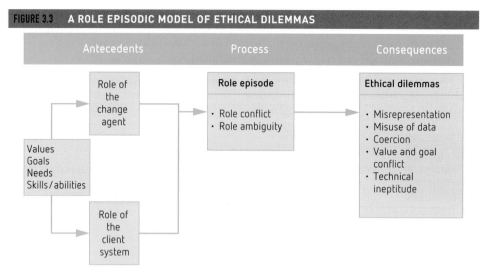

FIGURE 3.3   A ROLE EPISODIC MODEL OF ETHICAL DILEMMAS

Source: L. White and M. Rhodeback, 'Ethical dilemmas in organization development: a cross-cultural analysis', *Journal of Business Ethics*, 11 (1992): 663–70, Figure 1. With kind permission from Springer Science Business Media.

phase, there is an intention to address and clarify these differences. As a practical matter, however, it is reasonable to assume that these differences may or may not be addressed and clarified. Under such circumstances, the subsequent intervention process or role episode is subject to role conflict and role ambiguity. Neither the client nor the OD practitioner is clear about his or her respective responsibilities. Each party is pursuing different goals, and each is using different skills and values to achieve those goals. The role conflict and ambiguity can lead to five types of ethical dilemmas: (1) misrepresentation, (2) misuse of data, (3) manipulative dependency, (4) value and goal conflict and (5) technical ineptitude.

Misrepresentation

This occurs when OD practitioners claim that an intervention will produce results that are unreasonable for the change program or the situation. The client can contribute to this problem by portraying inaccurate goals and needs. In either case, one or both parties are operating under false pretences and an ethical dilemma exists. For example, in an infamous case called 'The undercover change agent', an attempt was made to use laboratory training in an organisation whose top management did not understand it and was not ready for it. The OD consultant sold 'T-groups' as the intervention that would solve the problems that faced the organisation. After the chairman of the business made a surprise visit to the site where the training was being held, the consultant was fired. The nature and style of the T-group was in direct contradiction to the chairman's concepts about leadership.[56] Misrepresentation is likely to occur in the entering and contracting phases of planned change when the initial consulting relationship is being established. To prevent misrepresentation, OD practitioners need to be very clear about the goals of the change effort and to explore openly with the client its expected effects, its relevance to the client system and the practitioner's competence in executing the intervention.

Misuse of data

This occurs when information gathered during the OD process is used punitively. Large amounts of information are invariably obtained during the entry and diagnostic phases of OD; although most OD practitioners value openness and trust, it is important that they be aware of how such data are going to be used. It is a human tendency to use data to enhance a power position. Openness is one thing, but leaking inappropriate information can be harmful to individuals and to the organisation as well. It is easy for a consultant, under the guise of obtaining information, to gather data about whether a particular manager is good or bad. When, how or if this information can be used is an ethical dilemma not easily resolved. To minimise misuse of data, practitioners should agree with organisation members up front about how data collected will be used. This agreement should be reviewed periodically in light of changing circumstances. Care should be taken regarding the use of data that could have public benefit.

Manipulative dependency

This ethical dilemma occurs when organisation members are forced to participate in an OD intervention. People should have the freedom to choose whether or not to participate in a change program if they are to gain self-reliance to solve their own problems. In team building, for example, team members should have the option of deciding not to become involved in the intervention. Management should not unilaterally decide that team building is good for members. However, freedom to make a choice implies knowledge about OD. Many organisation members have little information about OD interventions, what they involve and the nature and consequences of becoming involved with them. This makes it imperative for OD practitioners to educate clients about interventions before choices are made as to whether or not to implement them.

Coercion can also pose ethical dilemmas for the helping relationship between OD practitioners and organisation members. Inherent in any helping relationship are possibilities for excessive manipulation and dependency, two facets of coercion. Kelman pointed out that behaviour change 'inevitably involves some degree of manipulation and control, and at least an implicit imposition of the change agent's values on the client or the person he [or she] is influencing'.[57] This places the practitioner on two horns of a dilemma: (1) any attempt to change is in itself a change and thereby a manipulation, no matter how slight; and (2) there exists no formula or method to structure a change situation so that such manipulation can be totally absent. To attack the first aspect of the dilemma, Kelman stressed freedom of choice, seeing any action that limits freedom of choice as being ethically ambiguous or worse. To address the second aspect, Kelman argued that the OD practitioner must remain keenly aware of her or his own value system and alert to the possibility that these values are being imposed upon a client. In other words, an effective way to resolve this dilemma is to make the change effort as open as possible, with the free consent and knowledge of the individuals involved.

The second facet of coercion that can pose ethical dilemmas for the helping relationship involves dependency. Helping relationships invariably create dependency between those who need help and those who provide it.[58] A major goal in OD is to lessen the clients' dependency on consultants by helping them gain the knowledge and skills to address organisational problems and manage change themselves. In some cases, however, achieving independence from OD practitioners can result in the clients being either counterdependent or overdependent, especially in the early stages of the relationship. To resolve dependency issues, consultants can openly and explicitly discuss with the client how to handle the dependency problem, especially what the client and consultant expect of one another. Another approach is to focus on problem finding. Usually, the client is looking for a solution to a perceived problem. The consultant can redirect the energy to improved joint diagnosis so that both are working on problem identification and problem solving. This moves the energy of the client away from dependency. Finally, dependency can be reduced by changing the client's expectation – from being helped or controlled by the practitioner – to focusing on the need to manage the problem. This helps to reinforce the concept that the consultant is working for the client and offering assistance at the client's discretion.

Value and goal conflict

This ethical dilemma occurs when the purpose of the change effort is not clear or when the client and the practitioner disagree over how to achieve the goals. The important practical issue for OD consultants is whether it is justifiable to unilaterally withhold services from an organisation that does not agree with their values or methods. Lippitt suggested that the real question is the following: Assuming that some kind of change is going to occur anyway, doesn't the consultant have a responsibility to try to guide the change in the most constructive fashion possible?[59] The question may be of greater importance and relevance to an internal consultant or to a consultant who already has an ongoing relationship with the client.

According to the Career Industry Council of Australia (CICA),[60] independent OD practitioners and/or consultants, possibly through membership of entities such as CICA, have access to professional standards and/or ethics that protect them from compromising their own values when providing professional OD services to clients. Internal OD practitioners, while governed by organisational values, are able to refer to the same, if not similar, standards in an attempt to influence organisations, resulting in change or setting the baseline for new approaches to OD.

Technical ineptitude

This final ethical dilemma occurs when OD practitioners attempt to implement interventions for which they are not skilled or when the client attempts a change for which it is not ready. Critical to the success of any OD program is the selection of an appropriate intervention, which depends, in turn, on careful diagnosis of the organisation. Selection of an intervention is closely related to the practitioner's own values, skills and abilities. In solving organisational problems, many OD consultants tend to emphasise a favourite intervention or technique, such as team building, total quality management or self-managed teams.

Technical ineptitude: total lack of skill or knowledge of technology.

They let their own values and beliefs dictate the change method.[61] **Technical ineptitude** dilemmas can also occur when interventions do not align with the ability of the organisation to implement them. Again, careful diagnosis can reveal the extent to which the organisation is ready to make a change and possesses the skills and knowledge to implement it.

SUMMARY

This chapter examined the role of leaders in the change process. This concept applies to three kinds of people: individuals specialising in OD as a profession, people from related fields who have gained some competence in OD and managers who have the OD skills necessary to change and develop their organisations or departments. Comprehensive lists exist of core and advanced skills and knowledge that an effective OD specialist should possess, but a smaller set of basic skills and knowledge is applicable for all practitioners, regardless of whether they are OD professionals, related specialists or managers. These include four kinds of background: intrapersonal skills, interpersonal skills, general consultation skills and knowledge of OD theory.

The professional OD role can apply to internal consultants who belong to the organisation undergoing change, to external consultants who are members of universities and consulting firms or are self-employed and to members of internal–external consulting teams. The OD practitioner's role may be aptly described in terms of marginality and emotional demands. People with a tolerance for marginal roles seem especially adapted for OD practice because they are able to maintain neutrality and objectivity, and develop integrative solutions that reconcile viewpoints between opposing organisational departments. Similarly, the OD practitioner's emotional intelligence and awareness are keys to implementing the role successfully. Whereas, in the past, the OD practitioner's role has been described as falling at the client end of the continuum from client-centred to consultant-centred functioning, the development of new and varied interventions has shifted the role of the OD professional to cover the entire range of this continuum.

Although OD is still an emerging profession, most OD professionals have specific training in OD, ranging from short courses and workshops to graduate and doctoral education. No single career path exists, but internal consulting is often a stepping stone to becoming an external consultant. Because of the hectic pace of OD practice, OD specialists should be prepared to cope with high levels of stress and the possibility of career burnout.

Values have played a key role in OD, and traditional values promoting trust, collaboration and openness have recently been supplemented with concerns for improving organisational effectiveness and productivity. OD specialists may face value dilemmas in trying to jointly optimise human benefits and organisation performance. They may also encounter value conflicts when dealing with powerful external stakeholders, such as the government, shareholders and customers. Dealing with these outside groups may take political skills, as well as the more traditional social skills.

Ethical issues in OD involve how practitioners perform their helping role with clients. OD has always shown a concern for the ethical conduct of practitioners, and several ethical codes for OD practice have been developed by the various professional associations in OD. Ethical dilemmas in OD tend to arise around the following issues: misrepresentation, misuse of data, coercion, value and goal conflict, and technical ineptitude.

ACTIVITIES

REVIEW QUESTIONS

1   What are the core skills of an OD practitioner? How would these skills respond to a fluctuating environment? (LO1 & 2)

2   Can anybody be a change agent? Why/Why not? (LO2)

3   Developing a contract between a change agent and client is very complex. What would be the major problem encountered? (LO3)

4   Compare and contrast the advantages and disadvantages of internal and external change agents. (LO4)

5   Creating a dependency by a change agent may be considered unethical. Do you agree/disagree? Explain your answer. (LO5)

EXTEND YOUR LEARNING

1   The role of the OD practitioner is extremely complex and responsive to the organisation's circumstances at the time. Several change agents would have varied, or differing, perspectives. What would they be? How would you account for any variation in these perspectives? (LO1, 2 & 4)

2   A contract is a legal agreement that has many allocated responsibilities and accountabilities. Is it possible for such a legal agreement to be negotiated between a change agent and client? Explain your answer. (LO 3)

Search Me! Management

Explore **Search Me! Management** for articles relevant to this chapter. Fast and convenient, **Search Me! Management** is updated daily and provides you with 24-hour access to full text articles from hundreds of scholarly and popular journals, eBooks and newspapers, including *The Australian* and *The New York Times*. Visit http://login.cengagebrain.com and use the access code that comes with this book for 12 months access to the **Search Me! Management** database. Try searching for the following keywords:

Keywords:

- Humanistic values
- Diagnostic phase
- Contracting
- Ground rules
- Intrapersonal skills
- Interpersonal skills
- Marginality
- Ethical dilemmas
- Technical ineptitude

Search tip: **Search Me! Management** contains information from both local and international sources. To get the greatest number of search results, try using both Australian and American spellings in your searches; for example, 'globalisation' and 'globalization'; 'organisation' and 'organization'.

REFERENCES

1 See, for example, the website of Barry B. Grossman, http://www.hsod.net.
2 R. James, *Faith-Based Organisational Development (OD) with Churches in Malawi* (Praxis Note 47), INTRAC: International NGO Training and Research Centre, http://www.intrac.org/data/files/resources/584/Praxis-Note-47-Faith-Based-Organisational-Development-with-Churches-in-Malawi.pdf, 21 July 2009.
3 M. Touchstone, 'Professional development. Part 5: core humanistic values', *EMS*, 39 (May 2010): 29–30; T. Cummings and C. Cummings, 'Appreciating organization development: a comparative essay on divergent perspectives', *Human Resource Development Quarterly*, 25 (2014): 141–53.
4 A. Church and W. Burke, 'Practitioner attitudes about the field of organization development', in *Research in Organizational Change and Development*, eds W. Pasmore and R. Woodman (Greenwich, CT: JAI Press, 1995).
5 J. Kotter, *Leading Change* (Boston: Harvard Business Review Press, 2012).
6 D.S. Carlson, N. Upton and S. Seaman, 'The impact of human resource practices and compensation design on performance: an analysis of family-owned SMEs', *Journal of Small Business Management*, 44 (2006): 531–43.
7 V. Garrow, *OD: Past, Present and Future*, IES Working Paper: WP22, January 2009.
8 RMIT University, Centre for Sustainable Organisations and Work, https://www.rmit.edu.au/research/research-institutes-centres-and-groups/research-centres/centre-for-sustainable-organisations-and-work.
9 E.E. Lawler III and C.G. Worley, 'Winning support for organizational change: designing employee reward systems that keep on working', *Ivey Business Journal*, March/April 2006, http://iveybusinessjournal.com/publication/winning-support-for-organizational-change-designing-employee-reward-systems-that-keep-on-working.
10 C. Margerison, 'Consulting activities in organizational change', *Journal of Organizational Change Management*, 1 (1988): 60–7; P. Block, *Flawless Consulting: A Guide to Getting Your Expertise Used* (Austin, TX: Learning Concepts, 1981); R. Harrison, 'Choosing the depth of organizational intervention', *Journal of Applied Behavioral Science*, 6:11 (1970): 182–202.
11 M. Beer, *Organization Change and Development: A Systems View* (Santa Monica, CA: Goodyear, 1980); G. Lippitt and R. Lippitt, *The Consulting Process in Action*, 2nd edn (San Diego: University Associates, 1986).
12 L. Greiner and R. Metzger, *Consulting to Management* (Englewood Cliffs, NJ: Prentice Hall, 1983): 251–8; Beer, *Organization Change and Development*, op. cit.: 81–3.
13 F. Bevilacqua, 'The impact of organisational issues in the development of institutional repositories', University of Parma, October 2007, http://www.aepic.it/conf/DSUG2007/viewabstractcc46.html?id=203&cf=11.
14 Block, *Flawless Consulting*, op. cit.
15 J. Fordyce and R. Weil, *Managing with People: A Manager's Handbook of Organization Development Methods*, 2nd edn (Reading, MA: Addison-Wesley, 1979).

16 Beer, *Organization Change and Development*, op. cit.; Fordyce and Weil, *Managing with People*, op. cit.

17 N. Raab, 'Working with the client consultant relationship: why every step is an "intervention"', *OD Practitioner*, 36 (2004).

18 G. Lippitt, 'Criteria for selecting, evaluating, and developing consultants', *Training and Development Journal*, 28 (August 1972): 10–15.

19 Greiner and Metzger, *Consulting to Management*, op. cit.

20 Block, *Flawless Consulting*, op. cit.

21 Beer, *Organization Change and Development*, op. cit.

22 T. Cody, *Management Consulting: A Game Without Chips* (Fitzwilliam, NH: Kennedy and Kennedy, 1986): 108–16; H. Holtz, *How to Succeed as an Independent Consultant*, 2nd edn (New York: John Wiley and Sons, 1988): 145–61.

23 G. Bellman, *The Consultant's Calling* (San Francisco: Jossey-Bass, 1990).

24 M. Weisbord, 'The organization development contract', *Organization Development Practitioner*, 5:11 (1973): 1–4; M. Weisbord, 'The organization contract revisited', *Consultation*, 4 (Winter 1985): 305–15; D. Nadler, *Feedback and Organization Development: Using Data Based Methods* (Reading, MA: Addison-Wesley, 1977): 110–14.

25 Block, *Flawless Consulting*, op. cit.

26 ibid.

27 M. Lacey, 'Internal consulting: perspectives on the process of planned change', *Journal of Organizational Change Management*, 8 (1995): 75–84; J. Geirland and M. Maniker-Leiter, 'Five lessons for internal organization development consultants', *OD Practitioner*, 27 (1995): 44–8.

28 B. Glickman, 'Qualities of change agents' (unpublished manuscript, May 1974); R. Havelock, *The Change Agent's Guide to Innovation in Education* (Englewood Cliffs, NJ: Educational Technology, 1973): 5; R. Lippitt, 'Dimensions of the consultant's job', in *The Planning of Change*, eds W. Bennis, K. Benne and R. Chin (New York: Holt, Rinehart and Winston, 1961): 156–61; C. Rogers, *On Becoming a Person* (Boston: Houghton Mifflin, 1971); N. Paris, 'Some thoughts on the qualifications for a consultant' (unpublished manuscript, 1973); 'OD experts reflect on the major skills needed by consultants: with comments from Edgar Schein', *Academy of Management OD Newsletter* (Spring 1979): 1–4.

29 D. Harvey and D. Brown, *An Experiential Approach to Organization Development*, 5th edn (Englewood Cliffs, NJ: Prentice Hall, 1996): 94–6.

30 C. Worley, W. Rothwell and R. Sullivan, 'Competencies of OD practitioners', in *Practicing Organization Development*, 2nd edn, eds W. Rothwell and R. Sullivan (San Diego: Pfeiffer, 2005).

31 J. Esper, 'Core competencies in organization development' (independent study conducted as partial fulfilment of the MBA degree, Graduate School of Business Administration, University of Southern California, June 1987); E. Neilsen, *Becoming an OD Practitioner* (Englewood Cliffs, NJ: Prentice Hall, 1984); S. Eisen, H. Steele and J. Cherbeneau, 'Developing OD competence for the future', in *Practicing Organization Development*, eds W. Rothwell, R. Sullivan and G. McLean (San Diego: Pfeiffer, 1995).

32 B. Tannenbaum, 'Letter to the editor', Consulting Practice Communique, *Academy of Management Managerial Consultation Division*, 21 (1993): 16–17; B. Tannenbaum, 'Self-awareness: an essential element underlying consultant effectiveness', *Journal of Organizational Change Management*, 8 (1995): 85–6.

33 L. McKnight, 'Global consulting: the use of self to transfer OD values into national cultures', *Organization Development Journal*, 30 (2012).

34 M. Lacey, 'Internal consulting: perspectives on the process of planned change', *Journal of Organizational Change Management*, 8 (1995): 75–84.

35 E. Kirkhart and T. Isgar, 'Quality of work life for consultants: the internal–external relationship', *Consultation*, 5 (Spring 1986): 5–23.

36 J. Thacker and N. Kulick, 'The use of consultants in joint union/management quality of work life efforts', *Consultation*, 5 (Summer 1986): 116–26.

37 R. Ziller, *The Social Self* (Elmsford, NY: Pergamon, 1973).

38 D.W. Puchniak, 'Delusions of hostility: the marginal role of hostile takeovers in Japanese corporate governance remains unchanged', https://sydney.edu.au/law/anjel/documents/2010/DelusionsofHostility.pdf.

39 R. Ziller, B. Stark and H. Pruden, 'Marginality and integrative management positions', *Academy of Management Journal*, 12 (December 1969): 487–95; H. Pruden and B. Stark, 'Marginality associated with interorganizational linking process, productivity and satisfaction', *Academy of Management Journal*, 14 (March 1971): 145–8; W. Liddell, 'Marginality and integrative decisions', *Academy of Management Journal*, 16 (March 1973): 154–6; P. Brown and C. Cotton, 'Marginality, a force for the OD practitioner', *Training and Development Journal*, 29 (April 1975): 14–18; H. Aldrich and D. Gerker, 'Boundary spanning roles and organizational structure', *Academy of Management Review*, 2 (April 1977): 217–30; C. Cotton, 'Marginality – a neglected dimension in the design of work', *Academy of Management Review*, 2 (January 1977): 133–8; N. Margulies, 'Perspectives on the marginality of the consultant's role', in *The*

Cutting Edge, ed. W. Burke (La Jolla, CA: University Associates, 1978): 60–79.

40 P. Brown, C. Cotton and R. Golembiewski, 'Marginality and the OD practitioner', *Journal of Applied Behavioral Science*, 13 (1977): 493–506.

41 C. Lundberg and C. Young, 'A note on emotions and consultancy', *Journal of Organizational Change Management*, 14 (2001): 530–8; A. Carr, 'Understanding emotion and emotionality in a process of change', *Journal of Organizational Change Management*, 14 (2001): 421–36.

42 D. Goleman, *Emotional Intelligence* (New York: Bantam Books, 1995); R. Cooper and A. Sawaf, *Executive EQ: Emotional Intelligence in Leadership and Organisations* (New York: Grosset/Putnam, 1997); P. Salovey and D. Sluyter, eds, *Emotional Development and Emotional Intelligence* (New York: Basic Books, 1997).

43 Goleman, *Emotional Intelligence*, op. cit.

44 J. Sanford, *Fritz Kunkel: Selected Writings* (Mahwah, NJ: Paulist Press, 1984); Lundberg and Young, 'Note on emotions', op. cit.; Carr, 'Understanding emotion', op. cit.

45 J. Ciarrochi, J. Forgas and J. Mayer, *Emotional Intelligence in Everyday Life: A Scientific Inquiry* (New York: Psychology Press, 2001).

46 D. Kegan, 'Organization development as OD network members see it', *Group and Organization Studies*, 7 (March 1982): 5–11.

47 J. Lewis III, 'Growth of internal change agents in organizations', PhD Dissertation, Case Western Reserve University, 1970.

48 G. Edelwich and A. Brodsky, *Burn-Out Stages of Disillusionment in the Helping Professions* (New York: Human Science, 1980); M. Weisbord, 'The wizard of OD: or, what have magic slippers to do with burnout, evaluation, resistance, planned change, and action research?', *The OD Practitioner*, 10 (Summer 1978): 1–14; M. Mitchell, 'Consultant burnout', in *The 1977 Annual Handbook for Group Facilitators*, eds J. Jones and W. Pfeiffer (La Jolla, CA: University Associates, 1977): 145–56.

49 T. Isgar, 'Quality of work life of consultants', *Academy of Management OD Newsletter* (Winter 1983): 2–4.

50 A. Church and W. Burke, 'Practitioner attitudes about the field of organization development', in *Research in Organizational Change and Development*, eds W. Pasmore and R. Woodman (Greenwich, CT: JAI Press, 1995).

51 T. Cummings, 'Designing effective work groups', in *Handbook of Organizational Design*, eds P. Nystrom and W. Starbuck (Oxford: Oxford University Press, 1981): 250–71.

52 J. Schermerhorn, 'Interorganizational development', *Journal of Management*, 5 (1979): 21–38; T. Cummings, 'Interorganizational theory and organisation development', in *Systems Theory for Organization Development*, ed. T. Cummings (Chichester: John Wiley and Sons, 1980): 323–38.

53 Australasian Ethics Network (AEN), https://aenconference.com.

54 Australian Association for Professional and Applied Ethics, http://aapae.org.au.

55 D. Grace and S. Cohen, *Business Ethics: Australian Problems and Cases*, 2nd edn (Melbourne: Oxford University Press, 1998): 124–6.

56 W. Bennis, *Organization Development: Its Nature, Origins, and Prospects* (Reading, MA: Addison-Wesley, 1969).

57 H. Kelman, 'Manipulation of human behavior an ethical dilemma for the social scientist', in *The Planning of Change*, 2nd edn, eds W. Bennis, K. Bennie and R. Chin (New York: Holt, Rinehart and Winston, 1969): 584.

58 R. Beckhard, 'The dependency dilemma', *Consultants' Communique*, 6 (July–August–September 1978): 1–3.

59 G. Lippitt, *Organization Renewal* (Englewood Cliffs, NJ: Prentice Hall, 1969).

60 https://cica.org.au/wp-content/uploads/cica_prof_standards_booklet.pdf.

61 J. Slocum Jr, 'Does cognitive style affect diagnosis and intervention strategies?', *Group and Organization Studies*, 3 (June 1978): 199–210.

4

MANAGING RESISTANCE AND ORGANISATIONAL CULTURE

After studying this chapter, you should be able to:

1 Understand the complexity of resistance to change and apply the varying perceptions to contemporary change management situations.

2 Explain how resistance comes about and assess the effectiveness of various approaches to the management of resistance.

3 Summarise, and understand the implications of, the five key values that describe national cultures.

4 Explain how cultural context and economic development affect organisation development (OD).

KEY TERMS

Resistance

Mechanistic view

Social view

Conversational view

Sustaining momentum

Staying the course

Organisational culture

Cultural context

This chapter presents two contentious issues facing change management practitioners. First, resistance to change is an inevitable response to any attempt to alter the status quo but, rather than suppress, negate or discourage resistance, it should be managed and utilised as a resource. This chapter presents an overview of the research on resistance in the context of change management. A basic search through the literature returns a great number of articles, indicating a profound interest in resistance as a relevant – and important – area of focus for academic research and change management practitioners. In this chapter, we aim to outline the various perspectives and theories that have arisen over many years of research. You will see that there is not just one right approach, and some approaches suit certain situations, while a different approach will be appropriate for another situation.

As the general aim of organisational change is to adapt to the environment or to improve performance, either through incremental change or through strategic, transformational change,[1] it is perhaps unsurprising that resistance to change is often cited as the distinguishing feature of a failed change initiative. Individuals and groups will deal with and regard change in different ways depending on the situation.[2]

Second, in worldwide organisations, managers can use change management strategies, especially OD, to help firms operate in multiple countries. Referred to as international, global, multinational or transnational corporations, these firms must fit their organisational strategies, structures and processes to different cultures. Chapter 9 has a more detailed analysis of organisational culture as part of organisation transformation (OT), but OD can help members gain the organisational skills and knowledge needed to operate across cultural boundaries, enhancing organisational effectiveness through better alignment of people and systems with international strategy.

For a more detailed analysis of organisational culture as part of organisational transformation, see Chapter 9.

RESISTANCE TO CHANGE: REALITY OR MYTH?

Resistance is an often misunderstood component of change. The increasing rate of change, and uninvited changes in environment, determine an organisation's rise and fall.[3] Bruckman's[4] review of relevant literature found that there is no standard definition for resistance to change, and that perhaps the word 'change' is too big a word. Further, not all changes are necessarily worth resisting (few would resist a pay rise, for example).

Resistance: the refusal to accept or comply with something.

Bruckman's literature review of why resistance occurs includes:[5]

→ change in the status quo

→ increased fear and anxiety about the consequences of change – real or perceived[6]

→ altering of the way people see the world and calling into question their values and rationality

→ misunderstanding of the change itself

→ mistrust of those leading the change.

It is generally agreed that understanding the foundation of resistance aids an organisation's response to that type of resistance.

According to Falkenburg et al.,[7] much of the literature focuses on negative reactions to change, while more recent studies show this is an oversimplification and misleading. Studies suggest that people do not resist change per se; rather they resist the loss of pay or comfort or other benefits. Falkenburg et al. refer to Piderit's structure model of attitudes to change:

> Piderit uncovered three different emphases in conceptualisations of resistance: a cognitive state, an emotional state and a behavioural or intentional state. The cognitive

dimension of an attitude refers to an individual's beliefs about the attitude object. The emotional dimension of an attitude refers to an individual's feelings in response to the attitude object. The intentional dimension is a plan or resolution to take some action.[8]

Heffernan and Smythe[9] note that the research literature recognises that managing resistance is thought to be critical to successful change programs. Employees who are considered willing to initiate and respond positively to change are inherently valued by modern organisations.[10] The literature is divided, however, on whether resistance is positive or negative, whether it hinders or helps change, or whether it exists at all – for example, is resistance just a label or a category that means different things to different people?[11] Organisations that attempt change initiatives often find that the change efforts are stymied by individuals or groups who resist the changes.[12] As such, resistance to change is often cited as the reason for change failure.[13]

SOURCES OF RESISTANCE TO CHANGE

Most approaches to resistance are situation-based, but some research has focused on the individual difference perspective.[14] What is it about an individual that affects their adaptability to change? A significant amount of research has been conducted into the sources of resistance in individuals. **Table 4.1** describes many of these sources.

TABLE 4.1	SIX SOURCES OF GENERALISED DISPOSITION TO RESIST CHANGE
1 Reluctance to lose control	» The loss of control is considered a primary cause of resistance. » Control is lost because change is imposed rather than it being self-initiated. » Perspectives of resistance to change that advocate employee involvement in decision making generally focus primarily on loss of control.
2 Cognitive rigidity	» The trait of dogmatism may predict an individual's approach to change. » Dogmatic individuals are characterised by rigidity and closed-mindedness and therefore might be less willing and less able to adjust to new situations.
3 Lack of psychological resilience	» Organisational change can be a stressor, so less resilient individuals may have a lesser ability to cope with change. » Less resilient individuals may be reluctant to change because to change might be to admit past practices were faulty; that is, loss of face.
4 Intolerance to the adjustment period involved in change	» There may be resistance due to more work in the short term. » Resistance may come from those who support the need for change, but are reluctant to go through the adjustment period.
5 Preference for low levels of stimulation and novelty	» Those who prefer a lower level of stimulation may resist change, whereas those who are generally innovative show a greater need for novel stimuli. » A weaker need for stimuli may be shown by those who most resist change.
6 Reluctance to give up old habits	» Attachment to old habits is a common characteristic of an individual's resistance to change. » 'Familiarity breeds comfort.'

Source: Adapted from S. Oreg, 'Resistance to change: developing an individual differences measure', *Journal of Applied Psychology*, 88:4 (2003): 680–93.

Pardo del Val and Martinez Fuentes[15] conducted a similar study of sources of resistance; however, they linked the sources with the stage of the change process, as shown in **Table 4.2**. Taking another approach, Graetz et al.[16] align responses to change according to certain factors, as shown in **Table 4.3**.

TABLE 4.2 SOURCES OF RESISTANCE IN FIVE GROUPS	
Source of resistance	**The barrier**
Formulation stage	
The formulation stage is where the change strategy is developed.	
Perception of the need for change Resistance may form because the initial perception for the need for change is wrong or misguided	It may include: » myopia, or inability of the company to look into the future with clarity » denial or refusal to accept any information that is not expected or desired » perpetuation of ideas, meaning the tendency to go on with the present thoughts although the situation has changed » implicit assumptions, which are not discussed due to their implicit character and that therefore distort reality » communication barriers that lead to information distortion or misinterpretations » organisational silence, which limits the information flow with individuals who do not express their thoughts, meaning that decisions are made without all the necessary information
Low motivation for change	» Direct costs of change » Cannibalisation costs; that is, change that brings success to a product but at the same time brings losses to others, so it requires some sort of sacrifice » Cross-subsidy comforts, because the need for a change is compensated through the high rents obtained without change with another different factor, so that there is no real motivation for change » Past failures, which leave a pessimistic image for future changes » Different interests among employees and management, or lack of motivation of employees who value change results less than managers value them
Lack of creative response	» Fast and complex environmental changes, which do not allow a proper situation analysis » Reactive mindset, resignation or tendency to believe that obstacles are inevitable » Inadequate strategic vision or lack of clear commitment of top management to changes
Implementation stage	
This is the stage between the decision to change and the regular use of it in the organisation.	
Political and cultural deadlocks to change	» Implementation climate and relation between change values and organisational values, considering that a strong implementation climate when the values' relation is negative will result in resistance and opposition to change » Departmental politics or resistance from those departments that will suffer with the change implementation

»

»

	Implementation stage
	» Incommensurable beliefs or strong and definitive disagreement among groups about the nature of the problem and its consequent alternative solutions » Deep-rooted values and emotional loyalty » Forgetfulness of the social dimension of changes
A disparate group of sources of resistance with different characteristics	» Leadership inaction, sometimes because leaders are afraid of uncertainty, sometimes for fear of changing the status quo » Embedded routines » Collective action problems, especially dealing with the difficulty to decide who is going to move first or how to deal with free-riders » Lack of necessary capabilities to implement change – capabilities gap » Cynicism

Source: Adapted from M. Pardo del Val and C. Martinez Fuentes, 'Resistance to change: a literature review and empirical study', *Management Decision*, 41: (2003): 148–55.

TABLE 4.3	DRIVERS OF RESPONSES TO CHANGE
Factors	Indicators
Economic	» Job loss or job security and impact on self-image » Economic future for family » Reduction of value of existing skills for future promotion » Transfer of organisation or components of the organisation to less costly locations » Vested interests in position or salary benefits
Uncertainty	» Doubt about the stated benefits of the change » Doubt about ability to undertake new role or tasks » Rumours that destabilise the benefits of the change » Impact on relationships and values
Inconvenience	» Additional load to current role » Relocation of office or home » Loss of security of the familiar » Challenge to familiar routine
Threats to interpersonal relationships	» Status among employees » Threat to work team » Impact on morale of work team » Impact on organisation culture » Impact on social relationships
Impact on internal processes and systems	» Technology » Structure and dependencies » Inadequate communication to explain the change » Impact on resources
Impact on social functions	» Cognitive dissonance or incompatibility with new values » Fear of the unknown

Source: Adapted from F. Graetz, M. Rimmer, A. Lawrence and A. Smith, *Managing Organisational Change*, Wiley, 2006, p. 289. With permission from Emerald Group Publishing Limited.

Clarke and Clegg[17] propose that because continuous incremental change has been displaced by discontinuous change, organisation environments are less predictable and more complex to manage. Old ways of operating are no longer effective in dealing with the new levels of complexity and require new ways of thinking and practice, especially in the way that organisations manage change. This calls for new paradigms, deconstruction of the old order and development of new assets. Change managers should be mindful that implementing change is complex, and that multiple stakeholders have diverse needs and that no one change implementation strategy is going to satisfy them simultaneously.[18]

Apply your learning 4.1 comments on an ugly war that is being fought by traditional taxi companies against a new form of competition from Uber and other ride-share services.

APPLY YOUR LEARNING 4.1

REVOLUTIONARY CHANGE: UBER VS THE TAXI SERVICE INDUSTRY

Internationally, revolutionary changes have occurred in the people transport industry (generally referred to as the taxi service industry) because of the advent of the sharing economy platform. The development of Uber, and other new entrants to the competition environment such as 'Ola', has caused ongoing adverse reactions from those within the taxi service industry due to the pre-existing structure and deeply entrenched mindset of the industry.

Rather than examining why Uber is so popular to the detriment of the taxi service industry old guard, these traditional personal transport service providers have looked to government and legal intervention to solve the Uber problem. In many countries there has been industrial and legal action, against Uber in particular. The company has been banned in Germany and is currently facing Victorian Supreme Court proceedings in Australia, where the complainant – thousands of taxi and hire car drivers and other licence holders – are arguing that the company is running outside the existing regulations and is therefore operating illegally.

Regardless of its current fortunes, for some, the business plan of Uber is remarkable for a variety of reasons, and is also seen as a precursor to the way things might be done in the future. Uber exhibits three characteristics of revolutionary change strategies that can sustain them into the future:

→ Breaking the boundaries of pre-existing constraints – many industries are seen as 'prisoners of the system', whereby they are locked in monopolistic and over-regulated systems that have the effect of impeding any response to new technologies and changing customer demands. Companies like Uber disregard these constraints and see them as opportunities.

»

»

→ Embracing change – many companies have a strong resistance to change, and rather are financially and emotionally bound to the old ways of the industry and cannot adapt to the demands of a 'new' client base. Uber, however, has implemented technologically driven systems of booking and tracking, resulting in reduced costs to the customer and increased benefits to the individual driver.

→ Encouraging innovation – the community is evolving into a social network of communication, but the taxi service industry has not been responsive to the modern tools of connection. Uber and others stepped in to fill this void and to take advantage of new ideas and technology.

The challenges for this industry are many and varied, ranging from pay rates and employee entitlements to customer safety and security, and the future is shaping up to be a 'David and Goliath' battle, but ultimately the market will direct the future in this industry. The popularity of Uber and other market disrupters with customers has driven this form of sharing economy, and the reasons for this are not always clear. Interestingly, following protests against Uber by taxi drivers in London, Uber registered an 850 per cent increase in registration. It would appear that its business plan includes utilising the negative resistance to change within the industry. For the moment, Uber will continue to offer unique and innovative services to the community, and continue to inspire new entrants who are likely to follow their lead.

Critical thinking questions

1   What are the major reasons for resistance by the taxi service industry? How may they be overcome?

2   How is Uber continuing to innovate?

3   How will new entrants to the market (Ola, Sheba) affect the industry?

WHAT DO WE MEAN BY 'RESISTANCE'?

The term 'resistance' tends to be viewed in the pejorative sense, most likely because it can be difficult to manage. The following section describes the various meanings of resistance as understood by those who study resistance as a key aspect of change management.

Research into resistance to change has occurred over several years, beginning with Lewin, who introduced the term as a systems concept (a force affecting managers and employees equally), followed by other interpretations, including Dent and Goldberg's suggestion that people do not resist change but rather they resist the impact of change on their personal status quo. Other research, however, attempts to revisit Lewin's systems approach and critically appraise the interpretations that followed. Waddell, Cummings and Worley[19] describe change as a process that can 'hurt', even if we know that change is inevitable. Regardless of the organisation (even in public sector organisations), change and innovation are required in order to adapt and survive. Pardo del Val and Martinez Fuentes define resistance to change as follows:

> On the one hand, resistance is a phenomenon that affects the change process, delaying or slowing down its beginning, obstructing or hindering its implementation, and increasing its costs. On the other hand, resistance is any conduct that tries to keep the status quo, that is to say, resistance is equivalent to inertia, as the persistence to avoid change. So, inertia and thus resistance are not negative concepts in general, since change is not inherently beneficial for organisations. Even more, resistance could show change managers certain aspects that are not properly considered for the change process.[20]

Erwin and Garman[21] acknowledge that while there has been significant research into resistance to change, there still remains substantial variability in how its 'phenomena' are perceived. Resistance is still studied as either a problem or a positive factor for change.[22]

Ford and Ford[23] revisit the current understanding of resistance and suggest that new avenues of investigation into resistance are possible. They first break the current understanding into three views of resistance: mechanistic, social and conversational.

The mechanistic view

1   *Resistance is a natural, everyday phenomenon.* According to the **mechanistic view**, movement cannot occur without some form of resistance; in fact, resistance is evidence that something is moving. It is not exceptional.

Mechanistic view: explains phenomena in purely physical or deterministic terms.

Things move every day; therefore resistance is occurring every day. In an organisational context, these researchers identify common incidents of resistance: being late for meetings, forgetting a task, damaging equipment, being confused, complaining, declining requests, delaying the accomplishment of everyday goals.

2   *Resistance is neutral.* Resistance is neither good or bad, positive or negative, beneficial or detrimental.

3   *Resistance is a product of interaction.* The higher the resistance, the bigger the change. There are always two sides to the equation.

The social view

1   *Resistance is exceptional.* According to the **social view**, resistance is something extraordinary, and only happens in response to change.

Social view: perception of an organisation that includes multiple facets for consideration; for example, an organisation's culture and its impact on performance.

2   *Resistance is detrimental.* This is the pejorative sense of the word 'resistance'. Resistance is seen as detrimental to the success of a change. It is implied that all changes are inherently beneficial and should be implemented as planned. Ford and Ford[24] refer here to the notion that an individual can be 'tagged' as resistant, when in fact that individual considers themselves compliant. This is an important factor for the conversational view, mentioned below.

3   *Resistance is 'over there, in them/it'.* The social view refutes the interactive nature of resistance. It belongs over there; that is, resistance is 'in the workers' or the workers

are maladjusted. The error of locating it 'over there' is that it implies that resistance is not tied to movement, that the resistance is not caused by pressure elsewhere; that is, from the change itself. The response to change is isolated from the change process itself.

The conversational view

Conversational view: the articulation of various perspectives that can be shared among a group and act as a catalyst for further analysis.

1 *Conversations and change.* The **conversational view** recognises that organisations are made up of simultaneous, sequential and recursive conversations, undertaken by various networks within the organisation. There are different language communities, different language games and different approaches to texts. Therefore, a change agent cannot communicate with the assumption that there is a single language to which everyone has access. In order to remove potential misinterpretation of the key messages, the change agent will need to adopt a variety of delivery methods. The change agent cannot make his or her own language game dominant over others. The change agent must work within the message recipients' meanings.

2 *Resistance: the construction of a distinction.* The conversational view also recognises that individuals draw boundaries and make distinctions. They assign actions and events into categories of distinction. Each individual has their own reality. This is an important concept in the 'resistance is positive/negative' debate. What Ford and Ford[25] point out is that each person has a different meaning of resistance, and that resistance is therefore not a 'thing' that exists in its own right – it only exists in association with a language, which could be different among individuals. What could be interpreted as resistance could also be a request for more consultation and/or participation in the change process. Ford and Ford also point out that the labelling by a person of another individual as resistant is the result of that person making comparisons based on their point of view.[26] They advocate that the change agent should not be asking 'why is this person resisting?', rather 'why do I call that resistance?'[27]

3 *A construct of assertions and declarations.* Conversations are speech acts, and therefore resistance is brought into being through assertion and declaration, not before. If a change agent declares there is resistance, it is because he or she understands there to be resistance. The change agent is making a pronouncement. It is, in effect, the framing of the word 'resistance', and how this framing impacts on the change process. Think about how different the change process may be if the label was changed to 'cooperative' or 'compliant'.

MANAGERIAL RESPONSES TO RESISTANCE

In predicting where resistance to change will come from, managers should first identify who will win and who will lose from the proposed changes.[28] Change can generate deep resistance in people and in organisations, making it difficult, if not impossible, to implement organisational improvements.[29] At a personal level, change can arouse considerable anxiety about letting go of the known and moving to an uncertain future. Individuals may be unsure whether their existing skills and contributions will be valued in the future. They may have significant questions about whether they can learn to function effectively and to achieve benefits in the new situation. At the organisation level, resistance to change can come from three sources.[30] Technical resistance comes from the habit of following common procedures and the investment cost of resources invested in the status quo. Political resistance can arise when organisational changes threaten powerful stakeholders, such as top executive or staff personnel, and may call into question the past decisions of leaders. Organisation change often implies a different allocation of already scarce resources, such as capital, training budgets and good people. Finally, cultural resistance takes the form of systems and procedures that reinforce the status quo, promoting conformity to existing values, norms and assumptions about how things should operate.

There are at least three major strategies for dealing with resistance to change:[31]

1   *Empathy and support.* A first step in overcoming resistance is to know how people are experiencing change. This can help to identify those who are having trouble accepting the changes, the nature of their resistance and possible ways of overcoming it. Understanding how people experience change requires a great deal of empathy and support. It demands a willingness to suspend judgement and to try to see the situation from another's perspective, a process called 'active listening'. When people feel that those managing change are genuinely interested in their feelings and perceptions, they are likely to be less defensive and more willing to share their concerns and fears. This more open relationship not only provides useful information about resistance but also helps to establish the basis for the kind of joint problem solving that is necessary for overcoming barriers to change.

2   *Communication.* People tend to resist change when they are uncertain about its consequences. Lack of adequate information fuels rumours and gossip, and adds to the anxiety generally associated with change. Effective communication about changes and their likely consequences can reduce this speculation and allay unfounded fears. It can help members realistically prepare for change.

   However, communication is also one of the most frustrating aspects of managing change. Organisation members are constantly receiving data about current operations and future plans as well as informal rumours about people, changes and politics. Managers and OD practitioners must think seriously about how to break through this stream of information. One strategy is to make change information more salient by communicating through a new or different channel. If most information is delivered through memos and letters, then change information can be sent through meetings and presentations. Another method that can be effective during large-scale change is to deliberately substitute change information for normal operating information. One is embedding the need for change within the policies and processes (that is, standard operating procedures) that govern the functionality of the organisation. This sends a message that changing one's activities is a critical part of a member's job.

3   *Participation and involvement.* One of the oldest and most effective strategies for overcoming resistance is to involve organisation members directly in planning and implementing change.[32] Members can provide a diversity of information and ideas, which can contribute to making the innovations effective and appropriate to the

situation. They can also identify pitfalls and barriers to implementation. Involvement in planning the changes increases the likelihood that members' interests and needs will be accounted for during the intervention. Consequently, participants will be committed to implementing the changes as it is in their best interests to do so. Implementing the changes will contribute to meeting their needs. Moreover,[33] for people who have strong needs for involvement, the very act of participation can be motivating, leading to greater effort to make the changes work.[34]

How we manage resistance depends as much on the individual change practitioner as it does on established theories of resistance and subsequent recommendations for managing resistance. A consistent finding across much of the research into resistance is that without a clear strategy and well-defined key messages, effective management of change is unlikely.[35] As Ford and Ford[36] point out, resistance is a concept defined within an individual's own paradigm and experience. Therefore, it is inevitable that resistance to change continues to be considered a difficulty to overcome in change initiatives.

Calabrese[37] discusses change within a school administration context. He notes that a typical school administrator tasked with changing a school organisation can become fixed in a politically driven change process rather than one based on readiness, resulting in change that is temporary. The change in people, therefore, comes about from coercive power, although there remains a passive resistance. Calabrese refers to this process as one that never 'captures their soul', and refers to paradigms as a way to understand resistance:

> Paradigms affect personal and collective behaviour. As individuals, we use paradigms to interpret our environment. Our paradigms save us time from analysing every situation. As new situations appear, our minds quickly process these situations against a myriad of paradigms that our minds maintain on active duty. When the new situation conflicts with a paradigm, a warning signal sounds and subconsciously a defensive reaction develops ... The greater the mismatch between the new situation and our existing set of paradigms, the greater the level of resistance.[38]

From here, rigidity, lack of compromise, resentment and anger come into play. Calabrese builds on a four-step model proposed by Martin Luther King:

1 collection of the facts to determine whether injustices exist
2 negotiation
3 self-purification
4 direct action.

The answers to the questions raised in collection of the facts enables the change leader to determine whether anyone is likely to be hurt by the change, or if anyone is likely to benefit to a greater degree from the change.

In the negotiation stage, the change leader brings to the fore the existing paradigms of the organisation, and questions how these are relevant to the organisation currently. The self-purification stage refers to the analysis of one's motives before acting, a kind of self-reflective preparatory stage. In the direct action stage, the change leader responds to opponents through patience and understanding. A failure to take action means that they are complicit with those who resist the change; however, it is necessary to note that those who resist are not considered 'enemies' – rather, their opposition may stem from fear and reluctance to change. Calabrese uses this model to examine the school administrator as change leader, but it can be argued that it can be used in many other situations.

Another approach is Erwin and Garman's 2010 framework (outlined in **Table 4.4**), which is intended to be a starting point for practitioners in addressing resistance to change. What this framework lacks, however, is recognition that the need for change may be ill-advised. For example, Erwin and Garman refer to the personality trait of 'predisposition to resist'. Even if an individual has this trait, it nevertheless should be part of the change practitioner's resolve to understand the nature of the resistance rather than simply assigning it as a personality trait issue, a view supported by Ford, Ford and D'Amelio: 'This "change-agent-centric" view presumes that resistance is an accurate report by unbiased observers (change agents) of an objective reality (resistance by change recipients).'[39] Work with many practitioners, who have undertaken study through action learning and research-based leadership and management master's programs, strongly indicates that it is the adversarial and mixed message approach to resistance that still dominates the implementation of change programs in organisations.[40]

TABLE 4.4 ERWIN AND GARMAN'S (2010) FRAMEWORK FOR ADDRESSING RESISTANCE TO CHANGE	
Resistance research findings	**Practice guidance for change agents and managers**
What is resistance? Resistance to change Individuals may have negative thoughts, feelings and behaviours towards organisational change initiatives	Anticipate and plan for resistance
How do personality differences influence resistance? Predisposition to resist Openness to change	Provide additional support » Identify those inclined towards negative reactions and work to gain their trust. Engage the support of those more open to change. Gain support and help » Select and involve individuals with higher levels of resilience in leading change initiatives.
What are the key concerns and responses to change initiatives? Responses to change Competence	Address individuals' concerns » Recognise and be prepared to respond to concerns about change. » Provide meaningful opportunities for feedback. » Respond to valid resistance; use it for organisational improvement. Provide support and training » Provide adequate support and training in building employee confidence and their capabilities associated with the desired change.
What factors in the change process influence resistance? Communication Understanding Management consistency Participation	Communicate, communicate, communicate » Provide ample, clear and quality communications about change initiatives, associated implications and implementation actions. Ensure understanding of the change » Provide clear and appropriate details to ensure individuals understand the change, how it influences them and what is expected of them.

»

»

Resistance research findings	Practice guidance for change agents and managers
	Examine policies and behaviours for consistency
	» Be certain organisational policies, goals and management actions and behaviours are consistent with change initiatives.
	» Encourage and allow opportunities for participation in the change process.
	» Provide meaningful information about the change to individuals, solicit their input and opinions and encourage involvement in the decision process.
	» Provide individuals with the opportunity to participate in the change process, including identifying the need to change and developing and implementing change plans.
How do management relationships and styles influence resistance? Confidence and trust Management styles Employee relationships	Develop confidence and trust
	» Developing confidence and trust is a long-term endeavour involving gaining buy-in to the value of change and the probability of success; openness to constructive criticism and willingness to revise change plans if appropriate; transparency and clear articulation of the need, benefits and motivations behind change and that it is best for the organisation.
	Emphasise more effective management styles
	» Encourage collaboration, facts and logic in managing while avoiding the use of power and coercion.
	Develop quality manager–employee relationships
	» Assess manager–employee relationships and employee development opportunities to determine how they can be improved in a meaningful way, and follow through with the implementation of those initiatives.

Source: Adapted and summarised version of D. Erwin and A. Garman's framework in 'Resistance to organizational change: linking research and practice', *Leadership and Organization Development Journal*, 31:1 (2009): 39–56.

CONCRETE RESPONSES TO CHANGE

Change opponents also play an important and often underappreciated role. Those with day-to-day involvement and detailed knowledge may offer important insights into the proposed changes.[41] In managing a change process, managers should pay attention to broader concerns than that of the change program itself. It is thought that an individual's resistance to change is caused by deep-rooted values that do not necessarily 'fit' with the **organisational culture** or the change program's objectives.[42] Before the change process begins, managers who are acting as change agents need to analyse the organisational culture versus the change objectives, and if they find a disconnect between the two, work to establish a better alignment before the change process starts. Considered another key reason for change failure, organisational silence occurs, in part, when organisational culture does not align with the proposed change's objectives.[43] Silence can be perceived as vagueness and a lack of planning by change agents and top management. The change agent therefore must ensure that the organisation vocalises the change process.

Organisational culture: the ideas, customs and social behaviours within an organisation.

WHEN THERE IS EXCESSIVE CHANGE

Genuine resistance may be the result of too much organisational change. In a study by Falkenburg et al., excessive change caused individuals to resist – an expected outcome. The consequences were felt by both organisations and individuals. Managers experienced job rotation, middle managers were unable to function effectively and there were increased organisational inefficiencies.[44] Falkenburg et al. proposed a definition of excessive change that can be summarised as a movement that exceeds that which is normal, proper or reasonable, away from the present state towards a future state.[45]

Managers should be aware of the extent to which change becomes excessive. Excessive change may increase the level of resistance by employees due to 'change-fatigue' and most likely becomes excessive at the middle manager level because this is the level where most implementation activities occur.

> Individuals reacted to excessive change with frustration and anger. Some individuals expressed that they experienced stress and physical and psychological problems ...
>
> Employees also expressed feelings of uncertainty resulting from the change: uncertainty about their job, and about their competence and adequacy.[46]

Falkenburg et al. built on an existing framework by Porras and Robertson to manage the effects of excessive change. They found that individuals responded to excessive change in different ways, classified by whether the individual was active or passive in responding to the change. Some individuals worked to support the change: 'the response was active, take-charge, take-over attitude. When faced with many different change programs, or initiatives for new changes, they attempted taking control of the situation',[47] such as calling meetings with their managers or making decisions themselves. The passive employees followed orders without taking initiative on their own – where the change was probable. Where the change was improbable, the employees were overcome with paralysis and cynicism. According to Falkenburg et al. (see **Table 4.5**), the most serious behaviour was paralysis because 'employees become paralysed and cannot perform even their daily tasks. People were not unwilling, but unable, to carry through the changes, nor could they carry out the simple, routine tasks that they had always managed previously.'[48] The framework is broken down into four categories of implementation: diagnosis, planning, intervention and evaluation.

TABLE 4.5	MANAGING THE EFFECTS OF EXCESSIVE CHANGE
Diagnosis	The first step is to determine if the proposed change is necessary – or is it just change for change's sake? If the proposed change is necessary, limit it to only the necessary parts that are crucial to the organisation's prosperity, or in a difficult climate, an organisation's survival.
Planning	The planning phase involves the creation of discourse through conversations and discussions. The creation of discourse is fundamental to employees' understanding of the reason for change, particularly if it is a major or complex change. It can be argued that this should occur even when the change is not deemed excessive.

》

»

Intervention	The involvement of middle managers is crucial in the formulation and intervention stage. It is the middle managers who carry out the day-to-day operations and are closer to the organisation's internal and external stakeholders. Getting middle managers on board can help to visualise the expected change.
	Empowering individuals to make decisions may reduce resistance caused by excessive change. However, it is important to be careful when using empowerment and delegation as tools – excessive change can cause increased workload, and with increased workload there is a chance that employees may become paralysed. When this happens, empowerment and delegation may exacerbate an already tenuous situation.
	Equip individuals and teams with the necessary skills to carry out the change. One of the most basic reasons for resistance is that the individual or group does not feel they have the necessary skills with which to successfully respond to change. The skills are not just technical skills – interpersonal and conflict management skills are just as important.
Evaluation	Ensure employees know that the change process is completed. This can enable a sense of achievement and success.
	Following on from completion, it can be good practice to initiate a period of stability – free from major change.
	Build on the successes of the change process to develop the organisation's capacity for change. The perception of excessive change should be minimised to reduce the consequences of excessive change.

Source: Adapted from J. Falkenburg, I. Stensaker, C. Meyer and A. Haueng, 'When change becomes excessive', *Research in Organizational Change and Development*, 15 (2005): 31–62.

MANAGEMENT APPROACHES

Richard Cooke describes six reasons for employees to resist change:[49]

1 Employees may know something that you do not know, which may, in fact, make their resistance not only understandable, but even correct.

2 People who are happy with the status quo will fight to protect it.

3 If they can see no clear path between their current state and the new position, then they cannot begin to move forward.

4 If they do not believe they have the necessary skills to be successful in the new order or are heavily invested in the current order, then again they will resist.

5 They need to have clear and credible role models of the new behaviours.

6 They need to understand why the change is in their interests. Too many people make the mistake of saying why the company needs this, that and the other, but fail to make the link as to how these things benefit the individuals.

MANAGING RESISTANCE TO CHANGE

This chapter emphasises that resistance to change has been maligned by many and should be reconsidered by academics and practitioners alike. If people are to be successful in change management, resistance should be managed constructively and not feared or suppressed. This includes taking a fresh look at what resistance to change can offer the organisation.

THE IMPORTANCE OF TRAINING

Pardo del Val and Martinez Fuentes[50] advocate training as a key aspect in managing change. Often the reason for individual resistance is a lack of understanding and skills in those on whom change is imposed. Change programs imply that new capabilities will be required by employees, and it is by the acquisition of skills that individuals may embrace the change rather than resist. But the need for training does not just apply to those who may resist the change; it is also important to ensure that change agents are equipped with the appropriate skills and competencies. Waddell, Cummings and Worley[51] suggest change agent training encompass the following competencies (first described by Kotter and Schlesinger). These are:

1 *Education and communication.* This may need to be stratified through the organisation depending on department need, group norms within those departments and the capabilities of internal people to facilitate this.

2 *Participation and involvement of individuals and groups.* Even if change agents think they have all the answers, organisation member involvement will minimise resistance.

3 *Facilitation of support.* Participation and involvement of individuals and groups will assist in identifying which groups need priority support.

4 *Negotiation and agreement.* This may be needed if feedback from organisation members indicates the change plan is not feasible or is flawed.

5 *Manipulation and co-option.* This can be used if there are still people resisting the change and the change is systems-driven. Try to avoid this approach.

6 *Explicit and implicit coercion.* Avoid this approach at all costs unless there is the potential of physical risk for employees who do not adapt to the change. There is always a solution![52]

Organisations should also learn from the collective learnings of years of research. Bruckman summarises learnings based on observation of change processes in organisations:[53]

1 Work with the group.

2 Confront the fear of change.

3 Consider the group's perspective.

4 Build trust.

5 Avoid manipulating the work group.

6 Be willing to compromise.

7 Allow group ownership.

8 Actions versus words.

9 Reward new behaviours.

10 Financial rewards rarely reinforce behavioural change.

11 Manage the myths and realities.

12 Integrity – the most important variable.

SUSTAINING MOMENTUM

Once resistance has been identified and its management is under way, explicit attention must be directed to sustaining energy and commitment for implementing the change. The initial excitement and activity of changing often dissipate in the face of practical problems of trying to learn new ways of operating. As mentioned previously, a strong tendency exists among organisation members to return to old behaviours and well-known processes unless they receive sustained support and reinforcement for carrying the changes through to completion. The following five activities can help to **sustain momentum** for carrying change through to completion: providing resources for change, building a support system for change agents, developing new competencies and skills, reinforcing new behaviours and staying the course.

Sustaining momentum: continue for an extended period of time without interruption.

Providing resources for change

Implementing organisational change generally requires additional financial and human resources, particularly if the organisation continues day-to-day operations while trying to change itself. These extra resources are needed for such change activities as training, consultation, data collection and feedback, and special meetings. Extra resources also are helpful to provide a buffer as performance drops during the transition period. Organisations can underestimate the need for special resources devoted to the change process. Significant organisational change invariably requires considerable management time and energy, as well as the help of consultants. A separate 'change budget' that exists along with capital and operating budgets can earmark the resources needed for training members in how to behave differently and for assessing progress and making necessary modifications in the change program.[54] Unless these extra resources are planned for and provided, meaningful change is less likely to occur.

Building a support system for change agents

Organisation change can be difficult and filled with tension, not only for participants, but for change agents as well.[55] They often must give members emotional support, but they receive little support themselves. They must often maintain 'psychological distance' from others to gain the perspective needed to lead the change process. This separation can produce considerable tension and isolation, and change agents may need to create their own support system to help them cope with such problems. A support system typically consists of a network of people with whom the change agent has a close personal relationship – people who can give emotional support, serve as a sounding board for ideas and problems and challenge untested assumptions. For example, OD professionals often use trusted colleagues as 'shadow consultants' to help them think through difficult issues with clients and to offer conceptual and emotional support. Similarly, a growing number of organisations, such as law enforcement agencies in Australia, are forming internal networks of change agents to provide mutual learning and support and create a shift in the way the police force is perceived by the public.[56]

Developing new competencies and skills

Organisational changes frequently demand new knowledge, skills and behaviours from organisation members. In many cases, the changes cannot be implemented unless members gain new competencies. For example, employee-involvement programs often require managers to learn new leadership styles and new approaches to problem solving. Change agents must ensure that such learning occurs. They need to provide multiple learning opportunities, such as traditional training programs, on-the-job counselling and coaching and experiential simulations, covering both technical and social skills. Because it is easy to overlook the social component, change agents may need to devote special time and resources to helping members gain the social skills required to implement change.

Reinforcing new behaviours

In organisations, people generally do those things that bring them rewards. Consequently, one of the most effective ways to sustain momentum for change is to reinforce the kinds of behaviours needed to implement the changes. This can be accomplished by linking formal rewards directly to the desired behaviours. In addition, desired behaviours can be reinforced more frequently through informal recognition, encouragement and praise. Perhaps equally important are the intrinsic rewards that people can experience through early success in the change effort. Achieving identifiable early successes can make participants feel good about themselves and their behaviours, and this reinforces the drive to change.

Staying the course

Change requires time, and many of the expected financial and organisational benefits from change lag behind its implementation. If the organisation changes again too quickly or abandons the change before it is fully implemented, the desired results may never materialise. There are two primary reasons that managers do not keep a steady focus on change implementation. First, many managers fail to anticipate the decline in performance, productivity or satisfaction as change is implemented. Organisation members need time to practise, develop and learn new behaviours; they do not abandon old ways of doing things and adopt a new set of behaviours overnight. Moreover, change activities, such as training, extra meetings and consulting assistance, are extra expenses added on to current operating expenditures. There should be little surprise, therefore, that effectiveness declines before it gets better. However, perfectly good change projects are often abandoned when questions are raised about short-term performance declines. Patience and trust in the diagnosis and intervention design work are necessary.

Second, many managers do not keep focused on a change because they want to implement the next big idea that comes along. When organisations change before they have to (in other words, change for the sake of change), in response to the latest management fad, a 'flavour-of-the-month' cynicism can develop. As a result, organisation members provide only token support to a change under the (accurate) notion that the current change will not last. Successful organisational change requires persistent leadership that **stays the course** and does not waver unnecessarily.

Staying the course: continuing for a long term.

Apply your learning 4.2 reports on a McKinsey research project that reveals a wide gap between the aspirations of executives to innovate and their ability to execute. Organisational structures and processes are not the solution.

APPLY
YOUR
LEARNING
4.2

LEADERSHIP AND INNOVATION

... More than 70 percent of the senior executives in a survey we recently conducted say that innovation will be at least one of the top three drivers of growth for their companies in the next three to five years. Other executives see innovation as the most important way for companies to accelerate the pace of change in today's global business environment. Leading strategic thinkers are moving beyond a focus on traditional product and service categories to pioneer innovations in business processes, distribution, value chains, business models, and even the functions of management.

...

There are no best-practice solutions to seed and cultivate innovation. The structures and processes that many leaders reflexively use to encourage it are important, we find, but not sufficient. On the contrary, senior executives almost unanimously – 94 percent – say that people and corporate culture are the most important drivers of innovation.

Our experience convinces us that a disciplined focus on three people-management fundamentals may produce the building blocks of an innovative organization. A first step is to formally integrate innovation into the strategic-management agenda of senior leaders to an extent that few companies have done so far. In this way, innovation can be not only encouraged but also managed, tracked, and measured as a core element in a company's growth aspirations. Second, executives can make better use of existing (and often untapped) talent for innovation, without implementing disruptive change programs, by creating the conditions that allow dynamic innovation networks to emerge and flourish. Finally, they can take explicit steps to foster an innovation culture based on trust among employees. In such a culture, people understand that their ideas are valued, trust that it is safe to express those ideas, and oversee risk collectively, together with their managers. Such an environment can be more effective than monetary incentives in sustaining innovation.

Source: J. Barsh, M.M. Capozzi and J. Davidson, 'Leadership and innovation',
McKinsey Quarterly, January 2008.

| Critical thinking questions | 1 | How important is innovation to the success of businesses in the future? |
| | 2 | How can leaders use OD to assist with strategies to embed a culture of innovation? |

ORGANISATIONAL CULTURE

Because change management theories were developed predominantly by American and Western European practitioners, the practices and methods of change management are heavily influenced by the values and assumptions of those cultures. Thus, the 'traditional' approaches to planned change may promote management practices that conflict with the values and assumptions of other societies.[57] How should OD be conducted in an Indian firm operating in New Zealand? Alternatively, how should a global organisation with multiple offices employing locally engaged teams implement change universally? Some practitioners believe that OD can result in organisational improvements in any culture.[58] Despite different points of view on this topic, the practice of OD in international settings can be expected to expand dramatically. The rapid development of foreign economies and firms, along with the evolution of the global marketplace, is creating organisational needs and opportunities for change. How that change is implemented in a local setting is the challenge.[59]

In designing and implementing planned change for organisations operating outside the home country, OD practice must account for two important contingencies: alignment between the cultural values of the host country and traditional OD values, and the host country's level of economic development. Preliminary research suggests that failure to adapt OD interventions to these cultural and economic contingencies can produce disastrous results.[60] For example, several OD concepts, including dialogue, truthfulness and performance management, do not always work in all countries.[61] Dialogue assumes that 'all differences can be bridged if you get people together in the right context'. However, mediation, arbitration or traditional negotiations are more acceptable in some cultures than in others. Similarly, the notion of truthfulness is culturally relativistic and as a value depends on whether you are Australian, Asian, Middle Eastern or from some other culture. Finally, the process and content of performance evaluation can also depend on culture.[62]

OD interventions need to be responsive to the cultural values and organisational customs of the host country if the changes are to produce the kinds of positive results shown in Western cultures, such as the United States.[63] For example, team-building interventions in Latin American countries can fail if there is too much emphasis on personal disclosure and interpersonal relationships. Latin Americans typically value masculinity and a devotion to family, avoid conflict and are status conscious. They may be suspicious of human process interventions that seek to establish trust, openness and equality, and consequently they may resist them actively. The more a country's cultural values match the traditional values of OD, the less likely it is that an intervention will have to be dramatically modified.

CULTURAL CONTEXT

Researchers have proposed that applying OD in different countries requires a 'context-based' approach to planned change.[64] This involves fitting the change process to the organisation's **cultural context**, including the values held by members in the particular country or region. These beliefs inform people about behaviours that are important and acceptable in their culture. Cultural values play a major role in shaping the customs and practices that occur within organisations as well, influencing how members react to phenomena having to do with power, conflict, ambiguity, time and change.

Cultural context: the circumstances that form the setting for an event, statement or idea, and in terms of which it can be fully understood.

There is a growing body of knowledge about cultural diversity and its effect on organisational and management practices.[65] Researchers have identified five key values that describe national cultures and influence organisational customs: context orientation, power distance, uncertainty avoidance, achievement orientation and individualism (see **Table 4.6**).[66]

TABLE 4.6	CULTURAL VALUES AND ORGANISATION CUSTOMS		
Value	Definition	Organisation customs when the value is high	Representative countries
Context orientation	The extent to which words carry the meaning of a message; how time is viewed	Ceremony and routines are common. Structure is less formal; fewer written policies exist. People are often late for appointments.	*High*: Asian and Latin American countries *Low*: Scandinavian countries, United States
Power distance	The extent to which members of a society accept that power is distributed unequally in an organisation	Decision making is autocratic. Superiors consider subordinates as part of a different class. Subordinates are closely supervised. Employees are not likely to disagree. Powerful people are entitled to privileges.	*High*: Latin American and Eastern European countries *Low*: Scandinavian countries
Uncertainty avoidance	The extent to which members of an organisation tolerate the unfamiliar and unpredictable	Experts have status/authority. Clear roles are preferred. Conflict is undesirable. Change is resisted. Conservative practices are preferred.	*High*: Asian countries *Low*: European countries
Achievement orientation	The extent to which organisation members value assertiveness and the acquisition of material goods	Achievement is reflected in wealth and recognition. Decisiveness is valued. Larger and faster are better. Gender roles are clearly differentiated.	*High*: Asian and Latin American countries, South Africa *Low*: Scandinavian countries
Individualism	The extent to which people believe they should be responsible for themselves and their immediate families	Personal initiative is encouraged. Time is valuable to individuals. Competitiveness is accepted. Autonomy is highly valued.	*High*: Australia, New Zealand *Low*: Latin American and Eastern European countries

Context orientation

Context orientation[67] describes how information is conveyed and time is valued in a culture. In low-context cultures, such as Scandinavia and Australia, information is communicated directly in words and phrases. By using more specific words, more meaning is expressed. In addition, time is viewed as discrete and linear – as something that can be spent, used, saved or wasted. In high-context cultures, on the other hand, the communication medium reflects the message more than the words, and time is a fluid and flexible concept. For example, social cues in Japan and Venezuela provide as much, if not more, information about a particular situation than do words alone. Business practices in high-context cultures emphasise ceremony and ritual. How one behaves is an important signal of support and compliance with the way things are done. Structures are less formal in high-context cultures; there are few written policies and procedures to guide behaviour. Because high-context cultures view time as fluid, punctuality for appointments is less of a priority than maintaining relationships.

Power distance

This value concerns the way people view authority, status differences and influence patterns. People in high power-distance regions, such as Latin America and Eastern Europe, tend to accept unequal distributions of power and influence, and consequently autocratic and paternalistic decision-making practices are the norm. Organisations in high power-distance cultures tend to be centralised, with several hierarchical levels and a large proportion of supervisory personnel. Subordinates in these organisations represent a lower social class. They expect to be supervised closely and believe that power holders are entitled to special privileges. Such practices would be inappropriate in low power-distance regions, such as Scandinavia, where participative decision making and egalitarian methods prevail.

Uncertainty avoidance

This value reflects a preference for conservative practices and familiar and predictable situations. People in high uncertainty-avoidance regions, such as Asia, prefer stable routines over change and act to maintain the status quo. They do not like conflict and believe that company rules should not be broken. In regions where uncertainty avoidance is low, such as in many European countries, ambiguity is less threatening. Organisations in these cultures tend to favour fewer rules, higher levels of participation in decision making, more organic structures and more risk taking.

Achievement orientation

This value concerns the extent to which the culture favours the acquisition of power and resources. Employees from achievement-oriented cultures, such as Asia and Latin America, place a high value on career advancement, freedom and salary growth. Organisations in these cultures pursue aggressive goals and can have high levels of stress and conflict. Organisational success is measured in terms of size, growth and speed. On the other hand, workers in cultures where achievement is less of a driving value, such as those in Scandinavia, prize the social aspects of work, including working conditions and supervision, and typically favour opportunities to learn and grow at work.

Individualism

This value is concerned with looking out for oneself as opposed to one's group or organisation. In high-individualism cultures, such as Australia and the United States, personal initiative and competitiveness are valued strongly. Organisations in individualistic cultures often have high turnover rates and individual rather than group decision-making processes. Employee empowerment is supported when members believe that it improves the probability of personal gain. These cultures encourage personal initiative, competitiveness and individual autonomy. Conversely, in low individualism countries, such as China, Japan and Mexico, allegiance to one's group is paramount. Organisations operating in these cultures tend to favour cooperation among employees and loyalty to the company.

STUDIES ON THE FIVE VALUES DESCRIBING NATIONAL CULTURES

Research expanding the five key values discussed above could influence how change may be implemented. Hofstede et al. (2008) added two new dimensions: 'indulgence versus restraint' and 'monumentalism versus self-effacement'.[68]

1 *Indulgence versus restraint:* Indulgence stands for the social order that allows relatively free fulfilment of some desires and feelings, particularly those related to leisure, amusement with friends, spending, consumption and sex. Restraint stands for a society that controls such fulfilment, and where people feel less able to enjoy their lives.

2 *Monumentalism versus self-effacement:* Monumentalism stands for a society that rewards people who are, metaphorically speaking, like monuments: proud and unchangeable. Its opposite perspective, self-effacement, stands for a society that rewards humility and flexibility. Publications are emerging with the results from the Value Survey Module (VSM08), which is retesting the cultural dimensions using these new values.[69]

Apply your learning 4.3 is an article that gives recommendations about how to change workplace culture.

APPLY YOUR LEARNING
4.3

TURNING THE SHIP AROUND: A GUIDE TO CHANGING WORKPLACE CULTURE

One of the more difficult challenges facing the CEO, owner or manager of a failing company is changing the culture of the workplace.

People get stuck in their ways and often respond harshly to sudden calls for change. However, this resistance to change may be what has led the company astray in the first place.

...

Understanding that each business, culture, and person is unique in their own rights, here are a few tips for creating sustainable change in the workplace:

1 Consider the individual ...
2 Make the right hiring/firing decisions ...
3 Set short-term goals ...
4 Give employees a chance to be heard ...
5 Follow through with promises (good and bad) ...
6 Focus on the long-term goal ...

Source: A. Johansson, 'Turning the ship around: a guide to changing workplace culture', 20 March 2017, https://www.business.com/articles/a-guide-to-changing-workplace-culture, accessed 23 May 2018.

Critical thinking questions

1 The theme of this article is that someone in a position of leadership should facilitate sustainable change that allows each employee to flourish and succeed. Do you agree? Why/why not?

2 How may OD assist with the listed tips for sustainable change?

ECONOMIC DEVELOPMENT

In addition to cultural context, an important contingency affecting OD success internationally is a country's level of industrial and economic development. For example, although long considered an industrial economy, Russia's political and economic transformation, and the concurrent increases in uncertainties over infrastructure, corruption, cash flow and exchange rates, has radically altered assumptions underlying business practices. Thus, economic development can be judged from social, economic and political perspectives.[70] For example, it can be reflected in a country's management capability as measured by information systems and skills; decision-making and action-taking capabilities; project planning and organising abilities; evaluation and control technologies; leadership, motivational and reward systems; and human selection, placement and development levels. The United Nations' Human Development Programme has created a Human Development Index that assesses a country's economic development in terms of life expectancy, educational attainment and adjusted real income.

Subsistence economies

Countries such as Pakistan, Nepal, Nigeria, Uganda and Rwanda have relatively low degrees of development and their economies are primarily agriculture-based. Their populations consume most of what they produce, and any surplus is used to barter for other needed goods and services. A large proportion of the population is unfamiliar with the concept of 'employment'. Working for someone else in exchange for wages is not common or understood, and consequently few large organisations exist outside of the government. In subsistence economies, OD interventions emphasise global social change and focus on creating conditions for sustainable social and economic progress.

Industrialising economies

India, Iran, Malaysia, the People's Republic of China, the Philippines, Turkey and Venezuela are moderately developed and tend to be rich in natural resources. An expanding manufacturing base that accounts for increasing amounts of the country's gross domestic product fuels economic growth, no more evident than in India and China, which are fast becoming the powerhouses of economic development, much to the envy of industrialised nations. The rise of manufacturing also contributes to the formation of a class system, including upper-, middle- and low-income groups. Organisations operating in these nations generally focus on efficiency of operations and revenue growth. Consequently, OD interventions address strategic, structural and work design issues.[71] They help organisations identify domestic and international markets, develop clear and appropriate goals and structure themselves to achieve efficient performance and market growth.

Industrial economies

Highly developed countries, such as France, Japan, Sweden and the United States, emphasise non-agricultural industry. In these economies, manufactured goods are exported and traded with other industrialised countries; investment funds are available both internally and externally; the workforce is educated and skilled; and technology is often substituted for labour. Because the OD interventions described in this book were developed primarily in industrial economies, they can be expected to have their strongest effects in those contexts. However, their continued success cannot be ensured because these countries are advancing rapidly to post-industrial conditions. Here, OD interventions will need to fit into economies driven by information and knowledge, where service outpaces manufacturing, and where national and organisational boundaries are more open and flexible.

HOW CULTURAL CONTEXT AND ECONOMIC DEVELOPMENT AFFECT OD PRACTICE

The contingencies of cultural context and economic development can have powerful effects on the way OD is carried out in various countries.[72] They can determine whether change proceeds slowly or quickly; involves few or many members; is directed by hierarchical authority or by consensus; and focuses on business, organisational or human process issues. For example, planned change processes in Russia require more clarity in roles, the development of common understandings, changes in how an organisation's vision is communicated and the insightful use of symbols and signals.[73] When the two contingencies are considered together, they reveal four different international settings for OD practice, as shown in **Figure 4.1**. These different situations reflect the extent to which a country's culture fits with traditional OD values of direct and honest communication, sharing power and improving their effectiveness, and the degree to which the country is economically developed.[74]

| FIGURE 4.1 | THE CULTURAL AND ECONOMIC CONTEXTS OF INTERNATIONAL OD PRACTICE |

In **Figure 4.1**, the degree of economic development is restricted to industrialising and highly industrialised regions. Subsistence economies are not included because they afford little opportunity to practise traditional OD; in those contexts, a more appropriate strategy is global social change. In general, however, the more developed the economy, the more OD is applied to the organisational and human process issues described in this book. In less developed situations, OD focuses on business issues, such as procuring raw materials, producing efficiently and marketing successfully.[75] On the other hand, when the country's culture supports traditional OD values, the planned change process can be applied to organisational and human process issues with only small adjustments.[76] The more the cultural context differs from OD's traditional values profile, the more the planned change process will need to be modified to fit the situation.

Low cultural fit, moderate industrialisation

This context is least suited to traditional OD practice. It includes industrialising economies with cultural values that align poorly with OD values, including many Middle East nations, such as Iraq, Iran and the United Arab Emirates; the South Pacific region, including Malaysia and the Philippines; and certain Latin American countries, such as Brazil, Ecuador, Guatemala and Nicaragua. These regions are highly dependent on their natural resources and have a relatively small manufacturing base. They tend to be high-context cultures with values of high power distance and achievement orientation and of moderate uncertainty avoidance. Where they are not a bad fit with OD values is where these cultures tend towards moderate or high levels of collectivism, especially in relation to family.

These settings require change processes that fit local customs and that address business issues. As might be expected, little is written on applying OD in these countries, and there are even fewer reports of OD practice. Cultural values of high power distance and achievement are inconsistent with traditional OD activities emphasising openness, collaboration and empowerment. Moreover, executives in industrialising economies frequently equate OD with human process interventions, such as team building, training and conflict management. They perceive OD as too soft to meet their business needs. For example, Egyptian and Filipino managers tend to be autocratic, engage in protracted decision making and focus on economic and business problems. Consequently, organisational change is slow paced, centrally controlled and aimed at achieving technical rationality and efficiency.[77]

These contextual forces do not influence all organisations in the same way. A study of 20 large-group interventions in Mexico suggests that culture may not be as constraining as has been hypothesised.[78] Similarly, in an apparent exception to the rule, the president of Semco S/A (Brazil), Ricardo Semler, designed a highly participative organisation.[79] Most Semco employees set their own working hours and approve hires and promotions. Information flows downwards through a relatively flat hierarchy, and strategic decisions are made participatively by company-wide vote. Brazil's cultural values are not as strong on power distance and masculinity as in other Latin American countries, and that may explain the apparent success of this high-involvement organisation. It suggests that OD interventions can be implemented within this cultural context when strongly supported by senior management.

High cultural fit,[80] moderate industrialisation[81]

This international context includes industrialising economies with cultures that align with traditional OD values. Such settings support the kinds of OD processes described in this book, especially technostructural and strategic interventions that focus on business development. According to data on economic development and cultural values, relatively few countries fit this context. India's industrial base and democratic society are growing rapidly and may fit this contingency. Similarly, South Africa's recent political and cultural changes make it one of the most interesting settings in which to practise OD.[82]

South Africa is an industrialising economy. Its major cities are the manufacturing hubs of the economy, although agriculture and mining still dominate in rural areas. The country's values are in transition and may become more consistent with OD values. South Africans customarily have favoured a low-context orientation; relatively high levels of power distance; and moderate levels of individualism, uncertainty avoidance and achievement orientation. Organisations typically have been bureaucratic with authoritarian management, established career paths and job security primarily for Caucasian employees. These values and organisational conditions are changing, however, as the nation's political and governance structures are transformed. Formerly, apartheid policies reduced uncertainty and defined power differences among citizens. Today, free elections and the abolishment of apartheid have increased uncertainty drastically and established legal equality among the races. These changes are likely to move South Africa's values closer to those underlying OD. If so, OD interventions should become increasingly relevant to that nation's organisations.

A study of large South African corporations suggested the directions that OD is likely to take in that setting.[83] In the study internal OD practitioners were interviewed about key organisational responses to the political changes in the country at that time, such as the free election of Nelson Mandela, abolishment of apartheid and the Reconstruction and Development Program. Change initiatives at Spoornet, Eskom and Telkom, for example, centred around two strategic and organisational issues. First, the political changes opened up new international markets, provided access to new technologies and exposed these organisations to global competition. Consequently, these organisations initiated planned change efforts to create corporate visions and identify strategies for entering new markets and acquiring new technologies. Second, the political changes forced corporations to modify specific human resources and organisational practices. The most compelling change was mandated affirmative action quotas. At Spoornet, Eskom and Telkom, apartheid was thoroughly embedded in the organisations' structures, policies and physical arrangements. Thus, planned change focused on revising human resources policies and practices. Similarly, organisational structures that had fitted well within the stable environment of apartheid were outmoded and too rigid to meet the competitive challenges of international markets. Planned changes for restructuring these firms were implemented as part of longer-term strategies to change corporate culture towards more egalitarian and market-driven values.

Low cultural fit, high industrialisation[84]

This international setting includes industrialised countries with cultures that fit poorly with traditional OD values. Many countries in Central America, Eastern Asia and Eastern Europe fit this description. Reviews of OD practice in those regions suggest that planned change includes all four types of interventions described in this book, although the change process itself is adapted to local conditions.[85] For example, China, Japan, Korea, Mexico and Venezuela are high-context cultures where knowledge of local mannerisms, customs and rituals is required to understand the meaning of communicated information. To function in such settings, OD practitioners must know not only the language but the social customs as well. Similarly, cultural values emphasising high levels of power distance, uncertainty avoidance and achievement orientation foster organisations where roles, status differences and working conditions are clear; where autocratic and paternalistic decisions are expected; and where the acquisition of wealth and influence by the powerful is accepted. OD interventions that focus on social processes and employee empowerment are not favoured naturally in this cultural context and consequently need to be modified to fit the situations.

Japanese and Korean organisations, such as Nissan, Toyota, Fujitsu, NEC and Hyundai, provide good examples of how OD interventions can be tailored to this global setting. These firms are famous for continuous improvement and total quality management (TQM) practices; they adapt these interventions to fit the Asian culture. Roles and behaviours required to apply TQM are highly specified, thereby holding uncertainty to a relatively low level. Teamwork and consensus decision-making practices associated with quality improvement projects also help to manage uncertainty. When large numbers of employees are involved, information is spread quickly and members are kept informed about the changes taking place. Management controls the change process by regulating the implementation of suggestions made by the problem-solving groups. Because these interventions focus on work processes, teamwork and employee involvement do not threaten the power structure. Moreover, TQM and continuous improvement do not alter the organisation radically but produce small, incremental changes that can add up to impressive gains in long-term productivity and cost reduction.

In these cultures, OD practitioners also tailor the change process itself to fit local conditions. Mexican companies, for example, expect OD practitioners to act as experts and to offer concrete advice on how to improve the organisation. To be successful, OD practitioners need sufficient status and legitimacy to work with senior management and to act in expert roles.[86] Status typically is associated with academic credentials, senior management experience, high-level titles or recommendations by highly placed executives and administrators. As might be expected, the change process in Latin America is autocratic and driven downwards from the top of the organisation. Subordinates or lower-status people generally are not included in diagnostic or implementation activities because inclusion might equalise power differences and threaten the status quo. Moreover, cultural norms discourage employees from speaking out or openly criticising management. There is relatively little resistance to change because employees readily accept changes dictated by management.

In Asia, OD is an orderly process, driven by consensus and challenging performance goals. Organisational changes are implemented slowly and methodically, so trust builds and change-related uncertainty is reduced. Changing too quickly is seen as arrogant, divisive and threatening. At the China Association for International Exchange of Personnel, the move from a government bureau to a 'market-facing' organisation[87] has been gradual but consistent. Managers have been encouraged to contact more and more foreign organisations, to develop relationships and contracts and to learn marketing and OD skills. Because Asian values promote a cautious culture that prizes consensus, dignity and respect, OD tends to be impersonal and to focus mainly on work-flow improvements. Human process issues are rarely addressed because people are expected to act in ways that do not cause others to 'lose face' or to bring shame to the group.

High cultural fit, high industrialisation

This last setting includes industrialised countries with cultural contexts that fit well with traditional OD values. Much of the OD practice described in this book was developed in these situations, particularly in the United States.[88] To extend our learning, we will focus on how OD is practised in other nations in this global setting, including the Scandinavian countries – Sweden, Norway, Finland and Denmark – and countries with a strong British heritage, such as Great Britain, Australia and New Zealand.

Scandinavians enjoy a high standard of living and strong economic development. Because their cultural values most closely match those traditionally espoused in OD, organisational practices are highly participative and egalitarian. OD practice tends to mirror these values. Multiple stakeholders, such as managers, unionists and staff personnel, are involved actively in all stages of the change process, from entry and diagnosis to intervention and evaluation. This level of involvement is much higher than that typically occurring in the United States. It results in a change process that is heavily oriented to the needs of shop-floor participants. Norwegian labour laws, for example, give unionists the right to participate in technological innovations that can affect their work lives. Such laws also mandate that all employees in the country have the right to enriched forms of work.

Given this cultural context, it is not surprising that Scandinavian companies pioneered sociotechnical interventions[89] to improve productivity and quality of work life. Sweden's Volvo restructured automobile manufacturing around self-managed work groups. Denmark's Patent Office and Norway's Shell Oil demonstrated how union–management cooperative projects can enhance employee involvement throughout the organisation. In many cases, national governments were involved heavily in these change projects by sponsoring industry-wide improvement efforts. The Norwegian Government, for example, was instrumental in introducing industrial democracy to that nation's companies. It helped unions and management in selected industries implement pilot projects to enhance productivity and quality of work life. The results of these sociotechnical experiments were then diffused throughout the Norwegian economy. In many ways, the Scandinavian countries have gone further than other global regions in linking OD to national values and policies.

Countries associated with the United Kingdom tend to have values consistent with a low-context orientation, moderate to high individualism and achievement orientation, and moderate to low power distance and uncertainty avoidance. This cultural pattern results in personal relationships that often seem indirect to Americans. For example, a British subordinate who is told to think about a proposal is really being told that the suggestion has been rejected. These values also promote organisational policies that are steeped in formality, tradition and politics. The United Kingdom's long history tends to reinforce the status quo, and consequently resistance to change is high.

OD practice in the United Kingdom parallels the cultural pattern described above. For example, sociotechnical systems (STS) theory was developed by practitioners at the Tavistock Institute of Human Relations.[90] Applications such as self-managed work groups, however, have not readily diffused through British organisations. The individualistic values and inherently political nature of this culture tend to conflict with interventions emphasising employee empowerment and teamwork. In contrast, the Scandinavian cultures are far more supportive of sociotechnical practice and have been instrumental in diffusing it worldwide.

SUMMARY

Resistance is a complex and misunderstood concept that has often been blamed for the failure of a change process. It is crucial to have a thorough understanding as to the basis and form of resistance such that it may be managed in a constructive manner. By utilising the energy that is involved in contributing to the improvement of the change process, resistance can be perceived as more of a help, rather than a hindrance.

In organisations outside the country of origin (the home country), traditional approaches to OD need to be adapted to fit the cultural and economic development context in which they are applied in the country of destination (the host country). This adaptation approach recognises that OD practices may be culture bound: what works in one culture may be inappropriate in another. The cultural contexts of different geographical regions were examined in terms of five values: context orientation, power distance, uncertainty avoidance, achievement orientation and individualism. The adaptation approach also recognises that not all OD interventions may be appropriate in all cultures or in all organisations.

ACTIVITIES

REVIEW QUESTIONS

1   Explain your understanding of 'positive' and 'negative' resistance. (LO1 & 2)

2   There are many factors that would lead to resistance. Name two and explain your understanding in context with an example. (LO1 & 2)

3   Summarise, and give personal examples, of the five key values that describe national cultures. (LO3)

4   How does organisational culture affect OD planning and implementation? (LO4)

5   When can resistance be justified and constructive in a change process? (LO1, 2, 3 & 4)

EXTEND YOUR LEARNING

1   Can negative resistance be changed to positive so that change is more successful? Explain your answer using examples where relevant. (LO1 & 2)

2   Compare and contrast the various culture values. Give examples as evidence of your understanding. (LO3 & 4)

Search Me! Management

Explore **Search Me! Management** for articles relevant to this chapter. Fast and convenient, **Search Me! Management** is updated daily and provides you with 24-hour access to full text articles from hundreds of scholarly and popular journals, eBooks and newspapers, including *The Australian* and *The New York Times*. Visit http://login.cengagebrain.com and use the access code that comes with this book for 12 months access to the **Search Me! Management** database. Try searching for the following keywords:

Keywords:

- Resistance
- Mechanistic view
- Social view
- Conversational view
- Sustaining momentum
- Staying the course
- Organisational culture
- Cultural context

Search tip: **Search Me! Management** contains information from both local and international sources. To get the greatest number of search results, try using both Australian and American spellings in your searches; for example, 'globalisation' and 'globalization'; 'organisation' and 'organization'.

REFERENCES

1 M. Pardo del Val and C. Martinez Fuentes, 'Resistance to change: a literature review and empirical study', *Management Decision*, 41 (2003): 148–55.
2 A.D. Price and K. Chahal, 'A strategic framework for change management', *Construction Management and Economics*, 24 (2006): 237–51.
3 J.C. Bruckman, 'Overcoming resistance to change: causal factors, interventions, and critical values', *The Psychologist-Manager Journal*, 11 (2008): 211–19.
4 ibid.
5 ibid.
6 E. Disston, 'How to improve cross-departmental communication (we tried it, it works)', 23 January 2017, https://medium.com/@BetterCloud/how-to-improve-cross-departmental-communication-we-tried-it-it-works-53fb4af37e83.
7 J. Falkenberg, I. Stensaker, C. Meyer and A. Haueng, 'When change becomes excessive', *Research in Organizational Change and Development*, 15 (2005): 31–62.
8 ibid.: 44.
9 In D. Waddell, T. Cummings and C. Worley, *Organisation Development and Change*, 3rd edn (Australia: Nelson ITP, 2007).
10 S. Oreg, 'Resistance to change: developing an individual differences measure', *Journal of Applied Psychology*, 88 (2003): 680–93.

11 J. Ford and L. Ford, 'Resistance to change: a re-examination and extension', *Research in Organizational Change and Development*, 17 (2009): 211–39.
12 Oreg, 'Resistance to change: developing an individual differences measure', op. cit.
13 D. Erwin and A. Garman, 'Resistance to organizational change: linking research and practice', *Leadership and Organization Development Journal*, 31 (2009): 39–56.
14 Oreg, 'Resistance to change: developing an individual differences measure', op. cit.
15 Pardo del Val and Martinez Fuentes, 'Resistance to change', op. cit.: 149.
16 F. Graetz, M. Rimmer, A. Lawrence and A. Smith, *Managing Organisational Change* (Milton: Wiley, 2006): 289.
17 T. Clarke and S. Clegg, *Changing Paradigms: The Transformation of Management Knowledge for the 21st Century* (London: Harper Collins, 1998).
18 M. Heffernan and A. Smythe in Waddell, Cummings and Worley, *Organisation Development and Change*, op. cit.
19 Waddell, Cummings and Worley, *Organisation Development and Change*, op. cit.
20 Pardo del Val and Martinez Fuentes, 'Resistance to change: a literature review and empirical study', *Management Decision*, 41 (2003): 149.
21 Erwin and Garman, 'Resistance to organizational change', op. cit.

22 ibid.
23 Ford and Ford, 'Resistance to change', op. cit.
24 ibid.
25 ibid.
26 ibid.
27 ibid.
28 Price and Chahal, 'A strategic framework for change management', op. cit.
29 D. Garvin, *Learning in Action* (Cambridge: Harvard Business School Press, 2000).
30 M. McGill, J. Slocum and D. Lei, 'Management practices in learning organizations', *Organizational Dynamics* (Autumn 1993): 5–17; E. Nevis, A. DiBella and J. Gould, 'Understanding organizations as learning systems', *Sloan Management Review* (Winter 1995): 73–85.
31 J. Dewey, *How We Think* (Boston: DC Heath, 1933).
32 C. Argyris and D. Schon, *Organizational Learning II – Theory, Method and Practice* (Reading, Mass.: Addison-Wesley).
33 B. Bunker and B. Alban, *The Handbook of Large Group Methods* (San Francisco: Jossey-Bass, 2006); G. Bushe and R. Marshak, eds, *Dialogic Organization Development* (Oakland, CA: Berrett-Koehler, 2015).
34 Argyris and Schon, *Organizational Learning II*, op. cit.; P. Senge, *The Fifth Discipline* (New York: Doubleday, 1990); P. Senge, C. Roberts, R. Ross, B. Smith and A. Kleiner, *The Fifth Discipline Fieldbook: Strategies for Building a Learning Organization* (New York: Doubleday, 1995).
35 Waddell, Cummings and Worley, *Organisation Development and Change*, op. cit.
36 Ford and Ford, 'Resistance to change', op. cit.
37 R. Calabrese, 'The ethical imperative to lead change: overcoming the resistance to change', *The International Journal of Educational Management*, 17 (2003): 7–13.
38 ibid.: 7.
39 J. Ford, L. Ford and A. D'Amelio, 'Resistance to change: the rest of the story', *Academy of Management Review*, 33 (2008): 362–77.
40 M. Heffernan and A. Smythe in Waddell, Cummings and Worley, *Organisation Development and Change*, op. cit.
41 Price and Chahal, 'A strategic framework for change management', op. cit.
42 Pardo del Val and Martinez Fuentes 'Resistance to change', op. cit.
43 ibid.
44 J. Falkenberg, I. Stensaker, C. Meyer and A. Haueng, 'When change becomes excessive', *Research in Organizational Change and Development*, 15 (2005): 31–62.
45 ibid.
46 ibid.: 43.
47 ibid.: 31–62.
48 ibid.

49 Adapted from R. Cooke, 'Deflating resistance to change: or a quick guide to understanding resistance and moving forwards', *Human Resource Management International Digest*, 17 (2009): 3–4.
50 Pardo del Val and Martinez Fuentes, 'Resistance to change', op. cit.
51 Waddell, Cummings and Worley, *Organisation Development and Change*, op. cit.
52 M. Heffernan and A. Smythe in Waddell, Cummings and Worley, *Organisation Development and Change*, op. cit.
53 Adapted from Bruckman, 'Overcoming resistance to change', op. cit.: 214.
54 C. Worley, D. Hitch and W. Ross, *Integrated Strategic Change: How OD Helps to Build Competitive Advantage* (Reading, MA: Addison-Wesley, 1996).
55 M. Beer, *Organization Change and Development: A Systems View* (Santa Monica, CA: Goodyear, 1980).
56 E. Devroe, P. Ponsaers, L.G. Moor, J. Greene and L. Skinns, eds, *Tides and Currents in Police Theories*, 25, 2012–14.
57 E. Schein and P. Schein, *Organizational Culture and Leadership*, 5th edn (San Francisco: Jossey-Bass, 2016).
58 S. Camden-Anders and T. Knott, 'Contrasts in culture: practicing OD globally', in *Global and International Organization Development*, eds P. Sorensen, T. Head, T. Yaeger and D. Cooperrider (Chicago: Stipes Publishing, 2001).
59 F. Laloux, *Reinventing Organizations* (Brussels: Nelson Parker, 2014).
60 L. Bourgeois and M. Boltvinik, 'OD in cross-cultural settings: Latin America', *California Management Review*, 23 (Spring 1981): 75–81; L. Brown, 'Is organization development culture bound?', *Academy of Management Newsletter* (Winter 1982); P. Evans, 'Organization development in the transnational enterprise', in *Research in Organizational Change and Development*, 3, eds R. Woodman and W. Pasmore (Greenwich, CT: JAI Press, 1989): 1–38; R. Marshak, 'Lewin meets Confucius: a review of the OD model of change', *Journal of Applied Behavioral Science*, 29 (1997): 400–2; A. Chin and C. Chin, *Internationalizing OD: Cross-Cultural Experiences of NTL Members* (Alexandria, VA: NTL Institute, 1997); A. Shevat, 'Practicing OD with a technology-driven global company', *OD Practitioner*, 33 (2001): 28–35.
61 Shevat, 'Practicing OD', op. cit.
62 R. Kjar, 'A time of transition: lessons in global OD from a successful Japanese firm', *Organization Development Journal*, 25 (2007): 11–17; J. Schmuckler, 'Cross-cultural performance feedback', *OD Practitioner* 33 (2001): 15–20.
63 Evans, 'Organization development', op. cit.: 8–11; Brown, 'Is organization development culture bound?', op. cit.; Bourgeois and Boltvinik, 'OD in cross-cultural settings', op. cit.; W. Ouchi, *Theory Z* (Reading, MA: Addison-Wesley, 1981).

64 E. Schein, *Organization Culture and Leadership*, 2nd edn (San Francisco: Jossey-Bass, 1992); Evans, 'Organization Development', op. cit.: 11.

65 G. Hofstede, *Culture's Consequences* (Beverly Hills, CA: Sage Publications, 1980); A. Jaeger, 'Organization development and national culture: where's the fit?', *Academy of Management Journal*, 11 (1986): 178–90; A. Francesco and B. Gold, *International Organizational Behavior*, 2nd edn (Upper Saddle River, NJ: Prentice-Hall, 2004); R. Hodgetts, F. Luthans and J. Doh, *International Management: Culture, Strategy, and Behavior*, 6th edn (New York: McGraw-Hill, 2005).

66 G. Hofstede, *Culture's Consequences*, op. cit.; E. Hall and M. Hall, 'Key concepts: understanding structures of culture', in *International Management Behavior*, 3rd edn, eds H. Lane, J. DiStefano and M. Maznevski (Cambridge: Blackwell, 2000); F. Kluckhohn and F. Strodtbeck, *Variations in Value Orientations* (Evanston, IL: Peterson, 1961); F. Trompenaars, *Riding the Waves of Culture* (London: Economist Press, 1993).

67 H.A. von der Gracht, C.R. Vennemann and I. Darkow, 'Corporate foresight and innovation management: a portfolio-approach in evaluating organizational development', *Futures*, 42 (2010): 380–93.

68 G. Hofstede, G.J. Hofstede, M. Minkov and H. Vinken, 2008. *Value Survey Module 2008 Manual*, http://www.geerthofstede.nl/vsm-08.

69 E. Bergiel, B. Bergiel and J. Upson, 'Revisiting Hofstede's dimensions: examining the cultural convergence of the United States and Japan', January 2012, http://www.na-businesspress.com/AJM/BergielEB_Web12_1_pdf.

70 J. Sachs, *The End of Poverty* (New York: Penguin Books, 2005); A. Sen, *Development as Freedom* (New York: Anchor Books, 1999); K. Murrell, 'Management infrastructure in the Third World', in *Global Business Management in the 1990s*, ed. R. Moran (New York: Beacham, 1990); S. Fukuda-Parr, N. Woods and N. Birdsall, *Human Development Report 2002* (New York: United Nations Development Program, 2002).

71 B. Webster, 'Organization development: an international perspective' (unpublished master's thesis, Pepperdine University, 1995).

72 Jaeger, 'Organization development and national culture', op. cit.

73 S. Michailova, 'Contrasts in culture: Russian and Western perspectives in organization change', *Academy of Management Executive*, 14 (2000): 99–112.

74 The dearth of published empirical descriptions of OD in particular countries and organisations necessitates a regional focus. The risk is that these descriptions may generalise too much.

Practitioners should take great care in applying these observations to specific situations.

75 W. Woodworth, 'Privatisation in Belorussia: organizational change in the former USSR', *Organization Development Journal*, 3 (1993): 53–9.

76 K. Johnson, 'Estimating national culture and OD values', in Sorensen et al. eds, *Global and International Organization Development*, op. cit.: 329–44; Jaeger, 'Organization development and national culture', op. cit.

77 A. Shevat, 'The practice of organizational development in Israel', in Sorensen et al. eds, *Global and International Organization Development*, op. cit.: 237–41; W. Fisher, 'Organization development in Egypt', in Sorensen et al. eds, *Global and International Organization Development*, op. cit.: 241–9.

78 M. Manning and J. Delacerda, 'Building organization change in an emerging economy: whole systems change using large group methods in Mexico', in *Research in Organizational Change and Development*, 14, eds W. Pasmore and R. Woodman (Oxford, England: JAI Press, 2003): 51–97.

79 R. Semler, *Maverick* (New York: Random House, 2001); R. Semler, *The Seven Day Weekend: Changing the Way Work Works* (New York: Penguin Books, 2004).

80 'Strategic OD article', December 2003, http://lindasharkey.com/strategic-od-article.

81 G.M. Schwarz and G.P. Huber, 'Challenging organizational change research', *British Journal of Management*, 19 (March 2008): S1–S6.

82 J. Preston, L. DuToit and I. Barber, 'A potential model of transformational change applied to South Africa', in *Research in Organizational Change and Development*, 9, eds R. Woodman and W. Pasmore (Greenwich, CT: JAI Press, 1998); G. Sigmund, 'Current issues in South African corporations: an internal OD perspective' (unpublished master's thesis, Pepperdine University, 1996).

83 Sigmund, 'Current issues', op. cit.

84 Q. Yang, Y. Yu and W. Chen, 'Research on growing-up mechanism and fostering of venture enterprise based on knowledge management', in *Knowledge Discovery and Data Mining 2009* (WKDD 2009).

85 Webster, 'Organization development', op. cit.; I. Perlaki, 'Organization development in Eastern Europe', *Journal of Applied Behavioral Science*, 30 (1994): 297–312; J. Putti, 'Organization development scene in Asia: the case of Singapore', in Sorensen et al. eds, *Global and International Organization Development*, op. cit.: 275–84; I. Nonaka, 'Creating organizational order out of chaos: self-renewal in Japanese firms', *California Management Review* (Spring 1988): 57–73; K. Johnson, 'Organizational development in Venezuela', in Sorensen et al. eds, *Global and International Organization Development*,

op. cit.: 305–10; Fuchs, 'Organizational development', op. cit.; R. Babcock and T. Head, 'Organization development in the Republic of China (Taiwan)', in Sorensen et al. eds, *Global and International Organization Development*, op. cit.: 285–92; R. Marshak, 'Training and consulting in Korea', *OD Practitioner*, 25 (Summer 1993): 16–21.

86 Johnson, 'Organizational development', op. cit.; A. Mueller, 'Successful and unsuccessful OD interventions in a Venezuelan banking organization: the role of culture' (unpublished master's thesis, Pepperdine University, 1995).

87 M.F. Grace and R.W. Klein, 'Facing Mother Nature', *Regulation* (Fall 2007): 28–34, http://www.cato.org/ pubs/regulation/regv30n3/v30n3-5.pdf.

88 Webster, 'Organization development', op. cit.; B. Gustavsen, 'The LOM Program: a network-based strategy for organization development in Sweden', in *Research in Organizational Change and Development*, 5, eds R. Woodman and W. Pasmore (Greenwich, CT: JAI Press, 1991): 285–316; P. Sorensen Jr, H. Larsen, T. Head and H. Scoggins, 'Organization development in Denmark', in Sorensen et al. eds, *Global and International Organization Development*, op. cit.: 95–112; A. Derefeldt, 'Organization development in Sweden', in Sorensen et al. eds, *Global and International Organization Development*, op. cit.: 113–22.

89 D. Dulany and V. Pellettiere, 'Knowledge management process: a socio-technical approach', Aurora University, 2008, http://www.swdsi.org/ swdsi08/paper/SWDSI%20Proceedings%20 Paper%20S203.pdf.

90 E. Trist, 'On socio-technical systems', in *The Planning of Change*, 2nd edn, eds W. Bennis, K. Benne and R. Chin (New York: Holt, Rinehart and Winston, 1969): 269–72; A. Cherns, 'The principles of sociotechnical design', *Human Relations*, 19 (1976): 783–92; E. Jacques, *The Changing Culture of a Factory* (New York: Dryden, 1952).

5

THE PROCESS OF
ORGANISATIONAL CHANGE

LEARNING OUTCOMES

After studying this chapter, you should be able to:

1   Summarise the steps in the process of organisational change and apply them to current situations.

2   Describe the methods for designing change management processes and assess their relevance in the contemporary environment.

3   Explain the five kinds of processes used in the implementation of change.

4   Justify the feedback processes for implementation and evaluation of managed change programs.

5   Critically assess the concept of institutionalisation of the changed state.

KEY TERMS

Institutionalisation	Transformation
Diagnosis	Equifinality
Diagnostic model	Stratified sample
Open systems theory	

Intervention design, or action planning, derives from careful diagnosis and is meant to resolve specific problems and to improve particular areas of organisational functioning identified in the diagnosis. Organisation development (OD) interventions vary from standardised programs that have been developed and used in many organisations to unique programs tailored to a specific organisation or department.

Once diagnosis has revealed the causes of problems or opportunities for development, organisation members can begin planning, and subsequently implementing, the changes necessary for improving organisational effectiveness and performance. A large part of OD is concerned with interventions for improving organisations.

Planned change processes generally start when one or more key managers or administrators sense that their organisation, department or group could be improved or has problems that could be alleviated through OD. The organisation might be successful, yet have room for improvement. It might be facing impending environmental conditions (both internal and/or external) that necessitate a change in how it operates. This requires information gathering, processing and feedback. The quality of the information gathered is, therefore, a key part of the OD process. But perhaps the most important step in the diagnostic process – and often 'forgotten' – is feeding back diagnostic information to the client organisation. Although the data may have been collected with the client's help, the OD practitioner is usually responsible for organising and presenting the data to the client.[1] Properly analysed and meaningful data can have an impact on organisational change only if organisation members can use the information to devise appropriate action plans. A key objective of the feedback process is to be sure that the client has ownership of the data. This chapter introduces some basic methods of gathering data and emphasises the importance of gaining accurate and honest feedback before proceeding with the design, implementation and evaluation of change interventions.

This chapter finishes with the final stage of the OD cycle – evaluation and **institutionalisation**. Evaluation is concerned with providing feedback to practitioners and organisation members about the progress and impact of interventions. Such information may suggest the need for further diagnosis and modification of the change program, or it may show that the intervention is successful. Institutionalisation involves making OD interventions a permanent part of the organisation's normal functioning. It ensures that the results of successful change programs persist over time.

Institutionalisation: involves making OD interventions permanent and part of the organisation's normal functions.

DIAGNOSING ORGANISATIONS

When done well, diagnosis clearly points the organisation towards appropriate intervention activities that will improve organisation effectiveness.

Diagnosis is the process of assessing the functioning of the organisation, department, group or job to discover sources of problems and areas for improvement. It involves collecting pertinent information about current operations, analysing those data and drawing conclusions for potential change and improvement. Effective diagnosis provides the systematic understanding of the organisation necessary for the design of appropriate interventions. Thus, OD interventions derive from diagnosis and include the specific actions intended to resolve problems and improve organisational functioning.

Diagnosis: the process of assessing the functioning of an organisation, department, group or job and analysing pertinent data in order to discover sources of problems and propose areas for improvement.

Diagnostic models derive from conceptions about how organisations function and tell OD practitioners what to look for when diagnosing organisations, departments, groups or jobs. They represent a road map for discovering current functioning. A general, comprehensive diagnostic model is presented, based on open systems theory.[2]

WHAT IS DIAGNOSIS?

Diagnosis is the process of understanding how the organisation is functioning: it provides the information necessary for designing change interventions. It generally follows from successful entry and contracting.[3] The preliminary activities in planned change set the stage for successful diagnosis. Those processes help the OD practitioner and client jointly determine organisational issues to focus on, show how to collect and analyse data to understand them and how to work together to develop action steps. In another sense, diagnosis is happening all the time. Managers, organisations and OD practitioners are always trying to understand the drivers of organisational effectiveness as well as how and why the changes are occurring in a particular way.

Unfortunately, the term 'diagnosis' can be misleading when applied to organisations. It suggests a model of organisational change analogous to medicine: an organisation (patient) experiencing problems seeks help from an OD practitioner (doctor); the practitioner examines the organisation, finds the causes of the problems (as distinct from symptoms) and prescribes a solution. Diagnosis in OD is, however, much more collaborative than such a medical perspective implies. The values and ethical beliefs that underlie OD suggest that organisational members and change agents should be jointly involved in discovering the causes of organisational problems. Similarly, both should be actively involved in developing appropriate interventions and implementing them.

For example, a manager might seek OD help to reduce absenteeism in a department. The manager and consultant may jointly decide to diagnose the cause of the problem by examining company absenteeism records and by interviewing selected employees about possible reasons for absenteeism. Alternatively, they might examine employee loyalty and discover the aspects of the organisation that encourage people to stay. Analysis of these data could uncover causes of absenteeism, thus helping the manager and the practitioner to develop an appropriate intervention to address the issue.

The medical view of diagnosis also implies something is wrong with the patient and that one needs to uncover the cause of the illness. Where organisations have specific problems, diagnosis is problem-oriented. It seeks reasons for the problems. However, many managers involved with OD are not experiencing specific organisational problems. Rather, they want to improve the overall effectiveness of their organisation, department or group. Here, diagnosis is development-oriented. It assesses the current functioning to discover areas for future development. For example, a manager might be interested in using OD to improve a department already seemingly functioning well. Diagnosis might include an overall assessment of both the task-performance capabilities of the department and the department's impact upon its individual members. This process seeks to uncover specific areas for future development of the department's effectiveness.

In OD, diagnosis is used more broadly than a medical definition would suggest. It is a collaborative process between organisation members and the OD consultant to collect pertinent information, analyse it and draw conclusions for action planning and intervention.[4] Diagnosis may be aimed at uncovering the causes of specific problems or directed at assessing the overall functioning of the organisation or department to discover areas for future development. Diagnosis provides a systematic understanding of organisations so that appropriate interventions may be developed for solving problems and enhancing effectiveness.

Apply your learning 5.1 is a snippet of an article about environmental scanning in Western Australia.

IMPROVING RESILIENCE THROUGH ENVIRONMENTAL SCANNING IN WESTERN AUSTRALIA

APPLY YOUR LEARNING
5.1

The public sector's resilience to change is dependent at least in part on its capacity to anticipate change and its preparedness to respond. This is the case whether change occurs gradually and progressively or as major shocks. In the public sector, environmental scanning is a technique for identifying prospective policy challenges – and opportunities – that might arise from current and emerging issues and trends. It attempts to answer questions such as: how do we identify relevant issues and trends? How do we present these as snapshots? How can we translate that information into flexible strategies and priorities *and* prepare decision-makers for change?

The WA Department of Treasury introduced an environmental scanning process in the aftermath of the Global Financial Crisis that hit Australia in late 2008. A new strategic policy unit was created to 'make space' to provide advice on longer-term and crosscutting policy issues. Part of its remit was to start producing regular environmental scans. The unit developed its first environmental scan in 2009 on a fairly small scale. The approach was refined with two subsequent environmental scans conducted in 2010 and 2011, with a broadened consultation base within Treasury and across State public sector agencies.

...

The WA Department of Treasury's approach to environmental scans was initially informed by reviews of definitions, approaches and formats for environmental scans undertaken in other Australian jurisdictions and internationally. This informal desktop study suggested that the key features of environment scans were that they were outward looking, focused on change or possible change, considered the policy implications, explored the opportunities and challenges, and emphasised the issues that were most relevant to the organisation.

Over that past four years the WA Department of Treasury has developed its own, more prescriptive definition of environmental scanning that encompasses both the process and the use of such scans. First, environmental scanning is a formal and systematic exploration of the external environment to identify potential opportunities, challenges and likely relevant future developments that could or should inform government policy deliberations. Second, as a discipline, environmental scanning guides the development of flexible strategies and priorities that prepare the government and its decision-makers to respond quickly to change. This is an assertion of how the products of environmental scans might be used.

Environmental scans encompass both the potential for crises, which may include large-scale disasters, and softer, progressive processes of change. In this context, the essential nature of environmental scans is that they are

→ formal and systematic investigations
→ have an external focus

»

»

→ investigate likely relevant future developments
→ inform government policy deliberations
→ provide for flexible responses to change.
   The department's intentions in producing environmental scans were to use them to
→ raise awareness of key strategic issues, particularly crosscutting issues that
   might impact on Western Australia's public sector, either in the short term or
   over the longer term
→ inform the development of strategic plans and operational work plans, and
   policy development within Treasury
→ prepare the Government to respond quickly to change.

Scans have also proved a useful means of introducing new staff to a 'big picture'
view on key issues and trends that affect the public sector and more specifically
Treasury business. A further benefit is that they can pinpoint areas of risk, and
at the same time develop scenarios to test the impacts of change in external
parameters or policy conditions.

...

The WA Department of Treasury's approach to environmental scanning is
formal and systematic, outwardly focused and examines change that is relevant to
the WA public sector. Some of the lessons to be learned from this experience are
that environmental scanners should be encouraged to gather information from
a wide range of sources, and to incorporate consultation and awareness raising
as vital components of the process. They should think strategically. They should
construct a narrative that leads their audience to see opportunities for further
policy development, and that has the potential to manage policy challenges before
they become crises. Their product – the environmental scan – should be used as a
platform for debate rather than to communicate predetermined policy positions.

Environmental scans explore the potential to improve public sector resilience
in a softer setting of change, and should give the audience an appreciation of the
connections between public policy issues. Understanding these connections, and how
change in these connections influences government policy, is integral to the public
sector becoming more resilient to change.

Source: N. Eastough, 'Improving resilience through environmental scanning in
Western Australia', http://press-files.anu.edu.au/downloads/press/p283571/pdf/12.-Improving-Resilience-
through-Environmental-Scanning-in-Western-Australia.pdf, accessed 7 May 2018.

Critical thinking questions	
1	In this article, what is the importance of environmental scanning?
2	How does the WA Department of Treasury define environmental scanning?
3	What is the essential nature of environmental scanning?
4	How is environmental scanning best used?
5	Download the article and give an overview of how to conduct an environmental scan.

THE NEED FOR DIAGNOSTIC MODELS

Entry and contracting processes can result in a need to understand either a whole system or some part, process or feature of the organisation. To diagnose an organisation, OD practitioners and organisation members need to have some idea about what information to collect and analyse, based on intuitive hunches through to scientific explanations of how the organisation functions. Conceptual frameworks used to understand organisations are referred to as **diagnostic models**.[5] They describe the relationships between different features of the organisation, its context and effectiveness. As a result, diagnostic models indicate areas to examine and questions to ask when assessing how an organisation is functioning.

Diagnostic model: a conceptual framework describing the relationship between different features of the organisation, its context and effectiveness.

However, all models represent simplification of reality and therefore choose certain features as critical. Focusing attention on those features, to the exclusion of others, can result in a biased diagnosis. For example, a diagnostic model relating team effectiveness to the handling of interpersonal conflict[6] would lead an OD practitioner to ask questions about relationships among members, decision-making processes and conflict resolution methods. Although relevant, these questions ignore other group issues such as skills and knowledge composition, complexity of tasks performed by the group and member interdependencies. Thus, diagnostic models must be carefully chosen to address the organisation's presenting problems as well as ensuring comprehensiveness.

Potential diagnostic models are everywhere. Any collection of concepts and relationships that tries to represent a system or explain its effectiveness can potentially qualify as a diagnostic model. Major sources of diagnostic models in OD are the literally thousands of articles and books that discuss, describe and analyse how organisations function. They provide information about how and why certain organisational systems, processes or functions are effective. These studies often concern a specific facet of organisational behaviour, such as employee stress, leadership, motivation, problem solving, group dynamics, job design or career development. They also can involve the larger organisation and its context, including the environment, strategy, structure and culture. Diagnostic models can be derived from that information by noting the dimensions or variables that are associated with organisational effectiveness.

Another source of diagnostic models is the OD practitioner's own experience in organisations. This field knowledge is a wealth of practical information about how organisations operate. Unfortunately, only a small part of this vast experience has been translated into diagnostic models. These more clinical models represent the professional judgements of people with years of experience in organisational diagnosis. They generally link diagnosis with specific organisation processes, such as group problem solving, employee motivation or communication between managers and employees. The models list specific questions for diagnosing such processes.

Open systems model

This section introduces systems theory, a set of concepts and relationships that describes the properties and behaviours of things called *systems* – organisations, groups and people, for example.[7] Systems are viewed as unitary wholes composed of parts or subsystems;

they serve to integrate the parts into a functioning unit. For example, organisational systems are composed of departments such as sales, manufacturing and research. The organisation serves to coordinate the behaviours of its departments so that they function together. The general diagnostic model based on systems theory that underlies most of OD is called the **open systems theory**.

Open systems theory: a general comprehensive diagnostic model.

Systems can vary in how open they are to their outside environments. Open systems, such as organisations and people, exchange information and resources with their environments. They cannot completely control their own behaviour and are influenced in part by external forces. Organisations, for example, are affected by such environmental conditions as the availability of raw material, customer demands and government regulations. Understanding how these external forces affect the organisation can help to explain some of its internal behaviour.

Open systems display a hierarchical ordering. Each higher level of system is composed of lower level systems. Systems at the level of society are composed of organisations; organisations are composed of groups (departments); groups are composed of individuals; and so on. Although systems at different levels vary in many ways – in size and complexity, for example – they have a number of common characteristics by virtue of being open systems. These properties can be applied to systems at any level. The following key properties of open systems are described: (1) inputs, transformations and outputs; (2) boundaries; (3) feedback; (4) equifinality; and (5) alignment.

Inputs, transformations and outputs

Any organisational system is composed of three related parts: inputs, transformations and outputs, as shown in **Figure 5.1**. *Inputs* consist of human or other resources, such as information, energy and materials, coming into the system. They are acquired from the system's external environment. For example, a manufacturing organisation acquires raw materials from an outside supplier. Similarly, a hospital nursing unit acquires information about a patient's condition from the attending doctor. In each case, the system (organisation or nursing unit) obtains resources (raw materials or information) from its external environment.

Transformation: the process of converting inputs into outputs.

Transformations are the processes of converting inputs into outputs. In organisations, transformations are generally carried out by a production or operations function that is composed of social and technological components. The social component consists of people and their work relationships, whereas the technological component involves tools, techniques and methods of production or service delivery. Organisations have developed elaborate mechanisms for transforming incoming resources into goods and services. Banks, for example, transform deposits into mortgage loans. Schools attempt to transform students into more educated people. Transformation processes can also take place at the group and individual levels. For example, research and development departments can transform the latest scientific advances into new product ideas.

Outputs are the result of what is transformed by the system and sent to the environment. Thus, inputs that have been transformed represent outputs ready to leave the system. Health insurance funds receive money and medical bills, transform them through the operation of record keeping, and export payments to hospitals and doctors.

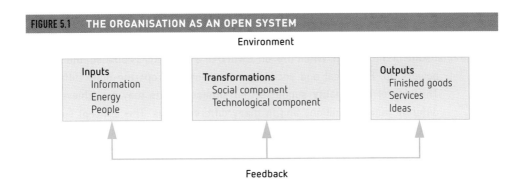

FIGURE 5.1   THE ORGANISATION AS AN OPEN SYSTEM

Boundaries

The idea of boundaries helps to distinguish between systems and environments. Closed systems have relatively rigid and impenetrable boundaries, whereas open systems have far more permeable ones. Boundaries – the borders or limits of the system – are easily seen in many biological and mechanical systems. Defining the boundaries of social systems is more difficult as there is a continuous inflow and outflow through them. For example, where are the organisational boundaries for call centres for various companies that are positioned offshore? The emergence of the information superhighway and worldwide information networks will continue to challenge the notion of boundaries in open systems.

The definition of 'boundary' is arbitrary, as a social system has multiple subsystems and one subsystem's boundary line may not be the same as that of another. As with the system itself, arbitrary boundaries may have to be assigned to any social organisation, depending on the variable to be stressed. The boundaries used for studying or analysing leadership may be quite different from those used to study intergroup dynamics.

Just as systems can be considered to be relatively open or closed, the permeability of boundaries also varies from fixed to diffuse. The boundaries of a community's police force are probably far more rigid and sharply defined than are those of the community's political parties. Conflict over boundaries is always a potential problem within an organisation, just as it is in the world outside the organisation.

Feedback

As shown in **Figure 5.1**, feedback is information about the actual performance or the results of the system. However, not all such information is feedback. Only information used to control the future functioning of the system is considered to be feedback. Feedback can be used to maintain the system in a steady state (for example, keeping an assembly line running at a certain speed) or to help the organisation adapt to changing circumstances. For example, a large organisation might implement a robust consumer feedback strategy in order to monitor quality standards across a number of outlets. However, this strategy would be flexible enough to allow employees to suggest different approaches or changes to that strategy to accommodate cultural and geographical considerations, all while not compromising on quality. This approach is then followed up by a market research study, which could lead the marketing department to recommend a change in the organisation's advertising campaign.

Equifinality

In closed systems, there is a direct cause-and-effect relationship between the initial condition and the final state of the system. When the 'on' switch of a computer is pushed, the system powers up. Biological and social systems, however, operate quite differently. The idea of **equifinality** suggests that similar results may be achieved with different initial conditions and in many different ways. This concept suggests that a manager can use varying forms of inputs into the organisation and can transform them in a variety of ways to obtain satisfactory outputs. Thus, the function of management is not to seek a single rigid solution but rather to develop a variety of satisfactory options (scenario planning). Systems and contingency theories suggest that there is no universal best way to design an organisation. Organisations and departments providing routine services should be designed differently from organisations specialising in research, for example.

Equifinality: a cause-and-effect relationship between the initial condition and the final state of a system.

Alignment

A system's overall effectiveness is determined by the extent to which the different parts are aligned with each other. This alignment or fit concerns the relationships between inputs and transformations, between transformations and outputs, and among the subsystems of the transformation process. Diagnosticians who view the relationships between the various parts of a system as a whole are taking what is referred to as a 'systemic perspective'.

Fit and alignment refer to a characteristic of the relationship between two or more parts. Just as the teeth in two wheels of a watch must mesh perfectly for the watch to keep time, so too do the parts of an organisation need to mesh for it to be effective. For example, Foster's Group attempts to achieve its goals through a strategy of diversification, and a divisional structure is used to support that strategy. A functional structure would not be a good fit with the strategy as it is more efficient for one division to focus on one product line than for one manufacturing department to try to make many different products. The systemic perspective suggests that diagnosis is the search for misfits among the various parts and subsystems of an organisation.

COLLECTING AND ANALYSING DIAGNOSTIC INFORMATION

Data collection involves gathering information on specific organisational features, such as the inputs, design components and outputs presented above. The process begins by establishing an effective relationship between the OD practitioner and those from whom data will be collected, and then choosing data-collection techniques. Four methods can be used to collect data: questionnaires, interviews, observations and unobtrusive measures. Data analysis organises and examines the information to make clear the underlying causes of an organisational problem or to identify areas for future development. The next step in the cyclical OD process is the feeding back of data to the client system. The overall process of data collection, analysis and feedback is shown in **Figure 5.2**.

FIGURE 5.2 THE DATA-COLLECTION AND FEEDBACK CYCLE

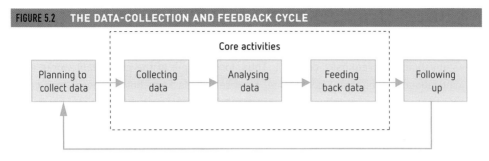

Source: D. Nadler, *Feedback and Organization Development* © 1977, p. 43. Reprinted by permission of Pearson Education, Inc., Upper Saddle River, New Jersey

THE DIAGNOSTIC RELATIONSHIP

In most cases of planned change, OD practitioners play an active role in gathering data from organisation members for diagnostic purposes. For example, they might interview members of a work team about causes of conflict among members, or they might survey employees at a large industrial plant about factors that contribute to poor product quality. Before collecting diagnostic information, practitioners need to establish a relationship with those who will provide and subsequently use it.[8] Because the nature of that relationship affects the quality and usefulness of the data collected, it is vital that OD practitioners provide organisation members with a clear idea of who they are, why the data are being collected, what the data gathering will involve and how the data will be used.[9] Answers to these questions can help to allay people's natural fears that the data might be used against them. Such answers also help to gain members' participation and support, which is essential for developing successful interventions.

Establishing the diagnostic relationship between the consultant and relevant organisation members is similar to forming a contract. It is meant to clarify expectations and to specify the conditions of the relationship. In those cases where members have been directly involved in the entering and contracting process, the diagnostic contract will typically be part of the initial contracting step. However, in situations where data will be collected from members who have not been directly involved in entering and contracting, OD practitioners will need to establish a diagnostic contract as a prelude to diagnosis. The answers to the following questions provide the substance of the diagnostic contract:[10]

1   *Who am I?* The answer to this question introduces the OD practitioner to the organisation, particularly to those members who do not know the consultant, but who will be asked to provide diagnostic data.

2   *Why am I here, and what am I doing?* These answers are aimed at defining the goals of the diagnosis and data-gathering activities. The consultant needs to present the objectives of the action research process and to describe how the diagnostic activities fit into the overall developmental strategy.

3   *Who do I work for?* This answer clarifies who has hired the consultant, whether it be a manager, a group of managers or a group of employees and managers. One way to build trust and support for the diagnosis is to have such persons directly involved in establishing the diagnostic contract. Thus, for example, if the consultant works for a joint labour–management committee, representatives from both sides of that group could help the consultant build the proper relationship with those from whom data will be gathered.

4   *What do I want from you, and why?* Here the consultant needs to specify how much time and effort people will need to give in order to provide valid data, and subsequently to work with these data in solving problems. Because some people may not want to participate in the diagnosis, it is important to specify that such involvement is voluntary.

5   *How will I protect your confidentiality?* This answer addresses member concerns about who will see their responses and in what form. This is especially critical when employees are asked to provide information about their attitudes or perceptions. The OD practitioner can either assure confidentiality or state that full participation in the change process requires open information sharing. In the first case, employees are frequently concerned about privacy and the possibility of being punished for their responses. To alleviate concern and to increase the likelihood of getting honest responses, the consultant may need to assure employees of the confidentiality of their information. This may require explicit guarantees of response anonymity. In the second case, full involvement of the participants in their own diagnosis may be a vital ingredient in the change process. If sensitive issues arise, assurances of confidentiality can restrict the OD practitioner and thwart meaningful diagnosis. The consultant is bound to keep confidential the issues that are most critical for the group or organisation to understand.[11] The OD practitioner must think carefully about how he or she wants to handle confidentiality issues.

6   *Who will have access to the data?* Respondents typically want to know whether or not they will have access to their data and who else in the organisation will have similar access. The OD practitioner needs to clarify access issues and, in most cases, should agree to provide respondents with their own results. Indeed, the collaborative nature of diagnosis means that organisation members will work with their own data to discover causes of problems and to devise relevant interventions.

7   *What's in it for you?* This answer is aimed at providing organisation members with a clear assessment of the benefits they can expect from the diagnosis. This usually entails describing the feedback process and how they can use the data to improve the organisation.

8   *Can I be trusted?* The diagnostic relationship ultimately rests on the trust that is established between the consultant and those providing the data. An open and honest exchange of information depends on such trust, and the practitioner should provide ample

time and face-to-face contact during the contracting process in order to build this trust. This requires the consultant to actively listen and openly discuss all questions raised by respondents.

Careful attention to establishing the diagnostic relationship helps to promote the three goals of data collection.[12] The first and most immediate objective is to obtain valid information about organisational functioning. Building a data-collection contract can ensure that organisation members provide information that is honest, reliable and complete.

Data collection can also rally energy for constructive organisational change. A good diagnostic relationship helps organisation members to start thinking about issues that concern them, and it creates expectations that change is possible. When members trust the consultant, they are likely to participate in the diagnostic process and to generate energy and commitment for organisational change.

Finally, data collection helps to develop the collaborative relationship necessary for effecting organisational change. The diagnostic stage of action research is probably the first time that most organisation members meet the OD practitioner. It can provide the basis for building a longer-term relationship. The data-collection contract and the subsequent data-gathering and feedback activities provide members with opportunities for seeing the consultant in action and for getting to know her or him personally. If the consultant can show employees that she or he is trustworthy, is willing to work with them and is able to help improve the organisation, then the data-collection process will contribute to the longer-term collaborative relationship so necessary for carrying out organisational changes.

METHODS FOR COLLECTING DATA

The four major techniques for gathering diagnostic data are questionnaires, interviews, observations and unobtrusive methods. **Table 5.1** briefly compares the methods and lists their major advantages and problems. No single method can fully measure the kinds of variables important to OD; each has certain strengths and weaknesses.[13] For example, perceptual measures, such as questionnaires and surveys, are open to self-report biases, such as the respondents' tendency to give socially desirable answers rather than honest opinions. Observations, on the other hand, are susceptible to observer biases, such as seeing what one wants to see rather than what is really there. Because of the biases inherent in any data-collection method, we recommend that more than one method be used when collecting diagnostic data. The data from the different methods can be compared and, if they are consistent, it is likely that the variables are being validly measured. For example, questionnaire measures of job discretion could be supplemented with observations of the number and kinds of decisions that the employees are making. If the two kinds of data support one another, job discretion is probably being accurately assessed. If the two kinds of data conflict, then the validity of the measures should be examined further – perhaps by employing a third method, such as interviews.

TABLE 5.1	DIFFERENT METHODS OF DATA COLLECTION	
Method	Major advantages	Major potential problems
Questionnaires	1 Responses can be quantified and easily summarised 2 Easy to use with large samples 3 Relatively inexpensive 4 Can obtain large volume of data	1 Non-empathy 2 Predetermined questions missing issues 3 Overinterpretation of data 4 Response bias
Interviews	1 Adaptive – allows data collection on a range of possible subjects 2 Source of 'rich' data 3 Empathic 4 Process of interviewing can build rapport	1 Expense 2 Bias in interviewer responses 3 Coding and interpretation difficulties 4 Self-report bias
Observations	1 Collects data on behaviour, rather than reports of behaviour 2 Real time, not retrospective 3 Adaptive	1 Coding and interpretation difficulties 2 Sampling inconsistencies 3 Observer bias and questionable reliability 4 Expense
Unobtrusive measures	1 Non-reactive – no response bias 2 High face validity 3 Easily quantified interviews	1 Access and retrieval difficulties 2 Validity concerns 3 Coding and interpretation difficulties

Source: D. Nadler, *Feedback and Organization Development* © 1977, p. 119.
Reprinted by permission of Pearson Education, Inc., Upper Saddle River, New Jersey.

Questionnaires

One of the most efficient ways of collecting data is through questionnaires. Because they typically contain fixed-response questions about various features of an organisation, these paper-and-pencil measures can be administered to large numbers of people simultaneously. Also, they can be analysed quickly, especially with the use of computers, thus permitting quantitative comparison and evaluation. As a result, data can easily be fed back to employees. Numerous basic resource books on survey methodology and questionnaire development are available.[14]

Questionnaires can vary in scope: some measure selected aspects of organisations and others assess more comprehensive organisational characteristics. They can also vary in the extent to which they are either standardised or tailored to a specific organisation. Standardised instruments are generally based on an explicit model of organisation, group or individual effectiveness. These questionnaires usually contain a predetermined set of questions that have been developed and refined over time. The questionnaire includes three items or questions for each dimension; a total score for each job dimension is computed simply by adding the responses for the three relevant items and arriving at a total score from 3 (low) to 21 (high). The questionnaire has wide applicability. It has been used in a variety of organisations with employees in both blue-collar and white-collar jobs.

Several research organisations have been highly instrumental in developing and refining surveys. The Australian Council for Educational Research is a prominent example. Two of the council's most recognised measures of organisational dimensions are 'Changing your management style' and 'Team climate inventory'.[15] Other examples include 'Organization change: orientation scale',[16] available from the Australian Institute of Management. In fact, so many questionnaires are available that rarely would an organisation have to create a totally new one. However, because every organisation has unique problems and special jargon for referring to them, almost any standardised instrument will need to have organisation-specific additions, modifications or omissions.

Customised questionnaires, on the other hand, are tailored to the needs of a particular client. Typically, they include questions composed by consultants or organisation members, receive limited use and do not undergo longer-term development. Customised questionnaires can be combined with standardised instruments to provide valid and reliable data focused on the particular issues that face an organisation.

Questionnaires, however, have a number of drawbacks that need to be taken into account when choosing whether to employ them for data collection. First, responses are limited to the questions asked in the instrument. They provide little opportunity to probe for additional data or ask for points of clarification. Second, questionnaires tend to be impersonal, and employees may not be willing to provide honest answers. Third, questionnaires often elicit response biases, such as the tendency to answer questions in a socially acceptable manner. This makes it difficult to draw valid conclusions from employees' self-reports.

Interviews

A second important measurement technique is the individual or group interview. These probably represent the most widely used technique for collecting data in OD. They permit the interviewer to ask the respondent direct questions, and further probing and clarification is possible as the interview proceeds. This flexibility is invaluable for gaining private views and feelings about the organisation and for exploring new issues that emerge during the interview.

Interviews may be highly structured, resembling questionnaires, or highly unstructured, starting with general questions that allow the respondent to lead the way. Structured interviews typically derive from a conceptual model of organisation functioning; the model guides the types of questions that are asked.

Unstructured interviews are more general and include broad questions about organisational functioning, such as:

→ What are the major goals or objectives of the organisation or department?

→ How does the organisation currently perform with respect to these purposes?

→ What are the strengths and weaknesses of the organisation or department?

→ What barriers stand in the way of good performance?

Although interviewing typically involves one-to-one interaction between an OD practitioner and an employee, it can be carried out in a group context. Group interviews save time and allow people to build on others' responses. A major drawback, however, is that group settings may inhibit some people from responding freely.

A popular type of group interview is the focus group or sensing meeting.[17] These are unstructured meetings conducted by a manager or a consultant.[18] A small group of 10 to 15 employees is selected, representing either a cross-section of functional areas and hierarchical levels or a homogeneous grouping, such as minorities or engineers. Group discussion is frequently started by asking general questions about organisational features and functioning, an intervention's progress or current performance. Group members are then encouraged to discuss their answers in some depth. Consequently, focus groups and sensing meetings are an economical way of obtaining interview data and are especially effective in understanding particular issues in some depth. The richness and validity of that information will depend on the extent to which the manager or consultant develops a trust relationship with the group and listens to member opinions.

Another popular unstructured group interview involves assessing the current state of an intact work group. The manager or consultant generally directs a question to the group, calling its attention to some part of group functioning. For example, group members may be asked how they feel the group is progressing on its stated task. The group might respond and then come up with its own series of questions about barriers to task performance. This unstructured interview is a fast, simple way of collecting data about group behaviour. It allows members to discuss issues of immediate concern and to engage actively in the questioning-and-answering process. This technique is, however, limited to relatively small groups and to settings where there is trust among employees and managers, and a commitment to assessing group processes.

Interviews are an effective method of collecting data in OD. They are adaptive, allowing the interviewer to modify questions and to probe emergent issues during the interview process. They also permit the interviewer to develop an empathetic relationship with employees, frequently resulting in frank disclosure of pertinent information. Such interviews can only be successful if both parties are prepared to listen.

A major drawback of interviews is the amount of time required to conduct and analyse them. They can consume a great deal of time, especially if the interviewers take full advantage of the opportunity to hear respondents out, and change their questions accordingly. Personal biases can also distort the data. Like questionnaires, interviews are subject to the self-report biases of respondents and, perhaps more importantly, to the biases of the interviewer. For example, the nature of the questions and the interactions between the interviewer and the respondent may discourage or encourage certain kinds of responses. These problems suggest that interviewing takes considerable skill to gather valid data. Interviewers must be able to understand their own biases, to listen and establish empathy with respondents and to change questions to pursue issues that develop during the course of the interview.

Observations

One of the more direct ways of collecting data is simply to observe organisational behaviours in their functional settings. The OD practitioner may do this by casually walking through a work area and looking around or by simply counting the occurrences of specific kinds of behaviours (for example, the number of times a phone call is answered after three rings in a service department). Observation can range from complete participant observation, in which the OD practitioner becomes a member of the group under study, to more detached observation, in which the observer is clearly not part of the group or situation itself and may use film, videotape or other methods to record behaviours.

Observations have a number of advantages. They are free of the biases inherent in self-report data. They put the practitioner directly in touch with the behaviours in question, without having to rely on others' perceptions. Observations also involve real-time data, describing behaviour that is occurring in the present rather than the past. This avoids the distortions that invariably arise when people are asked to recollect their behaviours. Finally, observations are adaptive in that the consultant can modify what she or he is observing according to the circumstances.

Among the problems with observations are difficulties in interpreting the meaning that underlies the observations. Practitioners may need to code the observations to make sense of them, and this can be expensive, take time and introduce bias into the data. Because the observer is the data-collection instrument, personal bias and subjectivity can distort data unless the observer is trained and skilled in knowing what to look for, how to observe, where and when to observe and how to record data systematically. Another problem concerns sampling. Observers must not only decide which people to observe but also choose the time periods, territory and events in which observations will be made. Failure to attend to these sampling issues can result in highly biased samples of observational data. When used correctly, observations provide insightful data about organisation and group functioning, intervention success and performance.

Unobtrusive measures

Unobtrusive data are not collected directly from respondents but from secondary sources, such as company records and archives. These data are generally available in organisations and include records of absenteeism or tardiness, grievances, quantity and quality of production or service, financial performance and correspondence with key customers, suppliers or governmental agencies.

Unobtrusive measures[19] provide a relatively objective view of organisational functioning. They are free from respondent and consultant biases and are perceived by many organisation members as being real. Moreover, unobtrusive measures tend to be quantified and reported at periodic intervals, permitting statistical analysis of behaviours occurring over time. Examination of monthly absenteeism rates, for example, might reveal trends in employee withdrawal behaviour.

The major problems with unobtrusive measures occur when collecting such information and drawing valid conclusions from it. Company records may not include data in a form that is usable by the consultant. If, for example, individual performance data are needed, the consultant may find that many companies only record production information at the group or departmental level. Unobtrusive data may also have their own built-in biases. Changes in accounting procedures and in methods of recording data are common in organisations; such changes can affect company records independently of what is actually happening in the organisation. For example, observed changes in productivity over time might be caused by modifications in methods of recording production, rather than by actual changes in organisational functioning.

Despite these drawbacks, unobtrusive data serve as a valuable adjunct to other diagnostic measures, such as interviews and questionnaires. Archival data can be used in preliminary diagnosis, indicating those organisational units that have absenteeism, grievance or production problems. Interviews can then be conducted or observations made in those units to discover the underlying causes of the problems. Conversely, unobtrusive data can be used to cross-check other forms of information. For example, if questionnaires reveal that employees in a department are dissatisfied with their jobs, company records might show whether that discontent is manifested in heightened withdrawal behaviours, lowered quality of work or similar counterproductive behaviours.

SAMPLING

Before discussing how to analyse data, the issue of sampling needs to be emphasised. Application of the different data-collection techniques invariably raises the following questions: 'How many people should be interviewed and who should they be?', 'What events should be observed and how many?' and 'How many records should be inspected and which ones?'[20]

In many OD cases, sampling is not an issue. Practitioners simply collect interview or questionnaire data from all members of the organisation or department in question, and so do not have to worry about whether the information is representative of the organisation or unit because all members of the population are included in the sample.

Sampling becomes an issue in OD, however, when data are collected from selected members, behaviours or records. This is often the case when diagnosing organisation-level issues or large systems. In these cases, it may be important to ensure that the sample of people, behaviours or records adequately represents the characteristics of the total population. For example, a sample of 50 employees might be used to assess the perceptions of all 300 members of a department, or a sample of production data might be used to evaluate the total production of a work group. OD practitioners often find that it is more economical and quicker to gather a sampling of diagnostic data than to collect all possible information. If done correctly, the sample can provide useful and valid information about the entire organisation or unit.

Sampling design involves considerable technical detail, and consultants may need to become familiar with basic references in this area or to obtain professional help.[21] The first issue to address is *sample size*, or how many people, events or records are needed to carry out the diagnosis or evaluation. This question has no simple answer: the necessary sample size is a function of size of the population, the confidence desired in the quality of the data and the resources (money and time) available for data collection.

First, the larger the population (for example, the number of organisation members or total number of work outcomes) or the more complex the client system (for example, the number of salary levels that must be sampled or the number of different functions), the more difficult it is to establish a 'right' sample size. As the population increases in size and complexity, the less meaning one can attach to simple measures, such as an overall average score on a questionnaire item. Because the population is composed of such different types of people or events, more data are needed to ensure an accurate representation of the potentially different subgroups. Second, the larger the proportion of the population that is selected, the more confidence one can have about the quality of the sample. If the diagnosis concerns an issue of great importance to the organisation, then extreme confidence may be needed, indicative of a larger sample size. Third, limited resources constrain sample size. If resources are limited but the required confidence is high, then questionnaires will be preferred to interviews because more information can be collected per member per dollar.

The second issue to address is sample selection. Probably the most common approach to sampling diagnostic data in OD is a simple random sample in which each member, behaviour or record has an equal chance of being selected. For example, assume that an OD practitioner would like to randomly select 50 people out of the 300 employees at a manufacturing plant. Using a complete list of all 300 employees, the consultant can generate a random sample in one of two ways. The first method would be to use a random number table in the back of almost any statistics text; the consultant would pick out the employees corresponding to the first 50 numbers under 300 beginning anywhere in the table. The second method would be to pick every sixth name (300 ÷ 50 = 6) starting anywhere in the list.

If the population is complex, or many subgroups need to be represented in the sample, a **stratified sample**[22] may be more appropriate than a random one. In a stratified sample, the population of members, events or records is segregated into a number of mutually exclusive subpopulations. Then, a random sample is taken from each subpopulation. For example, members of an organisation might be divided into three groups: managers, white-collar workers and blue-collar workers. A random sample of members, behaviours or records could be selected from each grouping in order to make diagnostic conclusions about each of the groups.

Stratified sample: the population of members, events or records is segregated into a number of mutually exclusive subpopulations.

Adequate sampling is critical when gathering valid diagnostic data, and the OD literature has tended to pay little attention to this issue. The OD practitioner should gain rudimentary knowledge in this area and use professional help if necessary.

Internal profile analysis

Choose any company with which you are familiar. If you are not familiar with any, consult magazines such as those from the United States (*Entrepreneur, Forbes, Fortune* and *Business Week*) and Asia Pacific (*Australian Financial Review, Business Review Weekly, Her Business, National Business Review, Unlimited*) or international magazines (*Economist, Far Eastern Economic Review, Financial Times, AsiaWeek, Asian Wall Street Journal*). Gather information on one company. Then complete the following internal profile analysis by placing a tick (✔) in the appropriate column.

Internal resource	Strong weakness	Slight weakness	Neutral	Slight strength	Strong strength
Financial					
Overall performance					
Ability to raise capital					
Working capital					
Position					

5.1

EXPERIENTIAL ACTIVITY

»

»

Internal resource	Strong weakness	Slight weakness	Neutral	Slight strength	Strong strength
Marketing					
Market performance					
Knowledge of markets					
Product					
Advertising and promotion					
Price					
Distribution					
Organisational and technical					
Location					
Production					
Facilities					
Access to suppliers					
Inventory control					
Quality control					
Organisation structure					
Rules, policies and procedures					
Company image					
Human					
Number of employees					
Relevancy of skills					
Morale					
Compensation package					

Based on your analysis, what three recommendations would you make to the company's management?

FEEDING BACK DIAGNOSTIC INFORMATION

As shown in **Figure 5.3**, the success of data feedback depends largely on its ability to arouse organisational action and to direct energy towards organisational problem solving. Whether or not feedback helps to energise the organisation depends on the content of the feedback data and on the process by which they are fed back to organisation members.

DETERMINING THE CONTENT OF THE FEEDBACK

Large amounts of data are collected in the course of diagnosing the organisation. In fact, there is often more information than the client needs or could interpret in a realistic period of time. If too many data are fed back, the client may decide that changing is impossible.

FIGURE 5.3   POSSIBLE EFFECTS OF FEEDBACK

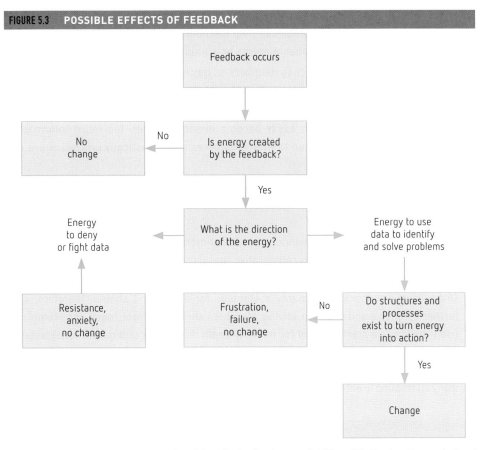

Source: D. Nadler, *Feedback and Organization Development* © 1977, p. 146. Reprinted by permission of Pearson Education, Inc., Upper Saddle River, New Jersey.

Therefore, OD practitioners need to summarise the data in ways that are useful for clients, so that they can both understand the information and draw action implications from it.

Several characteristics of effective feedback data have been described in the literature.[23] They include the nine properties listed below.

1 *Relevant.* Organisation members are more likely to use feedback data for problem solving if they find the information meaningful. Including managers and employees in the initial data-collection activities can increase the relevance of the data.

2 *Understandable.* Data must be presented to organisation members in a form that is readily interpreted. Statistical data, for example, can be made understandable through the use of graphs and charts.

3 *Descriptive.* Feedback data need to be linked to real organisational behaviours if they are to arouse and direct energy. The use of examples and detailed illustrations can help employees gain a better feel for the data.

4 *Verifiable.* Feedback data should be valid and accurate if they are to guide action. Thus, the information should allow organisation members to verify whether the findings really describe the organisation. For example, questionnaire data might include information

about the sample of respondents as well as frequency distributions for each item or measure. This kind of information can help members verify whether the feedback data accurately represent organisational events or attitudes.

5 *Timely.* Data should be fed back to members as quickly as possible after being collected and analysed. This will help ensure that the information is still valid and is linked to members' motivations to examine it.

6 *Limited.* Because people can easily become overloaded with too much information, feedback data should be limited to what employees can realistically process at any one time.

7 *Significant.* Feedback should be limited to those problems that organisation members can do something about. This will help energise them and direct their efforts towards realistic changes.

8 *Comparative.* Feedback data without some benchmark as a reference can be ambiguous. Whenever possible, data from comparative groups should be provided in order to give organisation members a better idea of how their group fits into a broader context.

9 *Unfinalised.* Feedback is primarily a stimulus for action and should, therefore, spur further diagnosis and problem solving. Members should be encouraged, for example, to use the data as a starting point for more in-depth discussion of organisational issues.

Apply your learning 5.2 gives a sample of how the Northern Territory Government assists with the provision of guidelines to giving and receiving performance feedback for a start-up company attempting to enter the international market and using feedback to guide its approach.

APPLY YOUR LEARNING 5.2

A GUIDE TO GIVING AND RECEIVING PERFORMANCE FEEDBACK

Feedback is critical for enhancing both individual and organisational performance.

There are 3 easy and important things [that can be done] to ensure performance is productive:

1 Set clear goals ...
2 Constantly review and keep detailed notes of performance ...
3 Provide regular feedback ...

...

... Both giving and receiving feedback are fundamental skills for managing and improving performance and link directly to the Performance Management Plan cycle. In this guide we'll explore:

→ Methods of collecting feedback;
→ How to give feedback;
→ Types of feedback; and
→ How to receive feedback.

It's important to provide regular, ongoing feedback to all staff against documented Performance Plans. The formal six and twelve monthly discussions are not a substitute for regular feedback that should occur on weekly, or even daily basis, but a formal addition to it. This ensures that the feedback provided is timely and immediate and ensures there are no surprises during the formal discussion. It also

»

»

ensures that the feedback is not delayed or reliant on memory, where it may lose its impact or significance.

There are many ways to gather information:
→ Observe an individual's performance in the workplace;
→ Review the individual's performance against the agreed work objectives;
→ Ask the individual to complete a self assessment; and
→ Undertake discussions/surveys with customers, colleagues, etc.

...

Everyone who supervises people should be skilled at giving feedback. It does take practice and if it is not done correctly, it can:
→ Result in conflict;
→ Impact an individual's self esteem;
→ Be destructive to the team and result in competitiveness; and
→ Be subjective.

To overcome these problems you need to ensure that you provide feedback that is:
→ Helpful ...
→ Specific rather than general ...
→ Immediate ...
→ Balanced ...
→ Constructive ...
→ Objective ...

...

It is important to note that regardless of the label we give to feedback, 'feedback is feedback' and to a large extent, it is in the eye of the beholder. Whether feedback is considered to be positive, constructive or negative is largely up to the person receiving it and the extent to which they accept it.

Source: Adapted from Northern Territory Government, 'A guide to giving and receiving performance feedback', Version 3.0, October 2015., https://ocpe.nt.gov.au/__data/assets/pdf_file/0004/247900/A_Guide_to_Giving_and_Receiving_Performance_Feedback.pdf, accessed 7 May 2018.

Critical thinking questions	
	1 The NT Government recognises the critical nature of feedback. Why is it important?
	2 How does the article recommend that you anticipate and overcome problems?
	3 Download the article and consider the prescriptive strategies to deal with feedback. Do you agree/disagree? Can it be improved?

CHARACTERISTICS OF THE FEEDBACK PROCESS

In addition to providing effective feedback data, it is equally important to attend to the process used to feed information back to people. Typically, data are provided to organisation members in a meeting or series of meetings. Feedback meetings provide a forum for discussing the data, drawing relevant conclusions and devising preliminary action plans.

Because the data might include sensitive material and evaluations of organisation members' behaviours, people may come to the meeting with considerable anxiety and fear about receiving the feedback. This anxiety can result in defensive behaviours aimed at denying the information or providing rationales. More positively, people can be stimulated by the feedback and the hope that desired changes will result from the feedback meeting.

Because people are likely to come to feedback meetings feeling anxiety, fear and hope, OD practitioners need to manage the feedback process so that constructive discussion and problem solving will occur. The most important objective of the feedback process is to ensure that organisation members own the data. Ownership is the opposite of resistance to change and refers to people's willingness to take responsibility for the data, its meaning and the consequences of using the data to devise a change strategy.[24] If the feedback session results in organisation members rejecting the data as invalid or useless, then the motivation to change is lost and members will have difficulty in engaging in a meaningful process of change.

Ownership of the feedback data is facilitated by the following five features of successful feedback processes:[25]

1   *Motivation to work with the data.* People need to feel that working on the feedback data will have beneficial outcomes. This may require explicit sanction and support from powerful groups so that people feel free to raise issues and identify concerns during the feedback sessions. If they have little motivation to work with the data or feel that there is little chance to use the data for change, the information will not be owned by the client system.

2   *Structure for the meeting.* Feedback meetings need some structure, or they may degenerate into chaos or aimless discussion. An agenda or outline and a discussion leader can usually provide the necessary direction. If the meeting is not kept on track, especially when the data are negative, ownership can be lost in conversations that become too general. When this happens, the energy gained from dealing directly with the problem is lost.

3   *Appropriate membership.* Generally, people who have common problems and can benefit from working together should be included in the feedback meeting. This may involve a fully intact work team, or groups made up of members from different functional areas or hierarchical levels. Without proper representation in the meeting, ownership of the data is lost because the participants cannot address the problem(s) suggested by the feedback.

4   *Appropriate power.* It is important to clarify the power possessed by the group. Members need to know on which issues they can make necessary changes, on which they can only recommend changes and on which they have no control. Unless there are clear boundaries, members are likely to have some hesitation about using the feedback data for generating action plans. Moreover, if the group has no power to make changes, the feedback meeting will become an empty exercise rather than a real problem-solving session. Without the power to address change, there will be little ownership of the data.

5   *Process help.* People in feedback meetings need help to work together as a group. When the data are negative, there is a natural tendency to resist the implications, deflect the

conversation onto safer subjects and the like. An OD practitioner with group process skills can help members stay focused on the subject and improve feedback discussion, problem solving and ownership.

When combined with effective feedback data, these features of successful feedback meetings enhance member ownership of the data. They help to ensure that organisation members fully discuss the implications of the diagnostic information and that their conclusions are directed towards organisational changes that are relevant and feasible.

DESIGNING INTERVENTIONS

The term 'intervention' refers to a set of sequenced planned actions or events that are intended to help an organisation increase its effectiveness. Interventions purposely disrupt the status quo; they are a deliberate attempt to move an organisation or subunit towards a different and more effective state. In OD, three major criteria define an effective intervention: (1) the extent to which it fits the needs of the organisation, (2) the degree to which it is based on causal knowledge of intended outcomes and (3) the extent to which it transfers competence to manage change to organisation members.

The first criterion concerns the extent to which the intervention is relevant to the organisation and its members. Effective interventions are based on valid information about the organisation's functioning. They provide organisation members with opportunities to make free and informed choices; and they gain members' internal commitment to those choices.[26]

Valid information is the result of an accurate diagnosis of the organisation's functioning. It must fairly reflect what organisation members perceive and feel about their primary concerns and issues. Free and informed choice suggests that members are actively involved in making decisions about the changes that will affect them. It means that they can choose not to participate and that interventions will not be imposed upon them. Internal commitment means that organisation members will accept ownership of the intervention and take responsibility for implementing it. If interventions are to result in meaningful changes, management, staff and other relevant members must be committed to implementing them.

The second criterion of an effective intervention involves knowledge of outcomes. Because interventions are intended to produce specific results, they must be based on valid knowledge that those outcomes can actually be produced. Otherwise there is no scientific basis for designing an effective OD intervention. Unfortunately, and in contrast to other applied disciplines, such as medicine and engineering, knowledge of intervention effects is in a rudimentary stage of development in OD. Much of the evaluation research lacks sufficient rigour to make strong causal inferences about the success or failure of change programs. Moreover, few attempts have been made to examine the comparative impacts of different OD techniques. This makes knowing whether one method is more effective than another difficult.

Despite these problems, more attempts are being made to systematically assess the strengths and weaknesses of OD interventions and to compare the impact of different techniques on organisation effectiveness.[27] Many of the OD interventions that will be discussed in this book have been subjected to evaluative research. This research is explored in the appropriate chapters, along with respective change programs.

The third criterion of an effective intervention involves the extent to which it enhances the organisation's capacity to manage change. The values underlying OD suggest that organisation members should be better able to carry out planned change activities on their own after an intervention. They should gain knowledge and skill in managing change from active participation in designing and implementing the intervention. Competence in change management is essential in today's environment, where technological, social, economic and political changes are rapid and persistent.

HOW TO DESIGN EFFECTIVE INTERVENTIONS

Designing OD interventions requires careful attention to the needs and dynamics of the change situation and to crafting a change program that will be consistent with the criteria of the effective interventions outlined above. Current knowledge of OD interventions provides only general prescriptions for change. There is little precise information or research about how to design interventions or how they can be expected to interact with organisational conditions to achieve specific results.[28] Moreover, the ability to implement most OD interventions is highly dependent on the skills and knowledge of the change agent. Thus, the design of an intervention will depend to some extent on the expertise of the practitioner.

Two major sets of contingencies that can affect intervention success have been discussed in the OD literature: those having to do with the change situation (including the practitioner) and those related to the target of change. Both kinds of contingencies need to be considered when designing interventions.

Contingencies related to the change situation

Researchers have identified a number of contingencies present in the change situation that can affect intervention success. These include individual differences among organisation members (for example, needs for autonomy), organisational factors (for example, management style and technical uncertainty) and dimensions of the change process itself (for example, the degree of top-management support). Unless these factors are taken into account when designing an intervention, the intervention will have little impact on organisational functioning or, worse, it might even produce negative results. For example, it is integral to understand what the sources are for gauging the level of motivation of employees in order to customise the intervention and how that will align with the demographics of the people who work there. In many cases, having knowledge of these contingencies might result in modifying or adjusting the change program to fit the setting. In applying a reward-system intervention to an organisation, the changes might have to be modified according to whether the company wants to reinforce individual or team performance.

Although knowledge and application of contingencies is still ongoing in the development of OD,[29] researchers have discovered several situational factors that can affect intervention success.[30] These include contingencies for many of the interventions reviewed in this book, and they will be discussed in the relevant chapters that describe the change programs. More generic contingencies that apply to all OD interventions follow, including the situational factors that must be considered when designing any intervention: the organisation's readiness for change, its change capability, its cultural context and the change agent's skills and abilities.

Readiness for change

Intervention success depends heavily on the organisation being ready for planned change. Indicators of readiness for change[31] include sensitivity to pressures for change, dissatisfaction with the status quo, availability of resources to support change and commitment of significant management time. When these conditions are present, interventions can be designed to address the organisational issues uncovered during diagnosis. When readiness for change is low, however, interventions need to focus on increasing the organisation's willingness to change.[32]

Capability to change

Managing planned change requires particular knowledge and skills. These include the ability to motivate change, lead change, develop political support, manage the transition and sustain momentum. If organisation members do not have these capabilities, then a preliminary training intervention may be needed before members can meaningfully engage in intervention design.

Cultural context

As discussed in Chapter 4, the national culture within which the organisation is embedded can have a powerful influence on members' reactions to change. Thus, intervention design needs to account for the cultural values and assumptions held by organisation members. Interventions may need to be modified to fit the local culture, particularly when OD practices developed in one culture are applied to organisations in another culture.[33] For example, a team-building intervention designed for top managers at an Australian company may need to be modified when applied to its foreign subsidiaries.

Capabilities of the change agent

Many failures in OD result when change agents apply interventions beyond their competence. In designing interventions, OD practitioners should assess their experience and expertise against the requirements needed to implement the intervention effectively. When a mismatch is discovered, practitioners can explore whether the intervention can be modified to fit their talents better, whether another intervention more suited to their skills can satisfy the organisation's needs or whether they should enlist the assistance of another change agent who can guide the process more effectively. The ethical guidelines under which OD practitioners operate require full disclosure of the applicability of their knowledge and expertise to the client situation. Practitioners are expected to intervene within their capabilities or to recommend someone more suited to the client's needs.

For a discussion on how national culture can influence organisational change, see Chapter 4.

Contingencies related to the target of change

OD interventions seek to change specific features or parts of organisations. These targets of change are the main focus of interventions, and researchers have identified two key contingencies related to change targets that can affect intervention success:

the organisational issues that the intervention is intended to resolve and the level of organisational system at which the intervention is expected to have a primary impact.

Organisational issues

Organisations need to address certain issues to operate effectively. **Figure 5.4** lists these issues along with the OD interventions that are intended to resolve them. It shows four interrelated issues that are key targets of OD interventions:

1   *Strategic issues.* Organisations need to decide what products or services they will provide and the markets in which they will compete, as well as how to relate to their environments and how to transform themselves to keep pace with changing conditions. These strategic issues are among the most critical facing organisations in today's changing and highly competitive environments. OD methods aimed at these issues are called 'strategic interventions'. They are among the most recent additions to OD and include integrated strategic change (ISC), transorganisational development (TD) and organisation transformation (OT).

2   *Technology and structure issues.* Organisations must decide how to divide work into departments and then how to coordinate them to support strategic directions. They must also make decisions about how to produce products or services and how to link people with tasks. OD methods for dealing with these structural and technological issues are called 'technostructural interventions'. They include OD activities relating to organisation design, employee involvement and work design.

3   *Human resource issues.* These issues are concerned with attracting competent people to the organisation, setting goals for them, appraising and rewarding their performance and ensuring that they develop their careers and manage stress. OD techniques aimed at these issues are called 'human resource management interventions'.

4   *Interpersonal issues.* These issues have to do with social processes occurring among organisation members, such as communication, decision making, leadership and group dynamics. OD methods focusing on these kinds of issues are called 'human process interventions'; included among them are some of the most common OD techniques, such as conflict resolution and team building.

These organisational issues are interrelated and need to be integrated with each other. The double-headed arrows connecting the different issues in **Figure 5.4** represent the fits or linkages among them. Organisations need to match answers to one set of questions with answers to other sets of questions to achieve high levels of effectiveness. For example, decisions about gaining competitive advantage need to fit with choices about organisation structure, setting goals for people, rewarding people, communication and problem solving.

The interventions presented in this book are intended to resolve these different concerns. As shown in **Figure 5.4**, particular OD interventions apply to specific issues. Thus, intervention design must create change methods appropriate to the organisational issues identified in diagnosis. Moreover, because the organisational issues are themselves linked, OD interventions need to be similarly integrated with one another. For example, a goal-setting intervention that attempts to establish motivating goals may need to be

FIGURE 5.4   TYPES OF OD INTERVENTIONS AND ORGANISATIONAL ISSUES

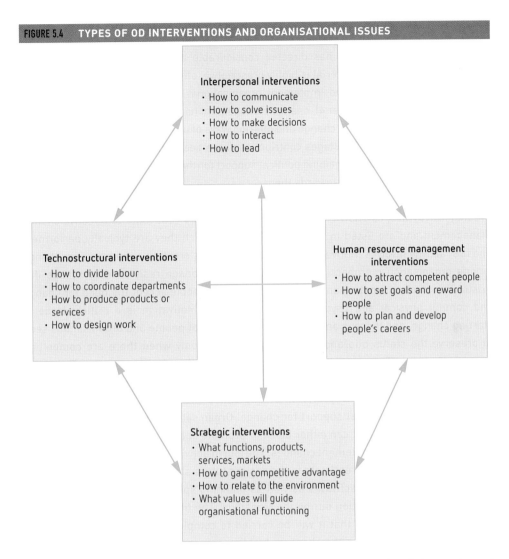

integrated with supporting interventions, such as a reward system that links pay to goal achievement. The key point is to think systematically. Interventions that are aimed at one kind of organisational issue will invariably have repercussions for other kinds of issues. This requires careful thinking about how OD interventions affect the different kinds of issues and how different change programs might be integrated to bring about a broader and more coherent impact on organisational functioning.

IMPLEMENTING CHANGE

Change can vary in complexity, from the introduction of relatively simple processes into a small work group to transforming the strategies and organisation design features of the whole organisation.

OVERVIEW OF CHANGE ACTIVITIES

For a comprehensive discussion on managing resistance to change, see Chapter 4.

The OD literature has directed considerable attention to managing change. Much of this material is highly prescriptive, offering advice to managers about how to plan and implement organisational changes. Traditionally (and as shown in Chapter 4), change management has focused on identifying sources of resistance to change and offering ways of overcoming or managing them.[34] From the early stages contributions have been aimed at creating visions and desired futures, gaining political support for them and managing the transition of the organisation towards them.[35]

The diversity of practical advice for managing change can be organised into five major activities, as shown in **Figure 5.5**. The activities contribute to effective change management and are listed in roughly the order in which they are typically performed. The first activity involves motivating change and includes creating a readiness for change among organisation members and helping them to manage resistance to change if it exists. This involves creating an environment in which people accept the need for change and commit physical and psychological energy to it. Motivation is a critical issue in starting change, and there is ample evidence to show that people and organisations seek to preserve the status quo and are willing to change only when there are compelling reasons to do so. The second activity is concerned with creating a vision. The vision provides a purpose and reason for change and describes the desired future state. Together, they provide the 'why' and 'what' of planned change. The third activity involves the development of political support for change. Organisations are made up of powerful individuals and groups that can either block or promote change, and change agents need to gain their support to implement changes. The fourth activity is concerned with managing the transition from the current state to the desired future state. It involves creating a plan for managing the change activities as well as planning special management structures for operating the organisation during the transition. The fifth activity involves sustaining momentum for change so that it will be carried to completion. This includes providing resources for implementing the changes, building a support system for change agents, developing new competencies and skills and reinforcing the new behaviours necessary for implementing the changes.

Each of the activities shown in **Figure 5.5** is important for managing change. Although little research on their relative contributions to change has been conducted, they all seem to demand careful attention when planning and implementing organisational change. Unless individuals are motivated and committed to change, unfreezing the status quo will be extremely difficult. In the absence of vision, change is likely to be disorganised and diffuse. Without the support of powerful individuals and groups, change is likely to be blocked and possibly sabotaged. Unless the transition process is carefully managed, the organisation will have difficulty functioning while it is moving from the current state to the future state. Without efforts to sustain the momentum for change, the organisation will have problems carrying the changes through to completion. Thus, all five activities must be managed effectively if organisational change is to be successful.

MOTIVATING CHANGE

Organisational change involves moving from the known to the unknown. Because the future is uncertain and may adversely affect people's competencies, worth and coping abilities, organisation members do not generally support change unless compelling reasons convince them to do so. Similarly, organisations tend to be heavily invested in the status quo, and they resist changing it in the face of uncertain future benefits. Consequently, a key issue in planning for action is how to motivate commitment to organisational change. As shown in **Figure 5.5**, this requires attention to two related tasks: creating readiness for change and managing resistance to change.

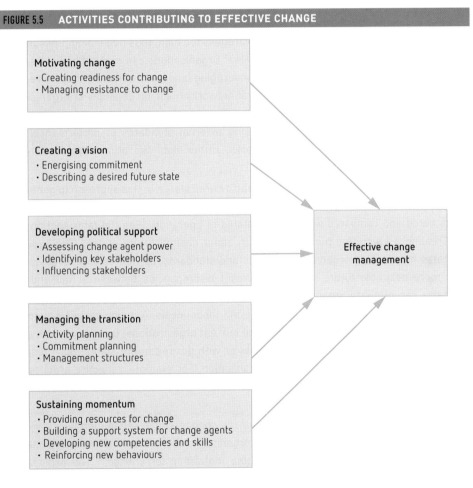

FIGURE 5.5   ACTIVITIES CONTRIBUTING TO EFFECTIVE CHANGE

Motivating change
- Creating readiness for change
- Managing resistance to change

Creating a vision
- Energising commitment
- Describing a desired future state

Developing political support
- Assessing change agent power
- Identifying key stakeholders
- Influencing stakeholders

Managing the transition
- Activity planning
- Commitment planning
- Management structures

Sustaining momentum
- Providing resources for change
- Building a support system for change agents
- Developing new competencies and skills
- Reinforcing new behaviours

Effective change management

Creating readiness for change

One of the more fundamental axioms of OD[36] is that people's readiness for change depends on creating a felt need for change. This involves making people so dissatisfied with the status quo that they are motivated to try new things and ways of behaving. Creating such dissatisfaction can be rather difficult, as evidenced by anyone who has tried to lose weight, stop smoking or change some other habitual behaviour. Generally, people and organisations need to experience deep levels of hurt before they will seriously undertake meaningful change. The following three methods can help generate sufficient dissatisfaction that change will be produced:

1   *Sensitise organisations to pressures for change.* Innumerable pressures for change operate both externally and internally to organisations. Modern organisations are facing unprecedented environmental pressures to change themselves, including heavy foreign competition, rapidly changing technology and global markets. Internal pressures to change include poor product quality, high production costs and excessive employee absenteeism and turnover. Before these pressures can serve as triggers for change, however, organisations must be sensitive to them. The pressures must pass beyond an organisation's threshold of awareness if managers are to respond to them. Many organisations set their thresholds of awareness too high, thus neglecting pressures for change until they reach disastrous levels.[37] Organisations can make themselves more sensitive to pressures for change by encouraging leaders to surround themselves with devil's advocates,[38] by cultivating external networks made up of people or organisations with different perspectives and views, by visiting other organisations to gain exposure to new ideas and methods and by using external standards of performance, such as competitors' progress or benchmarks, rather than the organisation's own past standards of performance.

2   *Reveal discrepancies between current and desired states.* In this approach to generating a felt need for change, information about the organisation's current functioning is gathered and compared with desired states of operation. (See the later section titled 'Creating a vision' for more information about desired future states.) These desired states may include organisational goals and standards, as well as a general vision of a more desirable future state.[39] Significant discrepancies between actual and ideal states can motivate organisation members to initiate corrective changes, particularly when members are committed to achieving those ideals. A major goal of diagnosis is to provide members with feedback about current organisational functioning so that this information can be compared with goals or with desired future states. Such feedback can energise action to improve the organisation. For example, reflective practices can be identified among the Australian allied health managers as well as within the tertiary education industry.

3   *Convey credible positive expectations for the change.* Organisation members invariably have expectations about the results of organisational changes, and those expectations can play an important role in generating motivation for change.[40] The expectations can serve as a self-fulfilling prophecy, leading members to invest energy in change programs that they expect will succeed. When members expect success, they are likely to develop greater commitment to the change process and to direct more energy into the kinds of constructive behaviour needed to implement change.[41] The key to achieving these positive effects is to communicate realistic, positive expectations about the organisational changes. Organisation members can also be taught about the benefits of

positive expectations and can be encouraged to set credible positive expectations for the change program.

CREATING A VISION

The second activity for managing change involves creating a vision of what members want the organisation to look like or become. Generally, the vision describes the desired future, towards which change is directed. It provides a valued direction for designing, implementing and assessing organisational changes. The vision can also energise commitment to change by providing a compelling rationale as to why change is necessary and worth the effort. It can provide members with a common goal and challenge. However, if the vision is seen as impossible or promotes changes that the organisation cannot implement, it can actually depress member motivation. For example, the former Prime Minister of Australia, Kevin Rudd, promised that every child in Years 9–12 would receive a government-sponsored computer. In contrast, US President John Kennedy's vision of 'putting a man on the moon and returning him safely to the earth' was only just beyond current engineering and technical feasibility. In the context of the 1960s, it was bold, alluring and vivid; it not only provided a purpose, but a valued direction as well.[42]

Creating a vision is considered a key element in most leadership frameworks.[43] Those leading the organisation or unit are responsible for its effectiveness, and they must take an active role in describing a desired future, and energising commitment to it. In many cases, leaders encourage participation in developing the vision in order to gain wider input and support. For example, they may involve subordinates and others who have a stake in the changes. The popular media include numerous accounts of executives who have helped to mobilise and direct organisational change. Although these people are at the senior executive level, providing a description of a desired future is no less important for those who lead change in small departments and work groups. At these lower organisational levels, ample opportunities exist to get employees directly involved in the visioning process.

People's values and preferences for what the organisation should look like, and how it should function, heavily drive the process of developing a vision. The vision represents people's ideals, fantasies or dreams of what they would like the organisation to look like or become.

Unfortunately, dreaming about the future is discouraged in most organisations.[44] It requires creative and intuitive thought processes that tend to conflict with the rational, analytical methods prevalent in organisations.[45] Consequently, leaders may need to create special conditions for describing a desired future, such as off-site workshops or exercises that stimulate creative thinking.

To be effective in managing change, creating a vision addresses two key aspects of organisation change: (1) describing the desired future and (2) energising commitment to moving towards it.

Describing the desired future

The visioning process is future-oriented. It generally results in a vision statement that describes the organisation's desired future state. Although the vision statement may be detailed, it does not generally specify how the changes will occur. These details are part of the subsequent activity planning that occurs when managing the transition towards the desired future.

A vision statement may include all or some of the following elements that can be communicated to organisation members:

1 *Mission.* Participants often define the mission of their organisation or subunit as a prelude to describing the desired future state. The mission includes the organisation's major strategic purpose or reason for existing. It may include specification of the following: target customers and markets, principal products or services, geographic domain, core technologies, strategic objectives and desired public image. LRN, a consulting company, ripped up its organisational chart and ignored entrenched processes in order to 'report' to its company mission.[46] The statements included the company's basic beliefs, values, priorities, competitive strengths and desired public image. Defining the mission can provide a sound starting point for envisioning what the organisation should look like and how it should operate. In some cases, members may have conflicting views about the mission, and surfacing and resolving those conflicts can help to mobilise and direct energy for the process.

2 *Valued outcomes.* Descriptions of desired futures often include specific performance and human outcomes that the organisation or unit would like to achieve. These valued outcomes can serve as goals for the change process and standards for assessing progress. Valued performance outcomes might include high levels of product innovation, manufacturing efficiency and customer service. Valued human outcomes could include high levels of employee satisfaction, development, safety and job security. These outcomes specify the kinds of values that the organisation would like to promote in the future.

Energising commitment

In addition to describing a desired future, creating a vision includes energising the commitment to change. This aspect of the visioning process is exciting, connected to the past and present, and compelling. It seeks to create a vision that is emotionally powerful to organisation members and that motivates them to change. To achieve excitement for change, organisations often create a slogan or metaphor that captures the essence of the changes. For example, part of Disneyland's return to prominence was guided by the motto 'Creating a place where people can feel like kids again'. The metaphor of feeling like a kid provided an important emotional appeal to Disney's change effort.

A vision that is clearly linked to the organisation's past and present can also energise commitment to change. It can provide a realistic context for moving towards the future and can enable members to develop realistic goals and maintain a temporal perspective of the 'big picture'. Apple's original vision of 'changing the way people do their work' provides a good example. Many employees had experienced the drudgery of a boring job, an uninspired boss or an alienating workplace. The notion that they could be a part of an organisation that is changing work into something more challenging, creative or satisfying was naturally alluring to many of them.

Finally, a compelling vision can energise commitment to change. By identifying a powerful reason or purpose for the change, the vision can provide meaning to the change activities that members will need to undertake during the transition. Thus, the words used in the vision can encourage behaviour towards the desired future as well as generate feelings of inclusiveness. Conversely, words can constrain people and leave them feeling controlled or manipulated. For example, 'shrewd' and 'creative' both imply innovative behaviour but have different connotations.

DEVELOPING POLITICAL SUPPORT

From a political perspective, organisations can be seen as loosely structured coalitions of individuals and groups with different preferences and interests.[47] For example, shop-floor workers may want secure, high-paying jobs, while top executives may be interested in diversifying the organisation into new businesses. The marketing department might be interested in developing new products and markets, and the production department may want to manufacture standard products in the most efficient way. These different groups or coalitions compete with one another for scarce resources and influence. They act to preserve or enhance their self-interest while managing to arrive at a sufficient balance of power to sustain commitment to the organisation and to achieve overall effectiveness.

Given this political view, attempts to change the organisation may threaten the balance of power among groups, resulting in political conflicts and struggles.[48] Individuals and groups will be concerned with how the changes affect their own power and influence, and they will act accordingly.[49] Some groups will become less powerful, while others will gain influence. Those whose power is threatened by the change will act defensively and seek to preserve the status quo; for example, they might attempt to present compelling evidence that change is unnecessary or that only minor modifications are needed. On the other hand, those participants who will gain power from the changes will tend to push heavily for them. They may bring in seemingly impartial consultants to legitimise the need for change. Consequently, conflicting interests, distorted information and political turmoil frequently accompany significant organisational changes.

Methods for managing the political dynamics of organisational change are relatively recent additions to OD. Traditionally, OD has tended to neglect political issues, mainly because its humanistic roots promoted collaboration and power sharing among individuals and groups.[50] Today, change agents are increasingly paying attention to power and political activity, particularly as they engage in strategic change that involves most parts and features of organisations. Some practitioners are concerned, however, about whether power and OD are compatible. A growing number of advocates suggest that OD practitioners can use power in positive ways.[51] They can build their own power base to gain access to other power holders within the organisation. Without such access, those who influence or make decisions may not have the advantage of an OD perspective. OD practitioners can use power strategies that are open and above board to get those in power to consider OD applications. They can facilitate processes for examining the uses of power in organisations and can help power holders devise more creative and positive strategies than political bargaining, deceit and the like. They can help power holders to confront the need for change and can help ensure that the interests and concerns of those with less power are considered. Although OD professionals can use power constructively in organisations, they will probably always be ambivalent and tense about whether such uses promote OD values and ethics or whether they represent the destructive, negative side of power. This tension seems healthy, and it is hoped that it will guide the wise use of power in OD.

As shown in **Figure 5.6**, managing the political dynamics of change includes the following activities:

1 *Assessing change agent power.* The first task is to evaluate the change agent's own sources of power. The change agent might be the leader of the organisation or department undergoing change, or he or she might be the OD consultant, if professional help is being used. By assessing their own power base, change agents can determine how to use it to influence others to support changes. They can also identify areas in which they might need to enhance their sources of power.

   Greiner and Schein, in the first OD book written entirely from a power perspective, identified three key sources of personal power in organisations (in addition to one's formal position): knowledge, personality and others' support.[52] Knowledge bases of power include having expertise that is valued by others and controlling important information. OD professionals typically gain power through their expertise in organisational change. Personality sources of power can derive from change agents' charisma, reputation and professional credibility. Charismatic leaders can inspire devotion and enthusiasm for change from subordinates. OD consultants with strong reputations and professional credibility can wield considerable power during organisational change. Others' support can contribute to individual power by providing access to information and resource networks. Others may also use their power on behalf of the change agent. For example, leaders in organisational units undergoing change can call on their informal networks for resources and support. They can encourage subordinates to exercise power in support of the change.

2 *Identifying key stakeholders.* Once change agents have assessed their own power bases, they can identify powerful individuals and groups who have an interest in the changes, such as staff groups, unions, departmental managers and top-level executives. These stakeholders can either thwart or support change, and it is important to gain broad-based support to minimise the risk that a single interest group will block the changes. Identifying key stakeholders can start from the simple question: 'Who stands to gain or lose from the changes?' Once stakeholders have been identified, creating a map of their influence may be useful.[53] The map could show relationships among the stakeholders in terms of who influences whom and what the stakes are for each party. This would provide change agents with information about which individuals and groups need to be influenced to accept and support the changes.

3 *Influencing stakeholders.* This activity involves gaining the support of key stakeholders to motivate a critical mass for change. There are at least three major strategies for using power to influence others in OD: playing it straight, using social networks and going around the formal system.[54] **Figure 5.6** links these strategies to the individual sources of power discussed above.

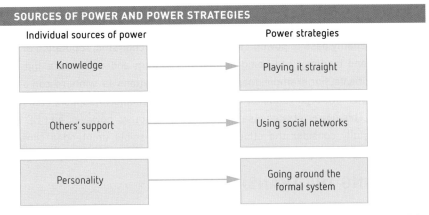

FIGURE 5.6   SOURCES OF POWER AND POWER STRATEGIES

Source: L. Greiner and V. Schein, *Power and Organization Development: Mobilizing Power to Implement Change*, © 1988, p. 52. Reprinted by permission of Pearson Education, Inc., Upper Saddle River, New Jersey.

The strategy of *playing it straight* is very consistent with an OD perspective, and so is the most widely used power strategy in OD. It involves determining the needs of particular stakeholders and presenting information as to how the changes can benefit them. This relatively straightforward approach is based on the premise that information and knowledge can persuade people about the need and direction for change. The success of this strategy relies heavily on the change agent's knowledge base. He or she must have the expertise and information necessary for persuading stakeholders that the changes are a logical way to meet their needs. For example, a change agent might present diagnostic data, such as company reports on productivity and absenteeism or surveys of members' perceptions of problems, to generate a felt need for change among specific stakeholders. Other persuasive evidence might include educational material and expert testimony, such as case studies and research reports, demonstrating how organisational changes can address pertinent issues.

The second power strategy, *using social networks*, is more foreign to OD and includes forming alliances and coalitions with other powerful individuals and groups, dealing directly with key decision makers and using formal and informal contacts to gain information. In this strategy, change agents try to use their social relationships to gain support for changes. As shown in **Figure 5.6**, they use the individual power base of others' support to gain the resources, commitment and political momentum needed for change. This social networking might include, for example, meeting with other powerful groups and forming an alliance to support specific changes. This would probably involve ensuring that the interests of the different parties – for example, labour and management – are considered in the change process. Many union and management quality-of-work-life efforts involve forming such alliances. This strategy might also include using informal contacts to discover key roadblocks to change and gain access to major decision makers that need to sanction the changes.

The power strategy of *going around the formal system* is probably least used in OD and involves deliberately circumventing organisation structures and procedures to get the changes implemented. Existing organisational arrangements can be roadblocks to change and, rather than taking the time and energy to remove them, working around the barriers may be more expedient and effective. As shown in **Figure 5.6**, this strategy relies on a strong personality base of power. The change agent's charisma, reputation or professional credibility lend legitimacy to going around the system and can reduce the likelihood of negative reprisals. For example, managers with reputations as 'winners' can often bend the rules to implement organisational changes. Those needing to support change trust their judgement. This power strategy is relatively easy to abuse, however, and OD practitioners should carefully consider the ethical issues and possible unintended consequences of circumventing formal policies and practices.

MANAGING THE TRANSITION

Implementing organisational change involves moving from the existing organisation state to the desired future state. This movement does not occur immediately but, as shown in **Figure 5.7**, requires a transition state during which the organisation learns how to implement the conditions needed to reach the desired future. Beckhard and Harris pointed out that the transition state may be quite different from the present state of the organisation and consequently may require special management structures and activities.[55] They identified three major activities and structures to facilitate organisational transition, listed below.

FIGURE 5.7   ORGANISATION CHANGE AS A TRANSITION STATE

1 *Activity planning.* This involves making a road map for change, citing specific activities and events that must occur if the transition is to be successful. Activity planning should clearly identify, temporally orient and integrate discrete change tasks and should link these tasks to the organisation's change goals and priorities. Activity planning should also gain top-management approval, be cost-effective and remain adaptable as feedback is received during the change process.

   An important feature of activity planning is that visions and desired future states can be quite general when compared with the realities of actually implementing change. As a result, it may be necessary to supplement them with midpoint goals as part of the activity plan.[56] These represent desirable organisational conditions between the current state and the desired future state. Midpoint goals are clearer and more detailed than desired future states, and so provide more concrete and manageable steps and benchmarks for change. Activity plans can use midpoint goals to successfully provide members with the direction and security for embarkation towards the desired future.

2 *Commitment planning.* This activity involves identifying key people and groups whose commitment is needed for change to occur and deciding how to gain their support. Although commitment planning is generally a part of developing political support (discussed above), specific plans for identifying key stakeholders and obtaining their commitment to change need to be made early in the change process.

3 *Management structures.* Because organisational transitions tend to be ambiguous and to need direction, special structures for managing the change process need to be created. These management structures should include people who have the power to mobilise resources to promote change, the respect of the existing leadership and advocates of change, and the interpersonal and political skills to guide the change process. Alternative management structures include the following:[57]

- The chief executive or head person manages the change effort.
- A project manager is given the temporary assignment of coordinating the transition.
- The formal organisation manages the change effort in addition to supervising normal operations.
- Representatives of the major constituencies involved in the change jointly manage the project.
- Natural leaders who have the confidence and trust of large numbers of affected employees are selected to manage the transition.
- A cross-section of people representing different organisational functions and levels manages the change.
- A kitchen cabinet representing people whom the chief executive consults and confides in manages the change effort.

SUSTAINING MOMENTUM

Once organisational changes are under way, explicit attention must be directed at sustaining energy and commitment for implementing them.[58] Often, the initial excitement and activity of changing dissipate in the face of the practical problems of trying to learn new ways of operating. A strong tendency exists among organisation members to return to what is well known and learned, unless they receive sustained support and reinforcement for carrying the changes through to completion.

The following four activities can help to sustain momentum for carrying change through to completion:

1 *Providing resources for change.* Implementing organisation change generally requires additional financial and human resources, particularly if the organisation continues day-to-day operations while trying to change itself. These extra resources are needed for such change activities as training, consultation, data collection and feedback, and special meetings. Extra resources are also helpful to provide a buffer as performance drops during the transition period. Organisations can seriously underestimate the need for special resources devoted to the change process. Significant organisational change invariably requires considerable management time and energy, as well as the help of consultants. A separate 'change budget' that exists along with capital and operating budgets can help to identify the resources needed for training members in how to behave differently and for assessing progress and making necessary modifications in the change program.[59] Unless these extra resources are planned for and provided, meaningful change is not as likely to occur.

2 *Building a support system for change agents.* Organisation change can be difficult and filled with tension, not only for participants but also for change agents.[60] Change agents

must often provide members with emotional support, yet they may receive little support themselves. They must often maintain 'psychological distance' from others in order to gain the perspective needed to lead the change process. This can produce considerable tension and isolation, and change agents may need to create their own support system to help them cope with these problems. This typically consists of a network of people with whom the change agent has close personal relationships. These people can provide emotional support and can serve as a sounding board for ideas and problems. They can challenge untested assumptions. For example, OD professionals often use trusted colleagues as 'shadow consultants' to help them think through difficult issues with clients and to offer conceptual and emotional support. Similarly, a growing number of companies, such as Boral, are forming internal networks of change agents to provide mutual learning and support.[61]

3   *Developing new competencies and skills.* Organisational changes frequently demand new knowledge, skills and behaviours from organisation members. In many cases, the changes cannot be implemented unless members gain new competencies. For example, employee-involvement programs often require managers to learn new leadership styles and new approaches to problem solving. Change agents need to ensure that such learning occurs. They need to provide multiple learning opportunities, such as traditional training programs, on-the-job counselling and coaching, and experiential simulations. This learning should cover both technical and social skills. Because it is easy to overlook the social component, change agents may need to devote special time and resources to helping members gain the social skills needed to implement changes.

4   *Reinforcing new behaviours.* People in organisations generally do those things that bring them rewards. Consequently, one of the most effective ways of sustaining momentum for change is to reinforce the kinds of behaviours needed to implement the changes. This can be accomplished by linking formal rewards directly to the desired behaviours. Desired behaviours can also be reinforced through recognition, encouragement and praise. These can usually be given more frequently than formal rewards, and change agents should take advantage of the myriad of informal opportunities available to recognise and praise changed behaviours in a timely fashion. Perhaps equally important are the intrinsic rewards that people can experience through early success in the change effort. Achieving identifiable, early successes can make participants feel good about themselves and their behaviours, thus reinforcing the drive to change.

EVALUATING ORGANISATION DEVELOPMENT INTERVENTIONS

Evaluation processes consider both the implementation success of the intended intervention and the long-term results it produces. Two key aspects of effective evaluation are measurement and research design. The institutionalisation or long-term persistence of intervention effects is examined in a framework that shows the organisation characteristics, intervention dimensions and processes that contribute to institutionalisation of OD interventions in organisations.

CONDUCTING ORGANISATION DEVELOPMENT EVALUATIONS

Assessing OD interventions involves judgements about whether an intervention has been implemented as intended and, if so, whether it is having desired results. Managers investing resources in OD efforts are increasingly being held accountable for the results. They are being asked to justify the expenditures in terms of hard, bottom-line outcomes. More and more, managers are asking for rigorous assessment of OD interventions and are using the results to make important resource allocation decisions about OD, such as whether to continue to support the change program, whether to modify or alter it, or whether to terminate it altogether and perhaps try something else.[62]

Traditionally, OD evaluation has been discussed as something that occurs after the intervention. This view can be misleading. Decisions about the measurement of relevant variables and the design of the evaluation process should be made early in the OD cycle so that evaluation choices can be integrated with intervention decisions.

There are two distinct types of OD evaluation: one intended to guide the implementation of interventions and the other to assess their overall impact. The key issues in evaluation are measurement and research design.

Implementation and evaluation feedback

Most discussions and applications of OD evaluation imply that evaluation is something done after intervention. It is typically argued that, once the intervention has been implemented, it should be evaluated to discover whether it is producing the intended effects. For example, it might reasonably be expected that a job-enrichment program would lead to higher employee satisfaction and performance. After implementing job enrichment, evaluation would involve assessing whether or not it did actually lead to positive results.

This after-implementation view of evaluation is only partially correct. It assumes that interventions have actually been implemented as intended and that the key problem for evaluation is to assess their effects. In many, if not most, OD programs, however, implementing interventions cannot be taken for granted.[63] Most OD interventions require significant changes in people's behaviours and ways of thinking about organisations, yet interventions typically offer only broad prescriptions for how such changes are to occur.[64] For example, job enrichment calls for adding discretion (freedom of judgement), variety and meaningful feedback to people's jobs. Implementing such changes requires considerable learning and experimentation as employees and managers discover how to translate these general prescriptions into specific behaviours and procedures. This learning process involves much trial and error and needs to be guided by information about whether behaviours and procedures are being changed as intended.[65] Consequently, we should expand our view of evaluation to include both during-implementation assessment of whether interventions are actually being implemented and after-implementation evaluation of whether they are producing expected results.

Both kinds of evaluation provide organisation members with feedback about interventions. Evaluation aimed at guiding implementation may be called *implementation feedback*, and assessment intended to discover intervention outcomes might be called *evaluation feedback*.[66] **Figure 5.8** shows how the two kinds of feedback fit with the diagnostic and intervention stages of OD. The application of OD to a particular organisation starts with a thorough diagnosis of the situation, which helps to identify particular organisational problems or areas for improvement, as well as likely causes underlying them. Next, from an array of possible interventions, one or more sets are chosen as a means of improving the organisation. This choice is based on knowledge that links interventions to diagnosis and change management.

FIGURE 5.8   IMPLEMENTATION AND EVALUATION FEEDBACK

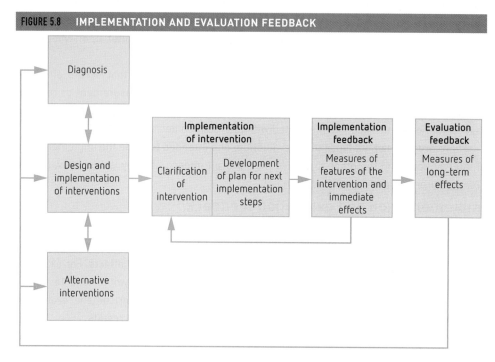

In most cases, the chosen intervention provides only general guidelines for organisational change, leaving managers and employees with the task of translating them into specific behaviours and procedures. Implementation feedback guides this process. It consists of two types of information: data about the different features of the intervention itself and data about the immediate effects of the intervention. These data are collected repeatedly and at short intervals. They provide a series of snapshots about how the intervention is progressing. Organisation members can use this information first to gain a clearer understanding of the intervention (the kinds of behaviours and procedures required to implement it) and, second, to plan for the next implementation steps. This feedback cycle might proceed for several rounds, with each round providing members with knowledge about the intervention and ideas for the next stage of implementation.

Once implementation feedback has informed organisation members that the intervention is sufficiently in place, evaluation feedback begins. In contrast to implementation feedback, it is concerned with the overall impact of the intervention and whether resources should continue to be allocated to it or to other possible interventions. Evaluation feedback takes longer to gather and interpret than implementation feedback. It typically includes a broad array of outcome measures, such as performance, job satisfaction, absenteeism and turnover. Negative results on these measures tell members that either the initial diagnosis was seriously flawed or that the choice of intervention was wrong. Such feedback might prompt additional diagnosis and a search for a more effective intervention. Positive results, on the other hand, tell members that the intervention produced the expected outcomes and might prompt a search for ways of institutionalising the changes, making them a permanent part of the organisation's normal functioning.

An example of a job-enrichment intervention helps to clarify the OD stages and feedback linkages shown in **Figure 5.8**. Suppose the initial diagnosis reveals that employee performance and satisfaction are low and that an underlying cause of this problem lies with jobs that are overly structured and routinised. An inspection of alternative interventions to improve productivity and satisfaction suggests that job enrichment might be applicable for this situation. Existing job-enrichment theory proposes that increasing employee discretion, task variety and feedback can lead to improvements in work quality and attitudes, and that this job design and outcome linkage are especially strong for employees with growth needs – needs for challenge, autonomy and development. Initial diagnosis suggests that most employees have high growth needs and that the existing job design prevents the fulfilment of these needs. Therefore, job enrichment seems particularly suited to this situation.

Managers and employees now start to translate the general prescriptions offered by job-enrichment theory into specific behaviours and procedures. At this stage, the intervention is relatively broad and needs to be tailored to fit the specific situation. To implement the intervention, employees might decide on the following organisational changes: job discretion can be increased through more participatory styles of supervision; task variety can be enhanced by allowing employees to inspect their job outputs; and feedback can be made more meaningful by providing employees with quicker and more specific information about their performances.

After three months of trying to implement these changes, the members use implementation feedback to see how the intervention is progressing. Questionnaires and interviews (similar to those used in diagnosis) are administered in order to measure the different features of job enrichment (discretion, variety and feedback) and to assess employees' reactions to the changes. Company records are analysed to show the short-term effects on productivity of the intervention. The data reveal that productivity and satisfaction have changed very little since the initial diagnosis. Employee perceptions of job discretion and feedback have also shown negligible change, but perceptions of task variety have shown significant improvement. In-depth discussion and analysis of this first round of implementation feedback help the supervisors gain a better feel for the kinds of behaviours needed to move towards a participatory leadership style. This greater clarification of one feature of the intervention leads to a decision to involve the supervisors in leadership training and so help them to develop the skills and knowledge needed to lead participatively. A decision is also made to make job feedback more meaningful by translating such data into simple bar graphs, rather than continuing to provide voluminous statistical reports.

After these modifications have been in effect for about three months, members institute a second round of implementation feedback to see how the intervention is progressing. The data now show that productivity and satisfaction have moved moderately higher than in the first round of feedback and that employee perceptions of task variety and feedback are both high. Employee perceptions of discretion, however, remain relatively low. Members conclude that the variety and feedback dimensions of job enrichment are sufficiently implemented but that the discretion component needs improvement. They decide to put more effort into supervisory training and to ask OD practitioners to provide online counselling and coaching to supervisors about their leadership styles.

After four more months, a third round of implementation feedback occurs. The data now show that satisfaction and performance are significantly higher than in the first round of feedback and moderately higher than in the second round. The data also show that discretion, variety and feedback are all high, suggesting that the job-enrichment interventions have been successfully implemented. Now evaluation feedback is used to assess the overall effectiveness of the program.

The evaluation feedback includes all the data from the satisfaction and performance measures used in the implementation feedback. Because both the immediate and broader effects of the intervention are being evaluated, additional outcomes are examined, such as employee absenteeism, maintenance costs and reactions of other organisational units not included in job enrichment. The full array of evaluation data might suggest that one year after the start of implementation, the job-enrichment program is having the expected effects and so should be continued and made more permanent.

Measurement

Providing useful implementation and evaluation feedback involves two activities: selecting the appropriate variables and designing good measures.

Selecting variables

Ideally, the variables measured in OD evaluation should derive from the theory or conceptual model that underlies the intervention. The model should incorporate the key features of the intervention as well as its expected results.

The job-level diagnostic model suggests a number of measurement variables for implementation and evaluation feedback. Whether or not the intervention is being implemented could be assessed by determining either how many job descriptions have been rewritten to include more responsibility, or how many organisation members have received cross-training in other job skills. Evaluation of the immediate and long-term impact of job enrichment would include measures of employee performance and satisfaction over time. Again, these measures would probably be included in the initial diagnosis, when the company's problems or areas for improvement are discovered.

The measurement of both intervention and outcome variables is necessary for implementation and evaluation feedback. Unfortunately, there has been a tendency in OD to measure only outcome variables while neglecting intervention variables altogether.[67] It is generally assumed that the intervention has been implemented, and attention is directed to its impact on organisational outcomes, such as performance, absenteeism and satisfaction. As argued earlier, implementing OD interventions generally takes considerable time and learning. It must be empirically determined that the intervention has been implemented; it cannot simply be assumed. Implementation feedback[68] serves this purpose, guiding the implementation process and helping to interpret outcome data. Outcome measures are ambiguous unless it is known how well the intervention has been implemented. For example, a negligible change in measures of performance and satisfaction could mean that the wrong intervention has been chosen, that the correct intervention has not been implemented effectively or that the wrong variables have been measured. Measurement of the intervention variables helps to determine the correct interpretation of outcome measures.

As suggested above, the choice of what intervention variables to measure should derive from the conceptual framework that underlies the OD intervention. OD research and theory have increasingly come to identify the specific organisational changes that are necessary for the implementation of particular interventions. These variables should guide not only the implementation of the intervention but also choices about what change variables to measure for evaluative purposes. Additional sources of knowledge about intervention variables can be found in the numerous references at the end of each of the intervention chapters in this book (Chapters 7 and 8) and in several of the books in the Wiley Series on Organisational Assessment and Change.[69]

INSTITUTIONALISING INTERVENTIONS

Once it has been determined that an intervention has been implemented and is effective, attention is directed at institutionalising the changes: making them a permanent part of the organisation's normal functioning. Lewin described change as occurring in three stages: unfreezing, moving and refreezing. Institutionalising an OD intervention concerns refreezing. It involves the long-term persistence of organisational changes. To the extent that changes persist, they can be said to be institutionalised. Such changes are not dependent on any one person but exist as part of the culture of an organisation: numerous others share norms about the appropriateness of the changes.

For discussion of OD interventions in relation to people and process, and strategy and structure, see Chapters 7 and 8 respectively.

How planned changes become institutionalised has not received much attention in recent years. Rapidly changing environments have led to admonitions from consultants and practitioners to 'change constantly', to 'change before you have to' and 'if it's not broke, fix it anyway'. Such a context has challenged the utility of the institutionalisation concept. Why endeavour to make any change permanent, given that it may require changing again soon? However, the admonitions have also resulted in institutionalisation concepts being applied in new ways. Change itself has become the focus of institutionalisation.[70] Total quality management, organisation learning (OL), ISC and self-design interventions are all aimed at enhancing the organisation's capability for change.[71] In this vein, processes of institutionalisation take on increased utility. This section presents a framework that identifies factors and processes contributing to the institutionalisation of OD interventions, including the process of change itself.

Institutionalisation framework

Figure 5.9 presents a framework that identifies organisation and intervention characteristics and institutionalisation processes affecting the degree to which change programs are institutionalised.[72] The model shows that two key antecedents – organisation and intervention characteristics – affect different institutionalisation processes operating in organisations. These processes in turn affect various indicators of institutionalisation. The model also shows that organisation characteristics can influence intervention characteristics. For example, organisations with powerful unions may have trouble gaining internal support for OD interventions.

Organisation characteristics

Figure 5.9 shows that three key dimensions of an organisation can affect intervention characteristics and institutionalisation processes.

1   *Congruence.* This is the degree to which an intervention is perceived as being in harmony with the organisation's managerial philosophy, strategy and structure; its current environment; and other changes taking place.[73] When an intervention is congruent with these dimensions, the probability is improved that it will be institutionalised. Congruence can facilitate persistence[74] by making it easier to gain member commitment to the intervention and to diffuse it to wider segments of the organisation. The converse is also true. Many OD interventions promote employee participation and growth. When applied in highly bureaucratic organisations with formalised structures and autocratic managerial styles, participative interventions are not perceived as being congruent with the organisation's managerial philosophy.

2   *Stability of environment and technology.* This involves the degree to which the organisation's environment and technology are changing. Unless the change target is buffered from these changes or unless the changes are directly dealt with by the change program, it may be difficult to achieve long-term stability of the intervention.[75] For example, decreased demand for the business's products or services can lead to reductions in personnel, which may change the composition of the groups involved in the intervention. Conversely, increased product demand can curtail institutionalisation by bringing new members on board at a rate faster than they can be effectively socialised.

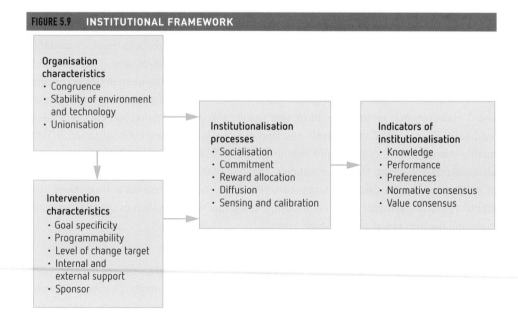

FIGURE 5.9   INSTITUTIONAL FRAMEWORK

3   *Unionisation.* Diffusion of interventions may be more difficult in unionised settings, especially if the changes affect union contract issues, such as salary and fringe benefits, job design and employee flexibility. For example, a rigid union contract can make it difficult to merge several job classifications into one, as might be required to increase task variety in a job-enrichment program. It is important to emphasise, however, that unions can be a powerful force for promoting change, especially when a good relationship exists between union and management.

Intervention characteristics

Figure 5.9 shows that five major features of OD interventions can affect institutionalisation processes:

1   *Goal specificity.* This involves the extent to which intervention goals are specific rather than broad. Specificity of goals helps to direct socialising activities (for example, training and orienting new members) to particular behaviours required to implement the intervention. It also facilitates operationalising the new behaviours so that rewards can be clearly linked to them. For example, an intervention aimed only at the goal of increasing product quality is likely to be more focused and readily put into operation than a change program intended to improve quality, quantity, safety, absenteeism and employee development.

2   *Programmability.* This involves the degree to which the changes can be programmed. This means that the different characteristics of the intervention are clearly specified in advance, thus facilitating socialisation, commitment and reward allocation.[76] For example, job enrichment specifies three targets of change: employee discretion, task variety and feedback. The change program can be planned and designed to promote these specific features.

3   *Level of change target.* This concerns the extent to which the change target is the total organisation, rather than a department or small work group. Each level possesses facilitators and inhibitors to persistence. Departmental and group change are susceptible to countervailing forces from others in the organisation, which can reduce the diffusion of the intervention, thus lowering its ability to improve organisation effectiveness. However, this does not necessarily preclude institutionalising the change within a department that successfully insulates itself from the rest of the organisation. This often manifests itself as a subculture within the organisation.[77]

    Targeting the intervention to wider segments of the organisation, on the other hand, can also help or hinder change persistence. It can facilitate institutionalisation by promoting a consensus across organisational departments exposed to the change. A shared belief about the intervention's value can be a powerful incentive to maintain the change. But targeting the larger system can also inhibit institutionalisation. The intervention can become mired in political resistance because of the 'not invented here' syndrome, or because powerful constituencies oppose it.

4   *Internal and external support.* Internal support refers to the degree to which there is an internal support system to guide the change process. Internal support, typically provided by an internal consultant, can help to gain commitment to the changes and help

organisation members to implement them. External consultants can also provide support, especially on a temporary basis during the early stages of implementation. For example, in many interventions aimed at implementing high-involvement organisations, both external and internal consultants provide support for the changes. The external consultant typically provides expertise on organisational design and trains members to implement the design. The internal consultant generally helps members to relate to other organisational units, to resolve conflicts and to legitimise the change activities within the organisation.

5   *Sponsor.* This concerns the presence of a powerful sponsor who can initiate, allocate and legitimise resources for the intervention. Sponsors must come from levels in the organisation high enough to control appropriate resources. They must have the visibility and power to nurture the intervention and see that it remains viable in the organisation. There are many examples of OD interventions that persisted for several years and then collapsed abruptly when the sponsor, usually a top administrator, left. There are also numerous examples of middle managers withdrawing support for interventions because top management did not include them in the change program.

Institutionalisation processes

The framework depicted in **Figure 5.9** shows five institutionalisation processes operating in organisations that can directly affect the degree to which OD interventions are institutionalised:

1   *Socialisation.* This concerns the transmission of information about beliefs, preferences, norms and values with respect to the intervention. Because implementation of OD interventions generally involves considerable learning and experimentation, a continual process of socialisation is necessary to promote persistence of the change program. Organisation members must focus attention on the evolving nature of the intervention and its ongoing meaning. They must communicate this information to other employees, especially new members. Transmission of information about the intervention helps to bring new members on board and allows participants to reaffirm the beliefs, norms and values that underlie the intervention.[78] For example, employee-involvement programs often include an initial transmission of information about the intervention, as well as the retraining of existing participants and training of new members. These processes are intended to encourage persistence with the program, as both new behaviours are learned and new members introduced.

2   *Commitment.* This binds people to behaviours associated with the intervention. It includes initial commitment to the program, as well as recommitment over time. Opportunities for commitment should allow people to select the necessary behaviours freely, explicitly and publicly. These conditions favour high commitment and can promote stability of the new behaviours. Commitment should derive from several organisational levels, including the employees directly involved and the middle and upper managers who can support or thwart the intervention. In many early employee-involvement programs, for example, attention was directed at gaining the workers' commitment to such programs. Unfortunately, middle managers were often ignored, resulting in considerable management resistance to the interventions.

3   *Reward allocation.* This involves linking rewards to the new behaviours required by an intervention. Organisational rewards can enhance the persistence of interventions in at least two ways. First, a combination of intrinsic and extrinsic rewards can reinforce new behaviours. Intrinsic rewards are internal and derive from the opportunities for challenge, development and accomplishment found in the work. When interventions provide these opportunities, motivation to perform should persist. Providing extrinsic rewards, such as money, for increased contributions can further reinforce this behaviour. Because the value of extrinsic rewards tends to diminish over time, it may be necessary to revise the reward system to maintain high levels of desired behaviours.

Second, new behaviours should persist to the extent that employees perceive rewards as equitable. When new behaviours are fairly compensated, people are likely to develop preferences for those behaviours. Over time, those preferences should lead to normative and value consensus about the appropriateness of the intervention. For example, many employee-involvement programs fail to persist because the employees feel that their increased contributions to organisational improvements are unfairly rewarded. This is especially true for interventions that rely exclusively on intrinsic rewards. People argue that an intervention that provides opportunities for intrinsic rewards should also provide greater pay or extrinsic rewards for higher levels of contribution to the organisation.

4   *Diffusion.* This refers to the process of transferring interventions from one system to another. Diffusion facilitates institutionalisation by providing a wider organisational base to support the new behaviours. Many interventions fail to persist because they run counter to the values and norms of the larger organisation. Rather than support the intervention, the larger organisation rejects the changes and often puts pressure on the change target to revert to old behaviours. Diffusion of the intervention to other organisational units reduces this counter-implementation strategy. It tends to lock in behaviours by providing normative consensus from other parts of the organisation. Moreover, the very act of transmitting institutionalised behaviours to other systems reinforces commitment to the changes.

5   *Sensing and calibration.* This involves detecting deviations from desired intervention behaviours and taking corrective action. Institutionalised behaviours invariably encounter destabilising forces, such as changes in the environment, new technologies and pressures from other departments to nullify changes. These factors cause some variation in performances, preferences, norms and values. To detect this variation and take corrective actions, organisations must have some sensing mechanism. Sensing mechanisms, such as implementation feedback, provide information about the occurrence of deviations. This knowledge can then initiate corrective actions to ensure that behaviours are more in line with the intervention. For example, the high level of job discretion associated with job enrichment might fail to persist. Information about this problem might initiate corrective actions, such as renewed attempts to socialise people or to gain commitment to the intervention.

Indicators of institutionalisation

Institutionalisation is not an all-or-nothing concept, but it does reflect degrees of persistence of an intervention. **Figure 5.9** shows five indicators that can be used to determine the extent of an intervention's persistence. The extent to which these factors are present or absent indicates the degree of institutionalisation.

1   *Knowledge*. This involves the extent to which organisation members have knowledge of the behaviours associated with an intervention. It is concerned with whether members know enough to perform the behaviours and to recognise the consequences of that performance. For example, job enrichment includes a number of new behaviours, such as performing a greater variety of tasks, analysing information about task performance and making decisions about work methods and plans.

2   *Performance*. This is concerned with the degree to which intervention behaviours are actually performed. It may be measured by counting the proportion of relevant people performing the behaviours. For example, 60 per cent of the employees in a particular work unit might be performing the job-enrichment behaviours described above. Another measure of performance is the frequency with which the new behaviours are performed. In assessing frequency, it is important to account for different variations of the same essential behaviour, as well as highly institutionalised behaviours that only need to be performed infrequently.

3   *Preferences*. This involves the degree to which organisation members privately accept the organisational changes. This contrasts with acceptance that is based primarily on organisational sanctions or group pressures. Private acceptance is usually reflected in people's positive attitudes towards the changes, and can be measured by the direction and intensity of these attitudes across the members of the work unit receiving the intervention. For example, a questionnaire that assesses members' perceptions of a job-enrichment program might show that most employees have a strong positive attitude towards making decisions, analysing feedback and performing a variety of tasks.

4   *Normative consensus*. This focuses on the extent to which people agree on the appropriateness of the organisational changes. This indicator of institutionalisation reflects the extent to which organisational changes have become part of the normative structure of the organisation. Changes persist to the degree that members feel they should support them. For example, a job-enrichment program would become institutionalised to the extent that employees support it and see it as appropriate to organisational functioning.

5   *Value consensus*. This is concerned with social consensus on values that are relevant to the organisational changes. Values are beliefs about how people should or should not behave. They are abstractions from more specific norms. Job enrichment, for example, is based on values promoting employee self-control and responsibility. Different behaviours associated with job enrichment, such as making decisions and performing a variety of tasks, would persist to the extent that employees widely share values of self-control and responsibility.

These five indicators can be used to assess the level of institutionalisation of an OD intervention. The more the indicators are present in a situation, the higher will be the degree of institutionalisation. Further, these factors seem to follow a specific development order: knowledge, performance, preferences, norms and values. People must first understand new behaviours or changes before they can perform them effectively. Such performance generates rewards and punishments, which in time affect people's preferences. As many individuals come to prefer the changes, normative consensus about their appropriateness develops. Finally, if there is normative agreement about the changes reflected in a particular set of values, over time there should be some consensus on those values among organisation members. This developmental view of institutionalisation implies that, whenever one of the last indicators is present, all the previous ones are automatically included as well; for example, if employees normatively agree with the behaviours that are associated with job enrichment, then they also have knowledge about the behaviours, can perform them effectively and prefer them. An OD intervention is fully institutionalised only when all five factors are present.

SUMMARY

This chapter presented an overview of the design, implementation and evaluation of interventions currently used in OD. An intervention is a set of planned activities intended to help an organisation improve its performance and effectiveness. Effective interventions are designed to fit the needs of the organisation, are based on causal knowledge of intended outcomes and transfer competence to manage change to organisation members.

'Designing interventions' discussed the selection of the most appropriate intervention, or series of interventions, which is an extremely difficult and sometimes risky venture. It is not only common to use more than one intervention but often tempting to choose the most familiar, thereby ignoring alternatives that may be more aligned with the needs of the organisation.

It is important to ask two primary questions when considering the multifaceted approach to change management. First, what is the type of change required? Is it behavioural (including people and process), structural, technical or a combination of these? Second, what is the impact of the change process? Will the impact be on individuals, groups or the organisation as a whole? By determining a response to these questions, it is possible to limit the choices and reduce the confusion that may occur.

'Implementing change' described five kinds of activities that change agents must carry out when planning and implementing changes. The first activity is motivating change, which involves creating a readiness for change among organisation members and managing their resistance. The second activity is about describing the desired future state, which may include the organisation's mission, valued performance and human outcomes, and valued organisational conditions to achieve those results, and creating a vision by articulating a compelling reason for implementing change. The third task for change agents is developing political support for the changes. Change agents must first assess their own sources of power, identify key stakeholders whose support is needed for change and then devise strategies for gaining their support. The fourth activity concerns managing the transition of the organisation from its current state to the desired future state. This calls for planning a road map for the change activities, as well as planning how to gain commitment for the changes. It may also involve creating special management structures for managing the transition. The fifth change task is sustaining momentum for the changes so that they are carried to completion. This includes providing resources for the change program, creating a support system for change agents, developing new competencies and skills, and reinforcing the new behaviours required to implement the changes.

'Evaluating OD interventions' discussed the final two stages of planned change – evaluating interventions and institutionalising them. Evaluation was discussed in terms of two kinds of necessary feedback. Implementation feedback is concerned with whether the intervention is being implemented as intended, and evaluation feedback indicates whether the intervention is producing expected results. The former is collected data about features of the intervention and its immediate effects, which are fed back repeatedly and at short intervals. The latter is data about the long-term effects of the intervention, which are fed back at long intervals.

Evaluation of interventions also involves decisions about measurement and research design. Measurement issues focus on selecting variables and designing good measures. Ideally, measurement decisions should derive from the theory that underlies the intervention and should include measures of the features of the intervention and its immediate and long-term consequences. Further, these measures should be operationally defined, valid and reliable and should involve multiple methods, such as a combination of questionnaires, interviews and company records.

Research design focuses on setting up the conditions for making valid assessments of an intervention's effects. This involves ruling out explanations for the observed results other than the intervention. Although randomised experimental designs are rarely feasible in OD, quasi-experimental designs exist for eliminating alternative explanations.

OD interventions are institutionalised when the change program persists and becomes part of the organisation's normal functioning. A framework for understanding and improving the institutionalisation of interventions identified organisation characteristics (congruence, stability of environment and technology, and unionisation) and intervention characteristics (goal specificity, programmability, level of change target, internal support and sponsor) affecting institutionalisation processes. It also described specific institutionalisation processes (socialisation, commitment, reward allocation, diffusion, and sensing and calibration) that directly affect indicators of intervention persistence (knowledge, performance, preferences, normative consensus and value consensus).

ACTIVITIES

REVIEW QUESTIONS

1   What/who are the primary targets of change programs? What is an intervention and how could it help a change program if the target of change is individuals? (L01)

2   Types of interventions are wide ranging and there are technical considerations in determining which intervention is acceptable. Consider the consequence of an inappropriate intervention and how it can be avoided. (L02)

3 Explain the five kinds of processes used in the implementation of change. What is most likely to impede its success? (LO3)

4 Feedback is crucial to determining accurate data and realistic performance. What other forms of assessment/evaluation would be advantageous? (LO4)

5 Institutionalisation may be regarded as good or bad. Provide reasons to justify both sides of the argument. What is your view of the value/contribution of institutionalisation? (LO5)

EXTEND YOUR LEARNING

1 The evaluation, or assessment of outcomes, of OD interventions is often neglected or manipulated. Why would this be the case, and what impact would it have on the change process? (LO1, 2, 3, 4 & 5)

2 'Machiavelli was the first OD practitioner.' Discuss. (LO1, 2, 3, 4 & 5)

3 'If change is constant, why is there the need to plan for every eventuality.' Discuss. (LO1, 2, 3, 4 & 5)

Search ✛ Me! **Management**

Explore **Search Me! Management** for articles relevant to this chapter. Fast and convenient, **Search Me! Management** is updated daily and provides you with 24-hour access to full text articles from hundreds of scholarly and popular journals, eBooks and newspapers, including *The Australian* and *The New York Times*. Visit http://login.cengagebrain.com and use the access code that comes with this book for 12 months access to the **Search Me! Management** database. Try searching for the following keywords:

Keywords:	Search tip: **Search Me! Management** contains information from both local and international sources. To get the greatest number of search results, try using both Australian and American spellings in your searches; for example, 'globalisation' and 'globalization'; 'organisation' and 'organization'.
• Institutionalisation	
• Diagnosis	
• Diagnostic model	
• Open systems theory	
• Transformation	
• Equifinality	
• Stratified sample	

REFERENCES

1 S. Parikh, *The Consultant's Handbook: A Practical Guide to Delivering High-value and Differentiated Services in a Competitive Marketplace* (New York: Wiley, 2015); E. Verlander, *The Practice of Professional Consulting* (San Francisco: Pfeiffer, 2012).

2 'Open systems model', Reflect and Learn, http://reflectlearn.org/discover/open-systems-model.

3 P. Block, *Flawless Consulting: A Guide to Getting Your Expertise Used*, 3rd edn (San Francisco: Jossey-Bass 2011); L. Greiner and F. Poulfelt,

Management Consulting Today and Tomorrow (New York: Routledge, 2010).

4 S. Whittle and R. Stevens, eds, *Changing Organizations from Within: Roles, Risks and Consultancy* (New York: Gower, 2016); A. Qureshi, M. Qureshi and S. Rathore, 'Dilemma in relationship of consultant and client', *Journal of Business Management*, 14 (2013): 109–13.

5 D. Nadler, 'Role of models in organizational assessment', in *Organizational Assessment*, eds E. Lawler III, D. Nadler and C. Cammann (New York:

John Wiley and Sons, 1980): 119–31; R. Keidel, *Seeing Organizational Patterns* (San Francisco: Berrett-Koehler, 1995); M. Harrison, *Diagnosing Organizations*, 2nd edn (Thousand Oaks, CA: Sage Publications, 1994).

6 A. Corney, 'Stanford MBA teaches executives how to master the "soft skills" that drive bottom line results', http://acorn-od.com/files/Andrea_Corney_Speaking_Resume.pdf.

7 M. Porter, *Competitive Advantage* (New York Free Press, 1985); M. Hitt, R.D. Ireland and R. Hoskisson, *Strategic Management*, 12th edn (Mason, OH: Cengage Learning, 2017).

8 D. Newman, 'Realizing the potential of big data analytics', *Forbes* (21 January 2017); T. Ashraf, 'Organizational development and big data: make the case for OD using big data as a change agent', *South Western Academy of Management Proceedings* (2016): 53–70; K. Pries and R. Dunnigan, *Big Data Analytics: A Practical Guide for Managers* (Boca Raton, FL: CRC Press, 2015).

9 S. Mohrman, T. Cummings and E. Lawler III, 'Creating useful knowledge with organizations: relationship and process issues', in *Producing Useful Knowledge for Organizations*, eds R. Kilmann and K. Thomas (New York: Praeger, 1983): 613–24; C. Argyris, R. Putnam and D. Smith, eds, *Action Science* (San Francisco: Jossey-Bass, 1985); E. Lawler III, A. Mohrman, S. Mohrman, G. Ledford Jr and T. Cummings, *Doing Research That Is Useful for Theory and Practice* (San Francisco: Jossey-Bass, 1985).

10 D. Nadler, *Feedback and Organization Development: Using Data-Based Methods* (Reading, MA: Addison-Wesley, 1977): 110–14.

11 W. Nielsen, N. Nykodym and D. Brown, 'Ethics and organizational change', *Asia Pacific Journal of Human Resources*, 29 (1991): 82–93.

12 Nadler, *Feedback and Organization Development*, op. cit.: 105–7.

13 W. Wymer and J. Carsten, 'Alternative ways to gather opinion', *HR Magazine* (April 1992): 71–8.

14 Examples of basic resource books on survey methodology include E. Ruel, W. Wagner and B. Gillespie, *The Practice of Survey Research: Theory and Applications* (Thousand Oaks, CA: Sage Publications, 2015); F. Fowler, *Survey Research Methods*, 5th edn (Thousand Oaks, CA: Sage Publications, 2014); L. Rea and R. Parker, *Designing and Conducting Survey Research: A Comprehensive Guide* (San Francisco: Jossey-Bass, 2012).

15 Australian Council for Educational Research, http://www.acer.edu.au.

16 J. Jones and W. Bearley, 'Organization change: orientation scale', *HRDQ* (King of Prussia, Pennsylvania, 1986).

17 J. Fordyce and R. Weil, *Managing with People*, 2nd edn (Reading, MA: Addison-Wesley, 1979); W. Wells, 'Group interviewing', in *Handbook of Marketing Research*, ed. R. Ferder (New York: McGraw-Hill, 1977); R. Krueger, *Focus Groups: A Practical Guide for Applied Research*, 2nd edn (Thousand Oaks, CA: Sage Publications, 1994).

18 R. Krueger and M. Casey, *Focus Groups: A Practical Guide for Applied Research*, 5th edn (Thousand Oaks, CA: Sage Publications, 2015).

19 'Unobtrusive measures', Research Methods Knowledge Base, http://www.socialresearchmethods.net/kb/unobtrus.php.

20 C. Emory, *Business Research Methods* (Homewood, IL: Richard D. Irwin, 1980): 146; J. Daniel, *Sampling Essentials: Practical Guidelines for Making Sampling Choices* (Thousand Oaks, CA: Sage Publications 2012).

21 W. Deming, *Sampling Design* (New York: John Wiley and Sons, 1960); L. Kish, *Survey Sampling* (New York: John Wiley and Sons, 1965); S. Sudman, *Applied Sampling* (New York: Academic Press, 1976).

22 H.A. Sánchez, B. Lai and M.E. Fayad, 'The sampling analysis pattern', IEEE International Conference on Information Reuse and Integration (October 2003).

23 S. Mohrman, T. Cummings and E. Lawler III, 'Creating useful knowledge with organizations: relationship and process issues', in *Producing Useful Knowledge for Organizations*, eds R. Kilmann and K. Thomas (New York: Praeger, 1983): 61–124.

24 C. Argyris, *Intervention Theory and Method: A Behavioral Science View* (Reading, MA: Addison-Wesley, 1970).

25 D. Nadler, *Feedback and Organization Development: Using Data-Based Methods* (Reading, MA: Addison-Wesley, 1977): 156–8.

26 Argyris, *Intervention Theory and Method*, op. cit.

27 T. Cummings, E. Molloy and R. Glen, 'A methodological critique of 58 selected work experiments', *Human Relations*, 30 (1977): 675–708; T. Cummings, E. Molloy and R. Glen, 'Intervention strategies for improving productivity and the quality of work life', *Organizational Dynamics*, 4 (Summer 1975): 59–60; J. Porras and P. Berg, 'The impact of organization development', *Academy of Management Review*, 3 (1978): 249–66; J. Nicholas, 'The comparative impact of organization development interventions on hard criteria measures', *Academy of Management Review*, 7 (1982): 531–42; R. Golembiewski, C. Proehl and D. Sink, 'Estimating the success of OD applications', *Training and Development Journal*, 72 (April 1982): 86–95.

28 A. Georges and L. Romme, 'Organizational development interventions: an artifaction

perspective', *Journal of Applied Behavioral Science*, 47 (2011): 8–32.

29 Nicholas, 'The comparative impact of organization development interventions', op. cit.; J. Porras and P. Robertson, 'Organization development theory: a typology and evaluation', in *Research in Organizational Change and Development*, 1, eds R. Woodman and W. Pasmore (Greenwich, CT: JAI Press, 1987): 1–57.

30 W. Pasmore, 'Tipping the balance: overcoming persistent problems in organizational change', in *Research in Organizational Change and Development*, vol. 19, eds W. Pasmore, A.B. Shani and R. Woodman (Howard House: Emerald Publishing, 2011), 259–92; G. Schwarz, 'Elephant on a treadmill: an evaluation of thematic narrowness in organizational change research', in *Research in Organizational Change and Development*, vol. 17, eds W. Pasmore, A.B. Shani and R. Woodman (Howard House: Emerald Publishing, 2009), 301–48.

31 B.J. Weiner, *A Theory of Organizational Readiness for Change* (Department of Health Policy and Management, Gillings School of Global Public Health, University of North Carolina, USA, 2009).

32 T. Stewart, 'Rate your readiness for change', *Fortune* (7 February 1994): 106–10.

33 G. Hofstede, *Culture's Consequences* (Beverly Hills, CA: Sage, 1980); K. Johnson, 'Estimating national culture and OD values', in *Global and International Organization Development*, eds P. Sorensen Jr, T. Head, K. Johnson, N. Mathys, J. Preston and D. Cooperrider (Champaign, IL: Stipes, 1995): 266–81.

34 J. Kotter and L. Schlesinger, 'Choosing strategies for change', *Harvard Business Review*, 57 (1979): 106–14; R. Ricardo, 'Overcoming resistance to change', *National Productivity Review*, 14 (1995): 28–39.

35 M. Weisbord, *Productive Work Places* (San Francisco: Jossey-Bass, 1987); R. Beckhard and R. Harris, *Organizational Transitions: Managing Complex Change*, 2nd edn (Reading, MA: Addison-Wesley, 1987); R. Beckhard and W. Pritchard, *Changing the Essence* (San Francisco: Jossey-Bass, 1991).

36 U. Majer and T. Sauer, *Intuition and the Axiomatic Method in Hilbert's Foundation of Physics* (Universität Göttingen, Germany and California Institute of Technology, Pasadena, USA, 2006).

37 N. Tichy and M. Devanna, *The Transformational Leader* (New York: John Wiley and Sons, 1986).

38 R. Cosier and C. Schwenk, 'Agreement and thinking alike: ingredients for poor decisions', *Academy of Management Executive*, 4 (1990): 69–74.

39 W. Burke, *Organization Development: A Normative View* (Reading, MA: Addison-Wesley, 1987).

40 D. Eden, 'OD and self-fulfilling prophecy: boosting productivity by raising expectations', *Journal of Applied Behavioral Science*, 22 (1986): 1–13.

41 ibid.: 8.

42 P. Senge, *The Fifth Discipline* (New York: Doubleday, 1990).

43 J. Kotter, *Leading Change* (Boston, MA: Harvard Business School Press, 1994); W. Bennis and B. Nanus, *Leadership* (New York: Harper and Row, 1985); J. O'Toole, *Leading Change: Overcoming the Ideology of Comfort and the Tyranny of Custom* (San Francisco: Jossey-Bass, 1995); F. Hesselbein, M. Goldsmith and R. Beckhard, eds, *The Leader of the Future* (San Francisco: Jossey-Bass, 1995).

44 Tichy and Devanna, *The Transformational Leader*, op. cit.

45 W. Bridges and S. Bridges, *Managing Transitions: Making the Most of Change* (Boston: Da Capo Press, 2017); W. Burke, *Organization Change: Theory and Practice*, 5th edn (Thousand Oaks, CA: Sage Publications, 2017).

46 D. Seidman, 'Letting the mission govern a company', *The New York Times* (24 June 2012).

47 J. Pfeffer, *Power in Organizations* (New York: Pitman, 1982); S. Piderit, 'Rethinking resistance and recognizing ambivalence: a multidimensional view of attitudes toward an organizational change', *Academy of Management Journal*, 25 (2000): 783–94; B. Mathews and C. Linski, 'Shifting the paradigm: reevaluating resistance to organizational change', *Journal of Organizational Change Management* 29 (2016): 963–72; E. Dent and S. Goldberg, 'Challenging "resistance to change"', *Journal of Applied Science* 35 (March 1999): 25; M. Weisbord, *Productive Workplaces* (San Francisco: Jossey-Bass, 1987); R. Beckhard and W. Pritchard, *Changing the Essence* (San Francisco, Jossey-Bass, 1991); J. Collins and J. Porras, *Built to Last* (New York: Harper Business, 1994); J. Conger, G. Spreitzer and E. Lawler, *The Leader's Change Handbook* (San Francisco: Jossey-Bass, 1999).

48 D. Nadler, 'The effective management of change', in *Handbook of Organizational Behavior*, ed. J. Lorsch (Englewood Cliffs, NJ: Prentice Hall, 1987): 358–69.

49 P. Tolchinsky, 'Accelerating change: new ways of thinking about engaging the whole system', *Organization Development Journal* 33 (2015): 45–63; R. Tenkasi, S. Mohrman and A. Mohrman, 'Accelerating learning during organizational transition', in *Tomorrow's Organization*, eds S. Mohrman, J. Galbraith, E. Lawler and associates (San Francisco: Jossey-Bass, 1998).

50 C. Alderfer, 'Organization development', *Annual Review of Psychology*, 28 (1977): 197–223.

51 T. Bateman, 'Organizational change and the politics of success', *Group and Organization Studies*, 5 (June 1980): 198–209; A. Cobb and

N. Margulies, 'Organization development: a political perspective', *Academy of Management Review*, 6 (1981): 49–59; A. Cobb, 'Political diagnosis: applications in organization development', *Academy of Management Review*, 11 (1986): 482–96; L. Greiner and V. Schein, *Power and Organization Development: Mobilizing Power to Implement Change* (Reading, MA: Addison-Wesley, 1988).

52 Greiner and Schein, *Power and Organization Development*, op. cit.

53 Nadler, 'The effective management of change', op. cit.; Beckhard and Pritchard, *Changing the Essence*, op. cit.

54 Greiner and Schein, *Power and Organization Development*, op. cit.

55 Beckhard and Harris, *Organizational Transitions*, op. cit.

56 ibid.

57 ibid.

58 M. Otto, 'Renewable energy financing issues in Africa' (paper presented at the International Conference on Renewable Energy in Africa: Making Renewable Energy Markets Work for Africa, United Nations Environment Programme, 16–18 April 2008).

59 C. Worley, D. Hitchin and W. Ross, *Integrated Strategic Change: How OD Helps to Build Competitive Advantage* (Reading, MA: Addison-Wesley, 1996).

60 M. Beer, *Organization Change and Development: A Systems View* (Santa Monica, CA: Goodyear, 1980).

61 B. Carter, 'Boral looks for new management style as CEO departs', *The Australian*, 23 May 2012.

62 D.M. Rousseau, ed., *The Oxford Handbook of Evidence-Based Management* (New York: Oxford University Press, 2012); J. Pfeffer and R.I. Sutton, *Hard Facts Dangerous Half-Truths and Total Nonsense: Profiting from Evidence-based Management* (Cambridge: Harvard Business School Press, 2006).

63 T. Cummings and E. Molloy, *Strategies for Improving Productivity and the Quality of Work Life* (New York: Praeger, 1977); J. Whitfield, W. Anthony and K. Kacmar, 'Evaluation of team-based management: a case study', *Journal of Organizational Change Management*, 8:2 (1995): 17–28.

64 W. Burke, *Organization Change: Theory and Practice*, 5th edn (Newbury Park, CA: Sage, 2018).

65 S. Mohrman and T. Cummings, 'Implementing quality-of-work-life programs by managers', in *The NTL Manager's Handbook*, eds R. Ritvo and A. Sargent (Arlington, VA: NTL Institute, 1983): 320–8; T. Cummings and S. Mohrman, 'Self-designing organizations: towards implementing quality-of-work-life innovations', in *Research in Organizational Change and Development*, 1, eds R. Woodman

and W. Pasmore (Greenwich, CT: JAI Press, 1987): 275–310.

66 T. Cummings, 'Institutionalising quality-of-work-life programs: the case for self-design', paper delivered at the Annual Meeting of the Academy of Management, Dallas, TX, August 1983.

67 M-Y. Cheung-Judge and L. Holbeche, *Organization Development* (Great Britain and United States: Kogan Page, 2011).

68 D. Waltrip, J. Maniscalco, C. Meinhard and A. Anderson, 'Implementation of an organizational development plan to create a learning organization', Water-Environment Federation, Virginia Beach, Virginia, USA, 2006.

69 P. Goodman, *Assessing Organizational Change: The Rushton Quality of Work Experiment* (New York: John Wiley and Sons, 1979); A. van de Ven and D. Ferry, eds, *Measuring and Assessing Organizations* (New York: John Wiley and Sons, 1985); E. Lawler III, D. Nadler and C. Cammann, eds, *Organizational Assessment: Perspectives on the Measurement of Organizational Behavior and Quality of Work Life* (New York: John Wiley and Sons, 1980); A. van de Ven and W. Joyce, eds, *Perspectives on Organizational Design and Behavior* (New York: John Wiley and Sons, 1981); S. Seashore, E. Lawler III, P. Mirvis and C. Cammann, eds, *Assessing Organizational Change: A Guide to Methods, Measures, and Practices* (New York: John Wiley and Sons, 1983).

70 M. Luppa, T. Luck, E. Brähler, H.H. König, S.G. Riedel-Heller, 'Prediction of institutionalisation in dementia: a systematic review', *Dementia and Geriatric Cognitive Disorders*, 26 (2008): 65–78.

71 D. Ciampa, *Total Quality: A User's Guide for Implementation* (Reading, MA: Addison-Wesley, 1992); P. Senge, *The Fifth Discipline* (New York: Doubleday, 1990); Cummings and Mohrman, 'Self-designing organizations', op. cit.; C. Worley, D. Hitchin and W. Ross, *Integrated Strategic Change* (Reading, MA: Addison-Wesley, 1996).

72 This section is based on the work of P. Goodman and J. Dean, 'Creating long-term organizational change', in *Change in Organizations*, ed. P. Goodman (San Francisco: Jossey-Bass, 1982): 226–79. To date, the framework is largely untested and unchallenged. Ledford's process model of persistence (see note 73) is the only other model proposed to explain institutionalisation. The empirical support for either model, however, is nil.

73 G. Ledford, 'The persistence of planned organizational change: a process theory perspective' (PhD dissertation, University of Michigan, 1984).

74 E. Vigoda, 'Internal politics in public administration systems: an empirical examination of its relationship with job congruence, organizational citizenship behavior, and in-role performance', *Public Personnel Management*, 29 (2000): 185–210.

75 L. Zucker, 'Normal change or risky business: institutional effects on the "hazard" of change in hospital organizations, 1959–1979', *Journal of Management Studies*, 24 (1987): 671–700.

76 S. Mohrman and T. Cummings, *Self-Designing Organizations: Learning How to Create High Performance* (Reading, MA: Addison-Wesley, 1989).

77 J. Martin and C. Siehl, 'Organizational cultures and counterculture: an uneasy symbiosis', *Organizational Dynamics* (1983): 52–64; D. Meyerson and J. Martin, 'Cultural change: an integration of three different views', *Journal of Management Studies*, 24 (1987): 623–47.

78 L. Zucker, 'The role of institutionalization in cultural persistence', *American Sociological Review*, 42 (1977): 726–43.

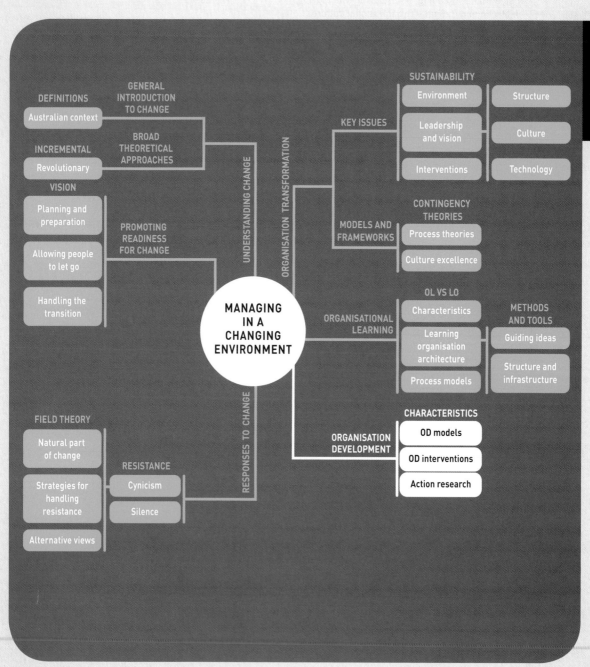

DEFINITIONS
Australian context

GENERAL
INTRODUCTION
TO CHANGE

INCREMENTAL
Revolutionary

BROAD
THEORETICAL
APPROACHES

VISION
Planning and
preparation

Allowing people
to let go

Handling the
transition

PROMOTING
READINESS
FOR CHANGE

UNDERSTANDING CHANGE

ORGANISATION TRANSFORMATION

SUSTAINABILITY

Environment

Structure

KEY ISSUES

Leadership
and vision

Culture

Interventions

Technology

CONTINGENCY
THEORIES

MODELS AND
FRAMEWORKS

Process theories

Culture excellence

OL VS LO

Characteristics

METHODS
AND TOOLS

ORGANISATIONAL
LEARNING

Learning
organisation
architecture

Guiding ideas

Structure and
infrastructure

Process models

MANAGING
IN A
CHANGING
ENVIRONMENT

CHARACTERISTICS

OD models

ORGANISATION
DEVELOPMENT

OD interventions

Action research

FIELD THEORY

Natural part
of change

RESPONSES TO CHANGE

Strategies for
handling
resistance

RESISTANCE

Cynicism

Alternative views

Silence

Source: Adapted from D. Waddell, *E-Business in Australia: Concepts and Cases*, Pearson Education Australia, 2002.

PART 3

ORGANISATION DEVELOPMENT

Part 3 comprises Chapters 6, 7 and 8. The main concepts and themes emerge as shown in the table below, which also indicates main chapter linkages. Note that the links are within Part 3 and extend into each of Parts 2, 4 and 5 because change concepts generally interrelate through their causes and effects.

THEME OR CONCEPT	CONNECTED WITH MATERIAL IN OTHER CHAPTERS
Learning organisations	Ch 5, 6, 7, 8
Design and planning	Ch 2, 5, 6, 7, 8, 11
People and performance	Ch 3, 4, 6, 7, 8, 9
Environment and structure	Ch 5, 8, 10, 11
Action research	Ch 1, 2, 6

Irene McAleese

Co-founder and Director of Marketing/
See.Sense

Source: Irene McAleese.

Seeing the sense in change

Change is a way of life for Aussie entrepreneur Irene McAleese, who now lives and works in Northern Ireland. Irene is the co-founder and director of marketing, business development and human resources at See.Sense, an innovative cycling technology start-up company.

See.Sense commenced business in 2013, producing a bicycle light designed to respond to the road, flashing brighter and faster than competitor lights to improve rider visibility when it is needed most. The product has captured imaginations and business awards ever since its inception. It is being increasingly adopted and saving lives along the way.

As with all success stories, Irene's was not an overnight event. She spent many years building skills to channel into See.Sense. For instance, in five and a half years with Queensland Rail (QR) in Brisbane, Irene held various roles, including:

→ Project Manager for the design and delivery of QR's People Leadership Program catering for the top 400 managers, and then for the design of the program tailored to front-line management

→ Change Management Project Officer for the Supply Division while a cultural change program was being implemented

→ Organisational Development Consultant in the Training and Development Unit

→ Administration Manager of the Legal Services Unit

→ Workplace Health and Safety Officer in the Corporate Services Unit

→ HR Strategy Project Officer, managing QR's human resources benchmarking program through InfoHRM.

During a two-year stint with the telecommunications company BT in London, Irene developed further in the following roles:

→ Employee Relations Manager – Performance Management Lead at BT Wholesale

→ Human Resources Manager – Field Operations at BT Wholesale, covering 3500 employees across the United Kingdom

→ Project Manager for the Delivering High Performance Program, in which 30 000 employees across BT Wholesale participated.

And she added another two years at Accenture in London, fulfilling roles such as:

→ Manager, Human Performance – Change Management Consulting, servicing key clients in the resources and financial services industries

→ Support to Accenture's UK Graduate Recruitment team

→ Consultant in the Human Performance team.

In other words, there are many experiences that have contributed to Irene's ability to foster a start-up company and to gain award-winning recognition of the company's product and approach. Consider the extent of success that See.Sense has achieved in a relatively short time, as evidenced by its awards:

→ Early Stage Company of the Year, Northern Ireland, December 2013
→ Winner of Global Jumpstart Competition, December 2013
→ Breakthrough Company of the Year, Invest NI Propel Programme, February 2014
→ InterTrade Ireland Ambassador Company, July 2014
→ Winner of Electronics Category of INVENT2014, NISPConnect, October 2014
→ National Finalist, Bank of Ireland Startup Awards, October 2014
→ National Finalist, Next Generation Digital Challenge Awards, October 2014
→ Ulster Finalist, Ulster Bank Business Achiever Awards, October 2014
→ National Finalist, UK Packaging Awards, October 2014
→ Winner of Best New Startup (Knowledge Economy), Women in Business Awards, NI Women in Business, November 2014
→ Winner of CIM Chair's Award for Marketing Excellence, Chartered Institute of Marketing Ireland, November 2014
→ The Duke of York's Pitch@Palace, November 2014
→ Winner of The Guardian Small Business Showcase Award for Marketing and PR Excellence, June 2015
→ Nominee for the BikeBiz Breakthrough Brand of the Year Award, July 2015
→ Winner of the BT Infinity Lab SME Awards, May 2016.

The very essence of innovation and entrepreneurship is an ability to change at the right time and in the right ways. Irene exemplifies the intuitive and trained entrepreneur with a skilled grounding. An understanding of systems and bureaucracies underpins the activities she now fulfils in a smaller, more speculative company.

See.Sense is continuing to do well. It is launching a second product, See.Sense ICON, after a successful Kickstarter campaign to raise the development funding. This new bike light connects to a smartphone app, providing the cyclist with crash detection and theft alerts. It can also provide cities with data on potholes as well as accident hot spot areas. It is this kind of clever design thinking that contributed to See. Sense ICON becoming featured in London's Design Museum. The See.Sense business has grown to a team of 15 and exports to over 70 countries around the world. The company raised £711 000 on equity crowdfunding platform Crowdcube in 2016 and investors included VC funds Techstart, and in 2017 raised a further £400 000 from existing investors plus new investor Clarendon VC. See.Sense has partnered with British Cycling in a four-year deal to be their 'Official Bike Light Supplier' and 'Official Crowdsourced Data and Insights Provider'. The company continues working with partners including TfGM, Manchester City Council and British Telecom. Irene became a speaker in demand at global conferences such as ITS (Intelligent Transport Systems) World Congress 2018 in Copenhagen, and Velo-City Global in Rio de Janeiro 2018. As See.Sense enjoys increased growth and success, Irene's vision and knowledge base is one of the key elements to temper and guide the changes.

6

ORGANISATION DEVELOPMENT AND CONTINUOUS CHANGE

After studying this chapter, you should be able to:

1 Define and discuss learning organisations.

2 Define and explain self-designing organisations.

3 Explain the goals and outcomes of knowledge management in changing organisational environments.

4 Discuss options for designing and building organisations for change.

KEY TERMS

Organisation learning (OL)
Knowledge management (KM)

Self-designing organisations

This chapter describes interventions that enable organisations to change themselves continuously. These change processes are contextual in organisation development (OD) and are still being developed and refined in theory and practice. They are aimed at the growing number of organisations facing highly turbulent environments, such as businesses in high-technology, entertainment and biotechnology industries, where timing is critical, technological change is rapid and competitive pressures are unrelenting and difficult to predict. In these situations, standard sources of competitive advantage – strategy, organisation design and core competencies – erode quickly and provide only temporary advantage. What is needed are dynamic capabilities[1] built into the organisation that enable it to renew forms of competitive advantage constantly to adapt to a rapidly shifting environment.

Continuous change approaches extend transformational change into a non-stop process of strategy setting, organisation designing and implementing the change.[2] Rather than focus on creating and implementing a particular strategy and organisation design, continuous change addresses the underlying structures, processes and activities for generating new forms of competitive advantage. Thus, the focus is on learning, changing and adapting – on how to produce a constant flow of new strategies and designs and not just on how to transform existing ones.

Learning organisations are those with the ability to learn how to change and improve themselves constantly. Distinct from individual learning, this approach and understanding helps organisations move beyond solving existing problems to gaining the capability to improve continuously. It results in the development of a learning organisation where empowered members take responsibility for changing the organisation and learning how to do this better and better.

Self-designing organisations have the capability to alter themselves fundamentally and continuously. Creating them is a highly participative process in which multiple stakeholders set strategic direction, design appropriate structures and processes and implement them. The self-designing approach builds on the learning organisation understanding and includes considerable innovation and learning as organisations gain the capacity to design and employ significant changes continually.

Built-to-change organisations include design elements and managerial practices that are all geared for change, not just normal operations. This approach is conceived from the ground up and provides design and implementation guidelines for building change capability into the structures, processes and behaviours of the organisation so that it can respond continually to a rapidly changing environment.

LEARNING ORGANISATIONS

The learning organisation field is aimed at helping organisations develop and use knowledge to change and improve themselves constantly. It includes two interrelated change processes: **organisation learning (OL)**, which enhances an organisation's capability to acquire and develop new knowledge, and **knowledge management (KM)**, which focuses on how that knowledge can be organised and used to improve performance. Both OL and KM are crucial in today's complex, rapidly changing environments. They can be a source of strategic renewal and can enable organisations to acquire and apply knowledge more quickly and effectively than competitors, thus establishing a sustained competitive advantage.[3] Moreover, when knowledge is translated into new products and services, it can become a key source of wealth creation for organisations.[4] OL and KM are among the most widespread and fastest-growing interventions in OD. They are the focus of an expanding body of research and practice and have been applied in such diverse organisations as the Australian Army, Minter Ellison, McKinsey, Microsoft and Boeing.

Organisation learning (OL): a system that enhances an organisation's capability to acquire and develop new knowledge.

Knowledge management (KM): the tools and techniques that enable organisations to collect, organise and translate information into useful knowledge.

CONCEPTUAL FRAMEWORK

Like many applied approaches in OD, there is some ambiguity about the concepts underlying OL and KM.[5] Sometimes the terms 'organisation learning' and 'knowledge management' are used interchangeably to apply to the broad set of activities through which organisations learn and organise knowledge; other times, they are used separately to emphasise different aspects of learning and managing knowledge. This confusion derives in part from the different disciplines and applications traditionally associated with OL and KM.[6]

OL interventions emphasise the organisational structures and social processes that enable employees and teams to learn and to share knowledge. They draw heavily on the social sciences for conceptual grounding and on OD concepts, such as team building, structural design and employee involvement, for practical guidance. In organisations, OL change processes are typically associated with the human resources function and may be assigned to a special leadership role such as chief learning officer.

KM approaches, on the other hand, focus on the tools and techniques that enable organisations to collect, organise and translate information into useful knowledge. They are rooted conceptually in the information and computer sciences and, in practice, emphasise electronic forms of knowledge storage and transmission, such as intranets, data warehousing and knowledge repositories. Organisationally, KM applications often are located in the information systems function and may be under the direction of a chief information or technology officer.

There is also confusion about the concept of OL itself, about whether it is an individual- or organisation-level process. Some researchers and practitioners describe OL as individual learning that occurs within an organisation context; thus, it is the aggregate of individual learning processes occurring within an organisation.[7] Others characterise it in terms of organisation processes and structures;[8] they emphasise how learning is embedded in routines, policies and organisation cultures.[9] Snyder has proposed an integration of the two perspectives that treats OL as a relative concept.[10] Individuals do learn in organisations but that learning may or may not contribute to OL. Learning is organisational to the extent that:

→ it is done to achieve organisational purposes

→ it is shared or distributed among members of the organisation

→ learning outcomes are embedded in the organisation's systems, structures and culture.

To the extent that these criteria are met, OL is distinct from individual learning. Thus, it is possible for individual members to learn while the organisation does not. For example, a member may learn to serve the customer better without ever sharing such learning with other members. Conversely, it is possible for the organisation to learn without individual members learning. Improvements in equipment design or work procedures, for example, reflect OL, even if these changes are not understood by individual members. Moreover, because OL serves the organisation's purposes and is embedded in its structures, it stays with the organisation, even if members change.

A key premise underlying much of the literature on OL and KM is that such interventions will lead to higher organisation performance. Although their positive linkage to performance is assumed, the mechanisms through which OL and KM translate into performance improvements are rarely identified or explained. Understanding those mechanisms, however, is essential for applying these change processes in organisations.

Based on existing research and practice, **Figure 6.1** provides an integrative framework for understanding OL and KM interventions,[11] summarising the elements of these change processes and showing how they combine to affect organisation performance. This framework suggests that specific characteristics, such as structure and human resources systems, influence how well OL processes are carried out. These learning processes affect the amount and kind of knowledge that an organisation possesses; in turn, that knowledge directly influences performance outcomes, such as product quality and customer service. As depicted in **Figure 6.1**, the linkage between organisation knowledge and performance depends on the organisation's competitive strategy. Organisation knowledge will lead to high performance to the extent that it is both relevant and applied effectively to the strategy. For example, customer-driven organisations require timely and relevant information about customer needs. Their success relies heavily on members having that knowledge and applying it effectively in their work with customers.

FIGURE 6.1   HOW ORGANISATION LEARNING AFFECTS ORGANISATION PERFORMANCE

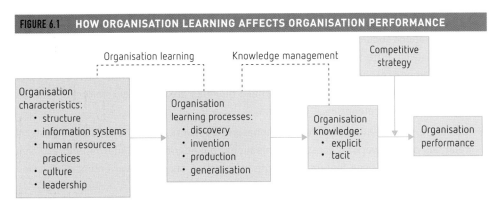

Source: Reprinted by permission of Sage Publications Ltd. from W. Snyder and T. Cummings, 'Organization learning disorders: conceptual model and intervention hypotheses', *Human Relations*, 51: 873–95. © The Tavistock Institute, 1998.

Figure 6.1 also shows how OL and KM are interrelated. OL interventions address how organisations can be designed to promote effective learning processes and how those learning processes themselves can be improved. KM interventions focus on the outcomes of learning processes, on how strategically relevant knowledge can be effectively organised and used throughout the organisation. Each of the key elements of OL and KM – organisation characteristics, OL processes and organisation knowledge – are described below, along with the interventions typically associated with them.

BUILDING ORGANISATION LEARNING FOR CONTINUOUS CHANGE

As shown in **Figure 6.1**, there are several organisation features that can promote effective learning processes, including structure, information systems, human resources practices, culture and leadership. Consequently, many of the interventions described in this book can help organisations develop more effective learning capabilities.[12] Human resources management interventions – performance appraisal, reward systems and career planning and development – can reinforce members' motivation to gain new skills and knowledge.

Technostructural interventions,[13] such as process-based and network structures, self-managing work teams and re-engineering, can provide the kinds of lateral linkages and teamwork needed to process, develop and share diverse information and knowledge. Human process changes, including team building, search conferences and intergroup relations interventions, can help members develop the kinds of healthy interpersonal relationships that underlie effective OL. Strategic approaches, such as integrated strategic change (ISC) and alliances, can help organisations gain knowledge about their environments and develop values and norms that promote OL.

Characteristics of a learning organisation

OL practitioners have combined many of these continuous change approaches into the design and implementation of what is commonly referred to as the 'learning organisation'. It is an organisation 'skilled at creating, acquiring, interpreting, transferring and retaining knowledge and at purposefully modifying its behaviour to reflect new knowledge and insights'.[14] Much of the literature on the learning organisation is prescriptive and proposes how organisations should be designed and managed to promote effective learning. Although there is relatively little systematic research to support these premises, there is growing consensus among researchers and practitioners about specific organisational features that characterise the learning organisation.[15] These qualities are mutually reinforcing and fall into five interrelated categories:

→ *Structure.* Organisation structures emphasise teamwork, fewer layers, strong lateral relations and networking across organisational boundaries both internal and external to the business. These features promote information sharing, involvement in decision making, systems thinking and empowerment.

→ *Information systems.* OL involves gathering and processing information and, consequently, the information systems of learning organisations provide an infrastructure for OL. These systems facilitate rapid acquisition, processing and sharing of rich, complex information and enable people to manage knowledge for competitive advantage.

→ *Human resources practices.* Human resources practices, including appraisal, rewards and training, are designed to account for long-term performance and knowledge development; they reinforce the acquisition and sharing of new skills and knowledge.

→ *Organisational culture.* Learning organisations have strong cultures that promote openness, creativity and experimentation among members. These values and norms provide the underlying social support needed for successful learning. They encourage members to acquire, process and share information; they nurture innovation and provide the freedom to try new things, risk failure and learn from mistakes.

→ *Leadership.* Like most interventions aimed at continuous change, OL and KM depend heavily on effective leadership throughout the organisation. The leaders of learning organisations actively model the openness, risk taking and reflection necessary for learning. They also communicate a compelling vision of the learning organisation and provide the empathy, support and personal advocacy needed to lead others in that direction.

Organisation learning processes

The organisation characteristics described above affect how well members carry out OL processes. As shown in **Figure 6.1**, these processes consist of four interrelated activities: discovery, invention, production and generalisation.[16] Learning starts with discovery when errors or gaps between desired and actual conditions are detected. For example, sales managers may discover that sales are falling below projected levels and set out to solve the problem. Invention is aimed at devising solutions to close the gap between desired and current conditions; it includes diagnosing the causes of the gap and creating appropriate solutions to reduce it. The sales managers may learn that poor advertising is contributing to the sales problem and may devise a new sales campaign to improve sales. Production processes involve implementing solutions and generalisation includes drawing conclusions about the effects of the solutions and extending that knowledge to other relevant situations. For instance, the new advertising program would be implemented and, if successful, the managers might use variations of it with other product lines. Thus, these four learning processes enable members to generate the knowledge necessary to change and improve the organisation.

Organisations can apply the learning processes described above to three types of learning.[17] First, *single-loop learning* or *adaptive learning*[18] is focused on improving the status quo. This is the most prevalent form of learning in organisations and enables members to reduce errors or gaps between desired and existing conditions. It can produce incremental change in how organisations function. The sales managers described above engaged in single-loop learning when they looked for ways to reduce the difference between current and desired levels of sales.

Second, *double-loop learning* or *generative learning*[19] is aimed at changing the status quo. It operates at a more abstract level than does single-loop learning because members learn how to change the existing assumptions and conditions within which single-loop learning operates. This level of learning can lead to transformational change, where the status quo itself is radically altered. For example, the sales managers may learn that sales projections are based on faulty assumptions and models about future market conditions. This knowledge may result in an entirely new conception of future markets, with corresponding changes in sales projections and product development plans. It may lead the managers to drop some products that had previously appeared promising, develop new ones that were not considered before and alter advertising and promotional campaigns to fit the new conditions.

The third type of learning is called *deuterolearning*,[20] which involves learning how to learn. Here, learning is directed at the learning process itself and seeks to improve how organisations perform single- and double-loop learning. For example, the sales managers might periodically examine how well they perform the processes of discovery, invention, production and generalisation. This could lead to improvements and efficiencies in how learning is conducted throughout the organisation.

Practitioners have developed change strategies designed specifically for OL processes. Although these interventions are relatively new in OD and do not follow a common change process, they tend to focus on cognitive aspects of learning and how members can become more effective learners. In describing these change strategies, we draw heavily on the work of Argyris and Schon and of Senge and his colleagues because it is the most developed and articulated work in OL practice.[21]

From this perspective, OL is not concerned with the organisation as a static entity but as an active process of sense making and organising. Based on the interpretive model of change, members socially construct the organisation as they continually act and interact with each other and learn from those actions how to organise themselves for productive achievement. This active learning process enables members to develop, test and modify mental models or maps of organisational reality. Called *theories in use*, these cognitive maps inform member behaviour and organising.[22] They guide how members make decisions, perform work and organise themselves. Unfortunately, members' theories in use can be faulty, resulting in ineffective behaviours and organising efforts. They can be too narrow and fail to account for important aspects of the environment; they can be too broad and include erroneous assumptions that lead to unexpected negative consequences. Effective OL can resolve these problems by enabling members to learn from their actions how to detect and correct errors in their mental maps, and thus it can promote more effective organising efforts.

The predominant mode of learning in most organisations is ineffective, however, and may even intensify errors. Referred to as *Model I learning*, it includes values and norms that emphasise unilateral control of environments and tasks, and protection of oneself and others from information that may be hurtful.[23] These norms result in a variety of defensive routines that inhibit learning, such as withholding information and feelings, competition and rivalry, and little public testing of theories in use and the assumptions underlying them. Model I is limited to single-loop learning, where existing theories in use are reinforced.

A more effective approach to learning, called *Model II learning*, is based on values promoting valid information, free and informed choice, internal commitment to the choice and continuous assessment of its implementation.[24] This results in minimal defensiveness, with greater openness to information and feedback, personal mastery and collaboration with others and public testing of theories in use. Model II applies to double-loop learning, where theories in use are changed, and to deuterolearning, where the learning process itself is examined and improved. Whether in partnership, or delivered in-house, organisational learning needs to deliver targeted outcomes to businesses. **Apply your learning 6.1** deals with some of the debates around learning in organisations.

Application stages

OL interventions are aimed at helping organisation members learn how to change from Model I to Model II learning. Like all learning, this change strategy includes the learning processes of discovery, invention, production and generalisation. Although the phases are described linearly below, in practice they form a recurrent cycle of overlapping learning activities.

Discover theories in use and their consequences

This first step involves uncovering members' mental models or theories in use and the consequences that follow from behaving and organising according to them. Depending on

IF LEARNING IS IMPORTANT, SHOW US THE MONEY!

APPLY YOUR LEARNING

6.1

Corporate education programs enable companies to link the development of their employees to business goals, and many have done so through education partnerships with universities and TAFEs. Reforms in the TAFE and university sectors have ensured the private training providers can capitalise on opportunities to assist corporations in Australasia with their learning needs. By aligning corporate education and training programs with corporate goals, and contracting with specialist education providers, organisations not only ensure greater accountability for their investment in corporate education, but they are also directly linking the development of their employees to the development of the organisation. Organisations with a strategic approach to corporate education provide a non-threatening environment in which employees can contribute ideas and explore innovative products, services and processes.

Corporate education programs delivered in partnership with a university, a TAFE or a private provider also benefit from stretching the level of thinking within an organisation. Some reasons for employer-sponsored corporate education programs include:

→ to provide a mechanism to identify and select leaders and enhance employee retention

→ to enhance an organisation's position as an 'employer of choice' to attract and retain the best available talent in a tight labour market

→ to improve an organisation's ability to compete by improving internal communication and understanding

→ to promote and strengthen the values and culture of an organisation.

A 2017 survey of 500 US corporations by LinkedIn showed reasonable budget commitment to training and development. Only 13 per cent were getting less money that year to train staff. But then only 27 per cent were getting an increase in training funding. Most companies were recommitting to staff learning activities at the same level as the previous year. There are a few ways of looking at this, and some questions arise about how important continuous learning really is to organisations, how much money should be spent on it, and whether the return on investment is real or idealistic.

Sources: Based on J. Ross, 'Training provider crowds out rivals', *The Australian*, 28 March 2012; J. Ross, 'TAFEs in danger of playing second fiddle', *The Australian*, 13 September 2012; K. Loussikian and J. Ross, 'New low for graduates of vocational training', *The Australian*, 10 December 2014; P. Petrone, 'Are you part of the 27% of orgs spending more on learning in 2017?', 17 February 2017, https://learning.linkedin.com/blog/learning-thought-leadership/27-of-companies-are-spending-more-on-learning-in-2017z-heres-wh; and M. Lamson, 'The Leadership Development Trends in 2018', 3 January 2018, https://www.inc.com/melissa-lamson/top-learning-development-trends-for-2018.html.

Critical thinking questions

1 Discuss the value of aligning corporate education and training programs with corporate goals. Is any other kind of education justifiable? Consider how vocational education reform may be linked to this issue.

»

»

2   Research further the theories espoused by Peter Senge and find examples within your own business areas of interest.

3   What kinds of education programs/projects are available within your organisation, or organisations you are familiar with? Do you consider them effective? Why or why not?

4   To what extent does your organisation, or an organisation you are familiar with, encourage staff to contribute ideas? In your opinion, are those encouragements effective? Why or why not?

the size of the client system, this may directly involve all members, such as a senior executive team, or it may include representatives of the system, such as a cross-section of members from different levels and areas.

OL practitioners have developed a variety of techniques to help members identify their theories in use. Because these theories generally are taken for granted and rarely examined, members need to generate and analyse data to infer the theories' underlying assumptions. One approach is called *dialogue*, a variant of the human process interventions described previously.[25] It involves members in genuine exchange about how they currently address problems, make decisions and interact with each other and relevant others, such as suppliers, customers and competitors. Participants are encouraged to be open and frank with each other, to behave as colleagues and to suspend individual assumptions as much as possible. OL practitioners facilitate dialogue sessions using many of the human process tools, such as process consultation and third-party intervention. As a result, group members are encouraged to inquire into their own and others' ways of thinking, to advocate for certain beliefs and to reflect on the assumptions that led to those beliefs. Dialogue can result in clearer understanding of existing theories in use and their behavioural consequences and enable members to uncover faulty assumptions that lead to ineffective behaviours and organising efforts.

A second method of identifying theories in use involves constructing an *action map* of members' theories and their behavioural consequences.[26] OL practitioners typically interview members about recurrent problems in the organisation, why they are occurring, actions that are taken to resolve them and outcomes of those behaviours. Based on this information, an action map is constructed showing interrelationships among the values underlying theories in use, the action strategies that follow from them and the results of those actions. Such information is fed back to members so that they can test the validity of the map, assess the effectiveness of their theories in use and identify factors that contribute to functional and dysfunctional learning in the organisation.

A third technique for identifying theories in use and revealing assumptions is called the *left-hand, right-hand column*.[27] It starts with each member selecting a specific example of a situation where he or she was interacting with others in a way that produced ineffective results. The example is described in the form of a script and is written on the right side of a page. For instance, it might include statements such as 'I told Larry that I thought his idea was good' or 'Joyce said to me that she did not want to take the assignment because her workload was too heavy'. On the left-hand side of the page, the member writes what he or she was thinking but not saying at each phase of the exchange; for example: 'When I told Larry that I thought his idea was good, what I was really thinking is that I have serious reservations about the idea, but Larry has a fragile ego and would be hurt by negative feedback'; 'Joyce said she didn't want to take the assignment because her workload is too heavy, but I know it's because she doesn't want to work with Larry'. This simple yet powerful exercise reveals hidden assumptions that guide behaviour and can make members aware of how erroneous or untested assumptions can undermine work relationships.

A fourth method that helps members identify how mental models are created and perpetuated is called the *ladder of inference*, as shown in **Figure 6.2**.[28] It demonstrates how far removed from concrete experience and selected data are the assumptions and beliefs that guide our behaviour. The ladder shows vividly how members' theories in use can be faulty and lead to ineffective actions. People may draw invalid conclusions from limited experience; their cultural and personal biases may distort meaning attributed to selected data. The ladder of inference can help members understand why their theories in use may be invalid and why their behaviours and organising efforts are ineffective. Members can start with descriptions of actions that are not producing intended results and then back down the ladder to discover the reasons underlying those ineffective behaviours. For example, a service technician might withhold from management valuable yet negative

FIGURE 6.2   THE LADDER OF INFERENCE

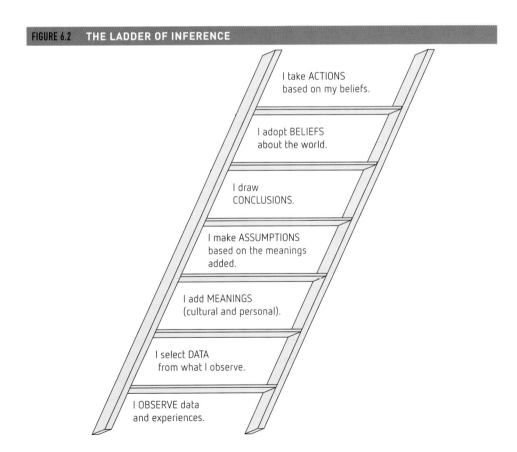

customer feedback about product quality, resulting in eventual loss of business. Backing down the ladder, the technician could discover an untested belief that upper management does not react favourably to negative information and may even 'shoot the messenger'. This belief may have resulted from assumptions and conclusions that the technician drew from observing periodic lay-offs and from hearing widespread rumours that the company is out to get troublemakers and people who speak up too much. The ladder of inference can help members understand the underlying reasons for their behaviours and help them confront the possibility that erroneous assumptions are contributing to ineffective actions.

Invent and produce more effective theories in use

Based on what is discovered in the first phase of this change process, members invent and produce theories in use that lead to more effective actions and that are more closely aligned with Model II learning. This involves double-loop learning as members try to create and enact new theories. In essence, members learn by doing; they learn from their invention and production actions how to invent and produce more effective theories in use. As might be expected, learning how to change theories in use can be extremely difficult. There is a strong tendency for members to revert to habitual behaviours and modes of learning. They may have trouble breaking out of existing mindsets and seeing new realities and possibilities. OL practitioners have developed both behavioural and conceptual interventions to help members overcome these problems.

Behaviourally, practitioners help members apply the values underlying Model II learning – valid information, free choice and internal commitment – to question their experience of trying to behave more consistently with Model II.[29] They encourage members to confront and talk openly about how habitual actions and learning methods prevent them from creating and enacting more effective theories. Once these barriers to change are discussed openly, members typically discover that they are changeable. This shared insight often leads to the invention of more effective theories for behaving, organising and learning. Subsequent experimentation with trying to enact those theories in the workplace is likely to produce more effective change because the errors that invariably occur when trying new things now can be discussed and hence corrected.

Conceptually, OL practitioners teach members *systems thinking* to help them invent more effective theories in use.[30] Systems thinking provides concepts and tools for detecting subtle but powerful structures that underlie complex situations. Learning to see such structures can help members understand previously unknown forces operating in the organisation. This information is essential for developing effective theories for organising, particularly in today's complex, changing world.

Systems thinking generally requires a radical shift in how members view the world: from seeing parts to seeing wholes; from seeing linear cause–effect chains to seeing interrelationships; from seeing static entities to seeing processes of change. Practitioners have developed a variety of exercises and tools to help members make this conceptual shift. These include systems diagrams for displaying circles of influence among system elements; system archetypes describing recurrent structures that affect organisations; computerised micro worlds where new strategies can be tried out under conditions that permit experimentation and learning; and games and experiential exercises demonstrating systems principles.[31]

Continuously monitor and improve the learning process

This final stage involves deuterolearning – learning how to learn. As described earlier, learning is directed at the learning process itself and at how well Model II learning characteristics are reflected in it. This includes assessing OL strategies and the organisational structures and processes that contribute to them. Members assess periodically how well these elements facilitate single- and double-loop learning. They generalise positive findings to new or changing situations and make appropriate modifications to improve OL. Because these activities reflect the highest and most difficult level of OL, they depend heavily on members' capabilities to do Model II learning. Members must be willing to openly question their theories in use about OL; they must be willing to test publicly the effectiveness of both their learning strategies and those of the wider organisation.

BUILDING KNOWLEDGE MANAGEMENT FOR CONTINUOUS CHANGE

The key outcome of OL processes is organisation knowledge. It includes what members know about organisation processes, products, customers and competitive environments. Such knowledge may be explicit and exist in codified forms such as documents, manuals and databases; or it may be tacit and reside mainly in members' skills, memories and intuitions.[32] Fuelled by innovations in information technology, KM approaches have focused heavily on codifying organisation knowledge so it can be readily accessed and applied to organisational tasks. Because tacit knowledge is difficult if not impossible to codify, attention has also been directed at how such knowledge can be shared informally across members and organisational units.

Knowledge and performance

Organisation knowledge contributes to organisation performance to the extent that it is relevant and applied effectively to the organisation's competitive strategy, as shown in **Figure 6.1**. Moreover, organisation knowledge is particularly valuable when it is unique and cannot easily be obtained by competitors.[33] Thus, organisations seek to develop or acquire knowledge that distinctly adds value for customers and that can be leveraged across products, functions, business units or geographical regions. For example, Wal-Mart excels at managing its unique distribution system across a wide variety of regional stores. Honda is particularly successful at leveraging its competence in producing motors across a number of product lines, including automobiles, motorcycles, generators, outboard motors and lawn mowers.[34]

Because organisation knowledge plays a crucial role in linking OL processes to organisation performance, increasing attention is being directed at how businesses can acquire and use it effectively. There are examples of organisations in Australia and around the world, such as IBM, ANZ Bank, Deakin University, Hewlett-Packard and Motorola, which aim to achieve competitive advantage through building and managing knowledge effectively.[35] These knowledge capabilities have been described as 'core competencies',[36] 'invisible assets'[37] and 'intellectual capital',[38] thus suggesting their contribution to organisation performance. Mohrman and her colleagues have looked at organisations through a knowledge lens.[39] They have shown how businesses can fine-tune their organisation designs so that each design element, such as structure, rewards, work design and managerial processes, contributes to creating and leveraging knowledge for competitive advantage.

There is growing emphasis in the accounting profession and in many industries on developing measures that capture knowledge capital.[40] For many organisations, the value of intellectual assets far exceeds the value of physical and financial assets; intellectual assets are usually worth three- to four-times tangible book value.[41] Moreover, the key components of cost in many of today's organisations are research and development, intellectual assets and services, rather than materials and labour, which are the focus of traditional cost accounting. Corporations from industries including but not limited to pharmaceuticals, telecommunications and biotechnologies have developed processes for measuring and managing intellectual capital.[42] When effectively implemented, this enables the firms to manage knowledge almost as rigorously as they manage their tangible assets. The growth of cloud computing has merged a number of issues around education and strategic knowledge, as the example in **Apply your learning 6.2** indicates.

APPLY
YOUR
LEARNING
6.2

MOOCs ARE MOVING

Massive Open Online Courses (MOOCs) have been growing in popularity and the top universities around the world are opening these unique variations of online learning to people everywhere. Advances in cloud technology, the spread of mobile computing and handheld devices, and the continuing relevance of university badging to people engaged in the workforce are some of the attractions of MOOCs. Such courses are also far less costly to students than traditional tertiary education courses, more flexible in delivery, and less disruptive to daily work. A staff member can pick up valuable vocational knowledge in a MOOC without being away from work or having the onerous demand of traditional assignments and exams. The downside is there is no formal qualification at the end of it. However, there are increasing signs that some employers are looking favourably upon the university-badged MOOCs, in addition to appreciating employees' initiative and motivation at gaining job-relevant knowledge from MOOCs. However, there remain some cynics who point out that lip service by employers about training their staff is more common than actually stumping up for staff to upskill by any means, including through MOOCs. Most people enrolled in MOOCs even today are paying their own way.

A *Harvard Business Review* study of 28 000 learners in 127 countries revealed in 2018 some trends relating to MOOCs. Only 15 per cent of people who start a course end up getting certificates of completion when the coursework is not included in performance evaluations. When their MOOC study is included in performance review, then over 50 per cent of students go through to completion, and higher when the company pays for enrolment in the MOOC. Overall, universities are starting to utilise MOOCs as part of their broader offering, but there is suspicion about their long-term benefits for education. Companies are interested in MOOCs to

»

the extent they can provide a cost-effective option for upskilling their staff in key areas. Working people like the flexibility and value MOOCs offer in fast-changing vocational settings.

Sources: Based on T. Dodd, 'Massive Online Open Courses are back and they're threatening universities', *Australian Financial Review*, 12 April 2017; and M. Hamori, 'Can MOOCs solve your training problem?' *Harvard Business Review*, January–February 2018.

Critical thinking questions

1   How could MOOCs be used by firms to manage knowledge almost as rigorously as they manage their tangible assets?

2   Could enrolling staff in MOOCs actually contribute to a firm's success or are they essentially a cost item? Explain your opinion.

3   If organisations are already under-investing in staff development, how might MOOCs help to change that emphasis, or will under-investment simply continue in your opinion?

Application stages

KM approaches are growing rapidly in OD and include a range of change strategies and methods. Although there is no universal approach to KM, the following change processes address the essential steps for generating, organising and distributing knowledge within organisations.

Generating knowledge

This stage involves identifying the kinds of knowledge that will create the most value for the organisation and then creating mechanisms for increasing that stock of knowledge. It starts with examination of the organisation's competitive strategy – how it seeks to create customer value to achieve profitable results. Strategy provides the focus for KM; it identifies those areas where knowledge is likely to have the biggest payoff. For example, competitive strategies that emphasise customer service, such as those found at McKinsey and Nordstrom, place a premium on knowledge about customer needs, preferences and behaviour. Strategies favouring product development, like those at Microsoft and Hoffman-La Roche, benefit from knowledge about technology and research and development. Strategies focusing on operational excellence, such as those at Motorola and Chevron, value knowledge about manufacturing and quality improvement processes.

Once the knowledge required for competitive strategy is identified, organisations need to devise mechanisms for acquiring or creating that knowledge. Externally, organisations can acquire other companies that possess the needed knowledge, or they can rent it from knowledge sources such as consultants and university researchers.[43] Internally, organisations can facilitate *communities of practice* – informal networks among employees performing similar work to share expertise and solve problems together.[44] They also can create more formal groups for knowledge generation, such as R&D departments, corporate universities and centres of excellence. Organisations can bring together people with different skills, ideas and values to generate new products or services. Called *creative abrasion*, this process breaks traditional frames of thinking by having diverse perspectives rub creatively against each other to develop innovative solutions.[45]

Organising knowledge

This phase includes putting valued knowledge into a form that organisation members can use readily. It may also involve refining knowledge to increase its value to users. KM practitioners have developed tools and methods for organising knowledge that form two broad strategies: codification and personalisation.[46]

Codification approaches[47] rely heavily on information technology. They categorise and store knowledge in databases where it can be accessed and used by appropriate members. This strategy works best for explicit forms of knowledge that can be extracted from people, reports and other data sources and then organised into meaningful categories called 'knowledge objects' that can be reused for various purposes. The economic rationale underlying this strategy is to invest once in a knowledge asset and then to reuse it many times. Management consulting firms such as McKinsey and Bain extract key knowledge objects from consulting reports, benchmark data and market segmentation analyses[48] and then place them in an electronic repository for people to use. This enables them to apply knowledge assets across various projects and clients, thus achieving scale in knowledge reuse to grow their business.

Personalisation strategies for organising knowledge focus on the people who develop knowledge and on how they can share it person-to-person. This approach emphasises tacit knowledge, which cannot be codified and stored effectively in computerised information systems. Such knowledge is typically accessed through personal conversations, direct contact and ongoing dialogue with the people who possess it. Thus, KM practitioners have developed a variety of methods for facilitating personal exchanges between those with tacit knowledge and those seeking it. For example, Ernst & Young has systems to openly share knowledge via online social networks with a structured knowledge sharing process that harnesses communities and community management tools. This approach encourages staff interaction with sharing of questions and answers in a community of practice setting, with the option of being private or public, moderated or open to everybody. Other companies have used tacit knowledge sharing in various settings. For instance, Bain and Company fostered networking among its employees through transferring people across offices, encouraging the prompt return of phone calls from colleagues, brainstorming sessions and cross-functional project teams. Hughes, Microsoft and Time-Life created 'knowledge maps' that identified valued competencies, skills and knowledge, and showed people where to go and whom to contact to access them.[49]

Distributing knowledge

This final stage of KM creates mechanisms for members to gain access to needed knowledge. It overlaps with the previous phase of KM and involves making knowledge easy for people to find and encouraging its use and reuse. KM practitioners have developed a variety of methods for distributing knowledge, generally grouped as three approaches: self-directed distribution, knowledge services and networks, and facilitated transfer.[50]

Self-directed distribution methods rely heavily on member control and initiative for knowledge dissemination. They typically include databases for storing knowledge and locator systems for helping members find what they want. Databases can include diverse information such as articles, analytical reports, customer data and best practices. Locator systems can range from simple phone directories to elaborate search engines. Self-directed knowledge transfer can involve either 'pull' or 'push' systems.[51] The former lets members pull down information they need, when they need it; the latter makes knowledge available to members by sending it out to them. Fluor Corporation, for example, placed job requirements and career ladder information on its intranet and let employees access the information on an 'as needed' basis.

Knowledge services and networks promote knowledge transfer by providing specific assistance and organised channels for leveraging knowledge throughout the organisation. KM services include a variety of support for knowledge distribution, such as help desks, information systems and knowledge packages. They may also involve special units and roles that scan the flow of knowledge and organise it into more useful forms, such as 'knowledge departments', 'knowledge managers' or 'knowledge integrators'.[52] Knowledge networks create linkages among organisation members for sharing knowledge and learning from one another. These connections can be electronic, such as those occurring in chat rooms, intranets and discussion databases, or they may be personal, such as those taking place in talk rooms, knowledge fairs and communities of practice.

Facilitated transfer of organisation knowledge involves specific people who assist and encourage knowledge distribution. These people are trained to help members find and transmit knowledge as well as gain access to databases and other knowledge services. They may also act as change agents helping members implement knowledge to improve organisation processes and structures. For example, BP's Shared Learning Program includes dedicated practitioners, called 'quality/progress professionals', who coach employees in best practices and how to use them. Other examples are found in diverse areas, such as the construction sector in Ghana.[53]

OUTCOMES OF ORGANISATION LEARNING AND KNOWLEDGE MANAGEMENT

Given the popularity of OL and KM interventions, research about their effects in organisations is growing. The Society for Organizational Learning (http://www.solonline.org) at MIT in the United States is engaged in a variety of research efforts that focus on capacity building, dialogue and other aspects of OL processes. For example, Volvo and IKEA applied learning processes in their implementation of environmentally sustainable organisation designs. Other organisations claim considerable success with the ladder of inference, the left-hand/right-hand column tool and systems thinking. The Canadian Broadcasting Corporation used the left-hand/right-hand column tool to increase collaboration between the English and French radio and TV organisations and to create a new vocabulary for sharing resources. Shani and Docherty reported how OD interventions aimed at designing and implementing OL mechanisms contributed to positive performance outcomes in companies in Israel, Sweden, the United Kingdom and the United States.[54] Studies of transfer of best practices and KM by the American Productivity and Quality Center reveal a number of performance improvements in such companies as Buckman Laboratories, Texas Instruments, CIGNA Property & Casualty and Chevron.[55] Among the reported outcomes were increases in new product sales, manufacturing capacity and corporate profits, as well as reductions in costs, service delivery time and start-up time for new ventures. A study of 40 firms in Europe, Japan and the United States found that in contrast to poorer performing companies, higher performing firms were better at creating, distributing and applying knowledge.[56] A recent study of KM in 131 Korean companies showed that those that combined strategies for managing both internal-oriented tacit knowledge and external-oriented objective knowledge performed the best.[57]

Despite these success stories, there appears to be considerable room for improving OL interventions. In the academic area, some questions have been raised about the diminishment of a sense of care and the loss of personal voice among researchers as they work at building organisational knowledge. A longitudinal analysis of Royal Dutch Shell described its rise and fall as a 'premier learning organisation' and questioned whether such a strategy could be institutionalised.[58] Argyris and Schon state that they are unaware of any organisation that has fully implemented a double-loop learning (Model II) system.[59] Accenture, a pioneer in KM, experienced problems applying a standardised KM system across its global operations primarily because it did not take into account local and regional differences in how knowledge is generated and used.[60] A comprehensive study of KM in 431 US and European firms also suggests that organisations may have more problems implementing KM practices than is commonly reported in the popular media.[61] Only 46 per cent of the companies reported above-average performance in 'generating new knowledge'. Ratings were even lower for 'embedding knowledge in processes, products and/or services' (29 per cent) and 'transferring existing knowledge into other parts of the organisation' (13 per cent). Another study of 31 KM projects across 20 organisations revealed that KM contributed to the fundamental transformation of only three of the firms studied.[62] Research continues in advancing economies such as United Arab Emirates and the challenges appear to be similar; low levels of KM awareness and few dedicated organisational positions are among the reasons for the problems.[63] Many of the companies, however, reported operational improvements in product development, customer support, software development, patent management and education and training. Because many of the existing reports of OL and KM outcomes are case studies or anecdotal reports, more systematic research is needed to assess the effects of these popular interventions.

SELF-DESIGNING ORGANISATIONS

Standing on a strong foundation of organisational learning theories, a growing number of researchers and practitioners have called for **self-designing organisations** that have the built-in capacity to transform themselves continually to achieve high performance in today's competitive and changing environments.[64] Mohrman and Cummings have developed a self-design change strategy that involves an ongoing series of designing and implementing activities carried out by

Self-designing organisations: organisations with the capability to alter themselves fundamentally and continuously.

managers and employees at all levels of the organisation.[65] The approach assists members to translate corporate values and general prescriptions for change into specific structures, processes and behaviours suited to their situations. It enables them to tailor changes to fit the organisation and helps them continually adapt the organisation to changing conditions.

THE DEMANDS OF ADAPTIVE CHANGE

Mohrman and Cummings developed the self-design strategy in response to a number of demands facing organisations having to adapt to turbulent environments. These demands strongly suggest the need for self-design, in contrast to more traditional approaches to organisation change that emphasise ready-made programs and see change as a periodic event. Although organisations prefer the control and certainty inherent in traditional change, the five requirements for adaptive change reviewed below argue against this strategy:

1   Adaptive change generally involves altering most features of the organisation and achieving a fit among them and with the organisation's strategy. This suggests the need for a systematic change process that accounts for these multiple features and relationships.[66]

2   Adaptive change generally occurs in situations experiencing rapid change and uncertainty. This means that changing is never totally finished as new structures and processes will have to be continually modified to fit changing conditions. Thus, the change process needs to be dynamic and iterative, with organisations continually changing themselves.[67]

3   Current knowledge about adaptive change provides only general prescriptions for change. Organisations need to learn how to translate that information into specific structures, processes and behaviours appropriate to their situations. This generally requires considerable on-site innovation and learning as members learn by doing – trying out new structures and behaviours, assessing their effectiveness and modifying them if necessary. Thus, adaptive change calls for constant organisational learning.[68]

4   Adaptive change invariably affects many organisation stakeholders, including owners, managers, employees and customers. These different stakeholders are likely to have different goals and interests related to the change process. Unless the differences are revealed and reconciled, enthusiastic support for change may be difficult to achieve. Consequently, the change process must attend to the interests of multiple stakeholders.[69]

5   Adaptive change needs to occur at multiple levels of the organisation if new strategies are to result in changed behaviours throughout the organisation. Top executives must formulate a corporate strategy and clarify a vision of what the organisation needs to look like to support it. Middle and lower levels of the organisation need to put those broad parameters into operation by creating structures, procedures and behaviours to implement the strategy.[70]

APPLICATION STAGES

The self-design strategy accounts for these demands of adaptive change. It focuses on all features of the organisation (for example, structure, human resources practices and technology) and designs them to support the business strategy. It is a dynamic and iterative process aimed at providing organisations with the built-in capacity to change and redesign themselves continually as circumstances demand. This approach promotes organisational learning among multiple stakeholders at all levels of the organisation, providing them with the knowledge and skills needed to transform the organisation and continually improve it.

Figure 6.3 outlines the self-design approach. Although the process is described in three stages, in practice those stages merge and interact iteratively over time. Each stage is described below.

FIGURE 6.3   THE SELF-DESIGN STRATEGY

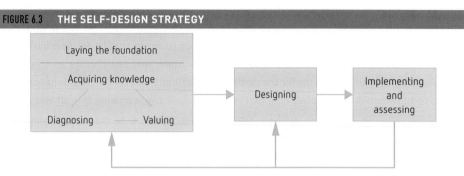

Source: S. Mohrman and T. Cummings, *Self-designing Organizations: Learning How to Create High Performance*, © 1989, p. 37. Reprinted by permission of Pearson Education, Inc., Upper Saddle River, New Jersey.

1 *Laying the foundation.* This initial stage provides organisation members with the basic knowledge and information needed to get started with adaptive change. It involves three kinds of activities. The first is acquiring knowledge about how organisations function, about organising principles for achieving high performance and about the self-design process. This information is generally gained through reading relevant material, attending in-house workshops and visiting other organisations that have adapted themselves successfully. This learning typically starts with senior executives or with those managing the change process and cascades to lower organisational levels if a decision is made to proceed with self-design. The second activity in laying the foundation involves valuing – determining the corporate values that will guide the change process. These values represent those performance outcomes and organisational conditions that will be needed to implement the corporate strategy. They are typically written in a values statement that is discussed and negotiated among multiple stakeholders at all levels of the organisation. The third activity is diagnosing the current organisation to determine what needs to be changed to enact the corporate strategy and values. Organisation members generally assess the different features of the organisation, including its performance. They look for incongruities between its functioning and its valued performances and conditions. In the case of an entirely new organisation, members diagnose constraints and contingencies[71] in the situation that need to be taken into account in designing the organisation.

2 *Designing.* In this second stage of self-design, organisation designs and innovations are generated to support corporate strategy and values. Only the broad parameters of a new organisation are specified; the details are left to be tailored to the levels and groupings within the organisation. Referred to as 'minimum specification design',[72] this process recognises that designs need to be refined and modified as they are implemented throughout the organisation.

3   *Implementing and assessing.* This last stage involves implementing the designed organisation changes. It includes an ongoing cycle of action learning: changing structures and behaviours, assessing progress and making necessary modifications. Information about how well implementation is progressing and how well the new organisational design is working is collected and used to clarify design and implementation issues and to make necessary adjustments. This learning process continues not only during implementation but indefinitely as members periodically assess and improve the design and alter it to fit changing conditions. The feedback loops shown in **Figure 6.3** suggest that the implementing and assessing activities may lead back to affect subsequent activities of designing, diagnosing, valuing and acquiring knowledge. This iterative sequence of activities provides organisations with the capacity to transform and improve themselves continually.

The self-design strategy is applicable to existing organisations requiring change, as well as to new organisations. It is also applicable to changing the total organisation or only some subunits. The way self-design is managed and unfolds can also differ. In some cases, it follows the existing organisational structure, starting with the senior executive team and cascading downwards across organisational levels. In other cases, the process is managed by special design teams that are sanctioned to set broad parameters for valuing and designing for the rest of the organisation. The outputs of these teams are then implemented across departments and work units, with considerable local refinement and modification.

Apply your learning 6.3 shows ways of alleviating stress within the workplace.

WORKPLACES DESIGNED FOR MENTAL HEALTH

APPLY
YOUR
LEARNING
6.3

Fifty of Australia's top corporate leaders met in Sydney in 2017 for Lifeline's National Stop Suicide Summit. Lifeline's CEO said at the Summit that 'not only do organisations have a real responsibility to support their people when they are struggling with life's challenges or thinking about suicide, but it also makes good business sense in creating safe, fulfilling and productive work environments'. The sentiment seemed to be shared by all who attended for discussions about workplace design and coping strategies for this growing corporate challenge.

One industry singled out recently has been mining in Australia, especially the fly-in fly-out (FIFO) workers who travel periodically to remote mining sites for intensive periods of work separated from their families and other communities. A *British Medical Journal* study noted in 2018 as many as one in six people are employed in FIFO positions in some Western Australian and Queensland communities. Furthermore, most FIFO workers are in the demographic of young or middle-aged men, workers who, in all sectors, are at increased risk of mental health problems and suicide. FIFO work is common in construction and mining but not so much in other industries. It involves employees travelling long distances to the worksite, living in company accommodation for the duration of their roster and travelling home between shifts. Work schedules are typically 12-hour shifts for one to four consecutive weeks. It takes the workers away from their home and family networks

»

for intense periods and often involves demanding work in isolated and challenging environmental conditions. The CFMEU recently reported on one company in Darwin subcontracted to the Inpex Ichthys gas project that had lost 14 FIFO staff to suicide since the project commenced in 2012. Surviving workers suggest the real rate could be higher and furthermore, related mental health and stress factors such as divorce rates and stress-related illnesses may not be fully tracked.

So, what are possible work design solutions? According to the 2018 *British Medical Journal* study, organisations should emphasise the importance of good mental health and wellbeing, maintain transparency regarding potential challenges of FIFO lifestyles, and offer professional support for managing multiple social roles and effective communication. According to the 2017 National Stop Suicide Summit, business leaders should publicly pledge to #stopsuicide, contribute to a cross-industry Suicide-Safe Workplaces Action Plan, become representatives in standing groups aimed at suicide prevention, and meet again regularly to review progress.

At the grass roots to minimise work stress, many leading companies have introduced in-house mindfulness, meditation and yoga programs. An earlier study by Ohio State University suggested a weekly combination of meditation and yoga can lower stress by more than 10 per cent, while Dr Ramesh Manocha, a researcher at the University of Sydney, reported in 2009 that meditation over a period of eight weeks reduced occupational stress by 26 per cent. But what can a workplace do, especially if the frontline workers are resistant to 'soft' remedies like yoga, meditation and mindfulness? The first challenge is to accept that mental health issues pose a financial or safety risk to their organisations and to implement counselling and support. Some companies offer employee assistance programs, but there is a level of stigma attached to mental health issues so not every worker will take advantage of such services. Workplace information and communication aimed at taking the cringe out of mental health and growing a culture of acceptance is important. The best-designed strategies to date ensure employees and managers know they can access support through their employee assistance program, as well as from other key resources such as **https://beyondblue.org.au** and **https://www.lifeline.org.au**. Given the high rates of stress-driven problems in many workplaces, managers should continue to consider the consequences of not responding appropriately.

Sources: Based on G. Jerums, 'The business of meditation', *Sunday Herald Sun*, 14 March 2010; P. McLeod, 'Mental disorders shadow the boom', *The Australian*, 4 August 2012; 'Top five: sources of stress', *The Australian*, 22 August 2014; Lifeline, 'Businesses pledge action at "Stop Suicide Summit"', media release, 2 May 2017, https://www.lifeline.org.au/about-lifeline/media-centre/media-releases/2017-articles-1/businesses-pledge-action-at-stop-suicide-summit; J. Thompson and A. Steer, 'Former Inpex worker lambasts FIFO workplace culture after recent death', ABC News, 9 March 2018; and B. Gardner et al., 'Mental health and well-being concerns of fly-in fly-out workers and their partners in Australia: a qualitative study', 2018, bmjopen.bmj.com/content/8/3/e019516.full.pdf.

Critical thinking questions

1 Imagine that you receive data showing the mental health problems described above are common and growing in your own organisation. What would you do, as a manager, at each stage of the self-design strategy diagram in **Figure 6.3** to try to stop the problem getting worse?

2 Is there any value in singling out an industry such as mining for issues of work stress and suicide? Aren't all workplaces undergoing change inherently stressful? Discuss.

BUILT-TO-CHANGE ORGANISATIONS

Another continuous change approach built on an underpinning of organisational learning and KM theory involves designing an entire organisation for change and not just for normal operations. Based on extensive action research at the University of Southern California's Center for Effective Organizations, Lawler and Worley have developed a built-to-change (B2C) approach to designing organisations.[73] It is based on the simple fact that most organisations are designed for stability and dependable operations. Their design elements and managerial practices reinforce predictable behaviours aimed at sustaining a particular competitive advantage. Lawler and Worley argue that many change efforts are unsuccessful, not because of human resistance or lack of visionary leadership, but because organisations are designed to be stable. Such built-in stability can be a recipe for failure in rapidly changing environments. In these situations, the ability to change constantly is the best sustainable source of competitive advantage. The B2C intervention helps organisations design themselves for change.

DESIGN GUIDELINES

The B2C intervention includes guidelines such as the following for how organisation design components can be configured to promote change:

→ *Managing talent.* B2C designs are geared to selecting, developing and managing the right talent for change. Selection practices seek quick learners who want to take initiative, desire professional growth and thrive on change. Employment contracts specify clearly that change is to be expected and support for change is a condition of employment and a path to success. Rather than specific job descriptions, members are encouraged to discover what needs to be done by frequent goal-setting reviews where tasks are constantly assessed and revised. Training and development are continuous and aimed at supporting change and gaining value-added skills and knowledge.

→ *Reward system.* Rewards play a key role in motivating and reinforcing change in B2C organisations. Individual or team bonuses are tied directly to change goals, learning new things and performing new tasks well. This establishes a clear line of sight between rewards and change activities. Bonuses can include one-time rewards given at the end of a particular change effort, or rewards targeted to different phases of the change process. B2C designs also shift the basis of rewards from jobs to people. Members are rewarded for what they can do, not for the particular job they perform. Because jobs and tasks are continually changing, people are motivated to learn new skills and knowledge, thus keeping pace with change and enhancing their long-term value to the organisation.

→ *Structure.* B2C designs emphasise flat, lean and flexible organisation structures that can be reconfigured quickly when the circumstances demand. These organic designs – process, matrix and network structures, for example – put decision making into the hands of those closest to the work and the environment. They enable members to process information, share it with relevant others and make decisions rapidly. Organic designs keep the organisation closely connected with the environment, so that it can detect external changes and create innovative responses to them.

→ *Information and decision processes.* In B2C organisations, information and decision making are moved throughout the organisation to wherever they are needed. These performance-based systems ensure that information is transparent and current and that it provides a clear picture of how the organisation is performing relative to its competitors. They enable organisations to make timely and relevant decisions to keep pace with changing conditions.

→ *Leadership.* B2C designs stress the importance of shared leadership throughout the organisation. Rather than having the organisation rely on centralised sources of power and control, these designs spread leadership across multiple levels of the organisation. This speeds decision making and response rates because those lower in the organisation need not have to wait for top-down direction. It provides leadership experience and skills to a broad array of members, thus developing a strong cadre of leadership talent. Shared leadership supports continuous change by spreading change expertise and commitment across the organisation. It increases the chances that competent leaders will be there to keep the change process moving forward. **Apply your learning 6.4** describes the experience of mentoring in a legal company.

APPLY
YOUR
LEARNING
6.4

MENTORING FOR CHANGE

Mentoring is noted for facilitating professional development and change in a variety of industry and professional settings.

The WA Chamber of Commerce and Industry is a champion of mentoring when it comes to ensuring training and development of apprentices is engaging and successful. The chamber's Apprenticeship Solutions Centre found during 2014 that mentoring programs in workplaces contributed to apprentice retention rates rising from 68.4 per cent to 89.7 per cent. Workforce development services manager at the WA Chamber of Commerce, Lena Constantine, said: 'Apprentices are a hugely important part of the business equation – they make up the talent pipeline and will provide future leaders to fulfil a company's workforce needs. More companies are recognising that you should never stop training regardless of the economic conditions.'

A similar story was found at the Chamber of Minerals and Energy where formal and informal mentoring of first-year apprentices reversed the situation of falling apprenticeship numbers, and instead increased numbers by 9.3 per cent in the 12 months to 30 September 2014. Manager of people strategies at the Chamber of Minerals and Energy, Emmanuel Hondros, observed: 'Many of the companies will pair young apprentices with older apprentices, while others will bring in high-profile mentors to attract and inspire under-represented sections of the community into trades that are critical to the sector. There are benefits for everyone when these types of programs are in place, particularly when it comes to soft skills such as relationship building.' The supplier and distributor of heavy earthmoving equipment to the mining and construction industry sectors, Komatsu Australia, has adopted the strategy of signing well-known champion race driver Jamie Whincup to take 200 apprentices under his wing. Whincup said: 'By mentoring them throughout this first

»

»

stage we are helping them to develop the skills they need to go on to be the best in their fields.'

Adelaide law firm Duncan Basheer Hannon has over 30 solicitors practising in a variety of corporate, commercial, hospitality and personal injury law, as well as approximately 40 professional and support staff.

Its most experienced consultant, Max Basheer, practised into his eighties, keeping up a case load and making a point to help less experienced staff.

His willingness to pass on his knowledge proved an invaluable asset to solicitor Stella Kassapidis. She said the move from Flinders University into working full-time in law had been a steep learning curve, but she was grateful for the support of the more experienced staff to help her move forward in her career, both personally and for the company.

The support included a strong working relationship with Mr Basheer, who made a point from day one to encourage her to seek his guidance if she needed it, she said.

She feels her skills and talents are valued by more experienced staff, 'It's a great place to work and I'm looking to stay here long-term. It's really going to benefit my career.'

General Manager Steve Nollis came to the firm with a few decades' experience from other fields.

He said the people and culture of the firm attracted him to the position. 'I'm impressed with the diversity of the group, the professionalism of the group and the can-do attitude.'

Sources: Based on C. Jenkin, 'Maximum rewards', *The Adelaide Advertiser*, 13 March 2010; and MyPrecinct, 'Mentors lead by example', *The West Australian*, 12 February 2015.

Critical thinking questions

1   How does this application support the 'built-to-change' intervention definition?

2   What difficulties can you anticipate arising in mentoring situations and how may they be avoided?

3   The examples outlined above illustrate mentoring in established organisations. How could a similar approach be applied in a start-up business?

APPLICATION STAGES

Lawler and Worley stress that not all organisations should be built to change, though most could benefit from applying some B2C principles. This intervention is mainly for organisations having problems adapting to complex and rapidly changing environments. For them, the following five initiatives can help the transition to a B2C organisation:

1   *Create a change-friendly identity.* This first stage addresses organisation identity – the established set of core values, norms and beliefs shared by organisation members. Similar to organisation culture, identity is the most stable part of an organisation; it is deep-seated, taken for granted and guides decisions and behaviours like an invisible hand.

Organisation identity can promote or hinder the transition to B2C depending on whether it supports change or stability. In many traditionally designed organisations, values and norms reinforce stability and predictability, thus making change difficult. To move towards a change-friendly identity requires surfacing existing values and norms, assessing their relevance to change and making appropriate adjustments. This typically involves highly interactive sessions where relevant stakeholders openly discuss and debate questions about the organisation's identity and how it can be 'reframed' to be more change friendly. Attention is directed at creating values and norms that focus behaviour on the organisation's environment and help members see change as necessary and natural. To enhance member commitment to a new change-friendly identity, these new or reframed values and norms are placed in the context of important external pressures facing the organisation and what these mean for its effectiveness. The organisation's existing design is also assessed in relation to the new identity and plans are made for changing specific components using the B2C guidelines outlined above.

2   *Pursue proximity.* This step helps the organisation get closer to current and possible future environments. Starting from the organisation's identity, the intervention looks outward to gain a clearer picture of environmental demands and opportunities. Rather than try to predict what is going to happen, attention is directed at developing scenarios of possible and desired future environments. Senior executives commit significant time to thinking about the future and to creating possible paths to future success using various scenario-planning methods. They identify how the organisation's core competencies and capabilities can contribute to making desired futures happen. This is then translated into a robust strategy for what needs to be done to move the organisation and the competitive environment in the desired directions.

3   *Build an orchestration capability.* This stage helps the organisation gain the ability to implement the strategy and to execute change effectively. It first specifies the events and decisions necessary to make the strategy happen, including how new competencies will be developed, if necessary. Then, based on the B2C belief that the ability to change is the key to competitive advantage, attention is directed at building this change capability into the organisation. This involves three related activities. First, change management skills are developed widely in the organisation by hiring people with those skills and by training existing managers and employees to acquire those skills. Second, an organisation effectiveness function is created with competencies in strategic planning, organisation design and change management. This centre of excellence is usually staffed by professionals from the strategic planning and human resources functions; they provide advice and facilitation for planning and executing change in the organisation. Third, organisation members learn how to apply their change capability by engaging in organisational changes and reflecting on that experience. This so-called 'learning by doing' is essential for building an orchestration capability. It provides members with the hands-on experience and reflective learning necessary to hone their change skills in action.

4   *Establish strategic adjustment as a normal condition.* This step involves creating dynamic alignment in implementing strategy, developing new capabilities and fitting

organisation design elements to emerging environmental demands. In fast-paced environments, the organisation must continually make strategic adjustments as part of normal operations. It must constantly work at changing and coordinating all of the organisation design elements so that they promote new strategies and capabilities and respond to shifting environmental demands and opportunities. Keys to making strategic adjustment a standard practice include pushing decision making downward in the organisation, sharing relevant information widely, giving members the relevant skills and knowledge, and measuring and rewarding the right things. These 'employee empowerment' practices reinforce the enormous value placed on human resources in B2C organisations; they also provide the structures, talent and systems to support continual change and adjustment.

5 *Seek virtuous spirals.* This last stage involves bringing all of the prior processes together to pursue a series of temporary competitive advantages. This so-called 'hit and run' approach rests on the logic that in turbulent environments success results from identifying future opportunities, organising to take advantage of them and then moving on to the next opportunity when things change. Because specific sources of competitive advantage do not last long, B2C organisations continually modify their capabilities and designs to take advantage of emerging prospects. They constantly work to balance the short and long runs, to keep close to an unfolding environment and to sustain dynamic alignment among their design elements and capabilities. When they do this for long periods of time, a virtuous spiral results. The organisation's design and capabilities support a successful strategy, which in turn provides the rewards and motivation to create even better designs and capabilities for newer strategies and so on. In rapidly changing environments, B2C organisations are more capable of seeking and creating virtuous spirals than traditional organisations.

SUMMARY

This chapter presented approaches for helping organisations change themselves continually. These change processes are particularly applicable for organisations facing turbulent environments where traditional sources of competitive advantage erode quickly. Building change capabilities directly into the organisation is essential to constantly renew forms of competitive advantage to keep pace with a rapidly shifting environment.

OL and KM approaches help organisations develop and use knowledge to change and improve themselves continually. OL interventions address how organisations can be designed to promote effective learning processes and how those learning processes themselves can be improved. An organisation designed to promote learning can create a continuous stream of valuable knowledge. KM focuses on how that knowledge can be organised and used to improve organisation performance. It is on this basis that other approaches have emerged in the field.

A self-design change strategy helps an organisation gain the capacity to design and implement its own continuous change. Self-design involves multiple levels of the organisation and multiple stakeholders and includes an iterative series of activities: acquiring knowledge, valuing, diagnosing, designing, implementing and assessing.

Built-to-change organisations are designed for change, not stability. They are based on design guidelines that promote change capability in the organisation's talent management, reward systems, structure, information and decision processes and leadership. In a rapidly changing environment, this change capability can be a source of sustained competitive advantage.

ACTIVITIES

REVIEW QUESTIONS

1 How does OL differ from individual learning? (LO1)

2 Explain 'single-loop' and 'double-loop' learning. (LO1)

3 Identify the steps for the application of KM. (LO3)

4 Define 'built-to-change'. Give an example of each component. (LO4)

5 What is the difference between OL and KM? Give an example of each. (LO1 & 3)

6 What are the five requirements for adaptive change? (LO1)

7 Is it easier to develop a self-design strategy for a new business or an existing business? Explain your answer. (LO2)

8 What are the series of activities involved in a self-design change strategy? (LO2)

9 Define and discuss learning organisations. (LO1)

10 What are the options available for designing and building organisations for change? (LO4)

11 Define and explain Model II learning. (LO1)

EXTEND YOUR LEARNING

1 'Self-design change strategies will facilitate optimum competitive advantage.' How may this occur? What difficulties do you envisage? (LO2)

2 'OL and KM are one and the same thing.' Do you agree? Why or why not? (LO1 & 3)

3 Is there a conflict between the concept of a built-to-change organisation and the establishment of long-term business goals? (LO4)

4 The text refers to the use of scenario planning as part of the adaptive process. What are the strengths and weaknesses of this technique, given the premise of this chapter that a growing number of organisations are facing highly turbulent environments? (LO1)

5 Explain the goals and outcomes of KM in changing organisational environments. (LO3)

6 In practice, the self-design process stages merge and interact iteratively over time. If this is so, then discuss why the process should be considered in three stages as outlined in **Figure 6.3**. (LO2)

Search ⊕ Me! **Management**

Explore **Search Me! Management** for articles relevant to this chapter. Fast and convenient, **Search Me! Management** is updated daily and provides you with 24-hour access to full text articles from hundreds of scholarly and popular journals, eBooks and newspapers, including *The Australian* and *The New York Times*. Visit http://login.cengagebrain.com and use the access code that comes with this book for 12 months access to the **Search Me! Management** database. Try searching for the following keywords:

Keywords:

- Organisation learning (OL)
- Knowledge management (KM)
- Self-designing organisations

Search tip: **Search Me! Management** contains information from both local and international sources. To get the greatest number of search results, try using both Australian and American spellings in your searches; for example, 'globalisation' and 'globalization'; 'organisation' and 'organization'.

REFERENCES

1 D. Teece, G. Pisano and A. Shuen, 'Dynamic capabilities and strategic management', *Strategic Management Journal*, 18 (1997): 509–33; O. Schilke, 'On the contingent value of dynamic capabilities for competitive advantage: the nonlinear moderating effect of environmental dynamism', *Strategic Management Journal*, 35 (2014): 179–203; D. Brozovic, 'Strategic flexibility: a review of the literature', *International Journal of Management Reviews*, 20 (2018): 3–31.

2 T. Lawrence, B. Dyck, S. Maitlis and M. Mauws, 'The underlying structure of continuous change', *Sloan Management Review*, 47 (2006): 59–66; S. Jurow, 'Change: the importance of process', *OLA Quarterly*, 8 (2014): 13–14; N. Jacobs, 'Creating enduring social impact: a model for multi-sector transformational change', *ISSS Journals – 60th Meeting*, 1:1 (2018): 1–26.

3 T. Lant, 'Organization learning: creating, retaining and transferring knowledge', *Administrative Science Quarterly* (Winter, 2000): 622–43; M. Crossan, H. Lane and R. White, 'An organizational learning framework: from intuition to institution', *Academy of Management Review*, 24 (1999): 522–37; S. Prokesch, 'Unleashing the power of learning: an interview with British Petroleum's John Browne', *Harvard Business Review* (September–October 1997): 147–68; J.C. Spender, 'Making knowledge the basis of a dynamic theory of the firm', *Strategic Management Journal*, 17 (1996): 45–62; R. Strata, 'Organizational learning: the key to management innovation', *Sloan Management Review*, 30 (1989): 63–74; J. Real, J. Roldán and A. Leal, 'From entrepreneurial orientation and learning orientation to business performance: analysing the mediating role of organizational learning and the moderating effects of organizational size', *British Journal of Management*, 25 (2014): 186–208.

4 D. Teece, 'Capturing value from knowledge assets: the new economy, market for know-how and intangible assets', *California Management Review*, 40 (Spring 1998): 55–79; E. Paiva, E. Revilla Gutierrez and A. Roth, 'Manufacturing strategy process and organizational knowledge: a cross-country analysis', *Journal of Knowledge Management*, 16 (2012): 302–28; L. Flores, W. Zheng, D. Rau and C.H. Thomas, 'Organizational learning: subprocess identification, construct validation, and an empirical test of cultural antecedents', *Journal of Management*, 38 (2012): 640–67.

5 G. Roth, 'The order and chaos of the learning organization', in *Handbook of Organization Development*, ed. T. Cummings (Thousand Oaks, CA: Sage Publications, 2008): 475–97; T. Van Ness, W. Mothersell and J. Motwani, 'Tweddle Group: a case study in blending lean and STS systems', *International Journal of Process Management and Benchmarking*, 5 (2015): 74–89.

6 D.A. Bray, 'Literature review – knowledge management research at the organizational level', May 2007, http://papers.ssrn.com/sol3/papers.cfm?abstract_id=991169.

7 C. Argyris and D. Schon, *Organizational Learning: A Theory of Action Perspective* (Reading, MA: Addison-Wesley, 1978); C. Argyris and D. Schon, *Organizational Learning II: Theory, Method and Practice* (Reading, MA: Addison-Wesley, 1996); Senge, *Fifth Discipline*, op. cit.

8 P. Adler and R. Cole, 'Designed for learning: a tale of two auto plants', *Sloan Management Review*, 34 (1993): 85–94; S. Cook and D. Yanow, 'Culture and organizational learning', *Journal of Management Inquiry*, 2 (1993): 373–90.

9 Cook and Yanow, 'Culture and organizational learning', op. cit.; G. Huber, 'The nontraditional quality of organizational learning', *Organization Science*, 2 (1991): 88–115.

10 W. Snyder, 'Organization learning and performance: an exploration of the linkages between organizational learning, knowledge and performance' (unpublished PhD dissertation, University of Southern California, Los Angeles, 1996); B. Shore and G. Zollo, 'Managing large-scale science and technology projects at the edge of knowledge: the Manhattan Project as a learning organisation', *International Journal of Technology Management*, 67 (2015): 26–46.

11 This framework draws heavily on the work of W. Snyder and T. Cummings, 'Organization learning disorders: conceptual model and intervention hypotheses', *Human Relations*, 51 (1998): 873–95.

12 K. Field, P. Holden and H. Lawlor, *Effective Subject Leadership* (London; New York: Routledge, 2000).

13 M. Kormanik, 'Organizational development (OD) interventions: managing systematic change in organisations', April 2009, http://armandojusto.blogspot.com.au/2009/04/organizational-development-od.html.

14 D. Garvin, *Learning in Action* (Cambridge: Harvard Business School Press, 2000); A. Örtenblad, 'What does "learning organization" mean?', editorial, *The Learning Organization*, 25:3 (2018): 150–8.

15 M. McGill, J. Slocum and D. Lei, 'Management practices in learning organizations', *Organizational Dynamics* (Autumn 1993): 5–17; E. Nevis, A. DiBella and J. Gould, 'Understanding organizations as learning systems', *Sloan Management Review* (Winter 1995): 73–85; G. Ramirez, 'Sustainable development: paradoxes, misunderstandings and learning organizations', *The Learning Organization*, 19:1 (2012): 58–76; J.H. Song, D.S. Chai, J. Kim and S.H. Bae, 'Job performance in the learning organization: the mediating impacts of self-efficacy and work engagement', *Performance Improvement Quarterly*, 30 (2018): 249–71.

16 J. Dewey, *How We Think* (Boston: DC Heath, 1933).

17 Argyris and Schon, *Organizational Learning*, op. cit.; Argyris and Schon, *Organizational Learning II*, op. cit.; Senge, *Fifth Discipline*, op. cit.

18 N.Y. Nikolaev and H. Iba, *Adaptive Learning of Polynomial Networks: Genetic Programming, Backpropagation and Bayesian Methods* (New York: Springer, 2006); A. Jain and A. Moreno, 'Organizational learning, knowledge management practices and firm's performance: an empirical study of a heavy engineering firm in India', *The Learning Organization*, 22 (2015): 14–39.

19 D.L. Cooperrider and M. Avital, *Constructive Discourse and Human Organization* (Amsterdam; London: Elsevier JAI, 2004); R. Chiva and J. Habib, 'A framework for organizational learning: zero, adaptive and generative learning', *Journal of Management and Organization*, 21 (2015): 350–68; B. Matthies and A. Coners, 'Double-loop learning in project environments: an implementation approach', *Expert Systems with Applications*, 96 (2018): 330–46.

20 'Looking at Radio's weblogData.root', Connectivity: Spike Hall's RU Weblog, 2 June 2004, http://radio-weblogs.com/0106698/2004/06/02.html.

21 Argyris and Schon, *Organizational Learning II*, op. cit.; Senge, *Fifth Discipline*, op. cit.; P. Senge, C. Roberts, R. Ross, B. Smith and A. Kleiner, *The Fifth Discipline Fieldbook: Strategies for Building a Learning Organization* (New York: Doubleday, 1995).

22 Argyris and Schon, *Organizational Learning II*, op. cit.

23 ibid.

24 Argyris and Schon, *Organizational Learning II*, op. cit.; C. Argyris, *Intervention Theory and Method* (Reading, MA: Addison-Wesley, 1970).

25 Senge, *Fifth Discipline*, op. cit.; B. Urban and E. Gaffurini, 'Social enterprises and organizational learning in South Africa', *Journal of Entrepreneurship in Emerging Economies*, 10:1 (2018): 117–33.

26 Argyris and Schon, *Organizational Learning II*, op. cit.

27 Argyris and Schon, ibid.; Senge et al., *Fifth Discipline Fieldbook*, op. cit.; B. Dumaine, 'Mr. learning organization', *Fortune* (17 October 1994): 147–57.

28 Senge et al., *Fifth Discipline Fieldbook*, op. cit.

29 Argyris and Schon, *Organizational Learning II*, op. cit.; Argyris, *Intervention Theory and Method*, op. cit.

30 Senge, *Fifth Discipline*, op. cit.

31 ibid.

32 M. Polanyi, *The Tacit Dimension* (New York: Doubleday, 1966); I. Nonaka and H. Takeuchi, *The Knowledge-Creating Company: How Japanese Companies Foster Creativity and Innovation for Competitive Advantage* (New York: Oxford University Press, 1995); J. Pollack, 'Transferring knowledge about knowledge management: implementation of a complex organisational change programme',

International Journal of Project Management, 30 (2012): 877–86.

33 M. Sarvary, 'Knowledge management and competition in the consulting industry', *California Management Review*, 41 (1999): 95–107; J. Barney, 'Looking inside for competitive advantage', *Academy of Management Executive*, 9 (1995): 49–61; M. Peteraf, 'The cornerstones of competitive advantage', *Strategic Management Journal*, 14:3 (1993): 179–92; V. Blanco-Mazagatos, E. de Quevedo-Puente and J.B. Delgado-García, 'Human resource practices and organizational human capital in the family firm: the effect of generational stage', *Journal of Business Research*, 84 (2018): 337–48.

34 Snyder, 'Organization learning and performance', op. cit.; M. Del Giudice, E. Carayannis and M. Peruta, 'Wal-Mart and cross-cultural approaches to strategic competitiveness', in *Cross-Cultural Knowledge Management, Innovation*, eds M. Del Giudice, E. Carayannis and M. Peruta, (New York: Springer Science+Business Media, 2012): 103–15.

35 D. Leonard-Barton, *Wellsprings of Knowledge: Building and Sustaining the Sources of Innovation* (Boston: Harvard Business School Press, 1995); Nonaka and Takeuchi, *The Knowledge-Creating Company*, op. cit.; E. Stewart, 'Watson, IBM's game-show winning computer that learns from its mistakes, being used by Australian businesses', ABC News, 2 November 2015, http://www.abc.net.au/news/2015-10-30/watson-ibm-computer-program-helping-australian-business/6898592.

36 C. Prahalad and G. Hamel, 'The core competencies of the corporation', *Harvard Business Review*, 68 (1990): 79–91; S. Tallman, 'Capabilities and capability development', *Wiley Encyclopedia of Management*, 6 (2015): 1–3.

37 H. Itami, *Mobilizing for Invisible Assets* (Cambridge, MA: Harvard University Press, 1987).

38 L. Edvinsson and M. Malone, *Intellectual Capital: Realizing Your Company's True Value by Finding Its Hidden Brainpower* (New York: Harper Business, 1997); T. Stewart, *Intellectual Capital: The New Wealth of Organizations* (New York: Doubleday, 1997); J. Nahapiet and S. Ghoshal, 'Social capital, intellectual capital and the organizational advantage', *Academy of Management Review*, 23 (1998): 242–66.

39 S. Mohrman, S. Cohen and A. Mohrman, 'An empirical model of the organization knowledge system in new product development firms', *Journal of Engineering and Technology Management*, 20 (2003): 7–38; S. Mohrman, 'Designing organizations to lead with knowledge', in *Handbook of Organization Development*, ed. T. Cummings (Thousand Oaks, CA: Sage Publications, 2008): 519–37.

40 Edvinsson and Malone, *Intellectual Capital*, op. cit.; Stewart, *Intellectual Capital*, op. cit.; R. Kaplan and D. Norton, *The Balanced Scorecard* (Boston: Harvard Business School Press, 1996); K. Svieby, *The New Organizational Wealth: Managing and Measuring Knowledge-Based Assets* (San Francisco: Berrett-Koehler, 1977); G. Mehralian, J.A. Nazari and P. Ghasemzadeh, 'The effects of knowledge creation process on organizational performance using the BSC approach: the mediating role of intellectual capital', *Journal of Knowledge Management*, 22:4 (2018): 802–23.

41 Edvinsson and Malone, *Intellectual Capital*, op. cit.; C. Handy, *The Age of Unreason* (Boston: Harvard Business School Press, 1991); R. Huggins and M. Weir, 'Intellectual assets and small knowledge-intensive business service firms', *Journal of Small Business and Enterprise Development*, 19 (2012): 92–113.

42 T. Stewart, 'Intellectual capital', *Fortune* (3 October 1994): 68–74; A. Mention, 'Intellectual capital, innovation and performance: a systematic review of the literature', *Business and Economic Research*, 2 (2012): 1–37; H. Ferenhof, S. Durst, M. Bialecki and P. Selig, 'Intellectual capital dimensions: state of the art in 2014', *Journal of Intellectual Capital*, 16 (2015): 58–100; V.M. Latilla, F. Frattini, A.M. Petruzzelli and M. Berner, 'Knowledge management, knowledge transfer and organizational performance in the arts and crafts industry: a literature review', *Journal of Knowledge Management*, 22:6 (2018): 1310–31.

43 V. Anand, C. Manz and W. Glick, 'An organizational memory approach to information management', *Academy of Management Review*, 23 (1998): 796–809; M. Friesl, 'Knowledge acquisition strategies and company performance in young high technology companies, *British Journal of Management*, 23 (2012): 325–43; J. Casillas, J. Barbero and H. Sapienza, 'Knowledge acquisition, learning, and the initial pace of internationalization', *International Business Review*, 24 (2015): 102–14.

44 E. Wenger, *Communities of Practice: Learning, Meaning and Identity* (Cambridge, UK: Cambridge University Press, 1999), J. Brown and P. Duguid, 'Organizational learning and communities of practice: towards a unified view of working, learning and innovation', *Organization Science*, 2 (1991): 40–57.

45 Leonard-Barton, *Wellsprings of Knowledge*, op. cit.; D. Leonard-Barton and S. Sensiper, 'The role of tacit knowledge in group innovation', *California Management Review*, 40 (Spring 1998): 112–32.

46 M. Hansen, N. Nohria and T. Tierney, 'What's your strategy for managing knowledge?', *Harvard Business Review* (March–April 1999): 106–16.

47 M.H. Boisot, I.C. MacMillan and K. Seok Han, *Explorations in Information Space: Knowledge, Agents and Organization* (Oxford: Oxford University Press, 2007).

48 D. Stroud, *The 50-plus Market: Why the Future is Age-neutral When it Comes to Marketing and Branding* (Sterling, VA: Kogan Page, 2005); J. Wu, J. Tseng, W. Yu, J. Yang, S. Lee and W. Tsai, 'An integrated proactive knowledge management model for enhancing engineering services', *Automation in Construction*, 24 (2012): 81–8.

49 T. Davenport and L. Prusak, *Working Knowledge: How Organizations Manage What They Know* (Boston: Harvard Business School Press, 1998); A. Padova and E. Scarso, 'Managing large amounts of knowledge objects: cognitive and organisational problems', *Knowledge Management Research and Practice*, 10 (2012): 287–95.

50 C. O'Dell and C. Grayson, *If Only We Knew What We Know* (New York: Free Press, 1998); A. Ramírez, V. Morales and D. Aranda, 'Knowledge creation and flexibility of distribution of information', *Industrial Management and Data Systems*, 112 (2012): 166–85.

51 D. Garvin and A. March, *A Note on Knowledge Management* (Boston: Harvard Business School Publishing, 1997).

52 O'Dell and Grayson, *If Only We Knew*, op. cit.

53 ibid.; D-G. Owusu-Manu, D.J. Edwards, E.A. Parn, M.F. Antwi-Afari and C. Aigbavboa, 'The knowledge enablers of knowledge transfer: a study in the construction industries in Ghana', *Journal of Engineering, Design and Technology*, 16:2 (2018): 194–210.

54 A.B. Shani and P. Docherty, *Learning by Design: Building Sustainable Organizations* (London: Blackwell, 2003); A.B. Shani and P. Docherty, 'Learning by design: key mechanisms in organization development', in *Handbook of Organization Development*, ed. T. Cummings (Thousand Oaks, CA: Sage Publications, 2008): 499–518.

55 O'Dell and Grayson, *If Only We Knew*, op. cit.

56 S. Hauschild, T. Licht and W. Stein, 'Creating a knowledge culture', *The McKinsey Quarterly*, 1 (2001): 74–81.

57 B. Choi, S. Poon and J. Davis, 'Effects of knowledge management strategy on organizational performance: a complementarity theory-based approach', *Omega*, 36 (2008): 235–51.

58 E. Boyle, 'A critical appraisal of the performance of Royal Dutch Shell as a learning organization in the 1990s', *The Learning Organization*, 9 (2002): 6–18; G.M. Schwarz, C. Cummings and T.G. Cummings, 'Devolution of researcher care in organization studies and the moderation of organizational knowledge', *Academy of Management Learning & Education*, 16:1 (2017): 70–83.

59 Argyris and Schon, *Organizational Learning II*, op. cit.: 112.

60 Y. Paik and D. Choi, 'The shortcomings of a standardized global knowledge management system: the case study of Accenture', *Academy of Management Executive*, 19 (2005): 81–4.

61 R. Ruggles, 'The state of the notion: knowledge management in practice', *California Management Review*, 40 (Spring 1998): 80–9; J. Connell, A. Kriz and M. Thorpe, 'Industry clusters: an antidote for knowledge sharing and collaborative innovation?', *Journal of Knowledge Management*, 18 (2014): 137–51.

62 Davenport and Prusak, *Working Knowledge*, op. cit.

63 C.M. Siddique, 'Knowledge management initiatives in the United Arab Emirates: a baseline study', *Journal of Knowledge Management*, 16 (2012): 702–23.

64 B. Hedberg, P. Nystrom and W. Starbuck, 'Camping on seesaws: prescriptions for a self-designing organization', *Administrative Science Quarterly*, 21 (1976): 41–65; K. Weick, 'Organization design: organizations as self-designing systems', *Organizational Dynamics*, 6 (1977): 30–46; C. Worley, 'Organizing for agile and sustainable health care: the Alegent Health case', in *Organizing for Sustainable Health Care* (Organizing for Sustainable Effectiveness, 2), eds S. Mohrman and A. Shani (Bingley, UK: Emerald Group Publishing Limited, 2012): 41–75; T. Voelker, K. Niu and G. Miles, 'Finding the best fit: considering the role of novelty in project selection for small businesses', *Small Business Institute Journal*, 7 (2011): 46–62; C.G. Worley, V. Zardet, M. Bonnet and A. Savall, 'The beginnings of agility at Brioche Pasquier', *Global Business and Organizational Excellence*, 35 (2016): 6–24.

65 S. Mohrman and T. Cummings, *Self-Designing Organizations: Learning How to Create High Performance* (Reading, MA: Addison-Wesley, 1989); T. Cummings and S. Mohrman, 'Self-designing organizations: towards implementing quality-of-work-life innovations', in *Research in Organizational Change and Development*, 1, eds R. Woodman and W. Pasmore (Greenwich, CT: JAI Press, 1987): 275–310; S. Mohrman and E. Lawler III, 'Designing organizations for sustainable effectiveness: a new paradigm for organizations and academic researchers', *Journal of Organizational Effectiveness: People and Performance*, 1 (2014): 14–34.

66 E. Beinhocker, 'The adaptable organization', *The McKinsey Quarterly*, 2 (2006): 77–87.

67 P. Lawrence and D. Dyer, *Renewing American Industry* (New York: Free Press, 1983).

68 C. Argyris, R. Putnam and D. Smith, *Action Science* (San Francisco: Jossey-Bass, 1985); C. Lundberg, 'On organizational learning: implications and

opportunities for expanding organizational development', in *Research in Organizational Change and Development*, 3, eds R. Woodman and W. Pasmore (Greenwich, CT: JAI Press, 1989): 61–82; P. Senge, *The Fifth Discipline* (New York: Doubleday, 1990); L.M. Randall, 'Transforming a university: a study of process leadership', *Academy of Educational Leadership Journal*, 16 (2012): 1–20.

69 M. Weisbord, *Productive Workplaces* (San Francisco: Jossey-Bass, 1987); R. Freeman, *Strategic Management* (Boston: Ballinger, 1984).

70 D. Miller and P. Friesen, *Organizations: A Quantum View* (Englewood Cliffs, NJ: Prentice Hall, 1984).

71 D. Byman, *Strengthening the Partnership: Improving Military Coordination with Relief Agencies and Allies in Humanitarian Operations* (Santa Monica, CA: Rand, 2000).

72 G. D'Antona and A. Ferrero, *Digital Signal Processing for Measurement Systems: Theory and Applications* (New York: Springer, 2006).

73 E. Lawler and C. Worley, *Built to Change: How to Achieve Sustained Organizational Effectiveness* (San Francisco: Jossey-Bass, 2006); C. Worley and E. Lawler, 'Designing organizations that are built to change', *Sloan Management Review*, 48 (2006): 19–23.

7

ORGANISATION DEVELOPMENT
INTERVENTIONS: PEOPLE AND PROCESS

After studying this chapter, you should be able to:

1 Discuss the human resource management processes of OD.
2 Describe performance management and appraisal from both individual and group perspectives.
3 Discuss the interpersonal processes of organisation development (OD).

KEY TERMS

Performance management

Performance appraisal

T-groups

Process consultation

This chapter discusses HRM and person-centred factors relating to OD interventions. These change programs are among the earliest in OD and represent attempts to improve people's working relationships with one another. The interventions are aimed at helping group members to assess their interactions and to devise more effective ways of working together. These interventions represent a basic skill requirement for an OD practitioner. In this chapter, we initially discuss HRM interventions that are concerned with the management of individual and group performance: goal setting, performance appraisal and reward systems. Later in the chapter we look at human process interventions aimed at interpersonal relations and group dynamics.

INDIVIDUAL AND GROUP PERFORMANCE

Performance management involves goal setting, performance appraisal and reward systems that align member work behaviour with business strategy, employee involvement and workplace technology. Here are the main elements of performance management explained.

Performance management: an integrated process of defining, assessing and reinforcing employee work behaviours and outcomes.

→ *Goal setting:* Describes the interaction between managers and employees in jointly defining member work behaviours and outcomes. Orienting employees to the appropriate kinds of work outcomes can reinforce the work designs and support the organisation's strategic objectives. Goal setting can clarify the duties and responsibilities associated with a particular job or work group. When applied to jobs, goal setting can focus on individual goals and reinforce individual contributions and work outcomes. When applied to work groups, goal setting can be directed at group objectives and reinforce members' joint actions, as well as overall group outcomes. One popular approach to goal setting is called 'management by objectives'.

→ *Performance appraisal:* Involves collecting and disseminating performance data to improve work outcomes. It is the primary HRM intervention for providing performance feedback to individuals and work groups. **Performance appraisal** is a systematic process of jointly assessing work-related achievements, strengths and weaknesses, but it can also facilitate career development counselling, provide information about the strength and diversity of human resources in the company and link employee performance with rewards.

Performance appraisal: a feedback system involving direct evaluation of individual or work group performance by a supervisor, manager or peers. It involves a systematic process of jointly assessing work-related achievements, strengths and weaknesses.

→ *Reward systems:* Concerned with eliciting and reinforcing desired behaviours and work outcomes. They can support goal-setting and feedback systems by rewarding the kinds of behaviours required, implementing a particular work design or supporting a business strategy. Like goal setting, reward systems can be oriented to individual jobs and goals or to group functions and objectives. Moreover, they can be geared to traditional work designs that require external forms of control or to enriched, self-regulating work designs that require employee self-control. Several innovative and effective reward systems are in use in organisations today.

The personnel or human resources departments of organisations traditionally implement performance management interventions, and personnel practitioners have special training in these areas. Because of the diversity and depth of knowledge required to successfully carry out these kinds of change programs, practitioners tend to specialise in one part of the personnel function, such as performance appraisal or compensation.

A MODEL OF PERFORMANCE MANAGEMENT

Performance management is an integrated process of defining, assessing and reinforcing employee work behaviours and outcomes.[1] Organisations with a well-developed performance management process tend to outperform organisations that don't have this element of organisation design.[2] As shown in **Figure 7.1**, performance management includes practices

FIGURE 7.1   A PERFORMANCE MANAGEMENT MODEL

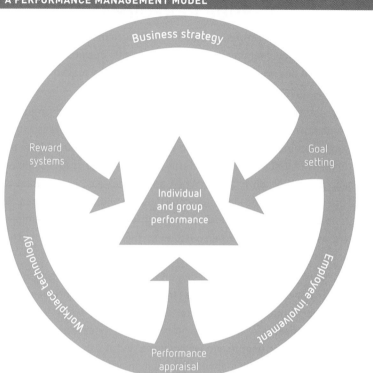

and methods for goal setting, performance appraisal and reward systems, all of which work together to influence the performance of individuals and work groups.

Goal setting specifies the kinds of performances that are desired; performance appraisal assesses those outcomes; and reward systems provide the reinforcers that ensure that desired outcomes are repeated. Because performance management occurs in a larger organisational context, at least three contextual factors determine how these practices affect work performance: business strategy, workplace technology and employee involvement.[3] High levels of work performance tend to occur when goal setting, performance appraisal and reward systems are jointly aligned with the following organisational factors:

→ *Business strategy.* This defines the goals and objectives that are needed if an organisation is to compete successfully. Performance management needs to focus, assess and reinforce member work behaviours towards those objectives, thus ensuring that work behaviours are strategically driven.

→ *Workplace technology.* This affects the decision as to whether performance management practices[4] should be based on the individual or the group. When technology is low in interdependence and work is designed for individual jobs, goal setting, performance appraisal and reward systems should be aimed at individual work behaviours. Conversely, when technology is highly interdependent and work is designed for groups, performance management should be aimed at group behaviours.[5]

→ *Employee involvement.* Finally, the level of employee involvement in an organisation should determine the nature of performance management practices. When organisations are highly bureaucratic with low levels of participation, goal setting, performance appraisal and reward systems should be formalised and administered by management and staff personnel. In high-involvement situations, on the other hand, performance management should be heavily participative, with both management and employees setting goals and appraising and rewarding performance. In high-involvement plants, for example, employees tend to participate in all stages of performance management. They are heavily involved in both designing and administering performance management practices.

GOAL SETTING

Goal setting involves managers and subordinates establishing and clarifying employee goals. In some cases, such as management by objectives, it can also facilitate employee counselling and support. The process of establishing challenging goals involves management in the level of participation and goal difficulty. Once goals have been established, how they are measured is an important determinant of member performance.[6] Goal setting can affect performance in at least three ways: it influences what people think and do as it focuses behaviour in the direction of the goals; goals energise behaviour, motivating people to make an effort to achieve difficult goals that are accepted; and, finally, goal setting leads to persistence in effort over time when goals are difficult but achievable.

Characteristics of goal setting

An impressive amount of research underlies goal-setting interventions and practices.[7] This research has resulted in identification of two major processes affecting positive outcomes:

1 establishment of challenging goals
2 clarification of goal measurement.
   Goal setting appears to work equally well in both individual and group settings.[8]

Establishing challenging goals

The first element of goal setting concerns the establishment of goals perceived as challenging, but which are realistic and will entail a high level of commitment. This can be accomplished by varying goal difficulty and the level of employee participation in the goal-setting process. Increasing the difficulty of employee goals, 'stretch goals' can increase their perceived challenge and enhance the amount of effort necessary for their achievement.[9] Thus, more difficult goals tend to lead to increased effort and performance, as long as they can be regarded as feasible. When set too high, however, goals may lose motivational potential, and employees will give up when failing to achieve them. Another aspect of establishing challenging goals is to vary the amount of employee participation in the goal-setting process. Having employees participate can increase motivation and performance, but only to the extent that members set higher goals than those typically assigned to them.

All three contextual factors play an important role in establishing challenging goals. First, there must be a clear 'line of sight' between the business strategy goals and the goals established for individuals or groups. Second, employee participation in goal setting is more likely to be effective if employee involvement policies in the organisation support it. Third, when tasks are highly interdependent and work is designed for groups, group-oriented participative goal setting tends to increase commitment.[10]

Clarifying goal measurement

The second element in the goal-setting process involves specification and clarification of the goals. Employees tend to perform better when given specific goals than when simply told to 'do their best', or when receiving no guidance at all. Specific goals reduce ambiguity about expectations, and focus the search for appropriate behaviours.

To clarify goal measurement, objectives should be operationally defined. For example, employees may agree to increase productivity by 5 per cent, a challenging and specific goal. Clarifying goal measurement also requires that employees and supervisors negotiate the resources necessary for their achievement. These may include time, equipment, raw materials or access to information.

Contextual factors also play an important role in the clarifying process. Goal specification and clarity can be difficult in high-technology settings. The work is often uncertain and highly interdependent. Increasing employee participation in the clarification of goal measurement can give employees ownership of a non-specific but challenging goal. Finally, the process of specifying and clarifying goals is extremely difficult if the business strategy is unclear. Under these conditions, attempting to gain consensus on the measurement and importance of goals can cause frustration and resistance to change.

Application steps

Based on these features of the goal-setting process, OD practitioners have developed specific approaches to goal setting. The following steps characterise those applications:

1 *Diagnosis.* This provides information about the nature and difficulty of specific goals, the appropriate types and levels of participation and the necessary support systems.

2 *Preparing for goal setting.* Preparation typically involves increased interaction and communication between managers and employees, as well as formal training in goal-setting methods.

3 *Setting goals.* Challenging goals are established and goal measurement is clarified. Employees participate in the process to the extent that contextual factors support such involvement, and because employees are likely to set higher goals than those assigned by management.

4 *Review.* Goal attributes are evaluated to see whether they are energising and challenging, and whether they support the business strategy and can be influenced by the employees.

Management by objectives

A common goal-setting method used in organisations is management by objectives (MBO). This mainly attempts to align personal goals with business strategy by increasing communications and shared perceptions between manager and subordinates, either individually or as a group, or by reconciling conflict.

All organisations have goals and objectives. However, often goals are unclearly stated, and managers and subordinates have different perceptions as to what those objectives are. Management by objectives seeks to resolve these differences in perceptions and goals. It can be defined as systematic and periodic manager–subordinate meetings designed to accomplish organisational goals by mutual work planning, periodic reviewing of accomplishments and mutual solving of problems arising in the course of getting the job done.

Management by objectives originated in two different backgrounds: organisational and developmental. The organisational root of MBO was developed by Drucker, who emphasised the need to establish objectives in eight key areas: 'market standing; innovation; productivity; physical and financial resources; profitability; manager performance and development; worker performance and attitude; and public responsibility'.[11] Drucker's work was expanded by Odiorne, whose first book on MBO stressed the need for quantitative measurement. There is some contention that MBO was a passing fad, but emerging research indicates a possible resurgence of the foundational principles of managing by objectives.[12]

According to Levinson,[13] MBO's second root lies in the work of McGregor, who stressed its qualitative nature, and use for development and growth on the job.[14] McGregor attempted to shift the emphasis from identifying weaknesses to analysing performance in order to define strengths and potentials. He believed this shift could be accomplished by having subordinates reach agreement with their manager on major job responsibilities. Afterwards, they could develop short-term performance goals and action plans for their achievement, allowing self-appraisal of their own performance. Subordinates would then discuss the results of this self-appraisal with their supervisors, thus developing a new set of performance goals and plans. This emphasis on mutual understanding and performance, rather than on personality, would change the supervisor's role from judge to helper, reducing both role conflict and ambiguity. This second MBO root reduces role ambiguity by making goal setting more participative and transactional,[15] as it increases communication between role incumbents and ensures individual and organisational goals are identified and achieved.

An MBO program often goes beyond the one-on-one, manager–subordinate relationship to focus on problem-solving discussions also involving work teams. Setting goals and reviewing individual performance are considered within the larger context of the job. In addition to organisational goals, the MBO process gives attention to individuals' personal and career goals, and tries to make these and organisational goals more complementary. The target-setting procedure allows real (rather than simulated) subordinate participation in goal setting, with open, problem-centred discussions among team members, supervisors and subordinates.

Effects of goal setting

Goal setting appears to produce positive results over a wide range of jobs and organisations. Tested on keypunch operators, logging crews, clerical workers, engineers and truck drivers, and adapted into contemporary team work contexts, goal setting has produced performance improvements of between 11 per cent and 27 per cent.[16] Moreover, four meta-analyses of the extensive empirical evidence supporting goal setting conclude that the proposed effects of goal difficulty, goal specificity and participation in goal setting are generally substantiated across studies and with both groups and individuals.[17] Longitudinal analyses support the conclusion that the profits in performance are not short-lived.[18] At least one major field study, however, failed to replicate the typical positive linear relationship between goal difficulty and performance, raising concern about the generalisability of the method from the laboratory to practice.[19] Additional research has tried to identify potential factors that might moderate the results of goal setting, including task uncertainty, amount and quality of planning, need for achievement, education, past goal successes and supervisory style.[20] Some support for the moderators has been found in this research. For example, when the technical context is uncertain, goals tend to be less specific and people need to engage in more search behaviour to establish meaningful goals.

PERFORMANCE APPRAISAL

Performance appraisal is a feedback system involving direct evaluation[21] of individual or work group performance by a supervisor, manager or peers. Most organisations use some kind of evaluation system for performance feedback, pay administration and, in some cases, counselling and developing employees. One recent study found multinational companies in Australia use performance feedback more than other companies relative to the largest occupational group.[22] An earlier survey of more than 500 companies found 90 per cent used performance appraisal to determine merit pay increases, 87 per cent to review performance and 79 per cent as the opportunity to set goals for the next period.[23] Thus, performance appraisal represents an important link between goal-setting processes and reward systems.

Abundant evidence, however, indicates that organisations do a poor job in appraising employees.[24] One study found that 32 per cent of managers surveyed rated their performance appraisal process as very ineffective and another study suggested that this ineffectiveness may be due to the complexity of tasks being conducted. For instance, services that rely for their production and experience on the clients, and other factors that are hard to control, are especially difficult to enmesh with performance appraisal systems. Companies such as Accenture, Microsoft and Deloitte have even begun eliminating annual performance reviews in favour of 'on demand' conversations between managers and employees.[25] **Apply your learning 7.1** provides commentary about some of the difficulties of providing performance feedback with appropriate sensitivity and in the right spirit. The issue of gender differences is discussed, but consider there are other factors in practice that align to make performance feedback quite a delicate balancing act for managers and staff.

As a consequence of problems associated with performance appraisal, increasingly organisations have sought ways of improving the process. Some innovations have enhanced employee involvement, balancing organisational and employee needs, and enlarging the number of raters (supervisors).[26] Such approaches have been used in organisations such as Levi Strauss, Intel and Monsanto.

The performance appraisal process

Table 7.1 summarises several common elements of performance appraisal systems.[27] For each element, two contrasting features – representing traditional bureaucratic approaches

APPRAISAL AS CRITICISM: A GENDER PERSPECTIVE

The #metoo movement is regarded as contributing to major breakthroughs in the ways that men and women interact, which extends into the workplace. The ways that work performance is perceived and even measured have historically been different for men and women. A Fortune.com study looking at 248 performance reviews made by managers from 28 different companies made some remarkable conclusions. Male staff tended to get far less negative feedback than females, and 76 per cent of the negative feedback given to females included personality criticism. Such criticisms were words like 'abrasive', 'judgemental' or 'strident'. Only 2 per cent of the far fewer negative reviews of males involved personalised comments of this nature.

There are obvious questions, deep ones, around why women in the workplace are receiving personalised appraisals from their managers, even when there is a blend of both female and male managers giving this kind of feedback. Where is the task focus that seems to be afforded mainly to males? Furthermore, while changes have to occur, this will obviously take some re-education and time; therefore, what tools can females deploy to cope and keep shining at work in the face of the challenge of personalised feedback?

The author of the study, linguist and tech entrepreneur Kieran Snyder, explains that many women are aware of the issue. One female consultant to businesses said, 'I know I need a thicker skin, but I have no idea how to get it.' The problem seems linked to generations of socialisation norms for women. Of course, males are also hurt by personal criticism, but historically, females have been socialised to be likable and more concerned with what others think about them. Today, popular media continue to portray those aspects of being female.

A more ingrained social and historical fact is that, for many centuries, females were disempowered physically, legally and financially. Males were the ones afforded the power to manage wealth, travel freely, engage in politics and make decisions on behalf of females.

The law was not designed to protect the individual safety of women, and money and property was not under their control. Therefore, being 'liked' by stronger, more powerful others was an essential protection and survival skill. Some parts of the world persist with such social structures. Today most women in modern economies inherit the psychological legacy of this disempowerment. Males and females alike, when observing a woman behaving in ways that are not traditionally 'likable', will tend to be more personally critical of her and inclined to suggest that she change her personal behaviours, rather than focusing on whether she has actually achieved her work tasks efficiently and effectively. The #metoo movement has highlighted the difficulties women have had pushing back against even the most overt abuses of power by males in the workplace. Of interest is that both men and women fall into the trap at times of marginalising the voices and performances of women at work.

So how can women cope with this reality? Snyder suggests it is important to consciously know that task achievement and working style bring both praise and critique. Avoid the socialised, unconscious expectation that good work will always be praised. The fact is that most good work, creativity and correct decisions are both

»

»

liked and disliked. The task is for women to retrain thinking to expect and accept this. There are some great role models for women who already demonstrate these modern abilities to cope; Snyder recommends observing and emulating them. Also it is useful to think differently about the nature of performance appraisal feedback. Try to interpret it as insights about the person giving the feedback, rather than information about themselves. In other words, a stinging reaction from a manager doesn't tell a woman anything about herself; it just tells her something about what customers and clients of the organisation may require. Such perspective helps filter the feedback required to achieve good work and avoid some of the difficult emotional highs and lows. Snyder believes when a female 'sees the roots of her beliefs and replaces them with a more accurate view of herself, she can free herself from the personal impact of the criticism'.

The contemporary world provides people with freedom and new opportunities; however, the legacy of previous socialisation patterns is everywhere. All genders should be alert, self-reflective and prepared to learn to change. Performance appraisal is a minefield and an opportunity all in one.

Sources: Based on T. Mohr, 'Learning to love criticism', *New York Times*, 28 September 2014; and B. Kessler, C. Corland and Z. Kinias, 'Gender balance: moving from awareness to action', *INSEAD Knowledge*, 27 April 2018.

Critical thinking questions	
1	Discuss why there is an apparent gender difference in the way appraisal feedback is provided to staff by managers.
2	Consider how a performance appraisal process might be modified or controlled to prevent a bias of feedback towards staff of different genders.
3	Think about the proposed solutions for females to cope with the different way they are appraised by their managers. Which ones are the best in your view, and also which solution overall do you think is best in the longer term?
4	Group activity: Form into two teams to debate the topic 'There is an appraisal bias in favour of males'. Appoint a moderator for the debate. Ensure the team arguing each side has a mixture of genders. Allow some preparation time in addition to presentation time. Ensure rules of courtesy are stated and applied throughout the debate.

TABLE 7.1	PERFORMANCE APPRAISAL ELEMENTS	
Elements	**Traditional approaches**	**Newer approaches**
Purpose	Organisational, legal, fragmented	Developmental, integrative
Appraiser	Supervisor, managers	Appraised, co-workers and others
Role of appraised	Passive recipient	Active participant
Measurement	Subjective, concerned with validity	Objective and subjective
Timing	Periodic, fixed and administratively driven	Dynamic, timely and employee- or work-driven

and newer, high-involvement approaches – are presented. Performance appraisals are conducted for several purposes, including affirmative action, pay and promotion decisions, as well as human resource planning and development.[28] Because each purpose defines what performances are relevant and how they should be measured, separate appraisal systems are often used. For example, appraisal methods for pay purposes are often different from systems assessing employee development or promotability. Employees also have several reasons for wanting appraisal, such as receiving feedback for career decisions, getting a raise and being promoted. Rather than expecting a few standard appraisal systems to meet these multiple purposes, the new approaches are more tailored to balance the multiple organisational and employee needs. This is accomplished by actively involving the appraised, their co-workers and managers in assessing the purposes of the appraisal when it takes place, and adjusting the process to fit that purpose. Thus, at one time the appraisal process might focus on pay decisions, another time on employee development and still another on employee promotability. Actively involving all relevant participants can increase the chances that the appraisal's purpose will be correctly identified and understood, and appropriate appraisal methods applied.

The new methods tend to expand the appraiser role beyond managers to include multiple raters, such as the appraised employee, co-workers and others having direct exposure to the employee's performance. Also known as 360-degree feedback, it is used more for member development than compensation purposes.[29] This wider involvement provides a number of different views of the appraised employee's performance. It can lead to a more comprehensive assessment of the employee's performance and increase the likelihood that both organisational and personal needs will be considered. The key task is to find an overall view of the employee's performance that incorporates all the different appraisals. Thus, the process of working out differences and arriving at an overall assessment is an important aspect of the appraisal process. This improves the appraisal's acceptance, accuracy of information and focus on activities critical to the business strategy.

The newer methods also expand the appraised employee's role. Traditionally, the employee is simply a receiver of feedback. The supervisor unilaterally completes a form about performance on predetermined dimensions – usually personality traits, such as initiative or concern for quality. The newer approaches actively involve the appraised in all phases of the appraisal process. The appraised joins with superiors and staff personnel in gathering data on performance and identifying training needs. This active involvement increases the likelihood that performance appraisal will include the employee's views, needs and criteria, along with those of the organisation. This newer role increases employees' acceptance and understanding of the feedback process.

Performance measurement is typically the source of many problems in appraisal as it is seen as subjective. Traditionally, performance evaluation focuses on the consistent use of pre-specified traits or behaviours. To improve consistency and validity of measurement, considerable training is used to help raters make valid assessments. This concern for validity stems largely from legal tests of performance appraisal systems and leads organisations to develop measurement approaches, such as the behaviourally anchored rating scale (BARS) and its variants. In newer approaches, validity is not only a legal or methodological issue but also a social issue, and all appropriate participants are involved in negotiating acceptable ways of measuring and assessing performance. Increased participation in goal setting is a part of this new approach. Rather than simply training the supervisor, all participants are trained in methods of measuring and assessing performance. By focusing on both objective and subjective measures of performance, the appraisal process is better understood, accepted and accurate.

The timing of performance appraisals is traditionally fixed by managers or staff personnel and is based on administrative criteria, such as annual pay decisions. Newer approaches now being used increase the frequency of feedback. Although it may not be practical to boost the number of formal appraisals, the frequency of informal feedback can increase, especially when strategic objectives change or when technology is highly uncertain. In these situations, frequent performance feedback is often necessary to ensure appropriate adaptations in work behaviour. The newer approaches increase the timeliness of feedback and allow employees to have more control over their work.

Effects of performance appraisal

Research strongly supports the role of feedback on performance. One study concluded that objective feedback as a means for improving individual and group performance has been 'impressively effective'[30] and has been supported by a number of literature reviews over the years.[31] Another researcher concluded that 'objective feedback does not usually work, it virtually always works'.[32] In field studies where performance feedback contained behaviour-specific information, median performance improvements were more than 47 per cent, and when the feedback concerned less specific information, median performance improvements were over 33 per cent. In a meta-analysis of performance appraisal interventions, feedback was found to have a consistently positive effect across studies.[33] In addition, although most appraisal research has focused on the relationship between performance and individuals, several studies have demonstrated a positive relationship between group performance and feedback.[34]

REWARD SYSTEMS

Organisational rewards are powerful incentives for improving employee and work group performance. OD has traditionally relied on intrinsic rewards, such as enriched jobs and opportunities for decision making, to motivate employee performance. Early quality-of-work-life interventions were mainly based on the intrinsic satisfaction to be derived from performing challenging, meaningful types of work. Also, OD practitioners have expanded their focus to include extrinsic rewards, such as pay, along with various incentives, such as stock options, bonuses and profit sharing, promotions and benefits. They have discovered that both intrinsic and extrinsic rewards can enhance performance and satisfaction.[35]

OD practitioners are increasingly attending to the design and implementation of reward systems. This attention to rewards has derived in part from research into organisation design and employee involvement. These perspectives treat rewards as an integral part of organisations. They hold that rewards should be congruent with other organisational systems and practices, such as the organisation structure, top-management's human resource philosophy and work designs. Many features of reward systems contribute to both employee fulfilment and organisational effectiveness.

How rewards affect performance

Considerable research has been done on how rewards affect individual and group performance. The most popular model to describe this relationship is the value expectancy theory. In addition to explaining how performance and rewards are related, it suggests requirements for designing and evaluating reward systems.

The value expectancy model[36] posits that employees will expend effort to achieve performance goals that they believe will lead to outcomes that they value. This effort will result in the desired performance goals as long as the goals are realistic, the employees fully understand what is expected of them and have the necessary skills and resources. Ongoing motivation depends on the extent to which attaining the desired performance goals actually results in valued outcomes. Consequently, key objectives of reward systems interventions are to identify the intrinsic and extrinsic[37] outcomes (rewards) that are highly valued and to link them to the achievement of desired performance goals.

Based on value expectancy theory, the ability of rewards to motivate desired behaviour depends on six factors:

1   *Availability.* For rewards to reinforce desired performance, they must be not only desired but also available. Too little of a desired reward is no reward at all.

2   *Timeliness.* A reward's motivating potential is reduced when it is separated in time from the performance that it is intended to reinforce.

3   *Performance contingency.* Rewards should be closely linked with particular performance. If the employees succeed in meeting the goal, the reward must be given; if the target is missed, the reward must be reduced or not given. The clearer the linkage between performance and rewards, the better rewards are able to motivate desired behaviour.

4   *Durability.* Some rewards last longer than others. Intrinsic rewards, such as increased autonomy and pride in workmanship, tend to last longer than extrinsic rewards.

5   *Equity.* Satisfaction and motivation can be improved when employees believe that the pay policies of the organisation are equitable or fair. Internal equity concerns a comparison of personal rewards to those holding similar jobs or performing similarly in the organisation. External equity concerns a comparison of rewards with those of other organisations in the same labour market.

6   *Visibility.* Organisation members must be able to see who is earning the rewards. Visible rewards – such as placement on a high-status project, promotion to a new job or increased authority – send signals to employees that rewards are available, timely and performance-contingent.

Reward systems interventions are used to elicit and maintain desired levels of performance. To the extent that rewards are available, durable, equitable, timely, visible and performance-contingent, they can support and reinforce organisational goals, work designs and employee involvement.

Reward-system process issues

Process refers to how rewards are typically administered in the organisation. At least two process issues affect employees' perceptions of the reward system:

→ who should be involved in designing and administering the reward system

→ what kind of communication should exist with respect to rewards.[38]

Traditionally, reward systems are designed by top managers and compensation specialists and then simply imposed on employees. Although this top-down process may result in a good system, it cannot ensure that employees will understand and trust it. In the absence of trust, workers are likely to have negative perceptions of the reward system. There is growing evidence that employee participation in the design and administration of a reward system can increase employee understanding and can contribute to feelings of control over, and commitment to, the plan.

Lawler and Jenkins described a small manufacturing plant where a committee of workers and managers designed a pay system.[39] The committee studied alternative plans and collected salary survey data. This resulted in a plan that gave control over salaries to members of work groups. Team members behaved responsibly in setting wage rates. They gave themselves 8 per cent raises, which fell at the fiftieth percentile in the local labour market. Moreover, the results of a survey administered six months after the start of the new pay plan showed significant improvements in turnover, job satisfaction and satisfaction with pay and its administration. Lawler attributed these improvements to employees having greater information about the pay system. Participation led to employee ownership of the plan and feelings that it was fair and trustworthy.

Communication about reward systems can also have a powerful impact on employee perceptions of pay equity and on motivation. Most organisations maintain secrecy about pay rates, especially in the managerial ranks. Managers typically argue that employees prefer secrecy. It also gives managers freedom in administering pay as they do not have to defend their judgements. There is evidence to suggest, however, that pay secrecy can lead to dissatisfaction with pay and to reduced motivation. Dissatisfaction derives mainly from people's misperceptions about their pay relative to the pay of others. Research shows that managers tend to overestimate the pay of peers and of people below them in the organisation, and that they tend to underestimate the pay of superiors.[40] These misperceptions contribute to dissatisfaction with pay because, regardless of the pay level of a manager, it will seem small in comparison to the perceived pay level of subordinates and peers. Perhaps worse, potential promotions will appear less valuable than they actually are.

Secrecy can reduce motivation by obscuring the relationship between pay and performance. For organisations that have a performance-based pay plan, secrecy prevents employees from testing whether the organisation is actually paying for performance, so employees come to mistrust the pay system, fearing that the company has something to hide. Secrecy can also reduce the beneficial impact of accurate performance feedback. Pay provides people with feedback about how they are performing in relation to some standard. Because managers tend to overestimate the pay of peers and subordinates, they will consider their own pay low and thus perceive performance feedback more negatively than it really is. Such misperceptions about performance discourage those managers who are actually performing effectively.

It is important to emphasise that both the amount of participation in designing reward systems and the amount of frankness in communicating about rewards should fit the rest of the organisation design and managerial philosophy. Clearly, high levels of participation and openness are congruent with democratic organisations. It is questionable whether authoritarian organisations would tolerate either one.

Apply your learning 7.2 highlights the implications of a reward system that does not adequately focus on the outcomes that matter most.

ROYAL REWARDS INDEED

APPLY YOUR LEARNING **7.2**

The Australian banking royal commission in 2018 provided some insights into problems linked to incentivised financial advice. Many advisers in a number of large financial institutions were found to be profiting from providing bad advice to customers. Commissioner Kenneth Hayne found that a chief challenge for the industry was to reward good behaviour without promoting sales. Performance objectives for financial advisers were not always focused on the quality of the financial product and instead on the quantity of fees that could be pocketed for steering customers towards certain investment decisions. Financial advisers were frequently identified to have given inappropriate advice in order to increase or maintain their share of revenue and increase their monthly bonuses. But, since financial systems are designed around profit and measured on this basis, some commentators pointed out the unsurprising link between performance pay and bad ethics in finance. Fairfax economics editor Ross Gittens observed how financial advisers have 'been jumping whatever hurdles they've had to clear to get the bonuses they were promised.' Many people watching the royal commission probably agreed based on their own work experiences. Bonuses, when offered, might be motivating but they can serve to take the focus off what the right thing to do is and put it instead on achieving, primarily, the stated target. When financial advisers emphasised financial products and targets, it may have been at the expense of less measurable performance outcomes of trust, reliability, veracity of advice, and so on. In the real world it is better to have both qualitative and quantitative performance objectives. The quote sometimes attributed to sociologist William Bruce Cameron was revived in the commentary around the findings of the banking royal commission, 'not everything that can be counted counts, and not everything that counts can be counted'. It would seem that appraising and rewarding the performances of workers is driven somehow by the perspective one takes on performance measurement.

Sources: Based on R. Gittens, 'Banks' misbehaviour shows power of KPIs', *The Sydney Morning Herald*, 24 April 2018; and C. Yeates, 'Westpac adviser's misconduct driven by bonus payments', *The Sydney Morning Herald*, 20 April 2018.

»

>>

Critical thinking questions	
1	Think about the two process issues affecting employee perceptions of the reward system: who should be involved in designing and administering the reward system; and what kind of communication should occur? Discuss the financial advisers example in relation to these questions.
2	What influence do secrecy and communication about remuneration have, whether positive or negative, on motivation in the workplace? Consider whether the workplace for financial advisers is different from other workplaces in this regard.
3	What does the quote by William Bruce Cameron mean in the context of workers in any organisation getting fair reward for work achieved?

INTERPERSONAL PROCESS APPROACH

T-groups: used mainly today to help managers learn about the effects of their behaviour on others, T-groups involve about 10 to 15 strangers who meet with a professional trainer to explore the social dynamics that emerge from their interactions.

Process consultation: a technique for helping group members to understand, diagnose and improve their behaviour. Through process consultation, the group should become better able to use its own resources to identify and solve interpersonal problems.

There are many OD interventions aimed at enhancing the development and empowerment of individuals within organisations. **T-groups** and team building are the techniques most often used to improve employees' communication ability, performance and interpersonal skills in an organisational context, although **process consultation** and third-party intervention can be used under particular circumstances.

→ *T-groups*, derived from the early laboratory training stem of OD, are used mainly today to help managers learn about the effects of their behaviour on others.

→ *Process consultation* is another OD technique for helping group members to understand, diagnose and improve their behaviour. Through process consultation, the group should become better able to use its own resources to identify and solve interpersonal problems that often block the solving of work-related problems.

→ *Third-party intervention* focuses directly on dysfunctional interpersonal conflict. This approach is used only in special circumstances and only when both parties are willing to engage in the process of direct confrontation.

→ *Team building* is aimed both at helping a team to perform its tasks better and at satisfying individual needs. Through team-building activities, group goals and norms become clearer. In addition, team members become better able to confront difficulties and problems and to understand the roles of individuals within the team. Among the specialised team-building approaches presented are interventions associated with ongoing teams as well as temporary teams, such as project teams and task forces.

T-GROUPS

As discussed in Chapter 1, sensitivity training, or the T-group, is an early forerunner of modern OD interventions. Its direct use in OD has lessened considerably, but

OD practitioners often attend T-groups to improve their own functioning. For example, T-groups can help OD practitioners become more aware of how others perceive them and thus increase their effectiveness with client systems. In addition, OD practitioners often recommend that organisation members attend a T-group to learn how their behaviours affect others, and to develop more effective ways of relating to people.

For more information on sensitivity training, see Chapter 1.

What are the goals?

T-groups are traditionally designed to provide members with experiential learning[41] about group dynamics, leadership and interpersonal relations. The basic T-group consists of about 10 to 15 strangers who meet with a professional trainer to explore the social dynamics that emerge from their interactions. Modifications of this basic design have generally moved in two directions. The first path has used T-group methods to help individuals gain deeper personal understanding and development. This intrapersonal focus is typically called an encounter group or a personal-growth group. It is generally considered outside the boundaries of OD and should be conducted only by professionally trained clinicians. The second direction uses T-group techniques to explore group dynamics and member relationships within an intact work group. Considerable training in T-group methods and group dynamics should be acquired before attempting these interventions.

After an extensive review of the literature, Campbell and Dunnette listed six overall objectives common to most T-groups, although not every practitioner need accomplish every objective in every T-group.[42] These objectives are:

1   increased understanding, insight and awareness of one's own behaviour and its impact on others
2   increased understanding and sensitivity about the behaviour of others
3   better understanding and awareness of group and intergroup processes
4   increased diagnostic skills in interpersonal and intergroup situations
5   increased ability to transform learning into action
6   improvements in individuals' ability to analyse their own interpersonal behaviour.

These goals seem to meet many T-group applications, although any one training program may emphasise one goal more than the others.

The results of T-groups

T-groups have been among the most controversial topics in OD, and probably more has been written about them than any other single topic in OD. A major issue of concern relates to the effectiveness of T-groups, and their impact on both the individual and the organisation. Campbell and Dunnette reviewed a large number of published articles on T-groups and criticised them for their lack of scientific rigour.[43] Argyris, on the other hand, criticised Campbell and Dunnette, arguing that a different kind of scientific rigour is necessary for evaluating T-groups.[44] Although there are obvious methodological problems, the studies generally support the notion that T-group training does bring about change in the individual back in his or her work situation.[45] Among the most frequently found changes are increased flexibility in role behaviour; more openness, receptivity and awareness; and more open communication, with better listening skills and less dependence on others. However, because the goals of many T-group designs are not carefully spelled out, because there are so many variations in design, and particularly because many of the research designs do not carefully measure an individual's real work climate and culture, the findings are not highly predictable. Further, some individuals do not attend T-group sessions voluntarily, and little knowledge is available about the differences between those who want to attend and those who are forced to attend.

In considering the value of T-groups for organisations, the evidence is even more mixed. One comparative study of different human process interventions showed that T-groups had the least impact on measures of process (for example, openness and decision making) and outcome (for example, productivity and costs).[46] Another comparative study showed, however, that structured T-groups had the most impact on hard measures, such as productivity and absenteeism.[47] The T-groups in this latter study were structured so that learning could be explicitly transferred back to the work setting. A third comparative study showed that, although T-groups improved group process, they failed to improve the organisational culture surrounding the groups and to gain peer and managerial support in the organisation.[48] Finally, in a meta-analysis of 16 studies, researchers concluded that laboratory training interventions had significant positive effects on overall employee satisfaction and other attitudes.[49]

In his review of the T-group literature, Kaplan concluded that, despite their tarnished reputation, such interventions 'can continue to serve a purpose they are uniquely suited for, to provide an emotional education and to promote awareness of relationships and group process'.[50]

Apply your learning 7.3 provides an example of the steps required to make an informed decision regarding the appropriateness of training.

APPLY YOUR LEARNING 7.3

T-GROUPS FOR HIGH PERFORMANCE

The development of high performance teams that use effective interpersonal relationships is a goal of most organisations and T-groups are one tool to try to achieve this. T-groups are challenging to work with because they are set up with no formal leader, no set task beyond the objective of creating a learning group, and no clear rules of procedure. Can you imagine the ambiguity when a T-group is first established? The Stanford Graduate School of Business has a model for establishing T-groups and provides some guidance in this approach.

A trainer or leader might commence the process with a T-group by stating a general purpose, such as the team is here to learn about itself. Natural thought leaders will start early with their contribution to discussion. Others will soon have thoughts and possible reactions as ideas and personalities of varying strength emerge during the discussion. In the course of a week or more, greater numbers of people interact and group dynamics intensify in complexity. Both positive and

»

»

negative communication exchanges are to be confronted and resolved, ultimately leading to improved awareness, learning and understanding of the individuals in the group. The feedback each individual gets and gives is among the most important outcomes of a T-group. Other benefits of engaging with the emergent process are learning how to raise difficult issues in a productive way, and also finding out how best to connect with others. Since this all happens among workmates who, regardless of real work roles, are not assigned any T-group roles but simply have to socialise and navigate to role agreement, it becomes a most democratic and participatory process. Stanford Graduate School of Business continues to provide its own training courses related to T-groups.

Sources: Based on C. Robin, 'The Power of T-Groups and Experiential Learning', Stanford Graduate School of Business, 2016; and Stanford Graduate School of Business, 'Introductory T-Groups', Stanford Graduate School of Business, 2018, https://www.gsb.stanford.edu/stanford-gsb-experience/learning/leadership/interpersonal-dynamics/facilitation-training-program/intro-tgroups.

Critical thinking questions

1 Do T-groups offer something different from the normal team building experiences common in organisations today? Discuss.

2 What sorts of reactions would you expect among team members in a T-group when it is first created and discussion starts?

3 How exactly would communication ability, performance and interpersonal skills be enhanced by participating in a T-group?

PROCESS CONSULTATION

Process consultation is a general model for carrying out helping relationships in groups.[51] It is oriented to helping managers, employees and groups assess and improve processes, such as communication, interpersonal relations, group performance and leadership. Schein argues that effective consultants and managers are good helpers, aiding others to get things done and achieve the goals they have set.[52] Process consultation is an approach to performing this helping relationship. It is aimed at ensuring that those who are receiving the help own their problems and gain the skills and expertise to diagnose and solve them themselves. Thus, it is an approach to helping people and groups to help themselves. Schein defines process consultation as 'a set of activities on the part of the consultant that helps the client to perceive, understand and act upon the process events which occur in the client's environment'.[53] The process consultant does not offer expert help in the sense of providing solutions to problems as in the doctor–patient model. Rather, the process consultant observes groups and people in action, helps them to diagnose the nature and extent of their problems, and helps them to learn to solve their own problems.

The stages of process consultation follow closely those described for planned change: entering, defining the relationship, selecting an approach, gathering data and making a diagnosis, intervening, reducing the involvement and terminating the relationship. However, when used in process consultation, these stages are not so clear-cut because any one of the steps constitutes an intervention. For example, the process consultant has intervened merely by conducting some preliminary interviews with group members. By being interviewed, the members may begin to see the situation in a new light.

Group process

Process consultation deals primarily with five important group processes:

1 communications
2 the functional roles of group members
3 the ways in which the group solves problems and makes decisions
4 the development and growth of group norms
5 the use of leadership and authority.

Communications

One of the process consultant's areas of interest is the nature and style of communication among group members, at both the overt and covert levels. At the overt level, communication issues involve who talks to whom, for how long and how often. By keeping a time log, the consultant can also note who talks and who interrupts. Watching body language and other non-verbal behaviour can also be a highly informative way of understanding communication processes.[54]

At the covert or hidden level of communication, sometimes one thing is said but another meant, thus giving a double message. Luft has described this phenomenon in what is called the Johari window.[55] **Figure 7.2**, a diagram of the Johari window, shows that some personal

FIGURE 7.2 JOHARI WINDOW	
Unknown to others	**Known to others**
2 Known to self, unknown to others	1 Known to self and others
4 Unknown to self or others	3 Unknown to self, known to others

Source: Adapted from J. Luft, 'The Johari window', *Human Relations Training News*, 5 (1961): 6–7.

issues are perceived by both the individual and others (cell 1). Other people are aware of their own issues, but they conceal them from others (cell 2). In this situation, a person may have certain feelings about themselves or about others in the work group that they do not share with others unless they feel safe and protected; by not revealing reactions that they feel might be hurtful or impolite, they lessen the degree of communication.

Cell 3 comprises personal issues that are unknown to the individual but that are communicated clearly to others. Cell 4 of the Johari window represents those personal aspects that are unknown to either the individual or others. Because such areas are outside the realm of the consultant and the group, focus is typically on the other three cells. The consultant can help people to learn about how others experience them, thus reducing cell 3. Further, the consultant can help individuals to give feedback to others, thus reducing cell 2. Reducing the size of these two cells helps to improve the communication process by enlarging cell 1, the 'self that is open to both the individual and others'.

The climate of the work group can have a great impact on the size of the quadrants in the Johari window, particularly cell 2. Gibb and others have outlined two basic types of climate: supportive and threatening.[56] Threatening climates (those that put the receiver on the defensive) can be of several types, and for each there is a corresponding supportive climate.

→ *Evaluative versus descriptive.* A listener who perceives a statement as evaluative is put on guard. If, on the other hand, the comment is perceived as descriptive and factual, the receiver is more likely to accept the communication.

→ *Control versus problem orientation.* One person's attempt to control another increases the latter's defensiveness. Problem orientation, by contrast, is supportive, as it does not imply that the receiver is somehow inferior.

→ *Strategy versus spontaneity.* Strategy implies manipulation, whereas spontaneity reduces defensive behaviour.

→ *Superiority versus equality.* To the extent that a person assumes a superior role, he or she arouses defensiveness in the other person. Equality is much more likely to result in joint problem solving.

→ *Certainty versus provisionalism.* The more dogmatic a person is, the more defensiveness will be aroused in others. Provisionalism, on the other hand, allows the other person to have some control over the situation and increases the likelihood of collaboration.

Functional roles of group members

The process consultant must be keenly aware of the different roles that individual members take on within a group. Both upon entering and while remaining in a group, the individual must determine a self-identity, influence and power that will satisfy personal needs while working to accomplish group goals. Preoccupation with individual needs or power struggles can severely reduce the effectiveness of a group, and unless the individual can, to some degree, expose and share those personal needs, the group is unlikely to be productive. Therefore, the process consultant must help the group confront and work through these needs.

Two other functions that need to be performed if a group is to be effective are: (1) task-related activities, such as giving and seeking information and elaborating, coordinating and evaluating activities; and (2) the group-maintenance function,[57] which is directed towards holding the group together as a cohesive team and includes encouraging, harmonising, compromising, setting standards and observing. Most ineffective groups do little group maintenance. This is a primary reason for bringing in a process observer. The process consultant can help by suggesting that some part of each meeting be reserved for examining these functions and periodically assessing the feelings of the group's members. The consultant's role is to make comments and assist with diagnosis, but the emphasis should be on facilitating the group's understanding and articulation of its own processes.

Problem solving and decision making

To be effective, a group must be able to identify problems, examine alternatives and make decisions. The first part of this process is the most important. Groups often fail to distinguish between problems (either task-related or interpersonal) and symptoms. Once the group has identified the problem, an OD consultant can help the group analyse its approach, restrain the group from reacting too quickly and making a premature diagnosis, or suggest additional options. The process consultant can help the group understand how it makes decisions and the consequences of each decision process, as well as help diagnose which type of decision process may be most effective in the given situation. Decision by unanimous consent, for example, may be ideal sometimes, but too costly or time-consuming at other times.

Group norms and growth

If a group of people works together over a period of time, it often develops group norms or standards of behaviour about what is good or bad, allowed or forbidden and right or wrong. There may be an explicit norm that group members are free to express their ideas and feelings, whereas the implicit norm is that one does not contradict the ideas or suggestions of certain members (usually the more powerful ones) of the group. The process consultant can be very helpful in assisting the group to understand and articulate its own norms and to determine whether those norms are helpful or dysfunctional. By understanding its norms and recognising which ones are helpful, the group can grow and deal realistically with its environment, make optimum use of its own resources and learn from its own experiences.[58]

Leadership and authority

A process consultant needs to understand the processes of leadership and how different leadership styles can help or hinder a group's functioning. In addition, the consultant can help the leader to adjust his or her style to fit the situation. An important step in that process is for the leader to gain a better understanding of his or her own behaviour and the group's reaction to that behaviour. It is also important that the leader become aware of alternative behaviours.

Basic process interventions

For each of the five group processes described above, a variety of interventions may be used. In broad terms, these interventions may be of the following types:[59]

1   Process interventions, including:
    → questions that direct attention to interpersonal issues
    → process-analysis periods

→ agenda review and testing procedures

→ meetings devoted to interpersonal processes

→ conceptual inputs on interpersonal-process topics.

Process interventions are designed to make the group sensitive to its own internal processes and to generate interest in analysing these processes.

2 Diagnostic and feedback interventions, including:

→ diagnostic questions and probes

→ forcing historical reconstruction, concretisation and process emphasis

→ feedback to groups during process analysis or regular work time

→ feedback to individuals after meetings or data-gathering sessions.

To give feedback to a group, the consultant must first observe relevant events, ask the proper questions and ensure that the feedback is given to the client system in a usable manner. The process consultant's feedback must be specific, timely and descriptive.

3 Coaching or counselling of individuals or groups to help them learn to observe and process their own data, accept and learn from the feedback process, and become active in identifying and solving their own problems.

4 Structural suggestions pertaining to the following:

→ group membership

→ communication or interaction patterns

→ allocation of work, assignments of responsibility or lines of authority.

When is process consultation appropriate?

Process consultation is a general model for helping relationships, and so has wide applicability in organisations. Because process consultation helps people and groups to own their problems and learn how to diagnose and resolve them, it is most applicable when:[60]

1 the client has a problem but does not know its source or how to resolve it

2 the client is unsure of what kind of help or consultation is available

3 the nature of the problem is such that the client would benefit from involvement in its diagnosis

4 the client is motivated by goals that the consultant can accept and has some capacity to enter into a helping relationship

5 the client ultimately knows what interventions are most applicable

6 the client is capable of learning how to assess and resolve his or her own problem.

Results of process consultation

A number of difficulties arise when trying to measure performance improvements as a result of process consultation. One problem is that most process consultation is conducted with groups that perform mental tasks (for example, decision making), and the outcomes of such tasks are difficult to evaluate. A second difficulty with measuring its effects occurs because, in many cases, process consultation is combined with other interventions in an ongoing OD program. Isolating the impact of process consultation from other interventions is difficult. A third problem with assessing the performance effects of process consultation is that much of the relevant research has used people's perceptions as the index of success, rather than hard performance measures. Much of this research shows positive results, including studies in which the success of process consultation was measured by questionnaires.

THIRD-PARTY INTERVENTION

Third-party intervention focuses on conflicts arising between two or more people within the same organisation. Conflict is inherent in groups and organisations and can arise from a variety of sources, including differences in personality, task orientation and perceptions among group members, as well as competition over scarce resources. To emphasise that conflict is neither good nor bad per se is important. It can enhance motivation and innovation and lead to greater understanding of ideas and views. On the other hand, conflict can prevent people from working together constructively; it can destroy necessary task interactions among group members. Consequently, third-party intervention is used primarily in situations in which conflict significantly disrupts necessary task interactions and work relationships among members.

Third-party intervention varies considerably according to the kinds of issues that underlie the conflict. Conflict can arise over substantive issues, such as work methods, pay rates and conditions of employment; or it can emerge from interpersonal issues, such as personality conflicts and misperceptions. When applied to substantive issues, conflict resolution interventions traditionally involve resolving labour–management disputes through arbitration and mediation. These methods require considerable training and expertise in law and labour relations and are not generally considered to be part of OD practice. When conflict involves interpersonal issues, however, OD has developed approaches that help to control and to resolve it. These third-party interventions help the parties to directly interact with each other, facilitating their diagnosis of the conflict and how to resolve it. The ability to facilitate conflict resolution is a basic skill in OD and applies to all of the process interventions discussed in this chapter. Consultants, for example, frequently help organisation members to resolve the interpersonal conflicts that invariably arise during process consultation and team building.

Third-party consultation interventions cannot resolve all interpersonal conflicts in organisations, and nor should they. Interpersonal conflicts are frequently not severe or disruptive enough to warrant attention. At other times, they may simply burn themselves out without any intervention.

An episodic model of conflict

Interpersonal conflict often occurs in iterative, cyclical stages known as 'episodes'. An episodic (or cyclical) model is shown in **Figure 7.3**. At times, the issues underlying the conflict are latent and do not present any manifest problems for the parties. Something triggers the conflict, however, and brings it into the open. For example, a violent disagreement or frank confrontation can unleash conflict behaviour. Because of the negative consequences of conflict behaviour, the disagreement usually becomes latent again, even though it is still unresolved. Once again, something triggers the conflict, making it overt, and so the cycle continues with the next conflict episode. Conflict has both costs and benefits for the antagonists and for those in contact with them. Unresolved conflict can proliferate and expand. An interpersonal conflict

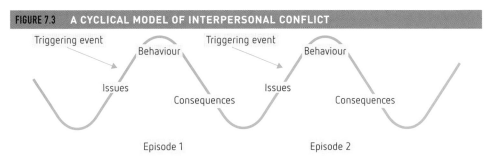

FIGURE 7.3   A CYCLICAL MODEL OF INTERPERSONAL CONFLICT

Source: R.G. Walton, *Managing Conflict*, 2nd edn © 1987, p. 67. Reprinted by permission of
Pearson Education, Inc., Upper Saddle River, New Jersey.

may be concealed under a cause or issue, serving to make the conflict more legitimate. Frequently, the overt conflict is only a symptom of a deeper problem.

The episodic model sets the stage for managers to apply four possible strategies for conflict resolution.[61] The first strategy is to prevent the ignition of conflict by arriving at a clear understanding of the triggering factors and thereafter avoiding or blunting them when the symptoms occur. This may not always be functional and may merely drive the conflict underground until it explodes. As a control strategy, though, this method may help to achieve a temporary cooling-off period.

The second control strategy is to set limits on the form of the conflict. Conflict can be constrained by informal gatherings before a formal meeting or by exploration of other options. It can also be limited by setting rules and procedures that specify the conditions under which the parties can interact.

The third control strategy is to help the parties cope differently with the consequences of the conflict. The third-party consultant may work with the individuals involved to help them devise new coping techniques, such as reducing their dependence on the relationship that is the source of the conflict, airing their feelings to friends and developing additional sources of emotional support. These methods can reduce the costs of the conflict without resolving the underlying issues.

The fourth method is to try to eliminate or resolve the basic issues causing the conflict.

Facilitating the conflict resolution process

Walton has identified a number of factors and tactical choices that can facilitate the use of the episodic model in resolving the underlying causes of conflict.[62] The following elements can help third-party consultants achieve productive dialogue between the disputants so that they examine their differences and change their perceptions and behaviours:

→ mutual motivation to resolve the conflict
→ equality of power between the parties
→ coordinated attempts to confront the conflict
→ relevant phasing of the stages of identifying differences and of searching for integrative solutions
→ open and clear forms of communication and productive levels of tension and stress.

Among the tactical choices identified by Walton are those that have to do with diagnosis, the context of the third-party intervention and the role of the consultant. One of the tactics in third-party intervention is the gathering of data, usually through preliminary interviewing. Group-process observations can also be used. Data gathering provides some understanding of the nature and type of conflict, the personality and conflict styles of the individuals involved, the issues and attendant pressures and the participants' readiness to work together to resolve the conflict.

The context in which the intervention occurs is also important. The neutrality of the meeting area, the formality of the setting, the appropriateness of the time for the meeting (that is, a meeting should not be started until a time has been agreed upon to conclude or adjourn) and the careful selection of those who should attend the meeting are all elements of this context and should be considered. In addition, the third-party consultant must decide on an appropriate role to assume in resolving conflict. The specific tactic chosen will depend on the diagnosis of the situation.

The third-party consultant must develop considerable skill at diagnosis, intervention and follow-up. The third-party intervener must:

→ be highly sensitive to his or her own feelings and to those of others

→ recognise that some tension and conflict are inevitable and that, although there can be an optimum amount and degree of conflict, too much conflict can be dysfunctional for both the individuals involved and the larger organisation

→ be sensitive to the situation and able to use a number of different intervention strategies and tactics when intervention appears to be useful

→ have professional expertise in third-party intervention and be seen by the parties as neutral or unbiased regarding the issues and outcomes of the conflict resolution.

TEAM BUILDING

Team building refers to a broad range of planned activities that help groups to improve the way they accomplish tasks and help group members to enhance their interpersonal and problem-solving skills. Organisations consist of many permanent and temporary groups. Team building is an effective approach to improving teamwork and task accomplishment in these situations. It can help problem-solving groups make maximum use of members' resources and contributions. It can help members to develop a high level of motivation to carry out group decisions. Team building can also help groups overcome specific problems, such as apathy and general lack of interest among members; loss of productivity; increasing complaints within the group; confusion about assignments; low participation in meetings; lack of innovation and initiation; increasing complaints from those outside the group about the quality, timeliness and effectiveness of services and products; and hostility or conflict among members.

Equally importantly, team building can facilitate other OD interventions, such as employee involvement, work design, restructuring and strategic change. These change programs are typically designed by management teams and implemented by various committees and work groups. Team building can help these groups design high-quality change programs. It can ensure that the programs are accepted and implemented by organisation members. Indeed, most technostructural, human resource management and strategic interventions depend on some form of team building for effective implementation.

Team building is not clearly differentiated from process consultation in the OD literature. This confusion stems mainly from the fact that most team building includes process consultation: helping the group to diagnose and to understand its own internal processes. However, process consultation is a more general approach to helping relationships than team building. Team building focuses explicitly on helping groups to perform tasks and to solve problems more effectively. Process consultation, on the other hand, is concerned with establishing effective helping relationships in organisations. It is seen as being essential for effective management and consultation, and can be applied to any helping relationship, from subordinate development[63] to interpersonal relationships to group development. Thus, team building consists of process consultation plus other, more task-oriented interventions.

Dyer has developed a checklist for identifying whether a team-building program is needed and whether the organisation is ready to start such a program (**Table 7.2**).[64] If the problem

TABLE 7.2	TEAM-BUILDING CHECKLIST					
I. Problem identification: To what extent is there evidence of the following problems in your work unit?						
		Low evidence		Some evidence	High evidence	
1	Loss of production or work-unit output	1	2	3	4	5
2	Grievances or complaints within the work unit	1	2	3	4	5
3	Conflicts or hostility between unit members	1	2	3	4	5
4	Confusion about assignments or unclear relationships between people	1	2	3	4	5
5	Lack of clear goals or low commitment to goals	1	2	3	4	5
6	Apathy or general lack of interest or involvement of unit members	1	2	3	4	5
7	Lack of innovation, risk taking, imagination or taking initiative	1	2	3	4	5
8	Ineffective staff meetings	1	2	3	4	5
9	Problems in working with the boss	1	2	3	4	5
10	Poor communications: people afraid to speak up, not listening to each other or not talking together	1	2	3	4	5
11	Lack of trust between boss and members or between members	1	2	3	4	5
12	Decisions made that people do not understand or agree with	1	2	3	4	5
13	People feel that good work is not recognised or rewarded	1	2	3	4	5
14	People are not encouraged to work together in a better team effort	1	2	3	4	5

Scoring: Add the score for the 14 items. If your score is between 14 and 28, there is little evidence that your unit needs team building. If your score is between 29 and 42, there is some evidence but no immediate pressure, unless two or three items are very high. If your score is between 43 and 56, you should seriously think about planning the team-building program. If your score is over 56, then team building should be the top priority for your work unit.

»

»

II. Are you (or your manager) prepared to start a team-building program? Consider the following statements. To what extent do they apply to you or your department?	Low		Medium	High	
1	You are comfortable in sharing organisational leadership and decision making with subordinates and prefer to work in a participative atmosphere	1	2	3	4	5
2	You see a high degree of interdependence as necessary among functions and workers in order to achieve your goals	1	2	3	4	5
3	The external environment is highly variable or changing rapidly and you need the best thinking of all your staff to plan for these conditions	1	2	3	4	5
4	You feel you need the input of your staff to plan major changes or develop new operating policies and procedures	1	2	3	4	5
5	You feel that broad consultation among your people as a group in goals, decisions and problems is necessary on a continuing basis	1	2	3	4	5
6	Members of your management team are (or can become) compatible with each other and are able to create a collaborative rather than a competitive environment	1	2	3	4	5
7	Members of your team are located close enough to meet together as needed	1	2	3	4	5
8	You feel you need to rely on the ability and willingness of subordinates to resolve critical operating problems directly and in the best interest of the company or organisation	1	2	3	4	5
9	Formal communication channels are not sufficient for the timely exchange of essential information, views and decisions among your team members	1	2	3	4	5
10	Organisation adaptation requires the use of such devices as project management, task forces or ad hoc problem-solving groups to augment conventional organisation structure	1	2	3	4	5
11	You feel it is important to bring out and deal with critical, albeit sensitive, issues that exist in your team	1	2	3	4	5
12	You are prepared to look at your own role and performance with your team	1	2	3	4	5
13	You feel there are operating or interpersonal problems that have remained unsolved too long and need the input from all group members	1	2	3	4	5
14	You need an opportunity to meet with your people to set goals and develop commitment to these goals	1	2	3	4	5

Scoring: If your total score is between 50 and 70, you are probably ready to go ahead with the team-building program. If your score is between 35 and 49, you should probably talk the situation over with your team and others to see what would need to be done to get ready for team building. If your score is between 14 and 34, you are probably not prepared to start team building.

Source: W. Dyer, *Team Building: Issues and Alternatives*, 2nd edn, copyright © 1987 by Addison-Wesley Publishing Company, Inc.

is a structural or technical one, an intergroup issue, an administrative mistake or a conflict between only two people, team building would not be an appropriate change strategy.

Team-building activities

A team is a group of interdependent individuals who share a common purpose, have common work methods and hold each other accountable.[65] The nature of that interdependence varies, creating the following types of teams:

→ groups reporting to the same supervisor, manager or executive

→ groups involving people with common organisational goals

→ temporary groups formed to do a specific, one-time task

→ groups consisting of people whose work roles are interdependent

→ groups whose members have no formal links in the organisation but whose collective purpose is to achieve tasks they cannot accomplish as individuals.

Just as there are various types of teams, there are a number of factors that affect the outcomes of a specific team-building activity: the length of time allocated to the activity; the team's willingness to look at the way that it operates; the length of time the team has been working together; and the permanence of the team. Consequently, the results of team-building activities can range from comparatively modest changes in the team's operating mechanisms (for example, meeting more frequently or gathering agenda items from more sources) to much deeper changes (for example, modifying team members' behaviour patterns or the nature and style of the group's management, or developing greater openness and trust).

In general, team-building activities can be classified as follows:

→ activities relevant to one or more individuals

→ activities specific to the group's operation and behaviour

→ activities that affect the group's relationship with the rest of the organisation.

The manager role

Ultimately, the manager is responsible for team functioning,[66] even though the team itself obviously must share this responsibility. Therefore, the development of a team group that can regularly stop to analyse and diagnose its own effectiveness and work process is management's task. The manager has the responsibility of diagnosing (with the team) the effectiveness of the team and taking appropriate action if the work unit shows signs of operating difficulty or stress.

However, many managers have not been trained to perform the data gathering, diagnosis, planning and action necessary for them to continually maintain and improve their teams. Thus, the issue of who should lead a team-building session is a function of managerial capability. The initial use of a consultant is usually advisable if a manager is aware of problems, feels that she or he may be part of the problem and believes that some positive action is needed to improve the operation of the unit, but is not exactly sure how to go about it. Dyer has provided a checklist for assessing the need for a consultant (**Table 7.3**). Some of the questions ask the manager to examine problems and to establish the degree to which the manager feels comfortable in trying out new and different things, the degree of knowledge about team building, whether the boss might be a major source of difficulty and the openness of group members.

Basically, the role of the consultant is to work closely with the manager (and members of the unit) until the manager is capable of actively engaging in team-development activities as a regular and ongoing part of overall managerial responsibilities. Assuming that the manager wants and needs a consultant, the two should work together as a team in developing the initial program, keeping in mind that: (1) the manager is ultimately responsible for all team-building activities, even though the consultant's resources are available; and (2) the goal of the consultant's presence is to help the manager to learn

TABLE 7.3 ADDRESSING THE NEED FOR A CONSULTANT			
Should you use an outside consultant to help in team building?	Circle the appropriate response		
1 Does the manager feel comfortable in trying out something new and different with the staff?	Yes	No	?
2 Is the staff used to spending time in an outside location working on issues of concern to the work unit?	Yes	No	?
3 Will group members speak up and give honest data?	Yes	No	?
4 Does your group generally work together without a lot of conflict or apathy?	Yes	No	?
5 Are you reasonably sure that the boss is not a major source of difficulty?	Yes	No	?
6 Is there a high commitment by the boss and unit members to achieving more effective team functioning?	Yes	No	?
7 Is the personal style of the boss and his or her management philosophy consistent with a team approach?	Yes	No	?
8 Do you feel you know enough about team building to begin a program without help?	Yes	No	?
9 Would your staff feel confident enough to begin a team-building program without outside help?	Yes	No	?

Scoring: If you have circled six or more 'yes' responses, you probably do not need an outside consultant. If you have four or more 'no' responses, you probably do need a consultant. If you have a mixture of 'yes', 'no' and '?' responses, you should probably invite a consultant to talk over the situation and make a joint decision.

Source: W. Dyer, *Team Building: Issues and Alternatives*, 2nd edn © 1987 by Addison-Wesley Publishing Co. Inc.

to continue team-development processes with minimum consultant help or without the ongoing help of the consultant. Thus, in the first stages, the consultant might be much more active in data gathering, diagnosis and action planning, particularly if a one- to three-day off-site workshop is considered. In later stages, the consultant takes a much less active role, with the manager becoming more active and taking on the role of both manager and team developer.

When is team building applicable?

Team building is applicable to a large number of team situations, from starting a new team and resolving conflicts among members to revitalising a complacent team. Lewis has identified the following conditions as best suited to team building:[67]

1   Patterns of communication and interaction are inadequate for good group functioning.

2   Group leaders desire an integrated team.

3   The group's task requires interaction among members.

4   The team leader will behave differently as the result of team building, and members will respond to the new behaviour.

5   The benefits outweigh the costs of team building.

6   Team building must be congruent with the leader's personal style and philosophy.

The results of team building

The research on team building has a number of problems. First, it focuses mainly on the feelings and attitudes of group members. There is little evidence to support the notion that group performance improves as a result of team-building experiences. One study, for example, found that team building was a smashing success in the eyes of the participants.[68] However, a rigorous field test of the results over time showed no appreciable effects on either the team's or the larger organisation's functioning and efficiency. Second, the positive effects of team building are typically measured over relatively short periods. Evidence suggests that the positive effects of off-site team building are short-lived and tend to fade after the group returns to the organisation. Third, team building rarely occurs in isolation. It is usually carried out in conjunction with other interventions that lead to, or result from, team building itself. For this reason, it is difficult to separate the effects of team building from those of the other interventions.[69]

Studies of the empirical literature present a mixed picture of the impact of team building on group performance. One review shows that team building improves process measures (such as employee openness and decision making) about 45 per cent of the time and improves outcome measures (such as productivity and costs) about 53 per cent of the time.[70] Another review reveals that team building positively affects hard measures of productivity, employee withdrawal and costs about 50 per cent of the time.[71] Still another review concludes that team building cannot be convincingly linked to improved performance. Of the 30 studies reviewed, only 10 attempted to measure changes in performance. Although these changes were generally positive, the studies' research designs were relatively weak, reducing confidence in the findings.[72] One review concluded that process interventions, such as team building and process consultation, are most likely to improve process variables, such as decision making, communication and problem solving.[73]

Boss has conducted extensive research on arresting the potential 'fade-out effects' of off-site team building.[74] He proposes that the tendency for the positive behaviours developed at off-site team building to regress once the group is back in the organisation can be checked by conducting a follow-up intervention called a 'personal management interview (PMI)'. This is done soon after the off-site team building and involves the team leader – who first negotiates roles with each member and then holds weekly or biweekly meetings with each member to improve communication – to resolve problems and increase personal accountability.

Buller and Bell have attempted to differentiate the effects of team building from the effects of other interventions that occur along with team building.[75] Specifically, they tried to separate the effects of team building from the effects of goal setting, an intervention aimed at setting realistic performance goals and developing action plans for achieving them. In a rigorous field experiment, Buller and Bell examined the differential effects of team building and goal setting on productivity measures of underground miners. The results show that team building affects the quality of performance, while goal setting affects the quantity of performance. This differential impact was explained in terms of the nature of the mining task. The task of improving the quality of performance was more complex, unstructured and interdependent than the task of achieving quantity. This suggests that team building can improve group performance, particularly on tasks that are complex, unstructured and interdependent.

ORGANISATION PROCESS APPROACHES

This second section of the chapter describes three system-wide process interventions – change programs directed at improving such processes as organisational problem solving, leadership, visioning and task accomplishment between groups – for a major subsystem or for an entire organisation.

1 The first type of intervention, the *organisation confrontation meeting*, is among the earliest organisation-wide process approaches. It helps to mobilise the problem-solving resources of a major subsystem or an entire organisation by encouraging members to identify and confront pressing issues.

2 The second organisation process approach is called *intergroup relations*. It consists of two interventions: the intergroup conflict resolution meeting and microcosm groups. Both interventions are aimed at diagnosing and addressing important organisation-level processes, such as conflict, the coordination of organisational units and diversity. The intergroup conflict intervention is specifically oriented towards conflict processes, whereas the microcosm group is a more generic system-wide change strategy.

3 A third organisation-wide process approach, the *large-group intervention*, has received considerable attention recently and is one of the fastest-growing areas in OD. Large-group interventions get a 'whole system into the room'[76] and create processes that allow a variety of stakeholders to interact simultaneously. A large-group intervention can be used to clarify important organisational values, develop new ways of looking at problems, articulate a new vision for the organisation, solve cross-functional problems, restructure operations or devise an organisational strategy. It is a powerful tool for addressing organisational problems and opportunities and for accelerating the pace of organisational change.

ORGANISATION CONFRONTATION MEETING

The confrontation meeting is an intervention designed to mobilise the resources of the entire organisation to identify problems, set priorities and action targets, and begin working on identified problems. Originally developed by Beckhard,[77] the intervention can be used at any time, but is particularly useful when the organisation is in stress and when there is a gap between the top and the rest of the organisation (such as a new top manager). General Electric's 'WorkOut' program and the approach of Kia Motors in Nigeria are among examples of how the confrontation meeting has been adapted to suit organisations.[78]

What are the steps?

The organisation confrontation meeting typically involves the following steps:

1 A group meeting of all involved is scheduled and held in an appropriate place. Usually the task is to identify problems about the work environment and the effectiveness of the organisation.

2 Groups are appointed, with representatives from all departments of the organisation. For example, each group might have one or more members from sales, purchasing, finance, manufacturing and quality assurance.

3   It must be stressed that the groups are to be open and honest and must work hard to identify problems they see in the organisation. No one will be criticised for bringing up problems and, in fact, the groups will be judged on their ability to do so.

4   The groups are given an hour or two to identify organisational problems. Generally, an OD practitioner goes from group to group, encouraging openness and assisting the groups with their tasks.

5   The groups then reconvene in a central meeting place. Each group reports the problems it has identified and sometimes offers solutions. Because each group hears the reports of all the others, a maximum amount of information is shared.

6   Either then or later, the master list of problems is broken down into categories. This process eliminates duplication and overlap, and allows the problems to be separated according to functional or other appropriate areas.

7   Following problem categorisation, participants are divided into problem-solving groups whose composition may (and usually does) differ from that of the original problem-identification groups.

8   Each group ranks the problems, develops a tactical action plan and determines an appropriate timetable for completing this phase of the process.

9   Each group then periodically reports its list of priorities and tactical plans of action to management or to the larger group.

10 Schedules for periodic (often monthly) follow-up meetings are established. The formal establishment of such follow-up meetings ensures both continuing action and the modification of priorities and timetables as needed.

Results of confrontation meetings

Because organisation confrontation meetings are often combined with other approaches, such as survey feedback, determining specific results is difficult. In many cases, the results appear dramatic in mobilising the total resources of the organisation for problem identification and solution.

Beckhard cites a number of specific examples in such varying organisations as a food-products manufacturer, a military-products manufacturer and a hotel.[79] Positive results were also found in a confrontation meeting with 40 professionals in a research and development firm.[80] The organisation confrontation meeting is a promising approach for mobilising organisational problem solving, especially in times of low performance.

INTERGROUP RELATIONS INTERVENTIONS

The ability to diagnose and understand intergroup relations is important for OD practitioners because:

→ groups must often work with and through other groups to accomplish their goals

→ groups within the organisation often create problems and demands on each other

→ the quality of the relationships between groups can affect the degree of organisational effectiveness.

Two OD interventions – microcosm groups and intergroup conflict resolution – are described here. A microcosm group uses members from several groups to help solve organisation-wide problems. Intergroup issues are explored in this context, and then solutions are implemented in the larger organisation. Intergroup conflict resolution helps two groups work out dysfunctional relationships. Together, these approaches help to improve intergroup processes and lead to organisational effectiveness.

Microcosm groups

A microcosm group consists of a small number of individuals who reflect the issue being addressed.[81] For example, a microcosm group made up of members who represent a spectrum of ethnic backgrounds, cultures and races can be created to address diversity issues in the organisation. This group, with the assistance of OD practitioners, can create programs and processes targeted to specific problems. In addition to addressing diversity problems, microcosm groups have been used to carry out organisation diagnoses, solve communications problems, integrate two cultures, smooth the transition to a new structure and address dysfunctional political processes.

Microcosm groups work through 'parallel processes', which are the unconscious changes that take place in individuals when two or more groups interact.[82] After two or more groups have interacted, members often find that their characteristic patterns of roles and interactions change to reflect the roles and dynamics of the group with whom they were relating. Put simply, one group seems to 'infect' and become 'infected' by the other groups.

What are the steps?

The process of using a microcosm group to address organisation-wide issues involves the following five steps:

1 *Identify an issue.* This step involves finding a system-wide problem to be addressed. This may result from an organisational diagnosis or may be an idea generated by an organisation member or task force.

2 *Convene the group.* Once an issue has been identified, the microcosm group can be formed. The most important convening principle is that group membership needs to reflect the appropriate mix of stakeholders related to the issue. For example, if the issue is organisational communication, then the group should contain people from all hierarchical levels and functions, including staff groups and unions, if applicable. Following the initial set-up, the group itself becomes responsible for determining its membership. It will decide whether to add new members and how to fill vacant positions. Convening the group also draws attention to the issue and gives the group status. Members also need to be perceived as credible representatives of the problem. This will increase the likelihood that organisation members will listen to, and follow, the suggestions they make.

3 *Provide group training.* Group training focuses on establishing a group mission or charter, working relationships between members, group decision-making norms and definitions of the problem to be addressed. Team-building interventions may also be appropriate. From a group-process perspective, OD practitioners may need to observe and comment on how the group develops. Because the group is a microcosm of the

organisation, it will tend, through its behaviour and attitudes, to reflect the problem in the larger organisation.

4 *Address the issue.* This step involves solving the problem and implementing solutions. OD practitioners may help the group to diagnose, design, implement and evaluate changes. A key issue is gaining wider organisation commitment to implementing the group's solutions. The following factors can facilitate such ownership. First, a communication plan should link group activities to the organisation. Second, group members need to be visible and accessible to management and labour. Third, problem-solving processes should include an appropriate level of participation by organisation members.

5 *Dissolve the group.* The microcosm group can be disbanded after the successful implementation of changes. This typically involves writing a final report or holding a final meeting.

The microcosm group intervention derives from an intergroup relations theory developed by Alderfer[83] and has been applied by him to communications and race-relations problems. A dearth of research exists on microcosm groups. This is partly due to the difficulty of measuring parallel processes and associating them with measures of organisational processes.

Resolving intergroup conflict

This intervention is specifically designed to help two groups or departments within an organisation resolve dysfunctional conflicts. Intergroup conflict is neither good nor bad in itself. In some cases, conflict among departments is necessary and productive for organisations. This applies in organisations where there is little interdependence among departments. Here, departments are independent, and conflict or competition among them can lead to higher levels of productivity. In other organisations, especially those with very interdependent departments, conflict may become dysfunctional.[84] Two or more groups may become polarised, and continued conflict may result in the development of defensiveness and negative stereotypes of the other group. It is particularly the case that, when intergroup communication is necessary, the amount and quality of communication usually drops off. Groups become defensive and begin seeing the others as 'the enemy', rather than in either positive or neutral terms. As the amount of communication decreases, the amount of mutual problem solving also falls off. The tendency increases for one group to sabotage the efforts of the other group, either consciously or unconsciously.

What are the steps?

A basic strategy for improving interdepartmental or intergroup relationships is to change the perceptions (perhaps, more accurately, misperceptions) that the two groups have of each other. One formal approach for accomplishing this consists of a 10-step procedure, originally described by Blake and his associates in their grid of OD.[85]

1 A consultant external to the two groups obtains their agreement to work directly on improving intergroup relationships. (The use of an outside consultant is highly recommended because, without the moderating influence of such a neutral third party,

it is almost impossible for the two groups to interact without becoming deadlocked and polarised in a defensive position.)

2 A time is set for the two groups to meet; preferably away from normal work situations.

3 The consultant, together with the managers of the two groups, describes the purpose and objectives of the meeting: the development of better mutual relationships, the exploration of the perceptions the groups have of each other and the development of plans for improving the relationship. The two groups are asked the following or similar questions: 'What qualities or attributes best describe our group?', 'What qualities or attributes best describe the other group?' and 'How do we think the other group will describe us?' Then the two groups are encouraged to establish norms of openness for feedback and discussion.

4 The two groups are then placed in separate rooms and asked to write their answers to the three questions. Usually, an outside consultant works with each group to help the members become more open and to encourage them to develop lists that accurately reflect their perceptions of their own image and of the other group.

5 After completing their lists, the two groups come together again. A representative from each group presents the written statements. Only the two representatives are allowed to speak. The primary objective at this stage is to make certain that the images, perceptions and attitudes are presented as accurately as possible and to avoid the arguments that might arise if the two groups openly confronted each other. Questions, however, are allowed to ensure that both groups clearly understand the written lists. Justifications, accusations or other statements are not permitted.

6 When it is clear that the two groups thoroughly understand the content of the lists, they again separate. By this time, a great number of misperceptions and discrepancies have already been brought to light.

7 The task of the two groups (almost always with a consultant as a process observer) is to analyse and review the reasons for the discrepancies. The emphasis is on solving the problems and reducing the misperceptions.

8 When the two groups have worked through the discrepancies, as well as the areas of common agreement, they meet to share both the identified discrepancies and their problem-solving approaches to those discrepancies.

9 The two groups are then asked to develop specific plans of action for solving specific problems and for improving their relationships.

10 When the two groups have gone as far as possible in formulating action plans, at least one follow-up meeting is scheduled so that the two groups can report on actions that have been implemented, identify any further problems that have emerged and, where necessary, formulate additional action plans.

In addition to this formal approach to improving interdepartmental or intergroup relationships, there are a number of more informal procedures. Beckhard asks each of the two groups to develop a list of what irritates or exasperates them about the other group and to predict what they think the other group will say about them.[86]

Different approaches to resolving intergroup conflict form a continuum varying from behavioural solutions to attitudinal change solutions.[87] Behavioural methods are oriented to keeping the relevant parties physically separate and specifying the limited conditions under which interaction will occur. Little attempt is made to understand or to change how members of each group see the other. Conversely, attitudinal methods – such as exchanging group members or requiring intense interaction with important rewards or opportunities clearly tied to coordination – are directed at changing how each group perceives the other. Here, it is assumed that perceptual distortions and stereotyping underlie the conflict and need to be changed to resolve it.

Most of the OD solutions to intergroup conflict reviewed in this section favour attitudinal change strategies. However, these interventions typically require considerably more skill and time than the behavioural solutions. Changing attitudes can be quite difficult in conflict situations, especially if the attitudes are deep-seated and form an integral part of people's personalities. Attitudinal change interventions should be reserved for those situations in which behavioural solutions might not work.

Results of intergroup conflict interventions

Several studies have been done on the effects of intergroup conflict resolution. In his original study, Blake reported vastly improved relationships between the union and management.[88] In a later study, Bennis used Blake's basic design to improve relationships between two groups of State Department officials: high-level administrative officers and officers in the Foreign Service.[89] Initially, there was much mutual distrust, negative stereotyping, blocked communication and hostility between the two groups: 'Each side perceived the other as more threatening than any realistic overseas enemy.'[90] Although no hard data were obtained, the intervention seemed to improve relationships so that the two groups 'at least understood the other side's point of view'.

Golembiewski and Blumberg used a modification of the Blake design that involved an exchange of 'images' among both organisational units and individuals in the marketing division of a large organisation.[91] An attitude questionnaire was used to make before-and-after comparisons. The results were found to be different for more or less 'deeply involved' individuals or units. In general, the more deeply involved individuals or units (promotion, regions and divisions, and sales) reflected more positive attitudes towards collaboration and had greater feelings of commitment to the success of the entire organisation. Less deeply involved positions or units (such areas as sales training, hospital sales and trade relations) did not show any particular trends in attitudinal changes, either positive or negative.

French and Bell, who used a somewhat similar design, reported that they were able to work successfully with three groups simultaneously.[92] They obtained positive results in their work with key groups in a Native American organisation: the tribal council, the tribal staff and the Community Action Program (CAP).[93] The researchers asked each group to develop perceptions of the other two, as well as of itself, and to share those perceptions in the larger group. The tribal council developed four lists: both favourable and unfavourable items about the tribal staff, a similar list about the CAP, and predictions as to what the staff and

CAP, respectively, would say about the council. Once each group had developed its lists, the results were shared in a three-group meeting, and the similarities and dissimilarities in the various lists worked through. According to the researchers, the use of this method reduces intergroup problems and friction while increasing communications and interactions.

Huse and Beer and others have described positive results arising from periodic cross-departmental meetings, whereby personnel within one department would meet, in sequence, with those from other departments to discuss perceptions, expectations and strong and weak points about one another.[94] In another study, Huse found that bringing representatives of different groups together to work on common work-related problems had a marked effect not only on relationships among a number of different manufacturing groups but also on the quality of the product, which increased by 62 per cent.[95] The basic tactic in this study was to ensure that representatives of two or more groups worked jointly on each work-related problem.

Based on their experience at TRW Systems, Fordyce and Weil developed a modified approach whereby each group builds three lists: one containing 'positive feedback' items (those things the group values and likes about the other group), a 'bug' list (those things the group dislikes about the other group) and an 'empathy' list (predictions about what the other group's list would contain).[96] When the groups come together, they build a master list of major concerns and unresolved problems, which are assigned priorities and developed into an agenda. When they have completed the task, the subgroups report the results of their discussions to the total group, which then develops a series of action steps for improving the relations between the groups and commits itself to following through. For each action step, specific responsibilities are assigned and an overall schedule developed for prompt completion of the action steps.

In conclusion, the technology for improving intergroup relations is promising. A greater distinction between attitudinal and behavioural changes needs to be made in planning effective intergroup interventions. A greater variety of interventions that address the practical difficulties of bringing two groups together is also necessary. Finally, a better background of knowledge must be developed as to when perceptions and behaviour need to be diverse and when they need to be brought more closely together. Growing knowledge and theory suggest that conflict can be either functional or dysfunctional, depending on the circumstances.[97]

LARGE-GROUP INTERVENTIONS

System-wide process interventions in the third group are called large-group interventions. These change programs have been variously referred to as 'search conferences', 'open space meetings' and 'future searches'.[98] They focus on issues that affect the whole organisation or large segments of it, such as budget cuts, introduction of new technology and changes in senior leadership. The defining feature of large-group interventions is bringing together large numbers of organisation members (often more than 100) for a two- to four-day meeting or conference. Here, members work together to identify and resolve organisation-wide problems, design new approaches to structuring and managing the organisation or propose future directions for it.

Large-group interventions are among the fastest-growing OD applications. Large-group interventions[99] can vary on several dimensions, including purpose, size, length, structure and number. The purposes of these change methods can range from solving particular organisational problems to envisioning future strategic directions. Large-group interventions have been run with groups of fewer than 50 to more than 2000 participants and have lasted between one and five days. Some large-group processes are relatively planned and structured, although others are more informal.[100] Some interventions involve a single large-group meeting, and others include a succession of meetings to accomplish system-wide change in a short period of time.[101]

Despite these differences, large-group interventions have similar conceptual foundations and methods. Large-group interventions have evolved over the past 25 years and represent a combination of open systems applications and 'futuring' and 'visioning' exercises. Open systems approaches direct attention to how organisations interact with, and are shaped by, their environments. A popular method used in large-group interventions is called 'environmental scanning', which involves mapping the pressures placed on the organisation by external stakeholders, such as regulatory agencies, customers and competitors.[102] This analysis helps members devise new ways of responding to, and influencing, the environment. Futuring and visioning exercises guide members in creating 'images of potential' towards which the organisation can grow and develop.[103] Focusing on the organisation's potential rather than on its problems can increase members' energy for change.

What are the steps?

Conducting a large-group intervention generally involves the following three steps:

1 *Preparing for the large-group meeting.* A design team consisting of OD practitioners and several members from the organisation is convened to organise the event. The team generally addresses three key ingredients for successful large-group meetings: a compelling meeting theme, appropriate members to participate and relevant tasks to address the theme. First, large-group interventions require a compelling reason or focal point for change. Although 'people problems' can be an important focus, more powerful reasons for large-group efforts include impending mergers or reorganisations, responding to environmental threats and opportunities or proposing radical organisational changes.

   A second issue in preparing for a large-group meeting includes inviting relevant people to participate. A fundamental goal of large-group interventions is to 'get the whole system in the room'. This involves inviting as many people as possible who have a stake in the conference theme, and who are energised and committed to conceiving and initiating change. The third ingredient for successful large-group meetings is to have a range of task activities that enable the participants to fully address the conference theme.

2 *Conducting the meeting.* The flow of events in a large-group meeting can vary greatly according to its purpose and the framework adopted. These gatherings, however, tend to involve three sequential activities: developing common ground among participants, discussing the issues and creating an agenda for change. First, participants develop

sufficient common ground among themselves to permit joint problem solving. This generally involves team-building activities. One exercise for creating teamwork is called 'appreciating the past'. It asks participants to examine the significant events, milestones and highlights of the organisation's previous 20 years.[104]

Second, members discuss the system-wide issue or theme. To promote widespread participation, members are typically organised into subgroups of eight to 10 people, representing as many stakeholder viewpoints as possible. The subgroups may be asked to address a *general* question. Subgroup members brainstorm answers to these questions, record them on flipchart paper and share them with the larger group. The responses from the different subgroups are compared, and common themes identified. The final task of large-group meetings is creating an agenda for change. Participants are asked to reflect on what they have learned at the meeting and to suggest changes for themselves, their department and the whole organisation. Members from the same department are often grouped together to discuss their proposals and to decide on action plans, timetables and accountabilities.

Action items for the total organisation are referred to a steering committee that addresses organisation-wide policy issues and action plans. At the conclusion of the large-group meeting, the departmental subgroups and the steering committee report their conclusions to all participants and seek initial commitment for change.

3 *Follow up on the meeting outcomes.* Follow-up efforts are vital if the action plans from large-scale interventions are to be implemented. These activities involve communicating the results of the meeting to the rest of the organisation, gaining wider commitment to the changes and structuring the change process.

Results of large-group interventions

The number of case studies describing the methods and results of large-group interventions has increased dramatically. Large-group interventions have been conducted in a variety of organisations around a variety of themes or issues, including natural resource conservation, community development and strategic change, and in countries around the world.[105] However, despite this proliferation of practice, little systematic research has been done on the effects of large-group interventions. Because these change efforts often set the stage for subsequent OD interventions, it is difficult to isolate their specific results from those of the other changes. Anecdotal evidence from practitioners suggests the following benefits from large-group interventions: increased energy towards organisational change, improved feelings of 'community', ability to see 'outside the boxes' and improved relationships with stakeholders. Clearly, systematic research is needed on this important system-wide process intervention.

SUMMARY

In this chapter, we presented human process interventions aimed at people and processes. In covering this area of OD – and some would suggest it is the most common form of change management – the chapter begins with the many strategies directed towards improving individual performance and group dynamics. Although many interventions may be appropriate under certain circumstances, a few were highlighted that are most commonly used: performance appraisal, goal setting, management by objectives and reward systems. As they are among the earliest OD interventions, these change programs also help people to gain interpersonal skills, work through interpersonal conflicts and develop effective groups.

The first interpersonal intervention discussed was the T-group, the forerunner of modern OD change programs. T-groups typically consist of a small number of strangers who meet with a professional trainer to explore the social dynamics that emerge from their interactions. OD practitioners often attend T-groups themselves to improve their interpersonal skills, or recommend that managers attend a T-group to learn more about how their behaviours affect others.

Process consultation is used not only as a way of helping groups become effective but also as a process whereby groups can learn to diagnose and solve their own problems and to continue to develop their competence and maturity. Important areas of activity include communications, roles of group members, difficulties with problem-solving and decision-making norms, and leadership and authority. The basic difference between process consultation and third-party intervention is that the latter focuses on interpersonal dysfunction in social relationships between two or more individuals within the same organisation, and is directed more towards resolving direct conflict between those individuals.

Team building is directed towards improving group effectiveness and the ways that members of teams work together. Teams may be permanent or temporary, but their members have either common organisational aims or work activities. The general process of team building, like process consultation, attempts to equip a group to handle its own ongoing problem solving.

The other organisation process interventions do not claim universal success; they work best only in certain situations. The organisation confrontation meeting is a way of mobilising resources for organisational problem solving and seems especially relevant for organisations undergoing stress.

The intergroup relations approaches are designed to help solve a variety of organisational problems. Microcosm groups can be formed to address particular issues and use parallel processes to diffuse group solutions to the organisation. The intergroup conflict-resolution approach involves a method for mitigating dysfunctional conflicts between groups or departments. Conflict can be dysfunctional in situations in which groups must work together. It may, however, promote organisational effectiveness when departments are relatively independent of each other.

Large-group interventions are designed to focus the energy and attention of a 'whole system' around organisational processes such as a vision, strategy or culture. It is best used when the organisation is about to begin a large-scale change effort or is facing a new situation.

ACTIVITIES

REVIEW QUESTIONS

1 Define 'process consultant' and discuss some applied examples of this role in organisations. (LO2 & 3)

2 Describe the two major components of group problem solving. (LO2)

3 What are the basic implications of the model for conflict resolution? (LO3)

4 In a third-party consultation, what skill must the third party develop in order to be successful? (LO1 & 3)

5 The results of team building can be classified into three main areas. What are they? (LO2)

6 Outline the four types of basic process intervention. When are they used? (LO1 & 3)

7 Explain the characteristics of a system-wide process intervention and provide a brief example to illustrate. (LO1 & 3)

8 Identify the characteristics of intergroup conflict resolution methods. (LO1 & 3)

9 What are the two basic assumptions about managerial behaviour in the management grid? (LO2)

10 What are the steps involved in improving interdepartmental/intergroup relationships? (LO1)

11 What are the components of the Johari window? (LO2 & 3)

12 What are the essential characteristics of 'large-group interventions'? (LO1)

13 Describe performance management and appraisal from both individual and group perspectives. (LO2)

14 Consider whether there are ever times when performance appraisal may be unnecessary or even counterproductive. (LO2)

EXTEND YOUR LEARNING

1 Locate and describe an example of an organisation that has used or is using T-groups to help develop its teams. (LO3)

2 Explore and describe the interpersonal processes of OD using examples from your own experiences or from publicly available organisational examples. (LO3)

3 Explore and describe the organisation processes of OD, including examples from your own experiences or from publicly available organisational examples. (LO1)

4 Form into a discussion group and discuss, one-by-one, each member's understanding of performance appraisal processes from their work experience. (If you have not had formal work, describe what you would expect or prefer the appraisal process to be like.) Allow the discussion to expand into finding what the group agrees would be the ideal performance appraisal process for most organisations to utilise. (LO2)

Search ⊕ Me! **Management**

Explore **Search Me! Management** for articles relevant to this chapter. Fast and convenient, **Search Me! Management** is updated daily and provides you with 24-hour access to full text articles from hundreds of scholarly and popular journals, eBooks and newspapers, including *The Australian* and *The New York Times*. Visit http://login.cengagebrain.com and use the access code that comes with this book for 12 months access to the **Search Me! Management** database. Try searching for the following keywords:

Keywords:

- Performance management
- Performance appraisal
- T-groups
- Process consultation

Search tip: **Search Me! Management** contains information from both local and international sources. To get the greatest number of search results, try using both Australian and American spellings in your searches; for example, 'globalisation' and 'globalization'; 'organisation' and 'organization'.

REFERENCES

1 A. Mohrman, S. Mohrman and C. Worley, 'High technology performance management', in *Managing Complexity in High Technology Organizations*, eds M. von Glinow and S. Mohrman (New York: Oxford University Press, 1990): 216–36; P. Buller and G. McEvoy, 'Strategy, human resource management and performance: sharpening line of sight', *Human Resource Management Review*, 22 (2012): 43–56; S. Albrecht, A. Bakker, J. Gruman, W. Macey and A. Saks, 'Employee engagement, human resource management practices and competitive advantage: an integrated approach', *Journal of Organizational Effectiveness: People and Performance*, 2 (1): 7–35.

2 H. Bird, 'Appraising clever people: lessons from introducing performance reviews for academics in a UK university', *Industrial and Commercial Training*, 47 (2015): 81–5; R.A. Mueller-Hanson and E.D. Pulakos, *Transforming Performance Management to Drive Performance: An Evidence-based Roadmap* (London: Taylor and Francis, 2018).

3 A. Mohrman, S. Resnick-West and E. Lawler III, *Designing Performance Appraisal Systems* (San Francisco: Jossey-Bass, 1990); P. Massingham and L. Tam, 'The relationship between human capital, value creation and employee reward', *Journal of Intellectual Capital*, 16 (2015): 390–418; P. Petrou, E. Demerouti and W. Schaufeli, 'Crafting the change: the role of employee job crafting behaviors for successful organizational change', *Journal of Management*, 44:5 (2016): 1766–92.

4 D.E. Detmer and E.B. Steen, *The Academic Health Centre: Leadership and Performance* (New York: Cambridge University Press, 2005); S. Kim. 'Managing millennials' personal use of technology at work', *Business Horizons*, 61:2 (2018): 261–70.

5 Mohrman, Mohrman and Worley, 'High technology performance management', op. cit.

6 E. Locke and G. Latham, *A Theory of Goal Setting and Task Performance* (Englewood Cliffs, NJ: Prentice Hall, 1990).

7 Locke and Latham, *A Theory of Goal Setting*, op. cit.; E. Locke, R. Shaw, L. Saari and G. Latham, 'Goal setting and task performance: 1969–1980', *Psychological Bulletin*, 97 (1981): 125–52; M. Tubbs, 'Goal setting: a meta-analytic examination of the empirical evidence', *Journal of Applied Psychology*, 71 (1986): 474–83; M. Arraya, R. Pellissier and I. Preto, 'Team goal-setting involves more than only goal-setting', *Sport, Business and Management: An International Journal*, 5 (2015): 157–74.

8 A. O'Leary-Kelly, J. Martocchio and D. Frink, 'A review of the influence of group goals on group performance', *Academy of Management Journal*, 37 (1994): 1285–301; G. Clissold, D. Buttigieg and H. De Cieri, 'A psychological approach to occupational safety', *Asia Pacific Journal of Human Resources*, 50 (2012): 92–109.

9 J. Kotlar, A. Massis, M. Wright, and F. Frattini, 'Organizational goals: antecedents, formation processes and implications for firm behavior and performance', *International Journal of Management Reviews*, 20 (2018): S3–S18.

10 D. Crown and J. Rosse, 'Yours, mine and ours: facilitating group productivity through the integration of individual and group goals', *Organizational Behavior and Human Decision Processes*, 64 (1995): 138–50; K. Yeager and F. Nafukho, 'Developing diverse teams to improve performance in the organizational setting', *European Journal of Training and Development*, 36 (2012): 388–408.

11 P. Drucker, *The Practice of Management* (New York: Harper and Row, 1954): 63.

12 G. Odiorne, *Management by Objectives* (New York: Pitman, 1965); G. Kyriakopoulos, 'Half a century of management by objectives (MBO): a review', *African Journal of Business Management*, 6 (2012): 1772–86; G. Kenny, 'From the stakeholder viewpoint: designing measurable objectives', *Journal of Business Strategy*, 33 (2012): 1–19; R. Kearney, *Public Sector Performance: Management, Motivation, and Measurement*, (London: Taylor and Francis, 2018).

13 H. Levinson, 'Management by objectives: a critique', *Training and Development Journal*, 26 (1972): 410–25.

14 D. McGregor, 'An uneasy look at performance appraisal', *Harvard Business Review*, 35 (May–June 1957): 89–94.

15 M.D. Tovey, M.L. Uren, and N. Sheldon, *Managing Performance Improvement*, 3rd edn (Frenchs Forest, NSW: Pearson Education, 2015).

16 Locke and Latham, *A Theory of Goal Setting*, op. cit.; V. Hinsz, 'Teams as technology: strengths, weaknesses, and trade-offs in cognitive task performance', *Team Performance Management*, 21 (2015): 18–30.

17 Tubbs, 'Goal setting', op. cit.; R. Guzzo, R. Jette and R. Katzell, 'The effects of psychologically based intervention programs on worker productivity: a meta-analysis', *Personal Psychology*, 38 (1985): 275–91; A. Mento, R. Steel and R. Karren, 'A meta-analytic study of the effects of goal setting on task performance: 1966–84', *Organizational Behavior and Human Decision Processes*, 39 (1987): 52–83; O'Leary-Kelly, Martocchio and Frink, 'A review of the influence of group goals on group performance', op. cit.

18 C. Pearson, 'Participative goal setting as a strategy for improving performance and job satisfaction: a longitudinal evaluation with railway track maintenance gangs', *Human Relations*, 40 (1987): 473–88; R. Pritchard, S. Jones, P. Roth, K. Stuebing and S. Ekeberg, 'Effects of group feedback, goal setting and incentives on organisational productivity', *Journal of Applied Psychology*, 73 (1988): 337–58; J. Olivella and R. Gregorio, 'A case study of an integrated manufacturing performance measurement and meeting system', *Journal of Manufacturing Technology Management*, 26 (2015): 515–35.

19 S. Yearta, S. Maitlis and R. Briner, 'An exploratory study of goal setting in theory and practice: a motivational technique that works?', *Journal of Occupational and Organizational Psychology*, 68 (1995): 237–52.

20 R. Steers, 'Task-goal attributes: achievement and supervisory performance', *Organizational Behavior and Human Performance*, 13 (1975): 392–403; G. Latham and G. Yukl, 'A review of research on the application of goal setting in organizations', *Academy of Management Journal*, 18 (1975): 824–45; S. Johnson, L. Garrison, G. Hernez-Broome, J. Fleenor and J. Steed, 'Go for the goal(s): relationship between goal setting and transfer of training following leadership development', *Academy of Management Learning and Education*, 11 (2012): 555–69; Y. Han. 'Is public service motivation changeable? Integrative modeling with goal-setting theory', *International Journal of Public Administration*, 41 (2018): 216–25.

21 P.J. Davis, 'Organisational development in local government: human resource issues and CEOs' (unpublished PhD thesis, Deakin University, 2006).

22 A. Parida, U. Kumar, D. Galar and C. Stenström, 'Performance measurement and management for maintenance: a literature review', *Journal of Quality in Maintenance Engineering*, 21 (2015): 2–33; T. Bartram, 'Performance and reward practices of multinational corporations operating in Australia', *Journal of Industrial Relations*, 57 (2015): 210–31.

23 C. Peck, 'Pay and performance: the interaction of compensation and performance appraisal', *Research Bulletin*, 155 (New York: Conference Board, 1984).

24 E. Lawler III, *Pay and Organization Development* (Reading, MA: Addison-Wesley, 1981): 113; Mohrman, Resnick-West and Lawler, *Designing Performance Appraisal Systems*, op. cit.

25 D. Antonioni, 'Improve the performance management process before discounting performance appraisals', *Compensation and Benefits Review*, 26:3 (1994): 29–37; M. Smith, J. Rasmussen, M. Mills, A. Wefald and R. Downey, 'Stress and performance: do service orientation and emotional energy moderate the relationship?', *Journal of Occupational Health Psychology*, 17 (2012): 116–28; J. Sahadi, 'Goodbye annual review, see ya performance ratings', CNNMoney, http://money.cnn.com/2015/09/25/pf/annual-review.

26 S. Mohrman, G. Ledford Jr, E. Lawler III and A. Mohrman, 'Quality of work life and employee involvement', in *International Review of Industrial and Organizational Psychology*, eds C. Cooper and I. Robertson (New York: John Wiley, 1986); G. Yukl and R. Lepsinger, 'How to get the most out of 360 degree feedback', *Training*, 32 (1995): 45–50;

W.J. Rothwell, C.K. Hohne and S. King, *Human Performance Improvement: Building Practitioner Performance* (London: Routledge, 2018).

27 Mohrman, Ledford, Lawler and Mohrman, 'Quality of work life and employee involvement', op. cit.

28 P. Cappelli and M. Conyon. 'What do performance appraisals do?', *ILR Review*, 71 (2017): 88–116; E.M. Mone, *Employee Engagement through Effective Performance Management: A Practical Guide for Managers* (Abingdon, UK: Routledge, 2018).

29 S. Gebelein, 'Employee development: multi-rater feedback goes strategic', *HR Focus*, 73 (1996): 1, 4; B. O'Reilly, '360 degree feedback can change your life', *Fortune* (17 October 1994): 93–100; M. Choi, H. Yoon and C. Jeung, 'Leadership development in Korea: a Delphi study, *Asia Pacific Journal of Human Resources*, 50 (2012): 23–42.

30 J. Fairbank and D. Prue, 'Developing performance feedback systems', in *Handbook of Organizational Behavior Management*, ed. L. Frederiksen (New York: John Wiley and Sons, 1982).

31 R. Ammons, *Knowledge of Performance: Survey of Literature, Some Possible Applications and Suggested Experimentation*, (Wright Patterson Air Force Base, Ohio: Wright Air Development Center, Aero Medical Laboratory, 1954); J. Adams, 'Response feedback and learning', *Psychology Bulletin*, 70 (1968): 486–504; J. Annett, *Feedback and Human Behavior* (Baltimore, MD: Penguin, 1969); J. Sassenrath, 'Theory and results on feedback and retention', *Journal of Educational Psychology*, 67 (1975): 894–9; F. Luthans and T. Davis, 'Behavioral management in service organisations', in *Service Management Effectiveness*, eds D. Bowen, R. Chase and T. Cummings (San Francisco: Jossey-Bass, 1989): 177–210; K. Potočanik and N. Anderson, 'Assessing innovation: a 360-degree appraisal study', *International Journal of Selection and Assessment*, 20 (2012): 497–509.

32 R. Kopelman, *Managing Productivity in Organizations* (New York: McGraw-Hill, 1986).

33 Guzzo, Jette and Katzell, 'The effects of psychologically based intervention programs', op. cit.

34 J. Chobbar and J. Wallin, 'A field study on the effect of feedback frequency on performance', *Journal of Applied Psychology*, 69 (1984): 524–30; P. White, 'Authentic appreciation creates a winning workforce: focus on the individual and watch the transformation take place', *Human Resource Management International Digest*, 23 (2015): 25–7; C.D. Parks and L.J. Sanna, *Group Performance and Interaction* (New York: Routledge, Taylor & Francis Group, 2018).

35 W. Scott, J. Farh and P. Podsakoff, 'The effects of "intrinsic" and "extrinsic" reinforcement contingencies on task behavior', *Organizational Behavior and Human Decision Processes*, 41 (1988): 405–25; E. Lawler III, *Strategic Pay* (San Francisco: Jossey-Bass, 1990).

36 J. Campbell, M. Dunnette, E. Lawler III and K. Weick, *Managerial Behavior, Performance and Effectiveness* (New York: McGraw-Hill, 1970).

37 I. Brooks, *Organisational Behaviour: Individuals, Groups and Organisation*, 2nd edn (Prentice Hall, 2002); M. Aamodt, *Industrial/organizational Psychology: An Applied Approach* (Belmont, CA: Wadsworth, Cengage Learning, 2013).

38 Lawler, *Pay and Organization Development*, op. cit.: 101–11.

39 E. Lawler III and G. Jenkins, *Employee Participation in Pay Plan Development* (unpublished technical report to US Department of Labor, Ann Arbor, MI: Institute for Social Research, University of Michigan, 1976).

40 W.G. Bennis, *American Bureaucracy* (London: Taylor and Francis, 2017).

41 C. Beard and J.P. Wilson, *Experiential Learning: A Best Practice Handbook for Educators and Trainers* (London, PA: Kogan Page, 2006); S. Hetzner, H. Heid and H. Gruber, 'Using workplace changes as learning opportunities: antecedents to reflection in professional work', *Journal of Workplace Learning*, 27 (2015): 34–50.

42 J. Campbell and M. Dunnette, 'Effectiveness of T-group experiences in managerial training and development', *Psychological Bulletin*, 70 (August 1968): 73–103.

43 ibid.

44 M. Dunnette, J. Campbell and C. Argyris, 'A symposium: laboratory training', *Industrial Relations*, 8 (October 1968): 1–45.

45 Campbell and Dunnette, 'Effectiveness of T-group experiences', op. cit.; R. House, 'T-group education and leadership effectiveness: a review of the empirical literature and a critical evaluation', *Personnel Psychology*, 20 (Spring 1967): 1–32; J. Campbell, M. Dunnette, E. Lawler III and K. Weick, *Managerial Behavior, Performance, and Effectiveness* (New York: McGraw-Hill, 1970): 292–8; B. Burnes and B. Cooke, 'The past, present and future of organization development: taking the long view', *Human Relations*, 4 (July 2012): 1–35.

46 J. Porras and P. Berg, 'The impact of organization development', *Academy of Management Review*, 3 (April 1978): 249–66.

47 J. Nicholas, 'The comparative impact of organization development interventions on hard criteria measures', *Academy of Management Review*, 7 (October 1982): 531–42.

48 D. Bowers, 'OD techniques and their results in 23 organizations: the Michigan IGL Study', *Journal of Applied Behavioral Science*, 9 (January–February 1973): 21–43.

49 G. Neuman, J. Edwards and N. Raju, 'Organizational development interventions: a meta-analysis of their effects on satisfaction and other attitudes', *Personnel Psychology*, 42 (1989): 461–83.

50 R. Kaplan, 'Is openness passe?', *Human Relations*, 39 (November 1986): 242; K. Hultman and J. Hultman, 'Self and identity: hidden factors in resistance to organizational change', *Organization Development Journal*, 36 (2018): 13–29.

51 E. Schein, *Process Consultation II: Lessons for Managers and Consultants* (Reading, MA: Addison-Wesley, 1987).

52 ibid.: 5–17.

53 ibid.: 34.

54 J. Fast, *Body Language* (Philadelphia: Lippincott, M. Evans, 1970).

55 J. Luft, 'The Johari window', *Human Relations Training News*, 5 (1961): 6–7.

56 J. Gibb, 'Defensive communication', *Journal of Communication*, 11 (1961): 141–8; P. Garrard, *The Leadership Hubris Epidemic: Biological Roots and Strategies for Prevention* (Cham: Springer International Publishing, 2018).

57 S.G. Krantz and L. Lee, *Explorations in Harmonic Analysis: With Applications to Complex Function Theory and the Heisenberg Group* (Boston: Birkhauser Verlag, c. 2009).

58 N. Clapp, *Work Group Norms: Leverage for Organizational Change, Theory and Application*, working paper (Plainfield, NJ: Block Petrella Weisbord, no date); R. Allen and S. Pilnick, 'Confronting the shadow organization: how to detect and defeat negative norms', *Organizational Dynamics* (Spring 1973): 3–18.

59 Schein, *Process Consultation*; *Process Consultation II*, op. cit.

60 ibid.: 32–4.

61 R. Walton, *Managing Conflict: Interpersonal Dialogue and Third-Party Roles*, 2nd edn (Reading, MA: Addison-Wesley, 1987).

62 ibid.: 83–110.

63 G. Syamala, 'Team building: a tool for organizational development', *International Journal on Global Business Management & Research*; Chennai 7(2), (Feb 2018): 44–9.

64 W. Dyer, *Team Building: Issues and Alternatives*, 2nd edn (Reading, MA: Addison-Wesley, 1987).

65 J. Katzenbach and D. Smith, *The Wisdom of Teams* (Boston: Harvard Business School Press, 1993).

66 M.A. West, *Effective Teamwork: Practical Lessons from Organizational Research* (Malden, MA: BPS Blackwell, 2004).

67 J. Lewis III, 'Management team development: will it work for you?', *Personnel* (July/August 1975): 14–25.

68 D. Eden, 'Team development: a true field experiment at three levels of rigor', *Journal of Applied Psychology*, 70 (1985): 94–100.

69 R. Woodman and J. Sherwood, 'The role of team development in organizational effectiveness: a critical review', *Psychological Bulletin*, 88 (July–November 1980): 166–86.

70 Porras and Berg, 'Impact of organization development', op. cit.

71 Nicholas, 'Comparative impact', op. cit.

72 Woodman and Sherwood, 'The role of team development', op. cit.

73 R. Woodman and S. Wayne, 'An investigation of positive-finding bias in evaluation of organization development interventions', *Academy of Management Journal*, 28 (December 1985): 889–913.

74 R. Boss, 'Team building and the problem of regression: the personal management interview as an intervention', *Journal of Applied Behavioral Science*, 19 (1983): 67–83.

75 R. Buller and C. Bell Jr, 'Effects of team building and goal setting: a field experiment', *Academy of Management Journal*, 29 (1986): 305–28.

76 M. Weisbord, *Productive Workplaces* (San Francisco: Jossey-Bass, 1987).

77 R. Beckhard, 'The confrontation meeting', *Harvard Business Review*, 4 (1967): 149–55; O.K. Ephraim, 'The effects of change process in managing organisational innovation (a case study of Kia Motors Nigeria Limited Emene Enugu)', MBA Thesis 2017, Department of Management, University of Nigeria.

78 B. Benedict Bunker and B. Alban, 'What makes large-group interventions effective?', *Journal of Applied Behavioral Science*, 28:4 (1992): 579–91; N. Tichy and S. Sherman, *Control Your Destiny or Someone Else Will* (New York: HarperCollins Publishers, 1993).

79 R. Beckhard, *Organization Development: Strategies and Models* (Reading, MA: Addison-Wesley, 1969).

80 W. Bennis, *Organization Development: Its Nature, Origins, and Prospects* (Reading, MA: Addison-Wesley, 1969): 7.

81 C. Alderfer, 'An intergroup perspective on group dynamics', in *Handbook of Organizational Behavior*, ed. J. Lorsch (Englewood Cliffs, NJ: Prentice Hall, 1987): 190–222; C. Alderfer, 'Improving organizational communication through long-term intergroup intervention', *Journal of Applied Behavioral Science*, 13 (1977): 193–210; C. Alderfer, R. Tucker, C. Alderfer and L. Tucker, 'The Race Relations Advisory Group: an intergroup intervention', in *Research in Organizational Change and Development*, 2, eds W. Pasmore and R. Woodman (Greenwich, CT: JAI Press, 1988): 269–321.

82 Alderfer, 'An intergroup perspective on group dynamics', op. cit.

83 Alderfer, 'Improving organizational communication', op. cit.

84 D. Tjosvold, 'Cooperation theory and organizations', *Human Relations*, 37 (1984): 743–67; M.L. Chang, 'Can intergroup conflict aid the growth of within- and between-group social capital?', *Journal of Management and Organization*, published online 27 October 2017, https://doi.org/10.1017/jmo.2017.51.

85 R. Blake, H. Shepard and J. Mouton, *Managing Intergroup Conflict in Industry* (Houston: Gulf, 1954).

86 Beckhard, *Organization Development*, op. cit.

87 E. Neilson, 'Understanding and managing intergroup conflict', in *Organizational Behavior and Administration*, eds P. Lawrence, L. Barnes and J. Lorsch (Homewood, IL: Richard Irwin, 1976): 291–305; D.E. Rast III, M.A. Hogg and D. van Knippenberg, 'Intergroup leadership across distinct subgroups and identities', *Personality and Social Psychology Bulletin* (11 March 2018), https://doi.org/10.1177/0146167218757466.

88 Blake, Shepard and Mouton, *Managing Intergroup Conflict*, op. cit.

89 W. Bennis, *Organization Development: Its Nature, Origins, and Prospects* (Reading, MA: Addison-Wesley, 1969)

90 ibid.: 4.

91 R. Golembiewski and A. Blumberg, 'Confrontation as a training design in complex organizations: attitudinal changes in a diversified population of managers', *Journal of Applied Behavioral Science*, 3 (1967): 525–47.

92 W. French and C. Bell, *Organization Development: Behavioral Science Interventions for Organization Improvement* (Englewood Cliffs, NJ: Prentice Hall, 1978).

93 P.D. Howard, *Building and Implementing a Security Certification and Accreditation Program: Official (ISC) Guide to the CAP CBK* (Boca Raton, FL: Auerbach Publications, 2006).

94 E. Huse and M. Beer, 'Eclectic approach to organizational development', *Harvard Business Review*, 49 (1971): 103–13; S. Long and Z. Liao, 'An investigation of bureaucratic influences on absorptive capacity-market responsiveness relationships', *Asian Journal of Technology Innovation*, 24:1 (2016): 142–58.

95 E. Huse, 'The behavioral scientist in the shop', *Personnel*, 44 (May–June 1965): 8–16.

96 J. Fordyce and R. Weil, *Managing WITH People* (Reading, MA: Addison-Wesley, 1971).

97 K. Thomas, 'Conflict and conflict management', in *Handbook of Industrial and Organizational Psychology*, ed. M. Dunnette (Chicago: Rand McNally, 1976): 889–936; S. Kauffeld and N. Lehmann-Willenbrock, 'Meetings matter: effects of team meetings on team and organizational success', *Small Group Research*, 43 (2012): 130–58; D. Parker, M. Holesgrove and R. Pathak, 'Improving productivity with self-organised teams and agile leadership', *International Journal of Productivity and Performance Management*, 64 (2015): 112–28.

98 Weisbord, *Productive Workplaces*, op. cit.; M. Weisbord, *Discovering Common Ground* (San Francisco: Berrett Koehler, 1993); B. Benedict Bunker and B. Alban, eds, 'Special issue: large-group interventions', *Journal of Applied Behavioral Science*, 28:4 (1992); H. Owen, *Open Space Technology: A User's Guide* (Potomac, MD: Abbott, 1992).

99 J. Smythe, *The CEO – the Chief Engagement Officer: Turning Hierarchy Upside Down to Drive Performance* (Aldershot, England; Burlington, VT: Gower, c. 2007); A. Sune and J. Gibb, 'Dynamic capabilities as patterns of organizational change: an empirical study on transforming a firm's resource base, *Journal of Organizational Change Management*, 28 (2015): 213–31.

100 H. Owen, *Open Space Technology*, op. cit.

101 D. Axelrod, 'Getting everyone involved', *Journal of Applied Behavioral Science*, 28 (1992): 499–509. E. Hopper, *Trauma and Organizations* (London: Karnac, 2012).

102 B. Holland, 'Scanning for blind spots', *Encyclopedia of Information Science and Technology*, 4th edn (Hershey, Pennsylvania: IGI Global, 2018).

103 R. Lippitt, 'Future before you plan', in *NTL Manager's Handbook* (Arlington, VA: NTL Institute, 1983): 38–41.

104 Weisbord, *Productive Workplaces*, op. cit.

105 Weisbord, *Discovering Common Ground*, op. cit.; P. Baloh, K. Desouza and R. Hackney, 'Contextualizing organizational interventions of knowledge management systems: a design science perspective', *Journal of the American Society for Information Science and Technology*, 63 (2012): 948–66; M. Festing, L. Knappert, P. Dowling and A. Engle, 'Global performance management in MNEs: conceptualization and profiles of country-specific characteristics in China, Germany, and the United States', *Thunderbird International Business Review*, 54 (2012): 825–43.

8 ORGANISATION DEVELOPMENT INTERVENTIONS: STRATEGY AND STRUCTURE

LEARNING OUTCOMES

After studying this chapter, you should be able to:

1   Explain the different ways an organisation can respond to its environment.

2   Describe the guidelines for open systems planning.

3   Discuss planned change initiatives, including transorganisational development, restructuring and re-engineering.

4   Explain the three approaches to work design.

KEY TERMS

Open systems planning (OSP)

Transorganisational development (TD)

Downsizing

Re-engineering

Sociotechnical systems (STS)

Self-managed work teams

This chapter is concerned with interventions that are aimed at organisational and environmental relationships. These change programs focus on helping organisations to relate better to their environments, and to achieve a better fit with those external forces that affect goal achievement and performance. Practitioners are discovering that additional knowledge and skills, such as competitive strategy, finance, marketing and political science, are necessary to conduct such large-scale change.

Because organisations are open systems, they must relate to their environments if they are to gain the resources and information needed to function and prosper. These relationships define an organisation's strategy and are affected by particular aspects and features of the environment. Organisations have devised a number of responses for managing environmental interfaces. The responses vary from creating special units to scan the environment to forming strategic alliances with other organisations.

The interventions described in this chapter are designed to help organisations to gain a comprehensive understanding of their environments and to devise appropriate responses to external demands. Open systems planning (OSP) is aimed at helping organisation members to assess the larger environment and to develop strategies for relating to it more effectively. The intervention results in a clear strategic mission for the organisation, as well as action plans for influencing the environment in favoured directions.

The final section is concerned with work design: creating jobs and work groups that generate high levels of employee fulfilment and productivity. This technostructural intervention[1] can be part of a larger employee involvement application, or it can be an independent change program. Work design has been extensively researched and applied in organisations. Organisations have tended to combine work design with formal structure and the support of changes in goal setting, reward systems, work environment and other performance management practices. These organisational factors can help to structure and reinforce the kinds of work behaviours associated with specific work designs.

ORGANISATIONAL AND ENVIRONMENTAL FRAMEWORK

This section provides a framework for understanding how environments affect organisations and, in turn, how organisations can impact on environments. The framework is based on the concept that organisations and their subunits are open systems existing in environmental contexts. Environments provide organisations with the necessary resources, information and legitimacy, and organisations must maintain effective relationships with suitable environments if they are to survive and grow. For example, a manufacturing firm must first obtain raw materials so that it can produce its products, and then use appropriate technologies to efficiently produce them, induce customers to buy them and satisfy the laws and regulations that govern its operations. Because organisations are dependent on environments, they need to manage all the external constraints and contingencies, while at the same time taking advantage of external opportunities. They also need to influence the environment in favourable directions through such methods as political lobbying, advertising and public relations.

In this section, we first describe the different environments that can affect organisations, and then identify those environmental dimensions that tend to influence the organisational responses to those external forces. Finally, we review the different ways in which an organisation can respond to the environment. This material provides an introductory context for describing the various interventions that concern organisational and environmental relationships: OSP and transorganisational development (TD).[2]

ENVIRONMENTS

Organisational environments consist of everything outside organisations that can affect, either directly or indirectly, their performance and outcomes. This could include external agents (such as suppliers, customers, regulators and competitors) and the cultural, political and economic forces in the wider societal and global context. These two classes of environments are called the 'task environment' and the 'general environment', respectively.[3] We will also describe the enacted environment, which reflects members' perceptions of the general and task environments.

The *general environment* consists of all external forces that can influence an organisation or department, and includes technological, legal and regulatory, political, economic, social and ecological components. Each of these forces can affect the organisation in both direct and indirect ways. For example, economic recessions can directly impact on the demand for a company's product. The general environment can also impact indirectly on organisations by virtue of the linkages between external agents. For example, an organisation may have trouble obtaining raw materials from a supplier because a consumer group has embroiled the supplier in a labour dispute with a national union, a lawsuit with a government regulator or a boycott. These members of the organisation's general environment can affect the organisation, even though they have no direct connection to it.

The *task environment* consists of those specific individuals and organisations that interact directly with the organisation and can affect goal achievement. The task environment consists of customers, suppliers, competitors, producers of substitute products or services, labour unions, financial institutions and so on. These direct relationships are the medium through which organisations and environments mutually influence one another. Customers, for example, can demand changes in the organisation's products, but the organisation can attempt to influence customers' tastes and desires through advertising.

The *enacted environment*[4] consists of the organisation's perception and representation of its environment. Weick suggested that environments must be perceived before they can influence decisions as to how to respond.[5] Organisation members must actively observe, register and make sense of the environment before their decisions as to how to act can be made. Thus, only the enacted environment can affect which organisational responses are chosen. The general and task environments, however, can influence whether those responses are successful or ineffective. For example, members may perceive customers as relatively satisfied with their products and may decide to make only token efforts at new-product development. If those perceptions are wrong and customers are dissatisfied with the products, the meagre efforts at product development can have disastrous consequences for the organisation. Consequently, an organisation's enacted environment should accurately reflect its general and task environments if members' decisions and actions are to be based on external realities.

ENVIRONMENTAL DIMENSIONS

Organisational environments can be characterised along a number of dimensions that can influence organisational and environmental relationships. One perspective views environments as information flows and suggests that organisations need to process information in order to discover how to relate to their environments.[6] The key feature of the environment to affect information processing is information uncertainty or the degree to which environmental information is ambiguous. Organisations seek to remove uncertainty from their environment so that they know how best to transact with it. For example, they try to discern customer needs through focus groups and surveys, and they attempt to understand competitor strategies by studying their press releases and sales force behaviours, and by learning about their key personnel. The greater the uncertainty, the more information processing is required to learn about the environment. This is particularly the case when environments are dynamic and complex. Dynamic environments change abruptly and unpredictably, while complex environments have many parts or elements that can affect organisations. These kinds of environments pose difficult information-processing problems for organisations. Global competition, technological change and financial markets, for example, have made the environments of many multinational firms highly uncertain and have severely strained their information-processing capacity.

Another perspective sees environments as consisting of resources for which organisations compete.[7] The key feature of the environment is resource dependence, or the degree to which an organisation relies on other organisations for resources. Organisations seek to manage critical sources of resource dependence, while remaining as autonomous as possible. For example, companies may contract with several suppliers of the same raw material so that they are not overly dependent on one vendor. Resource dependence is extremely high for an organisation when other organisations control critical resources that cannot easily be obtained elsewhere. Resource criticality and availability determine the extent to which an organisation is dependent on other organisations and must respond to their demands, as the 1970s oil embargo by the Organization of the Petroleum Exporting Countries (OPEC) clearly showed many Australian companies.

These two environmental dimensions – information uncertainty and resource dependence – can be combined to show the degree to which organisations are constrained by their environments and consequently must be responsive to their demands.[8] As shown in **Figure 8.1**, organisations have the most freedom from external forces when information uncertainty and resource dependence are both low. In this situation, organisations do not need to be responsive to their environments and can behave relatively independently of them. United States automotive manufacturers faced these conditions in the 1950s and operated with relatively little external constraint or threat. As information uncertainty and resource dependence become higher, however, organisations are more constrained and must be more responsive to external demands. They must accurately perceive the environment and respond to it appropriately. Modern organisations – such as financial institutions, high-technology businesses and health care facilities – are facing unprecedented amounts of environmental uncertainty and resource dependence. Their very existence depends on their recognition of external challenges and their quick and appropriate responses to them.

ORGANISATIONAL RESPONSES

Organisations employ many ways of responding to environmental demands. These help buffer the organisation's technology from external disruptions and link the organisation to sources of information and resources. Referred to as 'external structures', these responses are generally carried out by administrators and staff specialists who are responsible for setting corporate strategy and managing the environment. Three major external structures are described next.

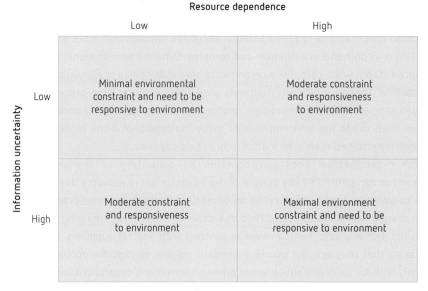

FIGURE 8.1 ENVIRONMENTAL DIMENSIONS AND ORGANISATIONAL TRANSACTIONS

Resource dependence

	Low	High
Low	Minimal environmental constraint and need to be responsive to environment	Moderate constraint and responsiveness to environment
High	Moderate constraint and responsiveness to environment	Maximal environment constraint and need to be responsive to environment

(Information uncertainty — vertical axis label)

Source: Howard E. Aldrich, *Organizations and Environments*, Copyright © 2008, by the Board of Trustees of the Leland Stanford Jr. University. All rights reserved. Used with the permission of Stanford University Press, http://www.sup.org.

SCANNING UNITS

Organisations must have the capacity to monitor and make sense of their environment if they are to respond to it appropriately. They must identify and attend to those environmental parts and features that are highly related to the organisation's own survival and growth. When environments have high information uncertainty, organisations may need to gather a diversity of information in order to comprehend external demands and opportunities. For example, they may need to attend to segmented labour markets,[9] changing laws and regulations, rapid scientific developments, shifting economic conditions, and abrupt changes in customer and supplier behaviours. Organisations can respond to these conditions by establishing special units for scanning particular parts or aspects of the environment, such as departments of market research, public relations, government relations and strategic planning.[10] These units generally include specialists with expertise in a particular segment of the environment, who gather and interpret relevant information about the environment, communicating it to decision makers who develop appropriate responses. For example, market researchers provide information to marketing executives about customer tastes and preferences. Such information guides choices about product development, pricing and advertising.

PROACTIVE RESPONSES

These involve attempts by organisations to change or modify their environments. Organisations are increasingly trying to influence external forces in favourable directions.[11] For example, they engage in political activity to influence government laws and regulations;

seek government regulation to control entry to industries; gain legitimacy in the wider society by behaving in accordance with valued cultural norms; acquire control over raw materials or markets by vertical and horizontal integration;[12] and introduce new products and services, using advertising to shape customer tastes and preferences. Although the range of proactive responses is almost limitless, organisations tend to be highly selective when choosing them. The responses can be costly to implement and can appear aggressive, thus evoking countervailing actions by powerful others, such as competitors and the government. For example, technology giants Microsoft, Apple and Samsung have had famous battles with each other and various government regulators over market dominance and intellectual property issues. Moreover, organisations are paying increased attention to whether their responses are socially responsible, sustainable and contribute to a healthy society. For example, Dow Jones maintains a Sustainability Index (DJSI) that identifies environmentally, financially and socially responsible companies around the world. With over a third of the criteria dedicated to social factors, the DJSI lists companies such as ANZ Bank, Stockland, Fujitsu, Unilever and Roche in its rankings. These corporations view their businesses as important arms of society and devote a considerable amount of time and corporate resources to charity and pressing social issues. Today, there is much global attention given to the ethical and moral implications of organisational behaviours.[13]

Collective structures

Organisations can cope with problems of environmental dependence[14] and uncertainty by increasing their coordination with other organisations. These collective structures help to control interdependencies among organisations and include such methods as bargaining, contracting, co-opting and creating joint ventures, federations, strategic alliances and consortia.[15] Contemporary organisations are increasingly turning to joint ventures and partnerships with other organisations in order to manage environmental uncertainty and perform tasks that are too costly and complicated for single organisations to perform. These multiorganisation arrangements are being used as a means of sharing resources for large-scale research and development, for reducing risks of innovation, for applying diverse expertise to complex problems and tasks and for overcoming barriers to entry into foreign markets. For example, defence contractors are forming strategic alliances to bid on large government projects; organisations from different countries are forming joint ventures to overcome restrictive trade barriers; and high-technology businesses are forming research consortia to undertake significant and costly research and development for their industries. Major barriers to forming collective structures in Australia are organisations' own drive to act autonomously and government policies that discourage coordination among organisations, especially in the same industry. Japanese industrial and economic policies, on the other hand, promote cooperation among organisations, thus giving them a competitive advantage in their responses to complex and dynamic global environments.[16] For example, starting in the late 1950s, the Japanese Government provided financial assistance and support to a series of cooperative research efforts among Japanese computer manufacturers. The resulting technological developments enabled the computer firms to reduce IBM's share of the mainframe market in Japan from 70 per cent to about 40 per cent in fewer than 15 years. Today there are many multilateral collaborations that cross borders at industry level; for instance, in 2015 the Japanese company Softbank announced a collaboration with IBM to deploy the supercomputer Watson to foster innovation among a wide range of partners, entrepreneurs and app developers throughout Japan.

OPEN SYSTEMS PLANNING

Open systems planning (OSP): involves an organisation systematically assessing its task environment and developing a strategic response to it.

Open systems planning (OSP) helps an organisation to systematically assess its task environment and to develop strategic responses to it. Like the other interventions in this book, OSP treats organisations or departments as open systems that must interact with a suitable environment in order to survive and develop. It helps organisation members develop a strategic mission for relating to the environment and influencing it in favourable directions. The process of applying OSP begins with a diagnosis of the existing environment and how the organisation relates to it. It then develops possible future environments, and action plans to bring about the desired future environment. A number of practical guidelines exist to apply this intervention effectively.

ASSUMPTIONS ABOUT ORGANISATION–ENVIRONMENT RELATIONS

OSP is based on four assumptions about how organisations relate, or should relate, to their environment.[17] These are:

1 *Organisation members' perceptions play a major role in environmental relations.* Members' perceptions determine which parts of the environment are attended to or ignored, as well as how much value is placed on those parts. Such perceptions provide the basis for planning and implementing specific actions in relation to the environment. For example, a production manager might focus on those parts of the environment that are directly related to making a product, such as raw material suppliers and available labour, while ignoring other, more indirect parts, such as government agencies. These perceptions would probably direct the manager towards talking with the suppliers and potential employees, while possibly neglecting the agencies. The key point is that organisational and environmental relations are largely determined by how members perceive the environment and choose to act towards it.

2 *Organisation members must share a common view of the environment to permit coordinated action towards it.* Without a shared view of the environment, organisation members would have trouble relating to it. Conflicts would arise about what parts of the environment are important and what value should be placed on different parts. Such perceptual disagreements make planning and implementing a coherent strategy difficult. For example, members of a top management team might have different views on the organisation's environment. Unless those differences are shared and resolved, the team will have problems developing a business strategy for relating to the environment.[18]

3   *Organisation members' perceptions must accurately reflect the condition of the environment if organisational responses are to be effective.* Members can misinterpret environmental information, ignore important forces or attend to negligible events. Such misperceptions can render organisational responses to the environment inappropriate, as happened to American car makers during the energy crisis of the mid-1970s. They believed that consumers wanted large automobiles and petroleum producers had plentiful supplies of relatively inexpensive petrol. The traditional strategy of manufacturing a high number of large-sized cars was quickly shown to be inappropriate to the actual environment; that is, consumers' growing preference for small, fuel-efficient cars and the decision of OPEC member nations to raise the price of crude oil. Such misperceptions typically occur when the environment exhibits high levels of complexity and unpredictable change. Such turbulence makes understanding the environment or predicting its future difficult.

4   *Organisations can not only adapt to their environment but also create it proactively.* Organisational and environmental relations are typically discussed in terms of organisations adapting to environmental forces. Attention is directed to understanding and predicting environmental conditions so that organisations can better react to them. A more proactive alternative is for organisations to plan for a desired environment and then to take action against the existing environment so as to move it in the desired direction. This active stance goes beyond adaptation because the organisation is trying to create a favourable environment rather than simply reacting to external forces. For example, when Alcoa first started to manufacture aluminium building materials, there was little demand for them. Rather than wait to see whether the market developed, Alcoa entered the construction business and pioneered the use of aluminium building materials. By being proactive, the company created a favourable environment.

IMPLEMENTATION PROCESS

Based on these premises about organisation and environment relations, OSP can help organisation members to assess their environment and plan a strategy for relating to it. After OSP, they may value differently the complexity of their environment and may generate a more varied range of response strategies.[19] OSP is typically carried out by the top management of an entire organisation, or by the management and key employees of a department. This group initially meets off-site for a two- to three-day period and may have several follow-up meetings of shorter duration. The organisation development (OD) practitioner helps guide the process. Members are encouraged to share their perceptions of the environment and to collect and examine a diversity of related data. Considerable attention is directed to the communication process itself. Participants are helped to establish sufficient trust and openness to share different views and work through differences.

OSP starts from the perspective of a particular organisation or department. This point of reference identifies the relevant environment. It serves as the focus of the planning process, which consists of the following steps:[20]

1   *Assess the external environment*[21] in terms of domains and the expectations that those domains have for the organisation's behaviour. This step maps the current environment facing the organisation. First, the different parts or domains of the environment are identified. Listing all the external groups that directly interact with the organisation – such as customers, suppliers or government agencies – usually does this. Then each domain's expectations of the organisation's behaviour are assessed.

2   *Assess how the organisation responds to the environmental expectations.* This step assesses the organisation's responses to the environmental expectations identified in step 1.

3   *Identify the core mission of the organisation.* This step helps to identify the underlying purpose or core mission of the organisation, as shown by how it responds to external demands. Attention is directed at discovering the mission as it is evidenced in the organisation's behaviour, rather than by simply accepting an official statement of the organisation's purpose. This is accomplished by examining the organisation and those environment transactions identified in steps 1 and 2, and then assessing the values that seem to underlie those interactions. These values provide clues about the actual identity or mission of the organisation.

4   *Create a realistic future scenario of environmental expectations and organisation responses.* This step asks members to project the organisation and its environment into the near future, assuming that there are no real changes in the organisation. It asks what will happen in steps 1, 2 and 3 if the organisation continues to operate as it does at present.

5   *Create an ideal future scenario of environmental expectations and organisational responses.* Here, members are asked to create alternative, desirable futures. This involves going back over steps 1, 2 and 3 and asking what members would ideally like to see happen in both the environment and the organisation in the near future. People are encouraged to fantasise about desired futures without worrying about possible constraints.

6   *Compare the present with the ideal future and prepare an action plan for reducing the discrepancy.* This last step identifies specific actions that will move both the environment and the organisation towards the desired future. Planning for appropriate interventions typically occurs in three time frames: tomorrow, six months from now and two years from now. Members also decide on a follow-up schedule for sharing the flow of actions and updating the planning process.

GUIDELINES FOR IMPLEMENTING OPEN SYSTEMS PLANNING

Practitioners who have applied OSP offer a number of suggestions for its effective use.[22] These rules of thumb include the following:

1   *Devote sufficient time and resources.* OSP is time-consuming and requires considerable effort and resources. There is much preparatory work in collecting environmental information, analysing it and drafting reports for group discussion. Also, participants

must be given sufficient time to develop healthy interpersonal relationships so that they can discuss the information openly, resolve conflicting viewpoints and arrive at a sufficient consensus to proceed effectively.

2 *Document all steps.* OSP generates considerable information and people can easily lose track of the data. Written reports of the various steps help to organise the diverse information. They can also keep other organisation members informed of the process and can provide them with a concrete focus for reacting to it.

3 *Deal only with key parts of the environment.* The tendency is to collect and examine too much information, losing track of what is important for organisational effectiveness. Mapping out the existing environment should start with an initial scanning that defines broad environmental domains. Only those domains considered important to organisational or departmental functioning are used for the remaining steps of the process.

4 *Follow the steps in order.* In using OSP, people tend to confuse the existing environment with the future environment. They also tend to mix the realistic future with the ideal future. If the steps are systematically followed, the process will logically lead from the present to the realistic future environment and then to the desired future environment.

5 *View planning as process, not outcome.* Probably the key value of OSP is helping organisation members develop an ongoing process for assessing and relating to the environment. While specific plans and action steps are important, they should be viewed as periodic outcomes of a larger process of environmental management.

TRANSORGANISATIONAL DEVELOPMENT

Transorganisational development (TD)[23] is an emerging form of planned change aimed at helping organisations develop collective and collaborative strategies with other organisations. Many of the tasks, problems and issues facing organisations today are too complex and multifaceted to be addressed by a single organisation. Multiorganisation strategies and arrangements are increasing rapidly in today's global, highly competitive environment. In the private sector, research and development consortia allow companies to share resources and risks associated with large-scale research efforts. For example, Sematech involves many large organisations – such as Intel, AT&T, IBM, Xerox, Motorola, universities and government entities – that have joined together to improve the competitiveness of the US semiconductor industry. Joint ventures between domestic and foreign companies help to overcome trade barriers and facilitate technology transfer across nations. For example, New United Motor Manufacturing, Inc. in Fremont, California, began as a joint venture between General Motors and Toyota to produce automobiles using Japanese teamwork methods. It reopened in 2010 as a Tesla Motors-operated facility, Tesla Factory. In the public sector, partnerships between government and business provide the resources and initiative to undertake complex urban renewal projects, such as the Docklands project in Melbourne. Alliances among public service agencies in a region – such as the Goulburn rural health

Transorganisational development (TD): an emerging form of planned change aimed at helping organisations develop collective and collaborative strategies with other organisations.

services in alliance with the local councils in Albury and Wodonga – can improve the coordination of services, promote economies and avoid costly overlap and redundancy.

TRANSORGANISATIONAL SYSTEMS AND THEIR PROBLEMS

Cummings has referred to these multiorganisation structures as transorganisational systems (TSs): groups of organisations that have joined together for a common purpose.[24] These are functional social systems midway between single organisations and societal systems. They are able to make decisions and perform tasks on behalf of their member organisations, although members maintain their separate organisational identities and goals. In contrast to most organisations, TSs tend to be underorganised: relationships among member organisations are loosely coupled; leadership and power are dispersed among autonomous organisations, rather than hierarchically centralised; and commitment and membership are tenuous as member organisations attempt to maintain their autonomy while performing jointly.

These characteristics make creating and managing TSs difficult.[25] Potential member organisations may not see the need to join with other organisations. They may be concerned with maintaining their autonomy or have trouble identifying potential partners. Australian companies, for example, are traditionally 'rugged individualists', preferring to work alone rather than to join with other organisations. Even if organisations do decide to join together, they may have problems managing their relationships and controlling joint performances. Because members are typically accustomed to hierarchical forms of control, they may have difficulty managing lateral relations among independent organisations. They may also have difficulty managing different levels of commitment and motivation among members, and sustaining membership over time.

APPLICATION STAGES

For more information on the stages of planned change, see Chapter 2.

Given these problems, TD has evolved as a unique form of planned change aimed at creating TSs and improving their effectiveness. In laying out the conceptual boundaries of TD, Cummings described the practice of TD as following the stages of planned change appropriate for underorganised systems (see Chapter 2).[26] These stages parallel other process models that have been proposed for creating and managing joint ventures, strategic alliances and interorganisational collaboration.[27] The four stages are shown in **Figure 8.2**, along with key issues that need to be addressed at each stage. The stages and issues are described next.

The initial stage of TD involves the identification of potential member organisations of the TS. It serves to specify the relevant participants for the remaining stages of TD. Identifying potential members can be difficult because organisations may not perceive the need to join together or may not know enough about each other to make membership choices. These problems are typical when trying to create a new TS. Relationships among potential members may be loosely coupled or non-existent, and so, even if organisations see the need to form a TS, they may be unsure about who should be included.

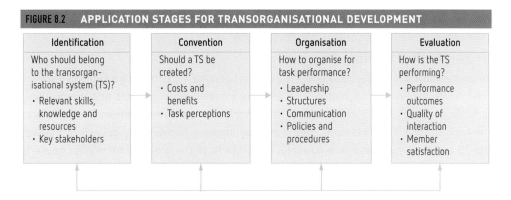

FIGURE 8.2   APPLICATION STAGES FOR TRANSORGANISATIONAL DEVELOPMENT

Identification	Convention	Organisation	Evaluation
Who should belong to the transorganisational system (TS)? • Relevant skills, knowledge and resources • Key stakeholders	Should a TS be created? • Costs and benefits • Task perceptions	How to organise for task performance? • Leadership • Structures • Communication • Policies and procedures	How is the TS performing? • Performance outcomes • Quality of interaction • Member satisfaction

The identification stage is generally carried out by one or a few organisations that are interested in exploring the possibility of creating a TS. Change agents work with these organisations to specify criteria for membership in the TS and identify organisations meeting those standards. Because TSs are intended to perform specific tasks, a practical criterion for membership is how much organisations can contribute to task performance. Potential members can be identified and judged in terms of the skills, knowledge and resources that they can bring to bear on the TS task. TD practitioners warn, however, that identifying potential members should also take into account the political realities of the situation.[28] Consequently, key stakeholders who can affect the creation and subsequent performance of the TS are identified as possible members.

During the early stages of creating a TS, there may be insufficient leadership and cohesion among participants to choose potential members. In these situations, participants may contract with an outside change agent who can help them to achieve sufficient agreement on TS membership. In several cases of TD, change agents helped members to create a special leadership group that could make decisions on behalf of the participants.[29] This leadership group comprised a small cadre of committed members and was able to develop enough cohesion among themselves to carry out the identification stage.

Convention stage

Once potential members of the TS have been identified, the convention stage is concerned with bringing them together to assess whether creating a TS is desirable and feasible. This face-to-face meeting enables potential members to mutually explore their motivations for joining and their perceptions of the joint task. They seek to establish sufficient levels of motivation and task consensus to form the TS.

Like the identification stage, this phase of TD generally requires considerable direction and facilitation by change agents. Existing stakeholders may not have the legitimacy or skills to perform the convening function, and change agents can serve as convenors if they are perceived as legitimate and credible by the different organisations. In many TD cases, conveners came from research centres or universities with reputations for neutrality and expertise in TD.[30] Because participating organisations tend to have diverse motives and views and limited means for resolving differences, change agents may need to structure and manage interactions to facilitate the airing of differences and arriving at consensus about forming the TS. They may need to help organisations work through differences and reconcile self-interest with those of the larger TS.

Organisation stage

When the convention stage results in the decision to create a TS, members begin to organise themselves for task performance. This involves establishing structures and mechanisms to facilitate communication and interaction among members and to direct joint efforts to the task at hand.[31] For example, members may create a coordinating council to manage the TS and they might assign a powerful leader to head the group. They might choose to formalise exchanges among members by developing rules, policies and formal operating procedures. In cases where members are required to invest large amounts of resources in the TS, such as might occur in an industry-based research consortium, the organising stage typically includes voluminous contracting and negotiating about members' contributions and returns. Here, corporate lawyers and financial analysts play key roles in structuring the TS. They determine how costs and benefits will be allocated among member organisations, as well as the legal obligations and contractual rights of members.

Evaluation stage

This final stage of TD involves assessing how the TS is performing. Members need feedback so that they can identify problems and begin to resolve them. Feedback data generally include performance outcomes and member satisfaction, as well as indicators of how well members are jointly interacting. For example, change agents can periodically interview or survey member organisations about various outcomes and features of the TS and feed those data back to TS leaders. Such information can enable leaders to make necessary modifications and adjustments in how the TS is operating. It may signal the need to return to previous stages of TD to make necessary corrections, as shown by the feedback arrows in **Figure 8.2**.

RESTRUCTURING ORGANISATIONS

Interventions aimed at structural design include moving from more traditional ways of dividing the organisation's overall work – such as functional, self-contained unit and matrix structures – to more integrative and flexible forms, such as process- and network-based structures. Diagnostic guidelines help determine which structure is appropriate for particular organisational environments, technologies and conditions.

Downsizing: reducing costs and bureaucracy by decreasing the size of the organisation.

Downsizing seeks to reduce costs and bureaucracy by decreasing the size of the organisation. This reduction in personnel can be accomplished by lay-offs, organisation redesign and outsourcing, which involves moving functions that are not part of the organisation's core competence to outside contractors. Successful downsizing is closely aligned with the organisation's strategy.

Re-engineering: a radical redesign of the organisation's core work processes to give tighter linkage and coordination among the different tasks.

Re-engineering radically redesigns the organisation's core work processes to give tighter linkage and coordination among the different tasks. This work-flow integration results in faster, more responsive task performance. Business process management is often accomplished with new information technology that permits employees to control and coordinate work processes more effectively.

DOWNSIZING

Downsizing refers to interventions that are aimed at reducing the size of the organisation.[32] This is typically accomplished by decreasing the number of employees through lay-offs, attrition, redeployment, redundancy or early retirement, or by reducing the number of organisational units or managerial levels through divestiture, outsourcing, reorganisation or delayering. An important consequence of downsizing has been the rise of the contingent workforce. These less expensive temporary or permanent part-time workers are often hired by the organisations that just laid off thousands of their employees. In many cases, terminated employees become independent contractors or consultants to the organisation that terminated them. Overall cost reduction is achieved by replacing expensive permanent workers with a contingent workforce.

Downsizing is generally a response to several factors, including product or service demand, pressure to focus on short-term profits or budget goals, a major change in organisation strategy and the belief that the slimmer the organisation, the better.[33] John Corrigan, former adviser to the Chartered Practising Accountants Australia Management Accounting Centre of Excellence, once said that cutting costs was important, but that there is evidence to suggest that the decimation of middle management ranks in organisations caused a loss of valuable experience and knowledge.[34] This view was supported by Professor Roger Collins, formerly of the Australian Graduate School of Management, who said that downsizing in Australia had very negative connotations and that, through downsizing, companies lost a lot of skills that were really needed.[35] These issues have cycled back into consciousness because global financial crises manifesting as local credit shortages continue to affect business activities and the labour market. One survival response by managers has been to restructure businesses and capitalise on advances in information and communication technology, which is to harness the capabilities of networks with associated advantages of resilience and adaptability. However, downsizing of staff is often a result of this and **Table 8.1** presents this and other issues for consideration in the network form of organisations.

Application stages

Successful downsizing interventions tend to proceed in the following steps:[36]

1 *Clarify the organisation's strategy.* In this initial stage, organisation leaders specify corporate strategy and clearly communicate how downsizing relates to it.

2 *Assess downsizing options and make relevant choices.* Once corporate strategy is clear, the full range of downsizing options can be identified and assessed. **Table 8.2** describes three primary downsizing methods: workforce reduction, organisation redesign and systemic changes. A specific downsizing strategy may use elements of all three approaches.

TABLE 8.1	ADVANTAGES, DISADVANTAGES AND CONTINGENCIES OF THE NETWORK-BASED FORM

Advantages

» Enables highly flexible and adaptive response to dynamic environments
» Creates a 'best of the best' organisation to focus resources on customer and market needs
» Each organisation can leverage a distinctive competency
» Permits rapid global expansion
» Can produce synergistic results

Disadvantages

» Managing lateral relations across autonomous organisations is difficult
» Motivating members to relinquish autonomy to join the network is troublesome
» Sustaining membership and benefits can be problematic
» May give partners access to proprietary knowledge/technology

Contingencies

» Highly complex and uncertain environments
» All sizes of organisations
» Highly uncertain technologies
» Goals of organisational specialisation and innovation
» Worldwide operations

TABLE 8.2	THREE TYPES OF DOWNSIZING TACTICS	
Downsizing tactic	Characteristics	Examples
Workforce reduction	Aimed at headcount reduction Short-term implementation Fosters a transition	Attrition Transfer and outplacement Retirement incentives Buyout packages Lay-offs
Organisation redesign	Aimed at organisational change Moderate-term implementation Fosters transition and, potentially, transformation	Eliminate functions Merge units Eliminate layers Eliminate products Redesign tasks
Systemic	Aimed at culture change Long-term implementation Fosters transformation	Change responsibility Involve all constituents Fosters continuous improvement and innovation Simplification Downsizing: a way of life

Source: K. Cameron, S. Freeman and A. Mishra, *Academy of Management Executive: The Thinking Manager's Source* © Academy of Management (NY), 1991. Reproduced with permission of Academy of Management (NY) in the format Textbook via Copyright Clearance Center.

From around the mid-1980s to today, it has become common for both private and public sector organisations to announce the elimination of thousands of jobs in the quest for quick productivity improvement. For example, in recent years Telstra, the state and federal public service, Rio Tinto, BHP Billiton, the big banks, Fairfax Media, Qantas and Ford Australia have each undergone major downsizing efforts involving hundreds or thousands of employees. The slowdown of the mining boom has brought challenges. Organisations going through downsizing have to be concerned about managing the effects of these cutbacks, not only for those who are being made redundant, but also for those who 'survive' – albeit with a reduced level of job security.

Unfortunately, organisations often choose obvious solutions for downsizing, such as lay-offs, that can be quickly implemented. This can produce a climate of fear and defensiveness as members focus on identifying who will be separated from the organisation. It is important to examine a broad range of options and to consider the entire organisation rather than certain areas. This can help allay fears that favouritism and politics are the basis for downsizing decisions. Moreover, the participation of organisation members in such decisions can have positive benefits. It can create a sense of urgency for identifying and implementing downsizing options other than lay-offs.

3 *Implement the changes.* This stage involves implementing methods for reducing the size of the organisation. Several practices characterise successful implementation. First, understand that downsizing is best controlled from the top down. Second, identify and target specific areas of inefficiency and high cost. Third, link specific actions to the organisation's strategy. Finally, communicate frequently, using a variety of media.

4 *Address the needs of survivors and those who leave.* When lay-offs occur, employees are generally asked to take on additional responsibilities and to learn new jobs, often with little or no increase in compensation. This added workload can be stressful, and when combined with anxiety over past lay-offs and possible future ones, can lead to what researchers have labelled the 'survivor syndrome'.[37] This involves a narrow set of self-absorbed and risk-averse behaviours that can threaten the organisation's survival. Organisations can address these survivor problems with communication processes that increase the amount and frequency of information provided. Communication should shift from explanations about who left (or why) to clarification of where the company is going, including its visions, strategies and goals.

Given the negative consequences typically associated with job loss, organisations have developed a number of methods to help employees who have been laid off. These include outplacement counselling, personal and family counselling, severance packages, office support for job searches, relocation services and job retraining. Each of these services is intended to help employees transition to another work situation.

5 *Follow through with growth plans.* Failure to move quickly to implement growth plans is a key determinant of ineffective downsizing.[38] For example, one study of 1020 human resource directors reported that only 44 per cent of the companies that had downsized in the previous five years had shared details of their growth plans with employees; only 34 per cent had told employees how they would fit into the company's new strategy.[39] The findings of this and related studies suggest that organisations need to ensure that employees understand the renewal strategy.

Results of downsizing

Research on the effects of downsizing has shown mixed results. Many studies have indicated that downsizing may not meet its intended goals, and there is mounting evidence that workforce reduction efforts were carried out in piecemeal fashion and failed to meet the objectives of the organisation.[40] Craig Littler studied 3500 companies across Australia and monitored downsizing patterns: in more than 60 per cent of those companies, the practice of downsizing had not led to any improvement in productivity. This finding is supported in some other studies and reminds managers of the need for critical thinking in strategic decision making.[41]

These research outcomes paint a rather bleak picture of the success of downsizing. However, the results must be interpreted cautiously, as they are subject to at least two major flaws. First, many of the surveys were sent to human resource specialists who might have been naturally inclined to view downsizing in a negative light. Second, the studies of financial performance may have included a biased sample of firms. If the companies selected for analysis had been poorly managed, then downsizing alone would have been unlikely to improve financial performance.

On the positive side, a number of organisations – such as Telstra, General Electric, Motorola, Texas Instruments, Boeing, Chrysler and Hewlett-Packard – have at times reported solid financial returns after downsizing. Although this evidence contradicts the negative findings described above, other research suggests that the way in which downsizing is conducted may explain these divergent outcomes. Studies of downsized firms in a range of industries show that those companies that effectively implement the application stages described above score significantly higher on several performance measures than firms that have no downsizing strategy or that implement the steps poorly.[42] Anecdotal evidence from case studies of downsized firms also shows that organisations that effectively implement the application stages are more satisfied with the process and outcomes of downsizing than are firms that do not. Thus, the success of downsizing efforts may depend as much on how effectively this intervention is applied as on the size of the lay-offs or the amount of delayering.

Apply your learning 8.1 is an example of a downsizing exercise in the telecommunications sector.

APPLY
YOUR
LEARNING
8.1

ONE-THIRD OF ALL TELSTRA JOBS LOST OVER THREE YEARS. REALLY?

Telstra surprised many in 2018 by announcing a large restructure that could result in up to 9500 jobs, almost a third of Telstra's workforce, being cut across the country in the subsequent three years. The Communication Workers Union immediately urged the federal government to become proactive in limiting the losses or at least supporting Telstra workers and their families involved in the redundancies. The union's view is that Telstra was once a publicly controlled asset and even today is a central infrastructure service for emergency calls and for connecting remote communities across the country. Telstra's view, as an independent telecommunications company in a fast-changing, global sector, is that efficiencies with available and emerging technology need to be harnessed. The reality is that information technology can consolidate large repeatable functions and effectively take the place of people, thereby delivering big cost savings. All of their competitors are likely to follow such approaches, so Telstra has to bite this bullet now if it is going to survive at the global level. Job losses are just one plank

»

in a larger restructure involving structural, process and strategic changes. Product range simplification, increases in online service and more digital solutions to service problems, embedding the new 5G network, and an overarching strategy to improve customer service are among the platitudes announced with the restructure. Will the restructure deliver the benefits Telstra aims for, and will the job losses help the company to speed towards those objectives? These are the yet unanswered questions the next few years will resolve.

Sources: Based on J. Henderson, 'Union begins to battle to save 9500 Telstra jobs', ARN, 27 June 2018; S. Letts, 'Telstra's big bang splits the company in two as 8,000 jobs go. Will it work?', ABC News, 21 June 2018; B. Grubb, 'Telstra overhaul to eliminate the human touch', *The Sydney Morning Herald*, 20 June 2018; and M. Gregory, 'Telstra may be simpler, but where will revenue come from?', Mumbrella, 27 June 2018.

Critical thinking questions

1   Discuss what can or should be done in the downsizing interventions application stages (specifically steps 3, 4 and 5 above) in the context of the announced Telstra restructure and downsizing over the next three years.

2   Does restructuring always have to include 'downsizing' in order to improve profitability and survival of the organisation?

RE-ENGINEERING

The final restructuring intervention is re-engineering: the fundamental rethinking and radical redesign of business processes in order to achieve dramatic improvements in performance.[43] Re-engineering seeks to transform how organisations produce and deliver goods and services. Beginning with the Industrial Revolution, organisations have increasingly fragmented work into specialised units, each focusing on a limited part of the overall production process. Although this division of labour has enabled organisations to mass-produce standardised products and services efficiently, it can be overly complicated and difficult to manage, as well as slow to respond to the rapid and unpredictable changes experienced by many organisations today. Re-engineering addresses these problems by breaking down specialised work units into more integrated, cross-functional work processes. This streamlines work processes and makes them faster and more flexible; consequently, they are more responsive to changes in competitive conditions, customer demands, product life cycles and technologies.[44] As might be expected, re-engineering requires an almost revolutionary change in how organisations design and think about work. It addresses fundamental issues about why organisations do what they do, and why they do it in a particular way.

In radically changing business processes, re-engineering frequently takes advantage of new information technology. Modern information technologies – such as teleconferencing, expert systems, shared databases and wireless communication – can enable organisations to re-engineer. They can help organisations break out of traditional ways of thinking about work and permit entirely new ways of producing and delivering products. Whereas new information technology can enable organisations to re-engineer themselves, existing technology can thwart such efforts. Many re-engineering projects fail because existing information systems do not provide the information needed to operate integrated business processes. The systems do not allow interdependent departments to interface with each other; they often require new information to be entered by hand into separate computer systems before people in different work areas can access it.

Re-engineering[45] is also associated with interventions that have to do with downsizing and work design. Although these interventions have different conceptual and applied backgrounds, they overlap considerably in practice. Re-engineering can result in production and delivery processes that require fewer people and layers of management. Conversely, downsizing may require subsequent re-engineering interventions. When downsizing occurs without fundamental changes in how work is performed, the same tasks are simply being performed by a smaller number of people. Thus, expected cost savings may not be realised because lower productivity offsets lower salaries and fewer benefits.

Re-engineering invariably involves aspects of work design, where tasks are assigned to jobs or teams. It identifies and assesses core business processes and redesigns work to account for key task interdependencies running through them. This typically results in new jobs or teams that emphasise multifunctional tasks, results-oriented feedback and employee empowerment – characteristics associated with motivational and sociotechnical approaches to work design. Regrettably, re-engineering has failed to apply attention to differences in individual people's reactions to work to its own work design prescriptions. It advocates enriched work and teams without consideration for the extensive research that shows that not all people are motivated to perform such work.

What are the steps?

Re-engineering is a relatively new intervention and is still developing applied methods. Early applications emphasised identifying which business processes to re-engineer and technical assessment of the work flow. Later efforts have extended re-engineering practice to address issues of managing change, such as how to manage resistance to change and how to manage the transition to new work processes.[46] The following application steps are included in re-engineering efforts, although the order may change slightly from one application to another.[47]

1 *Prepare the organisation.* Re-engineering begins with clarification and assessment of the organisation's strategic context, including its competitive environment, strategy and objectives.

2 *Fundamentally rethink the way work gets done.* This step lies at the heart of business process management and involves:
   → identifying and analysing core business processes
   → defining their key performance objectives
   → designing new processes.

These tasks are the real work of business process management and are typically performed by a cross-functional team that is given considerable time and resources to accomplish them.[48]

3   *Restructure the organisation around the new business processes.* An important element of this restructuring is the implementation of new information and measurement systems. They must reinforce a shift from measuring behaviours, such as absenteeism and grievances, to assessing outcomes, such as productivity, customer satisfaction and cost savings. Moreover, information technology is one of the key drivers of business process management because it can drastically reduce the cost and time associated with integrating and coordinating business processes.

Re-engineered organisations typically have the following characteristics:[49]

→   Work units change from functional departments to process teams.
→   Jobs change from simple tasks to multidimensional work.
→   People's roles change from controlled to empowered.
→   The focus of performance measures and compensation shifts from activities to results.
→   Organisational structures change from hierarchical to flat.
→   Managers change from supervisors to coaches; executives change from score keepers to leaders.

Results from re-engineering

The results from re-engineering vary widely. Industry journals and the business press regularly contain accounts of dramatic business results attributable to re-engineering. On the other hand, a best-selling book on re-engineering reported that as many as 70 per cent of the efforts failed to meet their cost, cycle time or productivity objectives.[50] Despite its popularity, re-engineering is only beginning to be evaluated systematically, and there is scope for further research to help unravel the disparate results.[51]

Evaluations of business process re-engineering are slowly emerging.[52] One of the foundational studies involved 100 companies and in-depth analysis of 20 re-engineering projects. It found that 11 cases had total business unit cost reductions of less than 5 per cent while six cases had total cost reductions averaging 18 per cent. The primary difference was the scope of the business process selected. Re-engineering key value-added processes significantly affected total business unit costs; re-engineering narrow business processes did not. Similarly, performance improvements in particular processes were strongly associated with changes in six key levers of behaviour, including structure, skills, information systems, roles, incentives and shared values. Efforts that addressed all six levers produced average cost reductions in specific processes by 35 per cent; efforts that affected only one or two change levers reduced costs by 19 per cent. Finally, the percentage reduction in total unit costs was associated with committed leadership.

Apply your learning 8.2 describes how technology can advance re-engineering efforts.

NEW WORLD BANK REPORT OUTLINES MALAYSIA'S SUCCESSES AND CHALLENGES IN TRANSFORMING LAND ADMINISTRATION

Malaysia's success in reforming land policies and land administration can help other developing countries striving to better manage their resources, says a new World Bank report.

The report, *Enhancing Public Sector Performance: Malaysia's Experience with Transforming Land Administration*, outlines the efforts made in peninsular Malaysia to improve systems for land administration.

Reforms that covered land policies and land administration services have been fundamental for peninsular Malaysia's secure land tenure, a well-functioning land market and sustainable management of land resources. This contributed to economic growth, efficient delivery of public services, environmental protection, as well as social cohesion and security.

Globally, more than 70 percent of the world's population do not have access to affordable systems to their secure land rights. Innovative and efficient mechanisms to improve land tenure security exemplified by peninsular Malaysia can help governments use land as a productive asset.

'A land administration system that works is a strategic goal for Malaysia. By providing reliable and affordable access to information on land rights, the land market has grown and become an important economic driver for the country,' said Tan Sri Dr Ali Hamsa, Chief Secretary to the Government of Malaysia.

Malaysia's cadaster and land registration system on peninsular Malaysia enables efficient delivery of land administration services, through both qualified and final titles, streamlining business processes, and using information communication technology (ICT) effectively. For example, the early adoption of qualified titles, which allowed land registration without a formal cadastral survey, facilitated the rapid and cost effective completion of national land administration data. The subsequent upgrading to formal titles and adoption of ICT solutions have further improved services and represent a fit-for-purpose approach to land administration.

'As our report shows, Malaysia offers important lessons in administering land – its successes as well as its challenges – enabling other countries to emulate what works and to learn from its pitfalls,' said Faris H. Hadad-Zervos, World Bank Country Manager for Malaysia.

The report also recognizes some of Malaysia's challenges. It recommends to avoid complex divisions of national and state land registries, and to integrate data systems in order to provide complete and accurate land data to public and private users. If a unified structure does not exist, it is critical to strengthen coordination between agencies and ensure data integration.

Knowledge and Research reports are flagship publications of the Malaysia Hub. This report is part of the Malaysia Development Experience Series, which strives to capture key learnings from Malaysia that are relevant for developing countries around the globe as they transition out of poverty and into shared prosperity.

Source: World Bank, 'Malaysia's land policies and administration offer useful examples to developing countries', press release, 15 November 2017, http://www.worldbank.org/en/news/press-release/2017/11/15/malaysias-land-policies-and-administration-offer-useful-examples-to-developing-countries.

»

Critical thinking questions	1	'If a unified structure does not exist, it is critical to strengthen coordination between agencies and ensure data integration.' Discuss this statement from the World Bank about the Malaysian government department experience in relation to the three main steps of re-engineering (discussed above).
	2	Speculate about performance improvements from this re-engineering approach in the government department using the six key levers of behaviour as your guide.

WORK DESIGN

This section examines three approaches to work design:

1   The *engineering approach* focuses on efficiency and simplification, and results in traditional job and work group designs.

2   A second approach to work design rests on *motivational theories and attempts to enrich the work experience*. Job enrichment[53] involves designing jobs with high levels of meaning, discretion and knowledge of results.

3   The third and most recent approach to work design derives from *sociotechnical systems methods*. This perspective seeks to optimise both the social and the technical aspects of work systems. It has led to the development of a popular form of work design called 'self-managed teams'.

The section describes each of these perspectives. Then, a contingency framework for integrating the approaches is presented, based on personal and technical factors in the workplace. When work is designed to fit these factors, it is both satisfying and productive.

THE ENGINEERING APPROACH

The oldest and most prevalent approach to work design is based on engineering concepts and methods. It proposes that the most efficient work designs can be determined by specifying the tasks to be performed, the work methods to be used and the work flow between individuals. The engineering approach is based on the pioneering work of Frederick Taylor, the father of scientific management. He developed ways of analysing and designing work and laid the groundwork for the professional field of industrial engineering.[54]

The engineering approach seeks to scientifically analyse the tasks performed by workers so as to discover those procedures that produce the maximum output with the minimum input of energies and resources.[55] This generally results in work designs with high levels of specialisation and specification. Such designs have several benefits: they allow workers to learn tasks rapidly, they permit short work cycles so that performance can take place with little or no mental effort and they reduce costs as lower-skilled people can be hired and trained easily and paid relatively low wages.

The engineering approach produces two kinds of work design: traditional jobs and traditional work groups. When one person can complete the work, as is the case with bank tellers and telephone operators, traditional jobs are created. They tend to be simplified, with routine and repetitive tasks having clear specifications concerning time and motion. When the work requires coordination between people, such as automobile assembly lines, traditional work groups are developed. They are composed of members who perform relatively routine, yet related, tasks. The overall group task is typically broken into simpler, discrete parts (often called jobs). The tasks and work methods are specified for each part, and the different parts are assigned to group members. Each member performs a routine and repetitive part of the group task. Members' separate task contributions are coordinated for overall task achievement through external controls, such as schedules, rigid work flows and supervisors.[56] In the 1950s and 1960s, this method of work design was popularised by the assembly lines of Australian automobile manufacturers, such as General Motors Holden, and was an important reason for the growth of Australian industry after the Second World War.

The engineering approach to job design is less an OD intervention than a benchmark in history. Critics of the approach argue that the method ignores the social and psychological needs of workers.[57] They suggest that the increasing educational level of the workforce and the substitution of automation for menial labour point to the need for more enriched forms of work, where people have greater discretion and challenge. Moreover, current competitive challenges require a more committed and involved workforce that is able to make online decisions and develop performance innovations. Work designed with the employee in mind is more humanly fulfilling and productive than that designed in traditional ways. However, it is important to recognise the strengths of the engineering approach. It remains an important work design intervention as its immediate cost savings and efficiency can easily be measured. It is also well understood and easily implemented and managed.

THE MOTIVATIONAL APPROACH

The motivational approach to work design views the effectiveness of organisational activities primarily as a function of members' needs and satisfaction. It seeks to improve employee performance and satisfaction by enriching jobs. This provides people with opportunities for autonomy, responsibility, closure (doing a complete job) and feedback about performance. Enriched jobs can be found in Australia at such companies as Golden Circle Limited and Rupnorth Cooperative Limited, among others.

The motivational approach is usually associated with the research of Herzberg, as well as that of Hackman and Oldham. Herzberg's two-factor theory of motivation proposed that certain attributes of work (such as opportunities for advancement and recognition, which he called 'motivators') help increase job satisfaction.[58] Other attributes (called 'hygiene' factors, such as company policies, working conditions, pay and supervision) do not produce satisfaction but prevent dissatisfaction. Only satisfied workers are motivated to produce.

Although Herzberg's motivational factors sound appealing, increasing doubt has been cast on the underlying theory. For example, motivation and hygiene factors are difficult to put into operation and measure, making implementation and evaluation of the theory difficult. Important worker characteristics that can affect whether or not people will respond favourably to job enrichment were also not included in the theory. Finally, Herzberg's failure to involve employees in the job enrichment process itself does not sit well with most current OD practitioners. Consequently, a second, well-researched approach to job enrichment has been favoured. It focuses on the attributes of the work itself and has resulted in a more scientifically acceptable theory of job enrichment than Herzberg's model. The research of Hackman and Oldham represents this more recent trend in job enrichment.[59]

A large company may have scope to offer employees motivation through the opportunity to take different positions, and therefore different challenges, as illustrated in **Apply your learning 8.3**.

CHANGING LANDSCAPE FOR THE GENERATIONS

How does the role of managing Generation Y (Gen-Y) employees differ from managing older generations? A 2017 research report about Gen-Y by University of Melbourne has some helpful insights. Their research has been tracking the lives of 515 Generation Y members, now aged 28–29, since 2005. Ominously, Gen-Y are trending towards giving up having a career, buying a house, and getting married and this is affecting their attitude and motivation towards work. Other survey research in 2017 by Global HR think-tank Reventure indicates there is major financial stress on Gen-Y that may be affecting their lives and work decisions. Great bosses make an honest effort to understand their people. The challenge is to leverage the unique characteristics, values and skills of people [independent of the category they belong to]. The evolving research of Gen-Y reveals they have a different mindset than Gen-X and the other generations. Each generation's attitudes and beliefs are shaped by cultural shifts, influential public personalities, politicians, economic pressures, world-shaping events, technological advances and so on. These differences in mindset play out in the workplace and that sets up an interesting dynamic: several generations with different views, attitudes, loyalties and skills. Such differences include relationships with the organisation, relationships with colleagues, work approaches, orientation towards leadership and orientation towards career. A main driver from Gen-Y is to create a life and find work that has a meaning. Stress minimisation and work–life balance are key issues for Gen-Y. Time off the job is important, even if it costs a promotion.

What are the main challenges that face today's managers when motivating and setting goals for Generation Y employees?

Employees of the different generations bring different values, attitudes towards work, work styles, job satisfaction criteria, learning styles and levels of commitment to the workplace. The role of the leader is to flex himself or herself and find ways to motivate these individuals, understanding that what might work for a Gen-X does not work for Gen-Y. But even two Gen-Yers can be different, so the leader must understand the psyche of the employee and see what truly motivates the employee.

And then the issue of the newest working generation, Gen-Z (millennials), also begins to loom. Gen-Zers have just begun coming to workplaces everywhere. Some early research suggests they may be strongly value driven, entrepreneurial, financially prudent and curious. How might these features affect how managers deal with them? In fact, the role of managers is getting quite complex today with, for

»

»

the first time in history, up to five generations sharing the workforce side by side – Veterans (pre-Second World War); Baby Boomers (Second World War to 1960s); Generation X (mid-1960s to late 1970s); Gen-Y (1979–91); and Gen-Z, born after 1992.

Motivational tools, rewards, recognition and retention tools will look different for each employee. A key question is how flexible is the organisation in its policies and practices to adjust to people from the different generations, and to cater to their needs and motivations? Or is a change required for us to become more flexible? This is a key question that organisations need to ask themselves, as success depends on the ability to recruit, retain, engage, manage and develop people.

Sources: Based on J. Nelder, 'Your millennial staff might be shopping for new jobs because of stress: here's how to retain them', SmartCompany, 20 December 2017; L. Ronnie, 'What industry will Generation Z work in?', *International Business Times*, 24 July 2017; and J. Wyn and H. Cahill, 'A generation dislodged: why things are tough for Gen Y', Pursuit, 18 September 2017.

Critical thinking questions

1   Should employers' motivational approach to work design include and consider differences between the mindsets of Gen-Y and Gen-X and any of the other generations? In your discussion, think about where you sit and what you want out of life.

2   If employers have to consider what motivates each generation in relation to work design, do you think universities, training organisations and in-house training programs also should consider how they deliver course content and teaching methods?

The core dimensions of jobs

Considerable research has been devoted to defining and understanding core job dimensions.[60] **Figure 8.3** summarises the Hackman and Oldham model of job design. Five core dimensions of work affect three critical psychological states, which in turn produce personal and job outcomes. These outcomes include high internal work motivation, high-quality work performance, satisfaction with the work, and low absenteeism and turnover.

Not all people react in similar ways to job enrichment interventions. Individual differences – such as a worker's knowledge and skill levels, growth need, strength and satisfaction with contextual factors – moderate the relationships between core dimensions, psychological states and outcomes. 'Worker knowledge and skill' refers to the education and experience levels that characterise the workforce. If employees lack the appropriate skills, for example, increasing skill variety may not improve a job's meaningfulness. Similarly, if workers lack the intrinsic motivation to grow and develop personally, attempts to provide them with increased autonomy may be resisted. (We discuss growth needs more fully in the last section of this chapter.) Finally, contextual factors include reward systems, supervisory style and co-worker satisfaction. When the employee is unhappy with the work context, attempts to enrich the work itself may be unsuccessful.

FIGURE 8.3   THE RELATIONSHIPS AMONG THE CORE JOB DIMENSIONS – THE CRITICAL INDIVIDUAL DIFFERENCES

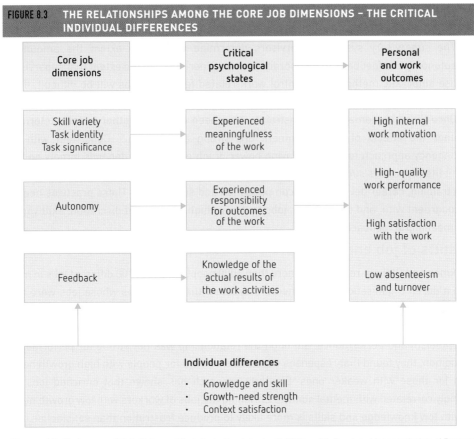

Source: J.R. Hackman and G.R. Oldham, *Work Redesign*, 1st edn, © 1980, p. 83. Reprinted by permission of Pearson Education, Inc., Upper Saddle River, New Jersey.

Barriers to job enrichment

As the application of job enrichment has spread, several obstacles to significant job restructuring have been identified. Most of these barriers exist in the organisational context within which the job design is executed. Other organisational systems and practices, whether technical, managerial or personnel, can affect both the implementation of job enrichment and the life span of whatever changes are made. At least four organisational systems can constrain the implementation of job enrichment:[61]

1   *The technical system.* The technology of an organisation can limit job enrichment by constraining the number of ways in which jobs can be changed. Technology may also set an 'enrichment ceiling'. Some types of work, such as continuous-process production systems, may be naturally enriched, so there is little more that can be gained from a job enrichment intervention.

2   *The personnel system.* Personnel systems can constrain job enrichment by creating formalised job descriptions that are rigidly defined and that limit flexibility in changing people's job duties.

3   *The control system.* Control systems, such as budgets, production reports and accounting practices, can limit the complexity and challenge of jobs within the system.

4   *The supervisory system.* Supervisors determine to a large extent the amount of autonomy and feedback that subordinates can experience. To the extent that supervisors use autocratic methods and control work-related feedback, jobs will be difficult, if not impossible, to enrich.

Once these implementation constraints have been overcome, other factors determine whether the effects of job enrichment are strong and lasting.[62] Consistent with the contingency approach to OD, the staying power of job enrichment depends largely on how well it fits with and is supported by other organisational practices, such as those associated with training, career development, compensation and supervision. These practices need to be congruent with, and to reinforce, jobs that have high amounts of discretion, skill variety and meaningful feedback.

Results of job enrichment

Hackman and Oldham reported on more than 1000 people in about 100 different jobs in more than a dozen organisations.[63] In general, they found that employees whose jobs were high on the core dimensions were more satisfied and motivated than those whose jobs were low on the dimensions. The core dimensions were also related to such behaviours as absenteeism and performance, although the relationship was not strong for performance. In addition, they found that responses were more positive for people with high growth needs than for those with weaker ones. Similarly, research has shown that enriched jobs are strongly correlated with mental ability.[64] Enriching the jobs of workers with low growth needs or with low knowledge and skills is more likely to produce frustration than satisfaction.

An impressive amount of research has been done on Hackman and Oldham's approach to job enrichment. In addition, several studies have extended and refined Hackman and Oldham's approach to both produce more reliable data[65] and incorporate other moderators, such as the need for achievement and job longevity.[66] In general, research has supported the proposed relationships between job characteristics and outcomes, including the moderating effects of growth needs, knowledge and skills, and context satisfaction.[67] In regard to context satisfaction, for example, research indicates that employee turnover, dissatisfaction and withdrawal are associated with dark offices, a lack of privacy and high worker densities.[68]

Reviews of the job enrichment research also report positive effects. An analysis of 28 studies concluded that the job characteristics are positively related to job satisfaction, particularly for people with high growth needs.[69] Another review concluded that job enrichment is effective at reducing employee turnover.[70] A different examination of 28 job enrichment studies reported overwhelmingly positive results.[71] Improvements in quality and cost measures were reported slightly more frequently than improvements in employee attitudes and quantity of production. However, the studies suffered from methodological weaknesses that suggest that the positive findings should be viewed with some caution. Another review of 16 job enrichment studies showed mixed results.[72] Thirteen of the programs were developed and implemented solely by management. These studies showed significant reduction in absenteeism, turnover and grievances, and improvements in quality of production in only about half of the cases where these variables were measured. The three studies with high levels of employee participation in the change program showed improvements in these variables in all cases where they were measured. These earlier studies combined with the emerging research of today indicate employee participation in the job enrichment program appears to enhance the success of such interventions.

THE SOCIOTECHNICAL SYSTEMS APPROACH

The **sociotechnical systems (STS)** approach is the most extensive body of scientific and applied work underlying employee involvement and innovative work designs today. Its techniques and design principles derive from extensive action research in both public and private organisations across a diversity of national cultures. This section reviews the conceptual foundations of the STS approach and then describes its most popular application: self-managed work teams.

Sociotechnical systems (STS): a sociotechnical system consists of two independent, yet related, parts: a social part that includes the people performing the tasks and the relationships among them, and a technical part consisting of the tools, techniques and methods for task performance.

Conceptual background

STS theory was originally developed at the Tavistock Institute of Human Relations in London in the early 1960s and has since spread to most industrialised nations. In Europe, and particularly Scandinavia, STS interventions are almost synonymous with work design and employee involvement. In Canada and the United States, STS concepts and methods underlie many of the innovative work designs and team-based structures that are so prevalent in today's organisations. Intel and Procter & Gamble are among the many organisations applying the STS approach to transform how work is designed and performed. STS theory is based on two fundamental premises:

→ that an organisation or work unit is a combined, social-plus-technical system

→ that this system is open in relation to its environment.[73]

Sociotechnical system

The first assumption suggests that whenever human beings are organised to perform tasks, a joint system is operating – a sociotechnical system. This system consists of two independent, yet related, parts: a social part that includes the people performing the tasks and the relationships among them, and a technical part consisting of the tools, techniques and methods for task performance. These two parts are independent of each other by virtue of each following a different set of behavioural laws. The social part operates according to biological and psychosocial laws, whereas the technical part functions according to mechanical and physical laws. Nevertheless, the two parts are related because they must act together to accomplish tasks. Hence, the term 'sociotechnical' signifies the joint relationship that must occur between the social and technical parts, and the word 'system' communicates that this connection results in a unified whole.

Because a sociotechnical system is composed of social and technical parts, it follows that it will produce two kinds of outcomes: products, such as goods and services, and social and psychological consequences, such as job satisfaction and commitment. The key issue is how to design the relationship between the two parts so that these outcomes are both positive (referred to as 'joint optimisation').

Sociotechnical practitioners design work and organisations so that the social and technical parts work well together, producing high levels of product and human satisfaction. This contrasts with the engineering approach to designing work, which tends to focus on the technical component and worries about fitting in people later. This often leads to mediocre performance at high social costs. This also contrasts with the motivation approach, which views work design in terms of human fulfilment. This approach can lead to satisfied employees, but inefficient work processes.

Environmental relationship

The second major premise underlying STS theory concerns the fact that such systems are open to their environments. Open systems need to interact with their environments to survive and develop. The environment provides the STS with necessary inputs of energy, raw materials and information, while the STS, in turn, provides the environment with products and services. The key issue here is how to design the interface between the STS and its environment so that the system has sufficient freedom to function while exchanging effectively with the environment. In what is typically referred to as boundary management, STS practitioners attempt to structure environmental relationships to both protect the system from external disruptions and to facilitate the exchange of necessary resources and information. This enables the STS to adapt to changing conditions and to influence the environment in favourable directions.

In summary, STS theory suggests that effective work systems jointly optimise the relationship between their social and technical parts. Moreover, such systems effectively manage the boundary that separates them from, while relating them to, the environment. This allows them to exchange with the environment while protecting themselves from external disruptions.

Self-managed work teams

Self-managed work teams: groups composed of members performing interrelated tasks. Members are given the multiple skills, autonomy and information necessary to control their own task behaviours with relatively little external control.

The most prevalent application of the STS approach is **self-managed work teams**.[74] Alternatively referred to as 'self-directed work teams', 'self-regulating work teams' or 'high-performance work teams', these work designs consist of members performing interrelated tasks.[75] Self-managed work teams are typically responsible for a whole product or service, or a major part of a larger production process. They control members' task behaviours and make decisions about task assignments and work methods. In many cases, the team sets its own production goals, within broader organisational limits, and may be responsible for support services, such as maintenance, purchasing and quality control. Team members are generally expected to learn many, if not all, of the jobs within the team's control and frequently are paid on the basis of knowledge and skills rather than seniority. When pay is based on performance, team rather than individual performance is used.

Figure 8.4 is a model explaining how self-managed work teams perform. It summarises current STS research and shows how teams can be designed for high performance. Although the model is mainly based on experience with teams that perform the daily work of the organisation (work teams), it also has relevance to other team designs, such as problem-solving teams, management teams, cross-functional integrating teams and employee involvement teams.[76]

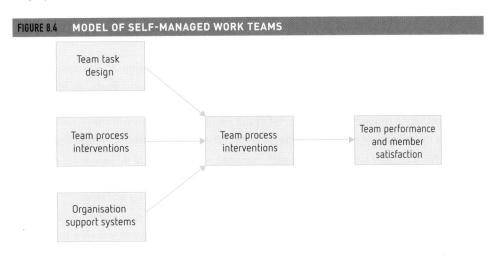

FIGURE 8.4   **MODEL OF SELF-MANAGED WORK TEAMS**

The model shows that team performance and member satisfaction follow directly from how well the team functions. This includes how well members communicate and coordinate with each other, resolve conflicts and problems, and make and implement task-relevant decisions. Team functioning, in turn, is influenced by three major inputs:

→ team task design

→ team process interventions

→ organisation support systems.

Because these inputs affect how well teams function and subsequently perform, they are key intervention targets for designing and implementing self-managed work teams.

Application steps

STS work designs have been implemented in a variety of settings, including manufacturing firms, hospitals, schools and government agencies. Although the specific implementation strategy is tailored to the situation, a common method of change underlies many of these applications. It generally involves high worker participation in the work design and implementation process. Such participative work design allows employees to translate their special knowledge of the work situation into relevant work designs. Because employees have ownership over the design process, they tend to be highly committed to implementing the work designs.[77] STS applications generally proceed in six steps:[78]

1   *Sanctioning the design effort.* In this stage, workers are provided with the necessary protection and support to diagnose their work system and to design an appropriate work design.

2   *Diagnosing the work system.* Knowledge of existing operations (or of intended operations, in the case of a new work system) is the basis for designing an appropriate

work design. STS practitioners have devised diagnostic models applicable to work systems making products or delivering services.

3   *Generating appropriate designs.* Although this typically results in self-managed work teams, it is important to emphasise that, in some cases, the diagnosis may reveal that tasks are not very interdependent and that an individual-job work design, such as an enriched job, might be more appropriate.

The output of this design step specifies the new work design. In the case of self-managed work teams, this would include the team's mission and goals, an ideal work flow, the skills and knowledge required of team members, a plan for training members to meet those requirements and a list of the decisions the team will make now, as well as the ones it should make over time as members develop greater skills and knowledge.

4   *Specifying support systems.* When self-managed work teams are designed, for example, the basis for pay and measurement systems may need to be changed from individual to team performance to facilitate necessary task interaction among workers.

5   *Implementing and evaluating the work designs.* For self-managing work teams, implementation generally requires considerable training to enable workers to gain the necessary technical and social skills to perform multiple tasks, and to control members' task behaviours. OD consultants often help team members carry out these tasks with a major emphasis on helping them gain competence in this area. Evaluation of the work design is necessary both to guide the implementation process and to assess the overall effectiveness of the design. In some cases, the evaluation information suggests the need for further diagnosis and redesign efforts.

6   *Continual change and improvement.* The ability to continually design and redesign work needs to be built into existing work designs. Members must have the skills and knowledge to continually assess their work unit and make necessary changes and improvements.

Results of self-managed teams

Research on STS design efforts is extensive. For example, a 1994 bibliography by researchers at Eindhoven University of Technology in the Netherlands found 3082 English-language studies.[79] By 2018, a Google Scholar search on the key term 'sociotechnical systems' returned research results numbering 21700. As with reports on job enrichment, most of the published reports on self-managed teams show favourable results.[80]

A series of famous case studies at General Foods' Gaines Pet Food/Topeka plant, the Saab-Scania engine assembly plant and Volvo's Kalmar and Uddevalla plants provides one set of positive findings. The Gaines Pet Food plant operated at an overhead rate some 33 per cent below that of traditional plants.[81] It reported annual variable cost savings of US$600000, one of the best safety records in the company, turnover rates far below average and high levels of job satisfaction. A long-term, external evaluation of the groups at the Gaines plant[82] attributed savings related to work innovation at about US$1 million a year, and, despite a variety of problems, productivity increased in every year but one over a decade of operation. The plant has maintained one of the highest product quality ratings at General Foods since its opening.

Extensive early research on self-managing groups was done by Saab-Scania.[83] The first group was established in 1969, and four years later there were 130 production groups. These groups generally showed improvements in production and employee attitudes and decreases in unplanned work stoppages and turnover rates. Interestingly, when workers from the United States visited Saab's engine assembly plant, they reported that work was too fast and that lunch breaks were too short.[84] A Saab executive commented that the visitors had not stayed long enough to become completely proficient, causing their complaint that the pace was too fast.

The widely publicised use of self-managing groups at Volvo's automotive plant in Kalmar, Sweden, also showed positive results.[85] The Kalmar factory opened in July 1974, and by the following year it was operating at 100 per cent efficiency. As a reference point, highly productive automobile plants normally operate at about 80 per cent of engineering standards. Interviews with workers and union officials indicated that the quality of work life was considerably better than in assembly jobs that they had in the past. In addition, Volvo's Uddevalla plant reported significant quality improvements and higher productivity than in comparable plants.[86]

A second set of studies supporting the positive impact of sociotechnical design teams comes from research comparing self-managed teams with other interventions. For example, probably one of the most thorough assessments of self-managing groups is a longitudinal study conducted in a food-processing plant in the Midwest of the United States.[87] Self-managing groups were created as part of an overall revamping of a major part of the plant's production facilities. The effects of the intervention were extremely positive. One year after start-up, production was 133 per cent higher than originally planned, while start-up costs were 7.7 per cent lower than planned. Employee attitudes were extremely positive towards the group design. These positive effects, however, did not result solely from the self-managing design. The intervention also included survey feedback for diagnostic purposes and changes in technology, the physical work setting and management. These kinds of changes are common in self-managing group projects. They suggest that such designs may require supporting changes in other organisational dimensions, such as technology, management style and physical setting, in order to facilitate the development of self-managed teams.

This study also permitted a comparison of self-managing groups with job enrichment, which occurred in another department of the company. Both interventions included survey feedback. The self-managing project involved technological changes, whereas the job enrichment program did not. The results showed that both interventions had similar positive effects in terms of employee attitudes. However, only the self-managing project had significant improvements in productivity and costs. Again, the productivity improvements cannot be totally attributed to the self-managed teams, but were also the result of the technological changes. Although the majority of studies report positive effects of self-managing groups, ongoing contemporary research suggests a more mixed assessment.[88]

DESIGNING WORK FOR TECHNICAL AND PERSONAL NEEDS

This section has described three approaches to work design: engineering, motivational and sociotechnical. However, trade-offs and conflicts among the approaches must be recognised. The engineering approach produces traditional jobs and work groups, and focuses on efficient performance. This approach tends to downplay employee needs and emphasise economic outcomes. The motivational approach strives to design jobs that are stimulating and demanding, and highlights the importance of employee need satisfaction. Research suggests, however, that increased satisfaction does not necessarily produce improvements in productivity. Finally, the STS approach attempts to optimise both social and technical aspects. Despite this integrative goal, STS has not produced consistent research results.

In this final section, we attempt to integrate the three perspectives by providing a contingency framework that suggests all three approaches can be effective when applied in the appropriate circumstances. Work design involves creating jobs and work groups for high levels of employee satisfaction and productivity. Considerable research shows that achieving such results depends on designing work to match specific factors that operate in the work setting. These factors have to do with the technology for producing goods and services and the personal needs of employees. When work is designed to fit or match these factors, it is most likely to be both productive and humanly satisfying.

Technical factors

Two key dimensions can affect change on the shop floor: technical interdependence, or the extent to which cooperation among workers is required to produce a product or service; and technical uncertainty, or the amount of information processing and decision making that employees must do in order to complete a task.[89] In general, the degree of technical interdependence determines whether work should be designed for individual jobs or work groups. With low technical interdependence and little need for worker cooperation – as, for example, in field sales and data entry – work can be designed for individual jobs. Conversely, when technical interdependence is high and employees must cooperate – as in production processes such as coal mining, assembly lines and software writing – work should be designed for groups composed of people who perform interacting tasks.

The second dimension, technical uncertainty, determines whether work should be designed for external forms of control, such as supervision, scheduling or standardisation, or for worker self-control. When technical uncertainty is low and little information has to be processed by employees, work can be designed for external control, such as might be found on assembly lines and in other forms of repetitive work. On the other hand, when technical uncertainty is high and people must process information and make decisions, work should be designed for high levels of employee self-control, such as might be found in professional work and troubleshooting tasks.

Figure 8.5 shows the different types of work designs that are most effective, from a purely technological perspective, for different combinations of interdependence and uncertainty. In quadrant 1, where technological interdependence and uncertainty are both low, such as might be found in data entry, jobs should be designed traditionally with limited amounts of employee interaction and self-control. When task interdependence is high yet uncertainty is low (quadrant 2), such as work occurring on assembly lines, work should be designed for traditional work groups in which employee interaction is scheduled and self-control is limited. In quadrant 3, where technological interdependence is low but uncertainty is high, as in field sales, work should be structured for individual jobs with internal forms of control, as in enriched jobs. Finally, when both technological interdependence and uncertainty are high (quadrant 4), such as might be found in a continuous-process chemical plant, work should be designed for self-managed teams in which members have the multiple skills, discretion and information necessary to control their interactions around the shared tasks.

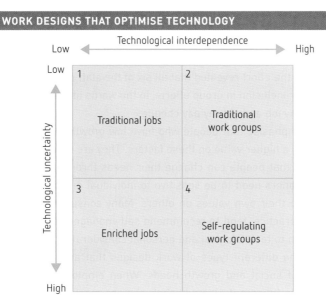

FIGURE 8.5   WORK DESIGNS THAT OPTIMISE TECHNOLOGY

Source: Reproduced by permission from Thomas G. Cummings, 'Designing work for productivity and quality of work life', *Outlook*, 6 (1982): 39.

Personal-need factors

Most of the research identifying individual differences in work design has focused on selected personal traits. Two types of personal needs can influence the kinds of work designs that are most effective: social needs, or the desire for significant social relationships; and growth needs, or the desire for personal accomplishment, learning and development.[90] In general, the degree of social needs determines whether work should be designed for individual jobs or work groups. People with low needs for social relationships are more likely to be satisfied working on individualised jobs than in interacting groups. Conversely, people with high social needs are more likely to be attracted to group forms of work than to individualised forms.

The second individual difference, growth needs, determines whether work designs should be routine and repetitive or complex and challenging. People with low growth needs are generally not attracted to jobs that offer complexity and challenge (that is, enriched jobs). They are more satisfied performing routine forms of work that do not require high levels of decision making. On the other hand, people with high growth needs are satisfied with work offering high levels of discretion, skill variety and meaningful feedback. Performing enriched jobs allows them to experience personal accomplishment and development.

That some people have low social and growth needs is often difficult for OD practitioners to accept, particularly in view of the growth and social values that underlie much OD practice. However, it is important to recognise that individual differences do exist. Assuming that all people have high growth needs or want high levels of social interaction can lead to inappropriate work designs. For example, a new manager of a clerical support unit was astonished to find the six members using typewriters when a significant portion of the work consisted of retyping memos and reports that were produced frequently, but changed very little from month to month. In addition, the unit had a terrible record for quality and on-time production. The manager quickly ordered new word processors and redesigned the work flow to increase interaction among members. Worker satisfaction declined, interpersonal conflicts increased and work quality and on-time performance remained poor. An assessment of the effort revealed that all six of the staff members had low growth needs and low needs for inclusion in group efforts. In the words of one worker: 'All I want is to come into work, do my job and get my pay cheque.'

It is important to emphasise that people who have low growth or social needs are not inferior to those placing a higher value on these factors. They are simply different. It is also necessary to recognise that people can change their needs through personal growth and experience. OD practitioners need to be sensitive to individual differences in work design and careful not to force their own values on others. Many consultants, eager to be seen on the cutting edge of practice, tend to recommend self-managed teams in all situations, without careful attention to technological and personal considerations.

Figure 8.6 shows the different types of work designs that are most effective for the various combinations of social and growth needs. When employees have relatively low social and growth needs (quadrant 1), traditional jobs are most effective. In quadrant 2, where employees have high social needs but low growth needs, traditional work groups, such as might be found on an assembly line, are most appropriate. These allow for some social interaction but limited amounts of challenge and discretion. When employees have low social needs but high growth needs (quadrant 3), enriched jobs are most satisfying. Here, work is designed for individual jobs that have high levels of task variety, discretion and feedback about results. A research scientist's job is likely to be an enriched one, as is that of a skilled craftsperson. Finally, in quadrant 4, where employees have high social and growth needs, work should be specifically designed for self-managed teams. Such groups offer opportunities for significant social interaction around tasks that are both complex and challenging. A team of astronauts in a space shuttle resembles a self-managing work group, as does a group managing the control room of an oil refinery or a group of nurses in a hospital unit.

Meeting both technical and personal needs

Satisfying both technical and human needs to achieve work design success is likely to occur only in limited circumstances. When the technical conditions of a company's production processes (as shown in **Figure 8.5**) are compatible with the personal needs of its employees (as shown in **Figure 8.6**), the respective work designs combine readily and can satisfy both. On General Motors' assembly lines, for example, the technology is highly interdependent, yet low in uncertainty (quadrant 2 in **Figure 8.5**). Much of the work is designed around traditional work groups in which task behaviours are standardised, and interactions among workers are scheduled. Such work is likely to be productive and fulfilling to the extent that

General Motors' production workers have high social needs and low growth needs (quadrant 2 in **Figure 8.6**).

FIGURE 8.6   WORK DESIGNS THAT OPTIMISE PERSONAL NEEDS

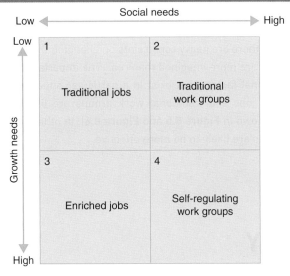

Source: Reproduced by permission from Thomas G. Cummings, 'Designing work for productivity and quality of work life', *Outlook*, 6 (1982): 40.

When technology and people are incompatible – for example, when an organisation has quadrant 1 technology and quadrant 4 worker needs – at least two kinds of changes can be made to design work to satisfy both requirements.[91] One strategy is to change technology or people to bring them more into line with each other. This is a key point underlying STS approaches. For example, technical interdependence can be reduced by breaking long assembly lines into more discrete groups. In Sweden, Volvo redesigned the physical layout and technology for assembling automobiles and trucks to promote self-managed teams. Modifying people's needs is more complex, and begins by matching new or existing workers to available work designs. For example, companies can assess workers' needs through standardised paper-and-pencil tests. The information from these can be used to counsel employees and to help them locate jobs that are compatible with their needs. Similarly, employees can be allowed to volunteer for specific work designs, a common practice in STS projects. This matching process is likely to require high levels of trust and cooperation between management and workers, as well as a shared commitment to designing work for high performance and employee satisfaction.

A second strategy for accommodating both technical and human requirements is to leave the two components alone and to design compromise work designs that only partially fulfil the demands of either. The key issue is to decide to what extent one contingency will be satisfied at the expense of the other. For example, when capital costs are high relative to labour costs (such as is found in highly automated plants) work design is likely to favour the technology. Conversely, in many service jobs where labour is expensive relative to capital, organisations may design work for employee motivation and satisfaction at the risk of short-changing their technology. These examples suggest a range of possible compromises based on different weightings of technical and human demands. Careful assessment of both types of contingencies and of the cost–benefit trade-offs is necessary to design an appropriate compromise work design.

Clearly, the strategy of designing work to bring technology and people more into line with each other is preferable to compromise work designs. Although the latter approach seems necessary when there are heavy constraints on changing the contingencies, in many cases those constraints are more imagined than real. The important thing is to understand the technical and personal factors that exist in a particular situation and to design work accordingly. Traditional jobs and traditional work groups are likely to be successful in certain situations (as shown in **Figure 8.5** and **Figure 8.6**); in other settings, enriched jobs and self-managed teams are likely to be more effective.

SUMMARY

In this chapter we presented interventions aimed at improving organisational and environmental relationships. Because organisations are open systems that exist in environmental contexts, they must establish and maintain effective linkages with the environment in order to survive and prosper. Three environments impact on organisational functioning: the general environment, the task environment and the enacted environment. Only the last of these can affect organisational choices about behaviour, but the first two impact on the consequences of those actions. Two key environmental dimensions affect the degree to which organisations are constrained by their environments and need to be responsive to them: information uncertainty and resource dependence. When both dimensions are high, organisations are maximally constrained and need to be responsive to their environment.

OSP helps an organisation to systematically assess its environment and develop strategic responses to it. This intervention is based on assumptions about the role of people's perceptions in environmental relations and the need for a shared view of the environment that permits coordinated action towards it. It begins with an assessment of the existing environment and how the organisation relates to it and progresses to possible future environments and action plans to bring them about. A number of guidelines exist for effectively applying this intervention.

TD is an emerging form of planned change that is aimed at helping organisations create partnerships with other organisations to perform tasks or to solve problems that are too complex and multifaceted for single organisations to carry out. Because these multi-organisation systems tend to be underorganised, TD follows the stages of planned change relevant to underorganised systems: identification, convention, organisation and evaluation.

We then presented interventions aimed at restructuring organisations. Two restructuring interventions were described: downsizing and re-engineering. Downsizing decreases the size of the organisation through workforce reduction or organisational redesign. It is generally associated with lay-offs where a certain number or class of organisation member is no longer employed by the organisation. Downsizing can contribute to OD by focusing on the organisation's strategy, using a variety of downsizing tactics, addressing the needs of all organisation members and following through with growth plans.

Re-engineering is the fundamental rethinking and radical redesign of business processes to achieve dramatic improvements in performance. It seeks to transform how organisations traditionally produce and deliver goods and services. A typical re-engineering project prepares the organisation, rethinks how work gets done and finally restructures the organisation around the newly designed core processes.

In the final section we discussed three different approaches to work design. In addition, a contingency framework was described to determine the approach most likely to result in high productivity and worker satisfaction, given certain workplace characteristics. The contingency framework reconciles the strengths and weaknesses of each approach. The engineering approach produces traditional jobs and traditional work groups. Traditional jobs are highly simplified and involve routine and repetitive forms of work. They do not require coordination among people to produce a product or service. Traditional jobs achieve high productivity and worker satisfaction in situations that are characterised by low technical uncertainty and interdependence, and low growth and social needs.

Traditional work groups are composed of members performing routine yet interrelated tasks. Member interactions are controlled externally, usually by rigid work flows, schedules and supervisors. Traditional work groups are best suited to conditions of low technical uncertainty, but high technical interdependence. They fit people with low growth needs but high social needs.

The motivational approach produces enriched jobs that involve high levels of skill variety, task identity, task significance, autonomy and feedback from the work itself. Enriched jobs achieve good results when the technology is uncertain but does not require high levels of coordination, and when employees have high growth needs and low social needs.

Finally, the STS approach is associated with self-managed teams. These groups are composed of members performing interrelated tasks. Members are given the multiple skills, autonomy and information necessary to control their own task behaviours with relatively little external control. Many OD practitioners argue that self-managed teams represent an ideal work design suited to the contemporary workforce. This is because high levels of technical uncertainty and interdependence are prevalent in today's workplaces and because today's workers often have high growth and social needs.

ACTIVITIES

REVIEW QUESTIONS

1   What constitutes the organisation's general environment? How would this impact on decisions made by a change agent? (LO1)

2   Through what strategies do organisations gain 'control' over their environments? What implications does this have for how change is managed? (LO1)

3 What is associated with a transorganisational system? Describe its stages and compare and contrast this with the OD process. (LO3)

4 Describe both downsizing and re-engineering, then compare and contrast them. (LO3)

5 What are the approaches to work design? Give an example of each. (LO4)

6 Why are the work design approaches more effective when integrated? (LO4)

7 What are the guidelines for OSP? (LO2)

8 Define TD and highlight an example of it happening in industry practice. (LO3)

9 Consider which aspects of the general environment would play a significant part in the success of TD activities. (LO1 & 3)

EXTEND YOUR LEARNING

Form a discussion group of friends, family or colleagues for the purpose of answering the questions that follow:

1 From your work experience, or from companies you have read about, describe an example of each of the approaches to work design discussing why you think that approach was chosen. (LO4)

2 'Downsizing has been the most successful change strategy for organisations in a turbulent environment.' Discuss this statement with emphasis on the practical experience of someone who is being 'downsized'. Compare this with the experience of a manager who must directly implement the downsizing. How do these two perspectives marry up with 'successful' change strategy? (LO3)

3 Refer to **Table 8.2** Three types of downsizing tactics. Take notice of the examples column of the table and open discussion to share direct or indirect knowledge of organisations that have followed one or other of these tactics. (LO3)

4 OSP is based on four assumptions about how organisations relate, or should relate, to their environment. Discuss these four assumptions by providing examples of each one and considering which ones may be more important than the others. (LO2)

5 In 2018 a $4 billion merger was announced between Fairfax Media and the Nine Network. Some news reports described it as a takeover rather than a merger. Review some of the facts of this story as reported by the ABC (**http://www.abc.net.au/news/2018-07-26/nine-announces-fairfax-takeover/10037712**) and then discuss what the two companies have to face in terms of TD. Summarise the pros and cons that TD forecasts may happen in such a situation. (LO3)

Search ⊕ Me! **Management**

Explore **Search Me! Management** for articles relevant to this chapter. Fast and convenient, **Search Me! Management** is updated daily and provides you with 24-hour access to full text articles from hundreds of scholarly and popular journals, eBooks and newspapers, including *The Australian* and *The New York Times*. Visit **http://login.cengagebrain.com** and use the access code that comes with this book for 12 months access to the **Search Me! Management** database. Try searching for the following keywords:

Keywords:

- Open systems planning (OSP)
- Transorganisational development (TD)
- Downsizing
- Re-engineering
- Sociotechnical systems (STS)
- Self-managed work teams

Search tip: **Search Me! Management** contains information from both local and international sources. To get the greatest number of search results, try using both Australian and American spellings in your searches; for example, 'globalisation' and 'globalization'; 'organisation' and 'organization'.

REFERENCES

1 N. Pupat, 'The impact of organisation development intervention on service process for curriculum development in Assumption University: a case study', 2009, http://www.graduate.au.edu/gsbejournal/5V/Journals/Nathaya.pdf; M.W. Stebbins, 'Abraham B. (Rami) Shani: a journey from action research and sociotechnical systems to collaborative management research and sustainable work systems', in *The Palgrave Handbook of Organizational Change Thinkers*, eds D. Szabla, W. Pasmore, M. Barnes and A. Gipson (Cham: Palgrave Macmillan, 2017).

2 D.M. Boje and M. Hillon, 'Transorganizational development', in *Handbook of Organizational Change*, ed. T. Cummings (Thousand Oaks, CA: Sage Publications, 2008): 651–4; A. O'Neill and R. Bent, 'The advantages of a transorganisational approach for developing senior executives', *Journal of Management Development*, 34 (2015): 621–31.

3 D. Samson, T. Donnet and R. Daft, *Management*, 6th Asia-Pacific edn (South Melbourne: Cengage Learning, 2018); D. Waddell, G. Jones and J. George, *Contemporary Management*, 3rd edn (North Ryde: McGraw-Hill Australia, 2013).

4 B. Barker Scott, 'Organization development primer: theory and practice of large group interventions', IRC Research Program, Queen's University IRC, June 2009, http://irc.queensu.ca/sites/default/files/articles/organization-development-primer-theory-and-practice-of-large-group-interventions.pdf.

5 K. Weick, *The Social Psychology of Organizing*, 2nd edn (Reading, MA: Addison-Wesley, 1979).

6 S. Alhawari, L. Karadsheh, A. Talet and E. Mansour, 'Knowledge-based risk management framework for information technology project', *International Journal of Information Management*, 32 (2012): 50–65; R. Bartnik and Y. Park, 'Technological change, information processing and supply chain integration: a conceptual model', *Benchmarking: An International Journal*, 25:5 (2018): 1279–301.

7 J. Pfeffer and G. Salancik, *The External Control of Organizations: A Resource Dependence Perspective* (New York: Harper and Row, 1978); H. Heizmann and M. Olsson, 'Power matters: the importance of Foucault's power/knowledge as a conceptual lens in KM research and practice', *Journal of Knowledge Management*, 19 (2015): 1–17.

8 H. Aldrich, *Organizations and Environments* (New York: Prentice Hall, 1979); R. Meinhardt, S. Junge and M. Weiss, 'The organizational environment with its measures, antecedents, and consequences: a review and research agenda', *Management Review Quarterly*, 68:2 (2018): 195–235.

9 Commission of the European Communities, 'Commission Recommendation of 3 October 2008 on the active inclusion of people excluded from the labour market', http://eur-lex.europa.eu/legal-content/EN/ALL/?uri=CELEX%3A32008H0867; M. Zollo, M. Minoja and V. Coda, 'Toward an integrated theory of strategy', *Strategic Management Journal*, 39:6 (2018): 1753–78.

10 Pfeffer and Salancik, *The External Control of Organizations*, op. cit.

11 Aldrich, *Organizations and Environments*, op. cit.

12 S. Pilsbury and A. Meaney, *Are Horizontal Mergers and Vertical Integration a Problem? Analysis of the Rail Freight Market in Europe*, discussion paper prepared on the part of the Joint Transport Research Centre, the OECD and the International Transport Forum, 2009, http://www.internationaltransportforum.org/jtrc/DiscussionPapers/DP200904.pdf; W.P. Wong, K.L. Soh, C.L. Chong and N. Karia, 'Logistics firms performance: efficiency and effectiveness perspectives', *International Journal of Productivity and Performance Management*, 64 (2015): 1–25.

13 F.J. de Graaf, 'Ethics and behavioural theory: how do professionals assess their mental models?', *Journal of Business Ethics* (2018), https://doi.org/10.1007/s10551-018-3955-6.

14 K.D. Heath and P. Tiffin, 'Context dependence in the coevolution of plant and rhizobial mutualists', *Proceedings of the Royal Society B: Biological Sciences*, 274 (August 2007): 1905–12; J. Bendickson, F.A. Gur and E.C. Taylor, 'Reducing environmental uncertainty: how high performance work systems moderate the resource dependence-firm performance relationship', *Canadian Journal of Administrative Sciences*, 35 (2018): 252–64.

15 Aldrich, *Organizations and Environments*, op. cit.

16 W. Ouchi, *The M-Form Society: How American Teamwork Can Recapture the Competitive Edge* (Reading, MA: Addison-Wesley, 1984); L. Thurow, *Head to Head: The Coming Economic Battle Among Japan, Europe and America* (New York: William Morrow, 1992); J. Stankiewicz, T. Tamagawa and N. Nakagawi, 'IBM, SoftBank alliance to bring Watson to all of Japan', IBM press release, 10 February 2015, http://www-03.ibm.com/press/us/en/pressrelease/46045.wss.

17 T. Cummings and S. Srivastva, *Management of Work: A Socio-Technical Systems Approach* (San Diego: University Associates, 1977): 112–16; M. Chen and X. Qi, 'Members' satisfaction and continuance intention: a socio-technical perspective', *Industrial Management and Data Systems*, 115 (2015): 1–19.

18 L. Bourgeois, 'Strategic goals, perceived uncertainty and economic performance in volatile environments', *Academy of Management Journal*, 28 (1985): 548–73; C. West Jr and C. Schwenk, 'Top management team strategic consensus, demographic homogeneity and firm performance: a report of resounding nonfindings', *Academy of Management Journal*, 17 (1996): 571–6.

19 R. Fry, 'Richard Beckhard: the formulator of organizational change', in Szabla et al. eds, *The Palgrave Handbook of Organizational Change Thinkers*, op. cit.

20 C. Krone, 'Open systems redesign', in *Theory and Method in Organization Development: An Evolutionary Process*, ed. J. Adams (Arlington, VA: NTL Institute for Applied Behavioral Science, 1974): 364–91; G. Jayaram, 'Open systems planning', in *The Planning of Change*, 3rd edn, eds W. Bennis, K. Benne, R. Chin and K. Corey (New York: Holt, Rinehart and Winston, 1976): 275–83; R. Beckhard and R. Harris, *Organizational Transitions: Managing Complex Change*, 2nd edn (Reading, MA: Addison-Wesley, 1987); Cummings and Srivastva, *Management of Work*, op. cit.

21 *Survey of Employee Engagement*, 2009, Institute for Organizational Excellence, University of Texas at Austin, http://www.utexas.edu/research/cswr/survey/new/wordpress/products/employee-engagement/survey-of-employee-engagement.

22 Jayaram, 'Open systems planning', op. cit.: 275–83; Cummings and Srivastva, *Management of Work*, op. cit.; R. Fry, 'Improving trustee, administrator and physician collaboration through open systems planning', in *Organization Development in Health Care Organizations*, eds N. Margulies and J. Adams (Reading, MA: Addison-Wesley, 1982): 282–92.

23 Prof. K.V. Bhanu Murthy, *Social Responsibility Standards and Global Environmental Accountability: A Developing Country Perspective* (MPRA Paper 2636, University Library of Munich, Germany, 2007).

24 T. Cummings, 'Transorganizational development', in *Research in Organizational Behavior*, 6, eds B. Staw and L. Cummings (Greenwich, CT: JAI Press, 1984): 367–422; P.S. Adler, 'Tom Cummings: a passion for people and learning', in Szabla et al. eds, *The Palgrave Handbook of Organizational Change Thinkers*, op. cit.

25 B. Gray, 'Conditions facilitating interorganizational collaboration', *Human Relations*, 38 (1985): 911–36; K. Harrigan and W. Newman, 'Bases of interorganization cooperation: propensity, power, persistence', *Journal of Management Studies*, 27 (1990): 417–34; Cummings, 'Transorganizational development', op. cit.; E. Delbufalo, 'Outcomes of inter-organizational trust in supply chain relationships: a systematic literature review and a meta-analysis of the empirical evidence', *Supply Chain Management: An International Journal*, 17 (2012): 377–402.

26 Cummings, 'Transorganizational development', op. cit.

27 C. Raben, 'Building strategic partnerships: creating and managing effective joint ventures', in *Organizational Architecture*, eds D. Nadler, M. Gerstein, R. Shaw and associates (San Francisco: Jossey-Bass, 1992): 81–109; B. Gray, *Collaborating: Finding Common Ground for Multiparty Problems* (San Francisco: Jossey-Bass, 1989); Harrigan and Newman, 'Bases of interorganization cooperation', op. cit.; P. Lorange and J. Roos, 'Analytical steps in the formation of strategic alliances', *Journal of Organizational Change Management*, 4 (1991): 60–72; S. Chua, 'Transformative thinking, transformative doing', *Journal of Public Procurement*, 17:3 (2017): 373–401.

28 D. Boje, *Towards a Theory and Praxis of Transorganizational Development: Stakeholder Networks and Their Habitats* (Working Paper 79–6, Behavioral and Organizational Science Study Center, Graduate School of Management, University of California at Los Angeles, February 1982); M. Martinsuo and P. Hoverfält, 'Change program management: toward a capability for managing value-oriented, integrated multi-project change

in its context', *International Journal of Project Management*, 36:1 (2018): 134–46.

29 L. Brès, E. Raufflet and J. Boghossian, 'Pluralism in organizations: learning from unconventional forms of organizations', *International Journal of Management Reviews*, 20 (2018): 364–86.

30 Cummings, 'Transorganizational development', op. cit.

31 Raben, 'Building strategic partnerships', op. cit.

32 W. Cascio, 'Downsizing: what do we know? what have we learned?', *The Academy of Management Executive*, 7 (1993): 95–104; F. Gandolfi and C. Littler, 'Downsizing is dead; long live the downsizing phenomenon: conceptualizing the phases of cost-cutting', *Journal of Management & Organization*, 18 (2012): 334–45; H. Sitlington, 'Knowledge sharing: implications for downsizing and restructuring outcomes in Australian organisations', *Asia Pacific Journal of Human Resources*, 50 (2012): 110–27.

33 ibid.

34 J. Corrigan, 'Corporate anorexia?', *Australian Accountant*, 67 (1997): 50–1.

35 A. Robb, 'Accountancy: trade or profession?', *The National Business Review* (New Zealand), 21 May 1999.

36 Adapted from Cameron, Freeman and Mishra, 'Best practices in white-collar downsizing: managing contradictions', op. cit.; and R. Marshall and L. Lyles, 'Planning for a restructured, revitalized organization', *Sloan Management Review*, 35 (1994): 81–91. See also L. Låstad, E. Berntson, K. Näswall, P. Lindfors and M. Sverke, 'Measuring quantitative and qualitative aspects of the job insecurity climate: scale validation', *Career Development International*, 20 (2015): 202–17.

37 J. Brockner, 'The effects of work layoffs on survivors: research, theory and practice', in *Research in Organizational Behavior*, 10, eds B. Staw and L. Cummings (Greenwich, CT: JAI Press, 1989): 213–55; T. Lynn, 'Organizational downsizing and the aftermath: survivors' perceptions of the impact on organizational commitment and personal professional development in the context of schools', dissertation, 2015, https://digital.library.txstate.edu/bitstream/handle/10877/5542/TAYLOR-DISSERTATION-2015.pdf?sequence=1; S.A.L. Bohle, M.J. Chambel and A. Diaz-Valdes Iriarte 'Job insecurity, procedural justice and downsizing survivor affects', *The International Journal of Human Resource Management* (2018), https://doi.org/10.1080/09585192.2018.1482939.

38 Marshall and Lyles, 'Planning for a restructured, revitalized organization', op. cit.

39 D. Todrin, 'The six biggest downsizing mistakes', Entrepreneur.com, 27 July 2011, http://www.entrepreneur.com/article/220074; L. Willcocks,

D. Feeny and M. Lacity, 'Transforming a human resource function through shared services and joint-venture outsourcing: the BAE Systems–Xchanging enterprise partnership 2001–2012, *Journal of Information Technology Teaching Cases*, 3 (2013): 29–42; D. Datta and D. Basuil, 'Does employee downsizing really work?', *Human Resource Management Practice* (2015): 197–221.

40 Kirby, 'Downsizing gets the push', op. cit.; I. Abbass, 'Restructuring in the oil and gas industry: implications for HR practitioners', *European Scientific Journal*, 8 (2012): 203–15.

41 ibid.; A. Schmitt, S. Borzillo and G. Probst, 'Don't let knowledge walk away: knowledge retention during employee downsizing', *Management Learning*, 43 (2012): 53–74; K. Day, A. Armenakis, H. Field and D. Norris, 'Other organizations are doing it, why shouldn't we? A look at downsizing and organizational identity through an institutional theory lens', *Journal of Change Management*, 12 (2012): 165–88.

42 Cameron, Freeman and Mishra, 'Best practices in white-collar downsizing: managing contradictions', op. cit.; D. van Dierendonck and G. Jacobs, 'Survivors and victims, a meta-analytical review of fairness and organizational commitment after downsizing', *British Journal of Management*, 23 (2012): 96–109; Schmitt, Borzillo and Probst, 'Don't let knowledge walk away', op. cit.

43 M. Hammer and J. Champy, *Reengineering the Corporation* (New York: HarperCollins, 1993); T. Stewart, 'Reengineering: the hot new managing tool', *Fortune* (23 August 1993): 41–8; J. Champy, *Reengineering Management* (New York: HarperCollins, 1994); D. Simchi-Levi, 'Reengineering *Management Science* for a sharper focus and broader appeal', *Management Science*, 64:2 (2018).

44 R. Kaplan and L. Murdock, 'Core process redesign', *The McKinsey Quarterly*, 2 (1991): 27–43; L. Sook-Ling, M.A. Ismail and Y. Yee-Yen, 'Information infrastructure capability and organisational competitive advantage: framework', *International Journal of Operations and Production Management*, 35 (2015): 1–33.

45 S. Sitalaksmi and Y. Zhu, 'The transformation of human resource management in Indonesian state-owned enterprises since the Asian Crisis', *Asia Pacific Business Review*, 16 (2010): 37–57; W. Pasmore, 'Deconstructing OD: a closer look at the emergence of OD values and their impact on the field', in *Enacting Values-based Change*, eds D. Jamieson, A. Church and J. Vogelsang (Cham: Palgrave Macmillan, 2018).

46 M. Habib and M. Wazir, 'Role of education and training in the successful implementation of business process reengineering: a case of public

sector of Khyber PakhtunKhwa (KPK)', *World Journal of Social Sciences*, 2 (2012): 172–85; A. Petrillo, G. Di Bona, A. Forcina and A. Silvestri, 'Building excellence through the Agile Reengineering Performance Model (ARPM): a strategic business model for organizations', *Business Process Management Journal*, 24:1: (2018): 128–57.

47 Kaplan and Murdock, 'Core process redesign', op. cit.; R. Manganelli and M. Klein, *The Reengineering Handbook* (New York: AMACOM, 1994).

48 J. Katzenbach and D. Smith, 'The rules for managing cross-functional reengineering teams', *Planning Review* (March–April 1993): 12–13; A. Nahavandi and E. Aranda, 'Restructuring teams for the reengineered organization', *The Academy of Management Executive*, 8 (1994): 58–68.

49 ibid.

50 Hammer and Champy, *Reengineering the Corporation*, op. cit.

51 Champy, *Reengineering Management*, op. cit.; K. Jensen, 'The effects of business process management on injury frequency' (unpublished master's thesis, Pepperdine University, 1993).

52 D. Glew, A. O'Leary-Kelly, R. Griffin and D. Van Fleet, 'Participation in organizations: a preview of the issues and proposed framework for future analysis', *Journal of Management*, 21:3 (1995): 395–421; H. Ngirande and A. Nel, 'The psychological impact of downsizing on employee survivors in the manufacturing industry', *African Journal of Business Management*, 6 (2012): 4371–5; R. Seethamraju, 'Business process management: a missing link in business education', *Business Process Management Journal*, 18 (2012): 532–47.

53 U. Hongchatikul, 'The impact of organizational development interventions on employee commitment and motivation and customer satisfaction: a case study', http://www.graduate.au.edu/gsbejournal/3V/Journals/5.pdf; A-M. Nisula, 'The relationship between supervisor support and individual improvisation', *Leadership and Organization Development Journal*, 36 (2015): 1–30.

54 F. Taylor, *The Principles of Scientific Management* (New York: Harper and Row, 1911).

55 ibid.

56 T. Cummings, 'Self-regulating work groups: a socio-technical synthesis', *Academy of Management Review*, 3 (1978): 625–34; G. Susman, *Autonomy at Work* (New York: Praeger, 1976); J. Slocum and H. Sims, 'A typology of technology and job redesign', *Human Relations*, 33 (1983): 193–212.

57 C.M. Burns, 'Automation and the human factors race to catch up', *Journal of Cognitive Engineering and Decision Making*, 12:1 (2018): 83–5.

58 F. Herzberg, B. Mausner and B. Snyderman, *The Motivation to Work* (New York: John Wiley and Sons, 1959); F. Herzberg, 'The wise old Turk',

Harvard Business Review, 52 (September–October 1974): 70–80; F. Herzberg and Z. Zautra, 'Orthodox job enrichment: measuring true quality in job satisfaction', *Personnel*, 53 (September–October 1976): 54–68.

59 J. Hackman and G. Oldham, *Work Redesign* (Reading, MA: Addison-Wesley, 1980); S. Wright, C. Adams, D. Nelson and J. Quick, *ORGB* (South Melbourne: Cengage Learning, 2011).

60 A. Turner and P. Lawrence, *Industrial Jobs and the Worker* (Cambridge: Harvard Graduate School of Business Administration, Division of Research, 1965); J. Hackman and G. Oldham, 'Development of the job diagnostic survey', *Journal of Applied Psychology*, 60 (April 1975): 159–70; H. Sims, A. Szilagyi and R. Keller, 'The measurement of job characteristics', *Academy of Management Journal*, 19 (1976): 195–212; J. Westover, 'Comparative international differences in intrinsic and extrinsic job quality characteristics and worker satisfaction, 1989–2005', *International Journal of Business and Social Science*, 3 (2012): 1–15; R. Ramos and T. Wehner, 'Failure in volunteer work: a call for strategic volunteer management', in *Strategies in Failure Management*, ed. S. Kunert (Cham: Springer, 2018).

61 G. Oldham and J. Hackman, 'Work design in the organizational context', in *Research in Organizational Behavior*, 2, eds B. Staw and L. Cummings (Greenwich, CT: JAI Press, 1980): 247–78; J. Cordery and T. Wall, 'Work design and supervisory practice: a model', *Human Relations*, 38 (1985): 425–41; G.Z. Neto, G.M. Pereira and M. Borchardt, 'What problems manufacturing companies can face when providing services around the world?', *Journal of Business and Industrial Marketing*, 30 (2015): 1–29.

62 Hackman and Oldham, *Work Redesign*, op. cit.

63 ibid.

64 M. Campion, 'Interdisciplinary approaches to job design: a constructive replication with extensions', *Journal of Applied Psychology*, 73 (1988): 467–81; R. Yeo and J. Li, 'In pursuit of learning: sensemaking the quality of work life', *European Journal of Training and Development*, 37 (2012): 1–20; A. Grant, 'Giving time, time after time: work design and sustained employee participation in corporate volunteering', *Academy of Management Review*, 37 (2012): 589–615.

65 C. Kulik, G. Oldham and P. Langner, 'Measurement of job characteristics: comparison of the original and the revised job diagnostic survey', *Journal of Applied Psychology*, 73 (1988): 426–66; J. Idaszak and F. Drasgow, 'A revision of the job diagnostic survey: elimination of a measurement artifact', *Journal of Applied Psychology*, 72 (1987): 69–74.

66 R. Steers and D. Spencer, 'The role of achievement motivation in job design', *Journal of Applied Psychology*, 62 (1977): 472–9; J. Champoux, 'A three sample test of some extensions to the job characteristics model', *Academy of Management Journal*, 23 (1980): 466–78; R. Katz, 'The influence of job longevity on employee reactions to task characteristics', *Human Relation*, 31 (1978): 703–25; S.K. Parker, F.P. Morgeson and G. Johns, 'One hundred years of work design research: looking back and looking forward', *Journal of Applied Psychology*, 102:3 (Mar 2017): 403–20.

67 R. Zeffane, 'Correlates of job satisfaction and their implications for work redesign', *Public Personnel Management*, 23 (1994): 61–76.

68 G. Oldham and Y. Fried, 'Employee reactions to workspace characteristics', *Journal of Applied Psychology*, 72 (1987): 75–80; H. Ren, M. Bolino, M. Shaffer and M. Kraimer, 'The influence of job demands and resources on repatriate career satisfaction: a relative deprivation perspective', *Journal of World Business*, 48 (2013): 149–59; S. Choi, K. Cheong and R. Feinberg, 'Moderating effects of supervisor support, monetary rewards, and career paths on the relationship between job burnout and turnover intentions in the context of call centers', *Managing Service Quality*, 22 (2012): 492–516.

69 B. Loher, R. Noe, N. Moeller and M. Fitzgerald, 'A meta-analysis of the relation of job characteristics to job satisfaction', *Journal of Applied Psychology*, 70 (1985): 280–9.

70 B. McEvoy and W. Cascio, 'Strategies for reducing employee turnover: a meta-analysis', *Journal of Applied Psychology*, 70 (1985): 342–53; R. Flower, D. Demir, J. McWilliams and D. Johnson, 'Perceptions of fairness in the psychological contracts of allied health professionals', *Asia-Pacific Journal of Business Administration*, 7 (2015): 106–16.

71 T. Cummings and E. Molloy, *Improving Productivity and the Quality of Work Life* (New York: Praeger, 1977).

72 J. Nicholas, 'The comparative impact of organization development interventions on hard criteria measures', *Academy of Management Review*, 7 (1982): 531–42. See also S. Al Haddad and T. Kotnour, 'Integrating the organizational change literature: a model for successful change', *Journal of Organizational Change Management*, 28 (2015): 234–62.

73 E. Trist, B. Higgin, H. Murray and A. Pollock, *Organizational Choice* (London: Tavistock, 1963); T. Cummings and B. Srivastva, *Management of Work: A Socio-Technical Systems Approach* (San Diego: University Associates, 1977); A. Cherns, 'Principles of sociotechnical design revisited', *Human Relations*, 40 (1987): 153–62.

74 Cummings, 'Self-regulating work groups', op. cit.: 625–34; J. Hackman, *The Design of Self-Managing Work Groups*, Technical Report No. 11 (New Haven: Yale University, School of Organization and Management, 1976); Cummings and Srivastva, *Management of Work*, op. cit.; Susman, *Autonomy at Work*, op. cit.; T. Cummings, 'Designing effective work groups', in *Handbook of Organizational Design: Remodeling Organizations and Their Environments*, 2, eds P. Nystrom and W. Starbuck (New York: Oxford University Press, 1981): 250–71; W. Weerheim, L. Van Rossum and W.D.T. Have, 'Successful implementation of self-managing teams', *Leadership in Health Services* (2018), https://doi.org/10.1108/LHS-11-2017-0066.

75 C. Manz, 'Beyond self-managing teams: toward self-leading teams in the work place', in *Research in Organizational Change and Development*, 4, eds W. Pasmore and R. Woodman (Greenwich, CT: JAI Press, 1990): 273–99; J. Yong-Kwan Lim, 'IT-enabled awareness and self-directed leadership behaviors in virtual teams', *Information and Organization*, 28:2 (2018): 71–88.

76 J.J. Jiang, G. Klein, J. Chia-An Tsai and Y. Li, 'Managing multiple-supplier project teams in new software development', *International Journal of Project Management*, 36:7 (2018): 925–39.

77 S. Benn, S.T.T. Teo and A. Martin, 'Employee participation and engagement in working for the environment', *Personnel Review*, 44 (2015): 492–510.

78 T. Cummings, 'Socio-technical systems: an intervention strategy', in *New Techniques in Organization Development*, ed. W. Burke (New York: Basic Books, 1975): 228–49; Cummings and Srivastva, *Management of Work*, op. cit.; Cummings and Molloy, *Improving Productivity and the Quality of Work Life*, op. cit.

79 F. van Eijnatten, S. Eggermont, G. de Goffau and I. Mankoe, *The Socio-technical Systems Design Paradigm* (Eindhoven, Netherlands: Eindhoven University of Technology, 1994).

80 J.S. Baek, S. Kim, Y. Pahk and E. Manzini, 'A sociotechnical framework for the design of collaborative services', *Design Studies*, 55 (2018): 54–78; S. Winby and S. Albers Mohrman, 'Digital sociotechnical system design', *The Journal of Applied Behavioral Science* (22 June 2018), https://doi.org/10.1177/0021886318781581.

81 R. Walton, 'How to counter alienation in the plant', *Harvard Business Review*, 12 (November–December 1972): 70–81.

82 R. Schrank, 'On ending worker alienation: the Gaines Pet Food plant', in *Humanizing the Workplace*, ed. R. Fairfield (Buffalo, NY: Prometheus Books, 1974): 119–20, 126; R. Walton, 'Teaching an old dog food new tricks', *The Wharton Magazine*, 4 (Winter 1978): 42; J. Wright, *State of*

the Masses: Sources of Discontent, Change and Stability (S.l.: Routledge, 2017).

83 J. Norsted and S. Aguren, *The Saab-Scania Report* (Stockholm: Swedish Employers' Confederation, 1975).

84 'Doubting Sweden's way', *Time* (10 March 1975): 40.

85 P. Gyllenhammär, *People at Work* (Reading, MA: Addison-Wesley, 1977): 15–17, 43, 52–3; B. Jönsson, 'Corporate strategy for people at work – the Volvo experience' (paper presented at the International Conference on the Quality of Working Life, Toronto, Canada, 30 August–3 September 1981); N. Tichy and J. Nisberg, 'When does work restructuring work? Organizational innovations at Volvo and GM', *Organizational Dynamics*, 5 (Summer 1976): 73; B. Hofmaier, 'Institutional and organizational perspectives on dialogue: lessons learned from Scandinavian experiences', in *Mindful Change in Times of Permanent Reorganization*, ed. G. Becke (Berlin: Springer, 2014)

86 J. Kapstein and J. Hoerr, 'Volvo's radical new plant: the death of the assembly line?', *Business Week* (28 August 1989): 92–3.

87 W. Pasmore, 'The comparative impacts of sociotechnical system, job-redesign and survey–feedback interventions', in *Sociotechnical Systems: A Source Book*, eds W. Pasmore and J. Sherwood (San Diego, University Associates, 1978): 291–300.

88 C. Magpili and P. Pilar, 'Self-managing team performance: a systematic review of multilevel input factors', *Small Group Research*, 49:1 (2018): 3–33; R. Page-Shipp, D. Joseph and C. van Niekerk, 'Conductorless singing group: a particular kind of self-managed team?', *Team Performance Management: An International Journal* (2018), https://doi.org/10.1108/TPM-09-2016-0041.

89 T. Cummings, 'Self-regulating work groups: a socio-technical synthesis', *Academy of Management Review*, 3 (1978): 625–34; G. Susman, *Autonomy at Work* (New York: Praeger, 1976); J. Slocum and H. Sims, 'A typology of technology and job redesign', *Human Relations*, 33 (1983): 193–212; M. Kiggundu, 'Task interdependence and job design: test of a theory', *Organizational Behavior and Human Performance*, 31 (1983): 145–72.

90 Hackman and Oldham, *Work Redesign*, op. cit.; K. Brousseau, 'Toward a dynamic model of job–person relationships: findings, research questions and implications for work system design', *Academy of Management Review*, 8 (1983): 33–45; G. Graen, T. Scandura and M. Graen, 'A field experimental test of the moderating effects of growth needs strength on productivity', *Journal of Applied Psychology*, 71 (1986): 484–91.

91 T. Cummings, 'Designing work for productivity and quality of life', *Outlook*, 6 (1982): 35–9.

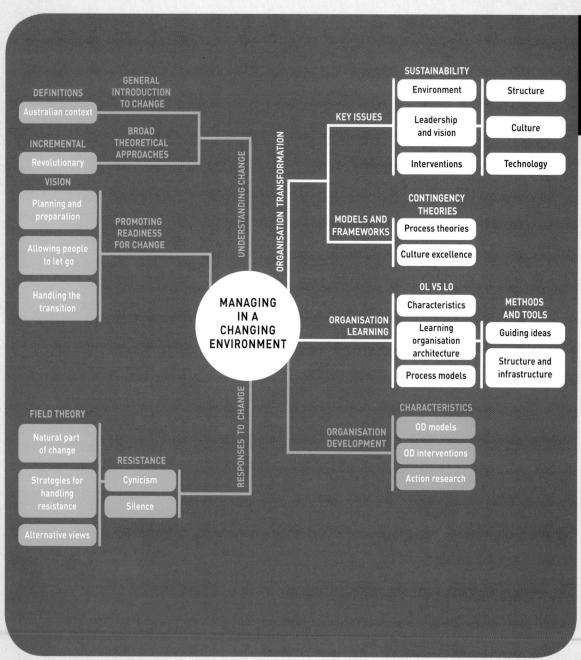

MANAGING IN A CHANGING ENVIRONMENT

UNDERSTANDING CHANGE

DEFINITIONS
- Australian context

GENERAL INTRODUCTION TO CHANGE

INCREMENTAL
- Revolutionary

BROAD THEORETICAL APPROACHES

VISION
- Planning and preparation
- Allowing people to let go
- Handling the transition

PROMOTING READINESS FOR CHANGE

RESPONSES TO CHANGE

FIELD THEORY
- Natural part of change
- Strategies for handling resistance
- Alternative views

RESISTANCE
- Cynicism
- Silence

ORGANISATION TRANSFORMATION

KEY ISSUES

SUSTAINABILITY
- Environment
- Leadership and vision
- Interventions
- Structure
- Culture
- Technology

MODELS AND FRAMEWORKS

CONTINGENCY THEORIES
- Process theories
- Culture excellence

ORGANISATION LEARNING

OL VS LO
- Characteristics
- Learning organisation architecture
- Process models

METHODS AND TOOLS
- Guiding ideas
- Structure and infrastructure

ORGANISATION DEVELOPMENT

CHARACTERISTICS
- OD models
- OD interventions
- Action research

Source: Adapted from D. Waddell, *E-Business in Australia: Concepts and Cases*, Pearson Education Australia, 2002.

PART

ORGANISATION TRANSFORMATION

4

Transformation and the future are impossible to keep separate. We have created the separation conceptually in the book to assist sequencing but, as our mapping indicates, Parts 4 and 5 relate very closely to each other. In addition, the main concepts and themes integrate within the two parts but also extend into each of Parts 1, 2 and 3.

THEME OR CONCEPT	CONNECTED WITH MATERIAL IN OTHER CHAPTERS
Nature of transformational change	Ch 1, 9
Integrated strategic change (ISC)	Ch 2, 5, 7, 8, 9
Culture change	Ch 4, 6, 7, 9
Global change	Ch 8, 10
Competition versus collaboration	Ch 3, 10, 11
Trends in organisation development (OD)	Ch 1, 12, 13

Source: Leanne Atkinson.

Leanne Atkinson

Manager/Salvation Army Thrift Shop

Angel of change gives plenty of food for thought

Leanne Atkinson has seen many stages in the life cycle of one of her projects, Warrnambool and District Food Share. In its infancy, she worked hard to get her food sharing idea off to a start. In its adolescence, she experienced the angst of conflict and the drive towards her project's independence from her. Now as a young adult, her food sharing concept is finding its own feet and beginning to fully emerge into the wider world.

Today, Leanne is manager of the Salvation Army Thrift Shop in Warrnambool, Victoria. She is a provider of resources and an angel of positive change in the lives of all who find their way to her door in their moments of greatest need. Her first claim to fame as a local legend was in her role in getting her food sharing idea into action. Over a decade ago, Leanne was employed as a Student Liaison Officer at the local TAFE college, and she admits she felt just a bit different from the other administrators. She was a single parent of six kids, which prompted an appreciation of thrifty ideas and clever use of resources. One thing she noticed was students at the college going without food, so she arranged to acquire free food from the Melbourne-based Foodbank to stock the student kitchenette. At that time there was no Foodbank in the burgeoning regional City of Warrnambool, so Leanne called a meeting of some key decision makers. They quickly realised there were many students (primary, secondary and tertiary) in the region going hungry, and it also became clear that others in the community were living without food at crucial times. Furthermore, there was significant food waste coming out of supermarkets and food businesses in the area just going to landfill and other wasteful destinations. In Leanne's words, 'I just did it ... I'd ask, and they'd send boxes in a truck, and I'd put the food in my car boot and drive it straight to the schools who needed it.' So, with the spiking demand for food through schools and more families approaching welfare agencies, Leanne knew she had to grow the area's food distribution capability.

Thinking that the word 'bank' implied that a deposit was required, Leanne coined a variation of the organisation's name, Warrnambool and District Food Share, in 2007 and arranged for the Worn Gundidj Aboriginal Cooperative to be an auspice and warehouse-providing local agency for the operation servicing people of all backgrounds in the community. There was no looking back as Leanne focused on leading numerous volunteers, managing day-to-day logistics, and keeping her communication going with every major community organisation, school and food waste supplier in the South West region, all the while liaising with Foodbank Victoria. The Warrnambool and

District Food Share model became distinguished under Leanne's leadership. The infant was fast becoming an adolescent keen to be part of the wider world.

While Leanne focused at the operational level on her angel of change mission feeding needy people, the managers of Worn Gundidj, state government funding sources for food waste services, politicians and the managers of various local agencies postured for change. Bureaucratic complexities, new funding opportunities, profile-raising activities for partner agencies and a terminal illness for the Worn-Gundidj CEO led to Food Share being separated from its Worn Gundidj relationship and going out entirely on its own. That's about when other interested parties marginalised Leanne from the major decisions of Food Share, and she was eventually replaced as its manager in 2013. The teen asserted independence and left home.

Leanne recalls it being a stressful time and yet remains proud to see the operation she nurtured in its infancy continuing on its way today and growing even more. The food rescue and sharing paradigm is widely understood now, and Warrnambool and District Food Share, under new management, is building its strength and becoming a fully fledged member of the community.

In her current role as manager of the Salvos Thrift Shop. Leanne remains absolutely central to the welfare community in Warrnambool and manages hundreds of volunteers every week. She is a true angel of positive change for people. Food Share was Leanne's baby in the beginning and represents her amazing contribution to the welfare of people who otherwise would be suffering were it not for her having such a compassionate vision and leading it through.

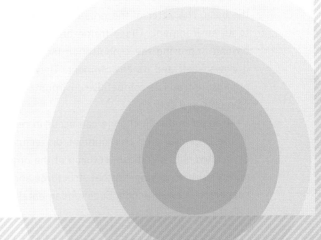

9

ORGANISATION TRANSFORMATION AND CHANGE

LEARNING OUTCOMES

After studying this chapter, you should be able to:

1   Define and explain transformational change.
2   Describe the systemic nature of transformational change.
3   Discuss integrated strategic change.
4   Define and explain organisational design.
5   Analyse the cultural aspects of change and organisational design.

KEY TERMS

Organisation transformation (OT)
Integrated strategic change (ISC)

Organisation design
Organisational culture

This chapter presents interventions for transforming organisations – that is, for changing the basic character of the organisation, including how it is structured and how it relates to its environment. These frame-breaking and sometimes revolutionary interventions go beyond improving the organisation incrementally, focusing instead on changing the way it views itself and its environment. They bring about important alignments between the organisation and its competitive environment and among the organisation's strategy, design elements and culture.

Transformational change can occur in response to or in anticipation of major changes in the organisation's environment or technology. In addition, these changes often are associated with significant revision of the organisation's business strategy, which, in turn, may require modifying internal structures and processes as well as its corporate culture to support the new direction. Such fundamental change entails a new paradigm for organising and managing organisations. It involves qualitatively different ways of perceiving, thinking and behaving in organisations. Movement towards this new way of operating requires senior executives to take an active leadership role. The change process is characterised by considerable innovation as members discover new ways of improving the organisation and adapting it to changing conditions.

Transformational change[1] is an emerging part of organisation development (OD) and there is some confusion about its meaning and definition. This chapter starts with a description of several major features of transformational change. Against this background, three kinds of interventions are discussed: integrated strategic change (ISC), organisation design and culture change.

ISC[2] is a comprehensive OD intervention aimed at a single organisation or business unit. It suggests that business strategy and organisation design must be aligned and changed together to respond to external and internal disruptions. An ISC plan helps members manage the transition between the current strategic orientation and the desired future strategic orientation.

Organisation design addresses the different elements that comprise the 'architecture' of the organisation, including structure, work design, human resources practices and management and information systems. It seeks to fit or align these components with each other so they direct members' behaviours in a strategic direction.

An organisation's culture is the pattern of assumptions, values and norms that are more or less shared by organisation members. A growing body of research has shown that culture can affect strategy formulation and implementation as well as the organisation's ability to achieve high levels of performance. Culture change involves helping senior executives and administrators diagnose the existing culture and make necessary alterations in the basic assumptions and values underlying organisational behaviours.

CHARACTERISTICS OF TRANSFORMATIONAL CHANGE

A large number of organisations are radically altering how they operate and relate to their environments.[3] Increased global competition is forcing many organisations to downsize or consolidate and become leaner, more efficient and flexible. Deregulation is pushing businesses in the financial services, telecommunications and airline industries to rethink business strategies and reshape how they operate. Public demand for less government intervention and lowered deficits is forcing public sector agencies to streamline operations and to deliver more for less. Rapid changes in technologies render many organisational practices obsolete, pushing businesses to be continually innovative and nimble.

Organisation transformation (OT) implies radical changes in how members perceive, think and behave at work. These changes go far beyond making the existing organisation better or fine-tuning the status quo. They are concerned with fundamentally altering the prevailing assumptions about how the organisation functions and relates to its environment. Changing these assumptions entails significant shifts in corporate values and norms and in the structures and organisational arrangements that shape members' behaviours. Not only is

Organisation transformation (OT): involves changing the basic character of the organisation, including how it is structured and how it relates to its environment.

the magnitude of change greater, but the change fundamentally alters the qualitative nature of the organisation.

CHANGE IS TRIGGERED BY ENVIRONMENTAL AND INTERNAL DISRUPTIONS

Organisations are unlikely to undertake transformational change unless significant reasons to do so emerge. Power, emotion and expertise are vested in the existing organisational arrangements and when faced with problems, organisations are more likely to fine-tune those structures than to alter them drastically. Thus, in most cases, organisations must experience or anticipate a severe threat to survival before they will be motivated to undertake transformational change.[4] Such threats arise when environmental and internal changes render existing organisational strategies and designs obsolete. These changes threaten the very existence of the organisation as it presently is constituted.

In studying a large number of OTs, Tushman, Newman and Romanelli showed that transformational change occurs in response to at least three kinds of disruption:[5]

1 *industry discontinuities* – sharp changes in legal, political, economic and technological conditions that shift the basis for competition within an industry

2 *product life cycle shifts* – changes in product life cycle that require different business strategies

3 *internal company dynamics* – changes in size, corporate portfolio strategy or executive turnover.

These disruptions severely jolt organisations and push them to question their business strategy and, in turn, their mission, values, structure, systems and procedures.

Apply your learning 9.1 describes an OT at the Australia Council for the Arts.

AUSTRALIA COUNCIL MAPS OUT ITS REFORM STRATEGY

The Australia Council for the Arts developed a strategic plan in 2015 delineating four main goals for the ensuing five years. It simultaneously revamped its grants model to link closely with the new priorities for the total of $189.8 million available to artists and organisations. This was a big change on the back of structural reform of the Australia Council in the previous year, but it was also done in the shadow of large overall government cuts to arts funding.

Among other items, the new strategic guidelines were supportive of established Indigenous performances and projects. A subsequent Statement of Intent 2017–18 reiterated the broad objectives for the Australia Council for the Arts being delivering Commonwealth arts funding, championing diversity and inclusion, supporting international engagement, providing targeted research and analysis, stimulating co-investment, and celebrating Australian arts. In practical terms, the strategic plan encouraged investment in Indigenous culture for intergenerational knowledge transfer. Still, there were some concerns about a lack of diversity targets for other important areas, such as, gender, location, ethnicity and disability. In fact, the

»

>>

disquiet has mounted as the next strategic plan is due from the Australia Council. In 2018, the *New York Times* ran a story questioning, 'Is the way Australia funds the Arts a recipe for mediocrity?' The article highlighted the Council's traditional approach to funding somewhat stagnating art forms through an unchanging and limited number of arts organisations in Australia.

The cycles of strategic planning always need to factor in the ongoing evaluative input of all stakeholders. The stage is now set for the Australia Council for the Arts to revisit strategic planning and lock into place its objectives and actions for a new cycle of the Arts in this country.

Sources: Based on M. Westwood, 'A culture of change', *The Australian*, 26 August 2014; C. Sebag-Montefiore, 'Is the way Australia funds the Arts a recipe for mediocrity?', *The New York Times*, 2 September 2018; and Australia Council for the Arts, 'Strategic Plan 2014 to 2019', http://www.australiacouncil.gov.au/strategic-plan.

Critical thinking questions

1   What form of disruption does the strategic plan in the article address?

2   As the Australia Council commences crafting a new strategic plan for the next few years, what kinds of resistance might emerge from current stakeholders?

3   The Australia Council is subject to political and budgetary factors that may create the need for transformational change on an annual basis. Check the media releases on the Council's website to see what has been announced most recently in terms of budget or strategy and consider the transformational change consequences that are likely to be experienced by the Council.

CHANGE IS SYSTEMIC AND REVOLUTIONARY

Transformational change involves reshaping the organisation's design elements and culture. These changes can be characterised as systemic and revolutionary because the entire nature of the organisation is altered fundamentally. Typically driven by senior executives, change may occur rapidly so that it does not get mired in politics, individual resistance and other forms of organisational inertia.[6] This is particularly pertinent to changing the different features of the organisation, such as structure, information systems, human resources practices and work design. These features tend to reinforce one another, thus making it difficult to change them in a piecemeal manner.[7] They need to be changed together and in a coordinated fashion so that they can mutually support each other and the new cultural values and assumptions.[8] Ultimately, these changes should motivate and direct people's behaviour in a new strategic direction. They are considered transformational when a majority of individuals in an organisation change their behaviours.[9]

Long-term studies of organisational evolution underscore the revolutionary nature of transformational change.[10] They suggest that organisations typically move through relatively long periods of smooth growth and operation. These periods of convergence or evolution are characterised by incremental changes. At times, however, most organisations experience severe external or internal disruptions that render existing organisational arrangements ineffective. Successful businesses respond to these threats to survival by transforming themselves to fit the new conditions. These periods of total system and quantum changes[11] represent abrupt shifts in the organisation's structure, culture and processes. If successful, the shifts enable the organisation to experience another long period of smooth functioning until the next disruption signals the need for drastic change.[12]

These studies of organisational evolution and revolution point to the benefits of implementing transformational change as rapidly as possible. The faster the organisation can respond to disruptions, the quicker it can attain the benefits of operating in a new way. Rapid change enables the organisation to reach a period of smooth growth and functioning sooner, thus providing it with a competitive advantage over those organisations that change more slowly.

CHANGE DEMANDS A NEW ORGANISING PARADIGM

Organisations undertaking transformational change are, by definition, involved in second-order or gamma types of change.[13] *Gamma change* involves discontinuous shifts in mental or organisational frameworks.[14] Creative metaphors, such as 'organisation learning' (OL) or 'continuous improvement', are often used to help members visualise the new paradigm.[15] Increases in technological change, concern for quality and worker participation have led many organisations to shift their organising paradigm. Characterised as the transition from a 'control-based' to a 'commitment-based' organisation, the features of the new paradigm include leaner, more flexible structures; information and decision making pushed down to the lowest levels; decentralised teams and business units accountable for specific products, services or customers; and participative management and teamwork. This new organising paradigm is well suited to changing conditions.

CHANGE IS DRIVEN BY SENIOR EXECUTIVES AND LINE MANAGEMENT

A key feature of transformational change is the active role of senior executives and line managers in all phases of the change process.[16] They are responsible for the strategic direction and operation of the organisation and actively lead the transformation. They decide when to initiate transformational change, what the change should be, how it should be implemented and who should be responsible for directing it. If it is perceived that existing executives lack the skill base, energy and commitment to undertake these tasks, they may be replaced by outsiders who are recruited to lead the change. Research on transformational change suggests that externally recruited executives are three times more likely to initiate such change than are existing executives.[17]

The critical role of executive leadership in transformational change is clearly emerging. Lucid accounts of transformational leaders describe how executives, such as Richard Branson (founder of Virgin Group), Ariana Huffington (Editor-in-Chief of The Huffington Post) and Dawn Casey (Chair of Indigenous Business Australia, the Indigenous Land Corporation and Director of the Museum of Applied Arts and Sciences), actively managed both the organisational and personal dynamics of transformational change.[18] The work of

Tushman, Newman and Nadler, and others points to three key roles for executive leadership of such change:[19]

1   *Envisioning.* Executives must articulate a clear and credible vision of the new strategic orientation. They also must set new and difficult standards for performance and generate pride in past accomplishments and enthusiasm for the new strategy.

2   *Energising.* Executives must demonstrate personal excitement for the changes and model the behaviours that are expected of others. Behavioural integrity, credibility and 'walking the talk' are important ingredients.[20] They must communicate examples of early success to mobilise energy for change.

3   *Enabling.* Executives must provide the resources necessary for undertaking significant change and use rewards to reinforce new behaviours. Executive leaders also must build an effective top-management team to manage the new organisation and develop management practices to support the change process.

CHANGE INVOLVES SIGNIFICANT LEARNING

Transformational change requires much learning and innovation.[21] Organisation members must learn how to enact the new behaviours required to implement new strategic directions. This typically involves trying new behaviours, assessing their consequences and modifying them if necessary. Because members usually need to learn qualitatively different ways of perceiving, thinking and behaving, the learning process is likely to be substantial and to involve much 'unlearning'. It is directed by a vision of the future organisation and by the values and norms needed to support it. Learning occurs at all levels of the organisation, from senior executives to lower-level employees.

Because the environment itself is likely to be changing during the change process, transformational change rarely has a delimited time frame, but is likely to persist as long as the organisation needs to adapt to change. Learning how to manage change continuously can help the organisation keep pace with a dynamic environment.

INTEGRATED STRATEGIC CHANGE

Integrated strategic change (ISC) extends traditional OD processes into the content-oriented discipline of strategic management. It is a deliberate, coordinated process that leads gradually or radically to systemic realignments between the environment and an organisation's strategic orientation, and that results in improvement in performance and effectiveness.[22]

The ISC process was initially developed by Worley, Hitchin and Ross in response to managers' complaints that good business strategies often are not implemented.[23] Research suggests that too little attention is given to the change process and human resource issues necessary to execute strategy.[24] The predominant paradigm in strategic management – formulation and implementation – artificially separates strategic thinking from operational and tactical actions; it ignores the contributions that planned change processes can make to implementation.[25] In the traditional process, senior

Integrated strategic change (ISC): a comprehensive OD intervention aimed at a single organisation or business unit. ISC requires business strategy and organisation design to be aligned and changed together to respond to external and internal disruptions.

managers and strategic planning staff prepare economic forecasts, competitor analyses and market studies. They discuss these studies and rationally align the organisation's strengths and weaknesses with environmental opportunities and threats to form the organisation's strategy.[26] Then, implementation occurs as middle managers, supervisors and employees hear about the new strategy through memos, restructuring announcements, changes in job responsibilities or new departmental objectives. Consequently, because participation has been limited to top management, there is little understanding of the need for change and little ownership of the new behaviours, initiatives and tactics required to achieve the announced objectives.

Key features

ISC, in contrast to the traditional process, was designed to be a highly participative process. It has three key features:[27]

1   The relevant unit of analysis is the organisation's *strategic orientation*, which comprises its strategy and organisation design. Strategy and the design that supports it must be considered as an integrated whole.

2   Creating the strategic plan, gaining commitment and support for it, planning its implementation and executing it are treated as one integrated process. The ability to repeat such a process quickly and effectively when conditions warrant is valuable, rare and difficult to imitate. Thus, a strategic change capability represents a sustainable competitive advantage.[28]

3   Individuals and groups throughout the organisation are integrated into the analysis, planning and implementation process to create a more achievable plan, maintain the organisation's strategic focus, direct attention and resources on the organisation's key competencies, improve coordination and integration within the organisation and create higher levels of shared ownership and commitment.

Application stages

The ISC process is applied in four phases: performing a strategic analysis, exercising strategic choice, designing a strategic change plan and implementing the plan. The four steps are discussed sequentially here but actually unfold in overlapping and integrated ways. **Figure 9.1** displays the steps in the ISC process and its change components. An organisation's existing strategic orientation, identified as its current strategy (S1) and organisation design (O1), is linked to its future strategic orientation (S2/O2) by the strategic change plan.

Performing the strategic analysis

The ISC process begins with a diagnosis of the organisation's readiness for change and its current strategy and organisation design (S1/O1). The most important indicator of readiness is senior management's willingness and ability to carry out strategic change. Greiner and Schein suggest that the two key dimensions in this analysis are the leader's willingness and commitment to change and the senior team's willingness and ability to follow the leader's initiative.[29] Organisations whose leaders are not willing to lead and whose senior managers are not willing and able to support the new strategic direction when necessary should consider team-building processes to ensure their commitment.

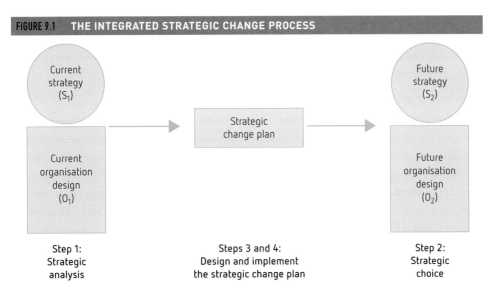

FIGURE 9.1   THE INTEGRATED STRATEGIC CHANGE PROCESS

The second stage in strategic analysis[30] is understanding the current strategy and organisation design. The process begins with an examination of the organisation's industry as well as its current financial performance and effectiveness. This information provides the necessary context to assess the current strategic orientation's viability. Porter's model of industry attractiveness[31] and the environmental framework are the two most relevant models for analysing the environment.

Next, the current strategic orientation is described to explain current levels of performance and human outcomes. Several models for guiding this diagnosis exist.[32] For example, the organisation's current strategy, structure and processes can be assessed according to the model and methods. A metaphor or other label that describes how the organisation's mission, objectives and business policies lead to improved performance can be used to represent strategy. 3M Company is known for applying a strategy of 'differentiation', leading to it supporting innovative behaviours by its engineers and technicians. An organisation's objectives, policies and budgets signal which parts of the environment are important and allocate and direct resources to particular environmental relationships.[33] Another example is Intel's new product development objectives and allocation of more than 20 per cent of revenue to research and development, which signal the importance of its linkage to the technological environment. Similar attention to properly resourcing for innovation is noted in other technology companies, such as Apple and Google.

The organisation's design is described by the structure, work design, information system and human resources system. Other models for understanding the organisation's strategic orientation include the competitive positioning model[34] and other typologies.[35] These frameworks assist in assessing customer satisfaction; product and service offerings; financial health; technological capabilities; and organisational culture, structure and systems.

The strategic analysis process actively involves organisation members. Large group conferences, employee focus groups, interviews with salespeople, customers and purchasing agents, and other methods allow a variety of employees and managers to participate in the diagnosis and increase the amount and relevance of the data collected. This builds commitment to and ownership of the analysis; should a strategic change effort result, members are more likely to understand why and be supportive of it.

Exercising strategic choice

Once the existing strategic orientation is understood, a new one must be designed. For example, the strategic analysis might reveal misfits among the organisation's environment, strategic orientation and performance. These misfits can be used as inputs for crafting the future strategy and organisation design. Based on this analysis, senior management formulates visions for the future and broadly defines two or three alternative sets of strategies and objectives for achieving those visions. Market forecasts, employees' readiness and willingness to change, competitor analyses and other projections can be used to develop the alternative future scenarios.[36] The different sets of strategies and objectives also include projections about the organisation design changes that will be necessary to support each alternative. Although participation from other organisation stakeholders is important in the alternative generation phase, choosing the appropriate strategic orientation ultimately rests with top management and cannot easily be delegated. Senior executives are in the unique position of viewing a strategy from a general management position. When major strategic decisions are delegated to lower-level managers, the risk of focusing too narrowly on a product, market or technology increases.

This step determines the content, or 'what', of strategic change. The desired strategy (S2) defines the products or services to offer, the markets to be served and the way these outputs will be produced and positioned. The desired organisation design (O2) specifies the structures and processes necessary to support the new strategy. Aligning an organisation's design with a particular strategy can be a major source of superior performance and competitive advantage.[37]

Designing the strategic change plan

The strategic change plan is a comprehensive agenda for moving the organisation from its current strategy and organisation design to the desired future strategic orientation. It represents the process or 'how' of strategic change. The change plan describes the types, magnitude and schedule of change activities, as well as the costs associated with them. It also specifies how the changes will be implemented, given power and political issues; the nature of the organisational culture; and the current ability of the organisation to implement change.[38]

Implementing the plan

The final step in the ISC process is the actual implementation of the strategic change plan.[39] This draws heavily on knowledge of motivation, group dynamics and change processes. It deals continuously with such issues as alignment, adaptability, teamwork and organisation and personal learning. Implementation requires senior managers to champion the different elements of the change plan. They can, for example, initiate action and allocate resources to particular activities, set high but achievable goals and provide feedback on accomplishments. In addition, leaders must hold people accountable to the change objectives, institutionalise the changes that occur and be prepared to solve problems as they arise. This final point recognises that no strategic change plan can account for all of the contingencies that emerge. There must be a willingness to adjust the plan as implementation unfolds to address unforeseen and unpredictable events and to take advantage of new opportunities.

Apply your learning 9.2 describes the strategic change process needed by the Miss Chu food business in light of its restructure.

MISS CHU AND LADY CHU RECONSTRUE

In 2015, Nahji Chu, founder of the Miss Chu tuckshop chain in Australia, was quoted while reflecting: 'There is no greater punishment than what I have been through and it will always be a lesson to me.'

This was in reference to how her restaurant chain almost went under in 2014 with business debts exceeding $4 million. Fast growth and an expensive effort at internationalisation via entry into the London market were the main cause of Miss Chu's troubles. Until then the store had captured a lucrative niche in Vietnamese food home delivery in Australia. Clever marketing, including their catchy slogan 'You ling, we bling', and a tasty menu of Vietnamese rice paper rolls were part of the growth formula. In addition, the use of Nahji Chu's life story as an immigrant who came to Australia with nothing and worked hard to build up a successful business was integrally tied to the operation. But financial management issues during expansion became a big problem for the chain.

To salvage the situation Miss Chu went into voluntary administration and the Mawson Group in Melbourne injected funds into the company and took on the task of restructure. In 2015 Miss Chu was sacked from the business and her former business partner Gabriel Machado bought out the company and continued trading using the same name and the original logo, which incorporates a photographic image of Nahji along with a reproduction of her original immigrant visa to Australia and trades strongly off her immigration success story. This has created an unusual legal situation for Miss Chu.

Nahji has started a new business of her own called Lady Chu, which effectively competes with the Miss Chu business no longer owned by her but which bears her image on its logo and refers to her life story. The Miss Chu business has sent Lady Chu legal letters telling them to not use Nahji's surname or an image of her that appears in the Miss Chu brand. They also want Lady Chu to stop using their new slogan. 'You Rrring We Bring', which sounds very similar to the original slogan Nahji created for the Miss Chu business.

So is it the established Miss Chu business that has the best strategic advantage here? Or does its founder, who has now started a competing business, hold the stronger strategic hand? How would you craft the plan for Miss Chu?

Sources: Based on T. Ooi, 'Mawson to get Miss Chu rolling again', *The Australian*, 18 May 2015; and D. McCauley, 'Miss Chu's outspoken founder defends her right to use her face and name after legal threats', news.com.au, 19 September 2017.

»

>>

Critical thinking questions	1	Analyse the possible positives and negatives of Nahji Chu being sacked from the business in 2015 according to steps 1 and 2 of the application stages in **Figure 9.1**, performing the strategic analysis and exercising strategic choice.
	2	Analyse the possible positives and negatives of Miss Chu legally challenging Lady Chu over trademark usage according to steps 3 and 4 of the application stages in **Figure 9.1**, designing the strategic change plan and implementing the plan.

ORGANISATION DESIGN

Organisation design:
configures the organisation's structure, work design, human resources practices, and management and information systems to guide members' behaviours in a strategic direction.

Organisation design configures the organisation's structure, work design, human resources practices, and management and information systems to guide members' behaviours in a strategic direction. This intervention typically occurs in response to a major change in the organisation's strategy that requires fundamentally new ways for the organisation to function and members to behave. It involves many of the organisational features discussed in previous chapters, such as restructuring organisations, work design and performance management. Because they all significantly affect member behaviour, organisation design constructs them to fit with each other so they all mutually reinforce the desired behaviour in the new strategic direction. This comprehensive intervention contrasts sharply with piecemeal approaches that address the design elements separately, and thus risk misaligning them with each other and sending mixed signals about desired behaviours. For example, many organisations have experienced problems implementing team-based structures because their existing information and reward systems emphasise individual-based performance.

CONCEPTUAL FRAMEWORK

A key notion in organisation design is 'fit', 'congruence' or 'alignment' among the organisational elements.[40] **Figure 9.2** presents a systems model showing the different components of organisation design and the interdependencies among them. It highlights the idea that the organisation is designed to support a particular strategy (strategic fit) and that the different design elements must be aligned with each other and all work together to guide members' behaviour in that strategic direction (design fit). Research shows that the better these fits, the more effective the organisation is likely to be.[41]

Most of the design components are reviewed briefly below.

→ *Strategy* determines how the organisation will use its resources to gain competitive advantage. It may focus on introducing new products and services (innovation strategy), controlling costs and reducing prices (cost-minimisation strategy) or some combination of both (imitation strategy). Strategy sets the direction for organisation design by identifying the criteria for making design choices and the organisational capabilities needed to make the strategy happen.

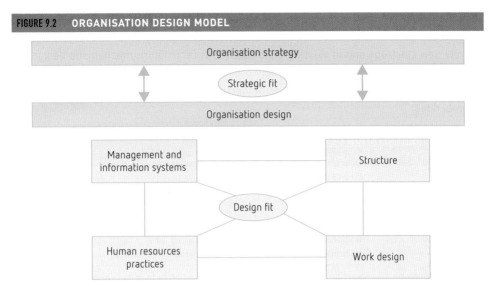

FIGURE 9.2 **ORGANISATION DESIGN MODEL**

→ *Structure* relates to how the organisation divides tasks, assigns them to departments and coordinates across them. It generally appears on an organisation chart showing the chain of command – where formal power and authority reside and how departments relate to each other. Structures can be highly formal and promote control and efficiency, such as a functional structure;[42] or they can be loosely defined and flexible, favouring change and innovation, such as a matrix, process or network structure.

→ *Work design* specifies how tasks are performed and assigned to jobs or groups. It can create traditional jobs and groups that involve standard tasks with little task variety and decision making, or enriched jobs and self-managed teams that involve highly variable, challenging and discretionary work.

→ *Human resources practices* involve selecting people and training, developing and rewarding them. These methods can be oriented to hiring and paying people for specific jobs, training them when necessary and rewarding their individual performance. Conversely, human resources practices can also select people to fit the organisation's culture, continually develop them and pay them for learning multiple skills and contributing to business success.

→ *Management and information systems*[43] have to do with how employees are led and the nature and kinds of information they are provided to guide their work. Managers can lead through command and control, relying on hierarchical authority and the chain of command; or they can be highly participative and facilitate employee involvement in decision making. Information systems can be highly centralised with limited access and data sharing; or they can be open and distribute copious information throughout the organisation.

Table 9.1 shows how these design components can be configured into two radically different organisation designs: *mechanistic*, supporting efficiency and control, and *organic*, promoting innovation and change.[44] Mechanistic designs have been prevalent in organisations for over a century; they propelled organisations into the industrial age. Today, competitive conditions require many organisations to be more flexible, fast and inventive.[45] Thus, organisation design is aimed more and more at creating organic designs, both in entirely new start-ups and in existing businesses that reconfigure mechanistic designs to make them more organic. Designing a new organisation is much easier than redesigning an existing one in which multiple sources of inertia[46] and resistance to change are likely to be embedded.

TABLE 9.1 ORGANISATION DESIGNS	Mechanistic design	Organic design
Strategy	Cost minimisation	Innovation
Structure	Formal/hierarchical Functional	Flat, lean and flexible Matrix, process and network
Work design	Traditional jobs Traditional work groups	Enriched jobs Self-managed teams
Human resources practices	Selection to fit job Up-front training Standard reward mix Pay for performance and individual merit Job-based pay	Selection to fit organisation Continuous training and development Individual choice rewards Pay for performance and business success Skill-based pay
Management and information systems	Command and control Closed, exclusive, centralised information	Employee involvement Open, inclusive, distributed information

As shown in **Table 9.1**, a mechanistic design supports an organisation strategy emphasising cost minimisation, such as might be found at Target and McDonald's or other businesses competing on price. The organisation tends to be structured into functional departments, with employees performing similar tasks grouped together for maximum efficiency. The managerial hierarchy is the main source of coordination and control. Accordingly, work design follows traditional principles with jobs and work groups being highly standardised with minimal decision making and skill variety. Human resources practices are geared towards selecting people to fit specific jobs and training them periodically when the need arises. Employees are paid on the basis of the job they perform, share a standard set of fringe benefits and achieve merit raises based on their individual performance. Management practices stress command and control with power concentrated at the top of the organisation and orders flowing downwards through the chain of command. Similarly, information systems are highly centralised, limited in access and do not permit sharing data widely in the organisation. When taken together, all of these design elements direct organisational behaviour towards efficiency and cost minimisation.

Table 9.1 shows that an organic design supports an organisation strategy aimed at innovation, such as might be found at 3M, Apple and Intel or other businesses competing on new products and services. All the design elements are geared to getting employees directly involved in the innovation process, facilitating interaction among them, developing and rewarding their knowledge and expertise and providing them with relevant and timely information. Consequently, the organisation's structure tends to be flat, lean and flexible like the matrix, process and network structures. Work design is aimed at employee motivation and decision making with enriched jobs and self-managed teams. Human resources practices focus on attracting, motivating and retaining talented employees. They send a strong signal that employees' knowledge and expertise are key sources of competitive advantage. Members are selected to fit an organisational culture valuing participation, teamwork and invention. Training and development are intense and continuous. Members are rewarded for learning multiple skills, have choices about fringe benefits and gain merit pay based on the business success of their work unit. Management practices are highly participative and promote employee involvement. Information systems are highly open and inclusive, providing relevant and timely information throughout the organisation. In summary, these design choices guide members' behaviours towards change and innovation.

Application stages

Organisation design can be applied to the whole organisation or to a major subpart such as a large department or stand-alone unit. It can start from a clean slate in a new organisation or reconfigure an existing organisation design. To construct the different design elements appropriately requires broad content knowledge of them. Thus, organisation design typically involves a team of change practitioners with expertise in corporate strategy, organisation structure, work design, human resources practices and management and information systems. This team works closely with senior executives who are responsible for determining the organisation's strategic direction and leading the organisation design intervention. The design process itself can be highly participative, involving stakeholders from throughout the organisation. This can increase the design's quality and stakeholders' commitment to implementing it.[47]

Organisation design generally follows the three broad steps outlined below.[48] Although they are presented sequentially, in practice they are highly interactive, often feeding back on each other and requiring continual revision as the process unfolds.

1 *Clarifying the design focus.* This preliminary stage involves assessing the organisation to create the overall framework for design. It starts with examining the organisation's strategy and objectives and determining what organisation capabilities are needed to achieve them. These become the design criteria for making choices about how to configure the design components. Then, the organisation is assessed against these design criteria to uncover gaps between how it currently functions and is designed and the desired capabilities. This gap analysis identifies current problems that the design intervention should address. It provides information for determining which design elements will receive the most attention and the likely magnitude and time frame of the design process.

2 *Designing the organisation.* This key step in organisation design involves configuring the design components to support the organisation's strategy and objectives. It starts with a broad outline of how the organisation should be structured and how the design components should fit together to form a particular design, usually falling somewhere along the continuum from mechanistic to organic. Senior executives responsible for the overall direction of the organisation typically design this overarching structure. Next, the design process addresses the specific details of the components, which involves

generating alternatives and making specific design choices. A range of organisational members often participate in these decisions, relying on their own as well as experts' experience and know-how, knowledge of best practice and information gained from visits to other organisations willing to share design experience. This stage results in an overall design for the organisation, detailed designs for the components and preliminary plans for how they will fit together and be implemented.

3 *Implementing the design.* The final step involves making the new design happen by putting into place the new structures, practices and systems. It draws heavily on the methods for leading and managing change and applies them to the entire organisation or subunit and not just limited parts. Because organisation design generally involves large amounts of transformational change, this intervention can place heavy demands on the organisation's resources and leadership expertise. Members from throughout the organisation must be motivated to implement the new design; all relevant stakeholders must support it politically. Organisation designs usually cannot be implemented in one step but must proceed in phases that involve considerable transition management. They often entail significant new work behaviours and relationships that require extensive and continuous organisation learning.

Apply your learning 9.3 describes an organisation design change at the Australian Human Rights Commission. It illustrates how the different design elements create sometimes conflicting priorities for managers to balance.

APPLY
YOUR
LEARNING
9.3

DESIGNING HUMAN RIGHTS CORRECTLY

The Australian Human Rights Commission (AHRC) had some possible issues with the way it was designed. These issues came to a head with the Gillian Triggs affair associated with the 2015 report into migrant children in detention. The AHRC was intended to function as a tribunal that resolves disputes over infringements of rights. Then President Gillian Triggs facilitated this function together with other AHRC roles.

Previous commission presidents tended to leave it to other commission members to conduct inquiries. The children in migration detention report saw Gillian Triggs mixing the two functions of lobbying for change and making independent decisions. This caused some confusion in the minds of the public, and of opposing political parties in the whole debate.

Some commentators wondered whether clearly separating those functions as was the case in the past would be a better way forward. A simple change such as removing the statutory requirement that defines 'human rights' in terms of unenforceable treaties that are not part of Australian domestic law may do the trick.

Source: Based on C. Merritt, 'Time to change act to reflect the reality', *The Australian*, 6 March 2015.

Critical
thinking
questions

1 What is the main structural design problem identified by the article?

2 What are the three steps in organisation design? How might these steps be applied in redesigning the organisation in the article above?

CULTURE CHANGE

The topic of **organisational culture** is very important to companies and the number of culture change interventions has grown accordingly. Organisational culture is also the focus of growing research and OD application and has spawned a number of best-selling management books, including *Theory S*, *The Art of Japanese Management*, *In Search of Excellence*, *Built to Last*, *Corporate Culture and Performance*, *Culture Code* and *Light a Fire Under Your Business: How to Build a Class 1 Corporate Culture Through Inspirational Leadership*.[49] Organisational culture is seen as a major strength of such companies as Intel, PepsiCo, Motorola, Hewlett-Packard and Levi Strauss. A growing number of managers appreciate the power of corporate culture in shaping employee beliefs and actions. A well-conceived and well-managed organisational culture, closely linked to an effective business strategy, can mean the difference between success and failure in today's demanding environments.

> **Organisational culture:** includes the pattern of basic assumptions, values, norms and artefacts shared by organisation members. It influences how members perceive, think and behave at work.

CONCEPT OF ORGANISATIONAL CULTURE

Despite the increased attention and research devoted to corporate culture, there is still some confusion about what the term 'culture' really means when applied to organisations.[50] Martin argues that culture can be viewed from an integrated, a differentiated or a fragmented perspective.[51] The integrated view focuses on culture as an organisationally shared phenomenon; it represents a stable and coherent set of beliefs about the organisation and its environment. In contrast to the integrated perspective, the differentiated view argues that culture is not monolithic but that it is best seen in terms of subcultures that exist throughout the organisation. While each subculture is locally stable and shared, there is much that is different across the subcultures. Finally, the fragmented view holds that culture is always changing and is dominated by ambiguity and paradox. Summarising an organisation's culture from a fragmented viewpoint has little meaning.

Despite these different cultural views, there is some agreement about the elements or features of culture that are typically measured. They include the artefacts, norms, values and basic assumptions that are more or less shared by organisation members. The meanings attached to these elements help members make sense out of everyday life in the organisation. The meanings signal how work is to be done and evaluated and how employees are to relate to each other and to other stakeholders such as customers, suppliers and government agencies.

As shown in **Figure 9.3**, organisation culture includes four major elements existing at different levels of awareness:[52]

1 *Artefacts*. Artefacts are the highest level of cultural manifestation.[53] They are the visible symbols of the deeper levels of culture, such as norms, values and basic assumptions. Artefacts include members' behaviours, clothing and language; and the organisation's structures, systems, procedures and physical aspects, such as decor, space arrangements and noise levels. At Nordstrom, a high-end retail department store in the United States, the policy and procedure manual is rumoured to be one

sentence: 'Do whatever you think is right.' In addition, stores promote from within; pay commissions on sales to link effort and compensation; provide stationery for salespeople to write personal notes to customers; and expect buyers to work as salespeople to better understand the customers' expectations. By themselves, artefacts can provide a great deal of information about the real culture of the organisation because they often represent the deeper assumptions. The difficulty in their use during cultural analysis is interpretation; an outsider (and even some insiders) has no way of knowing what the artefacts represent, if anything.

2   *Norms.* Just below the surface of cultural awareness are norms guiding how members should behave in particular situations. These represent unwritten rules of behaviour. Norms generally are inferred from observing how members behave and interact with each other. At Nordstrom, norms dictate that it's okay for members to go the extra mile to satisfy customer requests and it's not okay for salespeople to process customers who were working with another salesperson.

3   *Values.* The next-deeper level of awareness includes values about what ought to be in organisations. Values tell members what is important in the organisation and what deserves their attention. Because Nordstrom values customer service, the sales representatives pay strong attention to how well the customer is treated. Obviously, this value is supported by the norms and artefacts.

4   *Basic assumptions.* At the deepest level of cultural awareness are the taken-for-granted assumptions about how organisational problems should be solved. These basic assumptions tell members how to perceive, think and feel about things. They are non-confrontable and non-debatable assumptions about relating to the environment and about human nature, human activity and human relationships. For example, a basic assumption at Nordstrom is the belief in the fundamental dignity of people; it is morally right to treat customers with extraordinary service so that they will become loyal and frequent shoppers.

FIGURE 9.3   LEVELS OF CORPORATE CULTURE

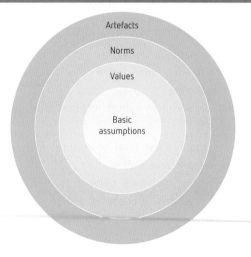

Culture is the pattern of artefacts, norms, values and basic assumptions about how to solve problems that works well enough to be taught to others.[54] Culture is a process of social learning; it is the outcome of prior choices about and experiences with strategy and organisation design. It is also a foundation for change that can either facilitate or hinder OT. For example, the cultures of many companies, such as IBM, Sony, Disney, Microsoft and Hewlett-Packard, are deeply rooted in the company's history. The cultures were laid down by strong founders and have been reinforced by top executives and corporate success into customary ways of perceiving and acting. These customs provide organisation members with clear and often widely shared answers to such practical issues as 'what really matters around here', 'how we do things around here' and 'what we do when a problem arises'.

ORGANISATIONAL CULTURE AND ORGANISATIONAL EFFECTIVENESS

The interest in organisational culture derives largely from its presumed impact on organisational effectiveness. Considerable speculation and increasing research suggest that organisational culture has both direct and indirect relationships with effectiveness.

Indirectly, culture affects performance through its influence on the organisation's ability to implement change. A particular pattern of values and assumptions that once was a source of strength for a company can become a major liability in successfully implementing a new strategy.[55] Case studies of OT are full of accounts where the change failed because the culture did not support the new strategy, including AT&T's failed integration of NCR, Daimler-Benz's troubles with Chrysler and Prudential Insurance's difficulties in diversifying into other financial services.

The growing appreciation that culture can play a significant role in implementing new strategy has fuelled interest in the topic, especially in those organisations needing to adapt to turbulent environments. A number of practitioners and academics have focused on helping organisations implement new strategies by bringing culture more in line with the new direction. Indeed, much of the emphasis in the 1970s on formulating business strategy shifted to organisational culture in the 1980s as businesses discovered cultural roadblocks to implementing a strategy. Along with this emerging focus on organisational culture, however, came the sobering reality that culture change is an extremely difficult and long-term process. Some experts doubt whether large organisations actually can bring about fundamental changes in their cultures; those who have accomplished such feats estimate that the process takes from six to 15 years.[56] For example, Telstra has struggled for years to change from a service-oriented telephone company to a market-oriented communications business. Its industrial conflict is thought to be partly the result of a dramatic shift in culture from a 'public sector' mindset to one that is more conducive to a market-competitive environment.

Indirectly, culture can also affect performance through its influence on an organisation's ability to operate in different countries. In the 1980s, Australia Post had a reputation for being a bureaucratic, stagnant organisation with poor customer service and increasing industrial unrest. The then federal government, as part of its microeconomic reform agenda, commercialised and corporatised the organisation. Beginning with a commitment from the managing director, culture change included turning the organisation into a customer service-focused business; building a committed and motivated workforce; and increasing productivity and profitability. Australia Post began a culture change intervention that took at least 15 years.

Multinationals may face problems doing business in other countries, especially when their corporate culture does not fit with the national culture. For example, Starbucks learned this when it had to close 70 per cent of its Australian stores. Australia has an entrenched coffee culture ranging from independents to local brands like Hudsons, which US-styled Starbucks found hard to enter. Customers were accustomed to stronger coffee brews brought in by European immigrants. Starbucks had failed, in part, to comprehend and value the uniqueness of the Australian coffee drinker. This cultural mismatch resulted in Starbucks closing down 61 cafes.[57]

Directly, evidence suggests that, in addition to affecting the implementation of business strategy, corporate culture can affect organisation performance. Comparative studies of Eastern and Western management methods suggest that the relative success of Japanese companies in the 1980s could be partly explained by their strong corporate cultures emphasising employee participation, open communication, security and equality.[58] A study of the productivity of university research departments in the United Kingdom showed a strong relationship between productivity and organisation cultures emphasising teamwork, information flow and employee involvement.[59] Another study of American companies showed a similar pattern of results.[60] Using survey measures of culture and Standard & Poor's financial ratios as indicators of organisational effectiveness, the results showed that companies whose cultures support employee participation in decision making, adaptable work methods, sensible work designs and reasonable and clear goals perform significantly higher (financial ratios about twice as high) than do companies scoring low on those factors. Moreover, the employee participation element of corporate culture showed differences in effectiveness among the companies after only three years; the other measures of culture showed differences in all five years. This suggests that changing some parts of corporate culture, such as participation, should be considered as a long-term investment.

Another study of 207 companies in 22 different industries examined relationships between financial performance and the strength of a culture, the strategic appropriateness of a culture and the adaptiveness of a culture.[61] First, there were no significant performance differences between organisations with widely shared values and those with little agreement around cultural assumptions. Second, there was a significant relationship between culture and performance when the organisation emphasised the 'right' values – values that were critical to success in a particular industry. Finally, performance results over time supported cultures that emphasised anticipating and adapting to environmental change.

These findings suggest that the strength of an organisation's culture can be both an advantage and a disadvantage. Under stable conditions, widely shared and strategically appropriate values can contribute significantly to organisation performance. However, if the environment is changing, strong cultures can be a liability. Unless they also emphasise adaptiveness, the organisation may experience wide swings in performance during transformational change. This line of thought has had empirical support.[62] In a study of over 150 large, publicly traded companies from 19 industries, organisations with strong cultures had more reliable performance outcomes – that is, the strength of the culture was related to the predictability of performance. However, when the environment was more uncertain and dynamic, this reliability faded. In stable environments, strong cultures can provide efficiency in decision making and operations. In volatile environments, the strength of the culture can become a weakness if it stunts creativity. Organisations with strong cultures are less able to exploit new environmental opportunities, unless, of course, the culture emphasises innovation and change.

DIAGNOSING ORGANISATIONAL CULTURE

Culture change interventions generally start by diagnosing the organisation's existing culture to assess its fit with current or proposed business strategies. This requires uncovering and understanding the shared assumptions, values, norms and artefacts that characterise an organisation's culture. OD practitioners have developed a number of useful approaches for diagnosing organisational culture. These approaches fall into three different yet complementary perspectives: the behavioural approach, the competing values approach and the deep assumption approach. Each diagnostic perspective focuses on particular aspects of organisational culture and together the approaches can provide a comprehensive assessment of these complex phenomena.

The behavioural approach

This method of diagnosis emphasises the surface level of organisational culture – the pattern of behaviours that produce business results.[63] It is among the more practical approaches to culture diagnosis because it assesses key work behaviours that can be observed.[64] The behavioural approach provides specific descriptions about how tasks are performed and how relationships are managed in an organisation. For example, **Table 9.2** summarises the organisational culture of an international banking division as perceived by its managers. In this classic case, the data were obtained from a series of individual and group interviews asking managers to describe 'the way the game is played', as if they were coaching a new organisation member. Managers were asked to give their impressions in regard to four key relationships (company-wide, boss–subordinate, peer and interdepartmental) and in terms of six managerial tasks (innovating, decision making, communicating, organising, monitoring and appraising/rewarding). These perceptions revealed a number of implicit norms for how tasks are performed and relationships managed at the division.

TABLE 9.2	SUMMARY OF CORPORATE CULTURE AT AN INTERNATIONAL BANKING DIVISION
Relationships	**Culture summary**
Company-wide	Preserve your autonomy Allow area managers to run the business as long as they keep the profit budget
Boss–subordinate	Avoid confrontations Smooth over disagreements Support the boss
Peer	Guard information; it is power Be a gentleman or lady
Interdepartment	Protect your department's bottom line Form alliances around specific issues Guard your turf
Tasks	**Culture summary**
Innovating	Consider it risky Be a quick second
Decision making	Handle each deal on its own merits Gain consensus Require many sign-offs Involve the right people Seize the opportunity
Communicating	Withhold information to control adversaries Avoid confrontation Be a gentleman or lady
Organising	Centralise power Be autocratic
Monitoring	Meet short-term profit goals
Appraising and rewarding	Reward the faithful Choose the best bankers as managers Seek safe jobs

Source: H. Schwartz and S.M. Davis, 'Matching corporate culture and business strategy', *Organizational Dynamics*, vol. 10, Summer © 1981. Reproduced with permission from Elsevier.

Cultural diagnosis derived from a behavioural approach also can be used to assess the cultural risk of trying to implement organisational changes needed to support a new strategy. Significant cultural risks result when changes that are highly important to implementing a new strategy are incompatible with the existing patterns of behaviour. Knowledge of such risks can help managers determine whether implementation plans should be changed to manage around the existing culture, whether the culture should be changed or whether the strategy itself should be modified or abandoned.

The competing values approach

This perspective assesses an organisation's culture in terms of how it resolves a set of value dilemmas.[65] The approach suggests that an organisation's culture can be understood in terms of two important 'value pairs'; each pair consists of contradictory values placed at opposite ends of a continuum. The two value pairs are (1) internal focus and integration versus external focus and differentiation and (2) flexibility and discretion versus stability and control. Organisations continually struggle to satisfy the conflicting demands placed on them by these competing values. For example, when faced with the competing values of internal versus external focus, organisations must choose between attending to the integration problems of internal operations and the competitive issues in the external environment. Too much emphasis on the environment can result in neglect of internal efficiencies. Conversely, too much attention to the internal aspects of organisations can result in missing important changes in the competitive environment.

The competing values approach commonly collects diagnostic data about the competing values with a survey designed specifically for that purpose.[66] It provides measures of where an organisation's existing values fall along each of the dimensions. When taken together, these data identify an organisation's culture as falling into one of the four quadrants: clan culture, adhocracy culture,[67] hierarchical culture and market culture. For example, if an organisation's values are focused on internal integration issues and emphasise innovation and flexibility, it manifests a clan culture. On the other hand, a market culture characterises values that are externally focused and emphasises stability and control.

The deep assumptions approach

This final diagnostic approach emphasises the deepest levels of organisational culture – the generally unexamined, but tacit and shared assumptions that guide member behaviour and that often have a powerful impact on organisation effectiveness. Diagnosing culture from this perspective typically begins with the most tangible level of awareness and then works down to the deep assumptions.

Diagnosing organisational culture at the deep assumptions level poses at least three difficult problems for collecting pertinent information.[68] First, culture reflects the more or less shared assumptions about what is important, how things are done and how people should behave in organisations. People generally take cultural assumptions for granted and rarely speak of them directly. Rather, the company's culture is implied in concrete behavioural examples, such as daily routines, stories, rituals and language. This means that considerable time and effort must be spent observing, sifting through and asking people about these cultural outcroppings to understand their deeper significance for organisation members. Second, some values and beliefs that people espouse have little to do with the ones they really hold and follow. People are reluctant to admit this discrepancy, yet somehow the real assumptions underlying idealised portrayals of culture must be discovered. Third, large, diverse organisations are likely to have several subcultures, including countercultures going against the grain of the wider organisation culture. Assumptions may not be shared widely and may differ across groups in the organisation. This means that focusing on limited parts of the organisation or on a few select individuals may provide a distorted view of the organisation's culture and subcultures. All relevant groups in the organisation must be identified and their cultural assumptions sampled. Only then can practitioners judge the extent to which assumptions are shared widely.

OD practitioners emphasising the deep assumptions approach have developed a number of useful techniques for assessing organisational culture.[69] One method involves an iterative interviewing process involving both outsiders and insiders.[70] Outsiders help members uncover cultural elements through joint exploration. The outsider enters the organisation and experiences surprises and puzzles that are different from what was expected. The outsider shares these observations with insiders and the two parties jointly explore their meaning. This process involves several iterations of experiencing surprises, checking for meaning and formulating hypotheses about the culture. It results in a formal written description of the assumptions underlying an organisational culture.

A second method for identifying the organisation's basic assumptions brings together a group of people for a culture workshop – for example, a senior management team or a cross-section of managers, old and new members, labour leaders and staff.[71] The group first brainstorms a large number of the organisation's artefacts, such as behaviours, symbols, language and physical space arrangements. From this list, the values and norms that would produce such artefacts are deduced. In addition, the values espoused in formal planning documents are listed. Finally, the group attempts to identify the assumptions that would explain the constellation of values, norms and artefacts. Because basic assumptions generally are taken for granted, they are difficult to articulate. A great deal of process consultation skill is required to help organisation members see the underlying assumptions.

Application stages

There is considerable debate over whether changing something as deep-seated as organisational culture is possible.[72] Those advocating culture change generally focus on the more surface elements of culture, such as norms and artefacts. These elements are more changeable than the deeper elements of values and basic assumptions. They offer change practitioners a more manageable set of action levers for changing organisational behaviours. Some would argue, however, that unless the deeper values and assumptions are changed, organisations have not really changed their culture.

Those arguing that implementing culture change is extremely difficult, if not impossible, typically focus on the deeper elements of culture (values and basic assumptions). Because these deeper elements represent assumptions about organisational life, members do not question them and have a difficult time envisioning anything else. Moreover, members may not want to change their cultural assumptions. The culture provides a strong defence against external uncertainties and threats.[73] It represents past solutions to difficult problems. Members also may have vested interests in maintaining the culture. They may have developed personal stakes, pride and power in the culture and may strongly resist attempts to change it. Finally, cultures that provide companies with a competitive advantage may be difficult to imitate, making it hard for less successful organisations to change their cultures to approximate the more successful ones.[74]

Given the problems with culture change, most practitioners in this area suggest that changes in corporate culture should be considered only after other, less difficult and less costly solutions have been applied or ruled out.[75] Attempts to overcome cultural risks when strategic changes are incompatible with the existing culture might include ways to manage around that culture. Consider, for example, a single-product organisation with a functional focus and a history of centralised control that is considering an ambitious product-diversification strategy. The company might manage around its existing culture by using business teams to coordinate functional specialists around each new product. Another alternative to changing culture is to modify strategy to bring it more in line with culture. The single-product organisation just mentioned might decide to undertake a less ambitious strategy of product diversification.

Despite problems in changing corporate culture, large-scale culture change may be necessary in certain situations: if the organisation's culture does not fit a changing environment; if the industry is extremely competitive and changes rapidly; if the company is mediocre or worse; if the business is about to become a very large company; or if the company is smaller and growing rapidly.[76] Organisations facing these conditions need to change their cultures to adapt to the situation or to operate at higher levels of effectiveness. They may have to supplement attempts at culture change with other approaches, such as managing around the existing culture and modifying strategy.

Although knowledge about changing corporate culture is in a formative stage, the following practical advice can serve as guidelines for culture change:[77]

1 *Formulate a clear strategic vision.* Effective culture change should start from a clear vision of the organisation's new strategy and of the shared values and behaviours needed to make it work.[78] This vision provides the purpose and direction for culture change. It serves as a yardstick for defining the organisation's existing culture and for deciding whether proposed changes are consistent with the core values of the organisation. A useful approach to providing clear strategic vision is the development of a statement of corporate purpose, listing in straightforward terms the basic values that the organisation believes in.

2 *Display top-management commitment.* Culture change must be managed from the top of the organisation. Senior executives and administrators have to be strongly committed to the new values and need to create constant pressures for change. They must have the staying power to see the changes through.[79]

3 *Model culture change at the highest levels.* Senior executives must communicate the new culture through their own actions. Their behaviours need to symbolise the kinds of values and behaviours being sought. In the few publicised cases of successful culture change, corporate leaders have shown an almost missionary zeal for the new values; their actions have symbolised the values forcefully.[80] For example, Toyota Australia's implementation of '360-degree performance appraisal' began at the top, giving even the most junior workers a chance to assess the performances of their bosses.

4 *Modify the organisation to support organisational change.* Culture change generally requires supporting modifications in organisation structure, human resources systems, information and control systems and management styles. These organisational features can help to orient people's behaviours to the new culture.[81] They can make people aware of the behaviours required to get things done in the new culture and can encourage performance of those behaviours. For example, when Ian McLeod became the managing director of Coles in 2008, he had a clear brief: refresh the stores, rather than focus on back-office operations. He realised that what the company needed was culture change: better customer service, better supply chains and less bureaucracy.

5   *Select and socialise newcomers and terminate deviants.* One of the most effective methods for changing corporate culture is to change organisation membership. People can be selected and terminated in terms of their fit with the new culture. This is especially important in key leadership positions, where people's actions can significantly promote or hinder new values and behaviours. For example, in trying to change from a car parts and battery company to a leader in electronics, Gould replaced about two-thirds of its senior executives with people more in tune with the new strategy and culture. Jan Carlzon of Scandinavian Airlines (SAS) replaced 13 out of 15 top executives in his turnaround of the airline. Another approach is to socialise newly hired people into the new culture. People are most open to organisational influences during the entry stage, when they can be effectively indoctrinated into the culture. For example, companies with strong cultures, such as Amcor, CSR and Westpac, attach great importance to socialising new members into the company's values.

6   *Develop ethical and legal sensitivity.* Culture change can raise significant tensions between organisation and individual interests, resulting in ethical and legal problems for practitioners. This is particularly pertinent when organisations are trying to implement cultural values promoting employee integrity, control, equitable treatment and job security – values often included in culture change efforts. Statements about such values provide employees with certain expectations about their rights and about how they will be treated in the organisation. The organisation needs to follow through with behaviours and procedures supporting and protecting these implied rights, or risk violating ethical principles and, in some cases, legal employment contracts. Recommendations for reducing the chances of such ethical and legal problems include setting realistic values for culture change and not promising what the organisation cannot deliver; encouraging input from throughout the organisation in setting cultural values; providing mechanisms for member dissent and diversity, such as internal review procedures; and educating managers about the legal and ethical pitfalls inherent in culture change and helping them develop guidelines for resolving such issues.

Apply your learning 9.4 presents an example of proposed culture change in the financial services industry. It demonstrates the complexity and challenges of such change.

APPLY
YOUR
LEARNING
9.4

ASIC IS SICK OF BAD CULTURE

The banking Royal Commission in 2018 laid bare some remarkable ethical problems within the banking system and specific institutions. The regulator largely responsible for banking, the Australian Securities and Investments Commission (ASIC), subsequently needed to improve the culture in the financial services industry.

Even before the Royal Commission had happened, in an interview with *The Australian*, ASIC chairman in 2015, Greg Medcraft, acknowledged the bad image of managers and staff in the financial services sector. 'You have to change the way

»

people think,' he said. Corporate scandals and ethical problems have been reported regularly and the problem has been that ASIC is limited in its ability to change things due to provisions in the Commonwealth *Crimes Act* concerning culture. Financial services and products are exempted from the provisions that criminalise the toleration of a company culture that leads to staff and managers breaking the law.

After the banking Royal Commission had exposed just how ruthless and cruel some banking practices had been for some customers, ASIC came under immense pressure to do more to clean up the industry. Treasurer Josh Frydenberg was quoted, 'The findings here go to a culture of negotiation rather [than] litigation.'

The Chairman of ASIC appointed by the government in 2018, James Shipton, was provided with a $70 million budget and Daniel Crennan, QC, to focus on litigation. Now it remains to be seen to what extent culture change can be driven in banking by the increased resourcing of enforcement.

Sources: Based on R. Gluyas, 'ASIC to target poor corporate culture', *The Australian*, 17 June 2015; and P. Durkin, 'Banking royal commission interim report: ASIC's role "unacceptable", *Australian Financial Review*, 28 September 2018.

Critical thinking questions

1 'The findings here go to a culture of negotiation rather [than] litigation.' Comment on this statement from Josh Frydenberg and what it means in relation to culture change.

2 In your opinion, should ASIC encourage further transformation in financial services organisations? Explain your answer.

3 Which of the six application stages of culture change may need to be considered by ASIC when making its recommendations to corporations?

SUMMARY

In this chapter, we presented interventions for helping organisations transform themselves. These changes can occur at any level in the organisation, but their ultimate intent is to change the total system. They typically happen in response to or in anticipation of significant environmental, technological or internal changes. These changes may involve alterations in the organisation's strategy, which, in turn, may lead to changing its design and culture.

ISC is a comprehensive intervention for responding to complex and uncertain environmental pressures. It gives equal weight to the strategic and organisational factors affecting organisation performance. These factors are highly integrated during the process of assessing the current strategy and organisation design, selecting the desired strategic orientation, developing a strategic change plan and implementing it.

Organisation design involves the organisation's structure, work design, human resources practices and management and information systems. It aligns these components with the organisation's strategy and with each other so they mutually direct behaviour to execute the strategy. This results in organisation designs that vary along a continuum from mechanistic to organic, depending on the requirements of the organisation's strategy. Organisation design typically starts with assessing the organisation to clarify the design focus. Then the design components are configured to support the organisation's strategy. Finally, implementation involves putting the new structures, practices and systems into place using many of the methods for leading and managing change.

Organisational culture includes the pattern of basic assumptions, values, norms and artefacts shared by organisation members. It influences how members perceive, think and behave at work. Culture affects whether organisations can implement new strategies and whether they can operate at high levels of excellence. Culture change interventions start with diagnosing the organisation's existing culture. This can include assessing the cultural risks of making organisational changes needed to implement strategy. Changing corporate culture can be extremely difficult and requires clear strategic vision, top-management commitment, symbolic leadership, supporting organisational changes, selection and socialisation of newcomers and termination of deviants, and sensitivity to legal and ethical issues.

ACTIVITIES

REVIEW QUESTIONS

1   Define OT. How is it different from OD? (L01)

2   What are the environmental and internal disruptions that can affect an organisation? Provide current examples of each and explain your selections. (L02)

3   What are the key features of ISC and how do they relate to each other? (L03)

4   What is organisation design? What difficulties would you expect if you intended to change an organisation in this manner? (L04)

5   Explain the difference between mechanistic and organic design and include examples. (L04)

6   Define organisational culture. What are the major elements at different levels of awareness? (L05)

7   What is the relationship between organisational culture and organisation effectiveness? (L05)

8   Define and explain transformational change. (L02)

9   Describe the deep assumptions approach to culture change with reference to examples. (L05)

EXTEND YOUR LEARNING

Review this case and read some of the current affairs articles relating to it, then answer the applied transformational change questions that follow:

In 2018, the Australian Broadcasting Corporation (ABC) experienced the loss of both its managing director and chairman as a result of the airing of dirty laundry during a transformational change process at the organisation (Sas, 2018). First it was the managing director, Michelle Guthrie, who was dismissed just halfway through her contract at the ABC. The chairman, Justin Milne, announced Guthrie's dismissal on the grounds that the working relationship of Guthrie with the board and ABC staff had broken down. The transformations that Guthrie had been hired to facilitate, and her style of implementation, had seemingly created too much angst. Within a few days, some revelations emerged about chairman Milne's part in applying pressure to managing director Guthrie to make some changes she felt were not needed. One change was Milne's repeated suggestions that Guthrie should get rid of high-profile political and economic commentator Emma Alberici due to her perceived biased reporting against the incumbent government. Guthrie resisted the change and was subsequently fired. Then some leaked emails emerged showing the internal communication about Guthrie's resistance to the chairman's pressure. Milne had to step down shortly after, as he was perceived to not be at 'arm's length' from political pressure from his friends in the government who may have encouraged him to press Guthrie for Alberici's sacking among other things.[82]

1   Transformational change occurs in response to at least three kinds of disruption, including industry discontinuities, product life cycle shifts and internal company dynamics. Discuss the ABC case and speculate about which of the changes are transformational, and which of the three types of disruption are at work in this instance, exploring some reasons why. (LO1 & 2)

2   'Organisations must experience or anticipate a severe threat to survival before they will be motivated to undertake transformational change.' Discuss how much you agree with this in the context of the ABC case. (LO1 & 2)

3   Using what you know about the ABC case, discuss the relationship between organisational culture and organisation effectiveness. (LO5)

4   Review the four phases of ISC: performing a strategic analysis, exercising strategic choice, designing a strategic change plan and implementing the plan. Referring to additional media reporting of the ABC turmoil at the time, explain where the four phases appear to have encountered difficulty. (LO3)

5   Discuss how the design of the ABC, as a government-funded media organisation with an independent board and a CEO in charge of overall operations, is intended to work strategically. What factors may have contributed to the organisational design not achieving strategic ends in this case of transformational change? (LO4)

Search Me! Management

Explore **Search Me! Management** for articles relevant to this chapter. Fast and convenient, **Search Me! Management** is updated daily and provides you with 24-hour access to full text articles from hundreds of scholarly and popular journals, eBooks and newspapers, including *The Australian* and *The New York Times*. Visit http://login.cengagebrain.com and use the access code that comes with this book for 12 months access to the **Search Me! Management** database. Try searching for the following keywords:

Keywords:

- Organisation transformation (OT)
- Integrated strategic change (ISC)
- Organisation design
- Organisational culture

Search tip: **Search Me! Management** contains information from both local and international sources. To get the greatest number of search results, try using both Australian and American spellings in your searches; for example, 'globalisation' and 'globalization'; 'organisation' and 'organization'.

REFERENCES

1 J. Hayes, *The Theory and Practice of Change Management* (London: Palgrave, 2018); S. Kurtmollaiev, A. Fjuk, P. Pedersen, S. Clatworthy and K. Kvale, 'Organizational transformation through service design: the institutional logics perspective', *Journal of Service Research* 21: 1 (2018): 59–74.

2 E. Flamholtz and Y. Randle, *Leading Strategic Change: Bridging Theory and Practice* (Cambridge, UK: Cambridge University Press, 2008); R. Torraco, 'Early history of the fields of practice of training and development and organization development', *Advances in Developing Human Resources* 18:4 (2016): 439–53.

3 L. Bryan and C. Joyce, 'The 21st century organization', *The McKinsey Quarterly* (2005): 24–33; R. Isaksson, R. Garvare, M. Johnson, C. Kuttainen and J. Pareis, 'Sustaining Sweden's competitive position: lean lifelong learning', *Measuring Business Excellence*, 19 (2015): 92–102.

4 F. Suares and R. Oliva, 'Environmental change and organisational transformation', *Industrial and Corporate Change*, 14 (2005): 1017–41; A. Grove, 'Churning things up', *Fortune* (11 August 2003): 115–18; J. Sorensen, 'The strength of corporate culture and the reliability of firm performance', *Administrative Science Quarterly*, 47 (2002): 70–91; G. Young, 'Managing organizational transformations: lessons from the Veterans Health Administration', *California Management Review*, 43 (2000): 66–82.

5 M. Tushman, W. Newman and E. Romanelli, 'Managing the unsteady pace of organizational evolution', *California Management Review* (Fall 1986): 29–44.

6 ibid.

7 A. Meyer, A. Tsui and C. Hinings, 'Guest co-editors introduction: configurational approaches to organizational analysis', *Academy of Management Journal*, 36 (1993): 1175–95.

8 J. Müller and S. Kunisch, 'Central perspectives and debates in strategic change research', *International Journal of Management Reviews*, 20:2 (2018): 457–82.

9 B. Blumenthal and P. Haspeslagh, 'Toward a definition of corporate transformation', *Sloan Management Review*, 35 (1994): 101–7; M.B. Goodman, 'Transformation and the corporate communication profession', *Corporate Communications: An International Journal*, 17 (2012): 241.

10 Tushman, Newman and Romanelli, 'Managing the unsteady pace', op. cit.; L. Greiner, 'Evolution and revolution as organizations grow', *Harvard Business Review* (July–August 1972): 37–46; M.

Yang, 'Transformational leadership and Taiwanese public relations practitioners' job satisfaction and organizational commitment', *Social Behavior and Personality: An International Journal*, 40 (2012): 31–46; N. Kaslow, C. Falender and C. Grus, 'Valuing and practicing competency-based supervision: A transformational leadership perspective', *Training and Education in Professional Psychology*, 6 (2012): 47–54.

11 J. Neal, *Handbook of Personal and Organizational Transformation*, (New York: Springer, 2018).

12 M. Tushman and E. Romanelli, 'Organizational evolution: a metamorphosis model of convergence and reorientation', in *Research in Organizational Behavior*, 7, eds L. Cummings and B. Staw (Greenwich, CT: JAI Press, 1985): 171–222.

13 L. Fitzgerald and A. McDermott, *Challenging Perspectives on Organizational Change in Health Care* (Florence: Taylor and Francis, 2017).

14 N. Gross and S. Geiger, 'Liminality and the entrepreneurial firm: practice renewal during periods of radical change', *International Journal of Entrepreneurial Behavior & Research*, 23:2 (2017): 185–209.

15 S. Haslam, J. Cornelissen and M. Werner, 'Metatheories and metaphors of organizational identity: integrating social constructionist, social identity, and social actor perspectives within a social interactionist model', *International Journal of Management Reviews* 19:3 (2017): 318–36.

16 E.K. Kelan and P. Wratil, 'Post-heroic leadership, tempered radicalism and senior leaders as change agents for gender equality', *European Management Review*, 15:1 (2018): 5–18; M. Sher, *The Dynamics of Change: Tavistock Approaches to Improving Social Systems*, (London: Taylor and Francis, 2018).

17 M. Tushman and B. Virany, 'Changing characteristics of executive teams in an emerging industry', *Journal of Business Venturing*, 2 (1986): 37–49; L. Greiner and A. Bhambri, 'New CEO intervention and dynamics of deliberate strategic change', *Strategic Management Journal*, 10 (Summer 1989): 67–86; N. Hill, M. Seo, J. Kang and M. Taylor, 'Building employee commitment to change across organizational levels: the influence of hierarchical distance and direct managers' transformational leadership', *Organization Science*, 23 (2012): 758–77.

18 S. Christopher, 'Which type of leader are you?', *Australian Financial Review*, 27 August 2015; D. Casey, 'How Woman of Influence Dawn Casey closed the gap on racism', *Australian Financial Review*, 10 February 2016.

19 P. Nutt and R. Backoff, 'Facilitating transformational change', *Journal of Applied*

Behavioral Science, 33 (1997): 490–508;
M. Tushman, W. Newman and D. Nadler,
'Executive leadership and organizational evolution:
managing incremental and discontinuous
change', in *Corporate Transformation: Revitalizing
Organizations for a Competitive World*, eds R.
Kilmann and T. Covin (San Francisco: Jossey-Bass,
1988): 102–30; W. Bennis and B. Nanus, *Leaders:
The Strategies for Taking Charge* (New York:
Harper and Row, 1985); Pettigrew, 'Context and
action', op. cit.; B. Burnes and R. By, 'Leadership
and change: the case for greater ethical clarity',
Journal of Business Ethics, 108 (2012): 239–52; A.
Stoughton and J. Ludema, 'The driving forces of
sustainability', *Journal of Organizational Change
Management*, 25 (2012): 501–17.

20 J. Kouses and B. Posner, *The Leadership
Challenge*, 3rd edn (San Francisco: Jossey-Bass,
2002); T. Simons, 'Behavioral integrity as a critical
ingredient for transformational leadership', *Journal
of Organizational Change Management*, 12 (1999):
89–105; S. Alavi and C. Gill, 'Leading change
authentically: how authentic leaders influence
follower responses to complex change', *Journal of
Leadership & Organizational Studies*, 24:2 (2016):
157–71.

21 T. Cummings and S. Mohrman, 'Self-designing
organizations: towards implementing quality-of-
work-life innovations', in *Research in Organizational
Change and Development*, 1, eds R. Woodman
and W. Pasmore (Greenwich, CT: JAI Press, 1987):
275–310.

22 L. Greiner and A. Bhambri, 'New CEO intervention
and the dynamics of strategic change', op. cit.;
K. Long, 'Employees first, customers second:
turning conventional management upside down',
Journal of Organizational Change Management,
24 (2011): 559–62; L. Jordan and T. Thatchenkery,
'Leadership decision-making strategies using
appreciative inquiry: a case study', *International
Journal of Globalisation and Small Business*, 4
(2011): 178–90; R. Newton, 'Strategic redesign for
globally distributed manufacturing: a case study',
International Journal of Technology Marketing, 7
(2012): 278–86.

23 C. Worley, D. Hitchin and W. Ross, *Integrated
Strategic Change: How Organization Development
Builds Competitive Advantage* (Reading, MA:
Addison-Wesley, 1996).

24 M. Jelinek and J. Litterer, 'Why OD must become
strategic', *Research in Organizational Change and
Development*, 2, eds W. Pasmore and R. Woodman
(Greenwich, CT: JAI Press, 1988): 135–62; A. Bhambri
and L. Pate, 'Introduction – the strategic change
agenda: stimuli, processes and outcomes', *Journal of
Organizational Change Management*, 4 (1991): 4–6;
D. Nadler, M. Gerstein, R. Shaw and associates,

eds, *Organizational Architecture* (San Francisco:
Jossey-Bass, 1992); C. Worley, D. Hitchin and W.
Ross, *Integrated Strategic Change: How Organization
Development Builds Competitive Advantage* (Reading,
MA: Addison-Wesley, 1996).

25 C. Worley, D. Hitchin, R. Patchett, R. Barnett
and J. Moss, 'Unburn the bridge, get to bedrock
and put legs on the dream: looking at strategy
implementation with fresh eyes' (paper presented
to the Western Academy of Management, Redondo
Beach, CA, March 1999).

26 H. Mintzberg, *The Rise and Fall of Strategic
Planning* (New York: Free Press, 1994).

27 Worley, Hitchin and Ross, *Integrated Strategic
Change*, op. cit.

28 P. Senge, *The Fifth Discipline* (New York:
Doubleday, 1990); E. Lawler, *The Ultimate
Advantage* (San Francisco: Jossey-Bass, 1992);
Worley, Hitchin and Ross, *Integrated Strategic
Change*, op. cit.

29 L. Greiner and V. Schein, *Power and Organization
Development* (Reading, MA: Addison-Wesley, 1988).

30 L.B. Ncube and M.H. Wasburn, 'Strategic analysis:
approaching continuous improvement proactively',
Review of Business, 29 (2008): 15–25.

31 M. Porter, *Competitive Strategy* (New York: Free
Press, 1980).

32 Grant, *Contemporary Strategy Analysis*, op. cit.

33 K. Kahn, *The PDMA Handbook of New Product
Development* (Hoboken, NJ: John Wiley and Sons,
2013); S. Nair, 'The idea hunter: How to find the
best ideas and make them happen', *Journal of
Product & Brand Management*, 21 (2012): 558–9;
J. Gauthier, 'Sustainable business strategies:
typologies and future directions', *Society and
Business Review*, 12:1 (2017): 77–93.

34 M. Porter, *Competitive Advantage* (New York: Free
Press, 1985).

35 R. Miles and C. Snow, *Organization Strategy,
Structure and Process* (New York: McGraw-
Hill, 1978); M. Tushman and E. Romanelli,
'Organizational evolution: a metamorphosis model
of convergence and reorientation', in *Research in
Organizational Behavior*, 7, eds L. Cummings and
B. Staw (Greenwich, CT: JAI Press, 1985).

36 J. Naisbitt and P. Aburdene, *Reinventing the
Corporation* (New York: Warner Books, 1985); A.
Toffler, *The Third Wave* (New York: McGraw-Hill,
1980); A. Toffler, *The Adaptive Corporation* (New
York: McGraw-Hill, 1984); M. Weisbord, *Productive
Workplaces* (San Francisco: Jossey-Bass, 1987).

37 E. Lawler, *The Ultimate Advantage*, op. cit.;
M. Tushman, W. Newman and E. Romanelli,
'Convergence and upheaval: managing the
unsteady pace of organizational evolution',
California Management Review, 29 (1987): 1–16;
Nadler et al., *Organizational Architecture*, op. cit.;

R. Bussell and B. Gale, *The PIMS Principles* (New York: Free Press, 1987).

38 L. Hrebiniak and W. Joyce, *Implementing Strategy* (New York: Macmillan, 1984); J. Galbraith and R. Kasanjian, *Strategy Implementation: Structure, Systems and Process*, 2nd edn (St Paul, Minnesota: West Publishing, 1986); T. Kuzhda, 'Organization development components, process and performance', [Електронний ресурс] / Tetiana Kuzhda, Volodymyr Gevko //Соціально-економічні проблеми і держава. – 2018. – Вип. 1 (18). – С. 61-69. – Режим доступу до журн.: http://sepd.tntu.edu.ua/images/stories/pdf/2018/18ktieor.pdf.

39 K. Long, 'Integrated strategic change and what it can do for you', Ezine Articles, 13 June 2010, http://ezinearticles.com/?Integrated-Strategic-Change-and-What-it-Can-Do-For-You&id=4473574.

40 J. Galbraith, *Organization Design* (Reading, MA: Addison-Wesley, 1977); D. Nadler, M. Tushman and M. Nadler, *Competing by Design: The Power of Organizational Architecture* (New York: Oxford University Press, 1997); R. Burton, B. Eriksen, D. Håkonsson and C. Snow, *Organization Design: The Evolving State-of-the-Art* (New York: Springer, 2006); A. Kates and J. Galbraith, *Designing Your Organization: Using The STAR Model to Solve 5 Critical Design Challenges* (San Francisco: Jossey-Bass, 2007); J. Galbraith, 'Organization design', in *Handbook of Organization Development*, ed. T. Cummings (Thousand Oaks, CA: Sage Publications, 2008): 325–52.

41 R.L. Daft, J. Murphy and H. Willmott, *Organization Theory & Design: An International Perspective* (Hampshire, UK: Cengage Learning, 2017); J. Müller and S. Kunisch, 'Central perspectives and debates in strategic change research', *International Journal of Management Reviews*, 20:2 (2018): 457–82.

42 N. Stanford, *Organization Design: A Practitioner's Guide* (New York: Routledge, 2018).

43 H. Ahmadi and P. Salami, 'Application of information systems in electronic insurance', *Research Journal of Information Technology*, 2 (2010): 1–6.

44 T. Burns and G. Stalker, *The Management of Innovation* (London: Social Science Paperbacks, 1961).

45 S. Mohrman, J. Galbraith and E. Lawler, eds, *Tomorrow's Organization: Crafting Winning Capabilities in a Dynamic World* (San Francisco: Jossey-Bass, 1998); J. Galbraith, D. Downey and A. Kates, *Designing Dynamic Organizations: A Hand-son Guide for Leaders at All Levels* (New York: AMACOM, 2001); E. Beinhocker, 'The adaptable corporation', *The McKinsey Quarterly*, 2 (2006): 76–87.

46 M. Moon, 'Bottom-up instigated organization change through constructionist conversation',

Journal of Knowledge Management Practice, 9 (December 2008), http://www.tlainc.com/articl169.htm.

47 S. Mohrman and T. Cummings, *Self-designing Organizations: Learning How to Create High Performance* (Reading, MA: Addison-Wesley, 1989); N. Stanford, *Organization Design: The Collaborative Approach* (Burlington, MA: Elsevier Butterworth-Heinemann, 2005); R. Chowdhury, 'Organizational design and firm-wide collaboration: retrospective appreciation of a change-led consulting intervention in India within a systems thinking paradigm', *Systems Research and Behavioral Science*, 29 (2012): 402–19.

48 Galbraith et al., *Designing Dynamic Organizations*, op. cit.; Kates and Galbraith, *Designing Your Organization*, op. cit.; Stanford, *Organization Design*, op. cit.

49 W. Ouchi, *Theory S: How American Business Can Meet the Japanese Challenge* (Reading, MA: Addison-Wesley, 1979); R. Pascale and A. Athos, *The Art of Japanese Management* (New York: Simon & Schuster, 1981); T. Deal and A. Kennedy, *Corporate Cultures* (Reading, MA: Addison-Wesley, 1982); T. Peters and R. Waterman, *In Search of Excellence* (New York: Harper & Row, 1982); T. Peters and N. Austin, *A Passion for Excellence* (New York: Random House, 1985); J. Pfeffer, *Competitive Advantage through People* (Cambridge, MA: Harvard Business School, 1994); J. Collins and J. Porras, *Built to Last* (New York: Harper Business, 1994); J. Kotter and J. Heskett, *Corporate Culture and Performance* (New York: Free Press, 1992); T. Pandola and J. Bird, *Light a Fire under Your Business: How to Build a Class 1 Corporate Culture through Inspirational Leadership* (Santa Barbara, CA: Praeger, 2015); D. Coyle, *Culture Code: The Hidden Language of Highly Successful Groups* (New York: Bantam, 2018).

50 J. Martin, *Organization Culture* (Newbury Park, CA: Sage Publications, 2002); D. Meyerson and J. Martin, 'Cultural change: an integration of three different views', *Journal of Management Studies*, 24 (1987): 623–47; D. Denison and G. Spreitser, 'Organizational culture and organizational development: a competing values approach', in *Research in Organizational Change and Development*, 5, eds R. Woodman and W. Pasmore (Greenwich, CT: JAI Press, 1991): 1–22; E. Schein, *Organizational Culture and Leadership*, 2nd edn (San Francisco: Jossey-Bass, 1992).

51 Martin, *Organization Culture*, op. cit.

52 Schein, *Organizational Culture*, op. cit.; R. Kilmann, M. Saxton and R. Serpa, eds, *Gaining Control of the Corporate Culture* (San Francisco: Jossey-Bass, 1985).

53 M. Thompson, R. Ellis and A.B. Wildavsky, *Cultural Theory* (New York: Routledge, 2018).

54 Schein, *Organizational Culture*, op. cit.

55 E. Abrahamson and C.J. Fombrun, 'Macrocultures: determinants and consequences', *Academy of Management Journal*, 19 (1994): 728–55; B. Dumaine, 'Creating a new company culture', *Fortune* (15 January 1990): 127–31; B. Boyle, S. Nicholas and R. Mitchell, 'Sharing and developing knowledge of organization culture during international assignments', *International Journal of Cross Cultural Management*, 12 (2012): 56; B. Uttal, 'The corporate culture vultures', *Fortune* (17 October 1983): 66–72; C.M. Lau, L. Kilbourne and R. Woodman, 'A shared schema approach to understanding organizational culture change', in *Research in Organizational Change and Development*, 14, eds W. Pasmore and R. Woodman (Greenwich, CT: JAI Press, 2003): 225–56; T. Gajendran, G. Brewer, A. Dainty and G. Runeson, 'A conceptual approach to studying the organisational culture of construction projects', *Australasian Journal of Construction Economics and Building*, 12 (2012): 1–26.

56 Uttal, 'The corporate culture vultures', op. cit.

57 D. Miletic, T. Arup and D. Emerson, 'Hundreds of jobs lost as Starbucks shuts 61 shops', *The Age* (30 July 2008); A. Turner, 'Why there are almost no Starbucks in Australia', CNBC (20 July 2018), https://www.cnbc.com/2018/07/20/starbucks-australia-coffee-failure.html.

58 Ouchi, *Theory S*, op. cit.; Pascale and Athos, *Japanese Management*, op. cit.

59 J. Ryan and J. Hurley, 'An empirical examination of the relationship between scientists' work environment and research performance', *R&D Management*, 37 (2007): 345–54.

60 D. Denison, 'The climate, culture and effectiveness of work organizations: a study of organizational behavior and financial performance' (unpublished PhD dissertation, University of Michigan, 1982).

61 Kotter and Heskett, *Corporate Culture*, op. cit.

62 J. Sorensen, 'The strength of corporate culture and the reliability of firm performance', *Administrative Science Quarterly*, 47 (2002): 70–91; A.J. Verdu-Jover, L. Alos-Simo and J-M. Gomez-Gras, 'Adaptive culture and product/service innovation outcomes', *European Management Journal*, 36:3 (2018): 330–40.

63 D. Hanna, *Designing Organizations for High Performance* (Reading, MA: Addison-Wesley, 1988); L. Hawke, 'Australian public sector performance management: success or stagnation?', *International Journal of Productivity and Performance Management*, 61 (2012): 310–28.

64 D. Lucy and D. Shepherd, 'Organisational resilience: developing change-readiness', Roffey Park (2018), https://www.roffeypark.com/wp-content/uploads2/Organisational-Resilience-Developing-Change-Readiness-Reduced-Size.pdf.

65 Denison and Spreitser, 'Organizational culture', op. cit.; R.E. Quinn, *Beyond Rational Management: Mastering the Paradoxes and Competing Demands of High Performance* (San Francisco: Jossey-Bass, 1988); K. Cameron and R. Quinn, *Diagnosing and Changing Organizational Culture* (San Francisco: Jossey-Bass, 2006).

66 M. Wiener, R. Gattringer and F. Strehl, 'Participation in inter-organisational collaborative open foresight: a matter of culture', *Technology Analysis & Strategic Management*, 30:6 (2018): 684–700.

67 C. Cheng and A. Liu, 'The relationship of organizational culture and the implementation of total quality management in construction firms', *Surveying and Built Environment*, 18 (June 2007): 7–16.

68 Schein, *Organizational Culture*, op. cit.

69 D. Brozovic, 'Strategic flexibility: a review of the literature', *International Journal of Management Reviews*, 20 (2018): 3–31.

70 Schein, *Organizational Culture*, op. cit.

71 E. Schein, *The Corporate Culture Survival Guide* (San Francisco: Jossey-Bass, 1999).

72 P. Frost, L. Moore, M. Louis, C. Lundberg and J. Martin, eds, *Organizational Culture* (Beverly Hills, CA: Sage Publications, 1985): 95–196; Martin, *Organizational Culture*, op. cit.

73 Meyerson and Martin, 'Cultural change', op. cit.

74 J. Barney, 'Organizational culture: can it be a source of sustained competitive advantage?', *Academy of Management Review*, 11 (1986): 656–65.

75 Uttal, 'Corporate culture vultures', op. cit.

76 ibid.: 70.

77 Schein, *Corporate Culture Survival Guide*, op. cit.; Schwarts and Davis, 'Matching corporate culture', op. cit.; Uttal, 'Corporate culture vultures', op. cit.; Davis, *Managing Corporate Culture*, op. cit.; Kilmann, Saxton and Serpa, *Gaining Control*, op. cit.; Frost et al., *Organizational Culture*, op. cit.; V. Sathe, 'Implications of corporate culture: a manager's guide to action', *Organizational Dynamics* (Autumn 1983): 5–23; B. Drake and E. Drake, 'Ethical and legal aspects of managing corporate cultures', *California Management Review* (Winter 1988): 107–23; K. Cameron, 'A process for changing organization culture', in *Handbook of Organization Development*, ed. T. Cummings (Thousand Oaks, CA: Sage Publications, 2008): 429–45.

78 C. Worley, D. Hitchin and W. Ross, *Integrated Strategic Change* (Reading, MA: Addison-Wesley, 1996); R. Beckhard and W. Pritchard, *Changing the Essence* (San Francisco: Jossey-Bass, 1992).

79 Dumaine, 'Creating a new company culture', op. cit.; C. O'Reilly, 'Corporations, culture and commitment: motivation and social control in organizations', *California Management Review*, 31 (Summer 1989): 9–25; Pettigrew, 'Context and action', op. cit.

80 Dumaine, 'Creating a new company culture', op. cit.

81 Tichy and Sherman, *Control Your Destiny*, op. cit.

82 See: N. Sas, 'ABC becomes the story after unprecedented week of accusations and high-profile departures', ABC News, 27 September 2018, http://www.abc.net.au/news/2018-09-27/abc-becomes-the-story-after-high-profile-departures/10310944; A. Patrick, 'Emma Alberici stands tall at ABC as Michelle Guthrie and Justin Milne tumble', *Australian Financial Review*, 1 October 2018, https://www.afr.com/opinion/emma-alberici-stands-tall-at-abc-as-michelle-guthrie-and-justin-milne-tumble-20181001-h162me; B. Brook, 'The mistakes Michelle Guthrie made that led to her sacking from $891k managing director role', News.com.au, 25 September 2018, https://www.news.com.au/finance/business/media/the-mistakes-michelle-guthrie-made-that-led-to-her-sacking-from-891k-managing-director-role/news-story/fc9ef1c147df93253bd30b22de8f84b7.

10

CHANGE IN A CHAOTIC AND UNPREDICTABLE ENVIRONMENT

After studying this chapter, you should be able to:

1   Recognise and relate examples of worldwide organisation development (OD).
2   Discuss global, multinational and transnational strategic orientation.

Worldwide OD

International orientation

Global orientation

Multinational orientation

Transnational orientation

This chapter describes the practice of change management in a chaotic and unpredictable environment, which is exhibited in international settings. It presents the contingencies and practice issues associated with change in organisations outside countries of origin (home countries), and worldwide organisations. At the same time, the applicability and effectiveness of change and cultures in countries of destination (host countries) are the subject of intense debate. Because many change theories were developed predominantly by Western practitioners, this has heavily influenced the perceptions and practices of change management in places throughout the world. Regardless of good intentions, many errors can be made by implementing strategies that are not congruent with existing cultures and norms. How will South-East Asian countries change when their next generation is being educated by Western universities with differing cultural values and behavioural norms? How would change practices be adapted by Malaysian companies establishing businesses in Australia? An alternative body of thought suggests that culture has a significant impact when change theory is internationalised, regardless of its origin. A wide range of studies have found particular challenges with regard to changes experienced by international business students at universities in Australia and elsewhere.[1] Recognising these current viewpoints, change management in an international setting will quickly become the norm rather than the exception.

There is significant evidence that change interventions need to be adapted before adoption in differing cultural settings, otherwise they can cause more damage than success.[2] Therefore, as part of the change management process there must be cultural and economic alignment with the values of the country of destination.

CHANGE MANAGEMENT THROUGHOUT THE WORLD

Change management is playing an increasingly important role in global social change. Practitioners using highly participative approaches are influencing the development of evolving countries, providing a voice to underrepresented social classes and bridging the gap between cultures facing similar social issues.

Survey feedback interventions have been used at Air New Zealand and Emirates Airlines (United Arab Emirates); work design interventions have been implemented in Gamesa (Mexico); large-group interventions have been used in Vitro (Mexico); structural interventions have been completed at Neusoft Corporation (China); and merger and acquisition integration interventions have been used at Akzo-Nobel (Netherlands).[3] This international diffusion of OD derives from three important trends: the rapid development of foreign economies, the increasing worldwide availability of technical and financial resources and the emergence of a global economy. All three are exemplified in research on the development of a globalised wine industry on La Palma Island.[4]

The dramatic restructuring of socialist and communist economies and the rapid economic growth of developing countries are astounding in scope and impact. Projected growth rates in East Asia, the Pacific and South Asia remain strong. Political transformations in the Middle East, China, Russia and South Africa are producing both uncertainty and new growth-oriented economies. The United States and Europe have both been languishing in debt and fiscal crises, but concerted negotiations and remedial packages are keeping economic activity at reasonable levels. Global economic growth in the years ahead should continue to be strong.

Organisations operating in the rejuvenated or newly emerging economies are increasingly turning to OD practices to embrace opportunities and improve effectiveness. In China, for example, economic reforms are breaking up the 'work units' – operational business units organised with housing, health care, education, food service and other infrastructure organisations – that used to dominate the Chinese economy. As these work units are disbanded so that the operational unit can address 'market facing' issues, the social fabric of China is being severely shocked. A variety of non-government organisations (NGOs) have formed to help China develop a 'civil society'. Many of these organisations, such as Global Village of Beijing, Friends of the Earth and the Green Earth Volunteers, are using appreciative inquiry interventions[5] to identify best practices and capacity-building processes. Ways of working together are being developed and networks of these NGOs are coming together to assist the homeless, build environmental awareness and deliver child care. Other interventions, including work design, survey feedback and leadership development, represent efforts to increase ownership, commitment and productivity in Chinese organisations.

The second trend contributing to OD applications in global settings is the unprecedented availability of technological and financial resources on a worldwide scale. The development of the internet and e-commerce has increased foreign governments' and organisations' access to enormous information resources and fuelled growth and development. The increased availability of capital and technology, for example, was cited as a primary reason for the rise of Chilean companies in the 1980s.[6] Information technology, in particular, is making the world 'smaller' and more interdependent. As organisations outside the United States adopt new technology, opportunities to apply techniques that facilitate planned change increase. OD interventions can smooth the transition to a new reporting structure, clarify roles and relationships and reduce the uncertainty associated with implementing new techniques and practices.

The final trend fuelling international OD applications has been the emergence of a global economy.[7] The continued growth of China's economy, the spread of terrorism on a worldwide basis and the impact of global warming aptly demonstrate how interdependent the world's markets have become. Many foreign organisations are maturing and growing by entering the global business community. Lowered trade barriers, deregulation and privatisation aid this international expansion. The established relationships and local knowledge that once favoured only a small number of worldwide organisations are no longer barriers to entry into many countries.[8] As organisations expand globally, they are faced with adapting structures, information systems, coordinating processes and human resources practices to worldwide operations in a variety of countries.

WORLDWIDE ORGANISATION DEVELOPMENT

An important trend facing many businesses is the consolidation and growth of the global marketplace.[9] Driven by competitive pressures, lowered trade barriers and advances in information technologies, the number of companies offering products and services in multiple countries is increasing rapidly. The organisational growth and complexity associated with managing worldwide operations is challenging. Executives must choose appropriate strategic orientations for operating across cultures and geographical locations and under diverse governmental and environmental requirements. They must be able to adapt corporate policies and procedures to a range of local conditions. Moreover, the need to control and coordinate operations in different nations places heavy demands on information and control systems as well as on managerial skills and knowledge.

Worldwide OD applies to organisations that are operating across multiple geographic and cultural boundaries. This contrasts with OD in organisations that operate outside a particular country but within a single cultural and economic context.

Worldwide OD: the application of OD principles and practices in organisations operating across multiple geographic and cultural boundaries.

WORLDWIDE STRATEGIC ORIENTATIONS

Worldwide organisations can be defined in terms of three key facets.[10] First, they offer products or services in more than one country and actively manage substantial direct investments in those countries. Consequently, they must relate to a variety of demands, such as unique product requirements, tariffs, value-added taxes, governmental regulations, transportation laws and trade agreements. Second, worldwide businesses must balance product and functional concerns with geographic issues of distance, time and culture. American tobacco companies, for example, face technological, moral and organisational issues in determining whether to market cigarettes in less-developed countries, and if they do, they must decide how to integrate manufacturing and distribution operations on a global scale. Third, worldwide companies must carry out coordinated activities across cultural boundaries using a wide variety of personnel, including expatriates, short-term and extended business travellers and local employees. Workers with different cultural backgrounds must be managed in ways that support the overall goals and image of the organisation.[11] The company must therefore adapt its human resources policies and procedures to fit the culture and accomplish operational objectives. From a managerial perspective, selecting executives to head foreign operations is an important decision in worldwide organisations.

How these three facets of products/services, organisation and personnel are arranged enables businesses to compete in the global marketplace.[12] Worldwide organisations can offer certain products or services in some countries and not in others; they can centralise or decentralise operations; and they can determine how to work with people from different cultures (for more detail, see Chapter 4). Despite the many possible combinations of characteristics, researchers have found that two dimensions are useful in guiding decisions about choices of strategic orientation.

For more detail on working cross-culturally, see Chapter 4.

As shown in **Figure 10.1**, managers need to assess two key success factors: the degrees to which there is a need for global integration or for local responsiveness. *Global integration* refers to whether or not business success requires tight coordination of people, plants, equipment, products or service delivery on a worldwide basis. For example, Intel's 'global factory' designs chips in multiple countries, manufactures the chips in a variety of locations around the world, assembles and tests the finished products in different countries and then ships the chips to customers. All of this activity must be coordinated carefully. *Local responsiveness*, on the other hand, is the extent to which business success is dependent on customising products, services, support, packaging and other aspects of operations to local conditions. Based on that information, worldwide organisations generally implement one of four types of strategic orientations: international, global, multinational or transnational. **Table 10.1** presents these orientations in terms of a diagnostic framework. Each strategic orientation is geared to specific market, technological and organisational requirements. OD interventions that support each orientation are also included in **Table 10.1**.

FIGURE 10.1	THE INTEGRATION–RESPONSIVENESS FRAMEWORK

Need for global integration	High	Global orientation	Transnational orientation
	Low	International orientation	Multinational orientation
		Low Need for local responsiveness High	

TABLE 10.1	CHARACTERISTICS AND INTERVENTIONS FOR WORLDWIDE STRATEGIC ORIENTATIONS				
Worldwide strategic orientation	Strategy	Structure	Information system	Human resources	OD interventions
International	Existing products Goals of increased foreign revenues	Centralised international division	Loose	Volunteer	Cross-cultural training Strategic planning
Global	Standardised products Goals of efficiency through volume	Centralised, balanced and coordinated activities Global product division	Formal	Ethnocentric selection	Career planning Role clarification Employee involvement Senior management team building Conflict management
Multinational	Tailored products Goals of local responsiveness through specialisation	Decentralised operations; centralised planning Global geographic divisions	Profit centres	Regiocentric or polycentric selection	Intergroup relations Local management team building Management development Reward systems Strategic alliances
Transnational	Tailored products Goals of learning and responsiveness through integration	Decentralised, worldwide coordination Global matrix or network	Subtle, clan-oriented controls	Geocentric selection	Extensive selection and rotation Cultural development Intergroup relations Building corporate vision

THE INTERNATIONAL STRATEGIC ORIENTATION

The **international orientation** exists when the key success factors of global integration and local responsiveness are low. This is the most common label given to organisations making their first attempts at operating outside their own country's markets. Success requires coordination between the parent company and the small number of foreign sales and marketing offices in

International orientation: the most common label given to organisations making their first attempts at operating outside their own country's markets.

chosen countries. Similarly, local responsiveness is low because the organisation exports the same products and services offered domestically. When an organisation has decided to expand internationally, it has most often determined that:

→ other country-markets appear to offer specific advantages large enough to exceed the tangible and intangible costs of implementing a new strategy

→ the organisation's products, services and value propositions are sufficiently powerful to counteract the initial disadvantages of operating in a foreign location

→ the organisational capabilities exist to extract value from the foreign operations in excess of simpler contracting or licensing of the organisation's technology, products or services in the foreign location.[13]

Characteristics of the international design

The goal of the international orientation is to increase total sales by adding revenues from non-domestic markets. By using existing products/services, domestic operating capacity is extended and leveraged. As a result, most domestic companies will enter international markets by extending their product lines first into nearby countries and then expanding to more remote areas. For example, most Australian-based companies first offer their products in New Zealand or Europe. After a certain period of time, they begin to set up operations in other countries.

To support this goal and operations strategy, an 'international division' is given responsibility for marketing, sales and distribution, although it may be able to set up joint ventures, licensing agreements, distribution territories/franchises and, in some cases, manufacturing plants. The organisation basically retains its original structure and operating practices. However, the information system governing the division is typically looser. While expecting returns on its investment, the organisation recognises the newness of the venture and gives the international division some 'free rein' to establish an international presence.

Finally, roles in the new international division are staffed with volunteers from the parent company, often with someone who has appropriate foreign language training, experience living overseas or eagerness for an international assignment. Little training or orientation for the position is offered as the organisation is generally unaware of the requirements for being successful in international business.

Implementing the international orientation

Changing from a domestic to an international organisation represents an incremental shift in scope for most organisations and is typically handled as a simple extension of the existing strategy into new markets. Despite the logic of such thinking, the shift is neither incremental nor simple and OD can play an important role in making the transition smoother and more productive. Apply your learning 10.1 highlights significant contemporary changes to the Australian student accommodation market precipitated by international organisations making strategic moves.

APPLY
YOUR
LEARNING
10.1

INTERNATIONALISED STUDENT ACCOMMODATION

A strategic investment by international partners with an eye on the large and lucrative student accommodation market in Australia has been successful and is still growing. Dutch pension fund APG and accommodation developer Scape Australia (a branch of London-based Scape Student Living) joined with Telopea Capital partners Craig Carracher and Stephen Gaitanos to make an initial outlay of $220 million. By 2018, the Melbourne assets alone are worth about $1 billion.

The investors still view the sector as relatively young and growing while contributing to a large portion (about $28 billion) of Australia's overall economy. Current shortages of purpose-built student accommodation and ongoing rises in international student numbers from Asian nations have given the group the strategic and financial payoff it is hoping for. Melbourne has been especially lucrative. The University of Melbourne alone has indicated a need for 6000 new beds for international students beyond 2018. Melbourne has a ratio of one bed to 10 students compared with London's one bed to four students, indicating more room for development. In the longer term, specialised attention to the unique features of the international student accommodation market will be required, especially if supply of non-purpose-built accommodation becomes available for student access. For now the market is relatively young and growing with strategic investment well under way.

Sources: Based on K. Loussikian, 'Student digs go Dutch', *The Australian*, 28 January 2015; and N. Lindsay and S. Johanson, 'Scape takes new stake in Melbourne student market', *The Sydney Morning Herald*, 30 June 2018.

Critical thinking questions

1   What are the strategic opportunities and risks being assumed by both the Dutch and UK companies in the venture described?

2   Identify and explain the range of international factors that may directly or indirectly either help or hinder the strategic goals of new ventures by international accommodation companies in Australia.

Strategic planning, technostructural and human resource interventions can help to implement an international orientation. Managers can use integrated strategic change (ISC) or an organisation redesign process to design and manage the transition from the old strategic orientation to the new one. Environmental scans, competitor analyses and market studies can be undertaken to calibrate expectations about revenue goals and determine the levels of investment necessary to support the division. Team building and large-group interventions, such as search conferences, can aid the process by allowing senior executives to gather appropriate information about international markets, distinctive competencies and culture and then choose a strategic orientation. Similarly, managers can apply technostructural interventions to design an appropriate organisation structure, define new tasks and work roles and clarify reporting relationships between corporate headquarters and foreign-based units. Based on these decisions, OD interventions can help the organisation to implement the change.

Managers and staff can also apply human resources management interventions to train and prepare managers and their families for international assignments and to develop selection methods and reward systems relevant to operating internationally.[14] Since these are the organisation's first experiences with international business, the OD practitioner can alert key managers and potential candidates for the international assignments to the need for cultural training. Candidates can be directed to outsourced offerings on cross-cultural skills, local country customs and legal/regulatory conditions. The OD practitioner can also assist the human resource organisation to design or modify existing compensation and benefits packages, or set up policies around housing, schooling and other expenses associated with the relocation.

This initial movement into the international arena enables domestic organisations to learn about the demands of the global marketplace, thus providing them with important knowledge and experience about the requirements for success in more sophisticated strategies. The OD practitioner should help the organisation set up learning practices and communication systems so that information about international experiences is shared with others, especially senior managers.

THE GLOBAL STRATEGIC ORIENTATION

Global orientation:
characterised by a strategy of marketing standardised products in different countries.

This orientation exists when the need for global integration is high but the need for local responsiveness is low. The **global orientation** is characterised by a strategy of marketing standardised products in different countries. It is an appropriate orientation when there is little economic reason to offer products or services with special features or locally available options. For example, manufacturers of office equipment, consumer goods, computers and semiconductors, tyres and containers can offer the same basic product in almost any country.

Characteristics of the global design

The goal of efficiency dominates this orientation. Production efficiency is gained through volume sales and a small number of large manufacturing plants; managerial efficiency is achieved by centralising product design, manufacturing, distribution and marketing decisions. Global integration is supported by the close physical proximity of major functional groups and formal control systems that balance inputs, production and distribution with worldwide demand. Many Japanese companies, such as Honda, Sony, NEC and Matsushita, used this strategy in the 1970s and early 1980s to grow in the international economy. In Europe, Nestlé exploits economies of scale in marketing by advertising well-known brand names around the world. The increased number of microwave-equipped and two-income families, for example, allowed Nestlé to push its Nescafé coffee and Lean Cuisine low-calorie frozen dinners to dominant market-share positions in Europe, North America, Latin America and Asia. Similarly, a Korean noodle maker, Nong Shim Company, avoided the 1999 Asian financial crisis by staying focused on efficiency. More recently, thanks to the global financial crisis (GFC) and ensuing US fiscal woes, Eurozone problems and fluctuations in

Chinese markets, business sentiments for efficiency and cost saving are again helping to drive organisation design. This is exemplified in recent research into factors affecting business leadership in China.[15]

In the global orientation, the organisation tends to be centralised with a global product structure. Presidents of each major product group report to the CEO and form the line organisation. Each of these product groups is responsible for worldwide operations. Information systems in global orientations tend to be quite formal, with local units reporting sales, costs and other data directly to the product president. The predominant human resources policy[16] integrates people into the organisation through ethnocentric selection[17] and staffing practices. These methods seek to fill key foreign positions with personnel from the home country where the corporation headquarters is located.[18] Key managerial jobs at Volvo, Siemens, Nissan and Michelin, for example, are often occupied by Swedish, German, Japanese and French citizens, respectively. Ethnocentric policies support the global orientation because expatriate managers are more likely than host-country nationals to recognise and comply with the need to centralise decision making and to standardise processes, decisions and relationships with the parent company. Although many Japanese automobile manufacturers have decentralised production, Nissan's global strategy has been to retain tight, centralised control of design and manufacturing, ensure that almost all of its senior foreign managers are Japanese and have even low-level decisions emerge from face-to-face meetings in Tokyo.

Implementing the global orientation

OD interventions can be used to refine and support the global strategic orientation as well as assist in the transition from an international orientation.

Planned change in the global orientation

Several OD interventions support the implementation of this orientation. Career planning, role clarification, employee involvement, conflict management and senior management team building help the organisation achieve improved operational efficiency. For example, role clarification interventions, such as job enrichment, goal setting and conflict management, can formalise and standardise organisational activities. This ensures that each individual knows specific details about how, when and why a job needs to be done. As a result, necessary activities are described and efficient transactions and relationships are created. Similarly, Intel has used training interventions to ensure consistent implementation of a variety of company-wide standard business practices, such as meeting protocols, performance management processes and reporting accountability.

Senior management team building can improve the quality of strategic decisions. Centralised policies make the organisation highly dependent on this group and can exaggerate decision-making errors. In addition, interpersonal conflict can increase the cost of coordination or cause significant coordination mistakes. Process interventions at this level can help to improve the speed and quality of decision making and improve interpersonal relationships.

Career planning can help home-country personnel develop a path to senior management by including foreign-subsidiary experiences and cross-functional assignments as necessary qualifications for advancement. At the country level, career planning can emphasise that advancement beyond regional operations is limited for host-country nationals. OD can help here by developing appropriate career paths within the local organisation or in technical, non-managerial areas. Finally, employee empowerment can support efficiency goals by involving members in efforts to achieve cost reduction, work standardisation and minimisation of coordination costs.

The transition to a global orientation

In addition to fine-tuning this strategic orientation, OD can help the organisation transition from an international to a global strategic orientation. The organisation's experience with the international strategic orientation has helped to build basic knowledge and skills in international business. The successful transition to a global strategy assumes that managers believe global integration is more important than local responsiveness and that the organisation has strong centralised operating capabilities. If the assessment of either key success factors or the organisation's competencies is inaccurate, implementation will be more difficult and performance will suffer.

The decision to favour global integration over local responsiveness must be rooted in a strong belief that the worldwide market is relatively homogeneous in character. That is, products and services, support, distribution or marketing activities can be standardised without negatively affecting sales or customer loyalty. This decision should not be made lightly and OD practitioners can help to structure rigorous debate and analysis of this key success factor.

In addition to information about the market, organisations must take into account their distinctive competencies when choosing a global strategy. The key organisational and operational competency necessary for success in a global strategy is the ability to coordinate a complex, worldwide organisation. The global strategy is facilitated when culture and core competencies are more suited to centralised decision making, when the organisation has experience with supply-chain management and when it is comfortable with enterprise resource and material resource planning processes. Centralisation favours a global orientation because the orientation favours tight, global coordination.

Once companies develop a strategic orientation for competing internationally, they create an organisation design to support it. Information like that found in **Table 10.1** is useful for designing structures, information systems and personnel practices for specific strategic orientations. An OD practitioner can help design change management programs to implement these features.

THE MULTINATIONAL STRATEGIC ORIENTATION

This strategic orientation exists when the need for global integration is low, but the need for local responsiveness is high. It represents a strategy that is conceptually quite different from the global strategic orientation.

Characteristics of the multinational design

A multinational strategy is characterised by a product line that is tailored to local conditions and is best suited to markets that vary significantly from region to region or country to country. At American Express, for example, charge card marketing is fitted to local values and tastes. The 'Don't leave home without it' and 'Membership has its privileges' themes seen in Australia and the United States had to be translated to 'Peace of mind only for members' in Japan because of the negative connotations of 'leaving home' and 'privilege'.[19]

The **multinational orientation** emphasises a decentralised, global division structure. Each region or country is served by a divisional organisation that operates autonomously and reports to headquarters. This results in a highly differentiated and loosely coordinated corporate structure. Operational decisions, such as product design, manufacturing and distribution, are decentralised and tightly integrated at the local level. For example, laundry

> **Multinational orientation:** characterised by a product line that is tailored to local conditions and is best suited to markets that vary significantly from region to region or country to country.

soap manufacturers offer product formulas, packaging and marketing strategies that conform to the different environmental regulations, types of washing machines, water hardness and distribution channels in each country. On the other hand, planning activities are often centralised at corporate headquarters to achieve important efficiencies necessary for the worldwide coordination of emerging technologies and of resource allocation. A profit-centre control system allows local autonomy as long as profitability is maintained. Examples of multinational corporations include Hoechst and BASF of Germany, IBM and Procter & Gamble of the United States and Fuji Xerox of Japan. Each of these organisations encourages local subsidiaries to maximise effectiveness within its geographic region.

People are integrated into multinational organisations through polycentric or regiocentric personnel policies because these businesses believe that host-country nationals can understand native cultures most clearly.[20] By filling positions with local citizens who appoint and develop their own staffs, the organisation aligns the needs of the market with the ability of its subsidiaries to produce customised products and services. The distinction between a polycentric and a regiocentric selection process is one of focus, as exemplified in recent research into the management of Chinese expatriates in multinational enterprises.[21] In a polycentric selection policy, a subsidiary represents only one country; in the regiocentric selection policy, a slightly broader perspective is taken and key positions are filled by regional citizens (people who might be called Europeans, as opposed to Belgians or Italians, for example).

Implementing the multinational orientation

The decentralised and locally coordinated multinational orientation suggests the need for a complex set of OD interventions. When applied to a subsidiary operating in a particular country or region, the OD processes described earlier in the chapter for organisations outside the home country are relevant. The key is to tailor OD to fit the specific cultural and economic context where the subsidiary is located.

Planned change in the multinational orientation

When OD is applied across different regions and countries, interventions must allow for differences in cultural and economic conditions that can affect its success. Appropriate interventions for multinational corporations include intergroup relations, local management team building, sophisticated management selection and development practices, and changes to reward systems. Team building remains an important intervention. Unlike team building for the senior management team in global orientations, the local management teams require attention in multinational organisations. This presents a challenge for OD practitioners because polycentric selection policies can produce management teams with different cultures at each subsidiary. Thus, a program developed for one subsidiary may not work with a different team at another subsidiary, given the different cultures that might be represented.

Intergroup interventions to improve relations between local subsidiaries and the parent company are also important for multinational companies. Decentralised decision making and regiocentric selection can strain corporate–subsidiary relations. Local management teams, operating in ways appropriate to their cultural context, may not be understood by corporate managers from another culture. An OD practitioner can help both groups understand these differences by offering training in cultural diversity and appreciation. The practitioner can also smooth parent–subsidiary relationships[22] by focusing on the profit-centre control system or other criteria as the means for monitoring and measuring subsidiary effectiveness.

Management selection, development and reward systems also require special attention in multinational organisations. Managerial selection for local or regional subsidiaries requires finding technically and managerially competent people who also possess the interpersonal competence needed to interface with corporate headquarters. Because these people may be difficult to find, management development programs can teach the necessary cross-cultural skills and abilities. Such programs typically involve language, cultural awareness and technical training; they can also include managers and staff from subsidiary and corporate offices to improve communications between the two areas. Finally, reward systems need to be aligned with the decentralised structure. Significant proportions of managers' total compensation could be tied to local profit performance, thereby aligning reward and control systems.

The transition to multinational

OD activities can help to facilitate the transition from an international to a multinational orientation. Much of the recommended activity in transitioning to a global orientation applies here as well, except that it must be customised to the issues facing a multinational strategy. For example, the successful transition to a multinational strategy assumes that managers believe local responsiveness is more important than global integration and that the organisation is comfortable with the ambiguity of managing decentralised operations.

The decision to favour local responsiveness over global integration must be made with the same analytic rigour described earlier. In this case, the analysis must support the belief that the worldwide market is relatively heterogeneous in character. That is, that products and services, support, distribution or marketing activities must be customised and localised to drive overall sales. Similarly, the organisation must have the managerial, technical and organisational competence to achieve profit margins from businesses operating around the globe. The multinational strategy is facilitated when culture and core competencies are more suited for decentralised decision making and when the organisation can manage high amounts of ambiguity and complexity.

Once companies develop a strategic orientation for competing internationally, they create an organisation design to support it. Information like that found in **Table 10.1** is useful for designing structures, information systems and personnel practices for specific strategic orientations. An OD practitioner can help design change management programs to implement these features.

THE TRANSNATIONAL STRATEGIC ORIENTATION

This orientation exists when the need for global integration and local responsiveness are both high. It represents the most complex and ambitious worldwide strategic orientation and reflects the belief that any product or service can be made anywhere and sold everywhere.[23]

Characteristics of the transnational design

The transnational strategy combines customised products with efficient and responsive operations; the key goal is learning. This is the most complex worldwide strategic orientation because transnationals can manufacture products, conduct research, raise capital, buy supplies and perform many other functions wherever in the world the job can be performed optimally. They can move skills, resources and knowledge to regions where they are needed.

The **transnational orientation** combines the best of global and multinational orientations and adds a third attribute – the ability to transfer resources both within the organisation and across national and cultural boundaries. Otis Elevator, a division of United Technologies, developed a new programmable elevator using six research centres in five countries: a US group handled the systems integration; Japan designed the special motor drives that make the elevators ride smoothly; France perfected the door systems; Germany created the electronics; and Spain produced the small-geared components.[24] Other examples of transnational companies include General Electric (GE), Asea Brown Boveri (ABB), Motorola, Electrolux and Hewlett-Packard.

Transnational orientation: combines the best of global and multinational orientations and adds a third attribute – the ability to transfer resources both within the organisation and across national and cultural boundaries.

Transnational companies organise themselves into global matrix and network structures especially suited for moving information and resources where they can best be used. In the matrix structure, local divisions similar to the multinational structure are crossed with product groups at the headquarters office. The network structure treats each local office, including headquarters, product groups and production facilities, as self-sufficient nodes that coordinate with each other to move knowledge and resources to their most valued place. Because of the heavy communication and logistic demands needed to operate these structures, transnationals have sophisticated information systems. State-of-the-art information technology is used to move strategic and operational information throughout the system rapidly and efficiently. Organisation learning (OL) and knowledge management (KM) practices gather, organise and disseminate the knowledge and skills of members who are located around the world.

People are integrated into transnational companies through a geocentric selection policy that staffs key positions with the best people, regardless of nationality.[25] This staffing practice recognises that the distinctive competence of a transnational business is its capacity to optimise resource allocation on a worldwide basis. Unlike global and multinational businesses, which spend more time training and developing managers to fit the strategy, the transnational business attempts to hire the right person from the beginning. Recruits at any of Hewlett-Packard's foreign locations, for example, are screened not only for technical qualifications, but for personality traits that match the company's cultural values.

Implementing the transnational orientation

There are two perspectives on change in a transnational strategy.

Planned change in the transnational orientation

Transnational companies require OD interventions that can improve their ability to achieve efficient global integration under highly decentralised decision-making conditions. These interventions include extensive management selection and development practices in support of the geocentric policies described above, intergroup relations and development, and communication of a strong corporate vision and culture. KM interventions help develop a worldwide repository of information that enables members' learning.

Effective transnational businesses have well-developed vision and mission statements that communicate the values and beliefs underlying the organisation's culture and guide its operational decisions. For example, ABB's mission statement went through a multicultural rewriting when the company recognised that talking about profit was an uncomfortable activity in some cultures.[26] OD processes that increase member participation in the construction or modification of these statements can help members gain ownership of them. Research into the development of corporate credos at software developer SAS and Apple showed that success was more a function of the heavy involvement of many managers than the quality of the statements themselves.[27]

Once vision and mission statements are crafted, management training can focus on clarifying their meaning, the values they express and the behaviours required to support those values. This process of gaining shared meaning and developing a strong culture provides a basis for social control. Because transnationals need flexibility and coordination, they cannot rely solely on formal reports of sales, costs or demand to guide behaviour. This information often takes too much time to compile and distribute. Rather, the corporate vision and culture provide transnational managers with the reasoning and guidelines for why and how they should make decisions.

This form of social control supports OD efforts to improve management selection and development, intergroup relationships and strategic change. The geocentric selection process can be supplemented by a personnel policy that rotates managers through different geographical regions and functional areas to blend people, perspectives and practices. At organisations such as GE, ABB, Coca-Cola and Colgate, a cadre of managers with extensive foreign experience has been developed. Rotation throughout the organisation also improves the chances that when two organisational units must cooperate, key personnel will know each other and make coordination more achievable. The corporate vision and culture can also become important tools in building cross-functional or interdepartmental processes for transferring knowledge, resources or products. Moreover, they can provide guidelines for formulating and implementing strategic change and serve as a social context for designing appropriate structures and systems at local subsidiaries.

The transition to the transnational orientation

In addition to implementing planned changes that support the development of the transnational orientation, OD can help businesses make the complex transition to a transnational strategy. Although many organisations take on the international orientation, a much smaller number are large enough to become global or multinational. The requirements for successfully operating a transnational orientation – global integration and local responsiveness – are sufficiently restrictive and demanding that only a small fraction of organisations should pursue this strategy. As a result, knowledge about the transition to transnational is still being developed.

Global and multinational organisations tend to evolve into a transnational orientation because of changes in the organisation's environment, markets or technologies.[28] In the global orientation, for example, environmental changes can challenge the logic of centralised and efficient operations. The success of Japanese car manufacturers employing a global strategy caused employment declines in the US car industry and overall trade imbalances. Consumer and government reactions forced Japanese companies to become more responsive to local conditions. Conversely, consumer preference changes can reduce the need for tailored products and locally responsive management that are characteristic of the multinational strategy. The typical response is to centralise many decisions and activities.

Thus, the evolution to a transnational orientation is a complex strategic change effort requiring the acquisition of two additional capabilities. First, global organisations must learn to trust distant operations and multinational organisations need to improve at coordination. Second, both types of organisations need to acquire the ability to transfer resources efficiently around the world. Much of the difficulty in evolving to a transnational strategy lies in developing these additional capabilities.

In the transition from a global to a transnational orientation, the business must acquire the know-how to operate a decentralised organisation and learn to transfer knowledge, skills and resources among disparate organisational units operating in different countries. In this situation, the administrative challenge is to encourage creative over centralised thinking and to let each functional area operate in a way that best suits its context. For example, if international markets require increasingly specialised products, then manufacturing needs to operate local plants and flexible delivery systems that can move raw materials to where they are needed, when they are needed. OD interventions that can help this transition include training efforts that increase the tolerance for differences in management practices; control systems; performance appraisals, policies and procedures; reward systems that encourage entrepreneurship and performance at each foreign subsidiary; and efficient organisation designs at the local level.

The global orientation strives to achieve efficiency through centralisation and standardisation of products and practices. In the case of organisational systems, this works against the establishment of highly specialised and flexible policies and resists the movement of knowledge, skills and resources. Training interventions that help managers develop an appreciation for the different ways that effectiveness can be achieved will aid the global organisation's move towards transnationalism.[29]

Changes in reward systems can also help the global business evolve. By moving from a highly quantitative, centralised, pay-for-performance system characteristic of a global orientation, the organisation can reward people who champion new ideas and provide incentives for decentralised business units. This more flexible reward system promotes coordination among subsidiaries, product lines and staff groups. In addition, the transition to a transnational orientation can be aided by OD practitioners working with individual business units, rather than with senior management at headquarters. Working with each subsidiary on issues relating to its own structure and function sends an important message about the importance of decentralised operations.

Finally, changing the staffing policy is another important signal to organisation members that a transition is occurring. Under the global orientation, an ethnocentric policy supported standardised activities. By staffing key positions with the best people, rather than limiting the choice to just parent-country individuals, the symbols of change are clear and the rewards for supporting the new orientation are visible.

In moving from a multinational to a transnational orientation, products, technologies and regulatory constraints can become more homogeneous and require more efficient operations. However, the competencies required to compete on a transnational basis may be located in many different geographic areas. The need to balance local responsiveness against the need for coordination among organisational units is new to multinational businesses. They must create interdependencies among organisational units through the flow of parts, components and finished goods; the flow of funds, skills and other scarce resources; or the flow of intelligence, ideas and knowledge. For example, as part of Ford's transition to a transnational company, the redesign of the US Tempo car was given to one person in the United Kingdom. He coordinated all features of the new car for both sides of the Atlantic and used the same platform, engines and other parts. Ford used teleconferencing and computer links, as well as extensive air travel, to manage the complex task of meshing car companies on two continents.[30]

In such situations, OD is an important activity because complex interdependencies require sophisticated and non-traditional coordinating mechanisms.[31] An OD intervention, such as intergroup team building or cultural awareness and interpersonal skills training, can help develop the communication linkages necessary for successful coordination. In addition, the inherently 'matrixed' structures of worldwide companies and the cross-cultural context of doing business in different countries tend to create conflict. An OD intervention, such as role clarification, third-party consultation and mediation techniques, can help to solve such problems.

The transition to a transnational business is difficult and threatens the status quo. Under the multinational orientation, each subsidiary is encouraged and rewarded for its creativity and independence. However, transnational businesses are effective when physically or geographically distinct organisational units coordinate their activities. The transition from independent to interdependent business units can produce conflict as the coordination requirements are worked through. An OD practitioner can help mitigate the uncertainty associated with the change by modifying reward systems to encourage cooperation and spelling out clearly the behaviours required for success.

SUMMARY

This chapter introduced the perspective that change management is complex and inevitable. From an OD perspective, a complex systems view enables strategic orientation to be monitored and adjusted in accordance with multinational, transnational or global influences on structural and strategic design.

OD activities to improve international, global, multinational and transnational strategic orientations are in increasing demand. Each of these strategies responds to specific environmental, technological and economic conditions. Interventions in worldwide organisations require a strategic and organisational perspective on change to align people, structures and systems.

ACTIVITIES

REVIEW QUESTIONS

1   Identify three significant political and economic changes in the past five years that would require businesses to adjust their practices to take into account the changes. (LO1)

2   Explain the three key facets in worldwide strategic orientation. Give examples that are not in the book. (LO2)

3   What are the characteristics of the global design? How do these differ from the characteristics of the multinational orientation and transnational design? (LO2)

4   Describe what is meant by 'worldwide organisational development' and offer some best-practice examples. (LO1)

EXTEND YOUR LEARNING

1   International diffusion of OD derives from three important trends: the rapid development of foreign economies, the increasing worldwide availability of technical and financial resources and the emergence of a global economy. Consider Trumpism in the United States, Brexit in the United Kingdom, and other protectionist trends in various economies around the world. If Australia's low barrier economy (fewer tariffs and subsidies) remains unchanged, what practical impacts will this have on the management of specific business organisations based here that are trying to engage in worldwide OD? Discuss two or three specific examples. (LO1)

2   Locate a handful of annual general reports from major listed companies. Individually or in groups, locate within the reports specific strategic statements or initiatives that clearly indicate a global, multinational or transnational strategic orientation. Find specific examples for each of the three kinds of orientation and explain why you believe each example fits with the definition. (LO2)

Search Me! management

Explore **Search Me! Management** for articles relevant to this chapter. Fast and convenient, **Search Me! Management** is updated daily and provides you with 24-hour access to full text articles from hundreds of scholarly and popular journals, eBooks and newspapers, including *The Australian* and *The New York Times*. Visit http://login.cengagebrain.com and use the access code that comes with this book for 12 months access to the **Search Me! Management** database. Try searching for the following keywords:

Keywords:

- Worldwide OD
- International orientation
- Global orientation
- Multinational orientation
- Transnational orientation

Search tip: **Search Me! Management** contains information from both local and international sources. To get the greatest number of search results, try using both Australian and American spellings in your searches; for example, 'globalisation' and 'globalization'; 'organisation' and 'organization'.

REFERENCES

1 S. Camden-Anders and T. Knott, 'Contrasts in culture: practicing OD globally', in *Global and International Organization Development*, eds P. Sorensen, T. Head, T. Yaeger and D. Cooperrider (Chicago: Stipes Publishing, 2001); E. Vaara, R. Sarala, G. Stahl and I. Björkman, 'The impact of organizational and national cultural differences on social conflict and knowledge transfer in international acquisitions', *Journal of Management Studies*, 49 (2012): 1–27; C. Gribble, J. Blackmore and M. Rahimi, 'Challenges to providing work integrated learning to international business students at Australian universities', *Higher Education, Skills and Work-Based Learning*, 5 (2015): 1–20; D.L. Ott, and S. Michailova, 'Cultural intelligence: a review and new research avenues', *International Journal of Management Reviews*, 20 (2018): 99–119.

2 L. Bourgeois and M. Boltvinik, 'OD in cross-cultural settings: Latin America', *California Management Review*, 23 (Spring 1981): 75–81; L. Brown, 'Is organization development culture bound?', *Academy of Management Newsletter* (Winter 1982); P. Evans, 'Organization development in the transnational enterprise', in *Research in Organizational Change and Development*, 3, eds R. Woodman and W. Pasmore (Greenwich, CT: JAI Press, 1989): 1–38; R. Marshak, 'Lewin meets Confucius: a review of the OD model of change', *Journal of Applied Behavioral Science*, 29 (1997): 400–2; A. Chin and C. Chin, *Internationalizing OD: Cross-Cultural Experiences of NTL Members* (Alexandria, VA: NTL Institute,

1997); A. Shevat, 'Practicing OD with a technology-driven global company', *OD Practitioner*, 33 (2001): 28–35; E. Briody, T. Pester and R. Trotter, 'A story's impact on organizational-culture change', *Journal of Organizational Change Management*, 25 (2012): 67–87.

3 B. Moore, 'The service profit chain – a tale of two airlines' (unpublished master's thesis, Pepperdine University, 1999). The other examples come from fieldwork projects in Pepperdine University's Master of Science in Organization Development program; Pepperdine University (2018), MS in Organization Development, https://bschool. pepperdine.edu/masters-degree/organization-development.

4 T. Friedman, *The World is Flat* (New York: Farrar, Straus and Giroux, 2006); T. Peters, 'Prometheus barely unbound', *Academy of Management Executive*, 4 (1990): 70–84; Evans, 'Organization development', op. cit.: 3–23; L. Thurow, *The Future of Capitalism* (New York: Morrow, 1996); A. Ogunyemi and K. Johnston, 'Exploring the roles of people, governance and technology in organizational readiness for emerging technologies', *The African Journal of Information Systems*, 4 (2012): 99–119; J. Mary, 'Innovation management for inclusive growth in India', *Advances in Management*, 5 (2012): 21–7; A.D. Alonso, 'Wine as a unique and valuable resource: an exploratory study of wine consumers on La Palma Island', *British Food Journal*, 117 (2015): 2757–76.

5 D.H. Burger, 'Logo-OD: the applicability of logotherapy as an organisation development intervention', *SA Journal of Industrial Psychology*, 34 (2008): 68–80.

6 C. Fuchs, 'Organizational development under political, economic and natural crisis', in Sorensen et al., eds, *Global and International Organization Development*, op. cit.: 248–58.

7 J. Bhagwati, *In Defense of Globalization* (New York: Oxford University Press, 2004); Friedman, *The World is Flat*, op. cit.

8 'A survey of multinationals: big is back', *Economist* (24 June 1995); M. Rastrollo-Horrillo and J. Martín-Armario, 'Internal orientation in the growth of born-globals: learning from inside', *Academy of Management Proceedings*, 2018:1 (July 2018).

9 *Organization Development Journal Special Edition: Best Global Practices in Internal OD*, Summer 2007, http://view2.fdu.edu/legacy/futodenablsusbus. pdf; E. Knight, D. Wojcik and P. O'Neill, 'Firm internationalization strategy: strategy-as-practice perspective on global production networks', *Academy of Management Proceedings*, 2018:1 (July 2018).

10 C. Bartlett and P. Beamish, *Transnational Management: Text and Cases in Cross-border Management* (New York: Cambridge University Press, 2018).

11 H. Lancaster, 'Global managers need boundless sensitivity, rugged constitutions', *Wall Street Journal* (13 October 1998): B1; E. Okoro, 'Cross-cultural etiquette and communication in global business: toward a strategic framework for managing corporate expansion', *International Journal of Business and Management*, 7 (2012): 130–8.

12 C. Bartlett and P. Beamish, *Transnational Management*, op. cit.; K. Rostek and D. Młodzianowski, 'The impact of conscious and organized change management on efficiency of functioning the network organization', *Management and Production Engineering Review*, 2018:3 (2018): 49–58.

13 C. Bartlett and P. Beamish, *Transnational Management*, op. cit.

14 H. Lee, 'Factors that influence expatriate failure: an interview study', *International Journal of Management*, 24 (2007): 403–15; L. Littrell, E. Salas, K. Hess, M. Paley and S. Riedel, 'Expatriate preparation: a critical analysis of 25 years of cross-cultural training research', *Human Resource Development Review*, 5 (2006): 355–89; L. Nishii, J. Khattab, M. Shemla and R.M. Paluch, 'A multi-level process model for understanding diversity practice effectiveness', *Academy of Management Annals*, 12:1 (2018): 37–82.

15 J. Soininen, K. Puumalainen, H. Sjögrén and P. Syrjä, 'The impact of global economic crisis on SMEs: does entrepreneurial orientation matter?', *Management Research Review*, 35 (2012): 927–44; J. Steinmetz, C. Bennett and D. Håkonsson, 'A practitioner's view of the future of organization design: future trends and implications for Royal Dutch Shell', *Journal of Organization Design*, 1 (2012): 7–11; S. Appelbaum, S. Keller, H. Alvarez and C. Bédard, 'Organizational crisis: lessons from Lehman Brothers and Paulson & Company, *International Journal of Commerce and Management*, 22 (2012): 286–305; S. Ren and Y. Zhu, 'Making sense of business leadership vis-à-vis China's reform and transition', *Leadership and Organization Development Journal*, 36 (2015): 867–84.

16 A.D. Kodwani, 'Human resource outsourcing: issues and challenges', *The Journal of Nepalese Business Studies*, IV (December 2007), http://www.nepjol. info/index.php/JNBS/article/viewFile/1028/1043.

17 J.W. Bernardzon, 'Staffing policies of Swedish MNCs' (unpublished master's thesis, Lulea University of Technology, Sweden, 2010).

18 C. Jiang and D. Yahiaoui, 'French multinational companies' HRM in China: strategic orientation and integration approaches', *Asia Pacific Business Review* (2018), https://doi.org/10.1080/13602381.20 18.1507283.

19 J. Main, 'How to go global – and why', *Fortune* (28 August 1989): 76.

20 Jiang and Yahiaoui, 'French multinational companies' HRM in China', op. cit.

21 M. Rozkwitalska, 'Cultural dilemmas of international management', *Journal of Intercultural Management*, 1 (April 2009): 91–9; Y. Zhong, C.J. Zhu, M.M. Zhang, 'The management of Chinese MNEs' expatriates: the current status and future research agenda', *Journal of Global Mobility*, 3 (2015): 289–302.

22 R. Reed and S. Dowd, *Nonprofit Merger as an Opportunity for Survival and Growth*, MAP for Nonprofits, 2009, http://www.nonprofitfinancefund. org/sites/default/files/images/initiatives/ mergeminnesota_mapfornonprofits.pdf.

23 Thurow, *The Future of Capitalism*, op. cit.

24 A. Borrus, 'The stateless corporation', *Business Week* (14 May 1990): 101–3.

25 Jiang and Yahiaoui, 'French multinational companies' HRM in China', op. cit.; S. Lowe, A. Kainzbauer, S.J. Magala and M. Daskalaki, 'International business and the Balti of meaning: food for thought', *Journal of Organizational Change Management*, 28 (2015): 177–93.

26 T. Stewart, 'A way to measure worldwide success', *Fortune* (15 March 1999): 196–8.

27 Evans, 'Organization development', op. cit.

28 J. Galbraith, *Designing the Global Corporation* (San Francisco: Jossey-Bass, 2000); C. Bartlett and

S. Ghoshal, 'Organizing for worldwide effectiveness: the transnational solution', *California Management Review* (Fall 1988): 54–74.

29 R. Sanders, 'In the twilight of two states: the "German House" in Tekmok, Kazakhstan', *Anthropological Notebooks*, 15 (2009): 37–47; M. Zhou and H. Liu, 'Transnational entrepreneurship and immigrant integration: new Chinese immigrants in Singapore and the United States', in *Immigration and Work*, 27, ed. J.A. Vallejo (Emerald Group Publishing Limited, 2015): 169–201.

30 Main, 'How to go global', op. cit.: 73.

31 Evans, 'Organization development in the transnational enterprise', op. cit.; A. DeCostanza, G. DiRosa, S. Rogers, A. Slaughter and A. Estrada, 'Researching teams: nothing's going to change our world', *Industrial and Organizational Psychology*, 5 (2012): 36–9; H. Haase, M. Franco and M. Félix, 'Organisational learning and intrapreneurship: evidence of interrelated concepts', *Leadership and Organization Development Journal*, 36 (2015): 1–23.

11

COMPETITIVE AND COLLABORATIVE STRATEGIES

After studying this chapter, you should be able to:

1   Apply an open systems view of the environment to strategic change management.

2   Define and describe competitive strategies.

3   Discuss a range of collaborative strategies.

4   Explain how to manage network change.

Environmental framework

Competitive strategies

Collaborative strategies

Transorganisational systems (TSs)

This chapter describes transformation interventions that help organisations implement strategies for both competing and collaborating with other organisations. These change programs are relatively recent additions to the organisation transformation (OT) field. They focus on helping organisations position themselves strategically in their social and economic environments and achieve a better fit with the external forces affecting goal achievement and performance. Practitioners are discovering that additional knowledge and skills in such areas as marketing, finance, economics, political science and complexity theory are necessary to implement these significant interventions.

Organisations are open systems and must relate to their environments. They must acquire the resources and information needed to function, and they must deliver products or services that customers value. An organisation's strategy – that is, how it acquires resources and delivers outputs – is shaped by particular aspects and features of the environment.

For example, cigarette manufacturers faced with increasing regulation and declining demand in Australia and New Zealand increased distribution to other countries and diversified into other industries, such as foods, beverages and consumer products. Thus, organisations can devise a number of competitive and collaborative responses for managing environmental interfaces. Competitive responses, such as creating or clarifying mission statements and goals, developing new strategies or creating special units to respond to the environment, help the organisation to outperform rivals. Collaborative responses, such as forming strategic alliances with other organisations and developing networks, seek to improve performance by joining with others. These often result in dramatic and chaotic change, which is called organisation transformation (OT).

The OT interventions described in this chapter help organisations gain a comprehensive understanding of their environments and devise appropriate responses to external demands. The chapter begins with an elaboration of the organisational environments; then two categories of interventions are described: competitive strategies and collaborative strategies.

Competitive strategies[1] include integrated strategic change (ISC) and mergers and acquisitions (M&As). ISC is a comprehensive OT intervention aimed at a single organisation or business unit. It suggests that business strategy and organisation design must be aligned and changed together to respond to external and internal disruptions. A strategic change plan helps members manage the transition between the current strategic orientation and the desired future strategic orientation. M&As represent a second strategy of competition. These interventions seek to leverage the strengths (or shore up the weaknesses) of one organisation by combining with another organisation. This complex strategic change involves integrating many of the interventions previously discussed in this text, including human process, technostructural and human resource management interventions. Research and practice in M&As strongly suggest that OT practices can contribute to implementation success.

Collaborative strategies include alliances and networks. Alliance interventions, including joint ventures, franchising and long-term contracts, help develop the relationship between two organisations that believe the benefits of cooperation outweigh the costs of lowered autonomy and control. These increasingly common arrangements require each organisation to understand its goals and strategy in the relationship, build and leverage trust, and ensure that it is receiving the expected benefits. Finally, and building on the knowledge of alliances, network development interventions are concerned with helping sets of three or more organisations engage in relationships to perform tasks or to solve problems that are too complex and multifaceted for a single organisation to resolve. These multiorganisational systems abound in today's environment and include research and development consortia, public–private partnerships and constellations of profit-seeking organisations. They tend to be loosely coupled and non-hierarchical, and consequently they require methods different from most traditional organisation development (OD) interventions that are geared to single organisations. These methods involve helping organisations recognise the need for partnerships and the development of coordinating structures for carrying out multiorganisational activities.

ENVIRONMENTAL FRAMEWORK

The framework is based on the concept that organisations and their subunits are *open systems*[2] existing in environmental contexts. Environments can be described in two ways. First, there are different types of environments consisting of specific components or forces. To survive and grow, organisations must understand these different environments, select appropriate parts to respond to and develop effective relationships with them. A manufacturing firm, for example, must understand raw materials markets, labour markets, customer segments and production technology alternatives. It then must select from a range of raw material suppliers, applicants for employment, customer demographics and production technologies to achieve desired outcomes effectively. Organisations are thus dependent on their environments. They need to manage external constraints and contingencies, and take advantage of external opportunities. They also need to influence the environment in favourable directions through such methods as political lobbying, advertising and public relations.

Second, several useful dimensions capture the nature of organisational environments. Some environments are rapidly changing and complex, and so require organisational responses different from those in environments that are stable and simple. For example, breakfast cereal manufacturers face a stable market and use well-understood production technologies. Their strategy and organisation design issues are radically different from those of software development companies, which face product life cycles measured in months instead of years, where labour skills are rare and hard to find and where demand can change drastically overnight.

In this section, we first describe different types of environments that can affect organisations. Then we identify environmental dimensions that influence organisational responses to external forces. This material provides an introductory context for describing two kinds of interventions – competitive strategies and collaborative strategies – that represent ways organisations can change dramatically in response to their environments.

ENVIRONMENTAL TYPES AND DIMENSIONS

Organisational environments are everything beyond the boundaries of organisations that can indirectly or directly affect performance and outcomes. There are three types of environments: the general and task environments; and the enacted environment, which reflects members' perceptions of the general and task environments.

The *general environment* consists of all external forces that can influence an organisation, including technological, legal and regulatory, political, economic, social and ecological components. The *task environment*[3] consists of the specific individuals and organisations that interact directly with the organisation and can affect goal achievement: customers, suppliers, competitors, producers of substitute products or services, labour unions, financial institutions and so on. The *enacted environment*[4] consists of the organisation members' perception and representation of its general and task environments. Only the enacted environment can affect which organisational responses are chosen. The general and task environments, however, can influence whether those responses are successful or ineffective.

Environments also can be characterised along dimensions that describe the organisation's context and influence its responses. The key dimension of the environment affecting information processing is *information uncertainty*, or the degree to which environmental information is ambiguous. Another key dimension is *resource dependence*, or the degree to which an organisation relies on other organisations for resources. These two environmental dimensions can be combined to show the degree to which organisations are constrained by their environments and consequently must be responsive to their demands.

Organisations must have the capacity to monitor and make sense of their environments if they are to respond appropriately. Organisations employ a number of methods to influence and respond to their environments, buffer their technology from external disruptions and link themselves to sources of information and resources. OT practitioners can help organisations implement competitive and collaborative responses.

Environmental framework:
the concept that organisations and their subunits are open systems existing in environmental contexts.

The two types of interventions discussed in this chapter derive from this **environmental framework**. Competitive interventions, such as ISC and M&As, focus on sets of administrative and competitive responses to help an individual organisation improve its performance. Collaborative interventions, such as alliances and networks, utilise a variety of collective responses to coordinate the actions of multiple organisations.

COMPETITIVE STRATEGIES

These interventions are concerned with choices organisations can make to improve their competitive performance. They include ISC and M&As. **Competitive strategies** use a variety of responses to better align the organisation with pressing environmental demands. To establish a competitive advantage, organisations must achieve a favoured position vis-à-vis their competitors or perform internally in ways that are unique, valuable and difficult to imitate. Research into the views of leaders about competitive strategies supports this.[5] Although typically associated with commercial firms, these competitive criteria can also apply to not-for-profit and governmental organisations. Activities that are unique, valuable and difficult to imitate enhance the organisation's performance by establishing a competitive advantage over its rivals.

Competitive strategies:
include integrated strategic change (ISC) and mergers and acquisitions (M&As).

→ *Uniqueness.* A fundamental assumption in competitive strategies is that all organisations possess a unique bundle of resources and processes. Individually or in combination, they represent the source of competitive advantage. An important task in any competitive strategy is to understand these unique organisational features. For example, resources can be financial (such as access to low-cost capital), reputational (such as brand image or a history of product quality), technological (such as patents, know-how or a strong research and development department) and human (such as excellent labour–management relationships or scarce and valuable skill sets). Bill Gates' knowledge of IBM's need for an operating system on the one hand and the availability of the disk operating system (DOS) on the other hand represent a powerful case for how resources alone can represent a unique advantage.

An organisation's processes – regular patterns of organisational activity involving a sequence of tasks performed by individuals[6] – use resources to produce goods and services. For example, a software development process combines computer resources, programming languages, typing skills, knowledge of computer languages and customer requirements to produce a new software application. Other organisational processes include new product development, strategic planning, appraising member performance, making sales calls, fulfilling customer orders and the like. When resources and processes are formed into capabilities that allow the organisation to perform complex activities better than others, a distinctive competence or 'hedgehog concept' is identified.[7] Collins found that a key determinant in an organisation's transition from 'good to great' was a clear understanding and commitment to the one thing an organisation does better than anyone else.[8]

→ *Value.* Organisations achieve competitive advantage when their unique resources and processes are arranged in such a way that products or services either warrant a higher-than-average price or are exceptionally low in cost. Both advantages are valuable according to a performance–price criterion. Products and services with highly desirable features or capabilities, although expensive, are valuable because of their ability to satisfy customer demands for high quality or some other performance dimension. BMW automobiles are valuable because the perceived benefits of superior handling exceed the price paid. On the other hand, outputs that cost little to produce are valuable because of their ability to satisfy customer demands at a low price. Hyundai automobiles are valuable because they provide basic transportation at a low price. BMW and Toyota are both profitable, but they achieve that outcome through different value propositions.

→ *Difficult to imitate.* Finally, competitive advantage is sustainable when unique and valuable resources and processes are difficult to mimic or duplicate by other organisations.[9] Organisations have devised a number of methods for making imitation difficult. For example, they can protect their competitive advantage by making it difficult for other businesses to identify their distinctive competence. Disclosing unimportant information at trade shows or forgoing superior profits can make it difficult for competitors to identify an organisation's strengths. Organisations also can aggressively pursue a range of opportunities, thus raising the cost for competitors who try to replicate their success. Finally, organisations can seek to retain key human resources through attractive compensation and reward practices, thereby making it more difficult and costly for competitors to attract such talent.

The success of a competitive strategy depends on organisation responses that result in unique, valuable and difficult-to-imitate advantages. This section describes two OT interventions that can assist individual organisations in developing these advantages and managing strategic change.

INTEGRATED STRATEGIC CHANGE

ISC is an intervention that extends traditional OD processes into the content-oriented discipline of strategic management. Discussed more fully in Chapter 9, ISC is a deliberate, coordinated process that leads gradually or radically to systemic realignments between the environment and a business's strategic orientation, and that results in improvement in performance and effectiveness.[10]

The ISC process was developed in response to managers' complaints that good business strategies often are not implemented. Implementation occurs as middle managers, supervisors and employees hear about the new strategy through memos, restructuring announcements, changes in job responsibilities or new departmental objectives. Consequently, because participation has been limited to top management, there is little understanding of the need for change and little ownership of the new behaviours, initiatives and tactics required to achieve the announced objectives.

For more detail on integrated strategic change, see Chapter 9.

MERGERS AND ACQUISITIONS

M&As involve the combination of two organisations. The term *merger* refers to the integration of two previously independent organisations into a completely new organisation, while *acquisition* involves the purchase of one organisation by another for integration into the acquiring organisation. M&As are distinct from the strategies of collaboration described later in this chapter because at least one of the organisations ceases to exist. The stressful dynamics associated with M&As led one researcher to call them the 'ultimate change management challenge'.[11]

Rationale for M&As

Organisations have a number of reasons for wanting to acquire or merge with other organisations, including diversification or vertical integration; gaining access to global markets, technology or other resources; and achieving operational efficiencies, improved innovation or resource sharing. Evidence from recent research into M&As supports this view.[12] As a result, M&As have become a preferred method for rapid growth and strategic change. In 2002, for example, over 6900 M&A deals worth $458.7 billion were conducted in the United States; globally, over 23 500 deals worth $1.4 trillion were registered. During the decade there were fluctuations, with the global financial crisis seeing the main contraction; however, by 2011 global M&As activity had rebounded to a total of $1.5 trillion.[13] Some examples of large transactions include Google, Oracle and PeopleSoft; HP and Compaq; AOL and Time Warner; Chrysler and Daimler-Benz; Ford and Volvo; and Boeing and McDonnell Douglas. Despite M&A popularity, they have a questionable record of success.[14] Among the reasons commonly cited for merger failure are inadequate due diligence processes, the lack of a compelling strategic rationale, unrealistic expectations of synergy, paying too much for the transaction, conflicting corporate cultures and failure to move quickly. This is true for M&As occurring in emerging economies as much as it is for those taking place in developed ones.[15]

An *M&A intervention* is typically preceded by an examination of corporate and business strategy. *Corporate strategy* describes the range of businesses within which the organisation will participate, while *business strategy* specifies how the organisation will compete in any particular business. Organisations must decide whether their corporate and strategic goals should be achieved through strategic change, such as ISC, an M&A or a collaborative response, such as alliances or networks. M&As are preferred when internal development is considered too slow, or when alliances or networks do not offer sufficient control over key resources to meet the organisation's objectives.

In addition to the OT issues described here, M&As are complex strategic changes that involve legal and financial knowledge beyond the scope of this text. OT practitioners are encouraged to seek out and work with specialists in these other relevant disciplines. The focus here is on how OT can contribute to M&A success. Apply your learning 11.1 describes a large merger in the Australian telecommunications industry.

CALLING IN A HUGE TELECOMMUNICATION MERGER

APPLY YOUR LEARNING

11.1

In 2018, TPG and Vodafone Australia announced both joint venture and merger plans in two separate announcements. The joint venture was to acquire a 5G spectrum at an auction by the federal government. The merger, however, was the biggest news with the new telecommunication organisation valued at $15 billion and taking a strategic position to compete head on with the established leaders, Telstra and Optus. Vodaphone Australia itself was the result of a joint venture between Hong Kong's Hutchison Whampoa and British parent Vodafone Group. But this new merger is another level again and the new organisation set to be running in 2019, under the name TPG Telecom Limited, brings together the continuing Vodaphone brand with the key TPG operations of iiNet and Internode. TPG's current CEO, a Singaporean billionaire, David Teoh, will lead the merged businesses. The effect of the merger on industry competitiveness will first be examined by the Australian Competition and Consumer Commission (ACCC), who stated they will, 'look at competitive impacts in mobile (and fixed line) services ... and ... likely impacts in related markets, such as spectrum acquisition markets, wholesale services, and mobile roaming'. The Foreign Investment Review Board will also take an interest in the proposal due to the Singapore ownership component of the merged organisation.

Source: Based on B. Kolavos, 'Vodafone, TPG merger to form $15b telco giant', *The West Australian*, 30 August 2018.

Critical thinking questions

1   Assess this merger according to the phases and activities listed in **Table 11.1.**

2   Discuss what the strategic rationale may have been for the Australian merger of TPG and Vodaphone.

3   To what extent do you think the joint venture announcement may be related to the merger announcement in terms of the longer-term change strategy for TPG Telecom Limited?

4   What do you think will be the future strategic direction of TPG Telecom Limited if the ACCC and the Foreign Investment Review Board require no major changes to the proposed arrangement?

TABLE 11.1	MAJOR PHASES AND ACTIVITIES IN MERGERS AND ACQUISITIONS	
Major M&A phases	Key steps	OD and change management issues
Precombination	Search for and select candidate Create M&A team Establish business case Perform due diligence assessment Develop merger integration plan	Ensure that candidates are screened for cultural as well as financial, technical and physical asset criteria. Define a clear leadership structure. Establish a clear strategic vision, competitive strategy and systems integration potential. Specify the desirable organisation design features. Specify an integration action plan.
Legal combination	Complete financial negotiations Close the deal Announce the combination	
Operational combination	Day 1 activities Organisational and technical integration activities Cultural integration activities	Implement changes quickly. Communicate. Solve problems together and focus on the customer. Conduct an evaluation to learn and identify further areas of integration planning.

Application stages

M&As involve three major phases, as shown in **Table 11.1**: precombination, legal combination and operational combination.[16] OT practitioners can make substantive contributions to the precombination and operational combination phases.

Precombination phase

This first phase consists of planning activities designed to ensure the success of the combined organisation. The organisation that initiates the OT change must identify a candidate organisation, work with it to gather information about each other and plan the implementation and integration activities. The evidence is growing that precombination activities are critical to M&A success.[17]

1 *Search for and select candidate.* This involves developing screening criteria to assess and narrow the field of candidate organisations, agreeing on a first-choice candidate, assessing regulatory compliance, establishing initial contacts and formulating a letter of intent. Criteria for choosing an M&A partner can include leadership and management characteristics, market-access resources, technical or financial capabilities, physical facilities and so on. An OT practitioner can add value at this stage of the process by encouraging screening criteria that include managerial, organisational and cultural components, as well as technical and financial aspects. In practice, financial issues tend to receive greater attention at this stage, with the goal of maximising shareholder value. Failure to attend to cultural and organisational issues, however, can result in diminished shareholder value during the operational combination phase.[18]

   Identifying potential candidates, narrowing the field, agreeing on a first choice and checking regulatory compliance are relatively straightforward activities. They generally involve investment brokers and other outside parties who have access to databases of organisational, financial and technical information. The final two activities – making initial contacts and creating a letter of intent – are aimed at determining the candidate's interest in the proposed merger or acquisition.

2   *Create an M&A team.* Once there is initial agreement between the two organisations to pursue a merger or acquisition, senior leaders from the respective organisations appoint an M&A team to establish the business case, oversee the due diligence process and develop a merger integration plan.[19] This team typically comprises senior executives and experts in such areas as business valuation, technology, organisation and marketing. An OT practitioner can facilitate formation of this team through human process interventions, such as team building and process consultation, and help the team establish clear goals and action strategies. The practitioner also can help members define a leadership structure, apply relevant skills and knowledge, and ensure that both organisations are represented appropriately. The group's leadership structure, or who will be accountable for the team's accomplishments, is especially critical. In an acquisition, an executive from the acquiring organisation is typically the team's leader. In a merger of equals, the choice of a single individual to lead the team is more difficult, but essential. The outcome of this decision and the process used to make it form the first outward symbol of how this strategic change will be conducted.

3   *Establish the business case.* The purpose of this activity is to develop a prima facie case that combining the two organisations will result in a competitive advantage that exceeds their separate advantages.[20] It includes specifying the strategic vision, competitive strategy and systems integration potential for the M&A. An OT practitioner can facilitate this discussion to ensure that each issue is fully explored. If the business case cannot be justified on strategic, financial or operational grounds, the M&A should be revisited or terminated, or another candidate should be sought.

Strategic vision represents the organisations' combined capabilities. It synthesises the strengths of the two organisations into a viable new organisation.

Competitive strategy describes the business model for how the combined organisation will add value in a particular product market or segment of the value chain, how that value proposition is best performed by the combined organisation (compared with competitors) and how it will be difficult to imitate. The purpose of this activity is to force the two organisations to go beyond the rhetoric of 'these two organisations should merge because it's a good fit'.

Systems integration specifies how the two organisations will be combined. It addresses how and if they can work together. It includes the following key questions: Will one organisation be acquired and operated as a wholly owned subsidiary? Does the transaction imply a merger of equals? Are lay-offs implied and, if so, where? On what basis can promised synergies or cost savings be achieved?

4   *Perform a due diligence assessment.* This involves evaluating whether the two organisations actually have the managerial, technical and financial resources that each assumes the other possesses. It includes a comprehensive review of each organisation's articles of incorporation, stock option plans, organisation charts and so on. Financial, human resources, operational, technical and logistical inventories are evaluated along with other legally binding issues. The discovery of previously unknown or unfavourable information can halt the M&A process.[21]

Although due diligence assessment traditionally emphasises the financial aspects of M&As, this focus is increasingly being challenged by evidence that culture clashes between two organisations can ruin expected financial gains.[22] Thus, attention to the cultural features of M&As is becoming more prevalent in due diligence assessment. The scope and detail of due diligence assessment depends on knowledge of the candidate's business, the complexity of its industry, the relative size and risk of the transaction and the available resources. Due diligence activities must reflect symbolically the vision and values of the combined organisations. An overly zealous assessment, for example, can contradict promises of openness and trust made earlier in the transaction. Missteps at this stage can lower or destroy opportunities for synergy, cost savings and improved shareholder value.

5   *Develop merger integration plans.* This stage specifies how the two organisations will be combined.[23] It defines integration objectives; the scope and timing of integration activities; organisation design criteria; Day 1 requirements; and who does what, where and when. The scope of these plans depends on how integrated the organisations will be. If the candidate organisation will operate as an independent subsidiary with an 'arm's-length' relationship to the parent, merger integration planning need only specify those systems that will be common to both organisations. A full integration of the two organisations requires a more extensive plan.

Merger integration planning starts with the business case conducted earlier and involves more detailed analyses of the strategic vision, competitive strategy and systems integration for the M&A. For example, assessment of the organisations' markets and suppliers can reveal opportunities to serve customers better and capture purchasing economies of scale. Examination of business processes can identify best operating practices; physical facilities that should be combined, left alone or shut down; and systems and procedures that are redundant. Capital budget analysis can show the investments that should be continued or dropped. Typically, the M&A team appoints subgroups composed of members from both organisations to perform these analyses. An OT practitioner can conduct team-building and process-consultation interventions to improve how those groups function.

Next, plans for designing the combined organisation are developed. They include the organisation's structure, reporting relationships, human resources policies, information and control systems, operating logistics, work designs and customer-focused activities.

The final task of integration planning involves developing an action plan for implementing the M&A. This specifies tasks to be performed, decision-making authority and responsibility, and timelines for achievement. It also includes a process for addressing conflicts and problems that will invariably arise during the implementation process.

Legal combination phase

This phase of the M&A process involves the legal and financial aspects of the transaction. The two organisations settle on the terms of the deal, register the transaction with and gain approval from appropriate regulatory agencies, communicate with and gain approval from shareholders and file appropriate legal documents. In some cases, an OT practitioner can provide advice on negotiating a fair agreement, but this phase generally requires knowledge and expertise beyond that typically found in OT practice.

Operational combination phase

This final phase involves implementing the merger integration plan. In practice, it begins during due diligence assessment and may continue for months or years following the legal combination phase. Research warns of the need for due diligence to avoid the potential pitfalls.[24] Successful OT implementation includes three kinds of activities:

1 *Day 1 activities.* These include communications and actions that officially start the implementation process. For example, announcements may be made about key executives of the combined organisation, the location of corporate headquarters, the structure of tasks, and areas and functions where lay-offs will occur. The OT practitioner pays special attention to sending important symbolic messages to organisation members, investors and regulators about the soundness of the merger plans and those changes that are critical to accomplishing strategic and operational objectives.[25]

2 *Operational and technical integration activities.* These involve the physical moves, structural changes, work designs and procedures that will be implemented to accomplish the strategic objectives and expected cost savings of the M&A. The merger integration plan lists these activities, which can be large in number and range in scope from seemingly trivial to quite critical. For example, Westpac's acquisition of the Bank of Melbourne involved changing Bank of Melbourne's employee uniforms, the signage at all banks, marketing and public relations campaigns, repainting buildings and integrating the route structures, among others. When these integration activities are not executed properly, the M&A process can be set back.

3 *Cultural integration activities.*[26] These tasks are aimed at building new values and norms in the combined organisation. Successful implementation blends both the technical and cultural aspects of the combined organisation.

The OT literature contains several practical suggestions for managing the operational combination phase.[27] First, the merger integration plan should be implemented sooner rather than later, and quickly rather than slowly. Integration of two organisations generally involves aggressive financial targets, short timelines and intense public scrutiny.[28] Moreover, the change process is often plagued by culture clashes and political fighting. Consequently, organisations need to make as many changes as possible in the first 100 days following the legal combination phase.[29] Quick movement in key areas has several advantages: it pre-empts unanticipated changes in the organisation that might thwart momentum in the desired direction; it reduces organisation members' uncertainty about when things will happen; and it reduces members' anxiety about the M&A's impact on their personal situation. All three of these conditions can prevent desired collaboration and other benefits from occurring.

Second, integration activities must be communicated clearly and in a timely fashion to a variety of stakeholders, including shareholders, regulators, customers and organisation members. M&As can increase uncertainty and anxiety about the future, especially for members of the involved organisations who often inquire: Will I have a job?

Will my job change? Will I have a new boss? These kinds of questions can dominate conversations, reduce productive work and spoil opportunities for collaboration. To reduce ambiguity, organisations can provide concrete answers through a variety of channels, including company newsletters, email and intranet postings, press releases, video and face-to-face presentations and one-on-one interaction with managers.

Third, members from both organisations need to work together to solve implementation problems and to address customer needs. Such coordinated tasks can clarify work roles and relationships, and they can contribute to member commitment and motivation. Moreover, when coordinated activity is directed at customer service, it can assure customers that their interests will be considered and satisfied during the merger.

Fourth, organisations need to assess the implementation process continually to identify integration problems and needs. The following questions can guide the assessment process:[30]

→ Have savings estimated during precombination planning been confirmed or exceeded?[31]

→ Has the new entity identified and implemented shared strategies or opportunities?

→ Has the new organisation been implemented without loss of key personnel?

→ Was the merger and integration process seen as fair and objective?

→ Is the combined company operating efficiently?

→ Have major problems with stakeholders been avoided?

→ Did the process proceed according to schedule?

→ Were substantive integration issues resolved?

→ Are people highly motivated (more so than before)?

M&As are among the most complex and challenging interventions facing organisations and OT practitioners.

COLLABORATIVE STRATEGIES

In the previous section, we explored strategies of competition: OT interventions that helped individual organisations cope with environmental dependence and uncertainty by managing their internal resources to achieve competitive advantage and improve performance. Organisations also can cope with environmental pressures by collaborating with other organisations. This section discusses **collaborative strategies** where two or more organisations agree to work together to achieve their objectives. This represents a fundamental shift in strategic orientation because the strategies, goals, structures and processes of two or more organisations become interdependent and must be coordinated and aligned.

Collaborative strategies: include alliances and networks.

The rationale for collaboration is discussed first. Then we describe the process of forming and developing alliances and networks. *Alliance interventions*[32] focus on the relationship between two organisations, while *network interventions* involve three or more organisations. As the number of organisations increases, the scope and complexity of the problems and issues that need to be addressed increase. Alliances can be building blocks for networks, however, and the lessons learned there can be applied to the development of network arrangements. Apply your learning 11.2 identifies a significant collaborative approach applied by an internet provider in the Northern Territory to improve service and systems.

COLLABORATION RATIONALE

More and more, organisations are collaborating with other organisations to achieve their objectives. These collaborative strategies can provide additional resources for large-scale research and development; spread the risks of innovation; apply diverse expertise to

APPLY
YOUR
LEARNING
11.2

REMOTE OPPORTUNITIES COME FROM COLLABORATION

The Northern Territory (NT) of Australia is known for being physically remote and that is exactly its attraction for tourists. However, modern tourists also like to remain connected to the internet and social media while travelling. It is a difficult conundrum that a new business collaboration in the NT is aiming to overcome. Free Wi-Fi access in places that seem like the edge of the known world is a seductive idea. Already, this business collaboration has brought free Wi-Fi to Uluru-Kata Tjuta National Park, Watarkka National Park (Kings Canyon), Desert Park, Karlu Karlu (Devil Marbles), Litchfield National Park, and Kakadu National Park. Tourism NT contracted Easyweb Digital on the basis of them having completed successful connectivity projects in other remote parts of Australia. Easyweb sought a collaboration with Ruckus Networks in the NT, with the latter providing the durable, hardy internet access equipment needed for extreme weather locations.

One of Ruckus Networks' managers, Carl Jefferys, was quoted, 'Not only is this a step towards making a huge difference in people's everyday lives, but it also creates new business opportunities for local organisations with limited means.' This is among the features of successful collaborations in business, that spinoff opportunities come out of the provision of the primary objective of the collaboration. In this case, a tourism project is likely to have benefits much broader than the tourism industry. Business is one and other social services and individuals are sure to benefit too.

The initial project to bring connectivity across the NT is targeting at least 25 communities and the extent of success and change brought by the enhanced service will be the driver of future projects in this vein.

Source: Based on 'Ruckus and Easyweb to roll out free WiFi across NT', *IT Brief*, 15 October 2018.

| Critical thinking questions | 1 | What is the primary strategic reason for Easyweb to seek a collaboration with Ruckus Networks? |
| | 2 | What are the advantages of Easyweb partnering with Ruckus Networks in this instance instead of simply purchasing the equipment needed for the project? |

complex problems and tasks; make information or technology available to learn and develop new capabilities; position the organisation to achieve economies of scale or scope; or gain access to new, especially international, marketplaces.[33] For example, pharmaceutical firms form strategic alliances to distribute non-competing medications and avoid the high costs of establishing sales organisations; businesses from different countries form joint ventures to overcome restrictive trade barriers; and high-technology firms form research consortia to undertake significant and costly research and development for their industries.

More generally, however, collaborative strategies allow organisations to perform tasks that are too costly and complicated for single organisations to perform.[34] These tasks include the full range of organisational activities, including purchasing raw materials, hiring and compensating organisation members, manufacturing and service delivery, obtaining investment capital, marketing and distribution, and strategic planning. The key to understanding collaborative strategies is recognising that these individual tasks must be coordinated with each other. Whenever a good or service from one of these tasks is exchanged between two units (individuals, departments or organisations), a *transaction* occurs. Transactions can be designed and managed internally within the organisation's structure, or externally between organisations. For example, organisations can acquire a raw materials provider and operate these tasks as part of internal operations or they can collaborate with a raw material supplier through long-term contracts in an alliance.

Economists and organisation theorists have spent considerable effort investigating when collaborative strategies are preferred over competitive strategies. They have developed frameworks, primarily transaction cost theory and agency theory, that are useful for understanding the interventions described in this chapter.[35] As a rule, collaborative strategies work well when transactions occur frequently and are well understood. Many organisations, for example, outsource their payroll tasks because the inputs (such as hours worked, pay rates and employment status), the throughputs (such as tax rates and withholdings) and the outputs occur regularly and are governed by well-known laws and regulations. Moreover, if transactions involve people, equipment or other assets that are unique to the task, then collaboration is preferred over competition. For example, Microsoft works with a variety of value-added resellers, independent software vendors, and small and large consulting businesses to bring its products to customers ranging in size from individual consumers to the largest business enterprises in the world. An internal sales and service department to handle the unique demands of each customer segment would be much more expensive to implement and would not deliver the same level of quality as the partner organisations. In general, relationships between and among organisations become more formalised as the frequency of interaction increases, the type of information and other resources that are exchanged become more proprietary and the number of different types of exchanges increases.[36]

Cummings has referred to groups of organisations that have joined together for a common purpose, including alliances and networks, as **transorganisational systems (TSs)**.[37] These are functional social systems existing intermediately between single organisations on the one hand and societal systems on the other. These multiorganisational systems can make decisions and perform tasks on behalf of their member organisations, although members maintain their separate organisational identities and goals. The separation distinguishes TSs from M&As.

In contrast to most organisational systems, TSs tend to be underorganised: relationships among member organisations are loosely coupled; leadership and power are dispersed among autonomous organisations, rather than hierarchically centralised; and commitment and membership are tenuous as member organisations act to maintain their autonomy while jointly performing. These characteristics make creating and managing TSs difficult.[38] Because members typically are accustomed to hierarchical forms of control, they may have difficulty managing lateral relations among independent organisations. They also may have

Developing as a change agent

There are many characteristics of a change agent. Some of these are reflected in the following list of actions. Write *yes* next to those that reflect collaborative characteristics and *no* next to those that would be considered competitive.

1 _____Create a change receptive climate.

2 _____Set implicit goals.

3 _____Provide feedback on performance.

4 _____Provide positive reinforcement.

5 _____Encourage structured activity.

6 _____Develop a well-defined hierarchical structure, and stick to it.

7 _____Tolerate failure.

8 _____Encourage a bias for action.

9 _____Make extensive use of formal meetings.

10 _____Allow bootlegging of ideas.

11 _____Reward successful personnel.

12 _____Terminate those who make mistakes as a way of creating a good example for others.

13 _____Make extensive use of informal meetings.

14 _____Encourage communication throughout the organisation.

15 _____Discourage joint projects and ventures among different departments.

16 _____Encourage brainstorming.

17 _____Encourage moderate risk taking.

18 _____Encourage networking with others in the enterprise.

19 _____Encourage personnel not to fear failing.

20 _____Encourage personnel to be willing to succeed even if it means doing unethical things.

Answers: 1 Y; 2 N; 3 Y; 4 Y; 5 N; 6 N; 7 Y; 8 Y; 9 N; 10 Y; 11 Y; 12 N; 13 Y; 14 Y; 15 N; 16 Y; 17 N; 18 Y; 19 Y; 20 N.

After reviewing your answers, consider whether some of the acts might have both collaborative *and* competitive characteristics. Discuss which ones would fit this dual category and explain why.

EXPERIENTIAL ACTIVITY 11.1

difficulty managing different levels of commitment and motivation among members and sustaining membership over time.

ALLIANCE INTERVENTIONS

An alliance is a formal agreement between two organisations to pursue a set of private and common goals through the sharing of resources, including intellectual property, people, capital, technology, capabilities and physical assets.[39] Alliances are an important strategy for such organisations as Corning Incorporated, FedEx, IBM and Starbucks. The term *alliance* generally refers to any collaborative effort between two organisations, including licensing agreements, franchises, long-term contracts and joint ventures. Franchising is a common collaborative strategy. Companies such as McDonald's, Jim's Mowing and Holiday Inn license their name and know-how to independent organisations that deliver the service and leverage the brand name for marketing. A *joint venture* is a special type of alliance where a third organisation, jointly owned and operated by two (or more) organisations, is created. Joint ventures between domestic and foreign companies, such as Fuji Xerox, can help overcome trade barriers and facilitate technology transfer across nations.

Application stages

The development of effective alliances generally follows a process of strategy formulation, partner selection, alliance structuring and start-up, and alliance operation and adjustment.

Alliance strategy formulation

The first step in developing alliances is to clarify the business strategy and understand why an alliance is an appropriate method to implement it. About one-half to two-thirds of alliances fail to meet their financial objectives, and the number-one reason for that failure is the lack of a clear strategy.[40] For example, Collins found that alliance success was heavily influenced by the alignment of the partner to the company's 'hedgehog concept'.[41] If the organisation understood its passion, distinctive capabilities and economic drivers, it was more likely to develop alliances that supported its strategy. Thus, it is important to pursue alliances according to a 'collaboration logic'.[42] The alliance must be seen as a more effective way of organising and operating than developing new capabilities to perform the work in-house, acquiring or merging with another organisation or buying the capabilities from another organisation in a transactional relationship.

Partner selection

Once the reasons for an alliance are clear, the search for an appropriate partner begins. Alliances always involve a cost–benefit trade-off; while the organisation typically gains access to new markets or new capabilities, it does so at the cost of yielding some autonomy and control over its activities.

Similar to the identification of M&A candidates discussed previously, this step involves developing screening criteria, agreeing on candidates, establishing initial contacts and formulating a letter of intent. A good alliance partnership will leverage both similarities and differences to create competitive advantage. Compatible management styles or cultures, goals, information technologies or operations are important similarities that can smooth alliance formation and implementation. However, different perspectives, technologies, capabilities and other resources can complement existing ones and be good sources of learning and value in the partnership. These differences can also be a source of frustration for the alliance. An OT practitioner can add value at this stage of the process by ensuring that the similarities and differences among potential alliance partners are explored and understood. In addition, the way the alliance begins and proceeds is an important ingredient in building trust, a characteristic of successful alliances explored more fully in the next step.

Alliance structuring and start-up

Following agreement to enter into an alliance, the focus shifts to how to structure the partnership and build and leverage trust in the relationship. First, an appropriate governance structure must be chosen and can include medium- to long-term contracts, minority equity investments, equal equity partnerships or majority equity investments. As the proportion of equity investment increases, the costs, risk and amount of required management attention also increase.[43] In general, partners need to know how expenses, profits, risk and knowledge will be shared.

Second, research increasingly points to 'relational quality' as a key success factor of long-term alliances.[44] Alliances shift the nature of the relationship from the simple exchange of goods, services or resources with no necessary expectation of a future relationship to one where there is a clear expectation of future exchange. The parties in the relationship must act in good faith to ensure the future. This requires trust – 'a psychological state comprising the intention to accept vulnerability based upon positive expectations of the intentions or behaviour' of another business or individual representing the organisation. It implies an expectation that the organisation will subordinate its self-interest to the 'joint interest' of the alliance under most conditions.[45]

Trust can increase or decrease over the life of the alliance. Early in the alliance formation process, it can serve as an initial reservoir of comfort and confidence based on perceptions of the organisation's reputation, prior success and other sources. These same factors can also contribute to a lack of initial trust. Trust can be increased or decreased by new assessments of the other's capabilities, competence and ethical behaviour. An OT practitioner can assist in this initial start-up phase by making implicit perceptions of trust explicit and getting both parties to set appropriate expectations.[46] During the structuring and start-up phase, trust can increase through direct activities as a function of the number, frequency and importance of interactions; differences between expectations and reality; the nature of mistakes and how they are resolved; and attributions made about partners' behaviour.

Alliance operation and adjustment

Once the alliance is functioning, the full range of OT interventions described in this text can be applied. Team building, conflict resolution, large-group interventions, work design, employee involvement, strategic planning and culture change efforts have all been reported in alliance work.[47] The OT practitioner should pay particular attention to helping each partner in the alliance clarify the capabilities contributed, the lessons learned and the benefits received.

Diagnosing the state of the alliance and making the appropriate adjustments is a function of understanding whether the environment has changed in ways that make collaboration unnecessary, whether partner goals and capabilities have changed the nature of the relationship and interdependence and whether the alliance is successfully generating outcomes. The long-term success of the Fuji Xerox joint venture, for example, has been due to the willingness and ability of the two organisations to adjust their relationship in terms of ownership, profit sharing, new product development responsibilities and market access.[48] **Apply your learning 11.3** provides a couple of examples of how companies can use alliances to achieve key strategies in particular industries.

APPLY YOUR LEARNING 11.3

ALLIANCES TAKE TWO

Alliances are increasingly common in this hyper-connected, technologically advanced, post-industrial era. The Australian corporate landscape is a frequent backdrop to many alliances as corporations and other organisations jostle to find synergies and advantages for serving markets and continuously improving their operations and investment portfolios. Two such examples emerged in 2018.

1   Straits Real Estate (SRE), a subsidiary of the Straits Trading Company of Singapore, and the Adelaide-based Commercial & General formed an alliance in order to acquire five new logistics assets worth A$130.5 million. This builds upon previous alliances between the two in which central commercial property was acquired in Sydney and Perth. The latest alliance focused upon operating assets and they specifically cited commercial entities Coca-Cola Amatil and Incitec Pivot as prime utilisers of the logistics assets, which are therefore perceived to have a strong cash flow and growth potential. SRE in particular seems interested in building its assets base through further alliances for similar acquisitions in Australia.

2   Two companies with deeply specialised experience in the gas and fluids components and supply chain network in Australia announced a joint venture in 2018. H.I. Fraser manufactures parts in Australia that are in critical systems on Collins Class submarines. Issartel also manufactures various gas and fluid components as part of the Naval Group in Australia. Both Issartel and H.I. Fraser plan to jointly qualify their supply chains and build a shared knowledge of the manufacture of submarine gas and fluid components with plans to consolidate Australia's contribution to the global submarine building industry.

Sources: Based on F. Chong, 'Straits Real Estate creates Australian logistics joint venture', *IPE International*, 20 September 2018; and 'H.I. Fraser and Issartel sign joint venture for Future Submarines' *Australian Defence Magazine*, 28 September 2018.

Critical thinking questions

1   What are the advantages and disadvantages of entering into the types of alliances described in the article?

2   Discuss what the strategic implications might be for the partners in each case example if the alliances were not entered into.

NETWORK INTERVENTIONS

Networks involve three or more organisations that have joined together for a common purpose, and their use is increasing rapidly in today's highly competitive global environment. For example, in the private sector, research and development consortia allow companies to share resources and risks associated with large-scale research efforts. Networks among airlines with regional specialisations can combine to provide worldwide coverage, while Japanese *keiretsu*, Korean *chaebols* and Mexican *grupos* can enable different organisations to take advantage of complementary capabilities among them. In the public sector, partnerships between government and business provide the resources and initiative to undertake complex urban renewal projects that promote economies, and avoid costly overlap and redundancy.[49]

Managing the development of multiorganisational networks involves two types of change: (1) creating the initial network and (2) managing change within an established network. Both change processes are complex and not well understood. First, the initial creation of networks recognises their underorganised nature. Forming them into a more coherent, operating whole involves understanding the relationships among the participating organisations and their roles in the system, as well as the implications and consequences of organisations leaving the network, changing roles or increasing their influence. Second, change within existing networks must account for the relationships among member organisations as a whole system.[50] The multiple and complex relationships involved in networks produce emergent phenomena that cannot be fully explained by simply knowing the parts. Each organisation in the network has goals that are partly related to the good of the network and partly focused on self-interest. How the network reacts over time is even more difficult to capture and is part of the emerging science of complexity.[51]

Creating the network

OT practitioners have evolved a unique form of planned change aimed at creating networks and improving their effectiveness. In laying out the conceptual boundaries of network development, also known as *transorganisation development*,[52] Cummings described the practice as following the phases of planned change appropriate for underorganised systems.[53] Due to their significance and the fact that they exemplify the fine line between OT and OD, the four stages are shown again in **Figure 11.1**, along with key issues that need to be addressed at each stage, and are described below.

Identification stage

This initial stage of network development involves identifying existing and potential member organisations best suited to achieving their collective objectives. Identifying potential members can be difficult because organisations may not perceive the need to join together or may not know enough about each other to make membership choices. These problems are typical when trying to create a new network. Relationships among potential members may be loosely coupled or non-existent; thus, even if organisations see the need to form a network, they may be unsure about who should be included.

The identification stage is generally carried out by one or a few organisations interested in exploring the possibility of creating a network. OT practitioners work with these initiating

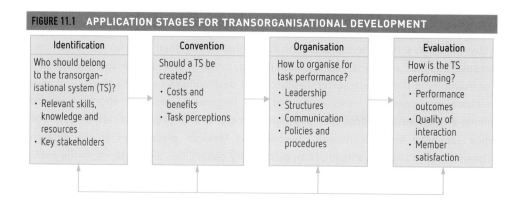

FIGURE 11.1   APPLICATION STAGES FOR TRANSORGANISATIONAL DEVELOPMENT

Identification	Convention	Organisation	Evaluation
Who should belong to the transorganisational system (TS)? • Relevant skills, knowledge and resources • Key stakeholders	Should a TS be created? • Costs and benefits • Task perceptions	How to organise for task performance? • Leadership • Structures • Communication • Policies and procedures	How is the TS performing? • Performance outcomes • Quality of interaction • Member satisfaction

organisations to clarify their own goals, such as product or technology exchange, learning or market access, and to understand the trade-off between the loss of autonomy and the value of collaboration. Change agents also help specify criteria for network membership and identify organisations meeting those standards. Because networks are intended to perform specific tasks, a practical criterion for membership is how much organisations can contribute to task performance. Potential members can be identified and judged in terms of the skills, knowledge and resources that they bring to bear on the network task. Practitioners warn, however, that identifying potential members also should take into account the political realities of the situation.[54] Consequently, key stakeholders who can affect the creation and subsequent performance of the network are identified as possible members.

An important difficulty at this stage can be insufficient leadership and cohesion among participants to choose potential members. In these situations, OT practitioners may need to adopt a more activist role in creating the network.[55] They may need to bring structure to a group of autonomous organisations that do not see the need to join together or may not know how to form relationships. In several cases of network development, change agents helped members create a special leadership group that could make decisions on behalf of the participants.[56] This leadership group comprised a small cadre of committed members and was able to develop enough cohesion among members to carry out the identification stage. The activist role requires strong leadership and direction. For example, change agents may need to educate potential network members about the benefits of joining together. They may need to structure face-to-face encounters aimed at sharing information and exploring interaction possibilities.

Convention stage

Once potential network members are identified, the convention stage is concerned with bringing them together to assess whether formalising the network is desirable and feasible. This face-to-face meeting enables potential members to explore mutually their motivations for joining and their perceptions of the joint task. They work to establish sufficient levels of motivation and task consensus to form the network.

Like the identification stage, this phase of network creation generally requires considerable direction and facilitation by OT practitioners. Existing stakeholders may not have the legitimacy or skills to perform the convening function, and practitioners can serve as conveners if they are perceived as legitimate and credible by the attending organisations. However, change agents need to maintain a neutral role, treating all members alike.[57] They need to be seen by members as working on behalf of the total system, rather than as being aligned with particular members or views. When practitioners are perceived as neutral, network members are more likely to share information with them and to listen to their inputs. Such neutrality can enhance change agents' ability to mediate conflicts among members. It can help them uncover diverse views and interests and forge agreements among stakeholders. OT practitioners, for example, can act as mediators, ensuring that members' views receive a fair hearing and that disputes are equitably resolved. They can help to bridge the different views and interests, and achieve integrative solutions. In many cases, practitioners came from research centres or universities with reputations for neutrality and expertise in networks.[58] Because participating organisations tend to have diverse motives and views and limited means for resolving differences, change agents may need to structure and manage interactions to facilitate airing of differences and arriving at consensus about forming the network. They may need to help organisations work through differences and reconcile self-interest with those of the larger network.

Organisation stage

When the convention stage results in a decision to create a network, members then begin to organise themselves for task performance. This involves developing the structures and mechanisms that promote communication and interaction among members and that direct joint efforts to the task at hand.[59] It includes the organisations to be involved in the network and the roles each will play; the communication and relationships among them; and the control system that will guide decision making and provide a mechanism for monitoring performance. For example, members may create a coordinating council to manage the network and a powerful leader to head it. They might choose to formalise exchanges among members by developing rules, policies and formal operating procedures. When members are required to invest large amounts of resources in the network, such as might occur in an industry-based research consortium, the organising stage typically includes voluminous contracting and negotiating about members' contributions and returns. Here, corporate lawyers and financial analysts play key roles in specifying the network structure. They determine how costs and benefits will be allocated among member organisations as well as the legal obligations, decision-making responsibilities and contractual rights of members. An OT practitioner can help members define competitive advantage for the network as well as the structural requirements necessary to support achievement of its goals.

Evaluation stage

This final stage of creating a network involves assessing how the network is performing. Members need feedback so that they can identify problems and begin to resolve them. Feedback data generally include performance outcomes and member satisfaction, as well as indicators of how well members are interacting jointly. Change agents can periodically interview or survey member organisations about various outcomes and features of the network, and feed that data back to network leaders. Such information will enable leaders to make necessary operational modifications and adjustments. It may signal the need to return to previous stages in the process to make necessary corrections, as shown by the feedback arrows in **Figure 11.1**.

Managing network change

In addition to developing new networks, OT practitioners may need to facilitate change within established networks. Planned change in existing networks derives from an understanding of the 'new sciences', including complexity, non-linear systems, catastrophe and chaos theories. From these perspectives, organisation networks are viewed as complex systems displaying the following properties:[60]

1   The behaviour of a network is sensitive to small differences in its initial conditions. How the network was established and formed – the depth and nature of trust among the partners, who was selected (and not selected) to be in the network and how the network was organised – plays a key role in its willingness and ability to change.

2   Networks display 'emergent' properties or characteristics that cannot be explained through an analysis of the parts: 'Given the properties of the parts and the laws of their interaction, it is not a trivial matter to infer the properties of the whole.'[61] The tools of systems thinking and the understanding of emergence in complex systems are still being developed and applied.[62]

3   A variety of network behaviours and patterns, both expected and unexpected, can emerge from members performing tasks and making decisions according to simple rules to which everyone agreed. This is amply demonstrated in Senge's 'beer game' simulation where a retailer, a wholesaler and a brewery each acts according to the simple rule of maximising its own profit. Participants in the simulation routinely end up with enormous inventories of poor-selling beer, delayed deliveries, excess capacity and other problems. Without an understanding of the 'whole' system, the nature of interdependencies within the system and timely and complete information, each part – acting in its own self-interest – destroys itself.[63] Apparently random changes in networks may simply be chaotic patterns that are not understood. These patterns cannot be known in advance but represent potential paths of change that are the result of the complex interactions among members in the network.

The process of change in complex systems such as networks involves creating instability, managing the tipping point and relying on self-organisation. These phases roughly follow Lewin's model of planned change. Change in a network requires an unfreezing process where the system becomes unstable. Movement in the system is described by the metaphor of a 'tipping point' where changes occur rapidly as a result of information processing. Finally, refreezing involves self-organisation. The descriptions below represent rudimentary applications of these concepts to networks; our understanding of them is still in a formative stage.

Create instability in the network

Before change in a network can occur, relationships among member organisations must become unstable. A network's susceptibility to instability is a function of members' motivations for structure versus agency.[64] *Structure* refers to the organisation's expected role in the network and represents a source of stability. All things being equal, network members tend to behave and perform according to their agreed-upon roles. For example, most routine communications among the network members are geared towards increasing stability and working together. A manufacturing plant in Nike's network is expected to produce a certain number of shoes at a certain cost with certain features. Nike headquarters in Beaverton, Oregon, has planned for its plant to behave this way. On the other hand, *agency* involves self-interest, which can create instability in the network. Each member of the network is trying to maximise its own performance in the context of the network. Changes in member goals and strategies, the ratio of costs and benefits in network membership and so on can affect the willingness and ability of members to contribute to network performance. When a plant in Nike's network grows to a sufficient size, it may decide to alter its role in the network. As the ratio of agency to structure increases, the instability of the network rises, thus enabling change to occur.

OT practitioners can facilitate instability in a network by changing the pattern of communication among members. They can, for example, encourage organisations to share information. Technology breakthroughs, new product introductions, changes in network membership or changes in the strategy of a network member all represent fluctuations that can increase the susceptibility of the network to change. Another important aspect of changing the pattern of information is to ask who should get the information. Understanding and creating instability is difficult because the nature of members' connectedness also influences the system's susceptibility. Some organisations are more connected than others; most organisations are closely connected to several others, but relatively unconnected to many. This makes creating a sense of urgency for change difficult. Diagnosis of the relationships among member organisations can provide important information about organisations that are central to network communications. It helps to better manage risk in global supply chains.[65]

Manage the tipping point

Although instability provides the impetus and opportunity for change, the direction, type and process of change are yet to be determined. An unstable network can move to a new state of organisation and performance or it can return to its old condition. At this point, network members, individually and collectively, make choices about what to do. An OT practitioner can help them through this change period. Recent studies suggest the following guides for facilitating network change:[66]

1   *The law of the few.* A new idea, practice or other change spreads because of relatively few but important roles in the network. Connectors, 'mavens' and salespeople help an innovation achieve sufficient awareness and credibility throughout the network to be considered viable. *Connectors* are individuals who occupy central positions in the network and are able to tap into many different network audiences. They have 'Rolodex' power; they are quickly able to alert and connect with a wide variety of people in many organisations. *Mavens* are 'information sinks'. They passionately pursue knowledge about a particular subject and are altruistically willing to tell anyone who is interested everything they know about it. The key to the maven's role is trust. People who speak

to mavens know that they are getting unbiased information; that there is no 'hidden agenda' – just good data. Finally, *salespeople* are the champions of change and are able to influence others to try new ideas, do new things or consider new options.

Thus, the first key factor in changing a network is the presence of communication channels occupied by connectors, mavens and salespeople. OT practitioners can fill any of these roles. They can, if appropriate, be mavens on a particular subject and act as a source of unbiased information about a new network practice, aspects of interpersonal relationships that network members agree is slowing network response or ideas about information systems that can speed communication. Less frequently, OT practitioners can be connectors, ensuring that any given message is seeded throughout the network. This is especially true if the change agent was part of the network's formation. In this case, the practitioner might have the relationships with organisations in the network.

Thus, networking skills, such as the ability to manage lateral relations among autonomous organisations in the relative absence of hierarchical control, are indispensable to practitioners of network change. Change agents must be able to span the boundaries of diverse organisations, link them together and facilitate exchanges among them.[67] The OT practitioner can also play the role of salesperson. Although it is in line with the 'activist' role described earlier in the practice of network creation, it is not a traditional aspect of OT practice. The wisdom of having a change agent as the champion of an idea rather than a key player in the organisation network is debatable. The change agent and network members must understand the trade-offs in sacrificing the OT practitioner's neutrality for influence. If that trade-off is made, the change agent will need the political competence to understand and resolve the conflicts of interest and value dilemmas inherent in systems made up of multiple organisations, each seeking to maintain autonomy while jointly interacting. Political savvy can help change agents manage their own roles and values in respect to those power dynamics.

2 *Stickiness.* The second ingredient in network change is stickiness. For a new idea or practice to take hold, the message communicated by the connectors, mavens and salespeople must be memorable. A memorable or sticky message is not a function of typical communication variables, such as frequency of the message, loudness or saliency. Stickiness is often a function of small and seemingly insignificant characteristics of the message, such as its structure, format and syntax, as well as its emotional content, practicality or sequencing with other messages. An OT practitioner can also help network members develop sticky messages. Brainstorming alternative phrases, using metaphors to symbolise meaning or enlisting the help of marketing and communications specialists can increase the chance of developing a sticky message. Since the ingredients of stickiness are not often obvious, several iterations of a message's structure with focus groups or different audiences may be necessary to understand what gets people's attention.

The power of context

Finally, a message must be meaningful. This is different from stickiness and refers to the change's relevance to network members. The source of meaning is in the context of the network. When network members are feeling pressure to innovate or move quickly in response to a customer request, for example, messages about new cost-cutting initiatives or new and exciting information systems that will allow everyone to see key financial data are uninteresting and can get lost. On the other hand, a message about how a new information system will speed up customer communication is more likely to be seen as relevant. When OT practitioners understand the network's current climate or 'conversation', they can help members determine the appropriate timing and relevance of any proposed communication.[68]

When the right people communicate a change, present and package it appropriately and distribute it in a timely fashion, the network can adopt a new idea or practice quickly. In the absence of these ingredients, there is not enough information, interest or relevance, and the change stalls.

Rely on self-organisation

Networks tend to exhibit 'self-organising' behaviour. Network members seek to reduce uncertainty in their environment, while the network as a whole drives to establish more order in how it functions. An OT practitioner can rely on this self-organising feature to refreeze change. Once change has occurred in the network, a variety of controls can be leveraged to institutionalise it. For example, communication systems can spread stories about how the change is affecting different members, diffusing throughout the network or contributing to network effectiveness. This increases the forces for stability in the network. Individual organisations can communicate their commitment to the change in an effort to lower agency forces that can contribute to instability. Each of these messages signifies constraint and shows that the different parts of the network are not independent of each other.

Apply your learning 11.4 portrays an innovative organisation that uses a proactive networking approach to help it survive in a turbulent environment.

FACEBOOK EDUCATION NETWORK?

APPLY YOUR LEARNING
11.4

Mark Zuckerberg of Facebook is one notable supporter of a software development in conjunction with a charter school network in the Silicon Valley area. Zuckerberg and one of his senior managers, Chris Cox, oversaw the creation of software that schools can deploy to help children learn at their own pace.

Summit Public Schools network first approached Zuckerberg for assistance with a pilot being undertaken in-house by a school network software engineer. The software enables the creation of tailored lessons and projects in which students and teachers share a view. Teachers can also administer individualised quizzes that the software can grade and track. The program has rolled out across the United States since then, and today approximately 380 districts and charter schools are involved nationwide.

The reactions among teachers, students and parents have been mixed. While the project is adhering to US federal government guidelines for ensuring student privacy, some observers are sceptical given Facebook's centrality in the debate around

»

»

transparency and how much personal information should be available about individuals. Children are, of course, required to be fully protected. Educators point out the lack of hard proof about the extent to which technology supports improved student learning. One school in Connecticut in 2017 experienced a strong backlash from parents who became suspicious of Facebook's commercial intentions. The conflict among the parents committee and other stakeholders culminated in the superintendent closing down the program. However, this was an extreme case. Facebook owns the rights to intellectual property it contributes to Summit's original software, but it asserts that profit is not an immediate goal. Just making education better for the kids and their teachers is the starting point. And yet, any service done well is one ultimately worth paying for.

Sources: Based on V. Goel and M. Rich, 'A Facebook education initiative targets students as individuals', *New York Times*, 4 September 2015; and N. Tabor, 'Mark Zuckerberg is trying to transform education. This town fought back', *Technology*, 11 October 2018.

Critical thinking questions	
1	In what ways might Facebook be able to participate in 'managing the tipping point' of network change in this example?
2	Networks tend to exhibit 'self-organising' behaviour. To what extent is Facebook, as a business, expressing itself in alignment with the network concept?

SUMMARY

In this chapter, we presented interventions aimed at implementing competitive and collaborative strategies. Organisations are open systems that exist in environmental contexts and they must establish and maintain effective linkages with the environment to survive and prosper. Three types of environments affect organisational functioning: the general environment, the task environment and the enacted environment. Only the last environment can affect organisational choices about behaviour, but the first two impact on the consequences of those actions. Two environmental dimensions – information uncertainty and resource dependence – affect the degree to which organisations are constrained by their environments and the need to be responsive to them. For example, when information uncertainty and resource dependence are high, organisations are maximally constrained and need to be responsive to their environments.

ISC is a comprehensive intervention for responding to complex and uncertain environmental pressures. It gives equal weight to the strategic and organisational factors affecting organisation performance and effectiveness. In addition, these factors are highly integrated during the process of assessing the current strategy and organisation design, selecting the desired strategic orientation, developing a strategic change plan and implementing it.

M&As involve combining two or more organisations to achieve strategic and financial objectives. The process generally involves three phases: precombination, legal combination and operational combination. The M&A process has been dominated by financial and technical concerns, but experience and research strongly support the contribution that OT practitioners can make to M&A success.

Collaborative strategies are a form of planned change aimed at helping organisations create partnerships with other organisations to perform tasks or solve problems that are too complex and multifaceted for single organisations to carry out. Alliance interventions describe the technical and organisational issues involved when two organisations choose to work together to achieve common goals.

Network development interventions must address two types of change. First, because multiorganisational systems tend to be underorganised, the initial development of the network follows the stages of planned change relevant to underorganised systems: identification, convention, organisation and evaluation. Second, the management of change within a network must acknowledge the distributed nature of influence and adopt methods of change that rely on the law of the few, the power of context and the stickiness factor.

ACTIVITIES

REVIEW QUESTIONS

1 What is the difference between open and closed systems? (LO1)

2 What are the three types of environments to consider when designing an OT change process? Include examples. (LO1)

3 What is the difference between general and task environments? Give three examples of each. (LO1)

4 The two environmental dimensions, information uncertainty and resource dependence, can be barriers to successful change. How may they be managed? (LO1)

5 Distinguish between competitive and collaborative strategies. What type of environment would be beneficial for each? (LO2)

6 Select two of the competitive strategies. After explaining the characteristics of each, compare and contrast them. (LO2)

7 What is ISC? Explain, using current examples. (LO2)

8 Why would an organisation choose to merge rather than acquire another company? (LO3)

9 Explain the difference between mergers and acquisitions. Why is this significant when considering a change process? (LO3)

10 What are TSs? Give four current examples. (LO4)

11 What are the advantages and disadvantages of alliances? Give examples where appropriate. (LO3)

12 What would the problems be if a manager's networks change? (LO4)

13 Are networks the current fad or fashion in management theory? Why or why not? (LO4)

14 Define and describe competitive strategies. (LO2)

15 What does it mean to say that an organisation is an open system? (LO1)

EXTEND YOUR LEARNING

1   Explain the importance of the activities (uniqueness, value and difficulty to imitate) in enhancing an organisation's performance. Choose an organisation that you are familiar with and describe how these activities give it a competitive advantage. (LO2)

2   Explain the 'law of the few' as part of managing network change by incorporating examples that you know from experience or cases you've read about. (LO4)

3   You are the manager of a not-for-profit or governmental organisation. Your colleague says collaborative strategies are all you need to focus on, as competitive strategies are not important in the non-profit context. Explain whether you agree with your colleague, giving specific examples to support your view. (LO2 & 3)

Search ⊕ Me! Management

Explore **Search Me! Management** for articles relevant to this chapter. Fast and convenient, **Search Me! Management** is updated daily and provides you with 24-hour access to full text articles from hundreds of scholarly and popular journals, eBooks and newspapers, including *The Australian* and *The New York Times*. Visit http://login.cengagebrain.com and use the access code that comes with this book for 12 months access to the **Search Me! Management** database. Try searching for the following keywords:

Keywords:

• Environmental framework

• Competitive strategies

• Collaborative strategies

• Transorganisational systems (TSs)

Search tip: **Search Me! Management** contains information from both local and international sources. To get the greatest number of search results, try using both Australian and American spellings in your searches; for example, 'globalisation' and 'globalization'; 'organisation' and 'organization'.

REFERENCES

1 K. Barnes and D. Francis, 'The OD practitioner as facilitator of innovation' (paper presented at OD Network Conference, San Francisco, CA, April 2006; H-T. Tsou, C.J. Cheng and H-Y. Hsu, 'Selecting business partner for service delivery co-innovation and competitive advantage', *Management Decision*, 53 (2015): 1–45; M. Geissdoerfer, D. Vladimirova and S. Evans, 'Sustainable business model innovation: A review', *Journal of Cleaner Production*, 198 (2018): 401–16.

2 R.V. Aguilera, 'An organizational approach to comparative corporate governance: costs, contingencies, and complementaries', *Organization Science*, 19 (2008): 475–92; M. Kodama, *Sustainable Growth through Strategic Innovation: Driving Congruence in Capabilities* (Northampton, MA: Edward Elgar Publishing, 2018).

3 S. Miller and A. Kirlik, 'Modeling the task environment: ACT-R and the lens model', *Proceedings of the Human Factors and Ergonomics Society 50th Annual Meeting* (University of Illinois, Aviation Human Factors Division, Savoy, Illinois, USA, 2006); A. van Mossel, F. van Rijnsoever and M. Hekkert, 'Navigators through the storm: a review of organization theories and the behavior of incumbent firms during transitions', *Environmental Innovation and Societal Transitions*, 26 (2018): 44–63.

4 S. Schick Case and T. Thatchenkery, 'Leveraging appreciative intelligence for positive enactment in times of uncertainty: a case study of a small investment firm', *American Journal of Economics and Business Administration*, 2 (2010): 147–52; R. Jing and A. Van de Ven, 'Toward a chance management view of organizational change', *Management and Organization Review*, 14:1 (2018): 161–78.

5 J. Barney, *Gaining and Sustaining Competitive Advantage* (Reading, MA: Addison-Wesley, 1996). S. Mantere, H. Schildt and J. Sillince, 'Reversal of strategic change', *Academy of Management Journal*, 55 (2012): 172–96. B. Saji, 'Strategic change initiatives in reward management in a merger – case study', *International Journal of Strategic Change Management*, 4 (2012): 139–48; A. Simon, C. Bartle, G. Stockport, B. Smith, J.E. Klobas and A. Sohal, 'Business leaders' views on the importance of strategic and dynamic capabilities for successful financial and non-financial business performance', *International Journal of Productivity and Performance Management*, 64 (2015): 908–31.

6 P. Saviotti and J. Metcalfe, *Evolutionary Theories of Economic and Technological Change: Present Status and Future Prospects* (New York: Routledge, 2018).

7 S. Flumerfelt, 'Leveraging system complexity for improvement', *Total Quality Management & Business Excellence* (2018), https://doi.org/10.1080/14783363.2018.1434769.

8 J. Collins, *Good to Great* (New York: HarperCollins, 2001); C. Rhoads and K. Gupta, 'Leadership lessons for the business community: strategies to maintain prosperity during a recession', *International Journal of Society Systems Science*, 4 (2012): 28–54.

9 R. Grant, *Contemporary Strategy Analysis*, 4th edn (Malden, MA: Blackwell, 2001); Barney, *Competitive Advantage*, op. cit.

10 L. Greiner and A. Bhambri, 'New CEO intervention and the dynamics of strategic change', *Strategic Management Journal*, 10 (1989): 67–87; K. Long, 'Employees first, customers second: turning conventional management upside down', *Journal of Organizational Change Management*, 24 (2011): 559–62.

11 T. Galpin and D. Robinson, 'Merger integration: the ultimate change management challenge', *Mergers and Acquisitions*, 31 (1997): 24–9.

12 M. Marks and P. Mirvis, *Joining Forces: Making One Plus One Equal Three in Mergers, Acquisitions, and Alliances* (San Francisco: Jossey-Bass, 1998); S. Rezvani, G. Dehkordi and A. Shamsollahi, 'Managing strategic change for organisations', *International Journal of Academic Research in Economics and Management Sciences*, 1 (2012): 112–21; A. Bansal, 'Understanding the integration mechanisms practiced during organizational change: evidence from five M&A transactions', *Journal of Organizational Change Management*, 28 (2015): 1–31.

13 G. Dixon, 'Merger and acquisition activity in Canada, world continues to decline in 2002', *The Canadian Press* (6 January 2003); A. Schmid, C. Sánchez and S. Goldberg, 'M&A today: great challenges, but great opportunities', *The Journal of Corporate Accounting and Finance*, 23 (2012): 3–8.

14 A variety of studies have questioned whether M&A activity actually generates benefits to the organisation or its shareholders, including M. Porter, 'From competitive advantage to corporate strategy', *Harvard Business Review* (May–June 1978): 43–59; 'Merger integration problems', *Leadership and Organization Development Journal*, 19 (1998): 59–60; 'Why good deals miss the bull's-eye: slow integration, poor communication torpedo prospects for creating value', *Mergers and Acquisitions*, 33 (1999): 5; Z. Rozen-Bakher, 'Comparison of merger and acquisition (M&A) success in horizontal, vertical and conglomerate M&As: industry sector vs. services sector', *The Service Industries Journal*, 38: 7-8 (2018): 492–518.

15 Zweig et al., 'Case against mergers', op. cit.; S. Munjal and V. Pereira, 'Opportunities and challenges for multiple-embeddedness through mergers and acquisitions in emerging economies', *Journal of Organizational Change Management*, 28 (2015): 817–31.

16 Marks and Mirvis, *Joining Forces*, op. cit.; R. Ashkenas, L. DeMonaco and S. Francis, 'Making the deal real: how GE capital integrates acquisitions', *Harvard Business Review* (January–February 1998); B. Brunsman, S. Sanderson and M. Van de Voorde, 'How to achieve value behind the deal during merger integration', *Oil and Gas Journal*, 96 (1998): 21–30; A. Fisher, 'How to make a merger work', *Fortune*

(24 January 1994): 66–70; K. Kostuch, R. Malchione and I. Marten, 'Post-merger integration: creating or destroying value?', *Corporate Board*, 19 (1998): 7–11; A. Kruse, 'Merging cultures: how OD adds value in mergers and acquisitions' (paper presented to the OD Network meeting, San Diego, CA, October 1999); M. Sirower, 'Constructing a synergistic base for premier deals', *Mergers and Acquisitions*, 32 (1998): 42–50; D. Jemison and S. Sitkin, 'Corporate acquisitions: a process perspective', *Academy of Management Review*, 11 (1986): 145–63.

17 Ashkenas, DeMonaco and Francis, 'Making the deal real', op. cit.; G. Ledford, C. Siehl, M. McGrath and J. Miller, *Managing Mergers and Acquisitions* (Los Angeles: Center for Effective Organizations, University of Southern California, 1985).

18 Ledford et al., 'Managing mergers and acquisitions', op. cit.; B. Blumenthal, 'The right talent mix to make mergers work', *Mergers and Acquisitions* (September–October 1995): 26–31; A. Buono, J. Bowditch and J. Lewis, 'When cultures collide: the anatomy of a merger', *Human Relations*, 38 (1985): 477–500; D. Tipton, 'Understanding employee views regarding impending mergers to minimize integration turmoil' (unpublished master's thesis, Pepperdine University, 1998).

19 Marks and Mirvis, *Joining Forces*, op. cit.; Ashkenas, DeMonaco and Francis, 'Making the deal real', op. cit.

20 Sirower, 'Constructing a synergistic base', op. cit.; Brunsman, Sanderson and Van de Voorde, 'How to achieve value', op. cit.; M.L. Marks and P.H. Mirvis, 'Managing the precombination phase of mergers and acquisitions', in *Advances in Mergers and Acquisitions*, 14, eds C.L. Cooper and S. Finkelstein (Bingley, UK: Emerald Group Publishing, 2015): 1–15.

21 Sirower, 'Constructing a synergistic base', op. cit.

22 Ledford et al., 'Managing mergers and acquisitions', op. cit.

23 Brunsman, Sanderson and Van de Voorde, 'How to achieve value', op. cit.

24 Ashkenas, DeMonaco and Francis, 'Making the deal real', op. cit.; R. Fiorentino and S. Garzella, 'Synergy management pitfalls in mergers and acquisitions', *Management Decision*, 53 (2015): 1469–503.

25 Ashkenas, DeMonaco and Francis, 'Making the deal real', op. cit.; Brunsman, Sanderson and Van de Voorde, 'How to achieve value', op. cit.

26 D. Rottig, J. Schappert and E. Starkman, 'Successfully managing the sociocultural integration process in international acquisitions: a qualitative analysis of Canon's acquisition of Océ', *Thunderbird International Business Review*, 59 (2017): 187–208.

27 Galpin and Robinson, 'Merger integration', op. cit.

28 ibid.; N. Rani, S.S. Yadav and P.K. Jain, 'Financial performance analysis of mergers and acquisitions:

evidence from India', *International Journal of Commerce and Management*, 25 (2015): 1–42.

29 Ashkenas, DeMonaco and Francis, 'Making the deal real', op. cit.

30 Kostuch, Malchione and Marten, 'Post-merger integration', op. cit.

31 This application was developed by Michael Krup. His contribution is gratefully acknowledged.

32 H.M. Krumholz, E.H. Bradley, B.K. Nallamothu, H.H. Ting, W.B. Batchelor, E. Kline-Rogers, A.F. Stern, J.R. Byrd and J.E. Brush Jr, 'A campaign to improve the timeliness of primary percutaneous coronary intervention door-to-balloon: an alliance for quality', *JACC: Cardiovascular Interventions*, 1 (2008): 97–104.

33 S. Heil and T. Bornemann, 'Creating shareholder value via collaborative innovation: the role of industry and resource alignment in knowledge exploration', *R&D Management*, 48 (2018): 394–409.

34 Aldrich, *Organizations and Environments*, op. cit.; L. Cruz and R. Fleming, 'Partnerships: the engaged university and library publishing', *OCLC Systems and Services: International Digital Library Perspectives*, 31 (2015): 1–7.

35 J.A. Fehrer, H.Woratschek and R.J. Brodie, 'A systemic logic for platform business models', *Journal of Service Management*, 29:4 (2018): 546–68.

36 P. Kenis and D. Knoke, 'How organisational field networks shape interorganisational tie-formation rates', *Academy of Management Review*, 27 (2002): 275–93.

37 T. Cummings, 'Transorganisational development', in *Research in Organizational Behavior* 6, eds B. Staw and L. Cummings (Greenwich, CT: JAI Press, 1984): 367–422.

38 B. Gray, 'Conditions facilitating interorganisational collaboration', *Human Relations*, 38 (1985): 911–36; K. Harrigan and W. Newman, 'Bases of interorganisation co-operation: propensity, power, persistence', *Journal of Management Studies*, 27 (1990): 417–34; Cummings, 'Transorganizational development', op. cit.; L. Lad, and C. Caldwell, Collaborative standards, voluntary codes and industry self-regulation, *Journal of Corporate Citizenship* (Fall 2009): 67–80.

39 A. Arino, J. de la Torre and P. Ring, 'Relational quality: managing trust in corporate alliances', *California Management Review*, 44 (2001): 109–31; M. Hitt, R. Ireland and R. Hoskisson, *Strategic Management* (Cincinnati, OH: South-Western College Publishing, 1999).

40 Bamford, Gomes-Casseres and Robinson, *Mastering Alliance Strategy*, op. cit.

41 Collins, *Good to Great*, op. cit.

42 Gomes-Casseres, 'Managing international alliances', op. cit.; J. Child and D. Faulkner, *Strategies of Cooperation: Managing Alliances,*

Networks, and Joint Ventures (New York: Oxford University Press, 1998); J. Bleijerveld, D.D. Gremler and J. Lemmink, 'Service alliances between unequals: the apple does not fall far from the better tree', *Journal of Service Management*, 26 (2015): 1–31.

43 Bamford, Gomes-Casseres and Robinson, *Mastering Alliance Strategy*, op. cit.

44 A. Arino, J. de la Torre and P. Ring, 'Relational quality', op. cit.

45 C. Rousseau, S. Sitkin, R. Burt and C. Camerer, 'Not so different after all: a cross-discipline view of trust', *Academy of Management Review*, 23 (1998): 395.

46 M. Hutt, E. Stafford, B. Walker and P. Reingen, 'Case study defining the social network of a strategic alliance', *Sloan Management Review*, Winter (2000): 51–62; H-T. Tsou, C. Cheng, H-Y. Hsu, 'Selecting business partner for service delivery co-innovation and competitive advantage', *Management Decision*, 53 (2015): 1–45.

47 Marks and Mirvis, *Joining Forces*, op. cit.; Child and Faulkner, *Strategies of Cooperation*, op. cit.

48 K. McQuade and B. Gomes-Casseres, *Xerox and Fuji-Xerox*, 9-391-156 (Boston: Harvard Business School, 1991).

49 M. Sartas, M. Schut, F. Hermans, P. van Asten and C. Leeuwis, 'Effects of multi-stakeholder platforms on multi-stakeholder innovation networks: implications for research for development interventions targeting innovations at scale', *PLoS ONE*, 13:6 (2018): e0197993, https://doi.org/10.1371/journal.pone.0197993.

50 D. Watts, *Six Degrees* (New York: WW Norton and Co., 2003); R. Beckett and M. Jones, 'Collaborative network success and the variable nature of trust', *Production Planning and Control: The Management of Operations*, 23 (2012): 240–51.

51 S. Strogatz, 'Exploring complex networks', *Nature*, 410 (March 2001): 268–76; E. Cameron and M. Green, *Making Sense of Change Management: A Complete Guide to the Models, Tools, and Techniques of Organizational Change* (London: Kogan Page, 2012).

52 P. Berthon, L. Pitt, D. Nel, E. Salehi-Sangari and A. Engstrom, 'The biotechnology and marketing interface: functional integration using mechanistic and holographic responses to environmental turbulence', *Journal of Commercial Biotechnology*, 14 (July 2008): 213–24; A.B. O'Neill and R. Bent, 'The advantages of a transorganisational approach for developing senior executives', *Journal of Management Development*, 34 (2015): 621–31.

53 Cummings, 'Transorganizational development', op. cit.; C. Raben, 'Building strategic partnerships: creating and managing effective joint ventures', in *Organizational Architecture*, eds Nadler et al. (San Francisco: Jossey-Bass, 1992):

81–109; B. Gray, *Collaborating: Finding Common Ground for Multiparty Problems* (San Francisco: Jossey-Bass, 1989); Harrigan and Newman, 'Bases of interorganisation cooperation', op. cit.; P. Lorange and J. Roos, 'Analytical steps in the formation of strategic alliances', *Journal of Organizational Change Management*, 4 (1991): 60–72; B. Gomes-Casseres, 'Managing international alliances', op. cit.

54 D. Boje, *Towards a Theory and Praxis of Transorganizational Development: Stakeholder Networks and Their Habitats* (Los Angeles: Behavioral and Organizational Science Study Center, Graduate School of Management, University of California, 1982); B. Gricar, 'The legitimacy of consultants and stakeholders in interorganizational problems' (paper presented at annual meeting of the Academy of Management, San Diego, CA, August 1981); T. Williams, 'The search conference in active adaptive planning', *Journal of Applied Behavioral Science*, 16 (1980): 470–83; B. Gray and T. Hay, 'Political limits to interorganisational consensus and change', *Journal of Applied Behavioral Science*, 22 (1986): 95–112.

55 Cummings, 'Transorganizational development', op. cit.

56 E. Trist, *Referent* organizations and the development of interorganizational domains (paper presented at annual meeting of the Academy of Management, Atlanta, August 1979).

57 Cummings, 'Transorganizational development', op. cit.

58 ibid.

59 Raben, 'Building strategic partnerships', op. cit.; C. Baldwin and K. Clark, 'Managing in an age of modularity', in *Managing in the Modular Age*, eds R. Garud, A. Kumaraswamy and R. Langlois (Malden, MA: Blackwell Publishing Ltd, 2003): 149–60.

60 P. Anderson, 'Complexity theory and organization science', *Organization Science*, 10 (1999): 216–32.

61 H. Simon, 'The architecture of complexity', in *Managing in the Modular Age*, eds R. Garud, A. Kumaraswamy and R. Langlois (Malden, MA: Blackwell Publishing Ltd, 2003): 15–37.

62 Senge, *The Fifth Discipline*, op. cit.; B. Lichtenstein, 'Emergence as a process of self-organizing: new assumptions and insights from the study of non-linear dynamic systems', *Journal of Organizational Change Management*, 13 (2000): 526–46.

63 Senge, *The Fifth Discipline*, op. cit.

64 Watts, *Six Degrees*, op. cit.

65 P. Monge and N. Contractor, *Theories of Communication Networks* (New York: Oxford University Press, 2003); E. Forsberg, 'Applying instruments for regional innovation – generating projects or legitimacy?', *International Journal of Innovation and Regional Development*, 4 (2012): 430–45; E. Noy and A. Luski, 'The multidisciplinary nature of business strategy: suggesting a rhizome

paradigm', *The Electronic Journal of Business Research Methods*, 10 (2012): 22–33; S. Prakash, G. Soni and A. Rathore, 'A grey based approach for assessment of risk associated with facility location in global supply chain', *Grey Systems: Theory and Application*, 5 (2015): 1–23.

66 This section relies on information in M. Gladwell, *The Tipping Point* (Boston: Little, Brown, 2000).

67 B. Gricar and D. Brown, 'Conflict, power, and organisation in a changing community', *Human Relations*, 34 (1981): 877–93.

68 S.K. Aros and D.E. Gibbons, 'Exploring communication media options in an inter-organizational disaster response coordination network using agent-based simulation', *European Journal of Operational Research*, 269:2 (2018): 451–65.

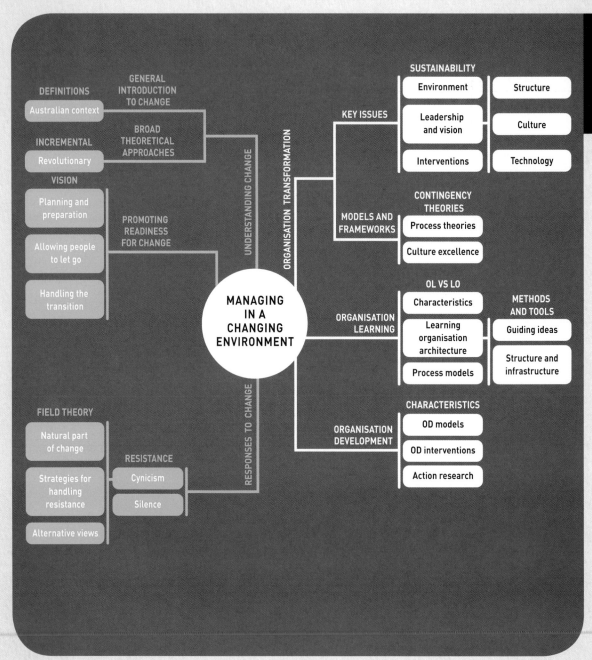

DEFINITIONS
Australian context

GENERAL
INTRODUCTION
TO CHANGE

INCREMENTAL
Revolutionary

BROAD
THEORETICAL
APPROACHES

VISION
Planning and
preparation

Allowing people
to let go

Handling the
transition

PROMOTING
READINESS
FOR CHANGE

UNDERSTANDING CHANGE

ORGANISATION TRANSFORMATION

MANAGING
IN A
CHANGING
ENVIRONMENT

KEY ISSUES

SUSTAINABILITY
Environment

Leadership
and vision

Interventions

Structure

Culture

Technology

MODELS AND
FRAMEWORKS

CONTINGENCY
THEORIES
Process theories

Culture excellence

ORGANISATION
LEARNING

OL VS LO
Characteristics

Learning
organisation
architecture

Process models

METHODS
AND TOOLS
Guiding ideas

Structure and
infrastructure

RESPONSES TO CHANGE

ORGANISATION
DEVELOPMENT

CHARACTERISTICS
OD models

OD interventions

Action research

FIELD THEORY
Natural part
of change

Strategies for
handling
resistance

Alternative views

RESISTANCE
Cynicism

Silence

Source: Adapted from D. Waddell, *E-Business in Australia: Concepts and Cases*, Pearson Education Australia, 2002.

PART 5

THE FUTURE OF CHANGE MANAGEMENT

It is evident that organisation transformation (OT), change management and organisation development (OD) are difficult to keep separate. We have created the delineation conceptually in the book to assist sequencing and clarity but, as our mapping indicates, there is often overlap.

Parts 4 and 5 encompass most trends and strategies for future scenarios, but focusing on OD. In addition, the main concepts and themes integrate within the two parts but also extend into each of Parts 1, 2 and 3.

THEME OR CONCEPT	CONNECTED WITH MATERIAL IN OTHER CHAPTERS
Nature of transformational change	Ch 1, 9
Integrated strategic change (ISC)	Ch 2, 5, 7, 8, 9
Culture change	Ch 4, 6, 7, 9
Global change	Ch 8, 10, 12
Competition versus collaboration	Ch 3, 10, 11
Trends in OD	Ch 1, 12, 13

It is important to note that change is not linear and certain approaches may apply to various aspects of change strategies. These may be evidenced in the integrative case studies (Part 6).

Laird Heffer

Business consultant/
Australian national radio

Source: Laird Heffer

Making change in the Australian radio industry

These days Laird Heffer is a business consultant. He's busy converting his considerable experience in business into excellent advice for up-and-coming entrepreneurs and the next generation of executive managers. With many management experiences under his belt, one particular skill set comes from the Australian national radio sector.

There was a time a few decades ago when commercial radio stations, as a matter of course, employed their own advertising sales teams to seek business from clients in their own geographic area. Often a single radio station would be owned by a large affiliated network, in which case it would engage a commission sales organisation owned by the network to represent the station with business clients in other parts of the country, especially capital city markets, from which additional advertising revenue could derive. The station's airtime would be sold to businesses and their advertising agencies, with 10 per cent commission paid to the advertising agency and 10 per cent to the commission sales organisation, both paid by the station. In practice what occurred was that a Sydney station that was part of an affiliation would use a national representation company in other capital cities, but employ its own sales team in Sydney. If the station was not a network affiliate, it might employ an independent sales company in other markets.

Embedded in the radio industry at the time, Laird identified a difficulty with using independent representatives, being that they often represented other media outlets, for instance, in newspaper and television. This made them essentially order takers rather than proactive representatives selling the benefits of the radio station to an advertiser. Furthermore, each representation company generally represented one radio station from each market. There were examples, therefore, of one city having multiple radio stations each employing separate representative companies that wound up selling against each other when an advertiser wanted to use radio in that city.

Laird's opportunity to create change emerged in 1988 when he was General Manager of 3KZ in Melbourne. This station was part of an affiliated network (including 2WS in Sydney), which had its own sales representation company, Wesgo National Sales, with bases in Melbourne and Sydney. When Wesgo National Sales began experiencing financial difficulty, Laird was offered the position of Executive Director in order to turn the sales operation around. Upon accepting the challenge, he worked out exactly what was going on at Wesgo National Sales. Operating margins were too small, regional stations in the network were not utilised effectively enough, the business model and the current Sydney manager were overdue for change, and the selling strategy was reactive instead of proactive. Further, the name Wesgo National Sales did not reflect the company's activities and it did not have a unique selling proposition, despite being the fourth biggest radio representative company in Australia.

Laird credits a few key things for creating the changes needed at Wesgo National Sales: a change of Sydney manager; a comprehensive analysis of strengths, weaknesses, opportunities and threats (SWOT); a business life cycle analysis; a redeveloped business plan; and a revised marketing approach. These fundamental initiatives were backed up with a couple of transformational ideas. One was the formulation of multi-station representation in a market, which removed the fight against other stations in the market and the endemic rate cutting. They could now sell a marketplace to an advertiser and determine advertising rates that in turn increased a radio station's yield. Such a change required Laird to develop communication strategies to convince the Board of both the parent company, Wesgo, and Wesgo National Sales, and their staff, the station owners and managers, and advertisers and their advertising agencies. The second big transformation was the introduction of an increased commission level for achieving a station's budget, which enabled Laird to provide incentives for the sales team.

With these big suggestions adopted, some other changes were implemented to ensure the new direction stayed in place. The name of the business was altered to reflect what it did – Radio Airtime Sales. With a new unique selling proposition and positioning statement, Radio Airtime Sales developed affiliate relationships with independent national sales companies in Brisbane, Adelaide and Perth to establish true national representation. Radio Airtime Sales was profitable after four months and became a benchmark for the industry. Reflecting on his profile and experiences in the Australian radio industry, and the new national reach of his organisation in particular, Laird observes that most of his staff were supportive of the changes being proposed. The hardest part of the change process was persuading station managers to accept the additional commission levels, as these would affect their profit in the short term. Of course, the longer-term rise in profitability was the vision that he was ultimately able to sell. Laird's legacy in improved performance and profitability for Radio Airtime Sales remains, even though the radio and broader media landscape have continued to transform.

12

ORGANISATION DEVELOPMENT FOR ECONOMIC, ECOLOGICAL AND SOCIAL OUTCOMES

LEARNING
OUTCOMES

After studying this chapter, you should be able to:

1 Describe organisation development (OD) interventions that help organisations balance economic, social and environmental objectives.

2 Describe sustainable management organisations (SMOs) and how OD can assist in their design and development.

3 Describe global social change organisations.

4 Explain how to adopt OD practices to develop global social change organisations.

5 Discuss the implications of adopting OD to global social change organisations.

6 Explain the role of change agents.

KEY TERMS	Sustainable effectiveness	Dynamic capability
	Sustainable management organisation (SMO)	Global social change organisation (GSCO)
	Corporate social responsibility (CSR)	Non-government organisation (NGO)

Sustainable effectiveness: the ability to reconfigure the organisation on an ongoing basis in order to deal with a rapidly changing environment.

Sustainable management organisation (SMO): a company that incorporates socially and environmentally responsible decision making into the planning, organisation and implementation of business strategies.

This chapter describes two relatively new interventions in OD aimed at enabling organisations to pursue **sustainable effectiveness**.[1] They are still being developed and refined but are intended for the growing number of organisations seeking balance in the achievement of economic, social and environmental outcomes.

The first intervention – **sustainable management organisations (SMOs)** – proposes that the central purpose of human systems should be *sustainable effectiveness*. These organisations are built to change and adapt in the service of positive economic, social and environmental results. This intervention describes the elements of a sustainable strategy and provides design and implementation guidelines for building these capabilities into the structures, processes and behaviours of the organisation.

Global social change organisations (GSCOs) engage in activities that give social and environmental outcomes relatively higher priority over economically oriented results. OD practitioners bring their processes and frameworks to facilitate the development of evolving countries, to change the practices of for-profit entities, to provide a voice to under-represented social classes and environmental issues, and to bridge the gap between cultures facing similar social issues. The application of planned change processes in these settings requires a new set of OD practitioner skills.

SUSTAINABLE MANAGEMENT ORGANISATIONS

A recent, global survey found that 90 per cent of executives believe sustainability issues are critical to the future success of their firms, but only 60 per cent have a sustainability strategy.[2] However, there is also clear evidence that both organisations and investors are acting proactively on this subject.[3] Sustainability initiatives focus on the environmental impact of business operations, including travel reductions, energy management, more environmentally sensitive product packaging, and recycling programs. **Corporate social responsibility (CSR)** programs also are increasingly common. More and more, however, firms are recognising that these positive actions are relatively short sighted; they are taking bigger steps to build financial, social and environmental performance into their organisation.[4] Loblaws, Canada's

Corporate social responsibility (CSR): a type of internationally private business self-regulation.

largest grocery chain, not only has packaging initiatives and energy-saving programs, but also has developing policies, including a sustainable seafood policy, that extend their organisation into supply chain relationships, coordinate with environmentally concerned non-government organisations (NGOs), educate consumers and contribute to financial performance.[5]

A variety of OD-related approaches that promote sustainability are being developed, including the Coalition for Environmentally Responsible Economies principles, the Natural Step, ISO 14000 and natural and climate capitalism.[6] These frameworks represent opportunities to make sustainability, especially ecological sustainability, a more deliberate and intentional value of OD. The SMO intervention asks a fundamentally different question about how to develop organisations compared to the strategic change interventions in Chapter 8. Those change programs asked, how can we develop organisations to improve their economic effectiveness – domestically or globally? SMO interventions ask, how can we develop organisations to achieve sustainable effectiveness? Based on action research at the University of Southern California's Center for Effective Organizations and an international collaborative research program, the features and processes for creating SMOs are emerging.[7]

SMOs are designed to achieve sustainable effectiveness. They can perform in three areas – people, planet and profit – and are agile enough to remain effective over time. This capability follows closely from the United Nations World Commission on Environment and

Development's description of sustainability: 'meeting the needs of the present without compromising the ability of future generations to meet their own needs'.[8] There are two important implications of this definition:

→ First, the organisation should generate sustainable outcomes. This means achieving a triple-bottom-line objective – positive economic, social and ecological results.[9] The organisation must be clear about its purpose and consider the needs of all stakeholders – shareholders, customers, employees, business partners, governments, the ecology, local communities and the public. The triple-bottom-line objective is also a normative value that guides how organisations should go about minimising harm or maximising benefits through their decisions and actions. This value is manifest in the day-to-day decisions that give social and ecological outcomes equal standing with economic concerns. SMOs are designed to do well in all three of these areas.

→ Second, SMOs should be able to sustain these outcomes over time. They must be adaptable, innovative and agile. Traditional organisations equate stability and reliability with effectiveness[10] and, in a world that is changing rapidly, they often find it difficult to maintain adequate levels of performance. SMOs assume that little about their environment will be stable even in the midterm. They are committed to having execution, innovation and implementation capabilities that support change.

DESIGN GUIDELINES

Consistent with the definition of sustainable effectiveness, the design of SMOs follows broad guidelines that are still being developed and refined. These guides have to do with setting strategies that support sustainability, determining sustainable objectives, establishing an organisation identity that is sustainability-friendly and creating an agile organisation.

Strategies that support sustainable effectiveness

Sustainable effectiveness – being effective along financial, social and environmental dimensions over a long period of time – requires an appropriately defined strategic intent.[11] As described in Chapter 8, a strategic intent consists of resource allocations that reflect choices of breadth, aggressiveness and differentiation. Each of these dimensions can support sustainable effectiveness.

→ *Breadth.* All things being equal, participation in multiple countries, markets, technologies or products and services increases an organisation's carbon footprint and social impact. The complexity of a broad strategy makes it difficult to understand the impact of the organisation on ecological and social outcomes. Over the years, Starbucks' scope of domestic and international operations, its product mix and ancillary services (for example, music, internet hot spots, food) has broadened dramatically. As it grew, the complexity of its operations required responses in its fair trade, water conservation, energy and recycling policies and systems to maintain an appropriate balance. On the other hand, some breadth and diversification makes it easier to make strategic changes that ensure reasonable profits over a long time frame. SMOs think hard about this balance.

→ *Aggressiveness.* In fast-changing markets, there are many appropriate opportunities to pursue objectives aggressively, but in general SMOs are wary of too much aggressiveness too often. While SMOs are effective competitors, their growth objectives are reasonable and reasoned. Tartan Yachts, a high-quality manufacturer of yachts, faced this dilemma in the early 2000s. Its success resulted in more orders than its single plant could produce in a timely fashion, and the growing overall economy provided a tempting opportunity to support the increased demand with increased production capacity. In the end, Tartan Yachts decided not to increase capacity. The organisation realised that a key differentiator was the special relationships it had built with customers and that quality was partly a function of keeping capacity sized appropriately. The wisdom of its conservative growth approach paid off handsomely during the 2008–10 economic downturn. Tartan Yachts did not have to go through the painful and disruptive downsizing that many of its competitors did, and it maintained its reputation for quality.

→ *Differentiation.* Understanding why customers make purchasing decisions and how the organisation's product and service features align with those choices is critical to success. SMOs build features into their offerings that reflect all three outcomes. For example, Volvo recently announced that all of its cars will use electric or hybrid-based engines by 2019. Such a decision clearly reflects an intent to offer a more sustainable product line, but it does not jeopardise Volvo's traditional reputation regarding safety.

Objectives that support sustainable effectiveness

In SMOs, social and ecological outcomes have equal standing with economic results. This is easier said than done. Greenpeace revealed that Nestlé, a well-respected and responsible company, was purchasing large quantities of low-priced palm oil from firms that were destroying rainforests to build even larger palm plantations. The news that Nestlé may have favoured economic over environmental objectives damaged its reputation and provoked a boycott of its products. SMOs deliberately integrate economic, social and ecological objectives.

First, SMOs must create positive *economic* outcomes to survive. Organisations that cannot operate in a way that leads to revenues meeting or exceeding expenses cannot survive, let alone create other types of valued outcomes. The difference between SMOs and traditional organisations is how much profit they make, how they make a profit and towards what end that profit is used.

SMOs understand that maximising profit or shareholder returns is not a requirement for a public company[12] and set sustainable goals for profitability and growth. Achieving social and environmental goals requires investment dollars that are difficult to acquire under a profit maximising philosophy. Former Johnson & Johnson CEO William Weldon argued that the firm had responsibilities to patients, customers, staff and the community that may prevent it from providing the best possible return, at least in the short term. Organisations are increasingly realising that maximising profits by leveraging debt, incentivising sales forces and executives to achieve 'big hairy audacious goals' or pursuing acquisitions to 'gain important synergies' that rarely materialise is a distraction from sustainable effectiveness.

As suggested above, SMOs take a less aggressive approach to growth.[13] Business strategies, in general, try to grow the organisation along some dimension, including size, profits, revenues, market share or influence. Aggressiveness that takes advantage of a short-term market opportunity is different from aggressiveness that consistently pursues organisational growth rates that greatly exceed the rate of market growth, the market's capacity to sustain growth or the organisation's capacity to support growth.

Align Technologies, for example, is the maker of Invisalign orthodontics, a series of customised mouthpieces that achieve the same results as metallic braces without the wires. Its technology challenges existing orthodontic suppliers as well as the skill sets and status of orthodontists. For Align Technologies to be successful, it must move aggressively to establish its position and technology as the incumbents defend their franchises. Nevertheless, Align Technologies must be careful to ensure that an aggressive growth strategy does not become its corporate identity. Expecting the firm to grow at the same rates after it has established its position in the market may not be reasonable.

Reasonable and sustainable profit and growth expectations mean that SMOs may never be the best performers in their industries at any particular point in time. Setting high, difficult-to-achieve economic goals requires dedicated resources and focus that can distract employees' attention from other goals and the creation of other kinds of value. SMOs recognise that the cost of sustainable profit and growth is a lower return on immediate financial performance but a more stable, long-term profitability with the ability to pursue social and environmental objectives.

Second, SMOs create positive *ecological* outcomes. They are keenly aware of their carbon footprint and their overall contribution to the planet's ecology. SMOs accept the logic of the Natural Step; for example, that current economic models of growth cannot reconcile the increasing demand for and decreasing supply of finite and fundamental natural resources.[14] This incompatibility is a central source of SMO strategies; how the organisation generates economic and social value without compromising the natural environment differentiates SMO strategies from those of other organisations. Creating ecological value suggests that business strategies built around the productive use of natural resources can solve environmental problems at a profit.

Most organisations pursuing sustainable effectiveness start by setting an initial goal of not destroying the environment. When profit maximising and growth-oriented worldwide organisations attempt to lower costs by placing activities in geographic areas with the lowest wage rates, such as Asia, large, complex sourcing and distribution supply chains are created. By some estimates, each of the largest tanker ships used in these supply chains can emit as much as 5000 tons of sulphur a year, the equivalent of 50 million typical automobiles.[15] As regulatory changes are being sought by environmental groups, these operating costs will likely increase. Thus, when the cost of pollution is factored into the cost of manufacturing and supply chain activities, SMOs begin to rethink the low wage rate decision. Instead, they seek ways to not only lower overall costs but also to reduce environmental damage as well.

Third, SMOs create positive *social* outcomes. This goal mandates that organisations contribute to human and cultural wellbeing and recognises the role social issues play in innovation and long-term adaptability. Social value includes the way an organisation treats its workforce and the communities, cultures, governments and countries in which it operates.

Organisations without a clear perspective on social issues are vulnerable to the profit maximisation motive. McDonald's noted the growing numbers of automobiles in Beijing, the attendant increase in driving times and stresses on family life, and concluded that opening drive-thru restaurants would be a good idea. The initial drive-thru restaurant struggled because the concept was unfamiliar to the Chinese. When a customer found the drive-thru lane, they didn't understand what to do at the ordering station, didn't know they had to drive up to the next window to pay and didn't know they needed to drive to the next window to pick up their food. After they picked up their food, they usually drove to a parking space, got out of the car and went into the restaurant to have their meal. In response, McDonald's made it easier to find the drive-thru lane and trained the workers to point cars to the next window, including holding the bag of food out of the last window to encourage drivers to move forward to get their meal.

When profit maximisation overrides the creation – or even the maintenance – of social and cultural values, organisations can unwittingly contribute to cultural homogenisation. The pursuit of economic growth by McDonald's may come at the expense of Chinese behaviours and culture. Does teaching them to behave like Westerners enhance cultural diversity?

Identities that are sustainability-friendly

SMOs' long-term success derives from their organisational identity.[16] Identity represents the 'central and enduring attributes of an organization that distinguish it from other organizations' and answers the question, 'Who are we as an organization?'[17] SMO identities are closely aligned with sustainable effectiveness, with balancing economic, ecological and social outcomes.

As shown in **Figure 12.1**, identity both flows from and helps to create an organisation's culture. Identity emerges from the values in use that define an organisation's culture, and in turn identity gives meaning to culture through the stories told to members. **Figure 12.1** also suggests that identity flows from and helps to create an organisation's brand, image and reputation. Identity drives the brand promises and messages that organisations make to customers and the market. Because all organisations must compete for resources, they must proactively communicate their mission and brand – what they offer, what markets they serve and what they stand for – to the marketplace. For example, Siemens, consistently rated as one of the most sustainable global companies by *Corporate Knights* magazine, uses the media tag line 'Ingenuity for Life' to reflect its commitment to pairing technology with purpose or how products can pursue economic, social and environmental objectives.

FIGURE 12.1   THE COMPONENTS OF ORGANISATION IDENTITY

Source: Adapted from Hatch and Schultz, 2002.

However, the image and reputation that external stakeholders hold about the organisation also influence identity. Customers and other stakeholders get to experience whether the organisation generally lives up to its brand promises. Experiences using the product or service, encounters with after-sales support services, stories from the business press or websites, and other sources of information provide feedback about the alignment between message and behaviours. For example, Citibank displayed advertisements in its offices that it was proud to be a part of programs that created jobs in America – and then announced it would cut 11 000 jobs. While there may be many reasons for this apparent contradiction, the poor and public 'optics' demonstrate how difficult managing a sustainable identity can be. Over time, the organisation builds up a reputation as reliable or unreliable, aggressive and litigious or relatively passive, a defender of human rights or a polluter, or a firm that stands behind its products or avoids publicity.

An SMO's identity should meet the standard of 'sustainability friendly'. A sustainability-friendly identity embraces the continuous pursuit of financial, social and environmental values as a core part of who the organisation believes it is. Thus, environmental initiatives and CSR programs would not be 'in addition to', but rather central to strategic and operational decisions. When decisions and actions are oriented towards integrating financial, social and environmental outcomes without the use of special incentives or projects, the organisation makes important contributions to sustainable effectiveness as a matter of course. For example, Nokia and Unilever do not emphasise efforts to market and produce a particular 'sustainable' product; rather, they are developing product portfolios that are financially successful, environmentally friendly and socially beneficial.

Organisation designs that support sustainable effectiveness

The final design guideline for SMOs is the need to create an organisation that can change and adapt routinely, such as agile organisations described in Chapter 13.[18] These kinds of organisations have a **dynamic capability**[19] that enables timely and effective responses to changing environments and multiple stakeholder demands. Here we discuss how the features of agile organisations contribute to sustainable effectiveness, including work systems, structures, management processes and human resource systems.

Dynamic capability: the capability of an organisation to purposefully adapt its resource base.

→ *Work processes.* An SMO's sustainability-friendly strategy and triple-bottom-line objectives are manifest in its work systems and processes. These work processes directly account for a large percentage of the organisation's economic, social and environmental impact. To achieve current and long-term economic performance, the organisation must design two types of work: (1) core and exploitative and (2) creative and exploratory.[20]

Core work in SMOs supports the current strategic intent and must be reliable, predictable and as efficient as practicable. Since the organisation's strategic intent can be subject to change, SMO core work may never be 100 per cent efficient, but it must be reliable enough to support the differentiators, meet demand and generate profit. It must also be designed to meet social and environmental objectives. For example,

DaVita Kidney Care is the dialysis division of the Fortune 500 DaVita, Inc. Its core work – delivering dialysis treatments to patients with kidney disease – is designed primarily for clinical quality and reliability. DaVita's 'we're a community first and a company second' identity drives it to address the core work quality first because effective dialysis processes generate the best economic and social outcomes. Thus, work efficiency is not at the expense of workforce, customer or community outcomes. Work processes are designed to generate positive work experiences for organisation members and DaVita's organisation identity encourages members to build strong personal relationships with patients and the local community through its 'wall of fame'. Moreover, a well-understood continuous improvement process works to increase efficiency and reduce the negative environmental by-products of dialysis.

Creative work in SMOs is designed to generate new projects, services and other disruptive innovations; it can make the current strategic intent obsolete and is fundamentally different from core work. Creative work is temporary and iterative; it is based on initiatives and activities not jobs, driven by shared goals and performed by cross-functional teams. In addition to its core work, DaVita must also build future leaders, understand the likely changes and implications of health care reform, identify potential acquisitions or perform due diligence activities, develop new business opportunities and other nonroutine and innovative activities.

For any activity that warrants attention, DaVita leaders create teams consisting of multiple functions and often including external stakeholders, such as regulators, legislators, patients, physicians and community representatives. These teams have clear goals and appropriate decision authority. Early in the team's work, members are expected to report out frequently on progress or obstacles. This creative work system enables DaVita to develop its members, to gather and charter resources quickly and to make resources available for other projects when a project is over.

Both core and creative work involve innovation. Core work must innovate to improve efficiency and effectiveness; creative work must innovate to develop future opportunities. Moreover, to achieve social and environmental outcomes, both types of work processes must carefully consider and adapt their input and throughput processes to ensure appropriate output characteristics.

→ *Structures.* Structures focus member attention and organisation resources on the most important aspects of getting core and creative work accomplished. The unique feature of SMO structures is their external focus and 'maximum surface area'.[21] As described in Chapter 13, maximum surface area structures support core and creative work with roles that are directly connected to some aspect of the external environment. To the extent possible, every role in an SMO should be a 'boundary spanning' role.[22] Externally focused roles enable organisation members to experience what is happening in professional, business, competitive and regulatory environments as well as community and environmental sectors and bring that information into the organisation as meaningful inputs to strategy and operations.

The surface area of almost any structure can be increased. For example, IBM and Siemens are different businesses with different structures but both have good external focus and surface area. In IBM's case, a 'front–back' structure puts cross-functional solution teams into direct contact with customers, and the back-office groups must stay current in their technical expertise to support the requested solutions. Both the front and back of the organisation work to support IBM's 'smarter planet' strategic intent. At Siemens, a divisional structure focuses on vertical industries, such as health care, financial services, transportation and power solutions, among others. Each business can stay connected to its relevant market, technology and environmental issues. The divisional structure is complemented by a regionally oriented go-to-market structure. Each region stays close to local issues, whether social, economic or environmental, and can assemble solutions that best fit customer needs.

→ *Management processes.* SMOs use flexible decision making and resource allocation processes to leverage information gathered by the externally focused roles. An important feature here is transparency. In SMOs, information is transparent and moved throughout the organisation to wherever it is needed and decision-making rights are assigned to the appropriate level and role in the organisation. This ensures that the right information is available and provides a clear picture of how the organisation is performing relative to triple-bottom-line objectives. It enables organisations to make timely and relevant decisions to keep pace with changing conditions.

→ *Human resource systems.* SMOs rethink the way that people are attracted, retained, developed, motivated and led. To attract the right kind of diverse workforce for the right period of time, SMOs use multiple employment deals and offer a wide variety of work arrangements, including contract labour, outsourcing and longer-term commitments to create the ability to treat employees as individuals. Individual treatment is necessary to match the skills, motives and lifestyles of individuals with the work that needs to be done. Accenture and Deloitte have career customisation programs that attract employees who want to choose and shape their own career tracks, lifestyles, work hours and work locations. Such systems mean that not everyone in the organisation is a career employee, has job security and can expect the organisation to provide them with stable employment. While stable employment might seem like a reasonable social sustainability practice, it may not be cost effective or even desired by individuals who prefer the flexibility of contract employment.

Aligning financial and nonfinancial reward systems to support sustainable effectiveness is critical. In general, financial and nonfinancial rewards should be given, based on the individual's triple-bottom-line performance. Executives, for example, need to be rewarded and recognised for achieving reasonable profit levels, CSR targets, lower carbon footprints and healthy relationships with the communities and countries in which they operate. In many cases, it makes sense to stress group or team performance because of the interdependencies that exist in organisations committed to sustainable effectiveness. For organisation members, SMOs shift the basis of rewards from jobs to people. Members are rewarded for what they can do with regard to sustainable effectiveness, not for the particular job they perform. Because jobs and tasks are continually changing, people are motivated to learn new skills and knowledge, thus keeping pace with change and enhancing their long-term value to the organisation.

Rewards also play a role in motivating and reinforcing change in SMOs. Individual or team bonuses are tied directly to change goals, learning new things and performing new tasks well. This establishes a clear line of sight between rewards and change activities. Bonuses can include one-time rewards given at the end of a particular change effort, or rewards targeted to different phases of the change process.

Finally, development and reward systems support the importance of a shared leadership philosophy; leadership in SMOs does not rest with jobs and is not restricted to executives. Rather than relying on centralised sources of power and control, SMOs spread leadership across multiple levels of the organisation. This approach speeds decision making and response rates because those lower in the organisation need not have to wait for top-down direction. It provides leadership experience and skills to a broad array of members, thus developing a strong cadre of leadership talent. Shared leadership supports continuous change by spreading change expertise and commitment across the organisation. It increases the chances that competent leaders will be there to keep the change process moving forward.

APPLICATION STAGES

Sustainable management design principles are being implemented in a growing number of organisations. Patagonia, Tom's Shoes and Ben & Jerry's are good examples of companies that were built from the ground up using SMO principles. UPS, Unilever, Gap Inc., GE, PepsiCo and P&G are continuing long-term efforts to make sustainable management an integral part of their identities. These companies are challenging long-held assumptions and making significant changes in their strategies and organisation designs. Like other strategic change interventions, SMO applications tend to involve systemic and revolutionary change processes driven by senior executives. Because these changes tend to be radical – they generally alter every feature of the organisation's design and challenge many of its long-held assumptions – they usually begin at a quick pace and remain a change initiative that never really ends. The following SMO application stages are broadly described; as OD practitioners gain more experience with this OD intervention, we can expect more detailed knowledge of how it works and produces results.[23]

Identifying and redefining organisation identity

Probably the biggest distinction between an SMO intervention and other strategic changes is the development of a new organisation identity. Almost every change initiative must support the emergence of a sustainable effectiveness identity. Identity change is both an outcome of the transformation process and a key measure of the change's effectiveness. It indicates that the organisation is applying new strategies and organisation principles to achieving triple-bottom-line results. Once identity redefinition is under way, continuous change interventions, such as those described in Chapter 6, can facilitate the change process.

Redefining organisation identity typically starts by discovering the organisation's existing identity. This involves assessing how well the organisation's values-in-use and brand promise and reputation support sustainable effectiveness and agility. OD practitioners can help organisation members conduct a cultural diagnosis (Chapter 4) along with an analysis of the firm's brand promises and reputation in the market. Then, change processes are directed at leveraging organisation values and reputational elements that already support sustained effectiveness rather than trying to 'fix' those values and brand images that are not aligned with it.

Building capabilities

Becoming an SMO involves identifying which existing organisation capabilities support sustainable effectiveness and determining which new abilities need to be built. Most organisations do not have sufficient resources to create all the necessary capabilities at once, so tough choices need to be made. These decisions are symbolically important; they signal to employees, owners, communities and NGOs how much the organisation actually supports a sustainability-friendly identity. Two capabilities that are essential to sustainability involve multi-stakeholder decision making and change management.

SMOs need to be good at multi-stakeholder decision making and take into account diverse perspectives in making choices.[24] Organisations like Gap, Inc., GE, Social Accountability International, Loblaw, Unilever and the World Wildlife Fund are working hard to develop this capability. It may require making changes in both the organisation and its external alliances and partnerships. First, training and development interventions can help organisation members learn collaborative decision making and 'systems thinking' skills that acknowledge the interdependencies and trade-offs necessary to meet triple-bottom-line objectives. Next, decision-making processes may need to be expanded to include nontraditional stakeholders, such as community and environmentally related NGOs. Team-building processes for developing trust, exploring alternatives and integrating perspectives among diverse participants can be helpful.[25] Lastly, organisational learning interventions can help the organisation apply its new skills and decision processes. Early experiences in trying to apply multi-stakeholder decision skills and systems are likely to be awkward and inefficient.[26] Organisation learning (OL) interventions can help members learn how to improve their multi-stakeholder decision-making capabilities.

SMOs also need to develop a change capability, which involves three related activities.[27] First, change management skills can be developed widely in the organisation by hiring people with those skills and by training existing managers and employees to acquire them. Most organisation members have a good understanding of technical and operational issues but are less familiar with managing change. Second, an organisation effectiveness function can be designed with competencies in strategic planning, organisation design and change management. Some SMOs have created a centre of excellence staffed by professionals from the strategic planning and human resources functions; they provide advice and facilitation for planning and executing change in the organisation. Third, organisation members can learn how to apply their change capability by engaging in organisational changes and reflecting on that experience. This so-called 'learning by doing' is essential for building a change capability. It provides members with the hands-on experience and reflective learning necessary to hone their change skills in action. Developing these change capabilities is likely to involve a significant investment in training and development.[28]

Sequencing the changes

Repurposing boards and building capabilities to support a sustainability-friendly identity are extensive and complex changes. The transformation to an SMO has to account for this complexity to positively move the organisation's identity. This involves a particular sequence of changes, starting with work system redesign. Then the strategy needs to be clarified and the organisation redesigned to promote agility. Large-group intervention techniques, described in Chapter 9, are particularly helpful to accelerate the transformation process because they can support the organisation's development of multi-stakeholder and change capabilities.

Work systems redesign

Work is the primary driver of an organisation's carbon footprint; it directly affects the workforce's wellbeing and is most connected to the creation of economic value. Thus, focusing on work redesign first ensures that the organisation's future aspirations are aligned with its past and current behaviours. It shows concretely that the organisation's commitment to sustainability is real, not just window-dressing. In many organisations today, there is growing pressure to 'do something' about sustainability. Organisations that develop marketing campaigns proclaiming support for green issues and social concerns before thinking through how their work processes affect those outcomes run a serious risk. If intentions of sustainable effectiveness are announced too early and with too much fanfare, an organisation's reputation can be damaged if marketing promises are not backed up by tangible actions. The organisation's efforts will be seen as 'greenwashing', and its ability to change identity is set back, perhaps permanently. It may take the firm a long time to rebuild trust in corporate sustainability promises.

Clarifying the strategy

Early in the change process, the organisation needs to meet with key stakeholders to clarify goals and to explore the implications of becoming an SMO on its capabilities and resources. This can be accomplished through a series of large-group interventions with key stakeholders. Large-group interventions are well suited for this part of the SMO change process. They enable organisation members to interact with multiple stakeholders in a transparent way, to learn new ways of behaving and deciding, and to gain clarity and commitment to becoming an SMO. The first large-group intervention, typically led by the board and the executive team, is concerned with fleshing out the organisation's sustainability strategy and future state. The focus is on gaining stakeholder support, determining how the different stakeholders will work together and clarifying the organisation's vision, mission and values. Subsequent large-group interventions address the design and implementation of particular aspects of strategy and organisation design.

Building an agile design

To move further towards being an SMO, an organisation needs to build an agile organisation design (see Chapter 13) that supports and reinforces the new sustainable-friendly work processes. Agile organisation designs have a 'maximum surface area' to support an external focus, strong collaboration capabilities, flexible resource allocation systems and transparent decision-making processes. They also include a talent management system with goals, performance appraisals and rewards that promote flexibility and sustainable effectiveness outcomes. In particular, people are retained or hired for their compatibility with an SMO; they are appraised and rewarded for sustainable behaviours. Performance management interventions (Chapter 7), talent development processes (Chapter 6) and organisation design interventions (Chapter 8) can help the organisation build an agile design.

Apply your learning 12.1 reports on the formulation of 17 Sustainable Development Goals (SDGs) in 2015 at a meeting of world leaders.

APPLY YOUR LEARNING 12.1

SUSTAINABLE DEVELOPMENT IN A DEVELOPED COUNTRY

The SDGs are relevant to developed countries like Australia in two ways.

First, they represent goals and targets that can make Australia itself more prosperous, fair and sustainable. Examples include improving gender equality and reducing non-communicable diseases.

Second, they encourage actions by Australia that will contribute to global sustainable development. Examples here are more sustainable consumption and production, reduced carbon emissions, and support for overseas development.

...

Australia faces major challenges in meeting the SDGs relating to sustainable energy (goal 7), sustainable consumption and production (goal 12), and climate change (goal 13).

Among other targets, these call for a doubling in the rate of improvement in energy efficiency (goal 7.3), implementing a 10-year framework on sustainable consumption and production (goal 12.1), and halving food waste by 2030 (goal 12.3). Australian households waste about 15% of the food they purchase per year – that's an estimated 361 kg of food waste per person per year, so there is plenty of scope for improvement.

We still have a way to go to meet the goals and targets for inequality within Australia. The gender-equality goal includes a target of ensuring that women have 'full and effective participation and equal opportunities for leadership at all levels of political and economic decision-making' (goal 5.5). This has proved elusive in Australia.

And the SDGs seek to raise incomes of the bottom 40% of the population faster than the rest – the opposite of what has been happening in Australia.

Perhaps one of the most significant applications of the SDGs to Australia will be in helping reduce the gap between Indigenous and non-Indigenous Australians. A core principle underpinning the SDGs is that 'no one is left behind': the goals and targets are to be met for all income and social groups, particularly disadvantaged groups.

Indigenous Australians have been well and truly left behind on health, education and employment indicators. The SDGs provide an opportunity to redress this.

»

»

...

Over the past three years, Monash Sustainability Institute and the UN Sustainable Development Solutions Network have held a series of workshops with business, government, non-government organisations and academia to identify which goals and targets are most important to Australia.

Source: J. Thwaites and T. Kestin, 'Sustainable Development Goals: a win-win for Australia', The Conversation, 24 September 2015. https://theconversation.com/ sustainable-development-goals-a-win-win-for-australia-47263. Creative Commons licence

| Critical thinking questions | 1 | Search the internet and list the 17 goals. |
| | 2 | Which of these goals has Australia already achieved and which are most likely never to be achieved (and why)? |

GLOBAL SOCIAL CHANGE

OD applied to global social change is one of the boldest and most consequential developments in the field.[29] This form of OD is generally practised in **global social change organisations (GSCOs)**, not-for-profit and NGOs that are tightly connected to grassroots efforts to help societies and communities address such important problems as unemployment, race relations, sustainable development, homelessness, poverty, hunger, disease, water quality and conservation, and political instability. Globally, GSCOs are heavily involved in the developing nations. Examples include the World Conservation Union (IUCN), BRAC (Bangladesh Rural Advancement Committee), the Society of Entrepreneurs and Ecology (China), Oceana, the Nature Conservancy, the Mountain Forum (Peru), International Physicians for the Prevention of Nuclear War, and the Clean Air Initiative for Asian Cities (Philippines). Many practitioners who help create and develop GSCOs come from OD backgrounds and have adapted their expertise to fit highly complex, political situations. This section describes GSCOs and how OD processes can be used for global social change.

Global social change organisations (GSCOs): part of a social innovation movement to foster the emergence of a global civilisation. They address complex social problems, including overpopulation and ecological degradation.

GLOBAL SOCIAL CHANGE ORGANISATIONS

GSCOs are part of a social innovation movement to foster the emergence of a global civilisation.[30] They exist under a variety of names, including development organisations (DOs), **non-government organisations (NGOs)**, social movement organisations, international private voluntary organisations and bridging organisations. They address complex social problems, including overpopulation, ecological degradation, the increasing concentration of wealth and power, the lack of management infrastructures to facilitate growth and the lack of fundamental human rights. The early efforts of many GSCOs to raise awareness and mobilise resources towards solving these problems culminated in the United Nations' Conference on Environment and Development in Rio de Janeiro in

Non-government organisation (NGO): usually a non-profit and sometimes international organisation independent of government that is active in humanitarian, educational, health care, public policy, social, human rights, environment and other areas to effect changes according to its objectives.

June 1992, where leaders from both industrialised and less-developed countries met to discuss sustainable development.[31] Since then, a number of conferences and agreements have occurred. The most notable are the 1997 Kyoto Protocol, which attempted to gain commitment from countries around the world to reduce greenhouse gas emissions, and the Global Compact, a strategic policy initiative that asks businesses to align their operations with 10 universally accepted principles related to human rights, labour, environment and corruption. The 2015 Paris Climate Accord committed signatory governments to collectively hold global warming to less than 2 degrees Centigrade. The work of individual GSCOs can be aided or constrained by these larger, governmental accords.

GSCOs have the following characteristics:[32]

→ They assert, as their primary task, a commitment to serve as an agent of change in creating environmentally and socially sustainable world futures; their transformational missions are articulated around the real needs of people and the earth.

→ They have discovered and mobilised innovative social-organisational architectures that make possible human cooperation across previously polarising or arbitrarily constraining boundaries.

→ They hold values of empowerment, or people-centred forms of action, in the accomplishment of their global change mission, emphasising the central role of people as both means and ends in any development process.

→ They are globally and locally linked in structure, membership or partnership and thereby exist, at least in identity and practice (perhaps not yet legally), as entities beyond the nation-state.

→ They are multiorganisational and often cross-sectorial. They can be business, government or not-for-profit organisations. Indeed, many of the most significant global change entities involve multiorganisation partnerships bridging sectorial boundaries in new hybrid forms of business, government and volunteerism.

GSCOs therefore differ from traditional for-profit firms on six dimensions.[33] First, they typically advocate a mission of social change – the formation and development of better societies and communities. 'Better' typically means more just (Amnesty International, the Hunger Project, World Vision, Occupy Movement), peaceful (Peace Direct, International Physicians for the Prevention of Nuclear War) or ecologically conscious (Nature Conservancy, the Global Village of Beijing, the Mountain Forum, IUCN, World Wildlife Fund, Friends of the Earth). In effective GSCOs, these missions tend to be focused over the long term as short-term protests and lobbying efforts tend to be less effective.[34]

Second, the mission is supported by a network structure. Most GSCO activity occurs at the boundary or periphery between two or more organisations.[35] Unlike most industrial firms that focus on internal effectiveness, GSCOs are directed at changing their environmental context. For example, World Vision operates microfinance institutions in 43 countries to boost the economic status of entrepreneurs, create jobs and develop local economies.

Third, GSCOs generally have strong values and ideologies that justify and motivate organisation behaviour. These 'causes' provide intrinsic rewards to GSCO members and a blueprint for action.[36] For example, the ideological position that basic human rights include shelter has directed Habitat for Humanity to erect low-cost homes in a wide variety of underdeveloped communities.

Fourth, GSCOs interact with a broad range of external and often conflicting constituencies. To help the poor, GSCOs often must work with the rich; to save the ecology, they must work with the polluters; and to empower the masses, they must work with the powerful few. This places a great deal of pressure on GSCOs to reconcile pursuit of a noble cause with the political reality of power and wealth.[37]

Fifth, managing these diverse external constituencies often creates significant organisational conflict.[38] On the one hand, GSCOs often need to be organised into departments to serve and represent particular stakeholders; on the other, they are strongly averse to bureaucracy and desire collegial and consensus-seeking cultures. The conflicting perspectives of the stakeholders, the differentiated departments and the ideological basis of the organisation's mission can produce a contentious internal environment. For example, the International Relief and Development Agency promotes grassroots development projects in developing countries using resources donated from developed countries. As the agency grew, departments were created to represent different stakeholders: a fundraising group handled donors, a projects department worked in the local offices, a public relations department directed media exposure and a policy information department lobbied the government. Each department adapted to fit its role. Fundraisers and lobbyists dressed more formally, took more moderate political positions and used more hierarchical forms of control than did the projects departments. These differences were often interpreted in political and ideological terms, creating considerable internal conflict. OD practitioners designed a series of feedback meetings to increase the understanding and relevance of the different groups.[39] Finally, GSCO membership often is transitory. Many people are volunteers, and the extent and depth of their involvement varies over time and by issue. Turnover can be quite high.

APPLICATION STAGES

GSCOs are concerned with creating sustainable change in communities and societies. This requires a form of planned change in which the practitioner is heavily involved, many stakeholders are encouraged and expected to participate, and 'technologies of empowerment' are used. Often referred to as 'participatory action research',[40] planned change in GSCOs typically involves three types of activities: building local organisation effectiveness, creating bridges and linkages with other relevant organisations, and developing vertical linkages with policymakers.[41]

Building the local organisation

Although GSCOs are concerned primarily with changing their environments, a critical issue in development projects is recognising the potential problems inherent in the GSCO itself. Because the focus of change is their environment, members of GSCOs are often oblivious to the need for internal development.[42]

Moreover, the complex organisational arrangements of a network make planned change in GSCOs particularly challenging.

OD practitioners focus on three activities in helping GSCOs build themselves into viable organisations: using values to create the vision, recognising that internal conflict is often a function of external conditions, and understanding the problems of success.

→ *Values to create vision.* For leadership to function effectively, the broad purposes of the GSCO must be clear and closely aligned with the ideologies of its members.[43] Singleness of purpose can be gained from tapping into the compelling aspects of the values and principles that the GSCO represents. For example, ActionAid has developed a 'human rights based approach' to development that is deeply rooted in the belief that poverty is a 'consequence of the denial or violation of human rights, and the result of unequal power dynamics in the process of claiming or realizing one's rights'.[44] In its third strategic review, a wide range of stakeholders were engaged to discuss three future-oriented scenarios designed to facilitate a deeper level of strategic discussion and exploration of the organisation's mission fundamentals.

Developing a shared vision can align individual and organisational values. Because most activities occur at the boundary of the organisation, members are often spread out geographically and are not in communication with each other. A clearly crafted vision allows people in disparate regions and positions to coordinate their activities. For example, ACDI/VOCA is a 'nonprofit that means business'. The organisation provides sustainable solutions that integrate approaches from agribusiness, community and enterprise development, financial services and food security perspectives. Its vision, 'A world in which people are empowered to succeed in the global economy', helps to coordinate the work of the people throughout the organisation. 'Our mission and a vision grow out of the farmer cooperative movement in the US going back 45 years. We know something about how you bring food from the farm to the table.' As one member put it, 'I'm part of helping a small farmer in a small village somewhere in the world be able to put food on their table and send their kids to school or to buy a net to protect themselves from malaria. I don't know how that couldn't impact you.' Another staff member noted, 'It's a privilege to have a job that is making a difference, and as a mom you feel that more. When I hear a story of a woman who's saying, "I couldn't feed my children", I think, oh my goodness. And now, because they got a loan, they got their business going, and they're connected with people who wanted to buy their stuff, you can just see it in their eyes and their voices. They have hope for the future. It's a fantastic thing.'

→ *Recognising conflict.* Because of the diverse perspectives of the different stakeholders, GSCOs often face multiple conflicts. In working through them, the organisational vision can be used as an important rallying point for discovering how each person's role contributes to the GSCO's purpose. The affective component of a GSCO vision gives purpose to members' lives and work. The Occupy Movement maintained its strong commitment to participatory democracy through a variety of processes at its general assemblies, including the 'stack' and the 'progressive stack' process.[45] In the stack process, people were invited to join a queue of speakers to comment on proposals, and to ensure that minority views had a clear opportunity to be heard, the progressive stack allowed marginalised groups to speak first. Another way to manage conflict is to prevent its occurrence. At the Hunger Project, the 'committed listener' and 'breakthrough' processes give GSCO members an opportunity to seek help before conflict becomes dysfunctional. Every member of the organisation has a designated person who acts as a committed listener. When things are not going well, or someone is feeling frustrated in their ability to accomplish a goal, they can talk it out with this colleague. The role of the committed listener is to listen intently, to help the individual understand the issues, and to think about framing or approaching the problem in new ways. This new perspective is called a 'breakthrough' – a creative solution to a potentially conflictual situation.[46]

→ *Problem of success.* Finally, a GSCO's success can create a number of problems. The very accomplishment of its mission can take away its reason for existence, thus causing an identity crisis. For example, a GSCO that succeeds in creating jobs for underprivileged youth can be dissolved because its funding is redirected towards organisations that have not yet met their goals, because its goals change, or simply because it has accomplished its purpose. During these times, the vital social role that these organisations play needs to be emphasised. GSCOs often represent bridges between the powerful and powerless, between the rich and poor, and between the elite and oppressed, and as such may need to be maintained as legitimate parts of the community.

Another problem can occur when GSCO success produces additional demands for greater formalisation. New people must be hired and acculturated; greater control over income and expenditures has to be developed; new skills and behaviours have to be learned. The need for more formal systems often runs counter to ideological principles of autonomy and freedom and can produce a profound resistance to change. Employees' participation during diagnosis and implementation can help them commit to the new systems. In addition, new employment opportunities, increased job responsibilities and improved capabilities to carry out the GSCO's mission can be used to encourage commitment and reduce resistance to the changes.

Supported by sponsors in industrialised countries, the International Child Sponsorship Agency (ICSA) delivers services that enhance children's welfare in developing countries. For many years, entrepreneurial leadership in the field led to growth in the number of programs and activities that were difficult to coordinate and monitor. The organisation brought in a new 'business-oriented' CEO to improve resource and program efficiencies. While everyone agreed that better coordination was necessary, they also believed that the new CEO's implementation of new accounting and information systems was too top-down. Tensions between headquarters and the field increased and turnover among key staff members led to an OD intervention. It started with a diagnosis that showed that the focus on control and efficiency conflicted with ICSA's traditional, entrepreneurial values. Changes were implemented to increase the involvement of the field in strategic planning, to increase and clarify the decisions that could be made in the field, and to reinforce the leadership and cultural styles that best represented the vision. The changes were viewed as a rebalancing of the organisation's priorities, giving fundraising and program development relatively equal influence over strategy and operations.[47]

Creating horizontal linkages

Successful GSCOs often require a network of local organisations with similar views and objectives.[48] Such projects as creating a civil society in China, turning responsibility for maintenance and control over small irrigation systems to local water users in Indonesia or teaching leadership skills in South Africa require that multiple organisations interact. Consequently, an important planned change activity in GSCOs is creating strong horizontal linkages to organisations in the community or society where the development project is taking place. The formation of 'support' organisations – value-added agencies that provide services to NGOs for their development – are an important part of these linkages.[49] For example, CANGO, the China Association for NGOs, is a government-sponsored NGO that provides capacity-building and project-execution services to support the emergence of a civil society in China. CANGO sponsors conferences and programs where like-minded NGOs can connect with each other and support common interests. Similarly, GSCOs aimed at job development not only must recruit, train and market potential job applicants but also must develop relationships with local job providers and government authorities. The GSCO must help these organisations commit to the GSCO's vision, mobilise resources and create policies to support development efforts.

The ability of GSCOs to sustain themselves depends on establishing linkages with other organisations whose cooperation is essential to preserving and expanding their efforts. Unfortunately, members of GSCOs often view local government officials, community leaders or for-profit organisations as part of the problem. Rather than interacting with these stakeholders, GSCOs often 'protect' themselves and their ideologies from contamination by these outsiders. Planned change efforts to overcome this myopia are similar to the trans-organisational development interventions discussed in Chapter 11. GSCO members are helped to identify, convene and organise these key external organisations. For example, hurricane Katrina in 2005 devastated many of New Orleans' oldest, poorest and culturally rich neighbourhoods. The rebuilding of neighbourhoods, such as Tremé or Holycross, was usually overseen by local NGOs, such as Esplanade Ridge/Tremé Neighborhood Association or Holy Cross Neighborhood Association. These groups connected with other NGOs, local and state government departments (other than Federal Emergency Management Agency [FEMA], which had lost credibility during the initial response), funding agencies and volunteers. Local coordination of the NGO activities allowed each neighbourhood to pursue locally relevant strategies for rehabilitation, to bring the right resources to the right places and to maintain local cultural and historical traditions.[50]

Developing vertical linkages

GSCOs also must create channels of communication and influence upward to governmental and policy-level decision-making processes. These higher-level decisions often affect the creation and eventual success of GSCO activities. For example, a centralised one-party government in Mali dominated the country's educational system and neglected teachers, schools, books and materials for decades, especially in the rural areas. When a new reformist government took control, a variety of GSCOs helped to organise grassroots groups to improve the schools. Supported by the GSCOs, local parent-teacher associations (PTAs) were organised, local members were elected and the groups were given training on how to manage the school. Although there was local improvement, the overall educational system remained fragmented. In response, GSCO-organised conferences brought PTAs from different villages together for dialogue and decision making. As regional PTA federations were formed, the GSCOs provided policy analysis and advocacy training to help them speak with one voice in negotiations over policy formulation with the Ministry of Education. These collective efforts have resulted in increased attention, influence and expenditures to rural schools.[51]

The Interchurch Organization for Development Cooperation (ICCO) increased the quality of its vertical linkages by deliberately changing its organisation design. Following a process of mission, vision and strategy reflection and noting a variety of development trends, ICCO set about decentralising operations and giving more local control and decision making to a newly formed regional office. The process increased the confidence and long-term financial commitment of the Dutch Government, built a stronger internal vertical organisation and empowered the regions to develop closer ties to governments and other partners.[52] **Apply your learning 12.2** describes how social change movements evolve as a result of a political drive emanating from the community.

APPLY YOUR LEARNING **12.2**

SOCIAL CHANGE MOVEMENTS

The 21st century has seen a proliferation of new social change movements driven by grassroots community activism. On the issue of climate change, for example, scores of community-based groups have formed in Australia over the past few years to provide forums for discussion, local action and public campaigns. Behind these movements is a growing body of 'concerned citizens' united by a sense of urgency, a vision of a better world and mapping a pathway for getting there.

...

Social movements are, fundamentally, about changing people's attitudes and behaviour, and so allowing – even forcing – governments to do more.

...

For example, WiserEarth ... is an online community space connecting the people, non-profit organisations and businesses working toward a just and sustainable world. GetUp in Australia and Avaaz internationally are using new technologies to mobilise public opinion on political issues.

Source: R. Eckersley, 'Social change movements', *ECOS*, 150, Aug–Sep 2009.

Critical thinking question

1   Research 'WiserEarth' and identify the vision and functions of the social change movement.

CHANGE-AGENT ROLES AND SKILLS

Planned global social change is a relatively new application of OD. The number of practitioners is small but growing, and the skills and knowledge necessary to carry out OD in these situations are being developed. The grassroots, political and ideological natures of many GSCOs require change-agent roles and skills that are quite different from those in more formal, for-profit settings.[53] GSCO change agents typically occupy stewardship and bridging roles. The *steward* role derives from the ideological and grassroots activities associated with GSCOs. It asks the change agent to be a co-learner or co-participant in achieving global social change. This type of change is 'sustainable', or ecologically, politically, culturally and economically balanced. Change agents must, therefore, work from an explicit value base that is aligned with GSCO activities. For example, change agents are not usually asked, 'What are your credentials to carry out this project?' Instead, practitioners are asked, 'Do you share our values?' or 'What do you think of the plight of the people we are serving?' Stewardship implies an orientation towards the development of sustainable solutions to local and global problems.

The second role, *bridging*, derives from the grassroots and political activities of many GSCOs. Bridging is an appropriate title for this role because it metaphorically reflects the core activities of GSCOs and the change agents who work with them. Both are mainly concerned with connecting and integrating diverse elements of societies and communities towards sustainable change, and with transferring ideas among individuals, groups, organisations and societies.

Carrying out the steward and the bridging roles requires communication, negotiation and networking skills. Communication and negotiation skills are essential for GSCO change agents because of the asymmetrical power bases that exist in grassroots development efforts. GSCOs are relatively powerless compared with governments, wealthy upper classes and formal organisations. Given the diverse social systems involved, there often is only a loose consensus about a GSCO's objectives. Moreover, different constituencies may have different interests, and there may be histories of antagonism among groups that make promulgation of the development project difficult. The steward and the bridging roles require persuasive articulation of the GSCO's ideology and purpose at all times, under many conditions, and to everyone involved.

The change agent must also be adept at political compromise and negotiation.[54] Asymmetrical power contexts represent strong challenges for stewardship and bridging. To accomplish sustainable change, important trade-offs often are necessary. The effective change agent needs to understand the elements of the ideology that can and cannot be sacrificed and when to fight or walk away from a situation.

Networking skills represent a significant part of the action research process as applied in GSCO settings. Networking takes place at two levels. First, in the steward role, practitioners bring to the GSCO specific knowledge regarding change, design and technologies of empowerment and participation that can be used to support a mission or ideological position.[55] The participants bring local knowledge of political players, history, culture and ecology. A 'co-generative dialogue' or 'collective reflection' process emerges when these two frames of reference interact to produce new ideas, possibilities and insights.[56] When both the practitioner and the participants contribute to sustainable solutions, the stewardship role is satisfied.

Second, in the bridging role, networking skills create conditions that enable diverse stakeholders to interact and solve common problems or address common issues. Change agents must be able to find common ground so that different constituencies can work together. Networking requires the capability to tap multiple sources of information and perspective, often located in very different constituencies. Action becomes possible through these networks.

The change agent in international GSCO settings must play a variety of roles and use many skills. Clearly, stewardship and bridging roles are important in facilitating GSCO accomplishment. Other roles and skills will likely emerge over time.

SUMMARY

In this chapter, we presented two interventions designed to help organisations generate positive social, environmental and economic outcomes. These change processes are fundamentally different from other OD interventions that focus primarily on the achievement of economic objectives.

SMO interventions are intended to achieve sustainable effectiveness. Organisations must be agile enough to sustain high levels of economic, social and environmental performance. Achieving these triple-bottom-line objectives relies on design guidelines that promote capabilities in change and multi-stakeholder decision making. The organisation's strategy must be realigned and clarified to support sustainability and the work systems, structure, management and information systems, and human resource systems must be oriented appropriately.

Finally, applications of OD to global social change were discussed. Typically carried out in GSCOs, these interventions promote the establishment of a global civilisation. Strong ideological positions regarding the fair and just distribution of wealth, resources and power fuel this movement. By strengthening local organisations, building horizontal linkages with other like-minded GSCOs and developing vertical linkages with policy-making organisations, a change agent can help GSCOs become more effective and alter their external context. To support roles of stewardship and bridging, change agents need communication, negotiation and networking skills.

ACTIVITIES

REVIEW QUESTIONS

1   Describe OD interventions that help organisations balance economic, social and environmental objectives. What are the advantages and disadvantages? (L01)

2   Describe SMOs and how OD can assist in their design and development. What problems may inhibit change from being successful? (L02)

3   Describe GSCOs and how to adopt OD processes to develop them. What other considerations are important for OD to be successful? (L03)

4   How do you adopt OD to an organisation focused on global social change? (L04)

5   What implications or consequences should you consider when adopting OD strategies to an organisation focused on global social change? (L05)

EXTEND YOUR LEARNING

1   Complete an external search on similar organisations that can be described as SMOs or exhibit global social change.
    a   What are their similarities and/or differences?
    b   What problems do they face and how can these problems be overcome?
    c   Can you predict (forecast) where these organisations will be in 20 years time? (L01, 2 & 3)

Search ✦ Me! **Management**

Explore **Search Me! Management** for articles relevant to this chapter. Fast and convenient, **Search Me! management** is updated daily and provides you with 24-hour access to full text articles from hundreds of scholarly and popular journals, eBooks and newspapers, including *The Australian* and *The New York Times*. Visit http://login.cengagebrain.com and use the access code that comes with this book for 12 months access to the **Search Me! Management** database. Try searching for the following keywords:

Keywords:

- Sustainable effectiveness
- Sustainable management organisation (SMO)
- Corporate social responsibility (CSR)
- Dynamic capability
- Global social change organisation (GSCO)
- Non-government organisation (NGO)

Search tip: **Search Me! Management** contains information from both local and international sources. To get the greatest number of search results, try using both Australian and American spellings in your searches; for example, 'globalisation' and 'globalization'; 'organisation' and 'organization'.

REFERENCES

1 S. Mohrman, J. O'Toole and E. Lawler, eds, *Corporate Stewardship: Achieving Sustainable Effectiveness* (New York: Routledge, 2015); S. Mohrman and A. Shani, 'Organizing for sustainable effectiveness: taking stock and moving forward', in *Organizing for Sustainability*, vol. 1, eds. S. Mohrman and A. Shani (Bingley, UK: Emerald Group Publishing, 2011): 1–40.

2 D. Kiron, G. Unruh, N. Kruschwitz, M. Reeves, H. Rubel and A.M. zum Felde, 'Corporate sustainability at a crossroads: progress toward our common future in uncertain times', *MIT Sloan Management Review*, May 2017.

3 R. Eccles, I. Ioannou and G. Serafeim, 'The impact of corporate sustainability on organizational processes and performance', *Management Science*, 60 (2014): 2835–57; C. Bhattacharya and P. Polman, 'Sustainability lessons from the front lines', *Sloan Management Review*, 58 (2017): 71–8; M. Epstein and A. Buhovac, *Making Sustainability Work: Best Practices in Managing and Measuring Corporate Social, Environmental, and Economic Impacts* (San Francisco: Berrett-Koehler Publishers, 2014).

4 E. Lawler and C. Worley, *Management Reset* (San Francisco: Jossey-Bass, 2011); J. Ludema, C. Laszlo and K. Lynch, 'Embedding sustainability: how the field of organization development and change can help companies harness the next big competitive advantage', in *Research in*

Organizational Change and Development, vol. 20, eds A. Shani, W. Pasmore and R. Woodman (Bingley, UK: Emerald Group Publishing, 2012): 265–99.

5 B. Steele and A. Feyerherm, 'Loblaw sustainable seafood: transforming the seafood supply chain through network development and collaboration', in *Organizing for Sustainable Effectiveness: Building Networks and Partnerships*, vol. 3, eds. C. Worley and P. Mirvis (Bingley: Emerald Group Publishing, 2013): 101–32.

6 P. Hawken, A. Lovins and L. Lovins, *Natural Capitalism: The Next Industrial Revolution* (New York: Earthscan, 2010); L. Lovins and B. Cohen, *Climate Capitalism* (New York: Farrar, Straus and Giroux, 2011); information on the Natural Step can be found at http://www.thenaturalstep.org and in B. Nattrass and M. Altomare, *The Natural Step for Business: Wealth, Ecology, and the Evolutionary Corporation* (Gabriola Island, British Columbia: New Society Publishers, 1999); information on CERES principles can be found at http://www.ceres.org.

7 Lawler and Worley, *Management Reset*, op. cit.; E. Lawler and C. Worley, *Built to Change: How to Achieve Sustained Organizational Effectiveness* (San Francisco: Jossey-Bass, 2006); C. Worley and S. Mohrman, 'Designing for sustainable effectiveness: the role of embeddedness and

agility', in *Corporate Stewardship: Achieving Sustainable Effectiveness*, eds. S. Mohrman, J. O'Toole and E. Lawler (New York: Routledge, 2015): 112–33; S. Mohrman, A. Shani and C. Worley (series editors), *Organizing for Sustainable Effectiveness*, vols 1–5 (Bingley, UK: Emerald Publishing, 2011, 2012, 2013, 2014, 2016).

8 G. Brundtland, ed., *Our Common Future: The World Commission on Environment and Development* (Oxford: Oxford University Press, 1987).

9 J. Elkington, 'Towards the sustainable corporation: win-win-win business strategies for sustainable development', *California Management Review*, 36:2 (1994): 90–100.

10 D. Katz and R. Kahn, *The Social Psychology of Organizations* (San Francisco: Wiley, 1978); M. Weber, *The Theory of Social and Economic Organization*, trans. A.M. Henderson and T. Parsons (London: Collier Macmillan Publishers, 1947).

11 A. Werbach, *Strategy for Sustainability: A Business Manifesto* (Cambridge: Harvard Business Review Press, 2009).

12 L. Stout, 'Corporations don't have to maximize profits', *The New York Times* (16 April 2015).

13 A. De Geus, *The Living Company* (Cambridge, MA: Harvard Business School Press, 1997).

14 H. Bradbury and J. Clair, 'Promoting sustainable organizations with Sweden's Natural Step', *Academy of Management Executive*, 13 (1999): 63–74.

15 Data last accessed from http://www.viewzone.com/sixteenships.html on 22 July 2017; additional data in J. Vidal, 'True scale of CO2 emissions from shipping revealed', *The Guardian* (13 February 2008).

16 M. Hatch and S. Majken, 'The dynamics of organizational identity', *Human Relations*, 55 (2002): 989–1018; J. Dutton and J. Dukerich, 'Keeping an eye on the mirror: image and identity in organizational adaptation', *Academy of Management Journal*, 34 (1991): 517–54; D. Whetten, 'Albert and Whetten revisited: strengthening the concept of organizational identity', *Journal of Management Inquiry*, 15 (2006): 219–34.

17 D. Whetten, 'Albert and Whetten revisited: strengthening the concept of organizational identity', Journal of Management Inquiry, 15 (2006): 219–34.

18 C. Worley, T. Williams and E. Lawler, *The Agility Factor* (San Francisco: Jossey-Bass, 2014).

19 I. Barreto, 'Dynamic capabilities: a review of past research and an agenda for the future', *Journal of Management*, 36 (2010): 256–80; S. Winter, 'Understanding dynamic capabilities', *Strategic Management Journal*, 24 (2003): 991–6.

20 C. O'Reilly and M. Tushman, *Lead and Disrupt: How to Solve the Innovator's Dilemma* (Palo Alto: Stanford University Press, 2016).

21 Lawler and Worley, *Built to Change*, op. cit.

22 H. Aldrich and D. Herker, 'Boundary spanning roles and organization structure', *Academy of Management Review*, 2 (1977): 217–30.

23 S. Benn, D. Dunphy and A. Griffiths, *Organizational Change for Corporate Sustainability* (New York: Routledge, 2014).

24 C. Worley, A. Feyerherm and D. Knudsen, 'Building a collaboration capability for sustainability', *Organizational Dynamics*, 39 (2010): 325–34.

25 ibid.

26 P. Kale and H. Singh, 'Managing strategic alliances: what do we know now and where do we go from here?', *Academy of Management Perspectives* (August 2009): 45–62.

27 C. Worley and E. Lawler, 'Building a change capability at Capital One Financial', *Organizational Dynamics*, 38 (2009): 245–51.

28 A. Hoffman, 'Climate change as a cultural and behavioral issue: addressing barriers and implementing solutions', *Organizational Dynamics*, 39 (2010): 295–305; Benn, Dunphy and Griffiths, *Organizational Change for Corporate Sustainability*, op. cit.

29 P. Gready, 'Organizational theories of change in the era of organizational cosmopolitanism: lessons from ActionAid's human rights-based approach', *Third World Quarterly*, 34 (2013): 1339–60; N. Banks and D. Hulme, *The Role of NGOs and Civil Society in Development and Poverty Reduction* (Manchester, UK: Brooks World Poverty Institute, 2012); P. Ronalds, *The Change Imperative: Creating the Next Generation NGO* (Sterling, VA: Kumarian Press, 2010); P. McMichael, *Development and Social Change: A Global Perspective* (Thousand Oaks, CA: Pine Forge Press, 2007); L. Brown and J. Covey, 'Development organizations and organization development: toward an expanded paradigm for organization development', in *Research in Organizational Change and Development*, vol. 1, eds R. Woodman and W. Pasmore (Greenwich, CT: JAI Press, 1987): 59–88.

30 J. Ehrenberg, *Civil Society*, 2nd edn (New York: NYU Press, 2017); Banks and Hulme, *The Role of NGOs*, op. cit.; P. Freire, *Pedagogy of the Oppressed* (Harmondsworth, England: Penguin, 1972); D. Cooperrider and W. Pasmore, 'Global social change: a new agenda for social science', *Human Relations*, 44 (1991): 1037–55; E. Boulding, 'The old and new transnationalism: an evolutionary perspective', *Human Relations*, 44 (1991): 789–805; P. Johnson and D. Cooperrider, 'Finding a path with a heart: global social change organizations and their challenge for the field of organizational development', in *Research in Organizational Change and Development*, vol. 5, eds. R. Woodman and W. Pasmore (Greenwich, CT: JAI Press, 1991): 223–84.

31 E. Smith, 'Growth vs. environment', *BusinessWeek*, 11 May 1992: 66–75.

32 D. Cooperrider and J. Dutton, eds., *Organizational Dimensions of Global Change* (Newbury Park, CA: Sage Publications, 1999), 12.

33 L. Brown, 'Bridging organizations and sustainable development', *Human Relations*, 44 (1991): 807–31; Johnson and Cooperrider, 'Finding a path', op. cit.; L.D. Brown, M. Leach and J. Covey, 'Organization development for social change', in *Handbook of Organization Development*, ed. T. Cummings (Thousand Oaks, CA: Sage Publications, 2008).

34 K. Rietig, 'The power of strategy: environmental NGO influence in international climate negotiations', *Global Governance*, 22 (2016): 269–88.

35 C. Worley and P. Mirvis, eds, *Organizing for Sustainable Effectiveness: Building Networks and Partnerships*, vol. 3 (Bingley, UK: Emerald Group Publishing, 2013).

36 D. Lewis, *Non-governmental Organizations, Management and Development* (New York: Routledge, 2014).

37 Banks and Hulme, *The Role of NGOs*, op. cit.

38 B. Jones, 'Looking good: mediatisation and international NGOs', *European Journal of Development Research*, 29 (2017): 176–91.

39 Brown and Covey, 'Development organizations', op. cit.; Brown, Leach and Covey, 'Organization development for social change', op. cit.

40 P. Reason and H. Bradbury, eds, *The SAGE Handbook of Action Research*, 2nd edn (Newbury Park, CA: Sage Publications, 2007).

41 U. Stephan, M. Patterson, C. Kelly and J. Mair, 'Organizations driving positive social change: a review and an integrative framework of change processes', *Journal of Management*, 4 (2016): 1250–81.

42 Gready, 'Organizational theories of change in the era of organizational cosmopolitanism', op. cit.: 1339.

43 G. Mitchell, 'The attributes of effective NGOs and the leadership values associated with a reputation for organizational effectiveness', *Nonprofit Management and Leadership*, 26 (2015): 39–57.

44 P. Gready, 'Organizational theories of change in the era of organizational cosmopolitanism', op. cit.: 1352.

45 A. Burtch, 'My hope for #occupy wall street', 4 October 2011, http://feministing.com/2011/10/04/guestpost-my-hope-for-occupy-wall-street, accessed 25 July 2017.

46 Johnson and Cooperrider, 'Finding a path with a heart', op. cit.: 237.

47 Brown, Leach and Covey, 'Organization development for social change', op. cit.

48 Mitchell, 'The attributes of effective NGOs', op. cit.

49 L.D. Brown and A. Kalegaonkar, 'Support organizations and the evolution of the NGO sector', *Nonprofit and Voluntary Sector Quarterly*, 31 (2002): 231–58.

50 R. Beech and B. Allen, *Dynamics of Disaster* (New York: Routledge, 2011).

51 Brown, Leach and Covey, 'Organization development for social change', op. cit.

52 W. Elbers and L. Schulpen, 'Reinventing international development NGOs: The case of ICCO', *The European Journal of Development Research*, 27 (2015): 1–18.

53 D. Bornstein, *How to Change the World: Social Entrepreneurs and the Power of New Ideas* (New York: Oxford, 2004); L.D. Brown and J.G. Covey, 'Action research for grassroots development: collective reflection and development NGOs in Asia' (presentation at the Academy of Management, Miami, 1990).

54 R. Saner and L. Yiu, 'Porous boundary and power politics: contextual constraints of organization development change projects in the United Nations organizations', *Gestalt Review*, 6 (2002): 84–94.

55 D. Cooperrider and S. Srivastva, 'Appreciative inquiry in organizational life', in *Research in Organizational Change and Development*, vol. 1, eds R. Woodman and W. Pasmore (Greenwich, CT: JAI Press, 1987): 129–69; Cooperrider and Dutton, *Organizational Dimensions of Global Change*, op. cit.

56 Brown and Covey, 'Action research', op. cit.; M. Elden and M. Levin, 'Cogenerative learning: bringing participation into action research', in *Participatory Action Research*, ed. W. Whyte (Newbury Park, CA: Sage Publications, 1991): 127–42.

13

FUTURE DIRECTIONS IN ORGANISATION DEVELOPMENT

After studying this chapter, you should be able to:

1   Describe current situations that exhibit organisation development (OD).

2   Explore OD's current state and several trends in its larger context.

3   Explore several implications for how OD will be practised in the future.

4   Discuss the likelihood of success with OD in the future.

Globalisation

Platform organisation

Agile organisation

Economic objectives

Social objectives

Ecological objectives

OD continues to evolve to meet the growing needs of organisations to adapt to rapid changes in the economy, technology and organisation practices. New methods and interventions are being applied, more complex and rigorous research is being conducted and organisations from diverse countries and industries are becoming involved. Yet, in the face of this growth and success, practitioners and researchers are concerned about the field's burgeoning diversity of concepts, interventions and valued outcomes. OD's conceptual and application boundaries are becoming more diffuse, making it more difficult to define the field's identity and to understand the nature and consequences of its practices and methods. OD's successful yet diffuse evolution makes it especially difficult, and foolhardy, to predict its future. Therefore, in this final chapter, we will step back and explore possible directions where OD might be headed, including crucial choices it may need to make in the coming years.[1]

THE CURRENT STATE OF ORGANISATION DEVELOPMENT

This text has described the current state of knowledge and practice in organisation development. OD is a field of applied behavioural science that is partly a reflection of its past, partly the result of its current engagement with organisations changing and developing themselves and partly an outcome of its emergent research.

OD mirrors key parts of its history. Many of the interventions described in this book, including team building, process consultation, survey feedback, diversity and inclusion, leadership development, work design and employee involvement, were developed and introduced early in OD's life cycle. They are widely accepted as best practice and testify to the enormous impact OD has had on organisational life.[2] These interventions reflect OD's traditional values and methods. They emerged in response to the overly bureaucratic organisational practices of the time. Many OD practitioners argue that these social problems persist in today's organisations and consequently, OD should continue to encourage the development of organisation processes and capabilities that are transparent, treat people with dignity and serve diverse stakeholders. OD's primary goals should still be to develop organisations that value human potential, trust and collaboration. The recent reemergence of positive organisational science among management scholars is a good example of this emphasis.

OD is also partly a reflection of its growing engagement with organisations seeking to adapt to highly complex and rapidly changing environments. The result is that the change management aspects of OD have seen tremendous growth over the past decade. In contrast to OD's 'softer' more humanistic side, change management is more pragmatic, aimed at helping organisations implement all kinds of changes regardless of whether they promote humanistic values or not.[3] Championed by many consulting firms and organisational centres of excellence, the success of change management has ignited debates about the differences between OD and change management, despite the existence of clear answers.[4] Today, many OD practitioners call themselves change management professionals, fearing that OD's soft reputation might damage their ability to be seen as relevant and practical.

Finally, OD is a product of active research. Led by universities and applied research centres, such as USC's Center for Effective Organizations (http://ceo.usc.edu), MIT's Society for Organizational Learning (http://www.solonline.org), the Tavistock Institute (http://www.tavinstitute.org), the Institut de Socio-Économie des Entreprises et des Organisations (Institute for Socio-Economic Enterprises and Organizations [ISEOR], http://www.iseor.com) and the Center for Leadership and Organizational Effectiveness (http://www.neoma-bs.fr/cleo), as well as practitioner-scholars around the world, OD's knowledge and practice base is constantly being refreshed. Researchers test the efficacy of different OD interventions and, by integrating knowledge from other disciplines, extend understanding of how and why organisations develop and change.[5] For example, action research, the primary change method used in OD, continues to be an active area of study, and the use of evidence-based management practices is growing rapidly.[6]

TRENDS IN THE CONTEXT OF ORGANISATION DEVELOPMENT

The broader context within which OD is practised is changing enormously. Current economic, technological and organisational trends suggest significant implications for organisations' future and OD's corresponding evolution.

THE ECONOMY

Researchers and futurists have described a variety of economic scenarios. There is substantial agreement that, while most of the world's economy is still adapting to the technological revolution, a new fourth industrial revolution – one that will blur the boundaries of the physical, digital and biological – is already emerging.[7] Although these economic scenarios differ in particulars, they share the rubric of **globalisation**. Brexit, successful and unsuccessful populist elections in the United States and Europe, escalating trade disputes among nations, and the emergence of African, Asian and Latin American economies are the latest signals that we are living in a complex global economy.

Globalisation: the process of interaction and integration between people, companies and governments worldwide.

The initial steps towards globalisation have fuelled price decreases in many consumer products, provided employment for people in less-developed nations and driven revenue growth in a variety of industries. Economists also cite examples of how music, art and other cultural artefacts have crossed boundaries and enriched people's experiences.[8] However, while the development of a global economy may well be under way, its promise and rationalisation are far from complete.[9] The transition to a global economy is for the most part unmanaged, and there is increasing concern over such social and ecological consequences as the concentration of wealth, climate change and geopolitical volatility.[10]

Globalisation is closely related to an increasing concentration of income and wealth in relatively few individuals, corporations and nations. Between the Second World War and the 1970s, incomes for the US population grew at about the same rate for all income classes. Since then, income growth for the top end of the distribution has been significantly higher.[11] A study by the Economic Policy Institute estimates that CEO pay increased 997 per cent between 1978 and 2014 compared to an increase of 10.9 per cent for workers, or 91.5 times faster.[12] In 2015, the upper 1 per cent of Americans accounted for about 22 per cent of the nation's income.[13] This pattern is similar when viewed globally. Of the 2043 billionaires in 2017 (up from 1210 in 2011 and 793 in 2006), 565 are in the United States (about 28 per cent). However, the 319 billionaires in China (about 16 per cent) is up from 115 billionaires in 2011, and the number of billionaires in Asia exceeds the number of billionaires in the United States. As Nobel Prize winner Joseph Stiglitz wrote, 'The more divided a society becomes in terms of wealth, the more reluctant the wealthy become to spend money on common needs.'[14] The Occupy Wall Street protest movement is an example of the social conflict that can arise when people fear that the wealthy act in their own self-interest and at expense of those who are financially less fortunate.

So far, globalisation has been powered mainly by fossil fuel. Reports from the Intergovernmental Panel on Climate Change and several follow-on studies support the conclusion that fossil-fuel driven industrialisation is not a controversial but a probable cause of global warming.[15] Failures to mitigate climate change or to adapt strategies to the realities of global warming were recently rated as the top economic threats in the World Economic Forum's 2016 global risk report.[16] Yet, strong financial and political pressures to support economic growth remain. President Donald Trump used such logic to reverse the cancellation of the Keystone Pipeline and to leave the Paris climate accord. In response, many entities have stepped up their conservation efforts, including states within the United States, most notably California; other countries, such as China, India and France; and industrial corporations, such as Volvo, Unilever, Gap, Suzuki, Honda, Ikea, illy and Google. Al Gore's latest documentary, *An Inconvenient Sequel*, argues that individuals and organisations are becoming more ecologically responsible, while others worry that there is not enough urgency to these efforts.[17]

Globalisation has also created significant geopolitical instability. Wars, terrorism, repression, peaceful or violent regime changes, and elections anywhere in the world can create uncertainty and wreak havoc on supply chain integrity, public and workforce safety and government services. These impacts affect consumer confidence, exchange rates, market volatility and the ability to recruit and retain a competent workforce. They can increase organisations' hesitancy to invest in people, technology or operations.

A 2015 McKinsey study found that, although executives rated these geostrategic risks as more threatening than ever before, most organisations had done little to address them: 'The inaction on geostrategic risks may owe to the fact that, since 2013, many companies haven't made much progress in developing capabilities or processes to manage the uncertainties that respondents foresee. Executives aren't any likelier now than two years ago to say political and geopolitical risks are well integrated into their companies' overall strategies.'[18] The McKinsey report describes a vicious circle where there is little investment in the capabilities to manage these risks because the weak and untrustworthy analyses of them do not support a threat-warranted investment. Thus, organisations remain vulnerable to these forces. HSBC, one of the largest financial institutions in the world, blamed 'largely unexpected economic and political events' for its 62 per cent drop in profitability in 2016.[19]

Apply your learning 13.1 is an example where nations are constantly aware of the economic status of the environment and the need to consult and negotiate.

PACIFIC NATIONS SEEK NEW WAY ON TRADE

Pacific Rim nations called for a new way forward on free trade amid the virtual collapse of global talks as they focused on keeping open fast-changing areas such as food and clean energy.

Senior trade officials from APEC – the 21-member body that accounts for more than half the world economy – voiced frustration on Friday at the standstill in the so-called Doha round that has tried for a decade to forge a global trade pact.

'All ministers agreed that we cannot simply keep doing what we have been doing in the Doha talks if we mean to move forward,' US Trade Representative Ron Kirk said after the talks in the snow-covered resort of Big Sky, Montana.

'At the same time, not one minister said we should throw in the towel. We should, instead, start a sober assessment of next steps,' Kirk said.

A senior Chinese official blamed unspecified countries' domestic politics and 'shortcomings of the multilateral system' for the dire state of the Doha talks led by the 153-member World Trade Organization.

But Assistant Commerce Minister Yu Jianhua said that China was committed to liberalisation both at home and abroad, acknowledging that the world's second largest economy was increasingly dependent on foreign trade.

'Opening up is our basic national policy and we will never change that,' Yu told reporters.

'We cannot go without the world economy. So we need Doha. The conclusion of the Doha round serves the best interest and long-term interest of China,' he said.

Yu said that the Doha round should fulfil the mission stated when the talks began in the Qatari capital in 2001 of trying to benefit the poorest countries that felt left out of previous rounds of liberalisation.

The fate of WTO talks will also be on the table next week in Paris at the 50th anniversary of the Organization for Economic Co-operation and Development, which groups 34 advanced or well-developed economies.

Australian Trade Minister Craig Emerson, who will lead a key session in Paris, warned that a complete collapse of trade negotiations would set off a damaging wave of protectionism around the world.

'It would be a great perversity that the world resisted protectionism during the deepest global recession since the Great Depression but might succumb to it during the recovery,' Emerson said.

Nine APEC members including the United States and Australia have been pursuing their own free trade pact, known as the Trans-Pacific Partnership, which they hope can create a template for larger agreements.

'It does have a lot of energy and momentum. The United States in particular is strongly committed and that's a good thing. We just need to ensure that it is a very high-quality agreement,' Emerson said.

Anti-globalisation activists have criticised negotiators for a lack of transparency, saying that little is known about the Trans-Pacific Partnership despite the goal of completing the framework in time for APEC's November summit in Hawaii.

»

Separately in Big Sky, APEC officials called in a statement for an 'open and transparent' trade of food amid concern that unstable prices would lead to export controls.

The statement asked the 21 economies to 'reduce unnecessary requirements in official export certificates for agricultural products' and to 'eliminate requirements that are not based on science'.

The language was requested by Japan, which has been alarmed at restrictions slapped on its food since its March 11 mega-earthquake that triggered a nuclear crisis at the Fukushima plant. Japanese foreign ministry official Chiaki Takahashi hailed the APEC statement, saying it rejected 'unfounded rumours' about radiation risks.

President Barack Obama's administration has made clean energy a key priority during the US chairmanship of APEC, believing that millions of jobs are waiting if green trade is opened up across the region.

The APEC statement set a November deadline to identify ways to 'streamline procedures and regulations' on the trade of alternative vehicles. But the statement was largely general in tone, with some officials seeking more clarity on the nature of products involved in green trade.

Source: S. Tandon, 'Pacific nations seek new way on trade', *The Age*, 21 May 2011.

Critical thinking questions

1   What countries are involved in APEC? What is meant by Pacific Rim nations?

2   What do you see as the major issues/problems facing negotiations?

3   Investigate the current status of APEC and the topics of mutual interest.

TECHNOLOGY

By almost any measure, information technology is a significant and increasingly pervasive fact of life. Its growth rate continues to boggle the mind. There were 7.5 billion mobile/smartphone subscriptions in 2017, up from 4.7 billion in 2009.[20] An estimated 2.4 billion worldwide internet users in 2012 grew to 3.7 billion in 2017, with Africa's usage growing 7722 per cent between 2000 and 2017.[21] Almost 50 per cent of the world's population is connected to the internet. It is the backbone of a global economy that enables us to interact on social media and supports innovations, such as artificial intelligence (AI), the Internet of Things (IoT), 3D printing, driverless cars, and a host of devices and solutions that are still emerging. These developments hold great promise for an enormous variety of personal, organisational and economic benefits.

There is a rising chorus of concern about this technological revolution, however. The increasing frequency and effectiveness of cyberattacks has ruined corporate reputations (for example, Sony, Target, Yahoo, Visa/Mastercard and Equifax), betrayed individual privacy and increased costs; it has completely changed the nature of warfare and appears to have played a role in elections around the world. The number of studies linking technology's growth to diminished human capability and development are now commonplace.[22] One study found that the average human attention span dropped from 12 seconds in 2000 to 8 seconds in 2015, while the 'Google effect' refers to our comfort in knowing the information we need is just a click away rather than having to rely on our memory.[23]

Moreover, the assumed positive relationship between technological change and productivity improvement has proven to be elusive. Despite the promises of time-saving efficiency and ease of use, technology has also been used to harm and humiliate.[24] Information technology's productivity gains and quality-of-work-life impacts remain fleeting. In line with sociotechnical systems (STS) research, evidence suggests that productivity improvements are a joint function of the technology itself and the organisation's adjustments in work skills and work design.[25] For example, UK bookmaker William Hill's investment in new electronic point-of-sale technologies didn't pay off until it addressed the retail managers' and customer-service advisers' work processes in its 1630 betting offices.[26] The implementation of electronic health records has been profitable for vendors but has yet to produce meaningful changes in the cost of health care for users or the public.[27] Sir Geoffrey Vickers' keen observations on technological consequences are as relevant today as they were when he voiced them in 1972: 'The technological system – especially with its strong connection to science – is now able to do things even if we do not understand the consequences of those actions. We approve of what it can do for us without knowing what it will do to us.'[28]

ORGANISATIONS

The final force shaping OD's future is organisations themselves. Although organisations will change and evolve in response to the economic and technology trends discussed above, they also proactively contribute to them. How organisations choose to organise and manage themselves, for example, can influence income equality, climate change and technological effectiveness.

A recent study by PwC explored how organisations' motivational and structural choices affect the direction of the larger economy.[29] It proposed that motivational choices about collectivism (versus individualism) and structural decisions about fragmentation (versus integration) influence the economy in particular ways. The PwC study described three alternative scenarios based on a combination of these choices. In the 'blue world' scenario, organisations choose individualism and integration in a logical extension of current economic and technological trends. This reinforces the economy's movement towards 'big company capitalism', where individual performance and achievement are valued. This choice of individualism motivation combines with the logics of scale and scope economies to reinforce an economy comprised of large organisations that are governed through tight and formal data, policies and rules. Concerns over the wellbeing of the collective economy are muted in favour of organisation results.

In the 'orange world' scenario, organisations seek a balance between individual and collective motivation and between integrated and fragmented structures, resulting in networks of specialised organisations. This specialisation contributes to structural fragmentation in the economy, with a variety of niches, segments and customers with unique demands. Here, small entrepreneurial firms and a mix of medium-sized businesses interact in a flexible ecosystem of suppliers and producers. Examples of this networked structure are **platform organisations**, such as Amazon, eBay and Travelocity, which use modern information technology and sophisticated software to link sellers to buyers. Gerald Davis' recent research on corporate America provides compelling evidence that the United States economy is currently headed towards an orange world scenario.[30]

Platform organisation: an organisation that uses modern information technology and sophisticated software to link sellers to buyers.

Finally, in the 'green world' scenario, organisations choose collective motivational schemes and integrative structures. These decisions are driven by consumer and employee beliefs and values and promote an economy focused on sustainability over market share and profitability. A 'green world' is designed from the ground up with a long-term view of social, economic and ecological balance.

These three scenarios suggest that organisations will face motivational and structural choices that set them and the larger economy on a path towards either big, centralised and controlling or small, networked and agile. They also suggest that organisations will face important choices about purpose and values. They will need to decide whether to embrace traditional individualistic, capitalistic and profit motives or more holistic and community purposes. These important value choices will significantly affect social, economic and ecological conditions at multiple levels of society worldwide.

IMPLICATIONS FOR OD'S FUTURE

These economic, technological and organisational trends strongly suggest that OD's applicability to organisations is unlikely to abate any time soon. Indeed, its fundamental purpose of helping organisations change and develop themselves may become even more relevant as these forces continue to unfold at an astonishing rate. Globalisation, the information revolution, and basic choices about organisational motivation and structure will have profound effects on how organisation members process information and make decisions, relate to each other, organise themselves for productive achievement and engage with their environment. While the substance of these activities will change with the times, the basic human and social processes underlying them will likely be similar to those OD has been addressing for decades. For example, organisational members will still need to deal with their cognitive and perceptual limitations and differences; they will need to integrate their personal characteristics and motivations with the needs of the organisation. Leaders will still need to develop strong interpersonal, strategic and change capabilities in their organisations. Teams will need to develop positive performance norms and practices and be able to address interpersonal issues. Organisations will still need to attract, develop and reward talent; they will need to design work and structure themselves for high performance; they will need to create strategies and cultures that enable them to engage proactively with the environment and adapt to change.

Thus, our sense of the future of OD borrows a page from its past. OD was founded on a set of beliefs about how organisations should change and develop. This book includes numerous examples demonstrating that an applied behavioural science focused on humanistic values of openness, trust, participation and collaboration can contribute to positive personal and organisational outcomes while enabling organisations to change and develop themselves. OD has created a powerful set of complementary interventions, such as team building, job enrichment, skill-based pay and **agile organisations**, for addressing human process, technostructural, human resource and strategic issues. These practices have shaped the way organisations are designed and managed and contributed to their effectiveness and change capability. Thus, borrowing a term from Peters and Waterman's best-selling book *In Search of Excellence*,[31] a strong argument can be made for OD to 'stick to its knitting'; that is, for OD to continue to do what it does well – to focus on its distinctive competencies to help organisations gain the capability to change and develop themselves.

Agile organisation: an organisation that has the ability to rapidly respond to change by adapting its initial stable configuration.

Sticking to its knitting does not mean that OD can simply rest on its past successes. Far from it. To help organisations adapt to the economic, technological and organisational trends described above, OD will need to make pertinent changes in its practices, objectives and values. It will need to align them to the emergent forces affecting organisations while retaining the core features that have contributed to its success.[32]

TOWARDS MORE INTEGRATED PRACTICES

To its credit, OD has long encouraged challenges to its status quo, debates about its essential nature and reflections on a broad range of issues and topics. Such open discussions are a healthy tradition that keep OD vibrant and moving forward. However, unless they lead to a shared resolution or integrative synthesis, they risk fragmenting the field and defusing its organisational relevance and effectiveness.

As described previously, OD is currently in the midst of a debate that is central to its identity and future direction: OD versus change management. We will briefly outline this ongoing discussion and suggest how it might lead to more integrative OD practices.

Our description of OD's current state highlighted organisations' increasing need to adapt to complex and changing environments, and the consequent favouring of the pragmatic practices of change management over the developmental processes of OD. Like this book, change management has commonly been treated as a discrete step in OD's planned change process (Chapter 5), following the stages of diagnosing the organisation (Chapter 5) and designing interventions (Chapter 6). Yet, as change management has grown in popularity, it has developed an identity apart from OD, contributing to fragmentation in the field's identity. Change management focuses on implementing organisational changes, with primary attention to the effectiveness and efficiency of the change process. It provides tools and methods for executing organisational changes proficiently, economically and expeditiously, traits that are especially prized in today's environments. Because change management focuses on the change process itself, it may pay scant attention to the diagnostic and design activities underlying the changes. This neglect is not problematic as long as the organisation has made a valid diagnosis and chosen appropriate changes to resolve problems or improve the situation. Then, implementing the changes effectively and efficiently is creditable. When organisational changes are based on faulty or inappropriate diagnosis and design choices, however, change management can inadvertently carry out changes that are ineffective, or worse, that exacerbate organisational problems. For example, effective implementation of an organisational change based on a defective diagnosis or a limited or inapt set of valued choices is likely to provide negligible benefits to the organisation while wasting its resources and time; it may draw attention away from addressing the underlying causes of organisational problems or identifying opportunities for improvement.

Perhaps more troublesome is the longer-term effect that can accrue to organisations that emphasise change management over OD. Even when change management helps organisations implement beneficial changes, it may do little to develop organisations' dynamic capabilities to manage future changes. Change management's pragmatic attention to executing changes effectively and efficiently can supplant longer-term, developmental considerations to help organisations gain the knowledge and skills to change themselves. Thus, organisations may become unduly dependent on change management practitioners each time a new organisational change is carried out. In today's environments, overreliance on change management expertise from practitioners, either outside or internal to the organisation, can impede organisations' long-term adaptability and success.

OD has unintentionally contributed to this growing separation from change management and the resulting fragmentation of the field. It has failed to forcefully clarify and show convincingly how its humanistic values and developmental practices can help organisations address the economic, technological and organisation trends described previously. Moreover, OD has not made a compelling and persistent case for the importance of careful diagnosis and consideration of multiple values in designing organisational changes *before* implementing the changes. Thus, in contrast to change management, organisations increasingly question OD's relevance to the demands facing them today; they see OD as limited to the softer side of organisations, to the psychosocial processes that are only indirectly related to hard performance outcomes. Similarly, organisations see OD's developmental approach to organisation change as too time-consuming and involving to keep pace with complex and rapidly changing conditions. For example, it is not uncommon for managers and administrators to voice that OD and its developmental practices are a luxury of earlier times when things were slower paced and less demanding. Also, given the high rate of executive turnover today, leaders may question, usually to themselves, the rationality of expending resources and time developing their organisations or subunits when the leader is unlikely to remain there long enough to reap the benefits.

Fortunately, practitioners of change management and OD and their client organisations are becoming more and more appreciative that a closer integration of the two approaches is the best path forward. It can provide a more strategic, robust and relevant approach to helping organisations address the economic, technological and organisational challenges facing them than application of either approach separately. OD can bring a broader orientation to change management beyond just implementation success. It can encourage organisations to address the prior, more strategic issue of what organisational changes are most relevant for moving the organisation ahead developmentally. What changes will provide the organisation with the necessary capabilities to solve emergent problems and to continually change and improve itself? Without a strategic and developmental perspective, change management can simply become a tool for implementing organisational changes, regardless of their purpose or intended effects.

Conversely, change management can bring to OD a more pragmatic, change-oriented perspective. It can provide the knowledge and methods for helping organisations execute changes that move them along their developmental path effectively and efficiently. For example, the change management chapter of each successive edition of this book has become longer and more detailed, with an increasing number of tools and processes for implementing organisational change. Many of these methods come from change management and other change approaches, such as industrial relations and strategic management that are not traditionally associated with OD. Without a strong capability to execute organisational change, OD risks becoming a developmental conversation and diagnostic process with little chance of putting those words or assessments into action.

The emergence of a more integrated view of the OD field seems not only desirable but likely. Change management practitioners increasingly ask how to get involved earlier in the change process when choices about which changes to implement are being made. OD practitioners question how their interventions can be implemented more effectively and efficiently. Applying behavioural science to improve organisations' effectiveness and capability to change and develop themselves requires an integrated body of theory and practice that addresses both the developmental and execution processes of planned change.

TOWARDS RESPONSIBLE PROGRESS

Traditionally, OD has supported personal and organisation growth. Personal growth is an OD watchword and remains a strength of the field. Organisation growth, usually measured economically, has also enjoyed unchallenged status and become embedded in many OD frameworks.[33] Attention to economic growth can overlook the scarce and limited resources that fuel it, however, with attendant social and ecological problems for organisations and society.

Consistent with rising societal concerns about economic growth's far-reaching and potentially negative consequences, OD is shifting from unquestioned support for organisations' economic growth to a vision of 'responsible progress'.[34] Progress for organisations has generally been defined in such terms as new products and services that make society better; the ability to put scarce resources to their most efficient use; the capacity to support full employment; and the equitable distribution of rewards in relation to the risks people take in productive enterprise. Although few people would argue with these criteria, the economic, technological and organisational trends discussed above suggest that criteria for organisation progress have gradually narrowed to a single metric: profitability for private and public firms and benefits exceeding costs for non-government organisations (NGOs) and governments. When organisation progress is measured solely in financial terms, it can lead to wider social and ecological problems, typically called 'externalities' by economists. Global warming, concentration of wealth, political instability and increasing dependency on technology are externalities that raise serious doubts that organisations' economic progress is making them or society 'better off'.

Responsible progress, on the other hand, proposes that organisations need to attend to a wide range of economic, social and ecological objectives that together contribute to organisation success. **Economic objectives** recognise the importance of productivity and efficiency. In any enterprise, there must be a 'net gain' of benefits to costs to justify survival. **Social objectives** include such outcomes as employee satisfaction and wellbeing, fair treatment of individual differences, work and home life balance, and community support. **Ecological objectives** embrace living within the environment's capacity to support life over the long run, enriching rather than depleting natural resources, and sustaining a healthy relationship among the elements of our ecosystem.

Economic objectives: objectives that recognise the importance of productivity and efficiency.

Social objectives: objectives that include such outcomes as employee satisfaction and wellbeing, fair treatment of individual differences, work and home life balance, and community support.

Ecological objectives: objectives that embrace living within the environment's capacity to support life over the long run, enriching rather than depleting natural resources, and sustaining a healthy relationship among the elements of our ecosystem.

Responsible progress requires organisations to seek a healthy balance or tension among these economic, social and ecological objectives. Because the objectives contribute to organisation success both independently and interactively, they operate as drivers of and constraints to each other. Consequently, to achieve responsible progress, organisations must *jointly optimise* the three objectives rather than maximise each one separately. Joint optimisation recognises that each of the three objectives alone is insufficient to produce responsible progress; the three must operate jointly to achieve overall success. For example, an organisation's profitability is partly determined by how well it treats employees and the extent to which its operations and products are ecologically sound. An organisation's social success depends in part on its economic results and on the ecological outcomes it produces. An organisation's ecological results are partially determined by how well its social values and norms support environmental responsibility and how economically its operations and products perform.

Learning how to jointly optimise economic, social and ecological objectives is not well understood nor is it an easy task. Organisations have traditionally maximised on a single objective, such as profitability or market capitalisation, and have pursued it aggressively. Expectedly, this singular focus on economic objectives leaves little time or motivation to address social and ecological outcomes. Thus, organisations can commit to narrow, economic objectives without appreciating or understanding their wider social and ecological impacts. In some ways, OD has unwittingly contributed to organisations' economic maximisation behaviour. It has promoted 'fast cycle' OD aimed at accelerating value creation; supported 'big hairy audacious goals' usually tied to economic outcomes; and helped organisations streamline supply chains and work flows to speed things up and produce more in less time.

Apply your learning 13.2 describes an example of responsible progress with an initiative to form consortiums of start-up organisations in rural cities.

THE PROBLEM WITH START-UPS CLUSTERING IN CAPITAL CITIES

Imagine if tens of thousands of entrepreneurs launched their venture in a regional centre instead of an east coast capital in the next decade.

Instead of starting in Sydney or Melbourne, they relocated to Newcastle, Geelong or Ipswich.

If a fraction of these start-ups flourished, the regional centre would in time have hundreds of high-growth ventures in emerging industries – ventures that create jobs and wealth for regional communities and draw workers and their families from capital cities.

I considered entrepreneurship's role in population planning amid news this week of Australia reaching 25 million residents. I see potential for a co-ordinated network of regional innovation clusters that compete with capital cities for high-growth start-ups.

Yes, entrepreneurship is only a small part of the population puzzle, but if governments are serious about encouraging people to move from the cities, we need a jump in higher-paid, knowledge-economy jobs in the regions. That's where entrepreneurship comes in.

Much good work in entrepreneurship is under way in the regions. Geelong, Newcastle and Wollongong, for example, understand the potential of innovation and start-up communities to help the transition from challenged older industries to the new.

Regional entrepreneurship initiatives, however, tend to be in isolation. Cities adopt innovation and start-up strategies on their own, sometimes with ad hoc support from federal, state and local government and other stakeholders. Rarely do they collaborate.

It's time to think bigger. The federal government should identify key innovation/ entrepreneurship clusters outside the east coast capitals and build policy to support their growth.

I would initially focus on Wollongong, Ipswich, Newcastle, Geelong and the Sunshine Coast (let's call them the 'WINGS' innovation network).

That's not to say innovation clusters in other states and territories are unimportant or that smaller regional centres do not deserve government support. Or that there are not dangers in governments trying to pick innovation-city winners.

But the focus of WINGS – each potentially a strong innovation cluster – is about supporting population decentralisation efforts from south-east Queensland to southern Victoria.

The WINGS strategy would require tiers of government and key stakeholders in those cities, such as regional universities, collaborating to create a powerful, branded innovation network: one that has the scale to encourage budding entrepreneurs to leave the capitals.

WINGS cities were chosen for five reasons. First, each is within two hours of an east coast capital, and history shows great innovation clusters often form an hour or so out of large cities; the cluster is far enough away to encourage collaboration but close enough to access cities.

Also, it's easier to encourage city-born entrepreneurs to move to nearby regional cities so they still have reasonable access to family, friends and their urban networks.

»

»

Second, each WINGS city has excellent university infrastructure. A strong regional university is central to regional innovation clusters. It develops local workforce skills and is often the central node in regional innovation/entrepreneurship efforts.

As an aside, I'm impressed with the work of the universities of Wollongong, Newcastle and other regional universities in driving local innovation.

It's a shame we mostly only hear from city-based Sandstone universities: several smaller universities are doing fantastic work and deeply understand their role in facilitating regional economic transformation. They deserve more government support for their innovation/entrepreneurship work.

The third factor is growth. Each WINGS city has strong projected population growth over the next two decades. Higher property and living costs will encourage the trend, well under way, of more people in Sydney, Melbourne and Brisbane moving to regional centres.

Ipswich in south-east Queensland, for example, is projected to have more than 430 000 residents by 2036 and Geelong more than 320 000. These and other WINGS cities will need many more jobs and thus many large and small employers.

Current innovation activity is the fourth factor. The WINGS cities have many innovation initiatives under way. With well-targeted government support, these networks could multiply, attracting and supporting more entrepreneurs who relocate from the city and build local ventures.

Necessity entrepreneurship is the fifth factor. I chose the WINGS cities because each needs to transform its economy. Geelong, Newcastle, Wollongong and Ipswich were affected by the downturn in traditional manufacturing and needed to change. The Sunshine Coast for many years has needed to diversify its economic base and is doing good things in innovation and start-up entrepreneurship.

The WINGS concept has several potential benefits. Unifying innovation clusters in these cities provides a starting point for co-ordinated support, collaboration and funding.

We should ask: what is needed from federal and state governments, local councils, regional universities and industry to create five great innovation clusters outside the capital cities in the next decade?

How can WINGS cities work together to strengthen their competitive position in attracting budding business from the capitals? How can a tech entrepreneur in Geelong be connected to a peer company in Wollongong? Can campaigns to attract start-ups in WINGS cities be co-ordinated to increase their reach and minimise cost?

Source: T. Featherstone, 'The problem with start-ups clustering in capital cities', *The Age*, 9 August 2018.

Critical thinking questions	
1	What is the primary focus of the author?
2	What are the five factors considered for selection?
3	What would be the benefits of such an arrangement?
4	What would be the major impediments to the establishment of such a consortium?

Moving ahead, OD can play a valuable role in helping organisations achieve responsible progress. It can use social-process tools and methods, such as process consultation, team building, conflict resolution and large-group interventions, to facilitate the kind of open and frank discussion needed for key organisational decision makers to recognise that joint optimisation trumps maximisation when considering economic, social and ecological objectives. OD can help organisations embed these discussions in their strategic decision-making processes through such interventions as integrated strategic change (ISC), dynamic strategy making and organisation learning (OL). This can provide the strategic direction for designing organisational structures and processes and implementing changes that enhance organisations' capability to achieve responsible progress. Moreover, these OD process and strategic interventions can enable a diversity of stakeholders to be involved in the discussions and decision-making processes, thus increasing the likelihood that responsible progress will be supported widely in the organisation.

TOWARDS MORE INCLUSIVE VALUES

OD has spent considerable time addressing the values that guide its practice. From the beginning, the field has embraced humanistic values as the foundation for developing organisations. They include personal self-determination and worth, growth and interpersonal openness, trust and collaboration. Many of OD's initial interventions were aimed at helping organisations actualise these values, such as process consultation, third-party interventions and team building. These changes helped organisations resolve many of the social problems resulting from overly bureaucratic structures and practices.

To continue to be applicable to organisations, OD's values have grown beyond personal and interpersonal outcomes to include organisation performance. Valuing economic outcomes, such as productivity, quality and efficiency, has given rise to interventions aimed at work design, performance management and organisation design. These changes have helped organisations better align their social and technical parts and environmental relationships. They have expanded criteria for judging OD and effectiveness to include both social and ecological criteria.

Moving forward, OD's continued relevance to organisations is likely to rest on how well its values guide organisations in addressing the economic, technological and organisational trends described previously. In line with our speculations that OD will move towards more integrated solutions and responsible progress, we believe that OD's values will become more inclusive and comprise economic, social and ecological objectives. More inclusive values will provide a broader set of criteria for defining what development means for organisations and assessing organisation effectiveness accordingly. They will provide more comprehensive guidelines for creating OD interventions that are likely to jointly optimise a wider, more varied set of objectives.

For example, the addition of 'diversity' as an OD value might involve the following scenario. The economic, technological and organisational trends identified above point to an increasing narrowness in organisations' and societies' objectives, processes and outcomes. The rising concentration of wealth and income stems partially from a limited focus on financial objectives, which constrains the variety of voices involved in deciding policy. Geopolitical instability is partly the result of people feeling they have little choice over their own destiny. Technological development can standardise behaviour and constrict human capability. Increased global warming confines our choices for amelioration. A few large firms dominate a considerable part of the global economy.

In response to this increasing narrowness, OD might embrace a broader and more strategic view of diversity as a value for developing organisations. It could encourage organisations to see diversity as a source of competitive advantage and sustainability. It might help them seek and listen to a variety of stakeholder opinions as well as explore multiple business strategies, organisation designs and ways of operating. In line with the movement towards responsible progress, OD could help organisations seek diversity in their economic, social and ecological objectives, providing a broader set of criteria to judge performance and to guide organisational change and development.

To increase diversity in a system that progressively reinforces narrowness, OD might persistently and convincingly remind organisation decision makers to ask these kinds of questions when making consequential decisions: 'Can we think more broadly about that?', 'What other criteria should we consider?' and 'Is there a way to achieve those economic ends as well as other outcomes through different means?'. OD could help organisations move beyond singular or remedial views of diversity, such as pluralism in race, gender or nationality, as ends in themselves. It can help them treat diversity more broadly as a strategy that fuels innovation, sustainability and economic success. The seeds for achieving responsible progress in all of its economic, social and ecological objectives are the innovative possibilities that exist when multiple viewpoints, values and beliefs are heard and nurtured over time.

In helping organisations fulfil the diversity value, OD would undoubtedly need to create new interventions, methods of change and ways of engaging with organisations. It would need to clearly and persistently make diversity a key criterion for organisations' development and success, making it an important focus of entering and contacting (Chapter 5), diagnosing (Chapter 5) and designing interventions (Chapter 6). OD practitioners would need to work closely with powerful stakeholders with different and likely conflicting interests to arrive at a sufficiently agreed on view of diversity to permit coordinated action to actualise it. OD's recent interventions that address economic, ecological and social outcomes (Chapter 12) are a step in this direction, and more will be needed as OD moves towards more inclusive values.

A scenario where the addition of diversity as a basic value in OD could be extended to the inclusion of other possible OD values, such as equity, family wellbeing, community enrichment and environmental sustainability. The key point is the fundamental values that OD promotes as essential to organisations' development and success are not just platitudes but important criteria and guides for practising OD and developing organisations. They have serious implications for how OD conceptualises organisations and helps to develop and improve them. In combination with more integrated solutions and greater attention to responsible progress, we expect more inclusive values to guide OD in the coming years.

SUMMARY

This concluding chapter summarises the current state of OD that was presented in detail throughout this book. Major economic, technological and organisational trends occurring in the broader context within which OD is practised were identified. They suggest that OD's relevance to organisations is likely to continue, if not increase, in the future. The field's basic values, concepts and practices address many of the challenges organisations are likely to face in the coming years. This suggests that OD should 'stick to its knitting', continuing to do what it does well by focusing on its distinctive competencies to help organisations gain the capability to change and develop themselves. OD cannot rest on its past successes, however. It must make pertinent changes in its practices, objectives and values to help organisations adapt to the emergent economic, technological and organisational forces identified previously. OD will need to better coordinate change management methods with its traditional developmental practices to provide organisations with more integrated solutions to their problems. OD will need to move beyond attention to personal and economic growth to helping organisations achieve responsible progress on economic, social and ecological objectives. This will require interventions that enable organisations to jointly optimise these outcomes. Finally, OD will need more inclusive values to provide organisations with more comprehensive criteria and guidance in measuring success and learning to adapt to an increasingly complex and changing environment.

ACTIVITIES

REVIEW QUESTIONS

1   What should be the primary goals of OD that will help it to survive into the future? (LO1)

2   Briefly describe and provide examples, of the three scenarios as provided by PwC (blue, orange and green worlds). (LO2)

3   What are the external forces (trends) for change? (LO2)

4   What role does motivation have in the change management process? What are the possible negative consequences of using motivation as a change strategy. (LO3)

5   What is an agile organisation? Give examples. (LO4)

EXTEND YOUR LEARNING

1   'Today, many OD practitioners call themselves change management professionals, fearing that OD's soft reputation might damage their ability to be seen as relevant and practical.' Do you agree or disagree with this statement? Give reasons and examples to support your answer. (LO1, 2 & 3)

2   Search the Australian Bureau of Statistics (ABS) data and update the current statistics on the number of millionaires in Australia. (LO4)

Search Me! **Management**

Explore **Search Me! Management** for articles relevant to this chapter. Fast and convenient, **Search Me! Management** is updated daily and provides you with 24-hour access to full text articles from hundreds of scholarly and popular journals, eBooks and newspapers, including *The Australian* and *The New York Times*. Visit http://login.cengagebrain.com and use the access code that comes with this book for 12 months access to the **Search Me! Management** database. Try searching for the following keywords:

Keywords:

- Globalisation
- Platform organisation
- Agile organisation
- Economic objectives
- Social objectives
- Ecological objectives

Search tip: **Search Me! Management** contains information from both local and international sources. To get the greatest number of search results, try using both Australian and American spellings in your searches; for example, 'globalisation' and 'globalization'; 'organisation' and 'organization'.

REFERENCES

1 W. Pasmore and R. Woodman, 'The future of research and practice in organizational change and development', in *Research in Organizational Change and Development*, vol. 25, eds A. Shani and D. Noumair (Bingley, England: Emerald Publishing, 2017): 1–32; T. Jick and K. Sturtevant, 'Taking stock of 30 years of change management: is it time for a reboot?', in *Research in Organizational Change and Development*, vol. 25, eds A. Shani and D. Noumair (Bingley, England: Emerald Publishing, 2017): 33–79; A. Church and W. Burke, 'Four trends shaping the future of organizations and organization development', *OD Practitioner*, 49 (2017): 14–22; B. Burnes and B. Cooke, 'The past, present and future of organization development: taking the long view', *Human Relations*, 65 (2012): 1395–429.

2 A. Kleiner, *The Age of Heretics*, 2nd edn (San Francisco: Jossey-Bass, 2008).

3 N. Worren, K. Ruddle and K. Moore, 'From organizational development to change management: the emergence of a new profession', *Journal of Applied Behavioral Science*, 35 (1999): 273–86; H. Hornstein, 'Organizational development and change management: don't throw the baby out with the bath water', *Journal of Applied Behavioral Science*, 37 (2001): 223–6; M. Davis, 'OD and change management consultants: an empirical examination and comparison of their values and interventions' (unpublished doctoral dissertation, George Washington University, 2002).

4 T. Cummings and C. Cummings, 'Appreciating organization development: a comparative essay on divergent perspectives', *Human Resource Development Quarterly*, 25 (2014): 141–54; C. Weidner and O. Kulick, 'The professionalization of organization development: a status report and look to the future', in *Research in Organizational Change and Development*, vol. 12, eds W. Pasmore and R. Woodman (Oxford, England: JAI Press, 1999); A. Church, 'The professionalization of organization development: the next step in an evolving field', in *Research in Organizational Change and Development*, vol. 13, eds R. Woodman and W. Pasmore (Oxford, England: JAI Press, 2001): 1–42.

5 A. Pettigrew, R. Woodman and K. Cameron, 'Studying organizational change and development: challenges for future research', *Academy of Management Journal*, 44 (2001): 697–714; L. Martins, 'Organizational change and development', in *APA Handbook of Industrial and Organizational Psychology*, vol. 3 (Washington, DC: American Psychological Association, 2011).

6 D. Coghlan and T. Brannick, *Doing Action Research in Your Own Organization* (Thousand Oaks, CA: Sage, 2014); D. Coghlan and A.B. Shani, 'Creating action research quality in organization development: rigorous, reflective and relevant', *Systemic Practice and Action Research*, 27 (2014): 523–36; A. Shani, D. Coghlan and P. Coughlan, *Handbook of Collaborative Management Research* (Thousand Oaks, CA: Sage Publications, 2008);

D. Coghlan, 'Seeking common ground in the diversity and diffusion of action research and collaborative management research action modalities: toward a general empirical method', in *Research in Organizational Change and Development*, vol. 18, eds W. Pasmore, A. Shani and R. Woodman (Bingley, UK: Emerald Group Publishing, 2010); S. Mohrman and E. Lawler, 'Generating knowledge that drives change', *Academy of Management Perspectives*, 26 (2012): 41–51; J. Pfeffer and R. Sutton, 'Evidence-based management', *Harvard Business Review*, 84 (2006): 62–74; D. Rousseau, 'Is there such a thing as "evidence-based management"?', *Academy of Management Review*, 31 (2006): 256–69.

7 K. Schwab, 'The fourth industrial revolution: what it means, how to respond', World Economic Forum, 14 January 2016, https://www.weforum.org/agenda/2016/01/the-fourth-industrial-revolution-what-it-means-and-how-to-respond, accessed 18 August 2017; A. Toffler, *The Third Wave* (New York: William Morrow, 1980); D. Korten, *When Corporations Rule the World* (West Hartford, CT: Kumarian Press; San Francisco: Berrett-Koehler, 1995); L. Thurow, *The Future of Capitalism* (New York: William Morrow, 1996); T. Friedman, *The World Is Flat* (New York: Farrar, Straus and Giroux, 2006); E. Lawler and C. Worley, *Management Reset* (San Francisco: Jossey-Bass, 2011); M. Young and S. Nair, 'Driving digital transformation: why culture and structure matter', The Conference Board Research Report R-1632-RR, June 2017, https://www.conference-board.org/publications/publicationdetail.cfm?publicationid=7525&centerId=10, accessed 20 August 2017.

8 J. Bhagwati, *In Defense of Globalization* (New York: Oxford University Press, 2004); T. Cowen, *Creative Destruction* (Princeton, NJ: Princeton University Press, 2002).

9 Friedman, *The World Is Flat*, op. cit.

10 A. Chua, *World on Fire* (New York: Anchor Books, 2003); The International Forum on Globalization, *Alternatives to Economic Globalization* (San Francisco: Berrett-Koehler, 2002); D. Cooperrider and J. Dutton, eds, *Organizational Dimensions of Global Change: No Limits to Cooperation* (Thousand Oaks, CA: Sage Publications, 1999); J. Perkins, *Confessions of an Economic Hit Man* (San Francisco: Berrett-Koehler, 2004); J. Stiglitz, *The Price of Inequality* (New York: W.W. Norton, 2012).

11 T. Piketty, *Capital in the Twenty-First Century* (Cambridge: Harvard Business Press, 2017); C. Stone, D. Trisi, A. Sherman and E. Horton, 'A guide to statistics on historical trends in income inequality', Center on Budget and Policy Priorities, 7 November 2016, https://www.cbpp.org/research/poverty-and-inequality/a-guideto-statistics-on-historical-trends-in-income-inequality, accessed 14 August 2017.

12 C. Isidore, 'CEO pay is 300 times greater than their employees', CNN, 22 June 2015, http://money.cnn.com/2015/06/22/news/companies/ceo-pay/index.html, accessed 14 August 2017.

13 Statistics reported based on a 2016 study by the Washington Center for Equitable Growth and reported in P. Martin, 'Economic inequality soars in US', https://www.wsws.org/en/articles/2016/07/02/rich-j02.html, accessed 21 August 2017.

14 J. Stiglitz, 'Of the 1%, by the 1%, for the 1%', *Vanity Fair*, May 2011, http://www.vanityfair.com/society/features/2011/05/top-one-percent-201105, accessed 16 August 2017.

15 IPCC, 'Summary for policymakers', in *Climate Change 2007: The Physical Science Basis. Contribution of Working Group I to the Fourth Assessment Report of the Intergovernmental Panel on Climate Change*, eds S. Solomon, D. Qin, M. Manning, Z. Chen, M. Marquis, K.B. Avery, M. Tignor and H.L. Miller (Cambridge: Cambridge University Press, 2007); NOAA National Centers for Environmental Information, State of the Climate: Global Climate Report for April 2017, published online May 2017, https://www.ncdc.noaa.gov/sotc/global/201704, accessed 16 August 2017.

16 World Economic Forum, 'The global risks report 2016', 11th edn, 2016, https://www.weforum.org/reports/the-global-risks-report-2016, accessed 16 August 2017.

17 L. Ross, K. Arrow, R. Cialdini, N. Diamond-Smith, J. Diamond, J. Dunne, M. Feldman et al., 'The climate change challenge and barriers to the exercise of foresight intelligence.' *BioScience*, 66 (2016): 363–70.

18 D. Erdmann, E. Greenberg and R. Harper, 'Geostrategic risks on the rise', McKinsey and Company, May 2016, http://www.mckinsey.com/business-functions/strategy-and-corporate-finance/our-insights/geostrategic-risks-on-the-rise, accessed 16 August 2017.

19 Reuters with CNBC, 'HSBC blames "largely unexpected economic and political events" for 62 percent drop in annual pre-tax profit', CNBC.com, 20 February 2017, https://www.cnbc.com/2017/02/20/hsbc-reports-results.html, accessed 18 August 2017.

20 R. Molla, 'Mobile broadband subscriptions are projected to double in five years', Recode.net, 18 June 2017, https://www.recode.net/2017/6/18/15826036/smartphone-subscriptions-basic-phones-globally-ericsson, accessed 15 August 2017.

21 Statistics accessed from http://www.internetworldstats.com/stats.htm on 15 August 2017. Internet users were for 31 March 2017.

22 R. Hiscott, '8 ways technology makes you stupid', *Huffington Post*, 25 July 2014, http://www.huffingtonpost.com/2014/07/25/technology-intelligence_n_5617181.html, accessed 31 August 2017; N. Carr, *The Shallows: What the Internet Is Doing to Our Brains* (New York: WW Norton & Company, 2011).

23 G. Roberts, 'Google effect: is technology making us stupid?', *Independent*, 15 July 2016, http://www.independent.co.uk/life-style/gadgets-and-tech/features/google-effect-is-technology-making-us-stupid-10391564.html, accessed 31 August 2017.

24 T. Wu, 'As technology gets better, will society get worse?', *The New Yorker*, 6 February 2014, http://www.newyorker.com/tech/elements/as-technology-gets-better-will-society-get-worse, accessed 15 August 2017; T. Wu, 'The problem with easy technology', *The New Yorker*, 21 February 2014, http://www.newyorker.com/tech/elements/the-problem-with-easy-technology, accessed 15 August 2017.

25 E. Sanders, 'Tech-driven efficiency spurs economic boom', *Los Angeles Times*, 22 February 2000, A-1; T. Kretschmer, 'Information and communication technologies and productivity growth: a survey of the literature', *OECD Digital Economy Papers*, No. 195, OECD Publishing, 2012, http://dx.doi.org/10.1787/5k9bh3jllgs7-en, accessed 15 December 2012.

26 D. Pollitt, 'William Hill backs a winner with EPoS training: employees embrace culture change and new working practices', *Human Resource Management International Digest*, 17 (2009): 18–20.

27 S. Lohr, 'Why the economic payoff from technology is so elusive', *New York Times*, 5 June 2016, https://www.nytimes.com/2016/06/06/business/why-theeconomic-payoff-from-technology-is-so-elusive.html, accessed 16 August 2017.

28 G. Vickers, *Freedom in a Rocking Boat* (New York: Penguin Books, 1972): 24.

29 C. Stubbings and J. Williams, *The Workforce of the Future: The Competing Forces Shaping 2030*; PwC, https://www.pwc.com/gx/en/services/people-organisation/publications/workforce-of-the-future.html, accessed 18 September 2017.

30 G. Davis, *The Vanishing American Corporation: Navigating the Hazards of a New Economy* (Oakland, CA: Barrett-Koehler, 2016).

31 T. Peters and R. Waterman, *In Search of Excellence* (New York: Harper and Row, 1982).

32 This section draws heavily from C. Worley and A. McCloskey, 'A positive vision of OD's future', in *The NTL Handbook of Organization Development and Change*, eds B. Jones and M. Brazzel (San Francisco: Pfeiffer, 2006): 501–13; J. Wirtenberg, L. Abrams and C. Ott, 'Assessing the field of organization development', *Journal of Applied Behavioral Science*, 40 (2004): 465–79; J. Wirtenberg, D. Lipsky, L. Abrams, M. Conway and J. Slepian, 'The future of organization development: enabling sustainable business performance through people', *Organization Development Journal*, 25 (2007): 11–27; R. Marshak, 'Organization development as a profession and a field', in *The NTL Handbook of Organization Development and Change*, eds B. Jones and M. Brazzel (San Francisco: Pfeiffer, 2006); Cummings and Cummings, 'Appreciating organization development', op. cit.; Church and Burke, 'Four trends shaping the future of organizations and organization development', op. cit.

33 G. Steiner and J. Miner, *Management Policy and Strategy* (New York: Macmillan Publishing, 1977).

34 C. Worley and E. Lawler, 'Built to change organizations and responsible progress: twin pillars of sustainable success', in *Research in Organizational Change and Development*, eds W. Pasmore, A. Shani and R. Woodman (Bingley, UK: Emerald Group Publishing, 2010).

PART

6

INTEGRATIVE CASE STUDIES

Nintendo Switch: Now you're playing with even more power!

Andrew Zur, University of Melbourne

INTRODUCTION

During the mid to late 2000s, Nintendo Co., Ltd ('Nintendo'), a Japanese multinational consumer electronics and software company headquartered in Kyoto, Japan, and home to some of the most iconic video game franchises of all time, including *Mario*, *Pokémon*, *Donkey Kong* and *The Legend of Zelda*, was at an all-time high in the video game industry with its incredibly popular hand-held game console, the Nintendo DS, and its home video game console, Wii (codenamed 'Revolution').

NINTENDO DS

The spiritual successor to the Game Boy, the Nintendo DS was a hand-held game console that was released by Nintendo in 2004 (2005 in Australia), with the original model backwards compatible with Game Boy Advance games. The Nintendo DS and its family, the Nintendo DS Lite, Nintendo DSi and Nintendo DSi XL, collectively sold 154.01 million units worldwide, 947.85 million units of software, and secured a 65.7 per cent market share. At the time, the Nintendo DS was competing with Sony's PlayStation Portable (PSP) (80.82 million worldwide sales, 34.3 per cent market share). Nintendo's previous hand-held video game console, the Game Boy Advance, released in 2001, commanded a formidable 90 per cent market share. The Nintendo DS had a clam shell design and was dual-screen: the top screen displayed the game and the bottom screen was a touch screen where players used a stylus to draw, move and access the game's menu. In Australia, the Nintendo DS launched with such titles as *Super Mario 64 DS* (a remake of the 1996 game *Super Mario 64* for the Nintendo 64 that showed off the hand-held's hardware capabilities) and *WarioWare: Touched!* (a compilation of microgames exclusively controlled with the Nintendo DS's touchscreen and microphone).

WII

Nintendo's home video game console, Wii (pronounced 'We'), sold 101.64 million units, 913.13 million software worldwide, and secured a 37 per cent share of the seventh generation of video game consoles. During this time, the Wii was competing with Microsoft's Xbox 360 (85.80 million worldwide sales, 31.2 per cent market share) and Sony's PlayStation 3 (PS3) (86.90 million worldwide sales, 31.6 per cent market share). Nintendo's market share for this generation of home video game consoles was significantly higher than its previous console, the GameCube, which, like the Game Boy Advance, launched in 2001 (2002 in Australia), was not considered a commercial success, with only 21.74 million units being sold worldwide and a 10.2 per cent share of the sixth generation of video game consoles. With the Wii, Nintendo chose not to compete with the PS3 and Xbox 360 on hardware and graphics. Instead, Nintendo introduced motion-sensor technology (through the Wii Remote and Sensor Bar), the Wii Shop Channel, DSi Shop, the now defunct WiiConnect24 service, and the original model was fully backwards compatible with all GameCube games. The Wii also introduced the Virtual Console, a game download service that focused on retro classics from Nintendo's past consoles, the Nintendo Entertainment System and Super Nintendo Entertainment System (known in Japan as the Family Computer ('Famicom') and Super Famicom respectively) as well as the Nintendo 64, Sega's Master System and Mega Drive (known as the Genesis in North America), the TurboGrafx-16 Entertainment SuperSystem (known as the PC Engine in Japan and France) and the Neo Geo. This enabled users a chance to replay (or play for the first time) popular Nintendo titles such as *Super Mario Bros. 3*, *The Legend of Zelda*, *Mega Man 2* and *Metroid* from the Nintendo Entertainment System, and *Super Mario World*, *Super Mario Kart* and *The Legend of Zelda: A Link to the Past* from the Super Nintendo Entertainment System, which had had only very limited re-releases outside of their original console release. The Wii launched with one of Nintendo's biggest franchises, *The Legend of Zelda*, in December 2006 with *The Legend of Zelda: Twilight Princess*. This game was simultaneously released on the GameCube and was Nintendo's final first party game for the console. Initial demand for the Wii outstripped supply, and hardware shortages were common early on after the system's launch. Nintendo debuted its other big franchise, *Super Mario Bros.*, on the Wii in November 2007 with *Super Mario Galaxy*.

The Wii was targeted towards families, with advertisements featuring young children, teenagers, parents and grandparents using the Wii Remote to play the games. Nintendo further supported this on its website at the time, stating that 'Wii sounds like "we", which emphasises this console is for everyone. Wii can be easily remembered by people around the world, no matter what language they speak' (Wired, 2006). The advertisements ('Wii would like to play') showed the ease of use of the console, with people of all ages able to effortlessly adapt to the concept of how the Nintendo Wii functioned. When the user moved the Wii Remote from the comfort of their lounge room, their on-screen character would mimic the same move in the game. The motion technology feature was ingeniously demonstrated through the pack-in game (excluding the Japanese and South Korean markets) *Wii Sports*, which 'sold' 82.68 million units worldwide, and is the fourth best-selling video game of all time. The game included five sports: bowling, tennis, baseball, golf and boxing. The rules of these sports titles were simplified for players and thus *Wii Sports* made both the sports titles and the Nintendo Wii video game console accessible to newcomers. The trust and confidence towards Nintendo from consumers grew as it became clear that there was truth in Nintendo's advertisements: the Wii really was as simple to use and play as what Nintendo was telling its audience. The motion sensor technology, at least initially, was not gimmicky or an expensive accessory or add-on that barely worked like the ill-fated Power Glove accessory released in 1989 for the Nintendo Entertainment System, which had difficult-to-use controls and imprecise virtual reality mechanics.

The easy-to-use features of the Wii contributed to its high sales figures (in fact, it is the best-selling Nintendo home video game console of all time), but outside of *Wii Sports* and related Nintendo-published titles like *Wii Sports Resort* (32.90 million units sold), *Wii Play* (28.92 million), *Wii Fit* (22.70 million), *Wii Fit Plus* (21.81 million) and *Wii Party* (8.41 million), which all had a strong focus on mini-games that were fun to play but short in duration, attachment rates to other games was relatively low. Aside from *Mario Kart Wii* (35.90 million sold), the Wii's other best-selling games included *New Super Mario Bros. Wii* (28.50 million sold), *Super Smash Bros. Brawl* (12.91 million sold) and *Super Mario Party 8* (8.30 million sold), again all with a focus on fun, short gameplay, and *Super Mario Galaxy* (11.40 million sold) and *The Legend of Zelda: Twilight Princess* (7.18 million sold), with a focus on exploration and longer gameplay. The popularity of the console ended up tarnishing the legacy of the console by attracting a series of lower-quality games, ports and shovelware rushed onto the console from developers whose focus was more on making a quick profit rather than fully utilising the Wii Remote motion technology in their games.

THIRD-PARTY DEVELOPERS

The video game industry sees strong third-party titles as a key sign of a gaming console's health. While the Wii console and first party Nintendo games and franchises sold incredibly well, this was not the case for the third-party developers. One commentator noted that 'the Wii landscape is bleak. Worse than it was on N64 [Nintendo 64]. Worse than on GameCube … the resulting third-party content is overwhelmingly bargain-bin trash' (Parish, 2008). Decline in third-party support for Nintendo consoles started in the mid-1990s with the company's third home video game console, the Nintendo 64 (32.93 million worldwide sales), with Nintendo choosing to continue using cartridges as the primary storage format. At this time, Nintendo's competitors, Sega's Saturn (8.82 million units sold) and Sony's PlayStation (104.25 million units sold), had moved to the CD-ROM format, which could hold a lot more data than cartridges. With their next home video game console release, the GameCube, Nintendo chose to use miniDVD optical discs, which were smaller in physical size and storage capacity than the more traditional discs used by their competitors: Sony's PlayStation 2 (PS2) (157.68 million worldwide sales), Microsoft's Xbox (24.65 million worldwide sales) and Sega's Dreamcast (8.20 worldwide sales). In particular, consumers were attracted to the PS2 (the highest selling video game console of all time) as the console, in addition to playing games, could also play DVDs. DVD players were relatively new to the industry when the PS2 was first released and consumers saw the purchase of the PS2 as a sensible choice: getting a game console and a DVD player in one. This was particularly the case in Japan, where the competition is almost exclusively between Nintendo and Sony, with Microsoft having less than 1 per cent market share of sales, and the popularity of the PS2 contributing in part to Sega exiting the video game industry after the failure of the Dreamcast.

Nintendo's decision to go against the industry trends and use proprietary game storage mediums gave the company a reputation as being difficult to work with. The lack of storage and the underpowered consoles drove many third-party developers to Nintendo's competitors, with many popular franchises (such as *Final Fantasy*, which was a staple on the Nintendo Entertainment System and Super Nintendo Entertainment System) disappearing completely from Nintendo's home video game consoles. Those games that were ported to Nintendo consoles from their competitors' more powerful machines (for example, *The Elder Scrolls V: Skyrim*, *Mass Effect 3*, *Call of Duty: Modern Warfare 3*, all on the Wii) arrived with missing features, scaled down graphics and scrapped gameplay. Even with the popularity of the Wii, third-party companies struggled to gain traction on the console, with nine of the top 10 best-selling software entries being Nintendo-published titles (277.69 million worldwide sales). If this is expanded to consider the top 20 Wii games by sales, Nintendo-published titles make up 14 entries (315.65 million worldwide sales), Ubisoft's *Just Dance* series make up four entries (33.69 million worldwide sales), with Sega's *Mario & Sonic at the Olympic Games* (8 million worldwide sales) and Majesco's *Zumba Fitness* (6.76 million worldwide sales) taking just one spot each. The trend of Nintendo-published titles dominating the sales charts is even more prevalent for the Nintendo DS, with Nintendo taking 18 of the top 20 entries. The top-selling Nintendo-published titles include: *New Super Mario Bros.* (29.85 million worldwide sales), *Nintendogs* (24.68 million), *Mario Kart DS* (23.2 million), *Brain Training* (20.16 million) and *Pokémon Diamond/Pearl* (18.25 million). Third-party publishers, Majesco's *Cooking Mama* (5.66 million worldwide sales) and Sega's *Mario & Sonic at the Olympic Games* (5.10 million worldwide sales), each took just one spot.

LEGACY OF THE WII

The Wii had a perception of being a console for the 'casual' gamer, with 'core' gamers owning either a PlayStation or Xbox as their main console, and Nintendo consoles being considered a 'secondary' console. The hardware, network infrastructure and graphics of the Wii were also underpowered compared to its rivals: the Xbox 360 and PlayStation 3. While game designer Shigeru Miyamoto initially defended Nintendo's decision to not include HD graphics in the Wii, he later admitted regret for their exclusion and cited the limited network infrastructure as a major reason why 'core' gamers considered the Wii separately from the Xbox 360 and PlayStation 3. The Wii's design was criticised as being 'short-sighted' as its hardware quickly become outdated and could not keep up with its rivals. The unique selling point of the Wii, the Wii Remote motion technology, was lost as it was quickly copied by Sony (Move) and Microsoft (Kinect) and incorporated into their controllers.

WII U

On 7 June 2011, after the Wii had been on sale for 4.5 years, Nintendo revealed the Wii U console (codenamed 'Project Cafe') at the E3 expo (Electronic Entertainment Expo) in

Los Angeles. The Wii U was released the following year and was the first Nintendo console to support high-definition graphics and utilised the touchscreen GamePad as part of play. The GamePad was similar to the bottom touchscreen on the Nintendo DS with the TV screen similar to the top screen on the Nintendo DS. Wii Designer Ken'ichiro Ashida stated that 'We had the DS on our minds as we worked on the Wii. We thought about copying the DS's touch-panel interface and even came up with a prototype' (Miller, 2011). While the idea was eventually rejected as it was believed that the two gaming systems would be identical, the concept was brought back and used for the Wii U. Nintendo had played with the idea of the dual screen function with the GameCube using the Game Boy Advance via the link cable, which turned the Game Boy Advance into a second screen and controller for select games. In theory the GamePad was a novel idea. It allowed players the ability to use the Wii U and play games even when the TV was in use. The GamePad could also be used as a remote control and users could even watch Netflix on the GamePad.

The Wii U launched in Australia with 25 games, and an additional 30 games were available during the first three months after the launch date. Nintendo-published titles at launch included *New Super Mario Bros. U* (which eventually went on to sell 5.61 million units worldwide, the console's second best-selling title) and *Nintendo Land* (4.63 million units sold worldwide, the console's sixth best-selling title). Third-party titles available at launch included Ubisoft's *ZombiU* (840 000 units sold worldwide), *Assassin's Creed III* (360 000 units sold worldwide) and *Just Dance 4* (380 000 units sold worldwide), Activision's *Call of Duty: Black Ops II* (420 000 units sold worldwide) and THQ's *Darksiders II* (160 000 units sold worldwide). The Wii U hardware had a moderately successful launch. It sold 557 901 units in Japan in the first three weeks (the Wii sold 544 034 units during the same period of time) and 636 000 units within the first month. In the United States, the Wii U sold 400 000 units in the first week of release (the Wii sold 600 000 during the same period of time) and 890 000 units within the first six weeks.

PROBLEMS WITH THE WII U

Initial reaction to the console was generally positive, but the launch of the Wii U was 'confusing at best and disappointing at worst' (Macdonald, 2013). The major issue was the confusion that stemmed from a lack of advertising leading up to the launch, which led to many consumers not understanding the differences between the Wii and the Wii U and thinking that the Wii U was simply an add-on to the Wii rather than a completely separate console. Up until this point, Nintendo consoles had console-specific controllers, meaning that the controller for the Nintendo 64 only worked for the Nintendo 64 and not, for example, with the Super Nintendo Entertainment System. However, with the Wii, for the first time Nintendo made the console backwards compatible with one of its past consoles: the GameCube. The Wii played GameCube discs and allowed GameCube controllers to be plugged into the Wii to play those games as Nintendo originally intended. On the Wii, the

GameCube controllers only worked with GameCube games and not with Wii games. With the Wii U, Nintendo allowed the Wii Remote to be used as another controller for Wii U games. The Wii U was also backwards compatible with the Wii. This meant that both Wii games and Wii Remotes could be used with the Wii U. The lack of a clear distinction between the two video game consoles was an issue even during the reveal of the Wii U at E3 the previous year, with even some commentators at the time unsure of the Wii U's status as a new stand-alone console or as a hardware update to the Wii. Dan Adelman, former head of Nintendo of America's indie program, commented that 'the name Wii U is abysmal. I think that cut sales in half right there' (Kuchera, 2014). Additionally, former President and CEO of Nintendo, Satoru Iwata, stated that 'Some have the misunderstanding that Wii U is just Wii with a pad for games, and others even consider Wii U GamePad as a peripheral device connectable to Wii ... We feel deeply responsible for not having tried hard enough to have consumers understand the product' (Makuch, 2013). While advertising for the Wii made it clear that the console was designed for everyone, the focus of the target customer in Wii U marketing was muddled further, leading to confusion for consumers.

Regarding the GamePad, many commentators believed that the technology was gimmicky and more 'innovation for innovation's sake' (Tassi, 2016). The second screen was cumbersome to use, as players needed to look down from the TV screen to the GamePad and then back up to the TV screen. This meant that players often missed critical gameplay that was taking place on the main TV screen as their focus was on the GamePad. At the time, Shigeru Miyamoto, Nintendo's Representative Director/Creative Fellow and the creator of the *Donkey Kong, Mario, The Legend of Zelda, Star Fox, F-Zero* and *Pikmin* series, defended the second screen hardware, stating that Nintendo was 'really focused on delivering content that takes advantage of that GamePad interaction and makes that second screen something that's very meaningful and so that's where we need to put our focus' (Crecente, 2015). The second screen was also difficult for third-party developers to produce games for the Wii U, with most developers choosing to skip the console and produce games for Nintendo's competitors: Sony's PlayStation 4 (PS4) and Microsoft's Xbox One. As outlined above, overall sales of third-party titles on the Wii U were dismal. Of the top 25 best-selling titles on the Wii U, 23 are Nintendo-published titles (24 if you include the Namco Bandi Games-published title *Pokken Tournament*, which featured *Pokémon* characters that, up until that point, were found exclusively on Nintendo video game consoles), with Mojang's *Minecraft* (1.45 million units sold worldwide and the console's 14th best-selling title overall) taking the other spot. The PS4 and Xbox One, both released in 2013, a year after the Wii U, were immensely more powerful machines than Nintendo's console and attracted a much bigger share of the total market for video game sales. The Wii U was also perceived to be competing with the PS4 and Xbox One rather than as a substitute to the other consoles as Nintendo had done with the Wii. Upon the Wii U's retirement in early 2017, the Nintendo console had managed a 14 per cent market share (13.8 million units sold worldwide) compared to the Xbox One with a 29 per cent market share (28.7 million units sold worldwide) and the PS4 with a 57 per cent market share (55.9 million units sold worldwide). Reflecting on the Wii U, Nintendo of America president Reggie Fils-Aimé commented that the Wii U simply did not have the games to support it at launch: 'This industry is all about content ... I can map out why the Wii took off at launch, it had two killer pieces at launch: *Twilight Princess*, *Wii Sports* ... So what happened with Wii U? Once the software came that showcased the capabilities of the system, guess what happened? The hardware took off' (Crecente, 2015). This was the major issue of the Wii U at launch: there weren't many games that truly showed off the system's hardware. The software that Fils-Aimé was referring to, and that fully utilised the GamePad, was almost exclusively Nintendo-published titles, which included the two aforementioned launch titles, *New Super Mario Bros. U* and *Nintendo Land*, as well as the Wii U's best-selling title *Mario Kart 8* (7.69 million worldwide sales), *Super Smash Bros. for Wii U* (5.07 million), *Super Mario 3D World* (4.99 million), *Splatoon* (4.70 million), *Super Mario Maker* (3.44 million) and *New Super Luigi U* (2.42 million).

NINTENDO AND SEGA'S PAST FAILURES

Third-party developers are not obligated to make games for every video game system. The design, manufacture, and marketing of even one game is very time-consuming and expensive. Publishers are therefore going to target video game consoles that are easy to develop for and guaranteed to sell games. Sega's second-to-last console, the Saturn, is an example of what can happen when a console is rushed out and difficult to program for. Sega's problems started during the Mega Drive (Genesis in North America) life cycle where multiple hardware add-ons were rushed out to prolong the life of the Mega Drive. Sega released two major add-ons: the Mega CD (Sega CD in North America) and the Mega Drive 32X (Genesis 32X in North America and Super 32X in Japan), which both plugged into the Mega Drive and had their own power adaptors. Games were released for the Mega Drive, the Mega-CD, Mega Drive 32X and the Mega-CD 32X, with the latter's games requiring the combination of the Mega Drive, Mega-CD and Mega Drive 32X to play the games. Sega was also considering releasing the Sega Neptune (a two-in-one Sega Mega Drive and Sega Mega Drive 32X) and the Sega Jupiter (a cartridge-based 32-bit console with similar specifications to the Sega Saturn). The Mega Drive 32X was released in late 1994 in North America and early 1995 in Europe and sold poorly (around 665 000 units). In Japan, the Mega Drive 32X was released on 3 December 1994, while the Sega Saturn was released a week prior on 22 November 1994. This caused both confusion and frustration to customers, as they were unsure of the purpose of the 32X, what differences, if any, the 32X offered over the existing hardware of the Mega Drive, and whether they should skip the 32X entirely and purchase the Sega Saturn instead. Developers also struggled with producing games for the 32X, with many titles being rushed out, not fully utilising the hardware improvements, not being marketed effectively, and being caught up and subsequently flying under the radar between the original Mega Drive games and the new Saturn games. Sega also launched the Saturn early in the United States (May 1995 rather than the planned September 1995) in an attempt to grab sales and market share before the launch of the upcoming PlayStation 2, catching many developers and retailers off guard. The console launched with a high price, few memorable games (*Virtua Fighter* being the exception), and a refusal by many retailers in the United States (including, Best Buy, Walmart and KB Toys) to even stock the console as they were not included in the retailers who received the initial May shipment of consoles. The difficult-to-program hardware, and the low-selling titles on the Mega Drive 32X, meant that many third-party developers skipped the Sega Saturn entirely. The console had low overall sales (8.82 million units worldwide) compared with the Mega Drive/Genesis (29.54 million units worldwide). These issues contributed to the Dreamcast, launched in 1999, being Sega's last video game console (8.20 million units sold worldwide) before the company made the decision to stop producing hardware and evolved into a third-party developer for its rival's systems. The Dreamcast, both retrospectively and at the time of release, was hailed as being a revolutionary console; well ahead of its competitors in innovation, and much easier to program for than its predecessor. However, the industry, developers and consumers often punish those companies that are innovative, preferring to maintain the status quo – with improved graphics being prioritised over gimmicky hardware innovations. Nintendo had previously attempted and failed with hardware innovations in the past. This is most notably with the Virtual Boy, a 'portable' video game console released in 1995 that endeavoured to display 3D graphics. The console was rushed to market at the end of the Super Nintendo Entertainment System's life to bridge the gap between that console and the delayed Nintendo 64. The Virtual Boy had a tiny library of games (22 games in total, with *Virtual Boy Wario Land* being the most regarded game) and was difficult to play due to the fact that the visual display was in black and red, which placed strain on the eyes of the player and caused motion sickness or dizziness for some consumers. Nintendo continued refining this technology with the Nintendo 3DS, which was a true portable video game console that mastered the 3D technology that the Virtual Boy earlier attempted. The Nintendo 3DS, released in 2011, is the successor to the Nintendo DS and allows users to play games in 3D without the need for additional add-ons such as 3D glasses. As of October 2018, the Nintendo 3DS family (the original Nintendo 3DS and 3DS XL (LL in Japan), Nintendo 2DS, New Nintendo 3DS and 3DS XL, and New Nintendo 2DS XL) has currently sold 72.74 million units worldwide and has an 81.9 per cent market share of the hand-held market.

Nintendo's Nintendo 64 Disk Drive (64DD) add-on to the Nintendo 64 was the other piece of hardware that the company pushed out to market. The 64DD, like the Family Computer Disk System released in 1986, was only released in Japan, exclusively via mail order, and sold 15 000 units from late 1999 to early 2001 before Nintendo retired the console. The purpose of the 64DD was part of Nintendo president Hiroshi Yamauchi's 'longtime dream of a network that connects Nintendo consoles all across the nation' and was deemed to be 'an appealing creativity package that delivered a well-designed user-driven experience' (Schneider, 2001). Games planned to utilise the expanded storage capabilities and the real-time clock for persistent game world design of the 64DD, most notably *The Legend of Zelda: Majora's Mask* (originally *Zelda Gaiden*), *Paper Mario* (originally *Super Mario RPG 2*) and *Donkey Kong 64* (originally *Ultra Donkey Kong*), which were released on Nintendo 64 cartridge format only, or cancelled completely, such as *Mother 3* (originally *Earthbound 64*), which was eventually released in Japan only on the Game Boy Advance.

NINTENDO SWITCH

Nintendo began work on its next video game console, the Nintendo Switch, in 2014 after the company suffered large financial losses as a result of the poor reception and sales of the Wii U. The Nintendo Switch (codenamed 'NX') was unveiled to the public in October 2016 and was released to the public in March 2017. The Nintendo Switch is considered a 'hybrid console' as it can be played in 'TV Mode' as a traditional home console by inserting the main console unit into the Nintendo Switch Dock station connected to a television; in 'Tabletop Mode' with the console being removed from the Switch Dock and the controllers detached from the console, played sitting on a table using the stand at the back of the device; and in 'Handheld Mode' as a traditional portable game console, similar to the Game Boy or Nintendo 3DS. The Nintendo Switch has a 15.75-centimetre LCD touchscreen and two Joy-Con controllers, which can be detached from the Nintendo Switch and held vertically or horizontally depending on the game being played. The Joy-Cons contain gyroscope and accelerometer technology, including a high-definition (HD) rumble feature, enabling the controllers to reproduce certain sensations like ice cubes rattling in a glass. The Joy-Cons also feature an infrared motion camera, NFC read/write functionality, which supports the existing Nintendo amiibo line of figures, and a capture button to save and share screenshots of game footage. These features are also available on the Pro Controller. The Nintendo Switch is Nintendo's first home console that is region free, meaning that games bought from any country can be played on the console, and charges via USB Type-C. The console can connect to up to 10 other Nintendo Switch devices over Wi-Fi for local multiplayer games and uses flash ROM cartridges and digital content for games and software.

REASONS FOR THE SUCCESS OF THE NINTENDO SWITCH

The Nintendo Switch had an incredibly successful launch, largely due to a combination of a number of different factors. First was the video game console's name: the Nintendo Switch. The name was chosen to demonstrate how quickly the console could 'switch' between being a dedicated home video game console that could be played in front of the TV to one that could be played on the go, such as in the office, at parties, in the car, while on a plane, at the airport, on the bus, in bed, at university and even on the toilet, with Nintendo giving a cheeky nod to its audience, acknowledging how many of its owners may use the console. Nintendo also reintroduced their name back into the console (which had been done with the Nintendo Entertainment System, Super Nintendo Entertainment System, Nintendo 64, and Nintendo GameCube) after dropping the 'Nintendo' name for the Wii and Wii U. Second was the carefully designed logo and related sound effect used in all marketing for the console. The red and white colours used in the Nintendo Switch logo are based on the colours associated with the long-standing Nintendo logo. Further, a click sound is used at the beginning of each commercial with a graphic showing the outline of two Joy Cons lining up above the Nintendo Switch name. The click sound is the sound that the Joy Cons make when attaching themselves to the Nintendo Switch console. Third was Nintendo's marketing campaign of play 'Anytime, anywhere, with anyone' (Nintendo, 2017), which, as in the Wii advertisements, showed the ease of using and playing the system. Even though there are multiple controller combinations to play the Nintendo Switch (such as with the Joy Cons attached to sides of the Nintendo Switch, in separate hands using the motion technology to detect movement, together in a Joy Con grip, or by using the Pro Controller), it is clearly conveyed to the consumer. Fourth, the commercials for the Nintendo Switch strategically focused on 20–30-year-olds with disposable income rather than the traditional children's market that Nintendo had previously always focused on. The final factor was the launch game: *The Legend of Zelda: Breath of the Wild*. *Breath of the Wild*, which was also simultaneously released on the Wii U as the last Nintendo-published title on the console, was a critically acclaimed title and considered one of the best video games of all time. The game has a Metacritic score of 97 per cent, was the highest rated game of 2017, and holds the largest number of perfect reviews of any game from any year. At launch, *Breath of the Wild* had a 102 per cent attach rate to Nintendo Switch hardware sales, meaning that each customer that bought a Nintendo Switch also bought a copy of *Breath of the Wild*. As of October 2018, *Breath of the Wild* has gone on to sell 9.32 million copies worldwide (and 1.31 million copies on the Wii U). Other critically and commercially successful Nintendo-published titles on the Nintendo Switch include *Super Mario Odyssey* (97 per cent on Metacritic and 11.17 million worldwide sales), *Mario Kart 8 Deluxe* (92 per cent; 10.35 million), an updated port of the Wii U title of the same name, and *Splatoon 2* (83 per cent; 6.76 million). The focus of the games on the Nintendo Switch had shifted to more in-depth exploration and longer gameplay.

Nintendo also fostered a much better relationship with third-party developers, which was demonstrated by the commitment of these developers during the initial reveal presentation for the Nintendo Switch as well as during E3 and official Nintendo Direct presentations. Nintendo also collaborated and allowed its intellectual property to be included in some third-party games, such as with *Super Mario* characters (Mario, Luigi, Peach, Yoshi, Toad, Toadette and Bowser) and *Donkey Kong* in Ubisoft's *Mario + Rabbids Kingdom Battle* (2.14 million worldwide sales) and *Starlink: Battle for Atlas* (released October 2018), which was released on all platforms but featured Star Fox characters (Fox McCloud, Slippy Toad, Falco Lombardi and Peppy Hare) exclusively on the Switch release. In addition, both the *Elder Scrolls V: Skyrim* and *Diablo III* Switch ports featured exclusive in-game content and costumes from Nintendo's *The Legend of Zelda* franchise. Further, the Nintendo Switch has been a 'fantastic platform' for indie developers with indie games, such as *Celeste* (Matt Makco Games), *Fast RMX* (Shin'en Multimedia), *Golf Story* (Sidebar Games), *Stardew Valley* (Chucklefish) and *Thimbleweed Park* (Terrible Toybox), selling more on the Nintendo Switch than on the PS4, Xbox One or on Steam. These indie games, which are released virtually via the Nintendo eShop, have become so popular that companies such as Limited Run Games, Super Rare Games and Signature Games have partnered with indie developers to release physical copies of the games. These companies have strategically targeted the lucrative 'core' gamer market who are collectors of physical games, spend large amounts of their disposable income on video game merchandise and like the tangible elements of games, cases, booklets and other content found in special-edition releases of games.

While the Wii U failed due to the gimmicky perception of the hardware, confusing branding and poor relationships with third-party developers, the Nintendo Switch has flourished and is seen as a spiritual evolution of the problematic Wii U. Aesthetically, the Nintendo Switch is essentially a slimmed-down version of the Wii U GamePad with the ability to detach the side controls. The ability to play the Nintendo Switch away from the TV was also inherited from the Wii U, except now you can literally play anywhere with the Nintendo Switch (as opposed to being close to the Wii U console with the GamePad). Further, many games and franchises, such as *The Legend of Zelda: Breath of the Wild*, *Mario Kart 8* (*Mario Kart 8 Deluxe* on Nintendo Switch), *Captain Toad: Treasure Tracker*, *Splatoon* (*Splatoon 2* on Nintendo Switch), *Xenoblade Chronicles X* (*Xenoblade Chronicles 2* and *Xenoblade Chronicles 2: Torna the Golden Country* on Nintendo Switch), *Donkey Kong Country: Tropical Freeze* and *New Super Mario Bros. U* (*New Super Mario Bros. U Deluxe* on Nintendo Switch), got their start on the Wii U and have been ported, remade, updated or received sequels on the Nintendo Switch console.

Despite all of the success surrounding the console, the Nintendo Switch does have some criticisms, most notably the delayed roll-out and poor reception of its paid subscription service, Nintendo Switch Online. The service launched in September 2018 and allows users to play online (a service that Nintendo had always provided to users for free on the Wii and Wii U and had up until that point been free for all users of Nintendo Switch) with compatible Nintendo Switch games as well as retro video games releases and upgrades (such as a 'souped-up' version of the original *The Legend of Zelda* from the NES subtitled *Living the Life of Luxury*) from Nintendo's past consoles, starting with the Nintendo Entertainment System. The Nintendo Switch Online service is the successor to Nintendo's Virtual Console service, and the new service will be the main way that users will play Nintendo's catalogue of retro video games moving forward in addition to playing select games featured on Nintendo's incredibly popular Nintendo Classic Mini consoles (as of October 2018, the NES and SNES versions have been released).

SALES OF THE NINTENDO SWITCH

Since its launch, sales of the Nintendo Switch have been impressive and console shortages were common, especially in the United States and Japan. As of October 2018, Nintendo currently has a 14.4 per cent market share of the eighth generation of video game consoles with 20.6 million sales. Nintendo's competitors, the PlayStation 4 (PS4) and Xbox One, have a 58.2 per cent (83 million units sold worldwide) and 27.3 per cent (39 million units sold worldwide) market share respectively (albeit some commentators argue that the Nintendo Switch's true competitor isn't the PS4 or the Xbox One but in fact the iPad). While Nintendo's overall market share is low, its competitors' products have been on sale since 2013, while the Nintendo Switch has been on sale since 2017. Looking at sales in 2017, Nintendo commanded a 30.4 per cent market share, with the PS4 on 55.5 per cent and Xbox One on 14.1 per cent. As of October 2018, Nintendo increased its market share in 2018, with the Nintendo Switch at 37 per cent, the Xbox One slightly increasing to 16.8 per cent, and the PS4 falling to 46.2 per cent market share by sales. Nintendo's competitors, Sony in 2016 with its PS4 Slim and PS4 Pro and Microsoft with its Xbox One S and Xbox One X in 2017, both updated their consoles to better compete in the industry and prolong the life of their existing machines, which had not seen a major update since their original launches. There are rumours that even Nintendo is considering a console update despite the fact that the Nintendo Switch was only launched in March 2017.

THE FUTURE OF NINTENDO

The Nintendo Switch succeeded where the Wii U failed, with Nintendo of America President Reggie Fils-Aimé explaining that the Wii U wasn't a 'beta test' but more of a learning experience, saying, 'Without our experiences on the Wii U, we would not have the Nintendo Switch in terms of what we learned and importantly what we heard from our consumers' (Doolan, 2018). The Nintendo Switch became the fastest selling video game console of all time, and some commentators are predicting that the sales of the Nintendo Switch will surpass those of the Wii. The Nintendo Switch mirrors many of the successful strategies of the Wii, notably a game from the *Zelda* franchise (*Breath of the Wild* on Nintendo Switch and *Twilight Princess* on Wii) as the Nintendo Switch's launch title and following that up with a game from the *Super Mario* franchise (*Odyssey* on Nintendo Switch and *Galaxy* for Wii) within the console's first year in the market. Whatever the final sales figures for the Nintendo Switch end up being, it is clear that Nintendo has learned its lessons that hurt the company in the past. Under the new leadership of Shuntaro Furukawa and through the combination of working with third-party developers and extending the Nintendo brand and intellectual property to mobile phones such as *Miitomo* and *Super Mario Run* (2016), *Fire Emblem Heroes* and *Animal Crossing: Pocket Camp* (2017), *Dragalia Lost* (2018) and *Mario Kart Tour* (2019), as well as its partnership with Niantic's incredibly successful *Pokémon GO* mobile game, Nintendo is setting itself up to remain relevant, fun and creative with both current and future generations.

REVIEW QUESTIONS

1 The video game industry has seen enormous change over the past three decades. What future changes to the industry do you believe will affect Nintendo and its competitors, Sony and Microsoft? Based on what you read in the case study, what internal changes should Nintendo make to best respond to these changes?

2 Has Nintendo's strategy regarding video game production truly changed after the dismal sales of the Wii U and the success of its new console, the Nintendo Switch? Or is Nintendo only as good as its next console release? Give examples from the case study to support your reasoning.

REFERENCES

Crecente, B. 2015, 22 June. 'Nintendo explains why the Wii U didn't take off at launch', https://www.polygon.com/2015/6/22/8823035/nintendo-explains-why-the-wii-u-didnt-take-off-at-launch, accessed 14 October 2018.

Doolan, L. 2018, 4 October. 'Reggie says Wii U's failure ultimately led to success of the Switch', http://www.nintendolife.com/news/2018/10/reggie_says_wii_us_failure_ultimately_led_to_success_of_the_switch, accessed 14 October 2018.

Kuchera, B. 2014, 5 August. 'The Wii U name is still hurting Nintendo', https://www.polygon.com/2014/8/5/5970787/wii-u-nintendo bad-name, accessed 14 October 2018.

Macdonald, K. 2013, 11 January. 'How successful was the Wii U launch?', https://au.ign.com/articles/2013/01/11/how-successful-was-the-wii-u-launch, accessed 14 October 2018.

Makuch, E. 2013, 24 April. 'Nintendo: Some believe Wii U is "just Wii with a pad for games"', https://www.gamespot.com/articles/nintendo-some-believe-wii-u-is-just-wii-with-a-pad-for-games/1100-6407527, accessed 14 October 2018.

Miller, R. 2011, 2 June. 'Nintendo's Wii successor (Project Café?) and other expectations for its E3 2011 keynote', https://www.theverge.com/2011/06/02/nintendo-wii-2-project-cafe-mario-e3-2011, accessed 14 October 2018.

Nintendo. 2017, 1 February. 'Nintendo Switch – Play anytime, anywhere, with anyone', https://www.youtube.com/watch?v=55vCzx-725Q, accessed 14 October 2018.

Parish, J. 2008, 29 January. '-3 in '07', https://web.archive.org/web/20110604143751/http://www.1up.com/do/blogEntry?bId=8601568&publicUserId= 5379721, accessed 14 October 2018.

Schneider, P. 2001, 9 February. 'Everything about the 64DD', https://au.ign.com/articles/2001/02/10/everything-about-the-64dd, accessed 14 October 2018.

Tassi, P. 2016, 20 April. '"Star Fox Zero" is what happens when Wii U Gamepad integration goes wrong', https://www.forbes.com/sites/insertcoin/2016/04/20/star-fox-zero-is-what-happens-when-wii-u-gamepad-integration-goes-wrong/#2619f8352b54, accessed 14 October 2018.

Wired. 2006, 27 April. 'Nintendo Revolution now called "Wii"', https://www.wired.com/2006/04/nintendo-revolu/, accessed 14 October 2018.

CASE STUDY 2

Implementing organisational transformation in Auzee Engineering Services (AES)[1]

Dr Shoaib Riaz, Dr Nell Kimberley and Dr Damian Morgan

BACKGROUND

Today's business environment is changing faster than ever before (Michel, By & Burnes, 2013; Nonaka, Kodama, Hirose & Kohlbacher, 2014). Business profiles, operations and even existence are in swift transformation. Ninety per cent of Fortune 500 companies existing in 1955 are now defunct, merged or reduced in size. And since 2000, 52 per cent of companies then listed in this same index have either gone bankrupt, been acquired or merged with other firms, or now exist in a reduced capacity. Companies are getting younger too. In 1960, the average company age on the Standard and Poor's 500 was 60 years. This average has continually shrunk since this time, and is forecast at just 12 years by 2020 (Novellino, 2015). At the current rate of replacement, 75 per cent of today's Standard and Poor's 500 companies will no longer exist by 2027 (Perry, 2015). Clearly, there has been a great deal of market disruption over the past 60 years and these changes are becoming increasingly rapid. These changes also reflect an increasingly unpredictable, dynamic and disruptive external environment that managers now face. The essential challenge is to maintain company prosperity to ensure continued viability. In response, managers commonly respond to external challenges by adopting large-scale organisational change, better known as organisation transformation (OT) (Hoyte & Greenwood, 2007; Rouse & Baba, 2006).

In Australia, previously held notions of once-a-decade change by managers have been replaced by new realisations where continuous and transformational change is considered the norm and is regarded as central to organisational success (Graetz & Smith, 2010; Smith, Oczkowski, Macklin & Noble, 2003). The willingness to adopt OT is evident in many large and successful Australian organisations, including Qantas and Coca-Cola Amatil (Coca-Cola Amatil, 2015; Qantas, 2013) and, as the focus of this case, AES.

INTRODUCTION TO AES

AES is a regional Australian subsidiary forming part of a global multinational group – Go Global Engineering Services – with headquarters in Europe; this multinational organisation is a leading global supplier of engineering technologies and services. The company has operated in Australia since 1918. The Australian group operations are divided into four business sectors: mobility solutions, industrial technology, consumer goods, and energy and building technology.

---

1   Auzee Engineering Services is a hypothetical organisation.

AES generates annual revenues totalling about A$1 billion per annum across Oceania. The Australian subsidiary employs over 1500 people, working primarily in Melbourne, Sydney and Brisbane locations. The organisation's activities cover a diverse range of product groups that include automotive components and engineering services, security systems, power tools and accessories, aftermarket parts, drive and control technology, solar energy, software innovations, hot water and heating systems, and communication centre services. **Table C2.1** summarises key facts about the size of AES operations within the parent company for financial year 2013–14.

TABLE C2.1	KEY FACTS ABOUT AES AND THE PARENT COMPANY, GO GLOBAL ENGINEERING SERVICES, FOR YEAR 2013–14	
Characteristics	AES	Parent company
Employees	>1500	≈400 000
Locations	3 (in Australia)	70 countries
Subsidiaries	–	≈550
Representation	–	≈150 countries
Annual sales	> A$1b	60b euros
Research and development cost	–	5b euros
Patent applications	–	5000

CHANGING WINDS FOR AES

Until the financial year 2009–10, AES was one of the largest suppliers of automotive components and technology to automotive manufacturers worldwide, along with Australia. From this time, the business landscape underwent rapid adjustments. Global and local trends in the automotive manufacturing industry, saw falling tariff barriers and new competition from manufacturers capitalising on relatively low-cost sources of labour. These external shifts placed financial pressures on the Australian automotive component manufacturing industry that resulted in closures among several automotive component manufacturers in Australia (Australian Government Productivity Commission, 2014).

More generally, global forces have driven dramatic changes in the demand for motor vehicles. Organisations have responded by increasing the size and scale of production in new locations. This new competition has placed relentless pressure on traditional automotive global manufacturers, who have focused on finding new ways to reduce manufacturing costs. In fact, motor vehicle producers in Australia have not survived these increasingly highly competitive global and domestic automotive markets. Australia has a long history of mass car production. Last century, Australia produced cars that were arguably the best available in the world (Mellor, 2014). Global car manufacturers including Ford, General Motors, Mitsubishi, Nissan and Toyota located subsidiaries in Australia to produce cars for the domestic and export markets (Australian Government

Productivity Commission, 2014). Production realised close to half a million units in the 1970s. However, by 2013, the total production of Australian-manufactured vehicles had fallen to around 200 000 units, with the Australian market becoming dominated by cars imported from Asia and Europe. At this time, Australia's share of global production was about 0.25 per cent, and of that, approximately 40 per cent of locally produced cars were exported (Australian Government Productivity Commission, 2014). Nevertheless, the remaining car manufacturers in Australia – Toyota, GM Holden and Ford – announced their intentions to cease Australian manufacturing operations. The last locally built Australian mass-produced car left the assembly line in 2017 (T. Davis, 2017).

The end of mass car production had flow-on effects on Australian automotive component manufacturing. This impacted AES directly. Due to the relatively high costs of Australian-based manufacture/supply of automotive components, AES was no longer competitive in global markets. This was due mainly to changing requirements and preferences of the automotive manufacturing industry globally, such as change in geographic patterns of demand for new vehicles; global production capacity exceeding demand of new vehicles; intense competition in local and global markets; changing consumer preferences; increased automotive manufacturing in developing countries, plus cost pressures associated with doing business in Australia. These factors necessitated that AES develop a new business model to remain financially viable.

SHIFT IN AES'S STRATEGY

The automotive components being manufactured at AES were primarily produced for export (up to 90 per cent), but due to global cost competition, it was no longer sufficiently competitive in export markets. To remain competitive in the global automotive components market, AES shifted approximately 70 per cent of automotive components manufacturing operations to overseas locations in Asia and Europe; these locations being geographically closer to end-point customers. This process, coinciding with reduced local car production, was completed in 2012.

AES's reduced Australian manufacturing operations had a profound impact on the company. After relocating 70 per cent of its automotive component manufacturing operations to offshore locations, current automotive components manufacturing activities represent just 5 to 10 per cent of its around A$1 billion business. As a result, approximately 400 employees were retrenched from the Melbourne facility and AES was on the verge of being shut down.

However, instead of shutting down, the company chose to transform itself by changing its business model. This process involved a redirection towards finding new businesses to replace the existing business.

The significant reductions in automotive component manufacturing operations in Australia necessitated diversification through the application of technologies into new products and industries, other than automotive component manufacturing. To achieve this, the company had to actively seek business diversification and subsequent business development outside the automotive industry. The diversification meant taking the existing automotive-style technology and applying it to a non-passenger motor vehicle environment; for example, adapting automotive radar and camera detection systems and finding their application to rail transport. Consequently, the company had to adopt a proactive model to explore and develop niche markets and new products. This was counter to past practices, where AES followed a reactive model determined by customers' demands.

CHALLENGES FACED BY AES IN IMPLEMENTING NEW BUSINESS MODEL

In 2012–13, AES's management considered diversification into other industries, products and markets. Finding alternative businesses was a significant change for AES. Traditionally, employees and management did little *upfront* work in order to gain new business. Customers were usually in-house or large original equipment manufacturers and that did not require matching or negotiating cut-throat competition to get the business. The strategic change of clientele now required significant effort to explore new markets and to find new customers. This added further complexity in understanding competitors and matching their needs to the employees' existing skills and technological expertise. AES had to focus on small customers, rather than being an equipment supplier to large companies, such as Bunnings. Success in these new markets required employees to be more customer-oriented and flexible to customer requirements.

AES's management faced huge challenges. In altering the way it operated, it had no real experience exploring new business fields. In order to do so, it had to address its employees' understanding of organisational purpose or, more simply, the way they looked at their work, work practices and organisational structure.

EMPLOYEES' UNDERSTANDING OF ORGANISATIONAL PURPOSE

To diversify the business, AES's employees had to change the way they interpreted and delivered the current business model, while understanding and accepting the purpose of a new business model. Almost all of AES's employees, except office coordinators, are engineers. To comply with the new business strategy, these engineers were required to source new business, to contribute to new ideas, to work on new opportunities and, overall, to become more flexible in their work practices. These activities required a fundamental shift in the way they perceived the nature of their work.

EMPLOYEES' WORK PRACTICES

Changes to work practices represented a significant shift for employees. Prior to the shift in their customer base, applications and systems (software) engineering were considered distinct areas. Now engineers had to work in both domains. Additionally, engineers were to be exposed to external clients, which presented them with technical and problem-solving challenges, along with a need for greater flexibility. Paralleling these changes to work practices were increased cost pressures and new processes. Engineers no longer waited for work to be allocated. Instead, they were required to conduct preliminary discussions and to work with potential clients before they could even hope to secure and start new projects.

ORGANISATIONAL STRUCTURE

The new business model also meant downsizing and creating a new organisational structure. In terms of organisational structure, a shift was required from a functional structure to a customer-focused matrix structure.

SUBSEQUENT EMPLOYEE RESISTANCE

Being a longstanding engineering organisation, AES used to employ engineers with penchant for stability and long-term horizons. In the past, these skilled employees focused exclusively on single projects having durations over several years. The new business model, encompassing short-term projects, created uncertainty and anxiety among employees. Not surprisingly, one-quarter of AES's remaining engineering employees took redundancy or retirement packages and left the organisation. Those employees who left the organisation did not find themselves fitting with the new business model and felt unsuited to work on new products and technologies.

Since most of the continuing employees in AES also had been working there for a long period (10 years or more), there was a level of dissatisfaction and implementing the new business model met with resistance from them.

LEADING AES THROUGH ROUGH WATERS

Like the employees, AES's management had little experience in implementing the new business model. However, instead of hiring external consultants, it adopted an organic approach to implementing change. Knowingly or unknowingly, it dealt with the change implementation challenges by adopting the following strategies.

MANAGEMENT WAS OPEN-MINDED

During the change implementation process, management exhibited openness to the uncertainty of its current situation and to inviting new possibilities from its employees.

In relation to business diversification efforts, management was not rigid in its approach to capturing new business. Instead, it was open to the idea of new business occurring from as yet unknown sources. It had understood that a significant proportion of new business would emerge from this area. As part of its strategy of being open to the unknown, management convinced its board, headquartered in Europe, that its new business plan should include approximately 15 per cent of turnover from unknown sources. It did not pursue any particular general business fields for new work.

In addition to management's comfort with an uncertain future, the senior management team was very receptive to new ideas generated by employees. Management's approach was to work closely with employees and to listen for new concepts. It encouraged employees to offer opinions with regard to opportunities and to explore these as far as possible. The engineers tended to follow a scientific approach towards testing new ideas and were more critical about the time spent on these tasks. Conversely, management was very responsive to new suggestions and opportunities, and developed a vision to materialise them. In order to encourage employees to generate new concepts, the management team actively implemented a continuous improvement program known as CIP; an intranet-based repository where employees could initiate and document a new idea for improvement. Ideas thought worthy of consideration were evaluated at management team meetings. One employee was assigned the task of monitoring the overall progress of ideas generated through the continuous improvement program.

MANAGEMENT PROMOTED ORGANISATIONAL AGILITY

AES's management demonstrated its ability to rapidly respond to changes in the operational environment. In order to make the organisation agile, management ensured that the company became more flexible, risk-taking and only minimally compliant with headquarters' strategic and operational plans.

Since the new business areas were different from the conventional activities previously engaged in by AES, management emphasised the need for the organisation to become more flexible both at individual and structural levels. Flexibility at the employee level included variable working arrangements, skill diversification, expanded job roles and employees having the freedom to drive their own careers. The flexibility in terms of organisational structure included achieving lean and therefore cost-effective structure through continuous structural adjustments.

During the business diversification process, management encouraged risk-taking to assist with business diversification. Furthermore, being a subsidiary of a European parent company, AES sometimes found itself in a conflicted situation. On the one hand, the company needed to be agile for success, but on the other hand, the multinational organisational structure, policies and procedures did not support agility. Central directives from headquarters made it difficult for the Australian subsidiary to act quickly in new business fields. Management improved organisational agility through the removal of its processes and procedures or by insisting that headquarters adopt central changes to meet AES's new business plans.

MANAGEMENT RELIED ON EMPLOYEES TO INITIATE AND ENACT CHANGE

Management valued its existing workforce, afforded them autonomy and acknowledged and/or acted upon their feedback.

To diversify the business, management aimed to extract maximum benefit from existing employees through motivation and support. It shunned hiring external consultants. The new team dynamic was sufficiently strong among the existing employees, so management did not wish to dilute their motivation by hiring employees from outside the organisation. In some cases, employees who had departed the company were approached and offered new roles with the organisation.

Management also encouraged employee autonomy. Autonomy here refers to the level of control that employees and teams had over their jobs and day-to-day work activities. Each team had its own project manager responsible for the work. Most of the decisions concerning new projects were decided by the project manager and/or project team, rather than management. Moreover, in terms of decision making, employees were generally independent. The engineers worked fairly autonomously in terms of deciding for themselves as to when they would attend the proving grounds or undertake testing. Only decisions that impacted on a larger proportion of the organisation were made with management's input.

Another form of management's reliance on employees related to feedback. The feedback here refers to employees' observations, suggestions and comments about the different processes and structures introduced by management during the change process. Feedback channels created an innovation mindset among employees and encouraged employees with an entrepreneurial spirit. Management acted upon employee feedback. Where management did not consider it viable to act on employee suggestions, feedback was at least acknowledged. Management acknowledged feedback by informing employees in subsequent meetings that it had listened to suggestions, analysed them and given them consideration, and it gave reasons for no action or later implementation. In some other instances, where management was not able to implement a whole idea, it considered some elements of the idea to acknowledge employee feedback.

MANAGEMENT SUPPORTED KNOWLEDGE-SHARING

Management supported knowledge-sharing by tapping into the deep pool of tacit knowledge within AES and its worldwide subsidiaries. The deep pool of knowledge refers to knowledge within the organisation, locally and globally, especially within the employees. It may be knowledge gained through personal interest in technical areas that were not related to the organisation's previous business activities. This encouraged the emergence of informal teams that would exchange information about how employees could work together on new and innovative technologies to win projects in different fields of business.

In order to learn from the experiences of other subsidiaries, AES also sent its employees overseas so that they could be cross-trained by these subsidiaries and could bring back knowledge about different areas of business that had not been previously pursued by AES. This further contributed to creating networks with employees in overseas subsidiaries and these networks later provided advice to AES. In situations where employees faced a specific problem in a new business field, the problem was opened up to subsidiaries worldwide where groups overseas with relevant experience could provide suitable advice. Employees formed weekend groups where they discussed how to take skills, such as sensor technology, to the next level when applied to rail projects. Management was aware of this and fully supported this approach. Thus, employees shared their ideas and knowledge and further refined them before presenting them to management. Another way of tapping into the deep pool of tacit organisational knowledge was to utilise the past experience of employees gained from previous jobs outside AES. Management respected the experience of employees gained in other organisations and let them apply this experience to assist diversification.

AES's executives understood the power and importance of informal teams as it tapped into previously underutilised skills and knowledge, such as monitoring software and mobile phone applications. As a way to demonstrate its support for the informal groups, senior management permitted informal groups to add the additional hours spent working on projects informally against their regular office hours.

MANAGEMENT EXERCISED LESS CONTROL

An interesting and unexpected management practice was the non-directive approach adopted by executives during the transformation. Management kept operations informal by promoting decentralisation and by not being overly critical about employees' mistakes.

As the organisation moved into diverse areas, it became relatively more relaxed in terms of how and with whom employees engaged to achieve work outcomes. As a consequence, power to make decisions was increasingly deferred to the employees. In the new organisational structure, many issues, such as budgetary approval processes, became ambiguous and depended on the employees' own interpretation rather than relying on clarification from management. Executives did not want to define everything for employees, thus allowing employees to decide on the best options as appropriate to specific situations. Employees had reasonable relationships with each other. In circumstances where guidance was needed, they preferred having informal discussions with their peers and management, rather than going through a formalised process. Thus, the working relationships among employees and between employees and management became less formal, with employees taking greater responsibility for decision making and outcomes.

Generally, instead of management providing constructive criticism to employees, management encouraged employees to evaluate their own shortcomings. This approach assisted employees to understand their own positions, to reflect upon their actions and their role, and to identify what they needed to do in future to learn from their mistakes.

MANAGEMENT ENLISTED EMPLOYEE COMMITMENT TO CHANGE

In order to make the transformation succeed, AES's management prioritised employee commitment to change. It achieved this through employee involvement in informal discussion, communicating decisions to employees proactively and through establishing a sense of stability and future certainty among employees.

Senior managers usually engaged with employees through informal discussions. Management considered informal meetings and a loose structure as an opportunity for employees to feel at ease and to discuss openly opportunities, success and failure. These opportunities also allowed employees to request support when needed.

During the transformation, management also adopted the policy of communicating openly and frequently. During regular departmental meetings, management kept employees informed about new initiatives within the organisation, why these initiatives were necessary, and how employees could play their role in ensuring these led to successful outcomes. In some cases, executives conveyed provisional information to employees with the proviso that the situation might change later on. This left employees with a sense of being consulted and included during the change process. Those employees on overseas assignments were also kept informed by management about the possible impacts of change on their roles. Meetings with employees on overseas assignments were conducted through teleconferencing. During those meetings, all expatriates from different locations around the world and AES management convened at the one time. Management remained transparent in making and communicating decisions to its employees.

After the closure of its manufacturing facility, employees became pessimistic about the future of the organisation. During this phase, management gave priority to creating stability and certainty. In order to minimise doubt among employees, executives exerted significant effort into positive statements received from the Board in Europe indicating that the jobs of remaining employees would be secure into the future. In an industry where bad news was often heard, executives motivated employees by showing them that there was 'light at the end of the tunnel'. Even if it won only relatively small projects in new business areas initially, management disseminated positive messages to motivate employees about the future possibilities and to reassure them that the organisation was on the right path with regard to defining and supporting a new business model.

RESULTS

Management practices adopted during transformation contributed to the co-creation of favourable organisational conditions. The confidence expressed by AES's directors and president in the media with regard to its change efforts, along with the other media reports about the organisation, provided the first indication of success in implementing OT. The second measure of success was reflected in the employees' changed attitudes and behaviours towards, and consistent with, the new business model (Schein, 2010; Waddell, Creed, Cummings & Worley, 2017). The third success indicator was the generally positive perception among the employees about the capability of transforming AES.

REVIEW QUESTIONS

1   Why is the organisational change in AES justified as organisational transformation? Elaborate.

2   Is there a definitive theory of organisational change that can be applied to all situations? Does this case support or contradict the idea of a definitive theory of change? Why or why not?

3   In the 21st century, what is the fundamental role of managers while implementing organisational change? What skills do they need to have while implementing change?

REFERENCES

Abdimomunova, L. and Valerdi, R. 2010. 'An organizational assessment process in support of enterprise transformation'. *Information Knowledge Systems Management*. 9(3/4): 175–95. doi:10.3233/IKS-2010-0165.

Australian Government Productivity Commission. 2014. *Australia's Automotive Manufacturing Industry: Productivity Commission Inquiry Report*. (Inquiry Report No. 70), http://www.pc.gov.au/inquiries/completed/automotive/report/automotive.pdf.

Bartunek, J.M. and Moch, M.K. 1987. 'First-order, second-order, and third-order change and organization development interventions: A cognitive approach'. *Journal of Applied Behavioral Science*. 23(4): 483–500.

Coca-Cola Amatil. 2015. 'Real possibilities real progress: 2015 annual report'. *Coca-Cola Amatil*.

David, F.R. 2011. *Strategic Management: Concepts and Cases*, 13th edn (Boston, Mass.; London: Pearson Education).

Davis, E.B., Kee, J. and Newcomer, K. 2010. 'Strategic transformation process: toward purpose, people, process and power'. *Organization Management Journal*. 7(1): 66–80. doi:10.1057/omj.2010.6.

Davis, T. 2017, Oct. 19. 'Australia was brilliant at making cars. Where did it all go wrong?'. *Australian Financial Review*, https://www.afr.com/lifestyle/cars-bikes-and-boats/cars/130-years-of-australian-carmaking--what-did-we-learn-20171018-gz33z2.

Fiol, C.M. and Lyles, M.A. 1985. 'Organizational learning'. *Academy of Management Review*. 10(4): 803–13. doi:10.5465/AMR.1985.4279103.

Ford, J.D. and Backoff, R.H. 1988. 'Organizational change in and out of dualities and paradox'. In R.E. Quin and K.S. Cameron (eds), *Paradox and Transformation: Toward a Theory of Change in Organization and Management* (Cambridge, MA: Ballinger): 81–121.

Fullan, M. 2001. *Leading in Culture of Change* (San Francisco, CA: Jossey-Bass).

Gary, J.S. 2000. 'Developing skills in strategic transformation'. *European Journal of Innovation Management*. 3(1): 45–52. doi:10.1108/14601060010305256.

Golembiewski, R.T. 1979. *Approaches to Planned Change Part II: Macro-level Interventions and Change-agent Strategies* (New York: Marcel Dekker).

Golembiewski, R.T., Billingsley, K. and Yeager, S. 1976. 'Measuring change and persistence in human affairs: types of change generated by OD designs'. *The Journal of Applied Behavioral Science*. 12(2): 133–57. doi:10.1177/002188637601200201.

Graetz, F. and Smith, A.C.T. 2010. 'Managing organizational change: a philosophies of change approach'. *Journal of Change Management*. 10(2): 135–54. doi:10.1080/14697011003795602.

Greenwood, R. and Hinings, C.R. 2006. 'Radical organizational change'. In S.R. Clegg, C. Hardy, T.B. Lawrence & W.R. Nord (eds), *The Sage Handbook of Organization Studies* (London: Sage): 814–42.

Hoyte, D.S. and Greenwood, R.A. 2007. 'Journey to the north face: a guide to business transformation'. *Academy of Strategic Management Journal*. 6: 91–104.

Kezar, A. 2001. 'Understanding and facilitating organizational change in the 21st century'. *ASHE-ERIC Higher Education Report*. 28(4): 147. doi:10.1002/aehe.2804.

Latham, J.R. 2013. 'A framework for leading the transformation to performance excellence part I: CEO perspectives on forces, facilitators, and strategic leadership systems'. *Quality Management Journal*. 20(2): 12–33.

McKnight, L.L. 2013. 'Transformational leadership in the context of punctuated change'. *Journal of Leadership, Accountability & Ethics*. 10(2): 103–12.

Mellor, J. 2014, 12 December. 'Australia's once vibrant auto industry crashes in slow motion'. *The New York Times*, https://www.nytimes.com/2014/12/14/automobiles/australias-once-vibrant-auto-industry-crashes-in-slow-motion.html.

Meyer, A.D. 1982. 'Adapting to environmental jolts'. *Administrative Science Quarterly*. 27(4): 515–37. doi:10.2307/2392528.

Michel, A., By, R.T. and Burnes, B. 2013. 'The limitations of dispositional resistance in relation to organizational change'. *Management Decision*. 51(4): 761–80. doi:10.1108/00251741311326554.

Nonaka, I., Kodama, M., Hirose, A. and Kohlbacher, F. 2014. 'Dynamic fractal organizations for promoting knowledge-based transformation – a new paradigm for organizational theory'. *European Management Journal*. 32(1): 137–46. doi:10.1016/j.emj.2013.02.003.

Novellino, T. 2015. 'Don't get cozy, Fortune 500: it's do-or-die time for digital disruption, says this author', http://upstart.bizjournals.com/resources/author/2015/06/04/fortune-500-must-disrupt-or-die-writes-r-ray-wang.html?page=all.

Perry, M.J. 2015. 'Fortune 500 firms in 1955 v. 2015; only 12% remain, thanks to the creative destruction that fuels economic prosperity', https://www.aei.org/publication/fortune-500-firms-in-1955-vs-2015-only-12-remain-thanks-to-the-creative-destruction-that-fuels-economic-growth.

Qantas. 2013. 'The transformation continues: Qantas sustainability review 2013', https://www.qantas.com.au/infodetail/about/investors/qantas-sustainability-review-2013.pdf.

Rouse, W.B. 2005. 'A theory of enterprise transformation'. *Systems Engineering*. 8(4): 279–95. doi:10.1002/sys.20035.

Rouse, W.B. and Baba, M.L. 2006. 'Enterprise transformation'. *Communications of the ACM*. 49(7): 67–72.

Schein, E.H. 2010. *Organizational Culture and Leadership*, 4th edn, vol. 2 (San Francisco, CA: John Wiley & Sons).

Smith, A., Oczkowski, E., Macklin, R. and Noble, C. 2003. 'Organisational change and the management of training in Australian enterprises'. *International Journal of Training & Development*. 7(1): 2–15. doi:10.1111/1468-2419.00167.

Viljoen, J.P. and Rothmann, S. 2002. 'Transformation in a tertiary-education institution: a case study'. *Management Dynamics*. 11(2): 2–10.

Virany, B., Tushman, M.L. and Romanelli, E. 1992. 'Executive succession and organization outcomes in turbulent environments: an organization learning approach'. *Organization Science*. 3(1): 72–91. doi:10.1287/orsc.3.1.72.

Waddell, D.M., Creed, A., Cummings, T.G. and Worley, C.G. 2017. *Organisational Change: Development and Transformation*, 6th edn (South Melbourne, VIC: Cengage Learning Australia).

Delivering your Aboriginal strategy: Using strategic change planning in a Victorian health and community support alliance

Zane Diamond, Monash University

> You cannot solve a problem with the same consciousness that created the problem in the first place.
>
> Attributed to Einstein.

INTRODUCTION

Over the preceding two decades, the Council of Australian Governments (COAG) has developed policies and adopted targets to improve the wellbeing of Aboriginal and Torres Strait Islander Australians. This work has become known as 'Closing the Gap' and its impact has been significant at the systemic level in guiding policy engagement and financial accountabilities between the government and the Australian health system regarding how services for Aboriginal and Torres Strait Islander people are provided. The Australian Government's new *National Strategic Framework for Aboriginal and Torres Strait Islander Peoples' Mental Health and Social and Emotional Wellbeing 2017–2023* (Commonwealth of Australia, 2017) has re-developed the agenda, building on the *National Strategic Framework for Aboriginal and Torres Strait Islander Health* (Commonwealth of Australia, 2003–07) for improving access to mainstream services by creating the *Health System Delivery Framework*. The earlier framework emphasised the need for a competent workforce as a key area, incorporating work done in 2004 by the Australian Health Ministers Advisory Council (AHMAC), which advocated the need for a *Cultural Respect Framework*, stating that:

> There is a growing understanding that a comprehensive response to addressing the marginalisation of Aboriginal and Torres Strait Islander peoples must sharpen the focus on improving the performance and accountability of mainstream services. (AHMAC, 2004: 5)

Arising from this early foundational work, the Cultural Competency Framework (NHMRC, 2004) was developed, building on these policy frameworks and moving the focus clearly to improving the cultural competency of organisations and their staff regarding the health and wellbeing of Aboriginal and Torres Strait Islander Australians. The result was the final adoption of the *National Strategic Framework for Aboriginal and Torres Strait Islander Health* (2003–2013), the framework that guided the work reported in this case study. It is important to note that while the most recent policy (2017–2023) suggests that the government has taken a new direction, it could be argued that programs such as described in this case study anticipated the aspirations of the new policy and provide practical guidance about how to operationalise these, namely: Be clinically appropriate; Be trauma-informed; Be culturally respectful; Develop culturally safe protocols; Employ workers, paraprofessionals and professionals who are culturally competent; Involve Aboriginal and Torres Strait Islander peoples in the design and assessment of mental health and related areas programs and services; and, Recognise carers as key partners in achieving better outcomes for people living with mental illness.

This integrative case study is based in Victoria, Australia; consequently, both the federal government and the Victorian state government significantly impact the way both primary health care and community health services account for the quality of their service delivery to local Aboriginal and Torres Strait Islander people. The focus is on organisations being better equipped to be responsive to the needs of Aboriginal and Torres Strait Islander people and to be able to provide evidence of increased participation by the First Peoples in the use of services and in the governance, leadership and management of primary health care and community health services. Funding is tied to those organisations providing evidence that they are engaging proactively with the 'Closing the Gap' agenda. This policy and funding nexus is creating a significant push for primary health care and community health services to change the way that they think about their work with Aboriginal and Torres Strait Islander clients and the employment of Aboriginal and Torres Strait Islander people within their organisations.

This case study will examine the work undertaken by a Health and Community Support Alliance to focus its role on developing and implementing an Aboriginal and Torres Strait Islander client strategy within its partner organisations (the Outer East Health and Community Support Alliance has been studied in this case study as the overarching sponsor of this initiative). The partners believed that, by combining their expertise and resources, they could work together to achieve an integrated regional response while also strengthening their respective organisational strategies and improving their reporting mechanisms.

After a developmental period of three years between 2009 and 2011, a strategic change management program was designed and implemented in 2012. This program aimed to improve individual and regional organisational capacity to embed strategies that would improve access to services for Aboriginal and/or Torres Strait Islander people in the Outer East region of Melbourne, Victoria. The approach undertaken to facilitate this program draws on complexity theory, applying intelligent complex adaptive systems theory to strategic change planning in a public health sector setting and using a participatory action research approach.

PROJECT BACKGROUND AND CONTEXT

The Outer East region of Melbourne comprises the local government areas of Maroondah, Knox and the Yarra Ranges (ABS, 2016). According to the most recent data available, there are now 2891 Aboriginal and Torres Strait Islander people living in the area, a significant increase on the 820 people identifying as Aboriginal and/or Torres Strait Islander people in 2012. The median age is now 23 years (down from 36 years). The median weekly household income is $1447 compared to the overall median of $1559. These, and other demographic information, such as languages spoken at home, numbers of people employed and levels of health and illness, are important statistics to know when one starts to consider the best way to develop a program to address the needs of this local population.

Beginning in 2006 and continuing through 2009, the partner organisations of the Outer East Health and Community Support Alliance (OEHCSA, also known as the Outer East Primary Care Partnership) developed an Integrated Health Promotion Plan committed to improving access to services for Aboriginal people living in the region. Initial work focused on the development of the OEHCSA's *Aboriginal Access and Engagement Policy*. To support the OEHCSA partner organisations in the implementation of this policy, the Outer East Training Model was designed. The Outer East Training Model ensures that OEHCSA partner organisations are able to provide measurable and/or demonstrable evidence of success of change at a systemic, organisational and individual level (Commonwealth of Australia, 2003–07).

The development of the OEHCSA Aboriginal Access and Engagement program was informed by the Cultural Competency Framework, the National Strategic Framework for Aboriginal and Torres Strait Islander Health and the Cultural Respect Framework.

A NOTE ON TERMINOLOGY

The term 'indigenous' is used internationally to recognise the rights of all indigenous peoples. As a legacy of colonisation, Australia's original inhabitants were called Aborigines. By distinction, the people of the Torres Strait were known as Torres Strait Islanders. A preference has been expressed by Australian First Peoples to be known collectively as Aboriginal and Torres Strait Islander peoples when discussing the broader Australian context; 'indigenous', when used in the Australia context, is capitalised. In Victoria, the site for this case study, there are Aboriginal people and Torres Strait Islander people living in the Outer East of Melbourne. In recognition of this area being the traditional lands of Aboriginal people, the preference is to use the word *Aboriginal* only while recognising that there are Torres Strait Islander people also using these services. Traditional Owners of this area identify as belonging to both the Wurundjeri and Boonwurrung peoples of the Kulin Nations and they are recognised in all matters relating to culture. The popular term for Victorian Aboriginal people is Koorie and this term is also used interchangeably with the phrase Aboriginal Victorian. In this case study, these various phrases and descriptors will be used as appropriate to the context.

PROGRAM DESIGN

The Organisational Leadership Program – Delivering Your Aboriginal Strategy was designed by the author in consultation with the Cultural Development Working Group of the OEHCSA, a group comprised of senior managers from the partnering community-based health services and community representatives.

THEORETICAL UNDERPINNINGS

The design of this program was informed by new developments in the field of change management and organisation development (OD) that are responding to change in unpredictable and sometimes chaotic environments. Small primary care and community health services are at the frontline of accountable service delivery. Their credibility and funding are increasingly tied to their effectiveness in undertaking organisational development that enables the government to achieve delivery on its 'Closing the Gap' promises.

COMPLEXITY THEORY

The ideas embedded in complexity theory are foundational to this work. The application of complexity theory in the human services proposes that these organisations are intelligent, complex, adaptive systems of interacting people, organisations, activities, resources and ideas (Bovaird, 2008; Palmberg, 2009; Sherif, 2006). Using complexity theory in the design of an organisational change strategy increases understanding of how these organisations operate, interact and cope with complexity and emergence. Bovaird (2008) proposed a new conceptual framework for strategic management in the public domain, advocating the use of strategic shaping and meta-planning as emergent strategic management mechanisms rather than relying on traditional linear approaches to strategic planning. He argues that, in the human services, predictability is inherently restricted. He proposes that designing change processes that harness complexity and emergence is the key to the successful integration of new ways of working.

PARTICIPATORY ACTION RESEARCH

The design of this project is underpinned by the participatory action research (PAR) approach. Designing an effective intervention often requires adapting available approaches and models to fit the context of the work. In this program it was important for the workshop participants to become partner researchers working with the facilitator to review and respond to the various aspects of the work, and to harness the complexity and emergence in 'real time', to ensure that the final objectives could be successfully reached by the conclusion of the program. This approach also offered a positive opportunity to develop the involvement of the local Aboriginal and Torres Strait Islander community at the organisational planning level, rather than at the client/consumer level that would be more common.

PAR, or action research as it is sometimes known, has change and action as embedded and critical elements of its approach and has, in its implementation and underpinning philosophies, an action purpose. (The term 'action research' was coined in 1946 by Kurt Lewin to describe a spiral action of research aimed at problem solving.) The concepts of participation and action are central to the method and have been used successfully in several Indigenous Australian community contexts to good effect. Walter (1998) suggests that the focus can be described as:

1 *Action:* Research should be more than just finding out; research should also involve an action component that seeks to engender positive change.

2   *Participation:* Research is a participatory process that requires the equal and collaborative involvement of the community of research interest.

Reason (1998) says that participatory action research has been defined as having a double objective: the first aim is to produce knowledge and action directly useful to a group of people through research, adult education or sociopolitical action; the second aim is to empower people at a second and deeper level through the process of constructing and using their own knowledge. McTaggart and Kemmis (1998), McTaggart (1997) and Wadsworth (1998) have developed an extensive body of work on this method.

In addition to working well with the intent of complexity theory to harness the professional expertise of those involved in leading the change, the PAR approach is also effective in responding to what we know about adult learners. We know that they are autonomous, self-directed, goal-oriented and relevancy-oriented – they need to know why they are learning something. Using PAR allows a process to manage emergence. It is similar to managing a linear strategic plan except that one is drawing on the synergy of talent in an organisation, or a facilitated process of change, and its clients/consumers.

PROJECT OBJECTIVES

The objective of the program was to develop a strategic change planning program designed to strengthen leadership and quality assurance in the improvement of access to services for Aboriginal people in OEHCSA organisations and to deliver this staged strategic change planning program to 25 executive officers, board members and managers of OEHCSA partners. Participants from each organisation then worked to develop organisation-specific strategic change plans that were designed to deliver measurable impacts by the end of the program.

PROJECT DELIVERABLES

Drawing on organisational change literature, there is an argument that any significant organisational change requires cascading sponsorship (Hofstede, 2001; Kotter, 2007; Kotter & Cohen, 2011; Kotter International, 2015). Therefore, it was important that representatives of the senior leadership team from each participating organisation be involved in some of the program to ensure that the projects developed for each had senior sponsorship and that there was agreement that the plans aligned with each organisation's overall strategic plans. Using the PAR cycle of 'Think, Plan, Act and Reflect', three workshops were staged throughout a 12-month period to enable input from the facilitator, with participants returning to their organisations, developing the necessary supports and structures for the work to proceed and implementing their ideas and actions between each workshop. The first, *Think/Plan*, was for CEOs, board members and selected project managers to agree on organisation-specific plans; the second, *Adjust/Plan*, was for project managers to develop and adjust organisational strategic change plans. The next phase, *Act*, which continued until the end of the project, provided mentoring/coaching support to participants outside the context of the structured sessions to support implementation at the local level. The third workshop, *Reflect*, was for the CEOs, board members and project managers to come together to assess the program impacts and plan for next phase of work.

COMMUNICATION STRATEGY

Once the program was developed, a communication strategy was implemented by the OEHCSA to invite, recruit and then manage the ongoing needs of the participants. This was seen as an important tool for ensuring that during the time between workshops the participants felt supported by and engaged with the OEHCSA about the work they were undertaking. Following the theory of cascading sponsorship, it was anticipated that the senior leadership of each organisation would identify the appropriate managers to become involved as the lead project managers for the Delivering Your Aboriginal Strategy program.

The OEHCSA continued to communicate by email and letter with the senior-level participants to ensure that they were informed of the ongoing work and that they felt supported to continue to provide senior leadership sponsorship. For the life of the program, communication to participants was also conducted by email and included the supply of relevant resources, academic articles, agendas for each workshop and additional correspondence where necessary.

One of the important aspects of a communication strategy is that it allows the organisation to receive information both actively and passively, a key element in the implementation of complexity theory to harness emerging organisational energy for the changes that are occurring.

METHODOLOGICAL APPROACH AND EVALUATION

As discussed above, it was important that the activities undertaken by each organisation were measurable and/or able to show demonstrable improvement and PAR was used to help achieve this. Each organisation agreed that it would attempt to establish the impact of the program on its capacity to influence or enact a change in its organisation regarding an Aboriginal policy or project activity. The overall measure was that at least 50 per cent of organisations participating in the program would be able to provide evidence of designing and implementing a strategic project that specifically contributed to improving Aboriginal use of their services. In each workshop, participants gave a presentation of their progress, discussed the obstacles they were encountering and adjusted their plans.

Using complexity theory, together with plans that had timelines and a participative action research approach, participants were able to troubleshoot their progress, respond to emerging changes and maximise opportunities as they arose. In this way, the work was always current and responsive to the changing demands on their organisation (for example, changes of senior personnel, in funding requirements and/or reporting requirements).

Qualitative evaluation techniques were used to collect data to evaluate the Delivering Your Aboriginal Strategy program. The methods of data collection used were qualitative surveys at the end of each workshop (formative evaluation) and semi-structured interviews at the end of the program (summative evaluation). The surveys included both process and impact questions and reflected the stages of the participatory action research model. At the end of the program, semi-structured interviews were conducted to capture the participant experience of the program and establish if the program had made a difference to implementing their chosen strategy.

HARNESSING COMPLEXITY AND EMERGENCE

All participating agencies were able to report that they had developed a strategic project and 70 per cent of agencies reported that they had either implemented their project or were about to implement their project. Of the 30 per cent that reported not implementing their project, their capacity to do so was influenced by other organisational conditions, such as organisational restructuring. The types of projects were varied and, while there were some common themes present, no two projects were the same. The analysis of the post-workshop qualitative surveys demonstrated that effective learning had taken place and that participants felt that they had been challenged to reorient themselves to a new way of approaching service delivery to Aboriginal and Torres Strait Islander clients using strategic planning tools.

Participants reported that the aspect that they found most valuable from the first workshop was that it supported them in 'challenging my current thinking' and 'rethinking our service', and that 'personalising the theory made it easy to connect to theory'.

The strongest responses were in relation to new knowledge of Indigenous Australian cultures. The responses were broad, ranging from understanding Traditional Owners and family connections to unconscious racism and information and insight into Indigenous Australian cultures based on personal experiences of the facilitators. The evaluations also highlighted participant demand for more information on Aboriginal and Torres Strait Islander cultures to be provided at the workshops, demonstrating that there is a gap in agency knowledge of the topic and the ways that this might influence effective service delivery, particularly at the middle-management level.

Following the second workshop, participants were asked if they felt 'more prepared and able to develop their organisational Aboriginal strategy'. All participants either agreed or strongly agreed that they felt they were prepared and able to develop their strategy. One participant observed that 'it was helpful to get input from a range of people developing projects and who were at different stages of engagement with Aboriginal communities'.

Overall, analysis of the feedback from organisations was that they could not have progressed with this work without having participated in the Delivering Your Aboriginal Strategy program. Specifically, they reported that the strength of the program was that it included:

1 a theoretical framework to contextualise organisational change and cultural competency principles

2 an accountability structure for the participants to their organisation and their peers

3 a strategic regional capacity building framework that acted as a catalyst for initiating individual projects – 'if it had been something I had said as a directive from inside the organisation I don't think it would have progressed, it was like permission to run something like that and the Delivering Your Aboriginal Strategy program was part of a wider movement … so you want to be part of it'

4 guidance through supervision and mentoring – 'we could talk about the smaller more detailed issues or ideas confidentially'; 'great reinforcing, gave us different ideas'; 'having access to that kind of unique expertise (mix of organisational theory and Aboriginal cultural content) was helpful to understand what was happening in our organisation'

5 a focus and action as a catalyst to 'start conversations' – 'it consolidated a lot of areas we were looking at and to see where we still needed to make changes' and 'helped us push along the project we knew we needed to do'

6 a dynamic learning environment that included working with participants from different sectors – 'having so many organisations there and having spelled out that you have to take a strategic approach'; 'the built-in processes of reflection across the workshops created the opportunity for the participants to discuss their projects in a critically reflective way with their peers'.

Analysis of the data also identified limitations to the effectiveness of the program. Two of these were:

1 Time allocation. This was by far the most significant obstacle and one that was common across all participating organisations. As one participant observed: 'The organisation valued our participation in the Delivering Your Aboriginal Strategy program, but this didn't translate into re-prioritising other work to enable us to contribute more time to it.' Specific issues were:

a unrealistic allocation of time to dedicate towards the project, given the scope of the changes envisaged by the process

b difficulties in quarantining time for workshops

c that the design of the project required work to be done between workshops – the additional time was not allocated within the organisation even though they had participated in developing the program. For example, there was board endorsement but no cascade into a strategic approach about how the work would be done.

2 Lack of information passed on from senior managers who failed to fully take on their role as sponsors. Some project managers saw little documentation or information about the Delivering Your Aboriginal Strategy program. One participant observed that they were unable to plan for how much time to contribute to the project because of this. Some reported that no information was passed on to them about the content/expectations of the program, only an authority to attend. This became an issue because the planning required to release staff to attend workshops and facilitate an organisational project is considerable. The issue of time, as noted above, was made more difficult because organisations were not planning for the demands placed on their nominated project manager through their participation in these types of workshops.

CONCLUSION

Overall, the Delivering Your Aboriginal Strategy program has been regarded as a success, with most participating organisations able to measure or demonstrate improved organisational capacity to address the provision of services to their Aboriginal and Torres Strait Islander clients. Complexity theory and PAR provided important theoretical and methodological underpinnings to the work of using strategic planning to improve service delivery, supporting an alliance of organisations that operated in particularly complex and ever-changing environments. As would be anticipated with the PAR approach, the reflection cycle has led to a new cycle of thinking about the next phase of their work in this vital area of 'Closing the Gap' and for many this means that they have the skills and knowledge to proactively engage with local Aboriginal and Torres Strait Islander people, to provide opportunity for partnership and employment and to improve access for Aboriginal Australian and Torres Strait Islander people within their organisations.

REVIEW QUESTIONS

1   In what ways can the objectives of your organisation be brought into alignment with the intentions of the Declaration on the Rights of Indigenous Peoples (2008) and the *National Strategic Framework for Aboriginal and Torres Strait Islander Peoples' Mental Health and Social and Emotional Wellbeing 2017–2023*?

2   Consider the chapters on strategic planning. How might your organisation develop a strategic plan that furthers Indigenous Australian peoples' aspirations for health and wellbeing?

3   Consider the chapters on organisational change and think about human resource development. What is your preferred style of intervention when thinking about undertaking organisational change to improve the way your organisation responds to the needs of Aboriginal and Torres Strait Islander people in your local area?

REFERENCES

Australian Bureau of Statistics (ABS). 2012. *Eastern Outer Melbourne – Victoria – Statistical Subdivision Community Profile* (Canberra, ACT).

Australian Bureau of Statistics (ABS). 2016. *Eastern Outer Melbourne – Victoria – Statistical Subdivision Community Profile* (Canberra, ACT).

Australian Health Ministers Advisory Council (AHMAC). 2004. *Cultural Respect Framework for Aboriginal and Torres Strait Islander Health* (Department of Health, South Australia).

Bovaird, T. 2008. 'Emergent strategic management and planning mechanisms in complex adaptive systems'. *Public Management Review*. 10(3): 319–40.

Commonwealth of Australia, 2003–07, *National Strategic Framework for Aboriginal and Torres Strait Islander Health 2003–2013: Australian Government Implementation Plan 2007–2013* (Commonwealth of Australia, ACT).

Commonwealth of Australia, 2017–23, *National Strategic Framework for Aboriginal and Torres Strait Islander Peoples' Mental Health and Social and Emotional Wellbeing 2017–2023: Australian Government Implementation Plan 2017–2023* (Commonwealth of Australia, ACT).

Hofstede, G. 2001. *Culture's Consequences: Comparing Values, Behaviors, Institutions, and Organizations Across Cultures*, 2nd edn (Thousand Oaks, CA: Sage).

Kemmis, S. and McTaggart, R. 1988. *The Action Research Planner*, 3rd edn (Deakin University, Geelong).

Kotter International. 2015. 'The eight-step process for leading change', http://www.kotterinternational.com/the-8-step-process-for-leading-change.

Kotter, J. 2007. 'Leading change: why transformation efforts fail'. *Harvard Business Review* (January 2007): 96–103.

Kotter, J. and Cohen, D.S. 2002. *The Heart of Change* (Boston: Harvard Business Review Press).

McTaggart, R. (ed.). 1997. *Participatory Action Research: International Contexts and Consequences* (New York: State University of New York Press).

Moore, B. 1999. 'The service profit chain – a tale of two airlines' (unpublished master's thesis, Pepperdine University).

National Health and Medical Research Council (NHMRC). 2004. *Cultural Competency in Health: A Guide for Policy, Partnerships and Participation* (Commonwealth of Australia, ACT).

Palmberg, K. 2009. 'Complex adaptive systems as metaphors for organizational management'. *Learning Organization*. 16(6): 483–98.

Reason, P. 1998. 'Towards a participatory world'. *Resurgence*. 168: 42–4.

Sherif, K. 2006. 'An adaptive strategy for managing knowledge in organizations'. *Journal of Knowledge Management*. 10(4): 72–80.

Wadsworth, Y. 1998. 'What is participatory action research?', http://www.aral.com.au/ari/p-ywadsworth98.html.

Walter, M. 1998. 'Participatory action research'. In A. Bryman (ed.), *Social Research Methods* (ch. 21) (Oxford: Oxford University Press).

Decolonising 'Closing the Gap': Changing the colonial mindset[1]

Zane Diamond, Monash University

> It is not only those who have been minoritised or deprivileged who can speak about oppression. Those in positions of power and privilege also have an obligation to speak about these issues. (Sefa Dei, 1999)

INTRODUCTION

In early 2012, Drug Rehab Australia (DRA)[2] contracted the author to work with them to develop an organisation-wide system that would frame its work with Indigenous Australians. DRA recognised that it had a fragmented response to service delivery and that it could do better. This case study will focus on a particular aspect of the work that enabled DRA to move from providing services to Aboriginal and Torres Strait Islander people as 'Closing the Gap'-funded clients towards implementing a fundamentally different approach; one that is needed into the future to ensure that the organisation is able to meet its government-funded commitments to Indigenous clients and also demonstrate best practice in this field.

Figure C4.1 is a copy of the initial contracting outline. It is included here because it represents the type of document that an organisation development (OD) specialist is commonly asked to address in the delivery of their services. Of itself, it does not do justice to the potential for effective change that existed in this organisation and, as this case study will suggest, the choice of interpretation rests with the OD specialist.

FIGURE C4.1 PROJECT SUMMARY: DEVELOPING SYSTEMS FOR INDIGENOUS AUSTRALIANS

Background:
Drug Rehab Australia (DRA) currently has fragmented responses to working with Indigenous Australians. This Project is to develop and implement systems, processes and standards that are organisation wide.

Strategic goals:
To develop and implement organisation-wide systems and process at DRA for working with Indigenous Australians

Key objectives:
Development and implementation of a comprehensive Indigenous Policy
Implementation of a Cultural Respect Framework
Completion of Closing the Gap Indigenous Access Plan for Federal Health Department[3]
Further develop working relationships with Indigenous organisations

»

---

1   Heinlein, 2002.
2   DRA is a pseudonym for the organisation that the author worked with.
3   The phrase 'Federal Health Department' indicates that this project is addressing federal-level health policies and funding drivers. The name is generalised because of the frequency with which these departments are changing their names and portfolio responsibilities.

»

From the outset of this discussion, I want you, the reader, to put yourself in the shoes of an OD specialist and think about your relationship to Aboriginal and/or Torres Strait Islander people in Australia and how you might work with organisations with whom you are contracted to engage with the 'Closing the Gap' narrative, to interrogate it and its requirements, and to develop a new type of change management response that recognises the sui generis rights of Indigenous Australians. Usually when a brief like this is developed, an organisation is not thinking about double-loop learning (Argyris, 1997), methods of achieving strategic change, participatory action research (McTaggart, 1991), complex adaptive systems (Bovaird, 2008) or the rights of Indigenous people (UNDRIP, 2008). Unfortunately, neither is the OD specialist. What I have found very valuable is to take the sound advice offered in this book and then think about it specifically regarding what this means for Indigenous people in postcolonial democracies such as Australia and what it means for you as an OD specialist in this field of work. I have successfully used this text with practitioners and students alike to bring everything together in the ways I will describe below.

So how might one go about thinking through a strategic change management process such as the one envisaged above at a drug rehabilitation organisation with respect to addressing the rights of Indigenous peoples? Why is this an issue? At its foundation, the way that human services have been delivered to both of Australia's Indigenous peoples, Aboriginal people and the people of the Torres Strait Islands, has been done 'to' these Indigenous peoples. This case study argues that the original colonial approach to development of health service provisions in Australia for Indigenous Australian citizens has not kept up with international best practice to work in partnership 'with' Indigenous people, and in part this is due to the colonial mindset that continues to be brought to such work by health services professionals. I am not suggesting that this is intentional but rather that such an approach saturates our thinking and stops us from developing new ways of engaging with the provision of such services.

The concept of the 'colonial mind' and the 'postcolonial mind' are useful theoretical constructs by which to examine the 'Closing the Gap' narrative in Australia, and here, with respect to the provision of effective and respectful drug rehabilitation services to Aboriginal and Torres Strait Islander people. Heinlein (2002) defines the 'official mind' of the colonial administrator as being the sum of ideas, perceptions and intentions of those policy makers who had a bearing on imperial policies. Robinson, Gallagher and Denny (1963), for example, observed that in India, 'The white rulers became increasingly absorbed with the mechanics of administration and sought to solve their problems less in social and more in narrow administrative terms'.

TOWARDS A POSTCOLONIAL MINDSET?

Australia endorsed the United Nations Declaration on the Rights of Indigenous Peoples (UNDRIP) in 2008. There are several articles that directly speak to the need for postcolonial democracies such as Australia to reset their relationship with Indigenous populations whose sui generis rights were not extinguished by colonisation. The right to control the approach to health and wellbeing outcomes is a key focus of the UNDRIP and the Australian Government has made the improvement of health outcomes one of its key priorities under the policy called 'Closing the Gap'. This policy recognises the issues of concern and seeks to develop administratively measurable metrics in order to improve the appalling health status of the Indigenous Australian population when compared to the non-Indigenous Australian population. I suggest that this deficit approach, while appealing to the majority and being administratively neat, fails to recognise the urgent need for a new approach – one that does not reinscribe the power relations that are so intrinsically embedded in the 'Closing the Gap' narrative.

PREPARATION: THINK AND PLAN

Mahood (2012) examines 'white workers on Australia's cultural frontier'. It is a sharp and thought-provoking indictment on how policies are not working and how Indigenous Australians speak about non-Indigenous Australians who work in their communities. She reflects on the lack of preparedness that most non-Indigenous Australians have when they become involved in the provision of services to Indigenous communities (2012), noting that:

> It is mandatory for anyone wishing to work in Antarctica to undergo a physical and psychological assessment to establish whether they will stand up to the stresses of isolation, the extreme environment, and the intense proximity to other people. All the same factors exist in remote Aboriginal communities, along with confronting cross-cultural conditions. Yet there don't appear to be any recognised training programs for people who aspire to work in a community, or screening criteria to weed out the mad, bad and incompetent who prowl the grey zone of Indigenous service delivery.

The initial aspects of this case study required a period of engaging and contracting that identified an agreed process. The OD specialist met with senior members of DRA across its service and corporate sections. The initial gathering of data ensured that the organisation came to the organisational change strategy with some understanding of the overall need for change. The first four steps of Kotter's *Eight Step Process for Leading Change* (2007; see also Kotter International, 2015; Kotter & Cohen, 2002) were employed. The readings referred to in this case study formed the basis for the readings given to all participants in a series of workshops. Along with Kotter, the process was underpinned by a participatory action research approach, drawing on some of the theoretical work being done in the field of complex adaptive systems as applied to human services (see, for example, Bovaird, 2008; Holland, 1995; Palmberg, 2009). The first meeting was designed around a 'Think' theme and the ideas outlined above were introduced to participants whose professional skills were well-honed in the specialist field of drug rehabilitation. Even so, they were willing to think about doing their work differently because they recognised that their organisation had a fractured and poorly integrated approach to service delivery for Aboriginal and/or Torres Strait Islander clients.

Part of the 'Thinking' stage involved them contributing to a guiding vision for the work. Their homework was to return to their part of the organisation and collect historical information and data about past Indigenous clients and to work with their teams to interrogate their work using SWOT analysis. For the second meeting of this group, in the 'Planning stage', each participant gave a presentation of their findings and collectively the group was surprised to see a pattern emerging of deficit-model thinking, of repeat clients, of a pattern of dependency and then disengagement by Indigenous clients and a sense of overwhelming powerlessness for the professionals involved, and a very small success rate despite a variety of measures used for such work. Plans were then discussed and agreed for each part of the organisation, with the decision that the overall approach needed to be integrated. A committee was formed to ensure that the work being undertaken was supporting the strategic goal to develop and implement organisation-wide systems and processes at DRA for working with Indigenous Australians and to enable each team to meet the key objectives underpinning the change management process.

A key aspect to these preparations was the approach adopted by the OD specialist, constantly asking questions of the 'normal' assumptions made about Indigenous clients during discussions and presenting participants with alternative views based on the UNDRIP and the concepts being revised into Australian federal health policies that were influenced by this international mechanism. This speaks to the question of the skills, knowledge and understanding of OD specialists who work in the broad human service field with respect to the provision of services to Indigenous Australians.

DISRUPTING 'NORMAL': ACT

The third part of the work, and the focus of the rest of this case study, involves only one part of the bigger organisation, its rural drug rehabilitation centre (RDRC). The author had been under the impression that there were few Indigenous clients involved as a proportion of the whole, and there were few if any Indigenous people employed there. It was not absolutely possible to say because the organisation did not collect this information.

With some surprise, my first field trip to RDRC revealed glimmers of what had been discussed in the first two parts of the process but about which the organisation seemed mostly unaware. During initial meetings with the manager, it became obvious that there had been involvement with Indigenous clients far beyond the organisational narrative. Further meetings with two key informants, 'Brian' who was the manager and 'Jason', an Indigenous person living in the area, revealed a precious process that had grown from their relationship; this provided a much-improved model of service delivery at the local level and possibly some lessons that could be expanded into the wider organisation. Subsequent to this work, the two leaders came together to record their story, which they gave permission to share.

Jason was undertaking a Certificate IV at the local TAFE and Brian, the manager of RDRC, was invited to speak to the students. The first thing to note here is that Indigenous people move in and out of the TAFE and university systems depending on their knowledge needs. Jason's presence in this group belied his vast community experience and life commitment to ensuring that local Aboriginal people were being well served by local services that were supposed to be there for them. He recalls his first meeting with Brian:

> I was doing a Cert 4 in Community Services and we chose to invite Brian the manager of RDA to come and talk to our class … he gave us a spiel about RDA and in particular RDRC, and come down to the Q&A time and I couldn't help me self of course and I put my hand up to bring up the subject of Indigenous affairs and he didn't answer me … So I actually come away from that meeting not thinking a whole lot of that man because he sort of brushed me off …

This first impression provides a graphic insight into how quickly impressions can be formed. Unwittingly, Brian had communicated that his service did not have the professional skills at the top to engage with Indigenous people, coming away with the impression that this was just another rural service that wasn't available to Indigenous clients in need. Jason then spoke about what happened next, something that surprised him and disrupted his first impressions:

> I was quite amazed a few days later when he rang me up and told me that it took three days to track me down [Brian: humph laugh] and he wanted to have a yak to me down at RDRC to see if we could sort something out … and that's pretty much how it started wasn't it?

This in itself is unusual in the field. Brian explained:

> [C]learly I'm from England and in some ways, I think that has been very useful for me. I'm an Australian citizen now and I've been here ten years – but this was many years ago – what four years, five years – anyway as an Englishman it's not so embarrassing not to know but as an Australian I think it is embarrassing not to know. I was able to ask questions, I was able to say 'I don't know' which was pretty much the answer you got from me at the TAFE, 'I don't know'. Whatever you asked me, I don't remember you asked me like 'what do you have for blackfellas out there?' I said, 'Look mate not much.' [Jason chuckles obligingly] But I was very happy and very pleased that you'd asked that question because I wanted to know. I'm interested in – I'm *genuinely* interested in different culture, I'm genuinely interested in Aboriginal and Indigenous culture … and also interested in not sticking my size ten boots in it and getting it wrong and doing it properly and coming from a position of – this is something we have talked about *a lot* – coming from a position of humility.

As Jason and Brian began their conversations, both were returning into their groups and speaking about the possibilities for engagement and partnership. Their discussions had led here because of the skills held by both Brian and Jason. Jason was not looking for a deficit approach and Brian was wanting to work *with* rather than *for* Indigenous clients, coming from his acknowledged place of ignorance. Interestingly, in my notes what stood out for me was their reflections about the need for humility on both sides.

Their reflections also provide insight into what could have been:

> [A]s the manager, you could have said no we are not going to do that here ... it's not part of the RDRC program ... (Jason)

Brian and Jason agreed that the first step would be to employ him at RDRC to ensure that the steps they took were taken together. In organisational terms, this is a very difficult first step. Commonly, organisations are wary of taking on the financial commitment of salaries on 'soft' program money so Brian employed Jason in a role that was advertised rather than setting up an Indigenous-specific position. He explains:

> [Y]ou came here initially to advise and then as it goes you know you came here as a worker on the same contract as anyone came. You're not here as an Indigenous worker you're here as a case manager. And we're not going to be giving you Indigenous clients ... you know it's what you're here to do and we all have to do what we have to do.

Again, in organisational terms, this approach can be very effective if the manager and other staff have the trust in the Indigenous worker's generic skills. Part of the colonial mindset commonly tries to push Aboriginal people into Aboriginal-specific jobs and block attempt for Indigenous people to contribute to an organisation beyond a limited brief. As an outcome of the developing trust between Jason and Brian, they had managed to circumvent such a mistake.

They then brought the staff together to discuss their ideas. Jason remembers:

> I think one of the greatest things was the time we had that staff meeting; Brian, you called everyone together and we had a little chat here in the office ... we actually had an Indigenous lady here that day who was a resident and I know that we talked here in the office and the suggestion was made that we should approach her to come to the meeting as an Aboriginal woman not as a resident because then the staff could get an answer to the question from a male and a female so I thought it was a great idea and I said to her 'when you are in this meeting you are an Auntie, a proud Indigenous woman. As soon as you come out that door again you are here as a resident again so do not get this mixed up'. What a proud woman she was there!

Jason was teaching Brian about Indigenous Australian protocol and together they were bringing the staff along with them slowly. The staff began to learn and ask questions. Changes started to become more obvious among the residents and importantly, members of the local Aboriginal community were starting to engage with RDRC, bringing their support and knowledge to the work of supporting all the residents, not just the Indigenous clients.

Most important, there was a greater integration of the services being offered by RDRC and word was getting out about their successes. In one example they recounted having a fire pit dug in the grounds as a place of healing and quiet reflection. In the ensuing months, Jason recalls a proud day:

> We developed an idea about having RDRC circuit breakers that gave us permission to change things ... so we had an open day here and I wanted to do a smoking ceremony and I asked Brian if we could contact that lady to ask her back [Brian: 'Yep she came with

her family'] ... so, she come back and the glow on her face for the honour of being the Indigenous Auntie to light our first fire I'll never forget. I'll never forget that. Seeing her coming up that drive and hopping out of that car however many years ago it's as fresh as if it happened today to me. What changes to that lady!

Such 'circuit-breaking' events are only possible with a considered organisational change strategy. Brian and Jason had such a vision and a plan. They engaged properly with the local community, both Indigenous and non-Indigenous, they made RDRC a place where Indigenous clients felt culturally safe, and they were inclusive of the needs of all staff and clients in a way that such new measures improved the provision of services for everyone involved.

During the 'Act' stage of the wider organisational process with which I was involved, I became concerned to capture a reliable picture of what these two leaders had done so that the wider organisation could develop and integrate the lessons they had learned.

REFLECT

As the OD specialist what I saw was that their work had gone virtually unrecognised in the larger organisation, which was mostly unaware of the depth and vision of the RDRC approach that had been developed by Jason and Brian. It was also a time for members of the participant group to bring back their successes and challenges to a final meeting, the 'Reflect' stage. From past experience, I knew this was going to be the stage where resistance to organisational change would be at its highest because this was the time for the agreements to be made about how to integrate the service provision model across quite disparate parts of the organisation. Jason and Brian made the presentation of the work they had been doing at RDRC. Such is their skill that they managed to create excitement in their vision and in their very practical suggestions. Many of their ideas became integrated into the final work of the process, a strategic management model that has become embedded. Indigenous people have been employed, there is better integration of services, engagement with Indigenous service providers and local communities has improved and RDA is meeting, and exceeding, its service agreements with both state and federal funding agencies.

LESSONS LEARNED?

In asking OD specialists to shift from a colonial, deficit to a postcolonial, rights-based mindset, the above example provides some glimmers of possibility for what can emerge, given the right circumstances. The role of the OD specialist is key here, but it is not the only determining feature. As has been posited throughout this book, from the contracting stage through to delivery and evaluation, there needed to be strong endorsement and cascading sponsorship from the senior leaders. There needed to be a strategic change management plan developed by all involved in the process to achieve buy-in. And there needed to be a willingness on the part of Indigenous and non-Indigenous Australians to step into a new type of arrangement that moved beyond replication of the colonial mindset.

The main lesson communicated clearly across the organisation was the need for humility, not something normally highlighted in organisational change management models. Some other aspects included:

- A need for all involved to have empathy for Indigenous matters, revolving around acceptance that Indigenous and non-Indigenous Australians are equal and should thus be treated equally – in other words, Indigenous Australians should have the same access to and outcomes from drug rehabilitation as non-Indigenous Australians have.
- A passionate and profound commitment held by participants, Indigenous and non-Indigenous Australians alike. This has commonly changed every corner of their lives, containing as it does a radical questioning of the traditional, colonial, civil service administrative mindset of privileged non-Indigenous Australians.
- A need for non-Indigenous Australian professionals (including the OD specialist) to have an understanding that Indigenous Australians suffer inequalities and injustices in society, while non-Indigenous Australians, particularly those in the administrative and governing classes, receive various forms of power and privilege.
- Recognition by all participants that the current, dominant model of drug rehabilitation fails to recognise the rights of Indigenous Australians and is therefore oppressive to them. This is even though Indigenous people themselves may collude in maintaining the colonial mindset, because this is perceived to have the best benefits in terms of its deficit approach.

All these lessons point to the need for a new class of OD specialists and health services providers who can work effectively in the complex interface of negotiated meaning that is undertaken in every part of the process of providing drug rehabilitation services to Aboriginal and Torres Strait Islander people. In doing so these OD professionals work to co-create new policy approaches that enable Indigenous understandings of health and wellbeing to come to the fore and complement contemporary holistic approaches to the difficult work of drug rehabilitation in postcolonial nations such as Australia.

REVIEW QUESTIONS

1   What is the colonial mindset that this case study identifies and why is it a problem?

2   Consider the material in the book on strategic planning. How might strategic planning for organisational change be useful in an organisation's engagement with Indigenous Australian clients?

3   What skills, knowledge and understanding do you consider are needed by an OD specialist in order for them to develop professional confidence to work effectively with Indigenous Australians?

REFERENCES

Argyris, C. 1977. 'Double loop learning in organisations'. *Harvard Business Review* (Sept–Oct 1977): 115–25.

Bovaird, T. 2008. 'Emergent strategic management and planning mechanisms in complex adaptive systems'. *Public Management Review*. 10(3): 319–40.

Heinlein, F. 2002. *British Government Policy and Decolonisation 1945–1963: Scrutinising the Official Mind* (London and Portland: Frank Cass).

Holland, J.H. 1995. *Hidden Order: How Adaptations Build Complexity* (Reading, MA: Addison-Wesley).

Kotter International. 2015. 'The eight-step process for leading change', http://www.kotterinternational.com/the-8-step-process-for-leading-change.

Kotter, J. 2007. 'Leading change, why transformation efforts fail', *Harvard Business Review* (January 2007): 96–103.

Kotter, J. and D.S. Cohen. 2002. *The Heart of Change* (Boston: Harvard Business Review Press).

McTaggart, R. 1991. 'Principles of participatory action research'. *Adult Education Quarterly*. 41(3): 168–97.

Mahood, K. 2012. 'Kartiya are like Toyotas: white workers on Australia's cultural frontier'. *Griffith Review*. 36: 43–60.

Palmberg, K. 2009. 'Complex adaptive systems as metaphors for organizational management'. *Learning Organization*. 16(6): 483–98.

Robinson, R., Gallagher, J. and Denny, A. 1963. *Africa and the Victorians: The Official Mind of Imperialism* (London: Macmillan).

Sefa Dei, G. 1999. 'George Sefa Dei'. Aurora Online, http://aurora.icaap.org/index.php/aurora/article/view/22/33.

United Nations. 2008. United Nations Declaration on the Rights of Indigenous Peoples (UNDRIP), http://www.un.org/esa/socdev/unpfii/documents/DRIPS_en.pdf.

CASE STUDY 5

Building a new brand culture for Burger U[1]

Scott Gardner, Murdoch University

BACKGROUND

In keeping with international trends, the profile of the quick service restaurant (QSR) market sector for burgers, pizzas, fish and chips, chicken dinners and hot sandwiches in New Zealand experienced rapid change after 2000.

By mid-2012, 75-year-old Auckland identity Bill Buckie (known as 'Wild Man Bill', for his tough-guy image and widely reported altercations with journalists, local councillors, difficult customers and New Zealand's Tax Department), was questioning his wisdom after 50 years in the burger business.

The tried-and-tested formula for his Wild Man Burgers (WMB) – 'Priced for value; tasty, quick, and plenty of it' – was clearly failing. Profits and market share were tanking as consumer expectations shifted to wider and healthier choices of food and beverages. The trend was also moving from functional seating, easy-wipe surfaces, garish livery and industrial-style lighting to comfortable modern decor and lighting, contemporary in-store designs and Wi-Fi connections. As the founder and managing director of the WMB parent company, BB Group (which had concerns in food wholesale, logistics and commercial property development), and majority (51 per cent) owner of both BB Group and WMB, Bill felt increasingly pressured to move with the times or risk destroying his dynasty.

THE SLIPPERY SLOPE FOR WMB, 2009–12

Revenue from WMB's 17 stores had been falling by an average of 12 per cent per annum (p.a.), with operational costs increasing well ahead of inflation at 9 per cent p.a. This trend had continued across three successive reporting periods – the fiscal years 2009–10, 2010–11 and 2011–12. This slide in revenue and profit was most pronounced in seven of the nine Auckland-based stores developed in the early 1980s in working-class areas. By 2012 these had become gentrified; abundant with caffe latte, organic food and yoga, they were trendy inner-city suburbs with traditional greasy spoon cafes a distant memory.

Bill's response to the rapidly changing demographics and plummeting sales was heightened by the members of BB Group's board, including the brass-necked South African venture capitalist Flick Du Plessis. Du Plessis had threatened 'severe consequences' at the last board meeting, in July, if 'immediate action was not undertaken to stem the blood oozing from this so called investment'. In December 2012, Du Plessis and the other board members finally ran out of patience. They told Bill, who had been absent from the meeting due to chest pains, that they had hired a Sydney-based strategic marketing and change specialist consultancy,

---

1   This case study is hypothetical, and draws upon hypothetical documentation.

Quadrant 47. Its brief was to 'review BB Group's investments, including a brand culture refresh and repositioning of WMB in the NZ QSR market'. Bill was unhappy with the decision but did not feel well enough to take on Du Plessis and the board.

THE OLD WMB BUSINESS MODEL

Bill had established his first store in a blue-collar suburb of Wellington in 1978, selling his famous 'Big Bro Burgers', fried fish and chicken. The store, which opened for breakfast at 6 a.m. and closed at 10 p.m. on weekdays and Saturdays, became a fixture with local tradespeople and other blue-collar workers wanting big breakfasts. It was also very popular for takeaway food for this clientele and family groups on the weekends. Using revenue generated from this venture, combined with the proceeds of some astute land purchases and sales, and his 'beat the odds' horse race-betting system, Bill had generated enough cash to underwrite a steady growth in the WMB empire in the 1980s and 1990s. By 1995, this extended to 17 stores across New Zealand's North and South Islands. Bill owned and controlled nine stores in Auckland, four in Wellington, two in Christchurch and two in his hometown of Dunedin. His diversified business, BB Group, also enjoyed significant growth in the 1980s and 1990s. With this cash-rich bonanza (which did not entirely escape the attention of the NZ Tax Department), Bill was able to reduce interest payments and costs of doing business. Significant economies of scale and process efficiencies were achieved through direct ownership of stores and control over supply chains for meat patties, vegetables and other consumables. Employing low-wage, part-time staff, aged 16 to 19 years, also kept operational costs down at WMB. These young people accounted for approximately 80 per cent of the 230 WMB managers and staff based across 17 stores and the BB Holdings headquarters in Auckland.

The WMB business model, which had worked so well in the 1980s and 1990s, came under severe pressure in the new millennium. This heralded an era of rising consumer expectations fuelled by lifestyle programs, social media, shifting inner-city demographics and increased competition for staff and upscale customers from big international players such as McDonald's. By 2009, a growing number of boutique and healthy-burger franchises were also capturing big chunks of Bill's market in the wealthy inner-city suburbs of Auckland, Wellington and Christchurch. WMB appealed primarily to a blue-collar male demographic. In 2009, it was not well positioned to capture the growing white-collar, health-conscious female and family markets. There was recognition that the brand needed to remain relevant in a dynamic market in which customer needs and wants and industry standards were constantly evolving.

DEVELOPING THE NEW BURGER U BRAND CULTURE AND BUSINESS PROFILE

In February 2013, the WMB brand was relaunched and communicated nationally in New Zealand through a new advertising campaign, and initial changes were made to in-store fit-out, menus, uniforms, product packaging, customer service messages, employee communications and training. The new brand characteristics included what the Sydney-based consultants termed a 'playful, cheeky, new name – Burger U'. This was intended to reposition the business from 'mass market' to 'boutique', appealing to a new generation of 'discerning customers seeking value, quality, friendly service and comfortable, pleasant surroundings'. Choice in this context meant incorporating healthier and lighter menu options with clear labelling to show calories and ingredients while retaining the traditional WMB proposition of value, taste and quality. The customer experience was to be enhanced through 'excellent service in a light-hearted fun atmosphere with groovy, comfortable "linger longer" retro decor, and smart upbeat staff who love and live the brand'. These service-value and brand-culture messages reached customers and staff through in-store promotions and TV, radio and social media advertising campaigns between January and October 2013.

The demands of the new brand culture led to the voluntary and involuntary departure of three senior managers, five store managers and 37 staff who did not 'fit with the new direction' by April 2013. Staff who displayed the 'right attitude and behaviours' were recruited internally and the newly rebranded stores in Auckland and Christchurch ran a recruitment campaign targeting tertiary students seeking better wages and working conditions than those offered by competing hotels, bars, cafes and QSRs. This shift from a low or minimum hourly wage culture to one of relatively good hourly rates, including team incentives and bonuses, would represent an increase of up to 8 per cent in payroll costs for Burger U in the 2013–14 fiscal year. The consultants estimated that this would be balanced out by higher margins, improved process efficiencies and a projected 4–9 per cent increase in market share in the 2014–15 fiscal year for the 'burgers and sundries' segment of New Zealand's QSR market. BB Group's chief financial officer, Frank Mazak, estimated that if this target was achieved it would amount to a NZ$4.5 million increase in annual turnover for the Burger U business.

COMMUNICATING NEW VALUES AND CULTURE AT BURGER U

At a special meeting of the BB Group board, held at the Auckland head office in February 2013, the Quadrant 47 consultants had pitched a big-bang brand-culture campaign to be rolled out nationally by the end of the year. This costly and aggressive launch into the boutique burger market was to comprise a NZ$280 000 TV, radio, in-store and social media advertising and promotions campaign. It was also to incorporate a series of culture-change workshops covering head office and all 11 stores. However, the prudent training manager at BB Group, Ciara Conti (Bill Buckie's sister-in-law), advised the board members to adopt a low-risk piloting approach to culture change. This would be implemented from March to December 2013 and embed changes to culture, infrastructure, brand and menu offerings in six selected stores. She also proposed a scaled-down version of the advertising and promotion campaign, focused on the localities of the pilot stores, arguing that low-cost social media promotions were sufficient to raise awareness of the Burger U brand in other locations. Her plan was approved by all members of the board, coming in at 40 per cent of the cost of the Quadrant 47 proposal. This decision came as a monumental disappointment to the two young consulting associates Nigel Roberts and Troy Creighton-Jones, who had been entrusted by the Quadrant 47 partners to service this unfashionable but cash-rich Trans-Tasman client. The recently appointed social media and online branding 'young guns' anticipated plenty of billable hours and profit from the Burger U Account, despite their limited understanding of change management design and implementation.

Dunedin-born and bred Ciara saw things differently. In her 'no nonsense' plan managers and staff in all 17 stores across New Zealand would be invited to provide feedback on the proposed changes during the pilot period. The national brand culture roll-out and associated NZ$35–60 000 per store refits would not be finalised until December 2014. Full national implementation of the new brand culture would also be subject to changes in the six pilot locations, translating into increased profitability. By consulting staff across all stores, she aimed to reality-check the application of new brand values in different locations. In doing so, she sought to ask 'What will work? What will not, and why?' with respect to different store localities and customer profiles (Dunedin stores and customers being somewhat different from those in inner-city Auckland).

Ciara anticipated that well-planned communication of the new brand value would translate into a new service culture at each store. This change communication initiative included regular group executive, store manager and supervisor briefings; change management workshops for management and staff representatives from pilot stores and head office; in-store Q&A sessions for staff and shift supervisors; website posts; and specially designed online 'live the brand' training for store staff.

The relaunched brand strategy encompassed a range of changes to customer service practices, product packaging, operating procedures and restaurant fit-out and appearance, with upgraded kitchens, new decor, installation of free Wi-Fi connectivity and changes to staff uniforms to reflect the new brand identity. Under the new 'Burger U' identity, healthier options, including a salad bar and organic and gluten-free items, appeared on the menu. The online presence of the company also changed, with an upgraded website reflecting the new brand values and designs, changes to the Facebook pages of all 17 stores and the development of a new 'Burger U App'.

In its efforts to create a new brand culture, the BB Group executive team was keen to retain the brand value that had brought competitive success to WMB over the years, combined with values that reflected a new brand culture and positioning. The amalgamated brand values promoted were '(1) playful, authentic and efficient customer engagement; (2) traditional, quality and value with assured high standards of hygiene; (3) groovy relaxing in-store atmosphere with supporting decor, layouts and lighting; (4) friendly and authentic engagement of customers to create loyal advocates who will recommend Burger U and return with friends and family'.

However, the question that had fuelled Ciara Conti's anxiety since her victory at the February board meeting remained: Would these changes translate into future competitive success for the organisation or impending disaster?

EMBEDDING BRAND VALUES AND CULTURE AT BURGER U

The new brand characteristics and cultural artefacts, such as store decor, signage, taglines, product packaging and customer engagement guidelines, represented important elements in the repositioning of WMB in the NZ QSR market and the minds of the consumer. However, bringing about real and lasting culture change across the national store network would take more than changes to taglines, advertising, packaging and in-store fit-outs. Persuading loyal, long-serving store and middle management to adopt new values and aligned working practices was one thing, but winning the hearts and minds of a predominantly casual (temporary) 16–19-year-old store-based workforce, already saturated with marketing messages through social media and other channels, was quite a different proposition. Designing a change process to encourage all managers and store staff to embrace the new brand and cultural values in their day-to-day work routines and customer service interactions was seen as a critical dimension of improving the Burger U long-term competitive position in the NZ QSR market. This balancing act of change implementation, brand recognition and sales growth was to prove a major challenge for Ciara in 2013 and 2014.

Ciara had worked at every level in the organisation over her 20 years with the company, including staff, management and senior management positions. She had an intimate understanding of the leadership style, management systems, in-store processes, working practices and cultural characteristics of the organisation. (Ciara also shared Bill's understanding of the customer base and harboured similar concerns about the risks associated with such a fundamental repositioning of the business.) She knew that it was imperative to establish the Burger U leadership team as champions of the new culture, and management at all levels as committed agents of change.

At the outset of the change management process, her challenge was threefold: (1) make the six-store pilot program a success in 2013; (2) roll out brand culture change to the remaining 11 stores no later than December 2014; and (3) work concurrently with the consultants, head-office marketing and promotions team, and store managers to monitor sales, attract new customers, retain existing 'high value' customers and brand advocates, and ensure that the sales targets set by the BB Group board were achieved for 2014–15.

GUIDING PRINCIPLES FOR CULTURE CHANGE

SCHEIN'S CULTURAL EMBEDDING MECHANISMS

According to Edgar Schein, a leading thinker in the field of organisation transformation (OT), adoption and maintenance of deep culture change requires attention to both primary and secondary (articulation and reinforcement) embedding mechanisms. Examples of primary embedding mechanisms include what leaders pay attention to, measure and control on a regular basis; how leaders allocate resources, rewards and status; and role-modelling teaching and coaching activity by senior management. Secondary embedding mechanisms typically include organisational design and structure, systems and procedures; physical design of the buildings; formal statements of organisational philosophy creeds and charters; rights, stories and rituals of the organisation (Schein, 2010).

CLAMPITT'S CULTURAL COMMUNICATION FRAMEWORK

Corporate communications specialist Philip Clampitt builds on Schein's principles, when explaining how leaders can effectively impart new cultural values and behaviours. He offers practical advice such as: 'Craft cultural statements which are thought through, developed by a broad representation of targeted staff, and made actionable on a day-to-day basis; reinforce the new cultural values in daily rituals and interactions; provide intense training at the outset with regular reminders of "what" is required and reflection on "why" things are done that way' (Clampitt, 2010). Clampitt's (2010) approach to imparting culture also emphasises highlighting specific examples of behaviours consistent with desired values and designing reward systems to reinforce these behaviours.

THE CHALLENGE OF REBRANDING AND CULTURE CHANGE

Nicholas Ind's work on corporate brand management and culture emphasises that brand values must be reflected in the work behaviours of staff and the impressions formed by customers and other external stakeholders. In his book *Living the Brand*, Ind (2011) reinforces the importance of creating internal brand champions, brand-loyal customer groups and positively oriented external audiences as the basis for successful culture building. These principles are reflected in the work of other leading writers on corporate branding, rebranding and identity, who acknowledge that alignment of brand and culture poses a major challenge for marketing, communications and organisational change specialists (De Chernatony & Cottam, 2008; Gotsi, Andriopoulos & Wilson, 2008; Cornelissen 2011).

TRANSLATING BRAND VALUES INTO ACTION USING ORGANISATION DEVELOPMENT AND TRANSFORMATION

Armed with an understanding of these principles and an understanding of the richness, complexity and multiple dimensions of organisational culture, Ciara realised that translating value statements into new patterns of behaviour and improved performance across WMB would require more than a brand communication campaign. To have any chance of success, she needed to understand two things: (1) the readiness of the organisation to introduce significant values-driven change; and (2) how to make the change implementation process manageable and scalable given the limited time and resources available. With these questions at the forefront of her mind, Ciara set out to design a change management and implementation plan incorporating organisation development (OD), OT, change communication and brand management principles. See Chapters 4 and 9 in this book. Also see Schein (2010) and Scharmer and Kaufer (2013), for a more detailed discussion of change leadership and communication in diverse, dynamic and emergent environments.

The change was to be implemented in all stores from April 2013 to December 2014. The brand relaunch and allied OT plan was driven 'top down', from the BB Group executive team and Burger U senior management team in response to changing market conditions and with a focus on achieving commercial and competitive outcomes. However, Ciara recognised that successful culture change should also incorporate systematic 'bottom up' OD methods. Combined with a communication and feedback cycle, this OD process directly involved managers and staff in the change implementation and associated improvements to operational systems and working practices. By respecting the knowledge and potential insights of managers and staff from across 17 store locations and head office, and using their feedback to shape the change process, Ciara aimed to reduce resistance and build advocacy for the new brand values and culture.

CHANGE IMPLEMENTATION AT BURGER U, APRIL 2013 TO OCTOBER 2013

Ciara dealt with her time, resources and scale-of-change challenges by identifying the six pilot stores with high-performing managers and staff willing to trial the brand adoption and cultural embedding process. She combined changes to in-store brand artefacts, such as decor, signage, taglines, product packaging and customer interaction points, with substantive changes to systems, roles, accountabilities, working practices and behaviours. To launch the pilot project in April 2013, managers and staff from the six representative stores – four from Auckland, and one each from Christchurch and Dunedin – came together with senior management and staff representatives from BB Group head office. They all participated in full-day workshops led by the Quadrant 47 consultants and the BB Group training and HR teams. At these workshops, the managers and staff were informed of the proposed change process, and asked to brainstorm and discuss ideas for implementing the brand values within their stores. Various measures were introduced to align pilot store systems, working practices and activities with the new brand values, including: creating a brand culture guide; rewriting position descriptions to reflect the new values; printing the new values on common documents, such as rosters; using the performance management systems to tie key performance indicators (KPIs) to the values; and rewarding managers, supervisors and teams whose behaviour embodies the brand culture.

Ciara also briefed the store managers to reinforce the values through local training sessions, and the new Facebook page and online training and internal communication system. Following the ideas of contemporary OD writer and Harvard professor Russel Beer (Beer, Eisenstat & Sector, 1991; Gardner, 1996), Ciara intended the pilot project to align systems, roles and working practices to the new brand values in the six trial stores. If successful, these examples would be used to demonstrate both the 'what' and 'how to' of culture change at the six pilot stores to managers and staff across the entire network.

Or at least that was the plan as it stood on 22 October 2013, when Bill Buckie collapsed with a fatal heart attack in the VIP tent at a country horse race meeting near Wellington.

POSTSCRIPT: OCTOBER 2013 TO CURRENT DAY

Despite some solid evidence that the brand culture was translating in the six pilot stores and promising signs of increased brand recognition for Burger U in the Auckland market, the steady slide in sales continued in the fiscal year 2013–14. Business was severely disrupted in the months following Bill's death, resulting in the pilot phase of the brand culture change being extended to July 2014. Family squabbles over shares in the estate and a divided board over the Du Plessis Venture Capital Group's plans to buy out Bill's majority interests in both BB Holdings and Burger U created significant uncertainty regarding the future of both companies. Throughout 2013, Ciara had constructed an elegant, informed and well-considered change strategy on paper that had been overtaken by events by the end of that year. As is often the case in today's dynamic market conditions, emergent changes had outstripped the speed, resource base and logic of planned change.

In view of these internal and external factors, what do you think would have happened to the Burger U brand, culture and business by the end of 2014, and later in the globally competitive, 'Uberised' food services industry of today?

REVIEW QUESTIONS

1   Did the WMB brand culture exercise led by Ciara represent the beginning of a deep culture change for WMB in 2013, or was it more of a superficial marketing exercise?

2   Explain your answer with reference to the text and relevant academic readings.

3   In your opinion, what aspects of the brand culture building and repositioning process should be undertaken by marketing and communications specialists and what aspects by OD and change management specialists? Explain your answer with reference to the text, this case study, the marketing literature and/or your own experience.

4   Do you think that Ciara did a good job? Explain your answer.

5   If you were Ciara, what would you have done differently between late 2012 and mid-2013?

6   Thinking about OD and OT approaches to organisational change and the internal and external factors impacting BB Group from October 2013 to July 2014, outline and discuss three brief 300–350-word scenarios on what may have happened to the Burger U brand culture change initiative by early 2015. Choose the most and least likely outcomes from your perspective and discuss with reference to the relevant reading from this text and other sources.

7   In light of your previous discussion and rapid changes in global food services and supporting technologies, what do you think would have happened to the Burger U business beyond 2015 until the present day? Support your answer with reference to the current literature on organisational transformation, and current and emerging business models in the global food services industry.

REFERENCES

Beer, M., Eisenstat, R. and Sector, B. 1991. 'Why change programs don't produce change'. In C. Mabey and B. Mayon-White (eds), *Managing Change*, 2nd edn (London: The Open University/Paul Chapman Publishing).

Clampitt, P.G. 2010. *Communicating for Managerial Effectiveness: Problems, Strategies and Solutions* (Thousand Oaks, CA: Sage Publications).

Cornelissen, J. 2011. *Corporate Communication: A Guide to Theory and Practice*, 3rd edn (London: Sage): 59–77.

De Chernatony, L. and Cottam, S. 2008. 'Interactions between organisational cultures and corporate brands'. *Journal of Product and Brand Management*. 17: 13–24.

Gardner, R.S. 1996. 'Revitalising change at the grassroots'. *HR Monthly* (October 1996): 14–16.

Gotsi, M., Andriopoulos, C. and Wilson, A. 2008. 'Corporate re-branding: is cultural alignment the weakest link?' *Management Decision*. 46: 46–57.

Ind, N. 2011. *Living the Brand: How to Transform Every Member of Your Organisation into a Brand Champion* (UK: Kogan Page).

Scharmer, O. and Kaufer, K. 2013. *Leading from the Emerging Future: From Egosystem to Ecosystem* (San Francisco: Berrett-Koehler).

Schein, E.H. 2010. *Organizational Culture and Leadership*, 4th edn (San Francisco: John Wiley and Sons).

Listening to the City: Rebuilding Ground Zero with the citizens of New York City

Karen Lin Mahar, Central Queensland University

On 11 September 2015, the world remembered the tragic events of the fateful day 14 years previously, when the collapse of the twin towers and the immense loss of life in a day changed how many saw the world forever.

In this ever-changing global environment, groups such as governments, communities and organisations struggle to keep up with the changes required by stakeholders within the system. Taking into consideration and processing an abundance of rich, complex information presents a significant challenge to these groups. Large-group intervention is an approach that has become an increasingly popular change management process method in the last 15 years. It incorporates the method of interactions between participants; this can involve stakeholders and other interested parties to enable them to work together to find options for a given social, civic or organisational issue. The approach seeks to actively involve interested parties in sourcing ideas and synthesising them to provide a sustainable list of outcomes. It provides the organisation with a democratic method to approach change that widely represents the stakeholders involved. It allows us to effectively utilise the knowledge and opinion of groups of five people to 5000 people. This democratic approach was used by the city of New York in 2002 in a project called 'Listening to the City'. The decision makers of Lower Manhattan wanted the citizens of New York City to help shape the change and development that would rebuild Ground Zero after the terrorist attack of 11 September 2001.

BACKGROUND

The events of 11 September 2001 had a profound effect on the citizens of New York City, both local and international. The devastating terrorist attack on the World Trade Center, commonly referred to as the 'twin towers', resulted in the deaths of almost 3000 individuals who were in the towers for work or tourist purposes. This event shattered the core of American and global societies and continues to leave a mark on the world, to this day. In rebuilding the site of this tragedy, referred to as 'Ground Zero', the city of New York and a coalition of organisations involved in the rebuilding of Lower Manhattan decided on a democratic civic approach to ensure the development and change of the location was reflective of all parties affected by September 11.

Large-group interventions are designed to work with groups of people and can accommodate large numbers in processing a feasible list of outcomes to meet the objectives required (Anderson, 2015). Large-group intervention is unique in organisational change methods as it provides top-down and bottom-up processes that encompass the views of the many stakeholders involved (van der Zouwen, 2011). The participation of over 5000 people in the 'Listening to the City' initiative was one of the biggest large-group interventions ever attempted. The Lower Manhattan Development Corporation, Port Authority and the Civic Alliance to Rebuild Lower Manhattan enlisted the services of America Speaks, an organisation with experience in facilitating large-group interventions, to manage and steer the initiative towards a democratic, yet effective result (Lukensmeyer & Brigham, 2005). The complexity and sensitivity of the issue meant that input across many sectors and stakeholders affected by September 11 was the preferred approach to ensure a peaceful rebuilding of the Ground Zero site (**Figure C6.1**).

FIGURE C6.1   PARTICIPANTS' CONNECTION TO SEPTEMBER 11

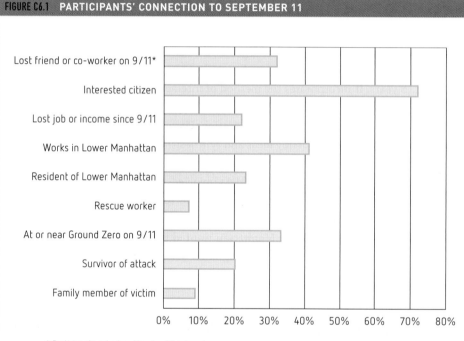

* Participants asked on Monday 22 July only.
Note: Participants could select multiple categories. This graph displays the combined participant results from Saturday 20 July to Monday 22 July.

Data source: The Civic Alliance to Rebuild Downtown New York, 'Listening to the City', *Report of Proceedings*, New York City, 2002, p. 6.

'LISTENING TO THE CITY'

A large-group intervention of this size was a huge project that was given a short time frame of three months to accomplish in 2002, a year after the tragedy (Lukensmeyer & Brigham, 2005). September 11 was still very raw in the minds of all participants and this large-group intervention was highly charged with emotion and passion. America Speaks structured this voice of change for Lower Manhattan in three sections: first, a large-group intervention, much like a town forum of 4500 participants; second, a smaller town forum with 200 participants; finally, an online two-week dialogue of 800 participants to fine-tune the ideas and outcomes from the first two town forums (Lukensmeyer & Brigham, 2005; Nabatchi, 2010).

The first town forum had 458 staff members to facilitate the 4500 participants. There was a facilitator on each table of 9–10 citizens. To ensure this process was successful in providing a cross-section of opinions representing the citizens of New York City, a diverse mix of participants was sourced (Lukensmeyer & Brigham, 2005). The demographic range was varied in all categories: race, ethnic background, income, geographic location and age (see **Table C6.1**). Participants were provided with voting remote controls, allowing them to vote and voice their opinions in real time (The Civic Alliance to Rebuild Downtown New York, 2002). These results were electronically tallied and projected on large screens to show the results from all participants, allowing the organisers to alter plans and provide new direction in accordance with the response from the participants. The six

TABLE C6.1   PARTICIPANTS' DEMOGRAPHIC MIX

Race		Age	
African–American	7%	19 or younger	4%
Asian/Pacific Islander	12%	20–34	27%
Caucasian	67%	35–54	45%
Native American	0%	55–64	14%
Mixed racial heritage	5%	65 or older	10%
None of the above	9%		
Income		**Location**	
Less than $25 000	17%	Manhattan	46
$25 000–$49 999	21%	Brooklyn	18
$50 000–$74 999	20%	Queens	10
$75 000–$99 999	14%	New Jersey	10
$100 000–$149 999	15%	Somewhere else in New York State	6
$150 000 or more	13%	Somewhere else in the US	5
		Bronx	3
		Staten Island	1
		From another country	1

Data source: The Civic Alliance to Rebuild Downtown New York, 'Listening to the City', *Report of Proceedings*, New York City, 2002, p. 7.

proposed plans were heavily rejected on the day by the majority of the participants and the organisers discovered that citizens wanted a memorial that would provide depth and respect to the events of September 11. They deemed the proposed six designs 'flat', 'uninspiring' and focused too much on commercial use (The Civic Alliance to Rebuild Downtown New York, 2002). The outcome indicated that people wanted a mixed use of affordable housing, community projects, commercial and retail use, upgrades in transport and a striking memorial that would look to the future but continue to remember the past. The second town forum of 200 participants indicated very similar responses towards the projected six designs and regarding the preferred ideas for the rebuild of Ground Zero (The Civic Alliance to Rebuild Downtown New York, 2002). These large-scale interventions highlighted the ability to focus on issues important to the people, retrieving the information in a large democratic process.

The final large-group intervention was an online dialogue of 800 participants using the same method of sourcing as the first two forums – that is, a diverse demographic range. This online dialogue continued for two weeks, allowing organisers to refine and respond to the ideas and directions generated from the first two (The Civic Alliance to Rebuild Downtown New York, 2002). The outcome was that they needed to go back to the drawing board and integrate a further 'mixed use' of Ground Zero, reflecting the growing needs and expectations of a large metropolis as well as the need to honour the victims of September 11.

OUTCOME OF 'LISTENING TO THE CITY'

The three large-group interventions provided clear directives for the rebuilding of Ground Zero. The citizens wanted a more diverse use of space that personified the tragedy but was also a mix of metropolis and community space attracting all New Yorkers (Lukensmeyer & Brigham, 2005). There were also strong expressions for the need for improved transport links and possibly a Lower Manhattan Grand Central Station. The Lower Manhattan Development Corporation, Port Authority and Civic Alliance to Rebuild Lower Manhattan decided to immediately launch an international competition to attract designs for the space that embodied the voices of the citizens. A key aspect of the competition was to include high rises to redefine the New York City skyline that was changed as a result of the terrorist attacks.

The overall results showed that 55 per cent of participants supported the need for affordable housing in the Lower Manhattan district, while 25 per cent preferred for the space to be devoted to community parks and greenery, improving the available public space (The Civic Alliance to Rebuild Downtown New York, 2002). The option of an entertainment and arts district was chosen by 20 per cent of respondents. In light of the fact that the participants rejected all six design proposals, organisers decided to ask who should design the rebuild of Ground Zero and an overwhelming 72 per cent said it should be architects and designers (The Civic Alliance to Rebuild Downtown New York, 2002).

Listening to the City showed a combination of change management and participating civic democracy redirecting the path of Ground Zero to a future change that reflected all parts of the New York community. New York architecture critic Paul Goldberger commented:

> Listening to the City would ultimately have a powerful, even profound effect on Ground Zero planning process, if not the entire direction of American urban planning itself. (Goldberger, 2004)

THE REBIRTH OF LOWER MANHATTAN

The revolutionary democratic process of bringing about the processes of change and development in the mass democratic fashion of Listening to the City provided stakeholders of Ground Zero with the tools, direction and spirit to rebuild New York City. Organisers of the large-scale intervention said the feedback of 68 per cent of people feeling that their voices had been heard was an overwhelmingly positive response (The Civic Alliance to Rebuild Downtown New York, 2002). This approach laid the blueprint for the rebirth of Lower Manhattan.

Since the unveiling of the Memorial Museum in 2011, there has been a determined effort by city officials to stop using the term 'Ground Zero' (Geoghegan, 2011). The $30 billion revival of Lower Manhattan has seen the resident population of the district triple (O'Connell, 2014). This growth was confirmed by the Alliance for Downtown New York, which was instrumental in the process of Listening to the City. The buildings that now adorn the former site are One World Trade Center, the National 11 September Memorial plaza, Museum Pavilion and the almost complete World Trade Center Transportation Hub designed by the Spanish architect Santiago Calatrava. Director of Port Authority Patrick Foye remarks on the rebuilding of the once devastated site: 'It makes the New York City skyline whole again' (Dobnik, 2014).

Direct input from the large-scale intervention of Listening to the City gave insight into the importance of a fitting memorial, use of green and public space, affordable housing and vital transit links over commercial and retail allocation. Businesses have also flocked to the rebuilt site, with Condé Nast, *Vanity Fair* and *The New Yorker* relocating to One World Trade Center. Having directly applied the feedback and witnessed the results of growth in residents, revival of the neighbourhood and acceptance of the site from tourists and locals alike, it is safe to conclude that the process and project have been a success. The more complete the rebuild becomes, the more 'Ground Zero' becomes 'Lower Manhattan Reborn'. 'The Lower Manhattan neighborhood is now booming and the site perimeter fences and wooden boards that have blocked many streets and intersections for more than a decade are coming down fast' (Walters, 2015).

REVIEW QUESTIONS

1   In your opinion, why have large-group interventions become a popular method in the process of change development?

2   Do you think using large-group interventions was an effective process of developing change for the rebuild of Ground Zero?

3   Listening to the City was held in 2002, a year after 9/11. Do you think the Alliance of Downtown New York needed to implement another large-scale intervention to further fine-tune ideas and approaches provided? For example, should it have held a large-scale intervention a year later, when the final designs were being selected?

4   Given the success of Listening to the City, in what other situations could a change agent apply the methods of the large-scale intervention to develop a change approach?

REFERENCES

Anderson, D.L. 2015. *Organization Development: The Process of Leading Organizational Change* (Thousand Oaks, CA: Sage Publications).

Dobnik, V. 2014. 'World Trade Center reopens for business 13 years after 9/11'. *The Sydney Morning Herald*, 5 November.

Geoghegan, T. 2011. 'Is it time to retire "Ground Zero"?', BBC News, 8 September, http://www.bbc.com/news/magazine-14827694.

Goldberger, P. 2004. *Up from Zero: Politics, Architecture and the Rebuilding of New York* (New York: Random House).

Lukensmeyer, C.J. and Brigham, S. 2005. 'Taking democracy to scale, large scale interventions for citizens'. *Journal of Applied Behavioral Science*. 41: 47–60.

Nabatchi, T. 2010. 'Addressing the citizenship and democratic deficits: the potential of deliberative democracy for public administration'. *The American Review of Public Administration*. 40: 376–99.

O'Connell, J. 2014. 'The Lower Manhattan Revival, now featuring One World Trade Center', *The Washington Post*, 31 October.

van der Zouwen, T. 2011. *Building an Evidence Based Practical Guide to Large Scale Interventions* (Delft, Netherlands: Eburon Delft Academic Publishers).

Walters, J. 2015. 'Ground Zero: no longer', *The Guardian*, 25 June.

Building an SMO at illycaffè

illycaffè is an Italian coffee producer and distributor. It was founded in 1933 by Francesco Illy, the developer of the modern espresso machine, in Trieste, Italy. The family still runs the company, which operates in 140 countries with more than 1100 employees worldwide. In 2016, it registered 460 million euros of gross revenue. The term 'distinctly illy' was coined by the company and its aficionados for illy's signature blend, a perfect balance of nine pure, sustainably grown Arabica beans from South America, Central America, India, Africa and China. Among coffee producers, illycaffè has a reputation for quality that is reflected in premium prices.

Sustainability is a core part of that reputation and embedded in illycaffè's mission, vision and values. Its guiding principles include producing the best coffee nature can provide, enhanced by the best available technologies and continuous improvement, to create long-term value and sustainability. The company's 2015 sustainable value report states that: 'The inspiring principle of illycaffè is the continuous striving for perfection. This driving force is expressed through two different founding values: the passion for excellence, intended as a love of beauty and a job well done; and ethics, the creation of long-term value through sustainability, transparency, the betterment of people, creating value, fostering social growth, and respecting the environment.'

Until the late 1980s, the world coffee market was governed by The International Coffee Agreement (ICA) cartel, which controlled prices and imposed quotas on coffee producers. As a result, the price of coffee was reasonably stable and contributed to steady and established supply chains throughout the industry. However, in 1989, the market changed drastically when the ICA collapsed and coffee prices tumbled from about US \$1.25 per pound to \$0.49 per pound in 1992. Small coffee producers were at a particular disadvantage as the huge price decreases decimated their income. The low prices spurred efforts to reduce costs, including the adoption of technology to automate the bean-picking process. Although the machines lowered harvest costs, they were not as selective as hand-picking. Machines could not distinguish the ripe from unripe coffee beans and lowered the overall quality of the harvest. Uneven quality was an acute threat to illycaffè's differentiated strategy. Moreover, the absence of the cartel introduced new actors into the supply chain, such as intermediaries and traders, which further diminished the coffee grower's ability to earn a decent living.

illycaffè's response was consistent with its mission, vision and values. By its own account, illycaffè is about creating shared stakeholder value, and the unregulated coffee prices required adaptations to the new dynamics of the international coffee market. This involved redefining both its supply chain and the way it governed that function. The change began with the network of relationships at the supply source. illycaffè built and leveraged social capital among the growers to improve the social, economic and environmental sustainability of the green coffee supply chain. These new practices were first developed in Brazil and are now being extended to other coffee growing regions.

In the first phase of the change process, illycaffè deliberately abandoned the traditional supply chain and created an integrated set of direct relationships with the farmers, bypassing the intermediaries. The main pillars of the integrated supply chain model included:

→ *Direct purchase.* illycaffè decided to enter into direct, long-term relationships with its suppliers. The relationships were founded on a belief in strong mutual benefit and did not rely on commodity exchanges for green coffee supply.

→ *Select the growers.* The decision about who to partner with was to be determined by the *on-the-ground* realities of each country. In Brazil, for example, growers were chosen through a competition, 'The Ernesto Illy Quality Prize for Espresso.' Although this competition had been established in 1991, involving more than 10 000 farmers and prizes worth over US$1.5 million, it became a vehicle for assuring a high-quality base of suppliers.

→ *Train and motivate the growers.* Agronomists from illycaffè's University of Caffè provided hands-on instruction at no cost to the coffee growers. The training developed competencies that supported the continuous improvement of product quality.

→ *Recognise quality, guarantee a profit.* Illy added a substantial mark-up over the international market prices for Arabica beans, directly paying farmers a premium to account for the greater cost and effort required to achieve superior quality.

→ *Build a community and culture of excellence.* illycaffè worked to develop a culture of coffee excellence throughout the region in a variety of creative ways. For example, il Clube illy do Café includes more than 450 growers. Through this program, the company establishes direct relationships with the growers based on the exchange of knowledge and mutual growth. Producers can acquire knowledge and competencies on new sustainable and responsible agricultural practices.

By leveraging existing systems and building new structures and processes, illycaffè built a more sustainable coffee grower community and supply chain. The grower acquired valuable information about the best cultivation techniques and technologies while taking into consideration product quality, the environment, trends in coffee growing, variability in weather and raw materials supply, and effective food safety controls in production and distribution.

The second phase of the change process involved establishing The Responsible Supply Chain Process (RSCP) certification. As the new, more sustainable, integrated green coffee supply chain was being established, illycaffè began developing specific guidelines to extend this approach and continuously improve it as a governance mechanism. The first step, completed in 2007 by Det Norske Veritas (DNV GL Business Assurance), an independent certification agency, was the definition of two protocols (for example, Protocols A and B) for deploying competencies, motivation and a culture of quality and responsibility along the entire supply chain. At the same time, the new system built in processes of continuous improvement. Specifically, Protocol A identified the systems and the impact areas needing development, such as organisation responsibilities, stakeholder roles and responsibilities, and sustainability communication processes. Each of these systems had to account for business ethics, environmental risks and social issues.

Protocol B concerned monitoring and mentoring continuous improvements in environmental and social issues and included awards for high performance. The company evaluated current performance along a triple-bottom-line objective and identified initiatives to support individual improvement plans or to disseminate sustainability and quality practices to other members of the network. Periodic evaluations were part of the process and helped illycaffè and its supply chain members improve their operating standards. In this way, coffee growers were not marginalised. The standards increased transparency and distributed power and wealth along the supply chain, thus changing the governance structure of the network.

While many of the monitoring and mentoring initiatives are driven by illycaffè, the award initiatives involved in Protocol B, such as the Ernesto Illy prize, stimulated a proactive attitude among growers towards sustainable innovation. Coffee growers now had more information and insight into how well distant parts of the industry and supply chain (with which the farmer did not have direct contact) were following 'good practice' as well as the problems they were facing or anticipating. In 2011, illycaffè complemented its own green coffee supply chain management system with the formal adoption of the standard requirements based on the protocols developed by DNV GL and received the 'Responsible Supply Chain Process' (RSCP) certification.

The benefits of illycaffè's supply chain and governance initiatives were felt beyond its own network. Other coffee growers in contact with illycaffè's coffee growers can learn the best techniques and build the capabilities necessary to become suppliers of green coffee for illycaffè. However, even if they do not immediately become part of illycaffè's supply base, they can incorporate this new knowledge and social capital into their operations and sell their green coffee to illycaffè's competitors or other traders. The overall sustainability of the system is improved.

Research on the decommoditisation of green coffee described this as the 'butterfly effect', where companies contributing to the modification of existing equilibriums in a market can trigger virtuous mechanisms that produce profit in a long-term strategy and integrate quality and sustainability. The research also concluded that creating awards can lead to a progressive revaluation of green coffee quality, and the development of a network of producers. The small modifications introduced to the Brazilian coffee market have produced significant long-term changes in the overall trends of the sector at the global level.

illycaffè's actions improved the company's internal commitment and external demonstration to environmental and social sustainability, ethical business practices and stakeholder involvement. In 2016, for the fourth consecutive year, illycaffè was included in the list of the World's Most Ethical Companies. Its approach also demonstrated awareness and effective management of the major risks and performance improvements associated with environmental pollution, product quality and safety, labour and human rights, and local community engagement. At the same time, business improvements through increased brand visibility, product credibility, quality standards achievement, increased connection with product origins, and illy's premium price on the final market were maintained.

illycaffè's implementation of an integrated supply chain and the corresponding governance system improved the company's internal commitment to create, over time, a system where individuals are treated with equity, dignity and respect; the environment is preserved and restored; and suppliers are compliant with rules and awarded for the quality and sustainability of their business.

REVIEW QUESTIONS

This case describes how illycaffè, an Italian coffee producer, responded in a sustainable way to disruptions in its environment and supply chain.

1   What were these disruptions?

2   illycaffè's changes were consistent with its mission and strategy, involved multiple stakeholders and addressed all three aspects of the triple-bottom-line objective. What in detail were these strategies and do you think they were appropriate and/or successful? Explain your answer.

This application was adapted from A. Longoni and D. Luzzini, 'Building social capital into the disrupted green coffee supply chain: Illy's journey to quality and sustainability', in *Organizing Supply Chain Processes for Sustainable Innovation in the Agri-Food Industry*, ed. R. Cagliano, F. Caniato, and C. Worley (Bingley, UK: Emerald Group Publishing Limited, 2016): 83–108; P. Andriani and C. Herrmann-Pillath, 'Transactional innovation and the de-commoditization of the Brazilian coffee trade', (12 March 2011), accessed from SSRN: https://ssrn.com/abstract=1784192 or http://dx.doi.org/10.2139/ssrn.1784192; http://worldsmostethicalcompanies.ethisphere.com/honorees/; illycaffè Sustainable Value Report 2015, accessed from http://valuereport.illy.com/pdf/isvr_EN_2015.pdf accessed on 29 July 2017.

Social and environmental change at LDI Africa

Landmark Development Initiative Africa (LDI Africa) is a non-profit social enterprise based in the United States. It builds the capacity of African corporations, small businesses and non-profits to compete in the global marketplace by recruiting skilled volunteers, especially young African professionals from outside of the continent. Through LDI Africa's partnerships with the Foundation Center in Nigeria and investors in five countries, African non-profits and businesses can access funding and business development services. LDI Africa also plans to send young professionals in Africa to the United States and around the world for overseas fellowships with non-profits and businesses seeking an international perspective on the challenges they face.

As a young professional in Nigeria, Gbenga Ogunjimi, LDI Africa's founder and CEO, had limited access to international management principles and professional development opportunities. Gbenga saw an opportunity to address development challenges facing his country and other parts of the African continent while working in the Washington, DC, headquarters of Atlas Corps, a non-profit organisation that sponsors international fellowships. He believed that by matching organisational needs for globally competitive expertise with a rapidly growing local workforce, he could create a virtuous cycle of social and economic development. He was motivated to establish a social enterprise based on his own experiences and developed the initial concept for LDI Africa.

Through volunteer placement services administered by LDI Africa, young professionals gain hands-on international experience helping African organisations launch and expand their operations. The youth fellows are able to hone their skills in a challenging work environment characterised by resource constraints, limited infrastructure and uncertain policies. The African organisations benefit from access to international business practices and skills, such as business planning, finance, marketing and management. When the three- to 12-month fellowship ends, LDI Africa also offers recruitment services for host organisations interested in hiring fellows. Thus, what separates LDI Africa from other non-profits is the fundamental goal of altering a status quo where African youth and organisations are struggling to obtain the capabilities needed to effectively compete in a global marketplace.

The organisation development (OD) process at LDI Africa started with a chance meeting between Gbenga and an OD practitioner, Kimberley Jutze. Kimberley, a graduate of Pepperdine University's Master of Science in Organization Development Program, was working to establish a consulting practice that addressed the resource and OD needs of social enterprises. After exchanging contact information, Gbenga and Kimberley met to discuss opportunities to work together on securing start-up capital, setting up an office in

Washington, DC, and developing partnerships with organisations involved in work abroad programs.

Once the consulting relationship was formalised, Kimberley conducted an informal assessment, which revealed that the planning documents in place were insufficiently detailed to prepare LDI Africa for a successful launch. Thus, before any of the initial requests for support could be addressed, LDI Africa needed a strategic plan to clearly define its mission, programs and operations. A business planning approach pioneered by the non-profit consulting firm Root Cause guided the development of a three-year strategy for launching and expanding LDI Africa. The plan described the social and financial returns that social impact investors could expect.

Over the next five months, Kimberley worked closely with Gbenga to facilitate the development of a social impact strategy. The strategy development process consisted of a series of meetings where each section of the social impact strategy outline (Need and Opportunity, Social Impact Model, Implementation Strategy and Action Plan) was reviewed and ideas were discussed. In between meetings, Gbenga prepared drafts of the social impact strategy.

Despite having a mutually agreed upon scope of work, differences in communication styles between Kimberley and Gbenga and expectations that were not clearly defined upfront posed challenges to the consulting relationship. For example, both parties had different assumptions about what level of detail was sufficient for addressing each section of the social impact strategy. Gbenga, who wanted to make the most of his limited time in the United States to launch LDI Africa as soon as possible, preferred a moderately detailed plan where he could address questions from social impact investors as they came up. In contrast, Kimberley believed that investing more time up front in addressing anticipated questions in the plan itself would facilitate smoother implementation later on. A final agreement was reached through ongoing feedback on drafts of the plan and open discussions about the quality and quantity of information needed to complete it. Attention also was given to establishing a collaborative relationship characterised by open and honest communication between Kimberley and Gbenga. This greatly improved communication between them as well as their working relationship.

By the time the social impact strategy was completed, Gbenga gained greater insight into the essential steps needed to transition LDI Africa from a concept to an operational organisation. He was better prepared to meet with prospective financial supporters and refer to details captured in the social impact strategy to fully explain LDI Africa's model.

After the social impact strategy was completed and LDI Africa was registered as a non-profit organisation, Gbenga asked Kimberley to help obtain seed funding. As a first step, they agreed to prepare a strategy to guide LDI Africa's resource development efforts. This consisted of meetings to review each section of the strategy outline and discuss ideas. Gbenga also drafted the strategy with support from Kimberley. After agreeing upon a funding target based on the organisation's annual operating budget, Kimberley used a strengths-based approach to assess LDI Africa's fundraising assets. She worked closely with Gbenga to determine which sources of funding the organisation was best prepared to cultivate as well as best and worst case scenarios for the amount of funding that LDI Africa could anticipate receiving from each source. A contingency plan was also developed that explained how LDI Africa would continue to operate in the event that the funding target was not fully reached during its first year of operation. The strategy also included an action plan with specific tasks, timeline and targets. Gbenga's active participation in the strategic planning process led him to appreciate the importance of thinking through different options to obtain funding and deploy LDI Africa's resources expediently rather than just pursuing whatever opportunities happened to come along. With an action plan in place, Gbenga was also better prepared to begin seeking start-up capital.

Most recently, Gbenga began forming a board of directors for LDI Africa and invited Kimberley to join as an adviser for resource and OD. Recognising the importance of an effective board, Kimberley coached Gbenga on board development issues, such as defining member roles and responsibilities, enlisting their support for fundraising activities, and facilitating board meetings. Through this informal consultation process, Gbenga is learning how to provide overall direction to the board and to obtain its support for LDI Africa's work. He is also addressing the challenge of board member engagement by managing expectations around each board member's role and time commitments.

As LDI Africa prepares to launch its pilot fellowship program in June 2013, it has recognised the need to develop partnerships with African organisations that have expressed interest in hosting young professionals, but are unable to cover fellowship costs, such as housing, transportation and insurance. Gbenga and Kimberley worked together to prepare a teaming agreement with an African foundation that provides micro-investments and mentorship to start-up enterprises. Their initial conversations with the African foundation involved explaining how the teaming process would work for preparing consortium grant applications to foundations, examining the pros and cons of joint fundraising before entering into an agreement, and drafting a teaming agreement for both parties to sign. As a result, Gbenga was better prepared to lead the partnership negotiation process. If LDI Africa is successful in obtaining grants for its pilot fellowship program, both organisations will benefit from the opportunity to contribute to the professional development of fellows and to the sustainability of newly formed African companies.

Throughout the process, Kimberley 'led from behind' by working one-on-one with Gbenga to enhance his leadership capabilities and serving as an observer in meetings so that he was consistently seen as leading LDI Africa's partnership and resource development efforts. Over the past 18 months, LDI Africa has made tremendous strides in its internal development. It has grown from a concept to a registered non-profit, hired four people to staff positions in Nigeria and the United States, and established an international board of directors. LDI Africa has also succeeded in obtaining an initial round of start-up capital that can help position the social enterprise to attract additional funding for its pilot program. Gbenga's strong personal commitment to LDI Africa and his dedication to developing it in a systematic way has poised the organisation for success within Nigeria and across Africa.

REVIEW QUESTIONS

1   Identify the need for change.

2   How did LDI Africa approach the change process? Do you think it was successful or could there be improvement or alternative approaches?

3   How will LDI Africa measure the outcomes of the change process? What would you expect to be its subsequent actions?

This application was developed with the kind assistance of Kimberley Jutze. Her contribution is gratefully acknowledged.

Diagnosis and feedback at Adhikar[1]

Adhikar[2] is a human rights-based, non-government organisation (NGO). Headquartered in Jharkhand, India, it was founded in 1985 to empower society's poor and marginalised populations. It has worked from within socially marginalised communities to organise against the unjust distribution of wealth, resources or power. Rajan Mishra founded the organisation and demonstrated the importance of self-determination by organising people into unions and other collectives. The organisation has grown from a handful of people inspired by Mishra's vision during its early days to over 200 employees.

Adhikar's scope of work and involvement are outlined in **Figure C9.1**. Under the umbrella of the Adivasi Sangathan unit, Adhikar organises regional labourers into unions. Adhikar also works in the area of budgetary analysis and expenditure monitoring of the state government through its financial education unit called Arthik Siksha. In addition, Adhikar administers a scholarship program that seeks to fund and train local-level leaders and an emergency response program that delivers relief services in times of natural disasters.

INITIATING A CHANGE PROCESS: ENTRY AND CONTRACTING

The Adhikar engagement began with contact between Ms Pia Mishra, an Adhikar regional coordinator and an organisation development (OD) practitioner with whom she had worked previously, to discuss the possibility of an intervention. The organisation had grown substantially, and its founder had recently joined the central government, necessitating his withdrawal from day-to-day management. A second meeting was arranged to explain the nature of the intended engagement and seek formal permission to enter the organisation, gather information and report back on the analysis and recommendations for action.

Together, Pia and the OD practitioners agreed to one- to two-hour interviews with each coordinator concerning their views of the organisation, its culture and any concerns or suggestions. All the respondents were to be assured of the confidentiality of their responses. In addition, the OD practitioner would visit a field location in Ghatsila to interact with the workers and interview the regional coordinator, Mr Dubey. During this visit, she would sit in on one of the regional meetings and interview the field workers in small groups of four or five. This was done to understand the organisation from the view of the field workers and gain insight into its issues through their lens.

Finally, the OD practitioner would make systematic observations of non-verbal behaviours, patterns of interaction and descriptions of the relationships among members during interviews, focus groups and the meetings she attended. This would provide indications of the organisation's climate.

---

1   This case was abridged and adapted from N. Nair and N. Vohra, 'The case of OD in an NGO in India', *Journal of Management Development*, 30 (2011): 148–59.
2   The names of the organisation, its location and the various individuals have been disguised to maintain confidentiality.

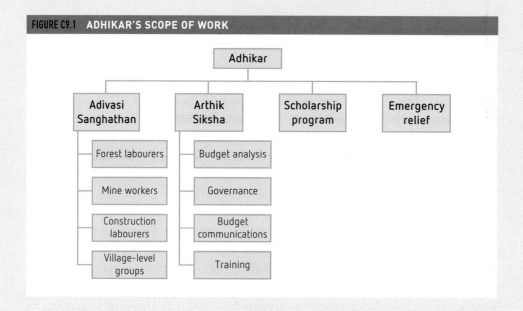

FIGURE C9.1   ADHIKAR'S SCOPE OF WORK

Following the data collection, a session would be held with all the coordinators to present the findings. This would serve as both a mirroring (feedback) activity as well as a forum for initiating dialogue and communication across the various units and members of the organisation.

Prior to the interviews, the OD practitioner familiarised herself with Adhikar and its activities through a study of various reports and publications, including annual reports, budget analysis reports of Arthik Siksha, newspaper clippings and other documents relating to the organisation. The OD practitioner then met each of the coordinators of Adhikar, starting with Pia, who served as the point of contact throughout. Most of the issues and concerns described below surfaced through these sessions. She observed that while most coordinators opened up freely to discuss their concerns, others, like Ms Devi (the Chaibasa Regional Coordinator), were less open and did not share much about their views on Adhikar and its functioning.

Most coordinators had been with the organisation since its inception. All of them echoed a strong sense of organisational identification and commitment. There was high regard for the founder, Mr Mishra. However, Pia has had to prove herself in the organisation, although she is professionally qualified and has been actively working in the field. Interestingly, during meetings with Pia, she never mentioned that she was the daughter of the founder. The OD practitioner came to know this only during the course of her later interviews.

DIAGNOSTIC DATA

The data from the interviews were categorised using Weisbord's six-box model (**Figure C9.2**) and are described below.

FIGURE C9.2   WEISBORD'S SIX-BOX MODEL

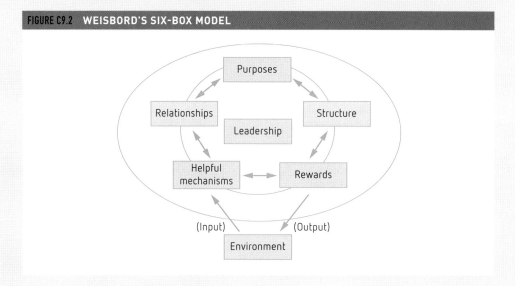

ISSUES RELATED TO PURPOSE

There was considerable agreement on the organisation's objective: facilitating social change through rights-based mobilisation and advocacy. However, some coordinators believed that the organisation needed to work more towards the *capacity building development* of the tribal/regional unions and not just their formation. The vision and future direction of Adhikar as either rights-based or developmental or a combination of both did not have a consensus among all the coordinators. The view posed by some was that it was time for Adhikar to move into developmental work, given that much of the rights-based work had been successful and the future lay in the area of capacity building.

ISSUES RELATED TO STRUCTURE

There appeared to be a lack of clarity regarding Adhikar's structure. As the organisation had grown, its structure had evolved. Adhikar was currently structured along both geographic and program dimensions (**Figure C9.3**). The various unions and programs were managed by different coordinators that all reported directly to the managing trustee, Mr Mishra. In addition, location coordinators in Chaibasa, Ghatsila and Saraikela worked to see that the programs were implemented locally and also reported to the managing trustee.

The structural confusion existed primarily because of considerable overlap in reporting relationships and responsibilities between programs and regions. Interviewees cited instances when this caused conflict regarding reporting relationships or precedence of command.

Coordinators had considerable autonomy. However, some felt that the sense of responsibility and accountability that comes with empowerment was lacking in Adhikar. Various coordinating mechanisms, such as periodic meetings among coordinators to make decentralisation effective, were absent. In such a scenario, the different units seemed to be operating in silos with little coordination and a total absence of centralisation at any level.

FIGURE C9.3   ADHIKAR REPORTING STRUCTURE

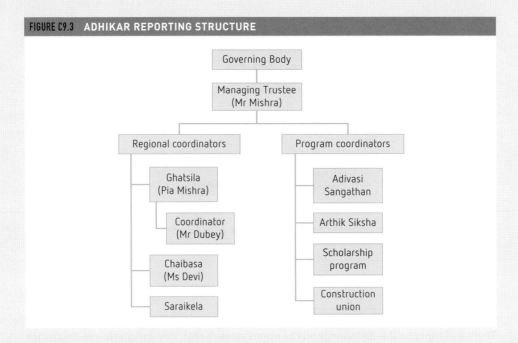

ISSUES RELATED TO RELATIONSHIPS

The most common theme in the interviews was the concern over a lack of coordination. Most of the program coordinators thought that there should be more integration among them. Each unit of Adhikar was performing well, but there was little sharing of information. Although there was a high degree of decentralisation and autonomy at the coordinator level, the coordinating mechanisms were absent. There had been a noticeable decline, over time, in the number of meetings when all the coordinators met, and many cited this as a reason for the disconnect they felt with Adhikar as a whole.

In talking with old versus new coordinators, the data supported the conclusion that there was little trust between the two groups. The new coordinators felt their professional growth and program initiatives were stymied by the old guard, who appeared to be protecting their turf. New coordinators did not feel welcomed by the more senior coordinators. On the other hand, the older members in the organisation believed that the new coordinators were over-ambitious and got right into the field without making an effort to understand the organisation. This concern was voiced by a few but not all coordinators, but the OD practitioner believed it had the potential to grow and create conflict if not properly addressed.

A related theme was that new entrants did not go through any formal socialisation process, which also manifested in a feeling of not being welcomed into the organisation. The interviewees provided examples where new entrants had to seek information and figure things out for themselves, which further created a feeling of isolation.

ISSUES RELATED TO REWARDS

Adhikar began as a rights-based organisation and most of the older employees chose to work there because of their dedication to the original cause. The newer employees (some better qualified professionally) were getting paid higher wages, which was perceived to be discriminatory and was a source of discontent among the older members.

As an NGO that depended on external funding, the issue of job security was also a matter of concern. With Mr Mishra's declining involvement, there was a palpable fear that Adhikar might close its doors in the not-too-distant future. The interviewees suggested that some form of assurance from the leadership of Adhikar might ease the sense of insecurity.

ISSUES RELATED TO HELPFUL MECHANISMS

Some coordinators were concerned about the irregularity of reporting. While some coordinators made progress reports on time, others were consistently tardy and this was pointed out as an example of inconsistency in leadership and authority. Most coordinators in the past had reported verbally on a regular basis to Mr Mishra, who was able to fill in gaps of information whenever required for other coordinators. Thus, the formal system of submitting and reading others' reports had never been emphasised.

ISSUES RELATED TO LEADERSHIP

Adhikar's founder and leader was considered dynamic and charismatic – a number of people had been attracted to the organisation by his personality. At the time of the interviews, Mr Mishra had taken a position in India's central government and was moving away from day-to-day management. This behaviour was interpreted as an appropriate response to keep political alignments transparent. However, it did create a leadership vacuum.

Perhaps because of his absence, many in the organisation were worried about a dearth of second-level leaders in the organisation. Even in his absence, Mr Mishra still appeared to be the de facto leader. The organisation seemed to be facing a crisis in terms of a leader who could command the same level of respect and following.

Two women, Ms Devi and Pia, were most often cited as potential future leaders of Adhikar. The Chaibasa coordinator, Ms Devi, had been with the organisation since its founding and was supported by the people in her region. In the eyes of some others, however, Ms Devi was a shadow of Mr Mishra and a surrogate leader for Pia. Ms Devi was viewed consistently as a good worker, but lacked the vision needed to lead a highly motivated team. Ms Devi had not been very forthcoming in the interview.

In the absence of her father, Pia appeared to be the chief decision maker. She had been with the organisation for five years as the program director of Ghatsila, and operated from the headquarters while Ms Devi preferred to work from her Chaibasa location.

Both women, independently, echoed reservations as potential next leaders and mentioned their gender as one of the reasons. They felt that the other male coordinators and the community they served might not be ready for a female leader. In discussions with most of the other coordinators, however, the OD practitioner got the sense that they were open to having a woman leader. Some of the coordination issues were expected to be addressed if a new leader was appointed.

REVIEW QUESTIONS

1   Based on the data provided in the case, what is your analysis of the situation at Adhikar? Is the organisation in trouble? If so, how big is the problem? Is the organisation 'doing fine?' That is, are all the data presented just symptoms of an organisation that is young and growing?

2   Design the feedback meeting. What is the purpose of the meeting, what is the agenda, and how will you present the data?

3   What actions do you believe the Adhikar organisation should take? What problems do you think these actions would solve?

Cultural and organisational integration at MMI: The Momentum and Metropolitan merger[1]

On an early, crisp March morning in 2017, Nicolaas Kruger, group CEO of MMI Holdings Ltd, was reminded of Charles Dickens' book *A Tale of Two Cities* when he arrived at the company's Parc du Cap office complex in Cape Town. MMI Holdings Ltd employed 14 697 people in South Africa and 2863 internationally. In 2016, its return on embedded value, a widely used industry measure of value creation, was 13 per cent compared to the industry average of 10.2 per cent, and the new business present value of future premiums (PVP) was R44.1 billion. (In September 2017, 1 South African Rand (ZAR) was 0.078 US Dollar; 1 US Dollar was 12.84 ZAR.)

Like the stark contrast between the strained Parisian lifestyle and the relaxed London setting of the 17th century, Cape Town had been the headquarters of Metropolitan, one of the two companies that merged to form MMI Holdings. Metropolitan's culture had been characterised by a more formal, traditional management style with top-down decision making. Momentum, the other firm in the merger, had been headquartered in the capital city of Pretoria and its proximity to the heart of South Africa's financial district influenced its culture. The Momentum culture was considered modern and more informal, with empowered high-performing employees and less power distance between staff and management.

With Table Mountain in the background and several cyclists and runners on the road, Kruger reflected on the different locations and rich history of each organisation as well as the merger's progress. For example, he noticed that there were no longer designated parking bays for executives in the Metropolitan building and inside, MMI and Metropolitan logos shared wall space. Before the merger, the top floor had been for the exclusive use of executives, but had been transformed into a staff cafeteria so that everyone could enjoy the view of Cape Town. To Kruger, this was significant progress towards aligning the two cultures around a common set of values. The question was, 'How could they capitalise on their progress to derive even more value from the merger?'

PRELUDE TO A MERGER

Metropolitan and Momentum were two of South Africa's top financial services companies. Metropolitan began as African Homes Trust in 1898 to help low-income earners build their own homes, and few companies had a history that so closely mirrored the progress of

[1] This case was co-authored by Caren Scheepers, Sonja Swart and Dieter von Staden at the Gordon Institute of Business Science, University of Pretoria, Johannesburg, South Africa. Some material was drawn from *Momentum and Metropolitan's Merger: Authentic Transformational Leadership* (2015) published by Richard Ivey School of Business Foundation, 9B15C004, https://www.iveycases.com/ProductView.aspx?id=70560.

South Africa and its people. In 1912, African Homes Trust took over an insurance company and in 1985 changed its name to Metropolitan Life. Life insurance was its primary product, sold through mass-market agents to primarily entry-level and middle-income markets. It was highly efficient at processing new business accounts, serving clients, processing claims and generally administering its policies. Metropolitan had sufficient scale in terms of the number of public and private sector clients in retirement fund administration to provide them with scale benefits and thus the ability to price competitively. It was also the leading player in private (closed) health care solutions administration.

Metropolitan was proud of its special emphasis on designing products for those who had previously, especially during the Apartheid years, been unable to participate in long-term savings. In the 1990s, Metropolitan expanded to Namibia, Lesotho and Botswana, and in 2006 it acquired a 60 per cent stake in a Ghana insurer. In 2010, Metropolitan had 5500 people and a market capitalisation of R9 billion.

Momentum, on the other hand, was a progressive company established in 1966 as 'Afrikaanse Verbond Lewens' (meaning 'Afrikaanse Life Bonds' in Afrikaans, one of South Africa's official languages). It acquired Monument Assurance in 1973 to form Momentum Life. Rand Merchant Bank Holdings (RMBH) invested in Momentum in 1992 and its growth benefited from a strong focus on middle and affluent market segments. In 1998, RMBH created FirstRand Limited, the largest financial services company on the JSE. Momentum had 9000 people and a market capitalisation of R16 billion. It had strong products in open health care solutions administration and umbrella retirement funds, both distributed through a strong broker channel. Momentum's life insurance product, Myriad, was a market leader in the industry due to its comprehensive coverage.

In 2010, Metropolitan and Momentum faced similar challenges. Looking for growth, each firm had developed insurance products aimed at the markets where the other was strong, and each had struggled to gain share. Momentum's Aspire product struggled to penetrate the lower income market, while Metropolitan's Odyssey Life Insurance product for the upper income market was unable to gain traction.

Both organisations started looking for corporate transactions as solutions to bridge these gaps. When Metropolitan's CEO Wilhelm van Zyl and Momentum's CEO Nicolaas Kruger talked about their respective challenges, they began to discuss whether a merger between them might solve both companies' challenges. On its face, their products and markets were complementary, and the operational risks from a merger were also lessened because there was little overlap in the broker and agency forces of the two companies.

Over the next three months, various discreet meetings with selected board members tested opinions about a possible merger. These meetings led to the formation of a merger committee.

THE CASE FOR CHANGE

The merger committee consisted of balanced representation of executive and non executive members from both companies, including the CEOs of both companies, the Chief Financial Officer of Metropolitan and the Chief Operating Officer of Momentum.

The merger committee's mandate was to formulate a clear business case for the boards. It became an important reference point in directing decision making. Whenever there was a question or choice, the team would invoke 'The business case must prevail' rule. In a time of great uncertainty, it offered direction and clarity.

The core of the business case recognised the complementary product lines and markets served. In addition, there were revenue and expense synergies to gain by integrating certain back-office functions. For example, Metropolitan ran a lower-cost health care insurance administration business than Momentum. On the other hand, Momentum had access to FirstRand's Rand Merchant Bank (RMB) asset management business, which had a much stronger third-party client franchise and could improve efficiencies in Metropolitan's business. Finally, Momentum's health insurance businesses and Metropolitan's life insurance business were well represented throughout Africa. Any regional expansion strategies into Africa would thus be complementary.

The business case also helped the merger committee to focus on MMI's long-term strategic direction, especially in the face of the immediate pressures for cost savings. An organisation development (OD) consultant, Dr Francois Hugo, facilitated some of the discussions to resolve differing views and offered input on building trust under conditions of uncertainty and conflicting perspectives. During several important decision points, the team members had to put the envisaged company's combined interest ahead of their own company's interest or their own individual interest. Nonetheless, there were still a number of occasions when the two parties had dissimilar views that could prevent the deal from going through.

An important point of contention early in the process was deciding on the combined entity's brand. Design consultants, for example, suggested names that combined parts of the two client-facing brands, like Metrum, Magma, Meridium and Emminent. Eventually, agreement was reached with the name MMI. MMI was positioned as the investor brand, while the strong and trusted brands of Momentum and Metropolitan would be used in client-facing businesses. This decision reflected the strong belief that the financial value of the merger would be maximised by leveraging the Metropolitan and Momentum brand names.

COMPETITION TRIBUNAL RULING

The merger application to South Africa's Competition Commission included the rationale of cost savings due to synergies from shared information technology platforms, combined locations and approximately 1500 (out of 13 000 positions) job redundancies. The transaction had to adhere to South Africa's rigorous company competition laws and regulations prescribed in the Competition Act, No. 18 of 1998. The high unemployment rate in South Africa created sensitivity to lay-offs, known as retrenchments in the South African environment. They were governed by strict labour laws, such as the Basic Conditions of Employment Act, No. 75 of 1997 and the Labour Relations Act, No. 66 of 1995. The Competition Tribunal ruled that the merger between the two companies would be approved on the condition that, during the first three years, there would be no employee retrenchments, except for senior managers. From a legal point of view, MMI could have appealed the ruling. However, the two boards decided not to challenge the decision in part due to the negative publicity this would cause. Kruger recalled:

> We decided to choose our battles. Instead, we focused on cost savings through consolidating our business units and used natural attrition to reduce staff numbers.

On 31 March 2010, Metropolitan issued 950 million new shares to FirstRand, in exchange for Momentum shares, aiming to list MMI Holdings Ltd on the JSE later in the year when agreement had been reached on the final terms of the merger transaction. Following implementation of the merger, FirstRand unbundled all its shares in Metropolitan and MMI was listed on the JSE on 1 December 2010. The combined entity was 15.6 per cent black-owned and, given South Africa's Broad Based Black Economic Empowerment (B-BBEE) Act No. 53 of 2003, it became one of the most empowered insurance companies in the country.

THE INTEGRATION PROCESS

The positioning of the transaction as a merger rather than a takeover was important in retaining key customer groups and talented employees from both organisations. However, while Momentum had more experience acquiring other companies, such as Lifegro, Southern Life and Sage Life, this was its first true merger. The idea of balancing representation on the board, as well as the executive committee and merger committees, made the process significantly more complex, and seeking consensus between the parties led to several iterations of decisions. Momentum's slightly larger embedded value resulted in 11 board members compared to Metropolitan's nine MMI board members. The chairperson was initially from Momentum, but there was an agreement that after one year, he would step down and the Metropolitan chairperson, J.J. Njeke, would become chairperson of the combined entity. Despite these efforts, some financial analysts, such as Tim Cohen of *Business Day*, questioned whether a true merger was possible. He insisted on calling it a 'soft takeover'.

Early in 2011, the two companies' executive teams were combined to form a new structure (**Figure C10.1**). The different cultural approaches in Metropolitan and Momentum became even more apparent during this time and required rigorous debate to reach compromises. The intent of achieving cost savings through synergies, while retaining the best of both organisations, required consultations and meticulous attention to creating space for both organisations to be heard. At times, the extensive consultation to ensure fairness in decision making slowed the integration process down. Kruger commented:

> We learned early in this merger process that the soft people issues were actually the hardest to deal with. There were a few months just prior to the merger where the senior executive roles in the new structure were not yet final. This difficult time experienced by executives gave us more empathy with what our staff were going through during the merger process.

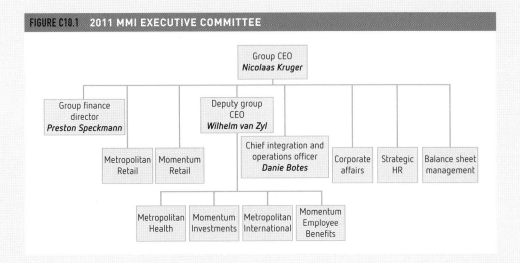

FIGURE C10.1   2011 MMI EXECUTIVE COMMITTEE

As Nicolaas Kruger, Momentum's former CEO, was appointed to the group CEO position, Metropolitan's former CEO, Wilhelm van Zyl, was appointed as deputy group CEO. Kruger was responsible for Momentum's and Metropolitan's retail businesses as well as the group-wide support functions. Van Zyl was accountable for Metropolitan Health, Momentum Investments, Metropolitan International and Momentum Employee Benefits.

The rationale for the new structure was to offer equal representation for both companies, and this structure purposefully balanced power between the two former CEOs. Moreover, a divisional structure made sense because the combined entity was too large for a functional structure and a matrix structure would have been too complex in the early days of the combined entity.

All executives were strong proponents of the long-term envisioned benefits of the merger and repeated the benefits to staff regularly. Leadership purposefully demonstrated their commitment to the merger by being highly visible and accessible during this period of uncertainty.

FORMULATING INTEGRATION PLANS

Following the merger's approval, the merger committee became responsible for finalising the due diligence process and establishing an integration program to manage the transition with a project approach. The composition of the merger committee was adjusted and comprised two non-executive board members from each company, including the CEOs. Johan Burger, representing Momentum's board, served as the committee's chair.

The merger committee had several debates to create a clear and common picture of the future that resulted in a jointly formulated vision: 'We will be a leader in meeting financial services' needs. We will meet clients' needs by providing a range of appropriate, value-for-money financial solutions in our market segments.' The finalisation date of the MMI Group strategy was February 2011. (See **Figure C10.2** for a summary of the action plan.)

FIGURE E10.2   HIGH-LEVEL TIMELINE OF MERGER INTEGRATION PROCEEDINGS

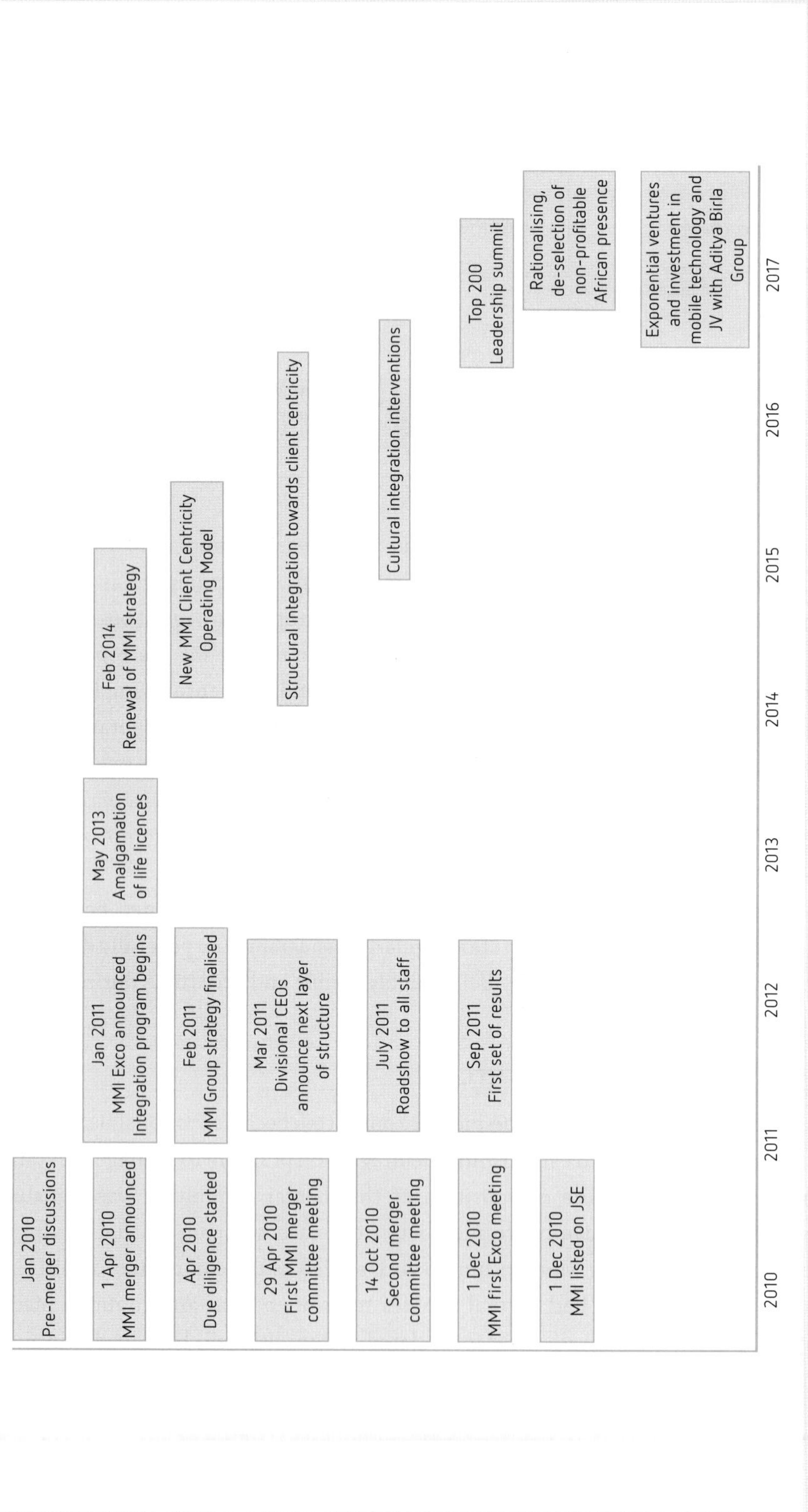

	2010	2011	2012	2013	2014	2015	2016	2017

Jan 2010
Pre-merger discussions

1 Apr 2010
MMI merger announced

Apr 2010
Due diligence started

29 Apr 2010
First MMI merger committee meeting

14 Oct 2010
Second merger committee meeting

1 Dec 2010
MMI first Exco meeting

1 Dec 2010
MMI listed on JSE

Jan 2011
MMI Exco announced Integration program begins

Feb 2011
MMI Group strategy finalised

Mar 2011
Divisional CEOs announce next layer of structure

July 2011
Roadshow to all staff

Sep 2011
First set of results

May 2013
Amalgamation of life licences

Feb 2014
Renewal of MMI strategy

New MMI Client Centricity Operating Model

Structural integration towards client centricity

Cultural integration interventions

Top 200 Leadership summit

Rationalising, de-selection of non-profitable African presence

Exponential ventures and investment in mobile technology and JV with Aditya Birla Group

The merger committee, in turn, appointed working groups to flesh out the details of the merger process. Danie Botes was appointed as the MMI chief integration officer to coordinate this process, based on his first-hand change management experience in the Sage and Southern Life integrations. One group, for example, focused on the integration of people processes and IT platforms. Other working groups paid attention to the combined organisational structures for the investments business unit, the international businesses, employee benefits and the health care administration business units. Structures for the lower income market life insurance business, called the emerging market retail division, and the upper income market life insurance retail division were also developed with equal representation from both organisations. Using working groups comprising both Metropolitan and Momentum employees increased understanding of each company's realities and aspirations.

The merger committee also retained a strategy consultancy that had worked in both organisations. The consultancy had central oversight and was ideally positioned to facilitate the working groups, which utilised an inclusive bottoms-up involvement process to formulate the implementation plans. Together, they developed strategies and integration plans that were presented to the merger committee for approval. Following approval by the merger committee, the working groups proceeded to implement their plans, taking into account top-down guidance from the merger committee.

Another important role of the merger committee was coordinating the communication of integration plans. For example, the two CEOs would formulate their communication messages and confirm consistency of messaging with each other prior to sending out combined media releases or external communications to shareholders, as prescribed by the JSE. Internal communications were also sent out by both CEOs, making sure the employees of both organisations received the communications at the same time. This enabled consistency in communication and prevented, to some extent, rumours in both the Gauteng and Western Cape provinces. These communications went out weekly to instil trust in leadership. When there was lack of progress, the CEOs gave honest feedback about unresolved issues and planned corrective actions.

In one of the first coordinated communications efforts, the newly formed executive committee in 2011 acknowledged that it would take a couple of years to bridge the vast differences in culture between the two organisations. As a result, they decided to focus on developing a common set of core values. The process commenced with an initial values assessment where all employees were invited to participate in a vote for the values they preferred. The assessment revealed that there were many similar preferred values across the two organisations. Behaviours associated with these values might differ, but the commonalities formed a strong foundation for the integration and alignment process, despite the different cultures. Six values emerged from this process, including integrity, accountability, diversity, innovation, teamwork and excellence.

The executive team also held countrywide roadshows, where as many staff as possible attended to hear first-hand what was planned for the merged entity. During these roadshows, the former CEOs acknowledged the past, offered updates on merger progress, shared success stories and reinforced the vision of the combined entity.

Finally, the merger committee initiated a Redeployment Centre (RDC) for those staff members whose jobs became redundant through the integration process. As jobs became available through natural attrition in the two organisations, employees were transferred back into these jobs. The RDC optimised resource redeployment and removed the need for lay-offs. It further contributed towards MMI ultimately exceeding its annual cost savings target of R500 million on completion of the merger integration.

STRATEGY REFORMULATION

By 2014, the initial vision of the combined entity needed updating. It had revolved around meeting financial services' needs and the strategy included such statements as 'We will use our insight into the needs of our clients, our strong client-facing brands, product innovation, and service excellence. Our game-changing strategy will establish MMI as a leader and enable us to deliver superior shareholder returns on a sustainable basis.'

The executive team embarked on a reformulation of their strategy with client-centricity as its driving force. They created a purpose, instead of a vision and mission, namely 'to enhance the lifetime financial wellness of people, their communities, and their businesses'. They believed the idea of 'financial wellness' was a continuous process of planning and managing clients' money so that they could handle everyday expenses and still reach their goals over a lifetime.

As part of the strategy reformulation, MMI explicitly wanted to enhance the financial wellness of a broad range of clients, including individuals as well as small and medium businesses, large companies and public enterprises. The executive team also confirmed the earlier strategic focus on South Africa, the rest of Africa, and selected international countries. MMI had strong capabilities in the full range of long- and short-term insurance for individuals and corporate clients, asset management, property management, investment and savings, health care insurance administration as well as health risk management. They summarised their strategic focus areas as client-centricity, growth and excellence. They defined their aspirations in both financial (growth in earnings, new business and embedded value) as well as client (financial wellness partner) terms (**Figure C10.3**). **Figure C10.3** also illustrates that MMI's executive team emphasised flexible and modular systems, innovation, culture and data analytics as enablers of the strategy.

A CLIENT-CENTRIC DESIGN

The executive committee introduced a major organisational redesign to support MMI's client-centric strategy in 2014. The reformulated strategy demonstrated a significant move away from a product-focused and siloed set of businesses. To support the new strategy, the executive committee proposed an operating model with a new client engagement solutions group at the centre of the design (**Figure C10.4**). With the support of the centres of excellence (shown on the right), the client engagement solutions group supported all segments and channels (shown on the left) by developing engagement tools to enhance client experiences. This operating model was designed

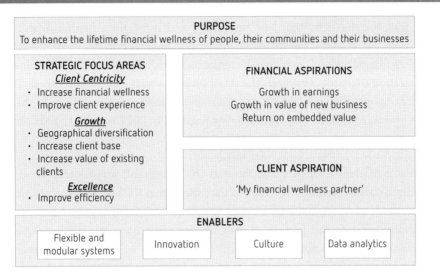

FIGURE C10.3 MMI'S REFORMULATED STRATEGY

PURPOSE
To enhance the lifetime financial wellness of people, their communities and their businesses

STRATEGIC FOCUS AREAS
Client Centricity
- Increase financial wellness
- Improve client experience

Growth
- Geographical diversification
- Increase client base
- Increase value of existing clients

Excellence
- Improve efficiency

FINANCIAL ASPIRATIONS
Growth in earnings
Growth in value of new business
Return on embedded value

CLIENT ASPIRATION
'My financial wellness partner'

ENABLERS

| Flexible and modular systems | Innovation | Culture | Data analytics |

FIGURE C10.4 MMI OPERATING MODEL

Group CEO

Segments
- Momentum Retail
- Metropolitan Retail
- Corporate and Public Sector
- International (Africa & India)
- UK

Client engagement solutions

Centres of excellence
- Health
- Investments and savings
- Life insurance
- Short-term insurance
- Lending solutions

Group-wide functions
- Finance
- Risk
- Operations
- Brand, corporate affairs and transformation

to optimise the execution of MMI's client-centric strategy. Segment and channel businesses used their intimate understanding of clients to build financial wellness client value propositions. The value propositions would use client engagement and experience tools designed by the client engagement solutions business (in the centre), as well as products provided by MMI's centres of excellence. Group-wide functions supported the entire organisation.

The MMI executive team consciously followed a phased approach to the merger integration. They wanted to take employees with them on the journey and sometimes had to wait for the right time and opportunity to integrate a further aspect of the organisation. For example, the structural integration kicked off in 2011 with the complete back-office integrations of employee benefits, asset management and health insurance administration divisions. However, the retail divisions were largely untouched. The new client-centric operating model with the client engagement solutions group in the centre was not envisaged in 2011. The restructuring initiated in 2014 was thus a next phase.

CULTURAL INTEGRATION INTERVENTIONS

By 2015, Dr Marlene Dippenaar, an internal OD consultant, was asked to head up the cultural integration process. She realised that the Group CEO and executive committee were invaluable in understanding the requirements of culture change and demonstrating their commitment to the process. During an executive team two-day breakaway, the executive committee acknowledged the cultural heritages of the original organisations and considered which aspects they wanted to retain. It was important for the executives that the aspired MMI culture would support the strategic direction of the organisation. They confirmed that the six values created earlier would be important enablers of living MMI's financial wellness purpose going forward and formulated specific behaviours that would characterise each value. They created a unifying narrative called *The MMI Way* to explain examples of the behaviours associated with each value.

The executive committee asked Blueprint Consultants from Canada to conduct a values assessment to establish the gap between the current and desired observed behaviours. The feedback revealed each business unit's performance on these values, and action plans were formulated to bridge the gap in each area. In some instances, they initiated leadership development or team-building interventions.

A highlight of this journey was a leadership summit for the top 200 leaders from all business units in September 2016. Participants were divided into focus groups and they discussed the organisational enablers that supported living the values as well as the challenges. This facilitated process assisted leaders in taking ownership of the process towards culture change. In addition, Dippenaar and her cultural integration team followed up the summit activities with facilitated sessions that involved each business unit executive team. Team members offered each other feedback on whether they practically lived the values; for example, holding others accountable. Each executive team identified its limiting beliefs and what prevented its members from living the values. Throughout the organisation, storytelling sessions were held, during which employees shared how they were living the MMI values. These illustrations assisted in bringing the values alive.

As part of the cultural intervention, Dippenaar and her team undertook an extensive project to align human resources (HR) practices to the MMI values. There were vast differences across the former Metropolitan and Momentum companies, and Dippenaar relied on the support of the MMI executive team because the actions created intense resistance. Their implementation required several iterative consultation processes with employees.

First, Dippenaar's team redesigned the on-boarding process for new employees, exposing them to the purpose, strategy and MMI way of conducting business. New employees received a document explaining each value with its associated behaviours. The team also audited whether HR policies, such as recruitment, selection and promotion, were aligned to the MMI values.

Second, in terms of talent management, the team ensured that MMI's Employee Value Proposition (EVP) was aligned to the values. For example, the Multiply wellness and rewards program – a fast-growing product that educated, engaged, empowered and encouraged clients to improve their physical wellness, education, safety and financial wellness – was made available to employees. It encouraged employees to make healthy changes through appropriate incentives. These actions contributed to establishing MMI's employee brand rather than Metropolitan's and Momentum's client-facing brands.

In addition, employees could be nominated for excellent performance and living MMI's values, and winners received an overseas vacation. The team also reviewed the bonus structure to ensure that employees were not awarded when they performed at the cost of others, as teamwork was one of the values. Employees were thus measured on task performance as well as value-aligned behaviour to influence promotion processes.

Third, the project team redesigned and renamed the MMI performance management system. The new 'performance excellence system' indicated that the approach was to inspire employees towards excellence, and leaders were trained to explain how individual employees' performance was aligned with MMI's purpose and strategy.

Finally, an important intervention at this time helped leaders assess their level of self-deception. The program asked if there were times when they knew they were not doing the right thing but justified their behaviour. All managers had to attend the training, presented by Arbinger, to move from a default mode of 'self-focus' (or in-the-box thinking) to the results-oriented and outward mindset found in a service leader culture. Another leadership development initiative, 'Enabling Change', was created to build a continuous change management capability in the organisation. Kruger believed that although corporate culture was driven by leadership, it was the actions and interactions of every MMI employee that shaped the shared culture.

REFLECTIONS, UPDATES AND OBSERVATIONS

In 2016 and 2017, MMI began to see additional benefits and results from the merger, and it continued to make adjustments. For example, 2016 was a year of several awards. Metropolitan Retail was rated the number one life insurer in the South African Consumer Satisfaction Index. Momentum Retail was rated second in this index. The Corporate and Public sector business won the Financial Intermediaries Association of South Africa (FIA) 2016 award for Product Supplier of the Year in the Employee Benefits category. MMI was the winner in the Media24 competition for financial results reporting, and its Corporate Social Investment spend reached R33 million in 2016.

TABLE C10.1 FIVE-YEAR FINANCIAL REVIEW					
	June 2016	June 2015	June 2014	June 2013	June 2012
New business premiums (PVP) (Rm)	44 090	50 396	41 739	35 357	32 053
Diluted core headline earnings	3 206	3 836	3 621	3 241	2 955
Dividend paid (Rm)	2 519	2 486	2 278	2 037	1 813
Diluted embedded value (Rm)	42 989	40 330	39 675	35 148	32 472
Return on embedded value (%) (annualised)	12.8%	9.6%	19.0%	17.4%	11.3%
Value of new business (Rm)	850	954	779	681	536

As shown in **Table C10.1**, MMI's financial performance showed steady improvement between 2012 and 2016. The value of new business was R850 million (up 13 per cent on a consistent basis). The total dividend paid during the 2016 financial year was R2519 million. Diluted core headline earnings were up compared to 2012, but down by 16 per cent to R3206 million from their 2015 peak. The contribution of each business to the diluted core headline earnings (as of 30 June 2016, comprising operating profit and investment income on shareholder assets) was as follows: Momentum Retail contributed 50 per cent and Metropolitan Retail, 21 per cent. The Corporate and Public sector contributed 19 per cent, while International contributed a small percentage at 1 per cent. Finally, shareholder capital contributed 9 per cent to diluted core headline earnings. MMI's diluted embedded value increased to R42 989 million at the end of the 2016 financial year.

The new operating model described above offered significant optimisation opportunities, and a number of group-wide optimisation projects supported the expense savings target of R750 million by 2019. Annual cost savings of R104 million was achieved during 2016 (slightly ahead of the target for the year).

Finally, the composition of the 2017 executive committee was again adjusted. It demonstrated the progress of the merger integration and pointed to MMI's subsequent development (**Figure C10.5**). For example, where the previous structure had separate executives for the Momentum and Metropolitan Retail Channels, the new design combined these positions.

MMI achieved a Level 2 status on South Africa's B-BBEE labour relations' scorecard, and MMI's executive committee of 2017 reflected the transformation efforts of the last couple of years. For example, Nicolaas Kruger's team includes four women, one of whom, Mary Vilakazi, is the Deputy Group CEO. In addition, more than half of the executive committee is now from previously disadvantaged groups.

STRATEGIC CHOICES GOING FORWARD

MMI believed that it was critical to embrace the advances in digitalisation and future-proof the organisation. An important strategy in this regard was the launch of MMI's

FIGURE C10.5 MMI EXECUTIVE COMMITTEE IN 2017

'Exponential Ventures' business in 2016. Partnering with leading Fintech players, they invested in innovative young businesses that held the potential to transform the life insurance industry by profitably reaching new markets, meeting new needs or leveraging new technologies and business models. Other African regions provided opportunities with respect to innovative technology-enabled micro-insurance products. For example, MMI entered into a joint venture (JV) with MTN, a South Africa-based multinational mobile telecommunications company, to offer innovative insurance solutions through MTN's significant telco distribution network on the continent. The JV was called 'aYo', which means Joy in Yoruba, a Nigerian language. MMI brought health, insurance systems and expertise to the venture.

As well, India's large population and economic growth rates were attractive and MMI received regulatory approval for its Health and Wellness JV with Aditya Birla Group, launching its first offering to a particular market segment in India. MMI will probably exit selected African countries, namely Zambia, Tanzania, Mauritius, Swaziland and Mozambique. The rationale for exiting these countries is to focus attention on more profitable countries in southern Africa with more attractive growth trajectories. MMI will also most likely scale down its presence in the United Kingdom. Going forward, MMI aimed to increase its focus on the organisation's large existing businesses in South Africa, as well as high potential growth initiatives in the country.

REVIEW QUESTIONS

1   How would you characterise the change initiatives during the MMI merger integration?
2   How effective was the roll-out of these initiatives in terms of timeline, sequence and impact?
3   What advice would you give Kruger to derive even more value from the merger?

Action research a process whereby research is needed to be closely linked to action and vice versa.

Agile organisation an organisation that has the ability to rapidly respond to change by adapting its initial stable configuration.

Behavioural science the scientific study of human behaviour.

Client a person/organisation using the services of a change agent either from within or outside the organisation.

Collaborative strategies include alliances and networks.

Competitive strategies include integrated strategic change (ISC) and mergers and acquisitions (M&As).

Conceptualisation the action or process of forming a concept or idea of a change process.

Consultant a person who provides expert advice professionally, usually outside an organisation.

Contracting entering into a formal and legally binding agreement.

Convention gathering of like-minded professionals.

Conversational view the articulation of various perspectives that can be shared among a group and act as a catalyst for further analysis.

Corporate social responsibility (CSR) a type of internationally private business self-regulation.

Cultural context the circumstances that form the setting for an event, statement or idea, and in terms of which it can be fully understood.

Diagnosis the process of assessing the functioning of an organisation, department, group or job and analysing pertinent data in order to discover sources of problems and propose areas for improvement.

Diagnostic model a conceptual framework describing the relationship between different features of the organisation, its context and effectiveness.

Diagnostic phase a process, practice or technique to identify change.

Downsizing reducing costs and bureaucracy by decreasing the size of the organisation.

Dynamic capability the capability of an organisation to purposefully adapt its resource base.

Ecological objectives objectives that embrace living within the environment's capacity to support life over the long run, enriching rather than depleting natural resources, and sustaining a healthy relationship among the elements of our ecosystem.

Economic objectives objectives that recognise the importance of productivity and efficiency.

Environmental framework the concept that organisations and their subunits are open systems existing in environmental contexts.

Equifinality a cause-and-effect relationship between the initial condition and the final state of a system.

Ethical dilemma a problem pertaining to the moral principles of the change process.

Global orientation characterised by a strategy of marketing standardised products in different countries.

Global social change organisation (GSCO) an organisation that aims to foster the emergence of a global civilisation. Examples include development organisations (DOs), international non-government organisations (INGOs), social movement organisations (SMOs), international private voluntary organisations and bridging organisations. GSCOs address complex social problems, including overpopulation and ecological degradation.

Globalisation (Chapter 1) the process by which businesses and other organisations develop international influence or start operating on an international scale; (Chapter 13) the process of interaction and integration between people, companies and governments worldwide.

Ground rules rules relating to the limits of actions during a change process.

Humanistic values a rationalist outlook of thought attaching prime importance to human matters.

Institutionalisation involves making OD interventions permanent and part of the organisation's normal functions.

Integrated strategic change (ISC) a comprehensive OD intervention aimed at a single organisation or business unit. ISC requires business strategy and organisation design to be aligned and changed together to respond to external and internal disruptions.

International orientation the most common label given to organisations making their first attempts at operating outside their own country's markets.

Interpersonal skills relate to relationships or communication between people.

Intrapersonal skills relate to activity taking place within a person's mind, including awareness of their personal inner dialogue; for example, meditation, prayer, visualisation.

Knowledge management (KM) the tools and techniques that enable organisations to collect, organise and translate information into useful knowledge.

Marginality an amount of change included to be sure of success.

Mechanistic view explains phenomena in purely physical or deterministic terms.

Metaphor for change   a figure of speech or a current-day example; not literally applicable. For example, change is like the weather, always changing.

Multinational orientation characterised by a product line that is tailored to local conditions and is best suited to markets that vary significantly from region to region or country to country.

Non-government organisation (NGO)   usually a non-profit and sometimes international organisation independent of government that is active in humanitarian, educational, health care, public policy, social, human rights, environment and other areas to effect changes according to its objectives.

Open systems planning (OSP)   involves an organisation systematically assessing its task environment and developing a strategic response to it.

Open systems theory   a general comprehensive diagnostic model.

Organisation design   configures the organisation's structure, work design, human resources practices, and management and information systems to guide members' behaviours in a strategic direction.

Organisation development (OD) a professional field of social action and an area of scientific inquiry.

Organisation learning (OL) a system that enhances an organisation's capability to acquire and develop new knowledge.

Organisation transformation (OT)   involves changing the basic character of the organisation, including how it is structured and how it relates to its environment.

Organisational culture   (Chapter 4) the ideas, customs and social behaviours within an organisation; (Chapter 9) includes the pattern of basic assumptions, values, norms and artefacts shared by organisation members. It influences how members perceive, think and behave at work.

Performance appraisal   a feedback system involving direct evaluation of individual or work group performance by a supervisor, manager or peers. It involves a systematic process of jointly assessing work-related achievements, strengths and weaknesses.

Performance management   an integrated process of defining, assessing and reinforcing employee work behaviours and outcomes.

Platform organisation   an organisation that uses modern information technology and sophisticated software to link sellers to buyers.

Positive model   a perspective of change that views change as constructive and uses an integrative approach to change. It uses current best practice from the organisation to help the change process.

Practitioner   a person actively engaged in the change process, usually a member of the organisation.

Process consultation   a technique for helping group members to understand, diagnose and improve their behaviour. Through process consultation, the group should become better able to use its own resources to identify and solve interpersonal problems.

Quasi-stationary equilibrium   appearing to be stable and unmoving but subtly changing.

Re-engineering   a radical redesign of the organisation's core work processes to give tighter linkage and coordination among the different tasks.

Resistance   the refusal to accept or comply with something.

Self-designing organisations organisations with the capability to alter themselves fundamentally and continuously.

Self-managed work teams   groups composed of members performing interrelated tasks. Members are given the multiple skills, autonomy and information necessary to control their own task behaviours with relatively little external control.

Sensitivity training   a program where small groups learn from their own interaction and evolving dynamics about particular issues.

Social objectives   objectives that include such outcomes as employee satisfaction and wellbeing, fair treatment of individual differences, work and home life balance, and community support.

Social view   perception of an organisation that includes multiple facets for consideration; for example, an organisation's culture and its impact on performance.

Sociotechnical systems (STS)   a sociotechnical system consists of two independent, yet related, parts: a social part that includes the people performing the tasks and the relationships among them, and a technical part consisting of the tools, techniques and methods for task performance.

Staying the course   continuing for a long term.

Strategic alliance   entering into an agreement between organisations for their mutual benefit.

Stratified sample   the population of members, events or records is segregated into a number of mutually exclusive subpopulations.

Sustainable effectiveness   the ability to reconfigure the organisation on an ongoing basis in order to deal with a rapidly changing environment.

Sustainable management organisation (SMO)   a company that incorporates socially and environmentally responsible decision making into the planning, organisation and implementation of business strategies.

Sustaining momentum   continue for an extended period of time without interruption.

Systematic collection   gathering data in an organised and planned determined manner.

T-groups   used mainly today to help managers learn about the effects of their behaviour on others, T-groups involve about 10 to 15 strangers who meet with a professional trainer to explore the social dynamics that emerge from their interactions.

Technical ineptitude   total lack of skill or knowledge of technology.

Transformation   the process of converting inputs into outputs.

Transnational orientation combines the best of global and multinational orientations and adds a third attribute – the ability to transfer resources both within the organisation and across national and cultural boundaries.

Transorganisational development (TD)   an emerging form of planned change aimed at helping organisations develop collective and collaborative strategies with other organisations.

Transorganisational systems (TSs)   functional social systems existing intermediately between single organisations and societal systems. These multi-organisational systems can make decisions and perform tasks on behalf of their member organisations, although members maintain their separate organisational identities and goals.

Worldwide OD   the application of OD principles and practices in organisations operating across multiple geographic and cultural boundaries.